THE COSTS AND FUNDING OF CIVIL LITIGATION

This book contains the first major comparative study of litigation costs and methods of funding litigation in more than 30 jurisdictions. It was linked with the most comprehensive review of costs ever carried out in England and Wales by Lord Justice Jackson in 2009 and benefited from the assistance of leading practitioners around the globe.

The study analyses the principles and rules that relate to paying courts, witnesses and lawyers, and the rules on cost shifting, if any. It also notes the major ways in which litigation can be funded, identifying the global trend on contraction of legal aid, the so far limited spread of contingency fees, and the growing new phenomenon of private third party litigation funding. The study also presents the results of nine case studies of typical claim types, so as to give a first overview comparison of which countries' legal systems are cheaper or more expensive.

The book further contains national chapters with in-depth analysis contributed by scholars in 18 jurisdictions (Australia, Belgium, Canada, China, Denmark, England & Wales, France, Germany, Japan, the Netherlands, New Zealand, Poland, Portugal, Russia, Spain, Switzerland, Taiwan and USA) and a further chapter on Latin American jurisdictions.

Civil Justice Systems

Series General Editor, Chris Hodges, Director, CMS Programme, CSLS, University of Oxford

This series covers new theoretical and empirical research on the mechanisms for resolution of civil disputes, including courts, tribunals, arbitration, compensation schemes, ombudsmen, codes of practice, complaint mechanisms, mediation, and various forms of Alternative Dispute Resolution. It examines frameworks for dispute resolution that comprise combinations of the above mechanisms, and the parameters and conditions for selecting certain types of techniques and procedures rather than others. It also evaluates individual techniques, against parameters such as cost, duration, accessibility, and delivery of desired outcomes, and illuminates how legal rights and obligations are operated in practice.

The Costs and Funding of Civil Litigation

A Comparative Perspective

Edited by

Christopher Hodges
Stefan Vogenauer

and

Magdalena Tulibacka

· HART ·
PUBLISHING

OXFORD AND PORTLAND, OREGON
2010

Published in the United Kingdom by Hart Publishing Ltd
16C Worcester Place, Oxford, OX1 2JW
Telephone: +44 (0)1865 517530
Fax: +44 (0)1865 510710
E-mail: mail@hartpub.co.uk
Website: http://www.hartpub.co.uk

Published in North America (US and Canada) by
Hart Publishing
c/o International Specialized Book Services
920 NE 58th Avenue, Suite 300
Portland, OR 97213-3786
USA
Tel: +1 503 287 3093 or toll-free: (1) 800 944 6190
Fax: +1 503 280 8832
E-mail: orders@isbs.com
Website: http://www.isbs.com

British Library Cataloguing in Publication Data
Data Available

ISBN: 978-1-84946-102-3 (Hart Publishing)
ISBN: 978-3-406-61701-0 (Verlag CH Beck)

Typeset by Hope Services, Abingdon
Printed and bound in Great Britain by
Antony Rowe Ltd, Chippenham, Wiltshire

FOREWORD

Dr Hodges, Professor Vogenauer and Dr Tulibacka have conducted an excellent and thorough comparative study of litigation costs and funding across a wide range of jurisdictions ('the Oxford study'). The Oxford study is important, because it provides both context and background for any critical examination of our own costs and funding rules.

The terms of reference set by the Master of the Rolls for the Review of Civil Litigation Costs last year included a requirement to compare the regime for England and Wales with the regimes operating in other jurisdictions. In the limited time available I looked at and wrote a summary of costs and funding regimes in ten jurisdictions only, namely Scotland, France, Germany, The Netherlands, Hong Kong (focusing on the HK Supplementary Legal Aid Scheme), Australia, New Zealand, the Eastern Caribbean, the USA and Canada.[1] Dr Hodges, Professor Vogenauer and Dr Tulibacka, working at the same time as myself, surveyed a much larger number of jurisdictions and made their findings available to my review. They also held a most informative two day seminar at Oxford in July 2009 on the subject, with speakers from both civil and common law jurisdictions. I took the findings of the Oxford study into account in reaching a number of my conclusions.[2]

The authors continued their work beyond 2009 and have now produced this excellent book, setting out the full findings of the Oxford study. I commend this book both for its breadth and detail and also for its percipient commentary. This work will make a valuable contribution to the debate which lies ahead about how the costs and funding rules of England and Wales should be reformed in order to promote access to justice.[3]

Rupert Jackson 16th July 2010
Royal Courts of Justice
Strand
London WC2A 2LL

[1] See chapters 18 and 54–62 of the Preliminary Report.

[2] See, for example, the Final Report at chapter 10 (re conditional fee agreements), paragraph 1.10; chapter 12 (re contingency fees), paragraph 1.4.

[3] At the time of writing this foreword the Coalition Government has not announced its conclusions on these matters or the timetable for any further consultation.

PREFACE

This book examines the approach to costs and funding of civil litigation from a comparative perspective. Its first part sets out the results of a major study that was carried out by two of the research Centres of the Faculty of Law of the University of Oxford, namely the Centre for Socio-Legal Studies and the Institute of European and Comparative Law, in 2009. The study is based on a number of reports that were prepared by scholars and practitioners from all over the world. Some of these national reports are reproduced in the second part of the book.

The study was conducted against the background of, and designed to feed into, a recent fundamental review of civil litigation costs in England and Wales. This was initiated by the then Master of the Rolls, Sir Anthony Clarke, in 2008. He appointed Lord Justice Jackson to conduct an enquiry with a view to making recommendations in order to promote access to justice at proportionate cost. The massive Final Report of the Jackson Review was published in December 2009 (a summary is provided in Chapter 8 of this book). It drew on a wide variety of sources, *inter alia* the preliminary results of our study, which had been published on the Social Sciences Research Network (SSRN). The Jackson Review sets forth a large number of suggestions for wide-ranging reforms of the English costs rules, and their implementation is currently discussed. We hope that this book can help to inform these discussions.

We are extremely grateful to all those who helped us in conducting the study and producing this book. First of all, warm thanks are due to the many academics and practitioners who, within very tight schedules, provided information, data and written contributions for the initial study in 2009 and for this book. They are listed at pages xiii to xviii, below. We are equally indebted to Mr Francis Denning for processing the figures on the case studies and creating the charts and to Mr James Reardon for copy editing. We are also much obliged to international law firm CMS EEIG. They provided generous funding of the Oxford conference in July 2009 at which the preliminary findings of this study were discussed. Finally, we are most grateful to Richard Hart and his team at Hart Publishing who have assisted with their usual expertise and unflappable flexibility, not least in producing this book within a very short time frame.

Oxford, 18 June 2010
Chris Hodges,
Stefan Vogenauer,
Magdalena Tulibacka

CONTENTS

GLOSSARY

ADR	alternative dispute resolution
ATE	after the event (insurance)
B2B	business to business
BTE	before the event (insurance)
CEPEJ	European Commission for the Efficiency of Justice
CFA	conditional fee agreement
CLAF	Contingency Legal Aid Fund
CPR 1999	Civil Procedure Rules 1999 (England and Wales)
LEI	legal expenses insurance
LF	litigation funding
OLAS	Ordinary Legal Aid Scheme
RTA	road traffic accident
SLAS	Supplementary Legal Aid Scheme
SME	small or medium sized enterprise
USD Intl	international dollar
VAT	value added tax

Further abbreviations used in Germany are explained in Chapter 11 of this book.

CONTRIBUTORS

Aránzazu Calzadilla Medina	University of La Laguna, Tenerife
Camille Cameron	Professor, Melbourne Law School
Helena HC Chen	Formosan Brothers, Taipei
Yvon Desdevises	Professor, University of Nantes
Kim Economides	Professor, Otago University
Alejandro Ferreres Comella	Uría & Menéndez, Barcelona
Manuel A Gómez	Assistant Professor, Florida International University College of Law, Miami
Paulien M M van der Grinten	Co-ordinating Legal Advisor, Ministry of Justice of the Netherlands
Deborah R Hensler	Judge John W Ford Professor of Dispute Resolution and Associate Dean, Graduate Studies, Stanford Law School
Burkhard Hess	Professor, University of Heidelberg
Christopher Hodges	Head of the CMS Research Programme on Civil Justice Systems, Centre for Socio-Legal Studies, University of Oxford
Rudolf Hübner	University of Heidelberg
Erik S Knutsen	Assistant Professor, Faculty of Law, Queen's University, Kingston, Ontario
Dmitry Maleshin	Vice-Dean, Associate Professor of Civil Procedural Law, Lomonosov Moscow State University
Anders Ørgaard	Professor, Aalborg University
Eri Osaka	Associate Professor, Toyo University
Michael Palmer	Professor, School of Oriental and African Studies, London
John Peysner	Professor, Lincoln Law School, Lincoln University
James F Reardon	University of Fribourg, Switzerland
Vincent Sagaert	Professor of Private Law, KU Leuven, Professor of Property Law, University of Antwerp, and Lawyer at the Brussels Bar
Ilse Samoy	Professor of Private Law, KU Leuven, Institute of the Law of Obligations
Kuan-Ling Shen	Professor, National Taiwan University

Henrique Sousa Antunes	Professor, Catholic University of Lisbon
Walter A S Stoffel	Professor of Commercial Law, Private International Law, and Bankruptcy Law, University of Fribourg, Switzerland; President of the Swiss Competition Commission
Ikuo Sugawara	Professor, Nagoya University
Kristine Svenningsen	Aalborg University
Jan-Erik Svensson	Partner, Gorrissen Federspiel Kierkegaard
Graham Taylor	Barrister
Carlos Trujillo Cabrera	University of La Laguna, Tenerife
Magdalena Tulibacka	Senior Lecturer, Westminster University, and Associate Fellow, Centre for Socio-Legal Studies, University of Oxford
Mark L L Tuil	Erasmus University, Rotterdam
Anne-Laure Villedieu	CMS Bureau Francis Lefebvre, Paris
Stefan Vogenauer	Professor of Comparative Law, Fellow of Brasenose College and Director of the Institute of European and Comparative Law, University of Oxford
Janet Walker	Professor of Law, Osgoode Hall Law School of York University, Toronto, Ontario
Chao Xi	The Chinese University of Hong Kong

AUTHORS OF REPORTS IN THE COSTS AND FUNDING OF CIVIL LITIGATION PROJECT[4]

Jurisdiction	Scholars	Practitioners
Austria	Professor Dr Georg E Kodek, Wirtschaftsuniversität Wienn, Institut für Bürgerliches Recht und Handelsrecht	Daniela Karollous-Bruner, CMS Reich-Rohrwig Hainz
Australia	Professor Camille Cameron, Melbourne University	Stuart Clark & Colin Loveday, Clayton Utz
Belgium	Professor Vincent Sagaert and Professor Ilse Samoy, Catholic University of Leuven	André Lombart, CMS De Backer
Bulgaria	Professor Ognyan Stambouliev, Sofia University	Kostadin Sirlestow, CMS Cameron McKenna
Canada	Professor Janet Walker, Osgoode Hall Law School of York University, Toronto and Assistant Professor Erik S Knutsen, Queen's University	John Morris, Borden Ladner Gervais LLP and W Daniel Newton, Carrel & Partners LLP
China	Professor Mike Palmer, School of Oriental and African Studies, London and Dr Chao Xi, The Chinese University of Hong Kong	Ulrike Glueck, CMS Hasche Sigle
Czech Republic	Professor doc JUDr Karel Klima CSc, and Tomas Krivka, Western Bohemian University, Pilsen and Charles University, Prague	Tomas Matejovsky and Kamila Rouckova, CMS Cameron McKenna

[4] National Reports are at www.csls.ox.ac.uk/COSTOFLITIGATIONDOCUMENTSANDREPORTS.php

Jurisdiction	Scholars	Practitioners
Denmark	Professor Anders Ørgaard, Aalborg University	Jan-Erik Svensson, Gorrissen Federspiel Kierkegaard
England & Wales	Dr Christopher Hodges, Centre for Socio-Legal Studies, Oxford University	Guy Pendell, CMS Cameron McKenna
Estonia	Dr Martin Käerdi, Tartu University and Raidla Lejins & Norcous	Marit Toom, Raidla Lejins & Norcous
Finland	Dr Eva Storskrubb, Diottmar & Indrenius	Pekka Puhakka, Asianajotoimisto Hammarström Puhakka Partners Oy
France	Professor Dr Loïc Cadiet, Paris University	Anne-Laure Villedieu, CMS Bureau Francis Lefebvre
Germany	Professsor Dr Burkhard Hess, Heidelberg University	Michael Molitoris, Nörr Stiefenhofer Lutz
Greece	Professor Konstantinos D Klamaris, Athens University	Dimitris Emvalomenos, Bahas, Gramatidis & Partners
Hong Kong	Professor Chao Xi, Chinese University of Hong Kong	Robert Clark and Karen Dicks, Deacons
Hungary	Professor Dr Zsuzsa Wopera and Adrienn Nagy, University of Miskolc	Milan Kohlrusz, CMS Cameron McKenna
Ireland		Stuart Margetson & Lisa Broderick, Matheson Ormsby Prentice
Italy	Professor Dr Elisabetta Silvestri, Pavia University	Laura Opilio & Paola Ghezzi, CMS Adonnino Ascoli & Cavasola Scamoni
Japan	Professor Ikuo Sugawara, Nagoya University and Assistant Professor Eri Osaka, Toyo University	Teruoki Ninomiya, Research and Training Institute of the Japanese Supreme Court

Jurisdiction	Scholars	Practitioners
Latin America	Professor Manuel A Gómez, Florida University	
Latvia	Professor Dr Kalvis Torgans, Latvia University	Toomas Vaher, Raidla & Partners, Tallinn
Lithuania	Dr Rimantas Simaitis, Vilnius University	Dr Rimantas Simaitis Raidla Lejins & Norcous
Netherlands	Professor mr Carla JM Klaassen, Radboud University and J Dammingh	Leonard Böhmer, CMS Derks Star Busmann NV
New Zealand	Professor Kim Economides, Otago University	Graham Taylor, Barrister, Wellington and Jim Guest, Downie Stewart
Norway	Sverre Blandhol, Oslo University	Magnus Hellesylt, Wiersholm, Mellbye & Bech
Poland	Dr Magdalena Tulibacka, Centre for Socio-Legal Studies, Oxford	Pawel Pietkiewicz, CMS Cameron McKenna
Portugal	Professor Henrique Sousa Antunes, Catholic University of Lisbon	Margarida Barrocas, Barrocas Sarmento Neves
Romania		Gabriel Sidere, CMS Cameron McKenna
Russia	Professor Dmitry Maleshin, Moscow University	Leonid Zubarev and Konstatin Kantyrev, CMS Cameron McKenna
Scotland		Rob Wilson, CMS Cameron McKenna
Singapore	Professor Jeffrey Pinsler, Singapore University	Lawrence Teh and Wendy Goh, Rodyk & Davidson
Spain	Dr Mª Aránzazu Calzadilla Medina and Carlos Trujillo Cabrera, University of La Laguna, Tenerife	Alejandro Ferreres Comella, Uría Menéndez

Jurisdiction	Scholars	Practitioners
Sweden		Peder Hammarskiöld & Sofia Englund, Advokatfirman Hammarskiöld & Co
Switzerland	Professor Dr Walter A Stoffel and James F Reardon, Fribourg University	Philipp Dickenmann, CMS von Erlach Henrici AG
Taiwan	Professor Kuan-Ling Shen, National Taiwan University	Helena Chen, FBLAW
USA	Professor Deborah R Hensler, Stanford University	Michael Hausfeld, Hausfeld LLP

Part I

The Oxford Study on Costs and Funding of Civil Litigation

CHRISTOPHER HODGES, STEFAN VOGENAUER AND MAGDALENA TULIBACKA

Introduction

I. The Purpose and Scope of This Study

The focus of this study is on how different jurisdictions approach the two linked subjects of litigation funding and costs. We seek answers to the following questions. What are the options for claimants to fund litigation to vindicate their rights? What court costs, lawyers' fees and other costs will litigants have to pay? What are the rules on costs, both in relation to initial payments and any rules on subsequent reimbursement, particularly in relation to such sums as may be a liability for a loser to reimburse a winner through cost-shifting rules? Are such sums predictable in advance? Are they proportionate to the work done or to the issues at stake? Overall, which jurisdictions are comparatively more or less expensive?

An important preliminary point is that these subjects can be difficult to grasp without a level of understanding of the national context, and particularly of the national rules and practices on civil procedure. However, the primary concern of this study is not with general civil procedure, and we have consciously omitted almost all description of national rules and practices on procedural issues beyond the costs and funding of litigation. This is for three reasons. First, it is assumed that readers of a book such as this will have sufficient familiarity with at least the broad distinctions between the basic common law and civil law models of procedure that are represented here. Secondly, whilst there are considerable variations on such issues between jurisdictions, not only in relation to general principles and architecture of the systems, but also in matters of detail, useful reference works already exist on such matters.[1] Thirdly, the length of this study would be considerably extended if such detailed descriptions were to be included and, more importantly, its focus on the issues of funding and costs, on which only limited other comparative research exists to date, would be diminished.

[1] AAS Zuckerman (ed), *Civil Justice in Crisis: Comparative Perspectives of Civil Procedure* (Oxford, Oxford University Press, 1999); A Layton and H Mercer (eds), *European Civil Practice* (2nd edn, London, Thomson, Sweet & Maxwell, 2004); N Trocker and V Varano (eds), *Civil Procedure Reform in Comparative Perspective* (Torino, Giappichelli, 2005); OG Chase, H Hershkoff, L Silberman, Y Taniguchi, V Varano and AAS Zuckerman, *Civil Litigation in Comparative Context* (St Paul/MN, Thomson West, 2007).

Nevertheless, although the focus of this study is not directly on civil procedure, the level and liabilities for costs and the opportunities for funding litigation ultimately raise fundamental questions about the architecture and efficiency of civil procedure within a given jurisdiction. This is because different procedural regimes will lead to different levels of cost. So the intrinsic level of the cost that a given system produces has significant implications not only for the efficiency of that system but also for its ability to deliver effective access to justice. The underlying policy issue is whether there is an inherent problem with the overall architecture of the legal system, or (merely) an issue of inefficiency within the internal operation of a given system. It may, after all, be a deliberate policy that a particular court procedure is expensive, in comparison with other possible dispute resolution options, so as to make the judicial route less attractive than, for example, a voluntary dispute resolution procedure or some other pathway such as a business scheme or ombudsman route.

II. The Importance of Litigation Costs

Why do costs matter? The answer is that issues raised by costs and funding are important for litigants, intermediaries (lawyers and experts) and system providers (governments and courts).

From the perspective of the claimant, the size and predictability of the costs of a dispute, and of a dispute resolution process, need to be evaluated to see whether the risks and benefits of using the process are favourable in pursuing a legal action, whether on its own or in comparison with any alternative procedures. If the costs or risk are too high, and there is no better alternative pathway, the result will be a denial of access to justice, and potential wrongs will not be remedied or compensated. Further, the extent of any shortfall in the recoverability of costs raises similar issues. From the defendant's perspective, similar risk-benefit calculations arise in relation to the decision to defend or admit a claim, influenced by the relative merits of a claim or defence.

From the perspective of lawyers or other intermediaries, such as experts, bailiffs or witnesses, the costs rules govern the amount of remuneration that can be earned or expenses that can be reimbursed, and this will affect the quality and quantum of supply of such services.

From the perspective of the state, there needs to be a balance between various, partly contradictory values. On the one hand, the promotion of the rule of law and the importance of social and economic stability demand that justice be sufficiently accessible, ie costs should be sufficiently low to allow individuals to vindicate their rights in the state courts. On the other hand, the very same values require that pointless claims be suppressed and settlements be promoted, ie costs should be sufficiently high to deter frivolous or vexatious litigants and incentivise the resolution of disputes without a formal judgment. There is another factor pulling in the same direction: given that public resources are limited, the cost of providing the civil justice system is normally covered from some combination of general public funds and/or of payments by individual litigants—the higher the costs born by the users of the court system, the lower the drain on the public purse.

The importance of costs issues within contemporary civil justice systems is readily apparent from the fact that several jurisdictions have given particular attention during the past decade to reforming civil procedure rules so as to reduce delays and costs. Indeed, when viewed holistically, one suspects that it would be difficult for almost every jurisdiction to maintain an assertion that its civil justice system is satisfactory from the perspectives of cost proportionality and a low level of affordability. Jurisdictions noted in this volume that have recently introduced significant reforms include the Netherlands (1992), England and Wales (1999 and proposals 2010), Taiwan (2003), China (2006), Belgium (2007), Portugal (2008), and Switzerland (2011). There is every possibility that further reforms will be made: this is a period of worldwide reflection on the role that litigation plays within civil justice dispute resolution systems.

In England and Wales, the influential Woolf reforms that resulted in the Civil Procedure Rules (CPR) 1999 brought about significant changes in the general culture of civil procedure, but are widely thought not to have resolved costs issues. A principal reason for the ongoing lack of stability in this respect arose not with the procedural rules but with the systems for funding litigation, and the fact that they changed at the same time as the procedural rules. The recent *Review of Civil Litigation Costs* by Lord Justice Jackson[2] sought solutions to these costs problems, possibly through reforms in costs rules and also through approaching different types of cases differently.

III. An Increased Focus on Costs

Costs and funding have been forgotten areas of civil procedure. The focus has traditionally been on the 'front end' of the design and rules of civil procedure, often based on certain doctrinal principles, rather than on an empirical evaluation of how well a system works by looking at the 'back end' of outcomes. But this is not true any more–systems are being evaluated against criteria of speed, cost, efficiency and appropriateness of the pathway for the type of case. As a consequence,

[2] Jackson LJ, *Review of Civil Litigation Costs: Final Report* (London, HMSO, 2010), available at http://www.judiciary.gov.uk/about_judiciary/cost-review/jan2010/final-report-140110.pdf.

[3] For exceptions, see A Paterson, 'Financing Legal Services: a Comparative Perspective' in DL Carey Miller and PR Beaumont (eds), *The Option of Litigating in Europe* (London, United Kingdom National Committee of Comparative Law, 1993) 149; V Maurer, RE Thomas and PA DeBooth, 'Attorney Fee Arrangements: the US and Western European Perspectives' (1998) 19 *Northwestern Journal of International Law and Business* 272. Various contributions in P Gottwald (ed), *Litigation in England and Germany: Legal Professional Services, Key Features and Funding* (Bielefeld, Gieseking, 2010) address costs and funding in the two respective jurisdictions.

whilst costs and funding have traditionally received relatively little attention by academic writers in general, and by comparative lawyers in particular,[3] there has recently been stronger interest in these subjects, and a number of important studies have been published.

First, scholars drew attention to the problem some ten years ago that certain civil procedure rules and the systems within which they operate can give rise to high and disproportionate costs. Adrian Zuckerman and others found in 1999 that the result was a widespread perception that the administration of justice was failing to meet the needs of the community.[4] They concluded that access to justice was so adversely affected by high litigation costs and long delays that in quite a few countries the courts no longer provide an adequate venue for seeking the protection of rights or for resolving disputes.

Secondly, the European Commission for the Efficiency of Justice (CEPEJ), an initiative of the Member States of the Council of Europe, published reports in 2006 and 2008 that contain data for the evaluation of judicial systems in Europe, with a focus on judicial and quasi-judicial institutions and their funding. They also include some information on court fees and legal aid.[5]

Thirdly, since 2006 the 'Measuring Access to Justice Project', a joint initiative of The Hague Institute for the Internationalisation of Law, Tilburg University and Utrecht University, has published a number of studies. Their common goal is to develop, validate and disseminate a standard methodology for measuring the costs and quality that users of justice may expect.[6] As a part of the project, a detailed analysis of litigation costs in the Netherlands, Bulgaria and Bolivia was undertaken. Its methodology includes not just the easily quantifiable costs but also aspects of time, delay, psychological and business cost. From the perspective of users, these 'costs' may be significant.

Fourthly, the European Commission obtained a large comparative study of litigation costs as part of its policy of building a European space of freedom, security and justice. The study was carried out by a Brussels based law firm, and its findings were published in 2007.[7] It found great variations in the costs and funding regimes of the Member States of the European Union.

[4] Zuckerman, *Civil Justice in Crisis* (n 1 above).

[5] European Commission for the Efficiency of Justice (CEPEJ), *European Judicial Systems: Edition 2006 (data 2004)* and *European Judicial Systems: Edition 2008 (2006 data)—Efficiency and Quality of Justice*, (Strasbourg, Council of Europe, 2006 and 2008), available at www.coe.int/T/dghl/cooperation/cepej/default_en.asp. See also P Albers, 'Judicial Systems in Europe Compared' in CH van Rhee and A Uzelac (eds), *Civil Justice between Efficiency and Quality: from Ius Commune to the CEPEJ* (Antwerp, Intersentia, 2008) 9.

[6] www.measuringaccesstojustice.com/index.php/Publications. See M Gramatikov et al, *A Handbook for Measuring the Costs and Quality of Access to Justice* (Apeldoorn et al, Maklu, 2010); M Gramatikov, M Laxminarayan and M Barendrecht, 'Assessment of the Validity and Reliability of a Methodology for Measuring the Costs and Quality of Access to Justice', TISCO Working Paper Series on Civil Law and Conflict Resolution Systems No 003/2010, available at http://ssrn.com/abstract=1559782.

[7] J Albert, *Study on the Transparency of Costs of Civil Judicial Proceedings in the European Union: Final Report* (Brussels; Hoche, Demolin, Brulard, Barthélémy; 2007), available at http://ec.europa.eu/justice_home/doc_centre/civil/studies/doc_civil_studies_en.htm.

Fifthly, in 2008 the Oxford Civil Justice Survey examined to what extent businesses in Europe were influenced by their perceptions of national civil justice systems and contract laws when choosing the applicable law and the forum of litigation for cross-border transactions. It emerged that the perception of costs was one of the important factors that influenced such choices, albeit slightly less important than might have been expected.[8]

Sixthly, a practitioners' review of costs rules in 56 jurisdictions was published by a major law firm just as this book went to press.[9]

Seventhly, 'cost and fee allocation rules' in civil procedure is one of the topics for the 18th International Congress of Comparative Law that will be held in Washington in July 2010.[9a]

Finally, this study on the costs and funding of civil litigation is part of the EU Civil Justice Project, which is a new pan-European academic initiative to research dispute resolution issues—whether using courts or alternative procedures and techniques—and build up empirical evidence to support policy decisions on best practice in dispute resolution for the twenty-first century.[10]

All these studies seem to reflect a general concern amongst (potential) litigants, practising lawyers, judges and governments that the costs of resolving a dispute through the courts are too high.

IV. Major Changes in Litigation Funding

In addition to a focus on costs, significant developments are occurring in relation to the means by which litigation is funded. The rule that a litigant has to pay something for the use of the public civil justice system, and in particular for using its intermediaries, is widely established (albeit not universal). However, increased costs have for many years given rise to concern over ensuring that playing fields within the civil justice system are level, and that those with limited resources should not be disadvantaged or even denied access to justice.

The traditional institutional approaches to this funding gap have been that lawyers waive their fees or that the state waives its fees and/or provides funding for a lawyer. Legal aid exists in various forms in different countries, ranging from lawyers acting on an unpaid *pro bono* basis to the state paying hourly rates for lawyers' work. It gained significant momentum in many Western societies from

[8] S Vogenauer, 'Perceptions of Civil Justice Systems in Europe and their Implications for Choice of Forum and Choice of Contract Law: an Empirical Analysis' in S Vogenauer and C Hodges (eds), *Civil Justice Systems in Europe: Implications for Choice of Forum and Choice of Contract Law* (Oxford, Hart Publishing, 2010) ch 1.

[9] Lovells, *At what cost? A Lovells multi jurisdictional guide to litigation costs* (London, 2010), available at http://www.hoganlovells.com/newsmedia/pubDetail.aspx?publication=6144.

[9a] M Reimann, *Cost and Fee Allocation in Civil Procedure: A Global Comparison Study* (forthcoming 2011).

[10] See summary at http://www.csls.ox.ac.uk/european_civil_justice_systems.php.

the 1950s onwards but governments have increasingly found it to be too expensive to provide on a comprehensive basis.

Funding of litigation by lawyers has a long history. Waiver of some or all fees is a common phenomenon, whether permitted or not. A 'conditional' or 'success fee' may be payable only upon successful conclusion of a case and may include an uplift over normal rates. In contrast, a 'contingency fee' is a fee that is based on a proportion of the sum recovered by the successful litigant (*pactum de quota litis*). Contingency fees have long been a main feature of litigation funding in the United States of America. Given a potential gap in access to justice, it is not surprising that interest in a contingency approach is also growing in legal systems where they are still limited or even prohibited.

A significant new development is the arrival of third party commercial funders in some countries, notably Australia, England and the United States. Insurers have been financing litigation for a long time, but funding from independent investment vehicles is a novel phenomenon. Long established prohibitions on a third party's financial involvement in litigation have been abolished in Australia and England in the face of a pragmatic need to maintain access to justice. Important issues over permissibility, legal ethics and regulation arise.

It is no exaggeration to observe that the potential consequences of these major changes in litigation funding are entirely uncertain. So far, the developments are unplanned and uncontrolled. Those jurisdictions in which reforms have been introduced by legislators or judges often give the impression of having undertaken limited consideration of the possible consequences.

V. The Oxford Study

This study was undertaken by two of the research Centres of the Faculty of Law of the University of Oxford, namely the Centre for Socio-Legal Studies and the Institute of European and Comparative Law. In conducting the enquiry, we had two particular aims that influenced its design.

The first aim was to cast the net wide. We intended to summarise the approach to costs and funding of civil litigation in a significant number of European jurisdictions, plus some other selected legal systems that we thought likely to have experienced distinct historical challenges and that might have developed innovative approaches to meet them. We therefore included, *inter alia*, jurisdictions from East Asia, Central and Eastern Europe and Scandinavia. Given the ambitious geographical reach of the study and our lack of familiarity with all, let alone the majority, of the legal systems under consideration, we had to rely on information provided by national experts in response to a questionnaire. This document is reproduced as an Appendix to this study.[11] We are of course aware of the method-

[11] See pp 110–13 below.

ological limitations of the use of questionnaires. However, we found it indispensable: the technique is bound to remain a hallmark of large scale comparative studies as long as omniscience has not descended upon comparatists. We tried to limit the inherent risks of relying on the answers of national correspondents by fine-graining the structure of our enquiry. We involved more than one respondent per legal system, we asked all of our correspondents to consider their respective responses, and we brought some of them together at a conference. How this was done is discussed in greater detail in the following paragraphs. At this stage, it may simply be noted that the involvement of a variety of participants was also linked to the second aim pursued with this study.

The second aim was to establish and compare the actual amounts of costs incurred by litigants in the jurisdictions surveyed, rather than just the abstract rules on cost and funding that prevail in different legal systems. To put it plainly, we sought initial answers to the questions 'how expensive are the litigation systems in different countries, and which are the cheapest and most expensive?' Our questionnaire was therefore designed to combine qualitative and quantitative approaches. Its first part sought information on funding and litigation in general. The second part set out nine case studies, and each respondent was asked to estimate the costs that the parties would incur in these hypothetical scenarios if they were litigated in his or her jurisdiction. The study therefore has a strong practice-related element. This led us to adopt a two-stage approach with regard to the addressees of our questionnaire which is, as far as we know, unprecedented in large-scale comparative studies. We first sent the questionnaire to experienced litigation practitioners in our target countries. They were asked to provide a first hand account of their national costs and funding regimes, as well as to assemble data for the case studies. At the second stage, we asked distinguished academics from the same jurisdictions to put the practitioners' accounts into historical and theoretical perspective and link them to broader features of civil procedure and the respective legal system in general. In doing so, we hope to have struck a balance between pragmatism and principle that will provide as accurate a picture of the law in action as possible.

The questionnaire was circulated to practitioners in 36 countries on 15 January 2009. Most of them had been identified through previous work with Christopher Hodges. We received responses from 34 jurisdictions, i.e. Australia, Austria, Belgium, Bulgaria, Canada, China, the Czech Republic, Denmark, England and Wales, Estonia, Finland, France, Germany, Greece, Hong Kong, Hungary, Ireland, Italy, Japan, Latvia, Lithuania, the Netherlands, Norway, Poland, Portugal, Romania, Russia, Scotland, Singapore, Spain, Sweden, Switzerland, and Taiwan. As a result of later contacts, we obtained a further practitioner's report from New Zealand and data on the case studies from Canadian practitioners. The original 34 reports were forwarded to legal scholars. In some cases, the recipients felt they had nothing to add. In others they did, and as a result we received 15 academic reports. Subsequently, we benefited from two further academic reports. One dealt with the United States of America, the other gave an overview of 14 Latin American jurisdictions. The names and affiliations of the national practitioners and academics who assisted with this study are listed on pp xiii ff of this book. Their reports are available on the project website,[12] together with any further materials received, such as legislative sources and statistics.

Some of the academic reporters involved in the study presented and discussed their findings at a conference held in Oxford on 6 and 7 July 2009. Other speakers at the conference included Lord Justice Jackson, who presented the Preliminary Report which he had issued two months before,[13] civil servants of the European Commission and the Dutch Ministry of Justice, the special advisor to CEPEJ, a commercial litigation funder, and representatives of business as well as consumer interest groups.[14]

Having reviewed the materials then assembled, we selected various countries and requested the scholars from those countries to contribute chapters for this book. The countries discussed in its Part II comprise seventeen national jurisdictions plus, in a single chapter, some twenty Latin American legal systems, not forgetting also that some countries, such as the United States of America and Switzerland, possess both federal and multiple state or cantonal jurisdictions. The omission of other countries should in no way be taken to mean that their solutions are irrelevant or not interesting. However, certain legal systems have broad similarities, and to include them all would have been somewhat repetitive, whereas those selected have specific features that seemed to be particularly worthy of illustration and comment. In view of the topical importance of reforms in England and Wales, which do seem to be of some ongoing international interest, we solicited three contributions on that jurisdiction (Chapters 7–9 below): the first is a national report in the same format as for other legal systems, the second a summary of the recent Jackson Costs Review, and the third offers some observations on possible future developments. We also received a second report on the Netherlands. Given the need to provide integrated policy reviews of national civil justice systems, we found this account, authored by Paulien van der Grinten of the Dutch Ministry of Justice, particularly interesting. It can be found in Chapter 15 below.

Contributors of the national chapters were asked to bear in mind a standard format, so as to ensure that the same basic information on funding options and cost rules is available, and to facilitate comparisons between national systems. However, we have not rigidly enforced the model format for each chapter: in the case of several countries, there is a particular national context that provided a justification or even the necessity to deviate from the standard pattern. In some cases, there are other reasons for a strict lack of uniformity: for example, the initial practitioner's perspective of the French rules by Anne-Laure Villedieu was sufficiently comprehensive for it to be reproduced here with some rearrangement to reflect

[12] See www.csls.ox.ac.uk/COSTOFLITIGATIONDOCUMENTSANDREPORTS.php.

[13] Jackson LJ, *Review of Civil Litigation Costs: Preliminary Report* (London, HMSO, 2009), available at http://www.judiciary.gov.uk/about_judiciary/cost-review/preliminary-report.htm. For the Jackson Review, see text at n 2 above.

[14] The programme of the conference and a summary of the discussion is available at http://www.csls.ox.ac.uk/documents/NoteoftheConferenceonLitigationCostsandFunding.doc.

the chapter format, with the addition at the start of an insightful academic commentary by Yvon Desdevises. This arrangement provides a clear overview of the French practice, theory and policy.

In sum, this study draws on three different and partially overlapping types of sources: the practitioners' reports, the academic reports and the scholarly country reports prepared for publication in Part II of this book. Whilst we have relied on the accuracy on the information received from our national reporters, we are fully responsible for the conclusions drawn and the policy recommendations made. These parts of the study will not necessarily reflect the views of those who provided us with information on their systems. Nor are they to be taken to represent the views of the conference sponsor CMS EEIG or indeed of any of the general funders supporting the Oxford Centre for Socio-Legal Studies[15] and the Oxford Institute of European and Comparative Law.[16]

We present the results of our study in four Sections. The first Section summarises the general approaches to costs and funding in the jurisdictions surveyed. These qualitative findings are supplemented with quantitative data in the second Section. The third Section attempts to tease out the underlying policy issues and to formulate some recommendations for law reform. A concise summary of our findings can be found in the fourth Section, at pp 100–110 below.

SECTION 1

NATIONAL APPROACHES TO COSTS AND FUNDING OF CIVIL LITIGATION

This Section describes the qualitative findings on national costs rules and funding arrangements for the jurisdictions studied. As explained in the Introduction above, it is a synthesis of the information provided in the national reports from practitioners and scholars, the information gathered at the Oxford conference in July 2009, and the information given in the national chapters included in Part II of this book. We refrain from giving footnote references to source materials, save in exceptional circumstances, since the cross-references would be too numerous: the substantiation is mostly readily available from the national chapters in this book.

Before presenting our findings we stress their *tentative* nature, given that this is a first attempt at collecting information on the subjects of costs and funding. Having said this, we are optimistic that the information assembled here is sufficiently reliable to support a number of important conclusions on matters of some significance to civil justice systems.

[15] Principally CMS EEIG and the European Justice Forum.

[16] A variety of national governments and foundations, as well as international law firms, particularly Clifford Chance LLP (for further information, see http://denning.law.ox.ac.uk/iecl/supporters.shtml).

I. Costs

A. General Points

(i) The universality of rules

Every jurisdiction has rules that regulate the economic consequences of litigation, ie rules on litigation costs. The basic *elements* that make up quantifiable costs (in economic terms, the cost centres) are the same in every jurisdiction. There are three elements:

a. Charges for use of the courts and their processes, including associated officers and bailiffs;
b. Evidential costs for witnesses and experts;
c. Lawyers' fees, where lawyers are involved, including the lawyers' cost of obtaining documentary evidence in common law jurisdictions.

(ii) A scarcity of principles

Few jurisdictions have formally codified the principles on which their rules on costs are based. Indeed, many jurisdictions have no readily-identifiable general theory on litigation funding and costs. An exception is Portugal, which stipulated in its 2008 reforms the principles that legal costs finance the legal system, guarantee access to the law, and discourage frivolous or excessive claims and dilatory judicial practices. In addition, Portuguese civil procedure is explicitly based on the principles of *victus victori* (or: *victus victori in expensis condemnatus est*—he who loses the suit pays costs to his adversary), causality, procedural advantage or benefit and proportionality.

Similarly, very few jurisdictions have expressly adopted a policy principle that costs should be *proportionate*, England and Wales being the leading example,[17] followed recently by Canada (although it remains to be seen whether the reforms will have an impact). The Portuguese Constitution also spells out principles of proportionality and access to justice.[18] Concern over cost proportionality has emerged in Australia but only some of the English-style cost management techniques have yet been adopted there. Of course, in some jurisdictions the application of the costs rules deliver a result that is in line with the principle of proportionality without that principle being stipulated in legislation.

[17] CPR, Part 1.1(2)(c).
[18] Art 20(1) of the Portuguese Constitution.

B. Costs Arising

(i) Court charges

Table 1 summarises the information supplied by national reporters in relation to the basis of charging for court fees and lawyers' fees (ie by tariff or otherwise) and the basis of computation of any costs that are shifted. It is reproduced as an Appendix to this study.[19] The findings can be summarised as follows.

All countries surveyed impose court fees on claimants who initiate proceedings, and sometimes on defendants for taking certain steps, apart from France and Sweden,[20] which impose no charge in most cases as a matter of principle, as occurs also in eight of twenty states in Latin America. After three decades of no court costs, China introduced them in 2006, but at the same time specified notably lower costs for targeted types of claims, namely those in matrimonial, labour and administrative matters.

All countries that impose court fees regulate the amounts by statute. The fees vary depending on the type of court, the specific instance of the proceedings, and type of case.[21] The majority of countries use a tariff system, either basing the fee on a specified fixed percentage of the claim value (either alone or together with some other flat fee, perhaps with the tariff applying to cases over a certain value) or on the basis of a detailed tariff that specifies certain bands of fees or percentages for cases of differing values. Many of the court charges in tariff-based systems taper so as to decrease with higher value cases. In the tariff-based countries there are usually flat fees for non-pecuniary claims and for some specific cases.

Some countries introduce flat fees for certain types of cases or types of activities (for instance China, Switzerland and Sweden) or for all cases (for instance Australia, Belgium, Finland, Hong Kong, Norway, Scotland, Singapore and the United States of America).

There is little information available on whether the charges levied are intended to cover all or some of the states' costs of running their court systems. Indeed, there is a suspicion that the fees are often selected on an arbitrary basis and that many courts' administrations are not transparent in relation to their actual costs. It is not clear to what extent governments actually compute what the costs are. The United Kingdom adopts a principle of 'full costs recovery', although it in fact only recovers around 80 per cent of the court budget through fees, with the remaining 20 per cent coming from Treasury funds.[22]

[19] See pp 114–31 below.

[20] In Sweden the state spends some SEK 4.3 billion on courts annually, and parties pay some SEK 47 million (1% of the total) on applications.

[21] Further details of the sums involved are given in Section 2 and Table 5 below.

[22] See the HM Courts Service website (http://www.hmcourtsservice.gov.uk/infoabout/fees/index.htm). Note that the full recovery policy was strongly criticized by Jackson LJ (n 13 above) ch 7; and see ch 8 below.

Two broad approaches might be adopted towards charging for court costs: a single fee at the start ('pay upfront') or a series of different fees applying to a sequence of procedural steps ('pay as you go'). The former approach is simple and easy to operate. It might be argued to discourage settlement, but whether that is so depends on a number of factors, including the overall size of the fee(s), and the number of steps and subsequent fees. A large initial fee may obviously deter access to the courts, but again that depends on the size of the fee relative to the resources of users. China introduced a single initial fee in 2006. Some jurisdictions refund part of the court charges if the case settles before the end of the formal process,[23] specifically in order to encourage settlement. Making access to the courts dependent on staged charges also theoretically encourages settlement, but in practice the incentive would be limited where, as is usually the case, the sums involved are comparatively low. A 'pay as you go' approach to court fees raises the issue of how many steps there are in the procedure, or might need to be taken before a case is resolved by the court or by settlement.

Some systems introduce complexity through costs for different actors who are used in various procedures which are employed to give legal notice to the parties involved ('service of process') (which might be by public or private officials or bailiffs) and in the enforcement of judgments (which might again be by private or public bailiffs). Other systems place the burden and cost of service and enforcement on the party personally. The latter solution saves public funds but increases personal costs. The former solution increases complexity but might be cheaper and more effective where carried out by a public official.

Court fees frequently include a tapering element: they may be related to the amount in dispute (where that is computable), whether on the basis of a percentage levy or incremental steps, but the percentage reduces for higher value claims, or is capped so as not to give rise to astronomical fees for very large cases. This tapering introduces an element of proportionality between claim value and costs. In 2008 the Portuguese government, having discovered that about half its cases related to small debt claims, controversially attempted to drive cases out of the courts by increasing court fees for those who bring over 200 cases a year.

There are indications from various jurisdictions that claimants adopt a number of strategies to avoid paying higher court costs than necessary. Thus, claimants might limit the issues in dispute, or the amounts claimed, or bring a test case. Examples include many continental European jurisdictions and Taiwan. This approach might deter unjustified inflation of claims, but it may equally deter the bringing of elements of justified but expensive claims. There is no empirical evidence to establish the actual position.

[23] Under the 2008 reforms in Portugal, 50% of the court fee is refunded if the case settles before the end of the court process. In Taiwan, as part of a specific policy of encouraging settlement and use of mediation, two-thirds of the court fees paid may be refunded when the claimant voluntarily dismisses the action prior to termination of the first oral session at first instance, when a settlement is reached, or where there was a successful mediation.

Although such matters are outside the scope of this study, there are some indications of a trend that governments and courts are seeking to reduce costs by creating specialist courts and tribunals, which should be more efficient and possibly reduce the need for expertise and possibly also factual evidence.[24]

Systems in which judges and courts are required to do significant amounts of work can lead to higher court fees than those systems in which the rules of procedure require judges to be more reactive.

In this respect, local perceptions of the size of costs can vary. The court fee tariff is considered high in Germany, and capped at a standard filing fee of €274,368 for any claim over €30 million.[25]

(ii) Reimbursement of witnesses

Every jurisdiction provides for reimbursement to witnesses of their costs of travel and other reasonable costs in giving evidence. Some systems also permit witnesses' time to be recompensed in some way. Central European states tend to reimburse employees or employers, but the sums paid for time are low. The award in Belgium is usually a total sum of €5! Witness costs are not a major cost centre within litigation.

(iii) Experts' fees

There are two different models in relation to the way in which expert evidence is obtained. The general civil law approach is that the court will appoint an expert (usually one). Persons appointed have a somewhat judicial function through being independent of the parties and resolving technical issues by way of answering the court's questions on particular issues. Such experts may, in many but not all jurisdictions, be university professors or other civil servants. In general, the party who requests such an expert must put up funds that will be used to pay the expert.[26] National systems of this type differ on whether such experts' fees are to be on an official scale, or are fixed through market forces or free negotiation with the court, but the amounts are almost always, under this model, approved by the court and the court transfers the money to the experts. The costs of such court-appointed experts will usually be payable or reimbursable by a losing opponent at the end of the case. In addition to such court-appointed experts, it may be possible in some (not all) civil law jurisdictions for parties to appoint and pay their own private experts, whose evidence might, or might not, be admissible in court, or

[24] The United Kingdom has a matrix of specialist courts and tribunals. For the reasons given, Taiwan has introduced small claims jurisdiction, an Intellectual Property Court and is considering the introduction of a construction court. Many other countries have similar examples.

[25] The recoverable lawyer's fee is similarly capped at €228,740 plus 19% VAT: see below.

[26] Belgium reformed its approach in 2007 after dissatisfaction over delays in obtaining court-appointed expert opinions, and following concern that the former system under which requesting parties paid experts direct led to perceptions of conflict of interest or bias on the part of the expert.

influential on the court-appointed expert. Such costs for private experts are rarely reimbursable.[27]

In contrast, in the common law jurisdictions, the traditional approach is that each party has to select and pay his own expert, whose evidence will be produced to the court. The rates are fixed by negotiation and market forces, rarely with any formal tariff (although some professional association tariffs might have influence). The costs will be reimbursed to a winning party if a loser pays rule applies in the jurisdiction, but the court has the power to review such amounts and reduce them if unreasonable.

(iv) Lawyers' fees

As shown in Table 1, in almost every state, the fees between lawyer and client can be freely agreed. Irrespective of the overwhelming application of the principle of freedom of contract, fees are subject to various control mechanisms: statutory or professional rules on lawyers' ethics, complaint mechanisms available to clients, and court assessment of reasonable costs in individual cases.

In many countries, the establishment by the bar of minimum fee levels would be an anticompetitive practice, and competition authorities have turned their attention to this issue in recent years. There has, however, been no competition objection to the setting of tariffs for lawyers' fees by statute, and many civil law jurisdictions have such tariffs. Nevertheless, it appears that no such tariffs are bindingly exclusive: lawyers in Germany, for example, may decide to charge the tariff sum or charge on some other basis, and the current state of the market is such that a lawyer who will be prepared to work on the tariff basis can always be found. In Greece, minimum fees for lawyers are established by statute but in practice lawyers often agree higher fees with clients. In Italy, lawyers' fees are regulated by statute, which used to establish minimum and maximum fees. Such fees in Italy vary depending on the value in dispute and on the specific activity that the lawyer carries out. The previous minimum fee levels are not applicable following the 2006 *Cippola* judgment of the European Court of Justice.[28] Maximum fee levels can also be declared contrary to the freedom to provide services within the EU.

Many jurisdictions have professional or legal rules on the regulation of lawyers' fees as between client and lawyer. These rules usually enumerate a series of factors that should be taken into account in deciding a fee for a given case. The list of such factors is frequently lengthy. As with court fees, claimants can adopt various strategies to keep lawyers' fees (initially) low, such as bringing only a part of the full claim to test their chances of success. In many jurisdictions, there is a rule that lawyers' fees should be reasonable (such as in Canada, Denmark, England and Wales, Finland and Sweden).

[27] Belgium changed the rule on this in 2007, and made the costs of private experts to be theoretically claimable, although this is expected to occur rarely. The 2004 Supreme Court case that sparked this reform illustrated a need for expert advice on quantification of the claim, and that was viewed as an essential consequence of the tort concerned.

[28] Joined Cases C-94/04 and C-202/04 *Cipolla* and *Capodarte* [2006] ECR I-11421.

The setting of factors and of tariff fee levels is usually subject to professional self-regulation rather than through entrusting the task to public or independent regulators. This observation should not be taken as criticism: how many suppliers of other services have their fees externally regulated in market economies? A peculiar system can be found in Belgium: there is in addition to a legal requirement to negotiate in 'good faith' (which is common in many other states as a matter of contract law), a professional bar obligation to 'calculate fees with modesty'.

Economic and regulatory theory indicates that an essential feature of a properly functioning market is transparent *information*. Many jurisdictions have a requirement for lawyers to provide their clients with information on fees, whether by law or under professional codes. We did not expressly seek information on this aspect, but examples include Australia, England and Wales, and Denmark. In Japan an estimate of fees must only be given on request. But in many jurisdictions parties often require information on rates, not predictions of work to be done, and therefore, importantly, not estimates of the cost of their own lawyer and the size of the risk (Ireland requires a reasonable estimate of both sides' costs at the start).

C. Cost Shifting

(i) Cost shifting regimes in general

Every jurisdiction studied has a rule on cost shifting. Almost everywhere *cost shifting (loser pays) is the general rule.* The only exceptions in the countries studied, where the general rule is that each side bears its own costs, are Lithuania and the United States of America (save for Alaska). In France, *dépenses* (roughly, official charges, although court fees are limited) are shifted but not *frais* (roughly, lawyers' costs). However, *dépenses* in France are so limited and low that the effect is that almost no costs are shifted.

There are five jurisdictions in our cohort where the general rule is that court costs are shifted but not lawyers' fees. This is so in China (save for certain exceptions, including intellectual property cases, where lawyers' fees are shifted), Russia, Japan (although shifting of court costs is the formal rule, it rarely happens in practice), Taiwan (court fees and witness costs are shifted, but not lawyers' fees, save in the Court of Third Instance and one other exception), and France (as mentioned above).

The EU Small Claims Procedure[29] includes a cost shifting rule. This Procedure is primarily of a written nature, unless an oral hearing is considered necessary by the court or tribunal or a party so requests, although the court or tribunal may refuse such a request. According to Recital 29 of the Regulation, the

> costs of the proceedings should be determined in accordance with national law. Having regard to the objectives of simplicity and cost-effectiveness, the court or tribunal should

[29] Regulation (EC) No 861/2007 of the European Parliament and of the Council of 11 July 2007 establishing a European Small Claims Procedure [2007] OJ L 199/1.

> order that an unsuccessful party be obliged to pay only the costs of the proceedings, including for example any costs resulting from the fact that the other party was represented by a lawyer or another legal professional, or any costs arising from the service or translation of documents, which are proportionate to the value of the claim or which were necessarily incurred.

Where general cost shifting (of court and lawyers' costs) applies, the following costs are shifted: court costs (at cost), witness and expert expenses (usually at cost but subject to court approval), and, in most jurisdictions, lawyers' fees and expenses (usually subject to reduction). In Spain and the United Kingdom,[30] costs cannot be awarded against the state where it has given legal aid support.

Almost every jurisdiction that has some cost shifting has rules on how to deal with the situation where the claimant only succeeds on part of the claim, or the defendant succeeds on part of a defence or counterclaim. The result, overall, is that both sides are partially successful. In general, the outcome is that the costs are apportioned between the parties. There are two opposing ways of looking at this apportioned result: either both the claimant and defendant pay some costs, or both are not awarded, or do not recover, all the costs to which they might otherwise have been entitled. In some countries such as Germany, the court states a proportion of the standard tariff costs that each party has to pay, and this results in a straightforward arithmetic calculation. In some jurisdictions, the approach might be less formulaic and the court might award a set sum to whichever parties have won on some aspects, based on a general and more impressionistic discretionary basis. Whichever approach is adopted partly depends on whether the court has a discretion to use costs awards as a sanction in respect of behaviour, which is discussed below.

Belgium changed from non-recoverability of lawyers' costs to their shiftability as recently as 2002. The change was brought about by, first, a desire to recognise the reality that numerous commercial sale agreements included a contractual right to recover the expenses of enforcement; secondly, re-examination of a view that lawyers' fees were not part of the damage to be compensated under contractual or extra-contractual liability; and thirdly, the impact of implementation of the Late Payment Directive, under which the creditor is entitled to claim reasonable compensation from the debtor for all relevant recovery costs incurred through the debtor's late payment.[31] Since the reform, there has been a dramatic fall in the number of cases brought. Pending further empirical research, it is as yet unclear whether there may have been 'too many' cases beforehand, or whether there are 'too few' now.

As shown in Table 1, for the purpose of shifting lawyers' fees, an established tariff system exists in many states, either in legislation (as is usually the case), in rules of courts, in rules for specific courts, or in lawyers' codes of conduct. These tariffs

[30] This is probably the case in a number of other states.

[31] Art 3(1)(e) of Directive 2000/35/EC of the European Parliament and of the Council of 29 June 2000 on combating late payment in commercial transactions [2000] OJ L 200/35.

are set out according to value of the case, specific tasks, and complexity of the case. Countries with tariff systems are: Austria, Australia (not all courts), Belgium, Czech Republic, Denmark, Estonia (a maximum recoverable), Germany, Hungary, Lithuania, the Netherlands, Poland,[32] and Scotland (partial). In Spain the voluntary tariff system established by the Bar is observed in practice. Use of a tariff by the Bar has been outlawed by the competition authorities in France and Japan. England and Wales have introduced fixed recoverable fees for some specific types of cases.[33]

Some jurisdictions that have a loser pays rule provide for some 'no costs' exceptions. Australia has a 'no costs' rule for public interest cases, and maximum recoverable costs in certain types of cases. England and Wales effectively has no cost shifting for small claims (under £5,000),[34] employment tribunal claims,[35] and family cases:[36] in the first two instances, the rules technically empower the court to award costs, but general practice is that costs are not awarded save in very exceptional cases. In the Netherlands courts are given a discretion on costs awards under the 'application procedure', which applies particularly in family cases. Some of these exceptions may have arisen fortuitously but a consistent feature appears to be an attempt to identify particular situations in which it makes no sense for individuals who have limited resources to find them depleted by unnecessary litigation, and to avoid incentivising proliferation of work within the process.

Where the cost shifting rule is applied, it is almost always not absolute, since the *court* almost always has general *discretion* over the award of costs, or at least a degree of discretion to alter the general loser pays rule. A justification for this is to enable the court to produce a just result. Some rules specify that a winner should be deprived of costs if he has put the loser to the expense of the litigation unnecessarily, when the proceedings could have been avoided and the case settled earlier. Some rules exempt a losing defendant from costs liability if it was reasonable to defend a case, such as if the true facts were unclear at the start, or the law required clarification, such as on a point of general public importance.

A justification for cost shifting that is seen in statements made in policy documents or rules is that the rule is intended to provide some equality of arms as between litigants of possibly widely differing resources. The cost shift cannot provide an increase in resources to an impecunious party, but it can to some extent deter (but not of itself prevent) a wealthy party from spending large sums on his case. As such, the rule encourages rationality and proportionate behaviour.

[32] Although there is a tariff in Poland, costs are not in practice predictable, since the rules permit lawyers to apply for the tariff sum to be multiplied in complex cases (and it is reported that the courts readily accede and do not tend to apply significant oversight) or be reduced in simple cases.

[33] See chs 7–9 below.

[34] CPR, Rule 27.14; see Jackson LJ (n 13 above) ch 49.

[35] Employment Tribunal Rules, Rule 38(1); see Jackson LJ (n 13 above) ch 50.

[36] Family Proceedings Rules 1991, Rule 2.71, effective from 3 April 2006; see Jackson LJ (n 13 above) ch 51.

(ii) The recoverability gap

In many jurisdictions where costs are shifted, there is a gap between the costs that the winner receives and his or her actual expenditure. Figures quoted by national reporters for the unrecovered percentages of total expenditure include Australia (30–45 per cent), Canada, England and Wales (25 per cent), Estonia, France, Germany, Hong Kong (up to 40 per cent), Latvia, the Netherlands, New Zealand (up to 80 per cent), Norway, Poland, Scotland, Singapore (33–50 per cent), and Switzerland.

The existence of the 'recoverability gap' has led to difficulties because its existence and effects are not always understood. Directive 2004/48/EC[37] aims to increase the number of enforcement actions of intellectual property infringements and provides that the loser shall pay the winner's costs in full. Those who were involved in the enactment of the Directive appear to have been acting on the assumption that all Member States had a 100 per cent cost shifting rule. The result of implementing this rule in the Netherlands has been that the number of intellectual property injunction claims has *fallen* because claimants are now concerned that they face an unacceptable risk if they lose a case.[38] Hence, the result of the implementation of the Directive has been the opposite of that intended, simply because the detailed operation of a national cost shifting rule was overlooked.

II. Funding

A. Funding regimes in general

In every legal system, the parties need to fund the costs of litigation that they are required to bear. The principal possible methods of funding litigation are:

a. Personal funds.
b. Funds or services provided as a benefit of membership of an association, such as a trade union.
c. Legal expenses insurance (LEI). The traditional type is before-the-event (BTE) insurance. In the past decade, after-the-event (ATE) bespoke litigation funding has become available for certain types of case in some states such as Germany, and in England and Wales after-the-event insurance has become available to cover the risk of loser pays liability in association with a conditional fee agreement.

[37] Directive 2004/48/EC of the European Parliament and of the Council of 29 April 2004 on the enforcement of intellectual property rights [2004] OJ L 157/32, with corrigendum at L 195/16.

[38] PMM van der Grinten, 'Challenges for the Creation of a European Law of Civil Procedure' 19 April 2009, available at http://papers.ssrn.com/sol3/papers.cfm?abstract_id=1392006.

d. Funding or services provided by the state (legal aid).
e. Funding by a lawyer for his own services and maybe disbursements to cover the services provided by experts or others. Funding may take various forms, such as acting on an unpaid basis (*pro bono*), a deferral of billing, or waiver of fees in the event of failure. A fee arrangement may also include a success fee, whether as part of a contingency fee or some other arrangement. Some states refer to *pro bono* work as 'legal aid'.
f. Funding by an independent third party.

These sources of funding are discussed in further detail below. Not all of them are available everywhere. There are historical reasons for the development or the absence of certain approaches and combinations of funding systems in a given jurisdiction.

Issues of funding are topical. Currently, almost all governments are refusing to make more money available for legal aid—quite the reverse.[39] However, the existence of proportionate, predictable and low costs regimes can at least tend to maintain an existing legal aid scheme. The most recent and interesting development concerns private funding.

B. Personal or association funding

Every country permits funding from personal resources, but such resources are unlikely to cover the cost of funding for many individuals or SMEs. Membership of trade or professional associations frequently provides LEI benefits. In some states, such membership is common: in Denmark 80 per cent of the working population belong to a union.

C. Legal Expenses Insurance (LEI)

In those jurisdictions where costs are predictable, insurance for legal expenses occurs frequently. The existence of wide pools of insured persons means that premiums can be low (the many pay for the few). Accordingly, (BTE) LEI is widespread in civil law systems, exemplified by Germany and Austria, where tariffs exist for lawyers' fees and, crucially, for shifted loser pays fees. LEI is reasonably or widely available in Denmark, England and Wales, Estonia, Finland, France, Germany (43 per cent of the population), Hungary, Ireland, Japan, the Netherlands and Spain.

ATE LEI arose in England and Wales[40] from 1995 to insure claimants against the adverse costs risk that appeared when conditional fee agreements (CFAs)

[39] The exceptions seem to be New Zealand, Japan and the Netherlands, noted below.
[40] See chs 7–9 below.

largely replaced legal aid. Premiums were initially paid for by the claimant through a reduction in damages, but the rules were changed from 1999 to make the full CFA fee and ATE premium recoverable from the defendant. This was intended to facilitate CFA funding but provoked huge costs wars, with insurers trying to reduce their exposure. The media industry has been particularly vocal in complaining against the combined disproportionate effect of having to reimburse CFA success fees and high ATE premiums in libel cases. Allegations of settlement blackmail arise. The recent *Review of Civil Litigation Costs* by Lord Justice Jackson, which recommends that CFA success fees and ATE premiums should not be shiftable, may signal the end of the ATE experiment, partly because ATE is inevitably expensive, with a limited pool of insured persons paying premiums and a limited number of insurers.

D. Legal aid

Some formal amelioration from litigation cost applies in every jurisdiction apart from Russia and the United States of America. In the United States, the availability of contingency fees (in addition to hourly or other negotiated fees) makes legal aid unnecessary, although there are situations where lawyers decline to act on contingency fees, such as in injunction cases, where public funding is necessary. Countries adopt different approaches to 'legal aid', and it can mean quite different things. The principal variants are:

a. The lawyer acts free to the party, but works *pro bono*. We discuss this funding mechanism in the next section. In some jurisdictions it is understood to be a part of the legal aid system. The difficulty to draw a clear borderline is apparent in countries where the state pays, in return for *pro bono* work, an annual sum to the Bar Association, which is allocated to pensions for lawyers, as is the case in Austria.
b. The lawyer is paid by the state. This is fairly common, but far from universal.
c. Assisted parties may be required to make a contribution towards the cost, either making a payment to their lawyer or to the state.
d. The assistance might only cover provision of the services of a lawyer, and not cover opponents' costs because the latter are not shifted, as in Taiwan of Japan. Hence the legal aid budget is potentially smaller than it might be in other states where costs are shifted and the fund indemnifies the liability.
e. Where costs are shiftable, the 'legal aid' assistance might cover opponents' costs if the case is lost, or it might not. Winning defendants cannot recover their costs against legally aided claimants in Spain and in England and Wales. Individuals remain liable for winning opponents' costs in Finland, Italy, the Netherlands, Sweden and Switzerland. This rule presumably applies whenever representation is *pro bono*, ie by a lawyer on an unpaid basis: this is certainly the case in Bulgaria. It is not entirely clear whether the rule acts as a barrier to justice, a

disincentive to bring unmerited claims or an incentive for settlement (whether justified or not).[41]

f. An application for legal aid might be determined by the court (Austria, Bulgaria, Germany, Greece, Norway, Poland, Romania, Taiwan), by the bar (Czech Republic, Spain), or by a public authority (England and Wales, Finland, France, Hong Kong, Ireland, Latvia, the Netherlands, New Zealand, Scotland, Singapore, Taiwan). Where a party has to apply to the court after the start of a case, the problem is that the applicant may not know, or be able to predict, whether he or she will be awarded legal aid, or how much assistance, without commencing a claim. In contrast, where the decision is taken by a separate administrative authority, some advance risk assessment can be undertaken confidentially before taking the decision to start proceedings.
g. A Supplementary Legal Aid Scheme (SLAS) exists in Hong Kong to supplement the state's Ordinary Legal Aid Scheme (OLAS). The SLAS was established with seed funding from a local charity, and is sustained by levying 10 per cent of the recoveries of funded claimants. It is fairly small in scope, with very small numbers, cost and risk.[42] There has been interest from the legal profession in England and Wales in establishing a CLAF that would operate independently, but it would not be viable as long as other forms of funding are more advantageous, and it would require initial capital from some source.

Almost all legal aid systems include means and merits tests. A notable exception is France. No government wishes to expend public funds on individuals who have sufficient resources to fund their own cases, or on cases that are meritless or risky.

China introduced some limited expansion in legal aid during the 1990s. New Zealand has recently expanded its scheme. In the Netherlands, legal aid continues to cover 40 per cent of the population. However, in nearly all other countries, the trend is significant contraction. Australia reduced its expenditure by 78 per cent since 1995–96. The United Kingdom radically deconstructed legal aid since the mid-1990s, and replaced it with privatised lawyer-funded arrangements, although total legal aid expenditure is still large compared with many other countries.

In advanced economies, public funding of legal services through legal aid was a significant plank in the strong consumer protection movement from the 1960s to

[41] The rule that the public funds will not indemnify an assisted person for opponents' costs if the case is lost is a striking and important feature. It is the opposite of the rule in England and Wales that had significant practical effect prior to the deconstruction of civil legal aid and introduction of conditional fee agreements (CFAs) around 1999. The non-indemnification rule should have a powerful effect on ensuring that claimants assess the merits of cases at the outset, but might also lead to under-claiming where the merits are unclear or cannot be investigated at that stage. A number of large English group actions that failed and cost legal aid large sums might not have been commenced if this non-indemnity rule had applied.

[42] In 2007, the OLAS, which funds individuals who have financial resources under HK$165,700, had an expenditure of HK$327 million and recovered for aided persons HK$740 million. It had 15,462 applicants, of whom 7,858 were granted support. In the same year, the SLAS, which funds individuals with resources between HK$165,700 and HK$460,300 and requires contribution of 10% of recoveries, paid out HK$4.8 million and recovered HK$39 million for claimants. It had 136 applicants, of which 79 were granted support.

2000, reflected in the European Legal Aid Directive[43] that set basic parameters for Member States in providing state funding for legal services. However, during the 2000s, and especially since the financial crisis of 2008, it has been clear that governments will not provide further public funds for legal services.[44] Legal aid, therefore, generally remains available only at a very limited level for the very poor that have cases with reasonable merits.

The challenge for governments thus is to provide access to justice for those in the population who do not qualify. In many jurisdictions, this middle-income group is significant and growing. In Western Europe, for example, legal costs are often so high that many cannot afford to bring or defend a claim: the United Kingdom coined the phrase 'middle-income-not-eligible-for-legal-aid' (MINELAs) for this group. In Central and Eastern Europe, the income level of the majority of the population has been low but the number of better paid people is rising, so a similar problem will increasingly arise there.

E. Funding by lawyers

(i) Pro bono services

Lawyers may provide working capital for their own work and even for disbursements through a number of mechanisms. One option is to agree at the start to work for nothing. It is not entirely clear to which extent *pro bono* advice and representation are provided and whether they have a future. There has been an interesting expansion of *pro bono* in Australia, and it is frequent in Canada. It may be the case that *pro bono* will be limited to provision by large commercial law firms, as part of their corporate social responsibility (and marketing) programmes. Small firms may have limited ability to afford significant *pro bono* service. The formal requirements of litigation processes have the result that claimants often need expert representation in at least some types of case, but that the inherent cost may inhibit both lawyers from providing free service and clients from accessing it.

(ii) Flexible billing

The practice of a lawyer funding litigation through deferring the presentation of bills is common. The working capital requirement is easier for the lawyer to carry where his investment in a particular case is small and he has a portfolio of cases that can produce regular cash flow. Although many lawyers prefer hourly rate billing, many who advise consumers operate on the basis of charging a modest or

[43] Council Directive 2002/8/EC of 27 January 2003 to improve access to justice in cross-border disputes by establishing minimum common rules relating to legal aid for such disputes [2002] OJ L 26/41.

[44] Civil legal aid was severely restricted in Sweden in 1997, see F Regan, 'The Swedish Legal Services Policy Remix: The Shift from Public Legal Aid to Private Legal Expense Insurance' (2003) 30 *Journal of Law and Society* 49.

nil file opening fee, coupled with awaiting the outcome of a case (a formal or informal success fee arrangement) before submitting a final account. Such deferral of fees can often be accompanied by a formal or informal agreement that a premium will be charged in the event of success: specific arrangements on success fees, contingency fees and similar arrangements are discussed below.

(iii) Success fees

Many jurisdictions permit success fees, payable only if the lawyer wins, as an element (but never a single element) in lawyers' remuneration. The success fee would typically be paid in addition to a basic fee. Sometimes, an initial fee is paid at the start of the case, and a success fee—or nothing further—is paid on conclusion. This approach clearly gives predictability.

Table 2 (an Appendix to this study[45]) summarises the available information on success and contingency fees. Success fees are banned in Austria, Singapore, and technically prohibited but used in practice in Russia. The success fee is capped in some states, such as 20 per cent of the sum awarded by the court in Greece, 25 per cent in Australia (Federal Court) and the Czech Republic, and 100 per cent of the basic fee (usually, work done multiplied by an hourly rate) in the United Kingdom (in employment cases a cap of 35 per cent of damages was introduced in 2010 on any fees based on a percentage of damages).[46]

(iv) Contingency fees

The term 'contingency fee' is used with different meanings. It usually refers to payment of an integral fee being a proportion of the recovery and solely dependent on success. However, this might be a single, integral fee, or it might be part of a total compensation arrangement that might also include other sums (eg a basic fee or a fee paid on a low hourly rate).

The difference between a success fee and a contingency fee is (normally) that the former may be any sum whereas the latter is specifically linked to the amount recovered. The latter is intended to incentivise the lawyer to maximize recovery, and to align the economic interests of the client and the lawyer.

There is a strong cultural resistance in many states to fees in which a lawyer can be paid a percentage of the money recovered (*pactum de quota litis*). Such an arrangement is banned in Australia (except for commercial cases), Austria, Belgium, Cyprus, the Czech Republic, Denmark, France, Greece, Ireland, Luxembourg, Malta, the Netherlands, New Zealand, Norway, Poland (but found in practice), Portugal, Romania, Russia (unenforceable but used), Singapore, Sweden (but permitted in special circumstances, eg class action), and United Kingdom. Contingency fees are permitted in Canada, Estonia, Finland (rarely

[45] See pp 132–33 below.

[46] The Damages-Based Agreement Regulations 2010/1206 at http://www.opsi.gov.uk/si/si2010/pdf/uksi_20101206_en.pdf. See Practice Note at http://www.lawsociety.org.uk/productsandservices/practicenotes/damagesbasedagreements.

used), Germany (in fairly rare circumstances), Hungary, Italy, Japan, Lithuania, Slovakia, Slovenia, Spain (rarely used), Taiwan and notably in the United States of America. In China, contingency fees were permitted until 2006, since when they have been prohibited in collective actions, criminal cases and administrative litigation. In other kinds of cases the contingency fee is now capped at 30 per cent of the recovery.

Few states provide a general statement of principle, such as that to be found in Norway, that a lawyer may not take an assignment where personal economic interests may come into conflict with the assignment and the client's interests.

Common law jurisdictions, apart from the United States of America, have traditionally banned anyone other than a principal party to litigation from having an interest in the proceeds of litigation or interfering in it, through the rules of maintenance and champerty.[47] However, such prohibitions have recently been amended (by legislation in England,[48] and by the courts in Australia[49]) as a matter of pragmatism, in order to facilitate the development of private funding so as to maintain access to justice in the face of the contraction of legal aid. Such prohibitions have not operated to ban insurance against liability and costs, nor the conduct of the defence of a case by an insurer or the prosecution of a case by an LEI insurer (for example in Germany, where rules on maintenance and champerty have not applied).

In Germany, contingency fees were permitted in 2008 as an exception in an individual case where the client would otherwise be prevented due to his financial circumstances from pursuing his legal rights (ie impecunious, or could not take the financial risk). Such agreements must be in writing. They may permit 'no win no fee', or a reduced fee, if there is a reasonable supplement payable for success.

Contingency fees were introduced recently in Canada as a means of increasing access to justice, especially in personal injury cases, where they are now widely used, but there have been no studies on whether the previous lack in efficiency and effectiveness of legal services has been remedied as a result of introducing them. The theoretical justification was to unlock funding by lawyers, and to align the lawyer's interests with those of the client in obtaining expeditious resolution of the matter with the maximum recovery. In 2006, the Canadian Supreme Court prohibited the practice of awarding a 'risk premium' for a lawyer who takes on a meritorious risky case as preventing predictability of cost exposure by defendants.[50] However, such awards continue to be made because risk is one of the factors taken into account in discretionary awards.

Contingency fees form an essential funding mechanism for litigation in the United States of America. But they are not the only device; attorneys there are free to accept work on whatever basis they choose, eg an hourly rate or fixed fee.

[47] Maintenance is the giving of assistance or encouragement to one of the parties to litigation by a person who has neither interest in the litigation nor any other motive recognised by law as justifying the interference. Champerty is a form of maintenance whereby the maintainer has an interest in the proceeds of the litigation. See *Giles v Thompson* [1993] All ER 321, HL.

[48] Courts and Legal Services Act 1990, s 58; Access to Justice Act 2000, s 27.

[49] *Campbells Cash and Carry Pty Ltd v Fostif Pty Ltd* [2006] HCA 41.

[50] *Walker v Ritchie* [2006] 2 SCR 428.

Certain types of case are less suitable for contingency fees, such as cases that do not involve quantifiable damages or do not have a statutory one way fee shifting rule. Attorneys tend to have a portfolio of contingency fee cases, comprising an acceptable mixture of individual risks. Claimant lawyers' fees in class actions are approved by the court, so they are not subject to contingency agreements with clients.

In Europe, debate over the extension of contingency fees has arisen in relation to the possible spread of collective actions. A proposal to introduce contingency fees for use in a new class action mechanism was rejected in Sweden in 2003, but permitted in Poland in 2010, although with success fees capped at 20 percent.

(v) Conditional Fee Agreements (CFAs) in England and Wales

After it became clear that significant public funding for lawyers was unsustainable, and legal aid had become successively restricted, the funding function largely privatized from 1995, through the creation of CFAs. There were many teething problems with CFAs, associated insurance (ATE), and with the coincidence of the new front-loading of work through pre-action protocols, manifested in a sequence of 'costs wars'. The Jackson Review signals a retreat from CFAs in favour of other forms of private funding, assisted by more fixed costs.[51]

F. Third Party Litigation Funders

An important recent development is the creation of third party funders (LFs), notably spreading from Australia (typically with a 20–40 per cent fee) and in some European jurisdictions (Austria, Germany, Ireland, the Netherlands (where the fee can be 25–40 per cent of the recovery) and the United Kingdom. The fee is not recoverable under the civil law tariff systems, so is deducted from the sum awarded or recovered. Some private funders have also existed in the United States for some years, and they appear to be expanding quickly.

III. Conclusions

The major findings with regard to the national costs and funding regimes are as follows.

The litigation system in every jurisdiction studied gives rise to the same basic elements of costs: charges for use of the court and its personnel, evidential costs for witnesses and experts, and lawyers' fees. In other words, there are costs for the use of the litigation process and costs for the services of intermediaries.

[51] See chs 7–9 below.

Almost every country levies some charge for use of its courts. This is always based on fixed rules, involving a tariff system, so is fully predictable. The charge usually varies with the sum in dispute, which introduces an element of proportionality, and tapers off as fees rise. The leading exception, where almost no cost is levied for access to the courts, is France.

Most countries do not seek to recover the full economic cost of the public justice system from user fees, but provide some funding from general taxation, although the proportion between user and general funding is rarely clear.

Witnesses of fact are reimbursed their expenses, but rarely otherwise paid. Expert witnesses are paid for their time, usually on an hourly rate basis regulated by the court.

Lawyers' fees to clients are almost always subject to open negotiation rather than regulation. Billing is frequently based on hourly rates. Some civil law jurisdictions have tariffs but they are rarely binding. Tariffs set by local Bars have been banned almost everywhere as anti-competitive.

In almost all jurisdictions, the general position is that the loser pays the costs of the court, evidence and lawyer. However, the court often has discretion over awarding costs in cases where each side wins some points. Court discretion is also intended to maintain an ability to sanction poor behavior during the litigation process. Some jurisdictions have rules on how costs are split when both sides have some success.

Some jurisdictions have exceptions to the general 'loser pays' rule in order to overcome funding barriers or encourage certain types of claims.

The United States of America are almost alone in maintaining a rule that each side pays their own costs.

In almost all jurisdictions there is a gap between the winner's recoverable and actual costs. The gap can be very high in some states, requiring a winning party to have significant finance.

There are several potential sources of funding for litigation, although options in individual cases may be limited. LEI has developed widely as a principal source of litigation finance in many civil law states as a result of the lower cost of their civil procedures and the predictable cost based on tariffs. Almost every jurisdiction has some form of independent support funding that is referred to as 'legal aid' but the modes of operation differ widely. Almost all state funding is subject to merits and means tests. Government funding for court and lawyers' fees is generally contracting, and this is placing greater emphasis on methods of funding by lawyers or others, especially in resolving low value disputes. Success fees are widely permitted, but there is strong resistance to fees in which damages are reduced. Independent commercial funders have emerged recently in some countries.

SECTION 2

THE PRICE OF LITIGATION: A COMPARISON OF JURISDICTIONS

I. Purpose and Presentation of the Case Studies

The central quantitative comparative challenge is to identify those jurisdictions and systems that are more or less expensive than others. Where is it cheap or expensive to litigate? There have been few previous attempts to undertake such a comparison, certainly not on a relatively large scale. The obvious follow-up questions are why certain systems produce higher or lower costs than others, and whether such systems should entertain some reform designed to lower costs or to provide alternative pathways for certain types of claims.

In order to be able to make such a comparison, albeit in broad terms, examples of cases were selected and sent to the practitioner correspondents involved in this study, each of whom is a noted expert in his or her jurisdiction. Since costs can vary significantly between different types of cases, nine characteristic scenarios were selected, to give a range of case types and costs. Typical fact patterns were chosen which, it was assumed, might arise in all jurisdictions concerned, such as a damages claim following a road traffic accident, a divorce, a wrongful dismissal, or larger commercial matters, and including injunctive and damages remedies. The contributing practitioners were asked to give their best estimates of the likely costs in the case studies.

The replies received from national practitioners are available in their national reports.[52] Summaries of those responses and data are set out below in the following tables:

—Table 3 (an Appendix to this study[53]) shows the total minimum cost of each case to the claimant, broken down into lawyers' fees and court fees (including other process costs where appropriate). It also notes where non-court alternative procedures would be preferred or would be available. These data are reproduced in the first four bar charts under each case study. In some instances, national reporters were unable to state total costs, or to itemise costs as between lawyers' and court costs: these instances are noted in the Table.

—Table 4 (an Appendix to this study[54]) shows the total costs of each case for both claimant and defendant. These data are reproduced in the fifth bar chart under each case study.

[52] See n 12 above.
[53] See pp 134–56 below.
[54] See pp 157–79 below.

The figures in the tables are stated in the currencies used by the national reporters and also in a hypothetical unit of currency, the so-called 'international dollar' (USD Intl). In comparing international data in different currencies, it is standard practice to calculate the Purchasing Power Parities (PPP), so as to reflect the differences in local price levels and purchasing power, and hence present a more realistic comparison of costs. The PPP is calculated according to a formula which takes into account the exchange rates as well as costs of living in the respective countries. The PPP factors for 2009 are based on data provided by the International Monetary Fund (IMF). The PPP conversion factors are calculated using these factors (constant values for 2009), and are defined as the number of national currency units per USD Intl Currency conversion rates, all as at 21 October 2009, are at Table 6 (an Appendix to this study).[55]

The nine case studies are set out sequentially below. For each case study, the relevant data from the tables is presented in the form of five charts:

1. Disaggregated total costs, showing lawyers' fees and court fees separately;
2. Aggregate total cost to a claimant of bringing a claim;
3. Lawyers' fees for the claimant only;
4. Court fees for the claimant only;
5. Comparison of total costs for claimant and defendant, ignoring any cost shifting.

Each case study is also accompanied by, first, our summaries on the general findings of the data and, secondly, comments from the national reporters on particular aspects that have not been included in the charts. Our summaries attempt to indicate results that are 'high' or 'low' in comparison with the data given for the other countries shown, but it must be recognised that such comments involve subjective interpretation and are made simply in order to assist in giving readers a general impression.

Data has only been included in a chart if the national reporter specified a figure. As a result, in some cases, one or the other country has been excluded from the charts because a single figure was not identified. In all these cases, the data and national reporter's comments have been included in the tables and usually in the explanatory notes, which make clear why a given country was excluded from inclusion in the chart. The usual reason why a national reporter was unable to specify a single accurate figure, particularly for lawyers' fees, was that the amount of the fee depended on the amount of work done, and such amount might vary considerably and be unquantifiable in advance. This proved to be generally the case in relation to any jurisdiction where lawyers' costs were not fixed by a tariff. National reporters usually quoted a range of costs in such circumstances, which often varied widely, and it would have been misleading to have included a single figure. However, the occurrence of such instances clearly indicates the level of unpredictability of costs that can occur in such jurisdictions, and raises issues over the proportionality of total costs to sums in dispute.

[55] See p 184 below.

In some cases the reporters indicated that litigation was not the recommended or popular route of obtaining redress, and in other cases it was expressly stated that litigation is not used as a response to the given legal problem: instead, the respondents suggested administrative or insurance routes. In some such cases, no costs of litigation were stated, and sometimes the costs of the alternative dispute resolution pathway could be stated, enabling comparisons to be drawn.

General conclusions on the findings from all the data are given at the end of this Section.

II. Features and Limitations of the Data

Our data set has the advantage of including a variety of civil law and common law jurisdictions. Attempts were made to obtain figures from further jurisdictions, notably the United States of America, but were unsuccessful.

Various limitations of the data presented here should be noted.[56] First, since civil procedure varies between jurisdictions, the case examples were described in broad terms, so as to avoid assumptions about the extent of work that would be necessary for final resolution of each case. This result inherently required national practitioner respondents to make a number of assumptions about a case, such as the extent of pleading, oral and documentary evidence, expertise, duration, amount and so on that would affect costs. Almost all responses involved some elements that are fixed costs and other elements that are estimates.

Further assumptions were sometimes required over the amount at stake: the case studies tended to avoid stating many precise figures or details, since the economic value of money or such matters as employment remuneration varies between jurisdictions. In order to reflect such differences, the PPP calculation described above was made.

Furthermore, the case studies did not specify information on the procedural conduct of the parties, which might again increase or reduce costs. The reason for this was that different legal systems have different responses to such behaviour (eg delaying tactics, calling of experts or offers of settlement). More importantly, the kinds of conduct that trigger such responses differ from one jurisdiction to another. Had information on procedural behaviour been included, there would have been a risk of distorting the picture.

We have already noted that in countries where lawyers' fees are calculated on a per-hour basis it was quite difficult to estimate the costs of a particular case. This was particularly clear in England and Wales; and Ireland is often excluded from the comparative tables whenever such tables include lawyers' fees.

[56] For an overview of the difficulties with studies such as this see CA Kern, 'Perception, Performance and Politics: Recent Approaches to the Qualitative Comparison of Civil Justice Systems' in S Vogenauer and C Hodges (eds), *Civil Justice Systems in Europe: Implications for Choice of Forum and Choice of Contract Law* (Oxford, Hart Publishing, 2010) ch 4.

Whilst reporters were asked to give figures for the costs of experts and witnesses, such figures are not always clear. Most court fees do not include remuneration for experts, witnesses, and other disbursements—some respondents indicated these costs if they are separate, others did not.

Accordingly, the data should be viewed as *preliminary*, giving a general impression, and not as a set of perfectly accurate figures. However, the results of the case studies provide a general overview and comparison of costs of roughly similar cases in the jurisdictions included in this study, based on the opinions of experienced national practitioners. The data make it possible to compare not only the overall costs in these case studies, but also specific elements of costs, such as court fees and lawyers' fees. Our study, with all its methodological difficulties, does produce data that may be considered to be at least indicative of the costs of civil litigation in a given jurisdiction, as compared to other jurisdictions. It also shows, as discussed below, that there are indeed both comparatively cheap and relatively expensive legal systems, and that the results sometimes differ from one type of case to another.

III. Case Studies

Case study 1: Small claim

Scenario

Repayment to a consumer of €200 price paid for product not delivered.

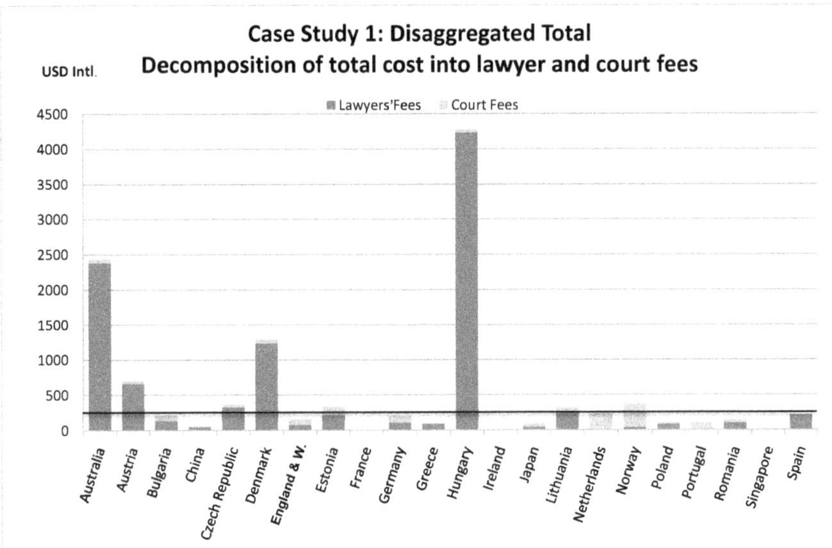

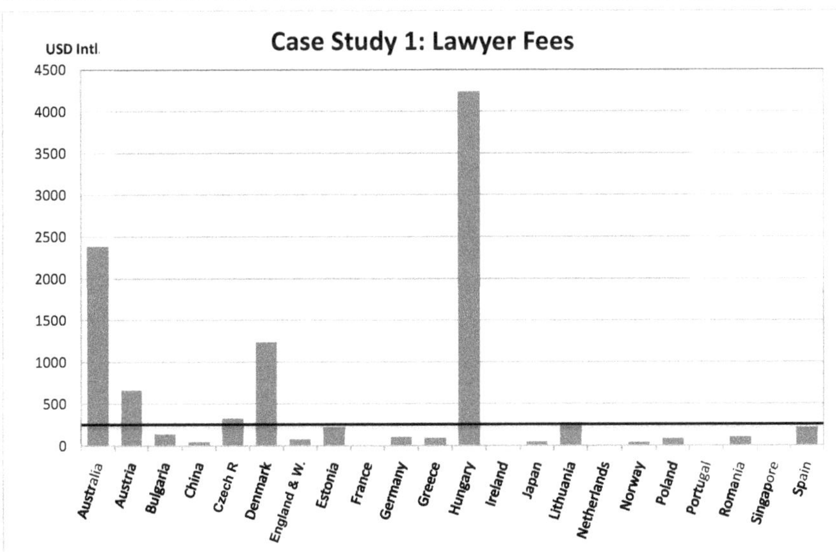

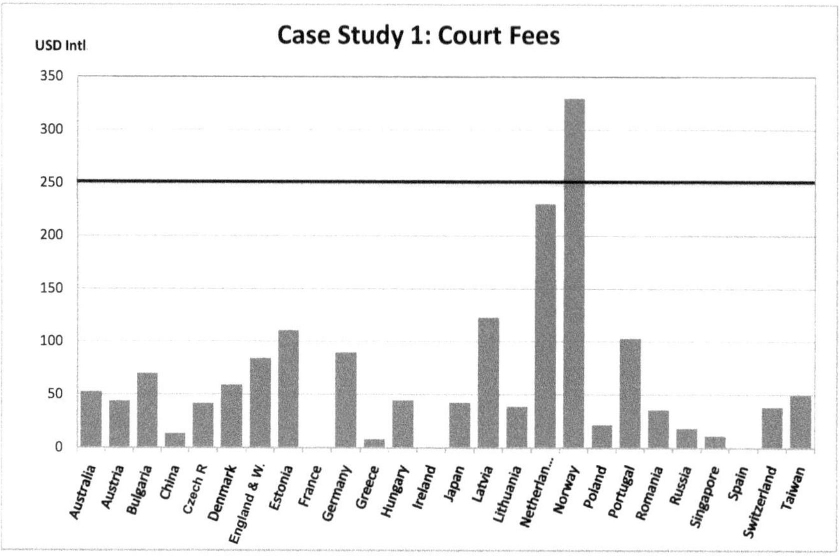
Case Study 1: Court Fees
USD Intl
350
300
250
200
150
100
50
0
Australia
Austria
Bulgaria
China
Czech R
Denmark
England & W.
Estonia
France
Germany
Greece
Hungary
Ireland
Japan
Latvia
Lithuania
Netherlan...
Norway
Poland
Portugal
Romania
Russia
Singapore
Spain
Switzerland
Taiwan

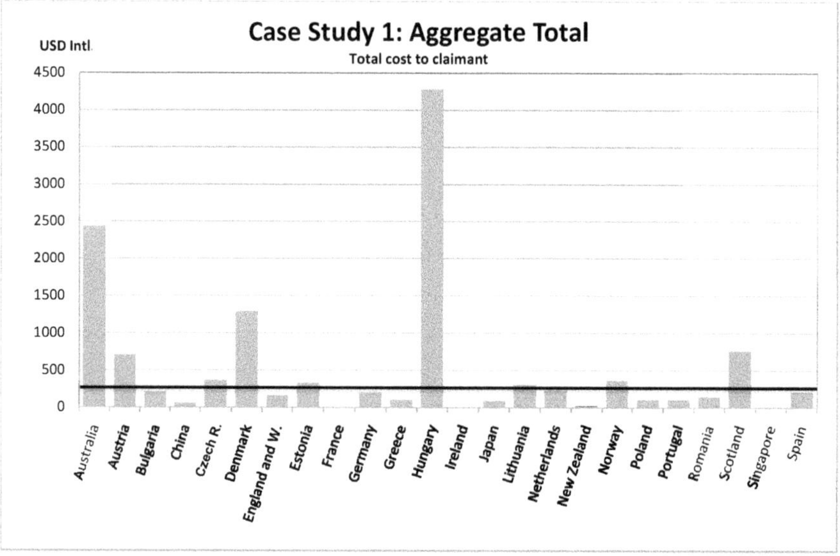
Case Study 1: Aggregate Total
Total cost to claimant
USD Intl
4500
4000
3500
3000
2500
2000
1500
1000
500
0
Australia
Austria
Bulgaria
China
Czech R.
Denmark
England and W.
Estonia
France
Germany
Greece
Hungary
Ireland
Japan
Lithuania
Netherlands
New Zealand
Norway
Poland
Portugal
Romania
Scotland
Singapore
Spain

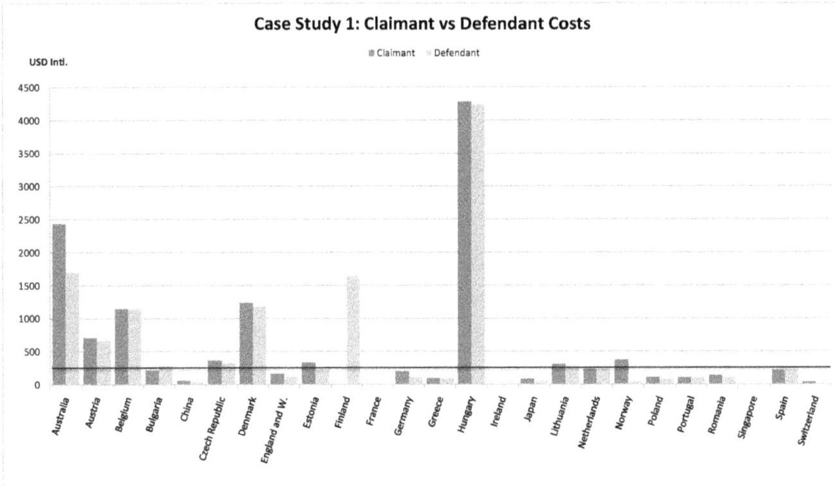

Findings

The black horizontal line in the charts shows the USD Intl equivalent of the value of the claim, €200. The most striking finding is that the cost to the claimant (and the total cost, whoever bears it) is not proportionate to the sum in dispute in a significant number of countries.

The charts show that the total costs fall into three categories: low and proportionate costs, costs that are approximately equal to the sum in dispute, and costs that are far in excess of the sum in dispute. In the first category are (in ascending order) France, Ireland, Singapore, China, Japan and Greece, followed by Poland, Portugal, England and Wales, Romania, Germany, Bulgaria and Spain. In the second category are Estonia, Lithuania, the Czech Republic, and Norway. Costs to claimants are much higher in Austria and Denmark, very high in Australia and extremely high in Hungary. The high amounts are due to lawyers' fees, which are notably higher than others for Hungary, Australia and Denmark. Lawyers' fees far exceed court fees in nearly all countries.

The same pattern of banding (low, slightly higher and very high bands) is apparent for court fees.

The court fees and lawyers' fees quoted are, however, misleading in that court proceedings would in most jurisdictions not be the pathway of choice for resolving such a small case. As appears from the explanatory notes below, many jurisdictions have alternative pathways that involve lower or minimal costs, ranging from small claims or expedited procedures (Estonia, France, Ireland, Singapore and Spain) to insurance (Denmark), to a dedicated consumer tribunal (Latvia, Norway), to a regulatory procedure (Russia).

Explanatory notes

Canada: litigation would not be a recommended route for such a case, but if a case was brought the total cost might be C$2,500.

Denmark: the consumer would probably have insurance and have to pay only DKK 0—DKK 2,000.

Estonia: this claim could be submitted in an expedited procedure as a payment order matter. In that case, the state fee would be EEK 750. If the matter is not resolved in an expedited procedure, the additional state fee (EEK 250) would have to be paid.

France: there would be no costs to parties as the case will be brought before *juridiction de proximité.*

Hong Kong: costs were quoted as being 'minimal'.

Ireland: the preferred option is a small claims procedure, which is free of charge.

Latvia: only court fees are quoted. Lawyers' costs depend on the amount of work involved. An alternative path is the Consumer Rights Protection Centre (free of charge to consumer).

New Zealand: the only fee would be the filing fee of NZ$30.

Norway: the costs quoted here are for the small claims court, but instead the preferred option would be the Consumer Dispute Committee, which is free of charge.

Russia: the respondents recommended the regulatory enforcement as the preferred path.

Singapore: the costs quoted here are for the Small Claims Tribunal.

Spain: the claim would be brought in a special procedure (*monitorio*: small debts proceedings) designed for claims under €30,000.

Case study 2: Divorce

Scenario

Divorce between husband on average income (say €50,000 pa), wife with no income, two children, living in an average home.

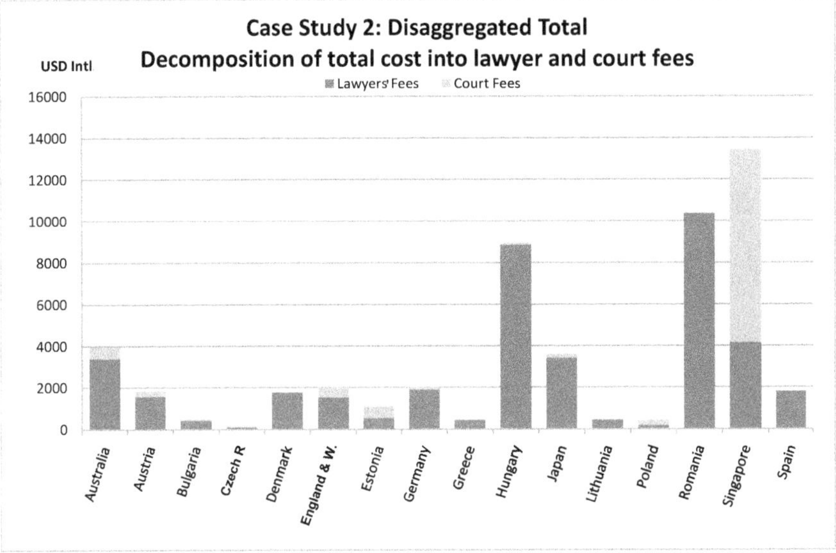

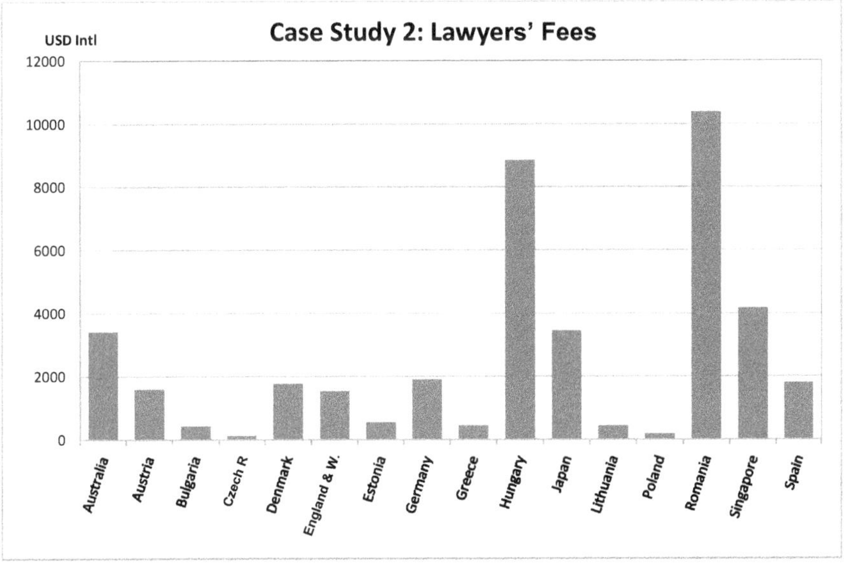

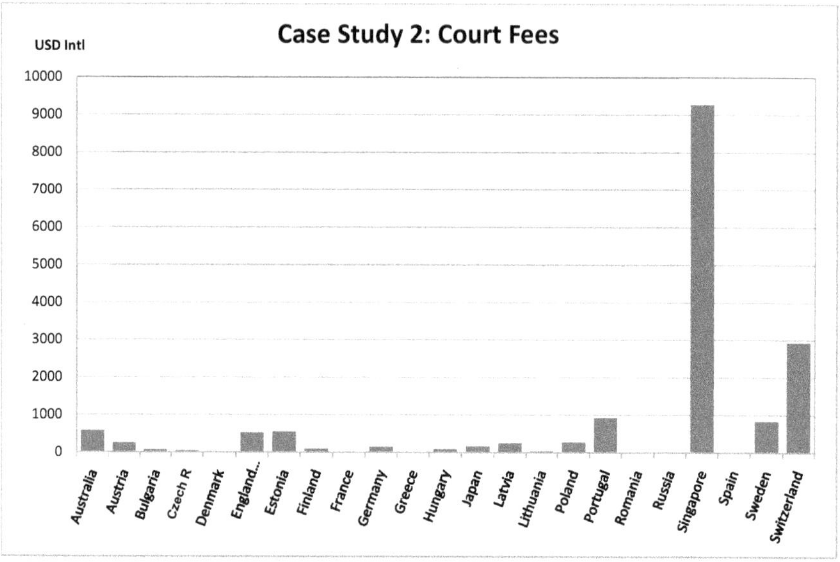
Case Study 2: Court Fees
USD Intl
10000
9000
8000
7000
6000
5000
4000
3000
2000
1000
0
Australia
Austria
Bulgaria
Czech R
Denmark
England...
Estonia
Finland
France
Germany
Greece
Hungary
Japan
Latvia
Lithuania
Poland
Portugal
Romania
Russia
Singapore
Spain
Sweden
Switzerland

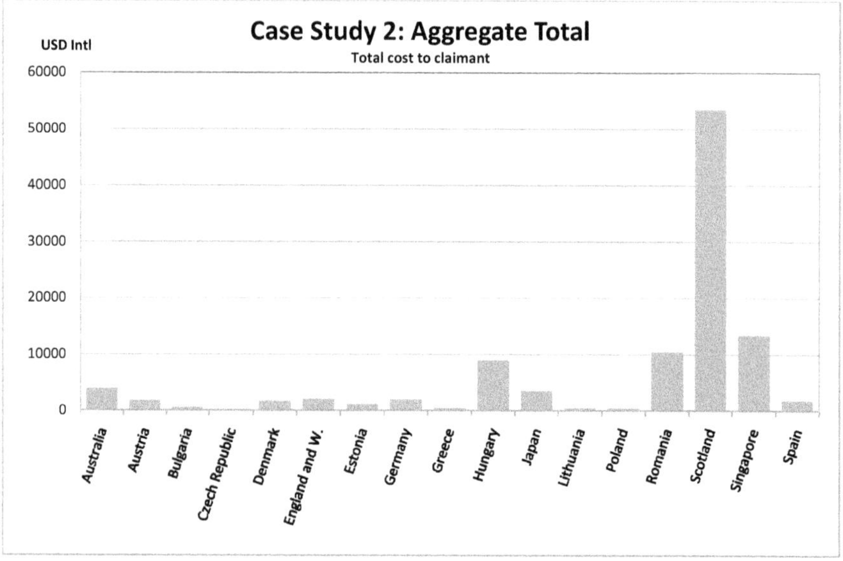
Case Study 2: Aggregate Total
Total cost to claimant
USD Intl
60000
50000
40000
30000
20000
10000
0
Australia
Austria
Bulgaria
Czech Republic
Denmark
England and W.
Estonia
Germany
Greece
Hungary
Japan
Lithuania
Poland
Romania
Scotland
Singapore
Spain

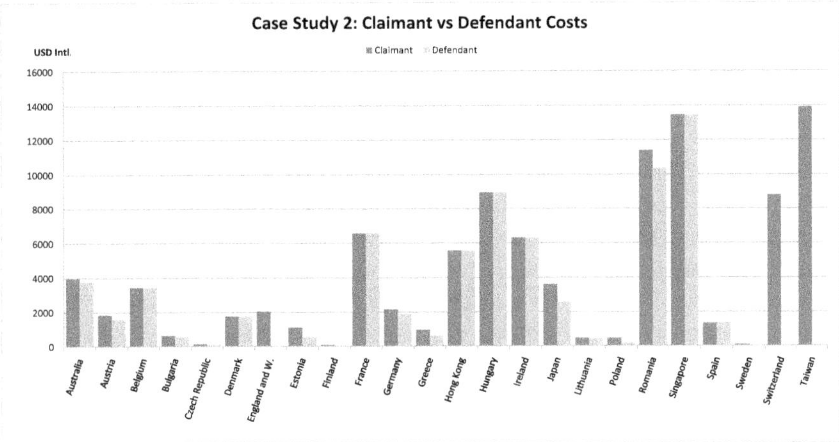

Findings

This case study illustrates that where lawyers' fees are based on hourly rates but the amount of work is difficult to predict, the final fees are impossible to establish in advance and may vary widely. The case study did not quote the value of the assets of either party (the significance of which might vary considerably in different jurisdictions), or whether the proceedings would involve extensive work for lawyers. However, the answers revealed that in several jurisdictions the procedure and substantive law could lead to variable and sometimes significant amounts of work for lawyers and hence in some jurisdictions significant and unpredictable cost (see comments below for Canada, Latvia, the Netherlands, Portugal, Russia, Scotland and Switzerland).

Where lawyers' fees have been quoted, they far exceed court costs save in Singapore and Estonia (but the latter are far lower sums than for Singapore). In Singapore, the court costs are twice as high as the lawyers' fees, and the court costs far exceed those of other countries. Total costs are low in the Czech Republic, Greece, Poland, Bulgaria and Lithuania. Total costs are notably higher in Australia and Japan, considerably higher in Hungary, Romania and Singapore.

Several countries regard mediation as a preferable route to litigation.

Explanatory notes

Canada: the range of possible costs might vary from C$2,000 to C$200,000: in view of this wide range, a figure has not been included in the charts.

Denmark: this type of case is normally dealt with out of court.

France: the amount quoted in the first chart covers only lawyers' fees, since no court fees are payable. It includes a fixed minimum fee of €4,000.

Japan: a case of this type would be mediated first, only after which is it possible to commence proceedings: the costs quoted here include both those of mediation and subsequent litigation.

Latvia: only court fees are quoted. Lawyers' costs depend on the amount of work involved and cannot be estimated.

Netherlands: since the lawyers' costs are based on hourly rates, the cost of this type of case would vary enormously, so the national reporter felt unable to state an accurate figure, and no figure has been included in the charts. The minimum costs might be €1,000 for each side.

New Zealand: this type of case is normally resolved through a negotiated settlement. Costs of litigation in case the settlement route fails might fall in the range of NZ$30,000 to NZ$60,000.

Norway: a case of this type is normally settled by administrative decision. Child custody cases are the only ones to go to court, and no court fee is payable in such cases. Lawyers' fees vary.

Portugal: it is not possible to estimate lawyers' fees, and hence total costs, since the amount of work done would be unpredictable. Alternative ways of proceeding would be either mediation (at a cost of €50 per party), or the registry procedure (€800 total cost for both parties).

Russia: only court fees can be quoted: lawyers' fees would vary considerably depending on the reputation of the lawyer.

Scotland: the general estimated costs for one party were quoted, but they could vary considerably.

Spain: the fees will increase if the divorce is contested. If the parties' incomes exceed €7,582.05, the fees will be proportionally increased.

Switzerland: The total is uncertain, and only court costs are included in the charts. The range of lawyers' fees quoted (between CHF 1,400 and CHF 16,000; in a case which goes all through the court process to a first judgment (without settlement), the final fee will be approximately twice the base fee, ie between CHF 2,800 and CHF 32,000).

Case study 3: Road traffic accident (RTA)

Scenario

Road traffic accident collision, in which the rear of the claimant's car and the front of the defendant's car are moderately damaged (i.e. rear and front respectively require total replacement panels, but engine is undamaged); cost of repair and replacement car €6,000.

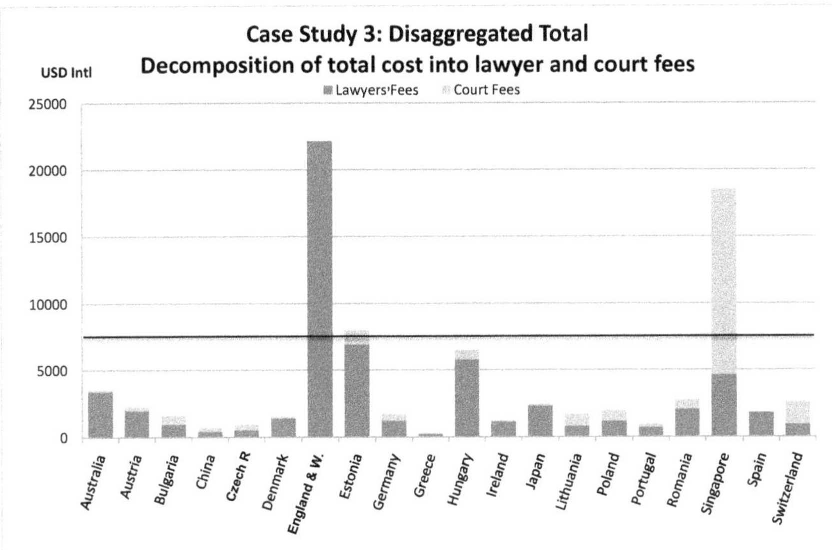

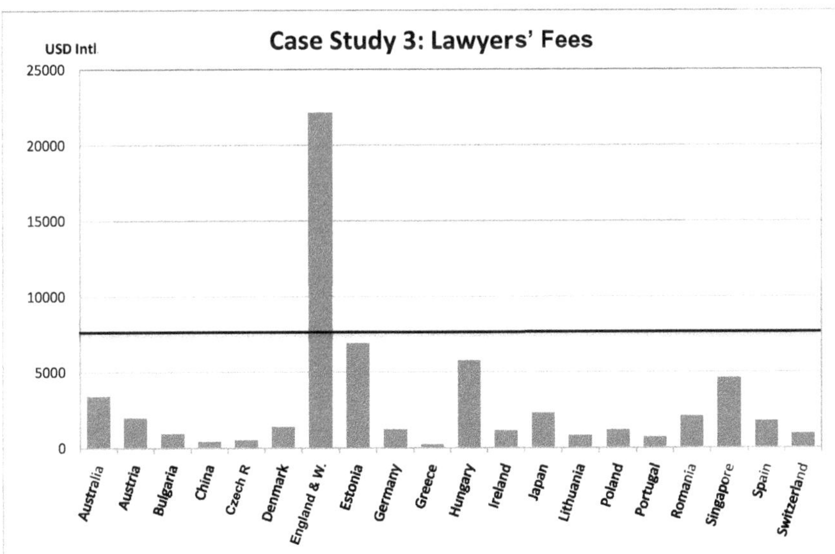

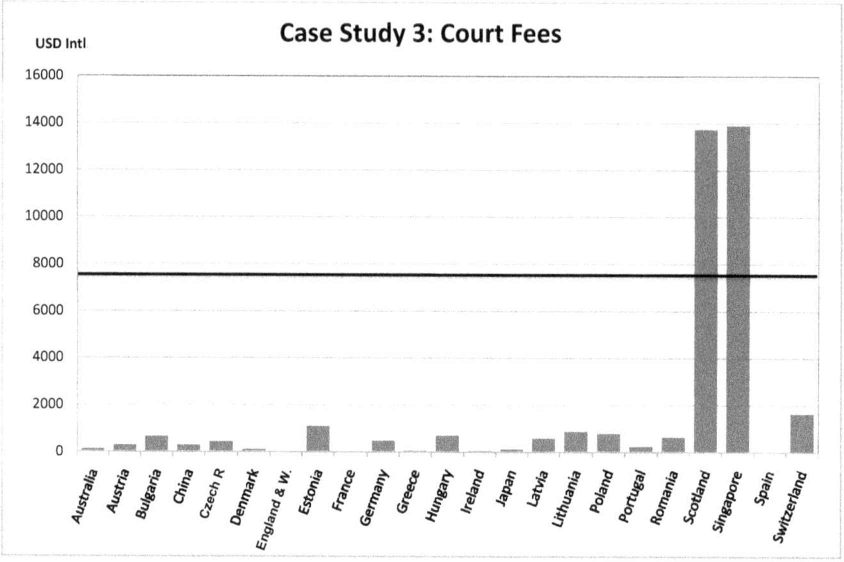
Case Study 3: Court Fees
USD Intl
16000
14000
12000
10000
8000
6000
4000
2000
0
Australia
Austria
Bulgaria
China
Czech R
Denmark
England & W.
Estonia
France
Germany
Greece
Hungary
Ireland
Japan
Latvia
Lithuania
Poland
Portugal
Romania
Scotland
Singapore
Spain
Switzerland

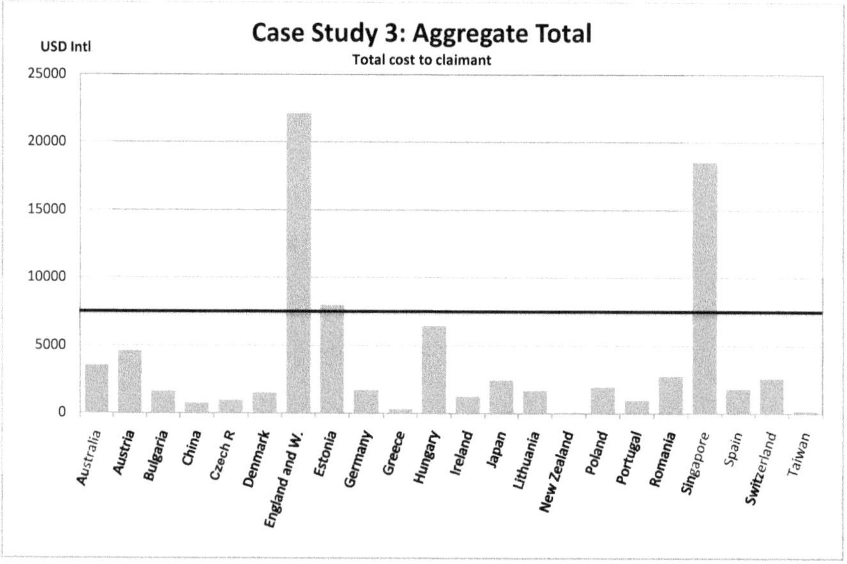
Case Study 3: Aggregate Total
Total cost to claimant
USD Intl
25000
20000
15000
10000
5000
0
Australia
Austria
Bulgaria
China
Czech R
Denmark
England and W.
Estonia
Germany
Greece
Hungary
Ireland
Japan
Lithuania
New Zealand
Poland
Portugal
Romania
Singapore
Spain
Switzerland
Taiwan

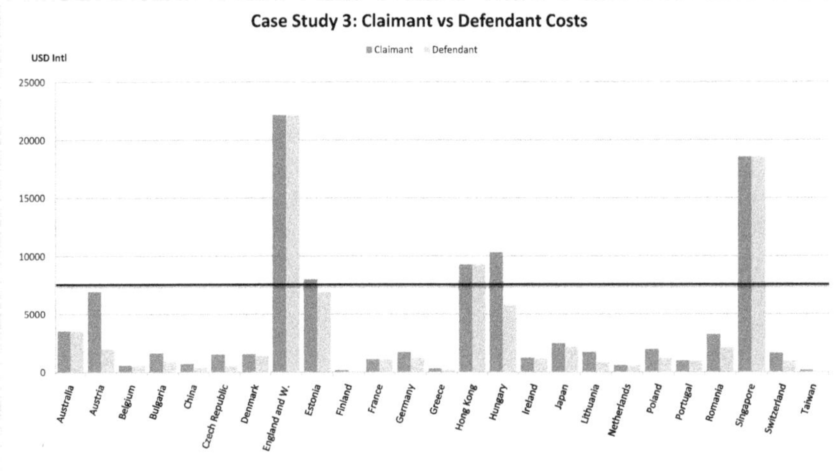

Findings

This case study illustrates that road traffic damage cases are frequently resolved through insurance arrangements rather than the courts (specifically mentioned for Canada, Finland, Norway, Russia and Sweden but probably used far more widely).

If a claim were to be brought in court (the case study quoted a loss of €6,000, indicated in the charts by the black line) total costs would arguably be disproportionate in Estonia and Hungary, and wholly disproportionate in Singapore (due to high court costs) and England and Wales (due to high lawyers' fees). Greece and China have the lowest total costs for a court procedure.

Explanatory notes

Canada: these claims are infrequent, since RTA cases are dealt with under administrative insurance arrangements: collision coverage, direct compensation and the Fault Determination Rules are specified under the Insurance Act.

Finland: these cases are settled by insurance, and the payment quoted in the chart goes to the insurance company.

Latvia: only court fees are quoted. Lawyers' costs depend on the amount of work involved.

New Zealand: this case would be regarded as uneconomic to pursue through the court (the costs ranging from NZ$10,000 to NZ$30,000), unless there were to be a simplified trial (costs NZ$5,000 to NZ$8,000), but the preferred option would be to persuade the parties to reduce the amount in dispute to NZ$15,000 so it could be dealt with in the Disputes Tribunal, in which case the only cost would be the filing fee of NZ$100.

Norway: cases of this type are settled through compulsory insurance arrangements.

Portugal: an alternative pathway would be preferable to the court. If the parties agree, they can submit the dispute to an arbitration centre, which will apply mediation, conciliation or arbitration. Both mediation and conciliation are free of charge; the arbitration will cost €190 or €310. Another alternative is to bring the claim before a magistrates' court, for which the cost will be €70.

Russia: cases of this type would be handled by insurance companies. If the case were pursued in court, the case acceptance fee (for a claim between €3,000 and €6,000) would be between €300 and €500, and the lawyer would charge €100 for each court hearing. An expert opinion would cost €60 to €200.

Sweden: cases of this type are normally settled by compulsory insurance arrangements.

Case Study 4: Employment

Scenario

Wrongful loss of employment by a middle-ranging manager (say salary €50,000 pa).

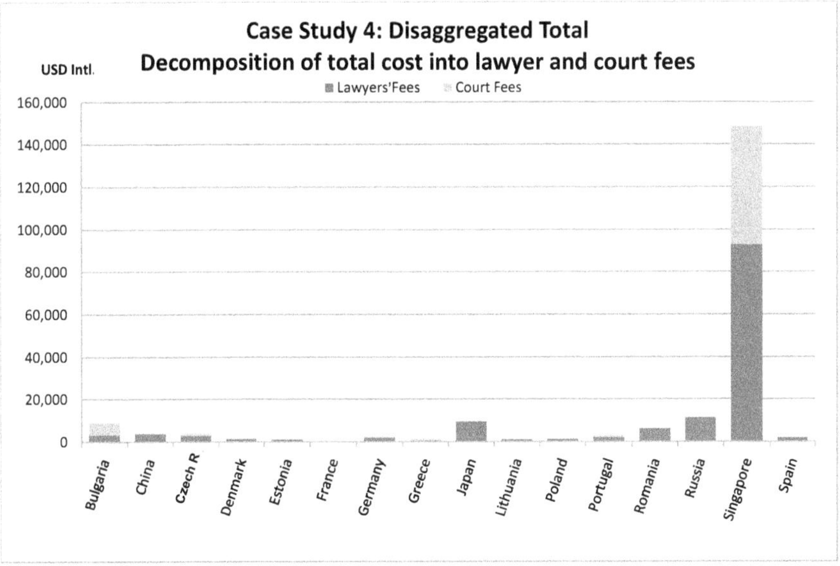

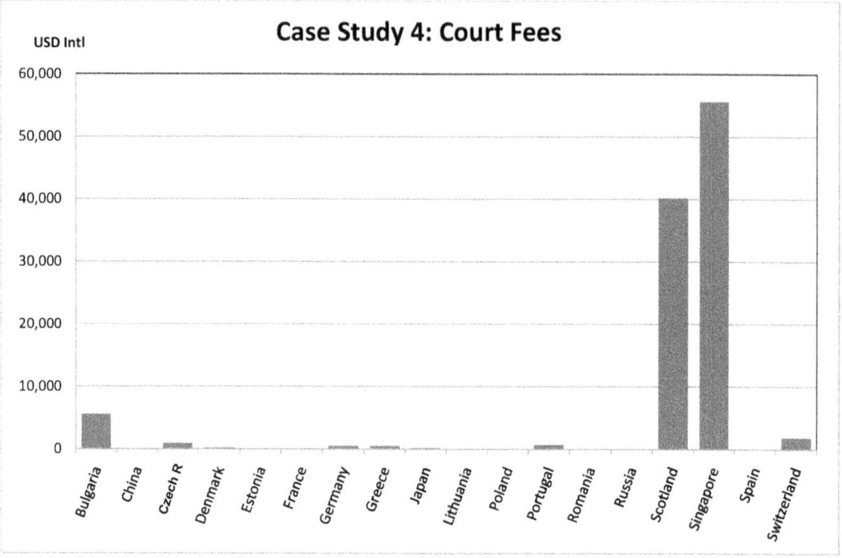
Case Study 4: Court Fees
USD Intl
60,000
50,000
40,000
30,000
20,000
10,000
0
Bulgaria
China
Czech R
Denmark
Estonia
France
Germany
Greece
Japan
Lithuania
Poland
Portugal
Romania
Russia
Scotland
Singapore
Spain
Switzerland

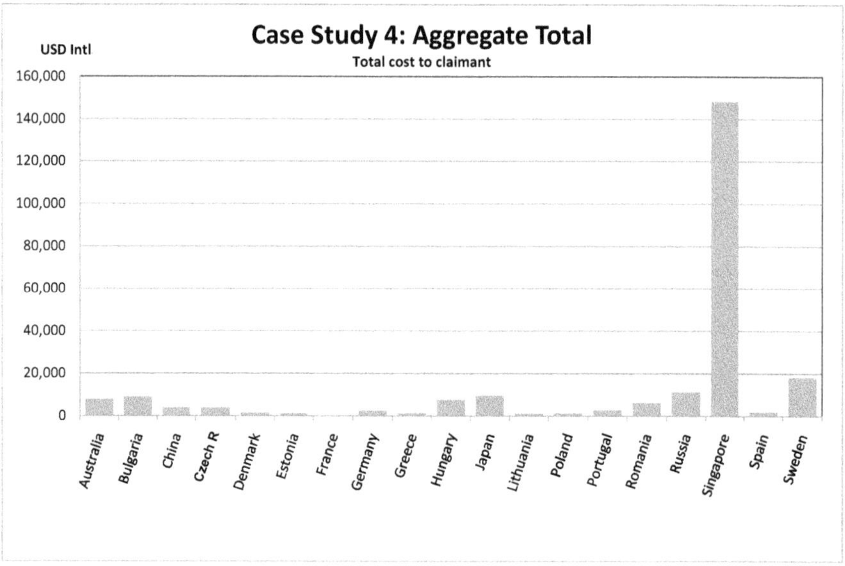
Case Study 4: Aggregate Total
Total cost to claimant
USD Intl
160,000
140,000
120,000
100,000
80,000
60,000
40,000
20,000
0
Australia
Bulgaria
China
Czech R
Denmark
Estonia
France
Germany
Greece
Hungary
Japan
Lithuania
Poland
Portugal
Romania
Russia
Singapore
Spain
Sweden

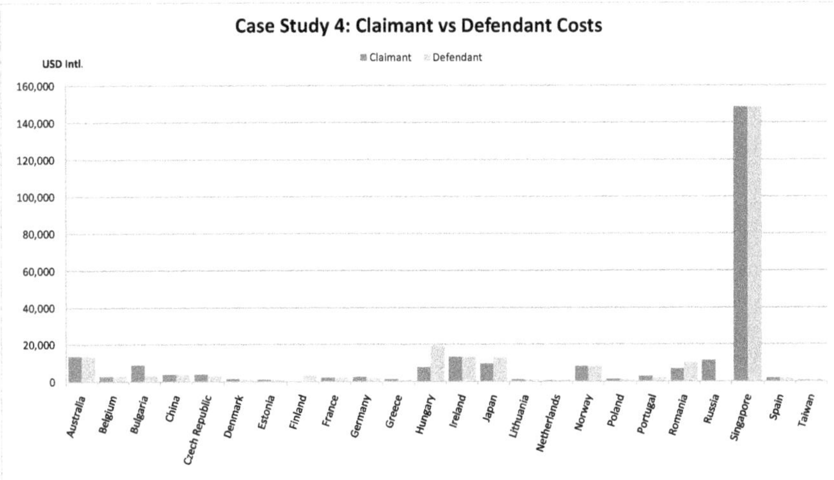

Findings

This case study illustrates that labour disputes in some jurisdictions are brought in specialist tribunals and/or subject to mediation (Australia, England and Wales, and New Zealand). The very low cost of mediation is illustrated by Portugal. Many countries prioritise and facilitate labour disputes by applying low or no court fees (China, Estonia, France, Lithuania, Latvia, Poland, Romania, Russia and Spain: in Hungary the state will advance the claimant's costs). Where cases have to proceed through normal court channels, some jurisdictions impose exceptionally high court costs, especially Singapore.

The effect of the result for Singapore as shown in the charts may disguise the variation in costs, and especially lawyers' fees, in other jurisdictions. Lawyers' fees may be disproportionate and constitute a barrier to justice depending on the amount at stake.

The notably low court costs for an employment claim are not generally mirrored by similar remission in lawyers' fees. Lawyers' fees far exceed court costs in every country except Bulgaria (where they are about equal) and Singapore (where lawyers' fees are about a third of court costs).

Explanatory notes

Austria: the costs would vary depending on the sum claimed, so it is not possible to generalize.

Australia: cases are settled in the Australian Industrial Relations Commission or in a state industrial relations commission (such as the NSW Industrial Relations Commission). In the latter, the first stage is conciliation. After that the case may proceed to an arbitrated hearing, for which the costs are quoted in the charts.

Canada: no precise amounts in response.

Denmark: it would be most likely that the claimant would either have insurance or be represented by a trade union. Whether the claimant wins or loses, he is therefore likely to pay only DKK 0 to DKK 2,000 in litigation costs depending on the deductible on his insurance.

England and Wales: the costs would vary depending on the amount of work done, so it is not possible to predict them. An employment claim would normally be brought in an Employment Tribunal, where contingency fees are permitted.

Germany: the costs quoted are for a claim of €12,500, which is the quarterly salary of the employee in the case.

Hong Kong: costs were quoted as 'minimal'.

Hungary: the state will advance the claimants' costs (and the loser will reimburse them).

Latvia: some employment cases are exempt from court costs. It is not possible to predict lawyers' fees, which would vary depending on whether they were agreed by the hour, or on a contingency or success fee.

New Zealand: the majority of cases settle through the Employment Mediation Service. If mediation fails and the case goes before the Employment Relations Authority, the cases might be between NZ$5,000 and NZ$20,000.

Portugal: an alternative approach is that the parties may provide that the claim be solved through labour mediation, which will cost €50 per party involved.

Switzerland: Uncertain total. A very wide bracket of lawyers' fees was given: 'between CHF 4,065 and CHF 8,135 (§ 3 of the Zurich Tariff for Lawyers' Fees). Where a case goes all through the court process to a first judgment (without settlement), the final fee will be approximately twice the base fee, ie between CHF 8,130 and CHF 16,270'.

Case study 5: Medical negligence

Scenario

Doctor's error results in permanent (a) loss of ability to walk (b) paraplegia, for male claimant aged 25 on salary of €25,000 pa, no current dependents, but likelihood of marriage and two children.

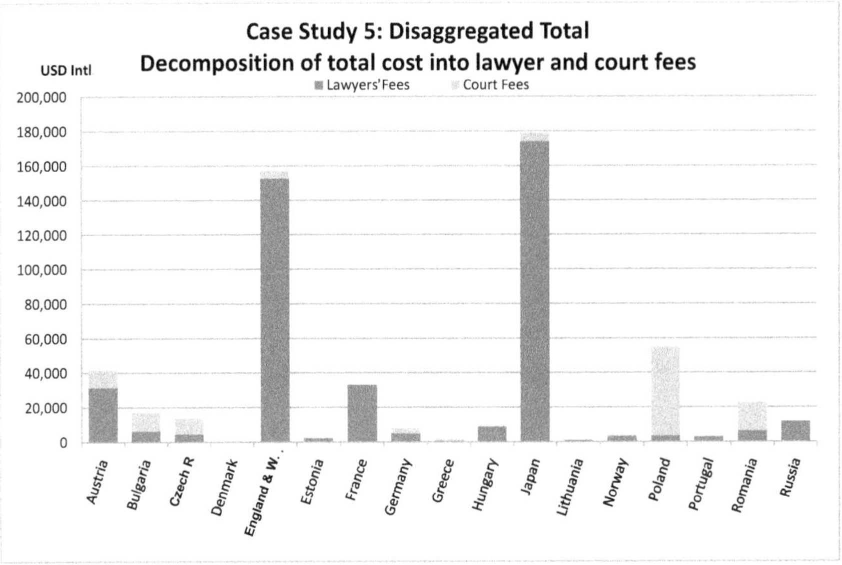

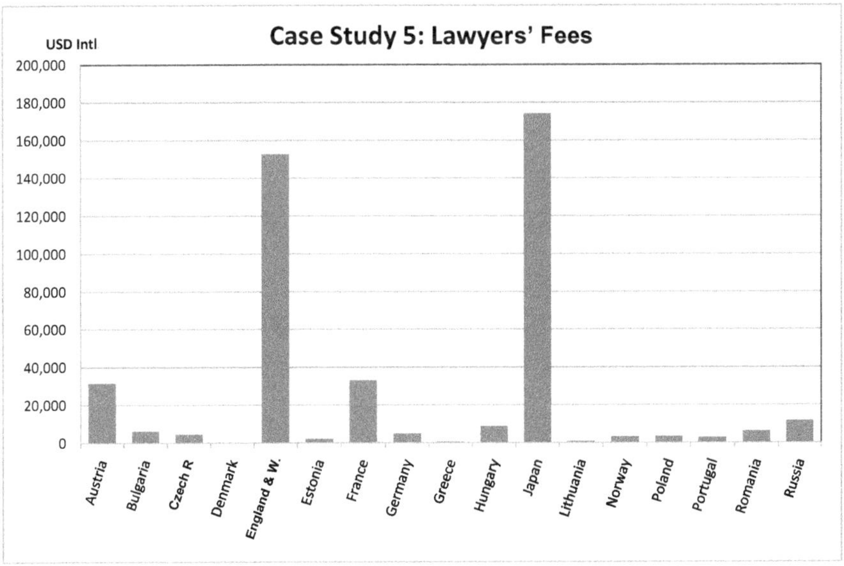

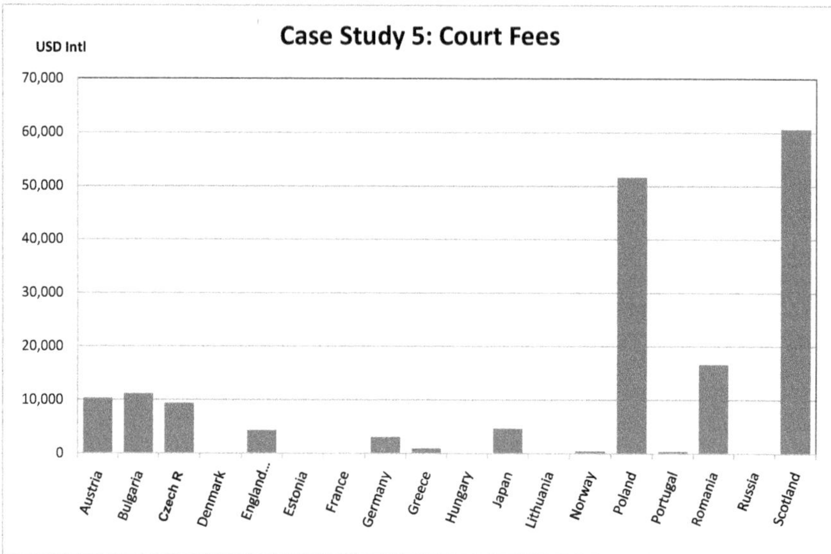
Case Study 5: Court Fees
USD Intl
70,000
60,000
50,000
40,000
30,000
20,000
10,000
0
Austria
Bulgaria
Czech R
Denmark
England...
Estonia
France
Germany
Greece
Hungary
Japan
Lithuania
Norway
Poland
Portugal
Romania
Russia
Scotland

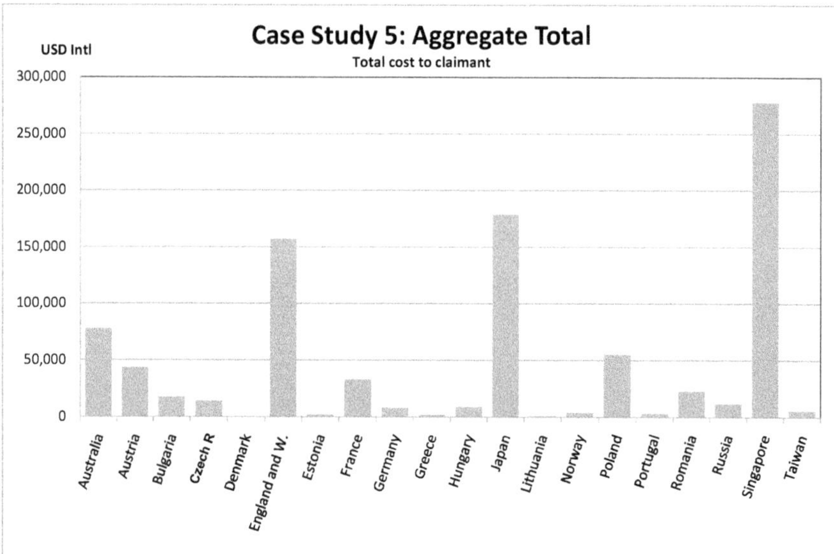
Case Study 5: Aggregate Total
Total cost to claimant
USD Intl
300,000
250,000
200,000
150,000
100,000
50,000
0
Australia
Austria
Bulgaria
Czech R
Denmark
England and W.
Estonia
France
Germany
Greece
Hungary
Japan
Lithuania
Norway
Poland
Portugal
Romania
Russia
Singapore
Taiwan

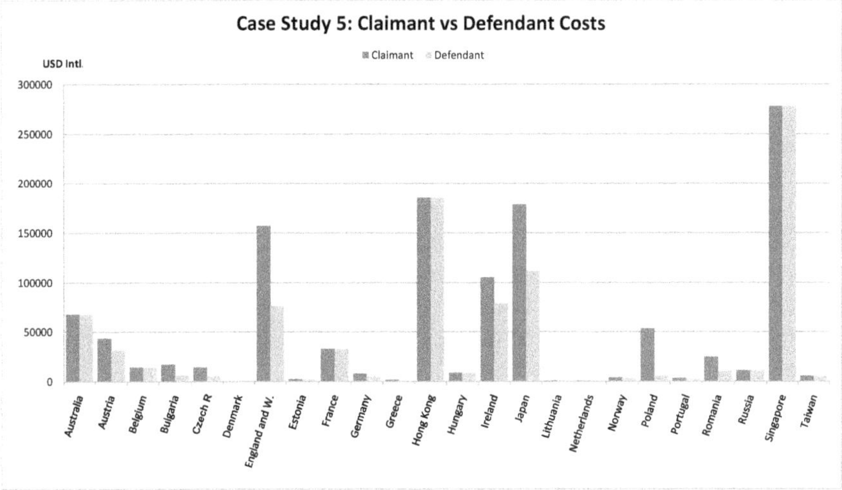

Findings

This case study illustrates two points. First, since medical negligence cases can be complex and involve detailed technical evidence, in some systems requiring an unpredictable amount of inquiry, several jurisdictions have introduced cheaper administrative and/or insurance-based solutions (notably Canada, Finland, Norway and Sweden).

Secondly, where the case has to go through the courts and requires extensive work by lawyers, the total costs (almost all comprising lawyers' fees) can be very high indeed (England and Wales, Japan). Court fees are particularly high in Poland and Scotland. However, lawyers' fees are lower than court costs in Poland, Romania, the Czech Republic and Bulgaria. Total costs of the court procedure are low in Denmark (because of legal aid), Lithuania, Greece, Estonia, Portugal and Norway, somewhat higher in Germany, Hungary and Russia, higher in the Czech Republic, Bulgaria and Romania, higher still in France, Austria and Poland, and very high in England and Wales and Japan. That list does not include Canada, where the success fee elements of a contingency fee, as with the English conditional fee, will drive up the total cost.

Explanatory notes

Canada: the case would be handled on a contingency fee, with a success fee of 35–40 per cent: it is not possible to specify an amount.

China: both court fees and lawyers' fees depend on the amount in dispute (the latter would be between 3 and 10 percent of the amount in dispute, for each party). It is not possible to predict exact amounts.

Denmark: The costs to the claimant will be nil, irrespective of the outcome of the case, since the claimant is covered by legal aid. The defendant is the state.

England and Wales: the data quoted for solicitors' and barristers' fees assumes that both act on a CFA basis (otherwise the amounts will be half those quoted, since they will not involve success fees). The sums include £2,500 in respect of disbursements (largely medical reports).

Finland: the bracket of costs given by the reporter was very wide: between €4,000 and €50,000. Accordingly, no figure has been included in the charts.

Latvia: medical negligence cases are exempt from court costs. It is not possible to predict lawyers' fees, which would vary depending on whether they were agreed by the hour, or on a contingency or success fee.

New Zealand: cases are settled through the Accident Compensation Scheme.

Norway: cases are first referred to the Patient Injury Committee; only in exceptional circumstances are appeals brought to court.

Portugal: an alternative is to bring the claim before a magistrates' court, for which the cost will be €70.

Spain: either a civil or criminal procedure could be used, the costs varying between each. The costs would depend on the amount of damages, so precise amounts are stated.

Sweden: these cases do not go to court but are dealt with through administrative insurance arrangements. The county councils provide public medical care and have insurance with a mutual insurance company, which has contracted an independent entity, PSR Personskadereglering AB, that processes claims. If a patient hires a lawyer to represent him before the PRS, the lawyer's costs will not normally be reimbursed by the insurance.

Case Study 6: Small or medium sized enterprise (SME)

Scenario

Small company claim for unpaid debt of €8,000

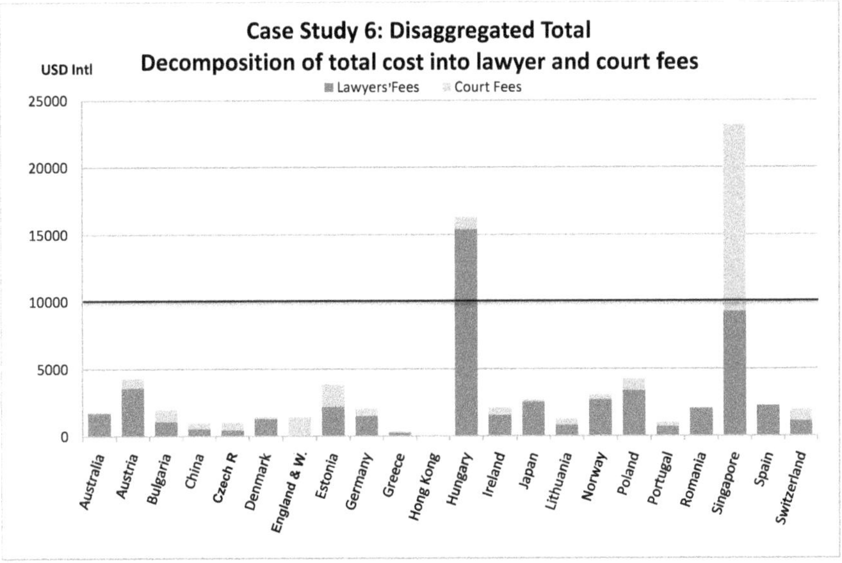

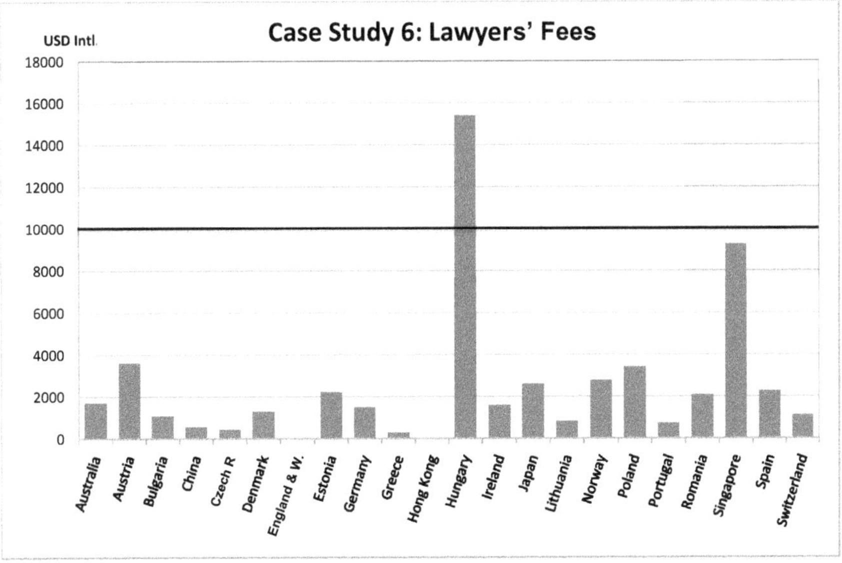

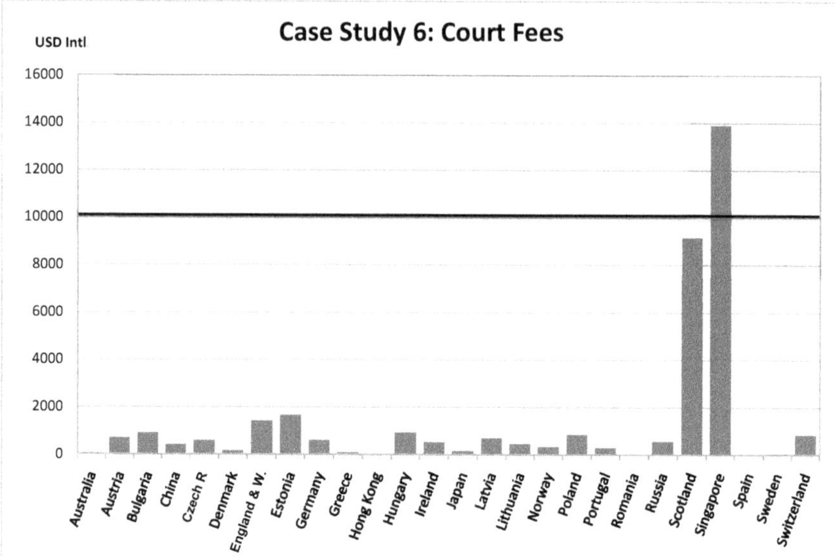
Case Study 6: Court Fees
USD Intl
16000
14000
12000
10000
8000
6000
4000
2000
0
Australia
Austria
Bulgaria
China
Czech R
Denmark
England & W.
Estonia
Germany
Greece
Hong Kong
Hungary
Ireland
Japan
Latvia
Lithuania
Norway
Poland
Portugal
Romania
Russia
Scotland
Singapore
Spain
Sweden
Switzerland

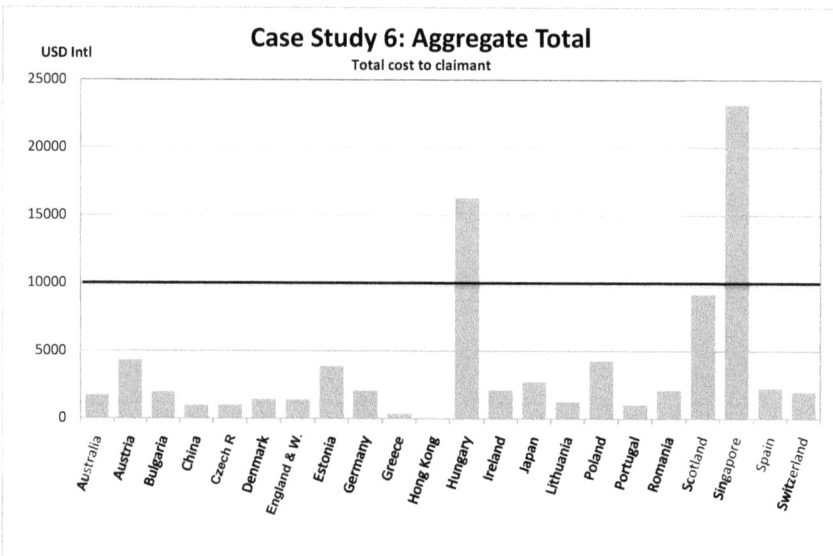
Case Study 6: Aggregate Total
Total cost to claimant
USD Intl
25000
20000
15000
10000
5000
0
Australia
Austria
Bulgaria
China
Czech R
Denmark
England & W.
Estonia
Germany
Greece
Hong Kong
Hungary
Ireland
Japan
Lithuania
Poland
Portugal
Romania
Scotland
Singapore
Spain
Switzerland

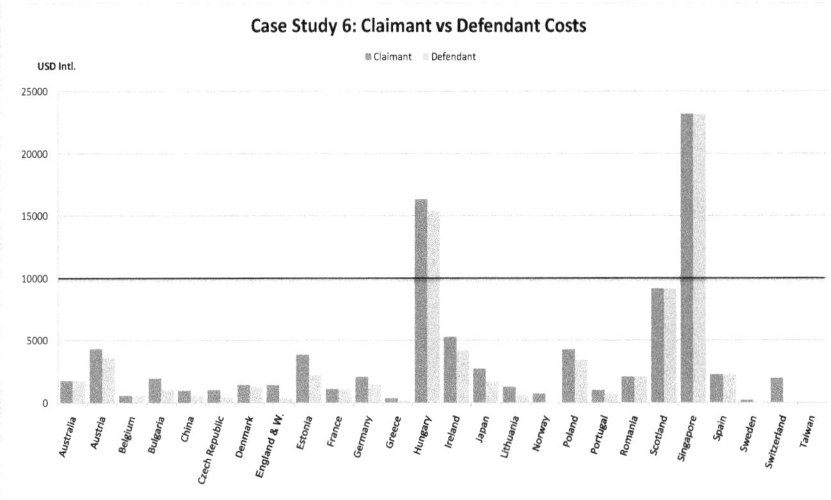

Findings

Two features appear from this case study. First, several jurisdictions have small claims procedures that involve lower than normal costs. Hence, secondly, the overall level of costs is notably more proportionate than for small claims in case studies 1 and (in part) 2 above, as can be seen by comparing the costs with the sum in dispute, indicated by the black line (€8,000).

The significant unusual comparative features are the large size of court costs quoted for Singapore and Scotland, and the high level of lawyers' costs quoted for Hungary. In many cases, lawyers' fees far exceed court costs, save in England and Wales, and Singapore.

Explanatory notes

Canada: this would be dealt with as a small claim and cost C$3,000–5,000. If it were brought in court under the Simplified Rules it would cost C$10,000–C$15,000.

France: a very wide bracket of costs was given by the reporter (between €2,000 and €20,000) so no figure has been included in the charts.

Hong Kong: the claim would probably be brought in the Small Claims Tribunal, for which there are no legal fees. The claimant would probably abandon any excess claim over the HK$50,000 ceiling on jurisdiction of the Small Claims Tribunal.

Latvia: only court fees are quoted. Lawyers' costs depend on the amount of work involved.

Netherlands: the costs would depend on the amount of work done by the lawyers. The winner would probably be awarded €2,500 as shifted costs.

New Zealand: a simplified administrative debt collection procedure would be pursued in the District Court, and the costs of the lawyers' clerk would be NZ$1,000–2,000.

Norway: the sums quoted are for the Small Claims procedure. The amount payable to lawyers is difficult to predict and will depend on agreement with the client. The amount quoted here for lawyers' fees is the maximum permitted for cost-shifting purposes. Accordingly, a sum for lawyers' fees is not included in the charts. An alternative pathway would be a direct enforcement procedure, for which the costs would be NKK 1,581 plus NKK 5,000.

Portugal: an alternative is the magistrates' court procedure, which costs €70.

Case study 7: Large commercial case

Scenario

Substantial and complex breach of contract claim between two large companies over supply of defective machinery worth €2 million, with €5 million loss of profit.

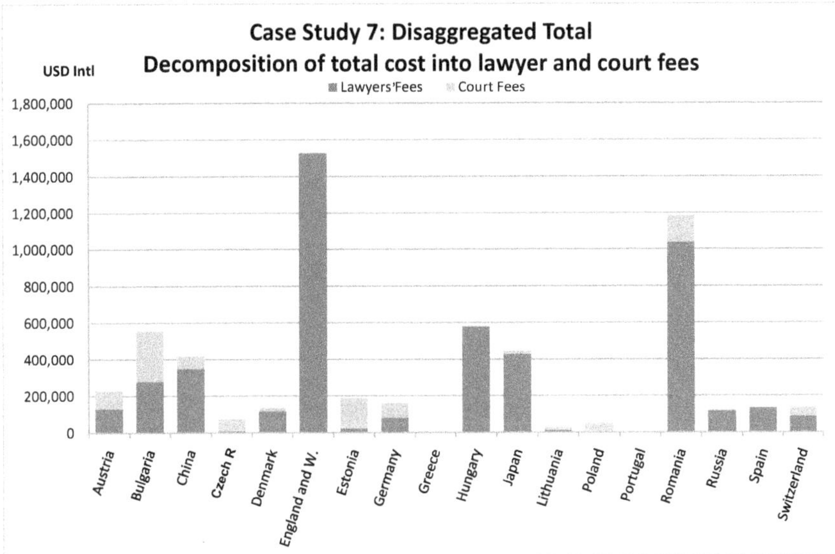

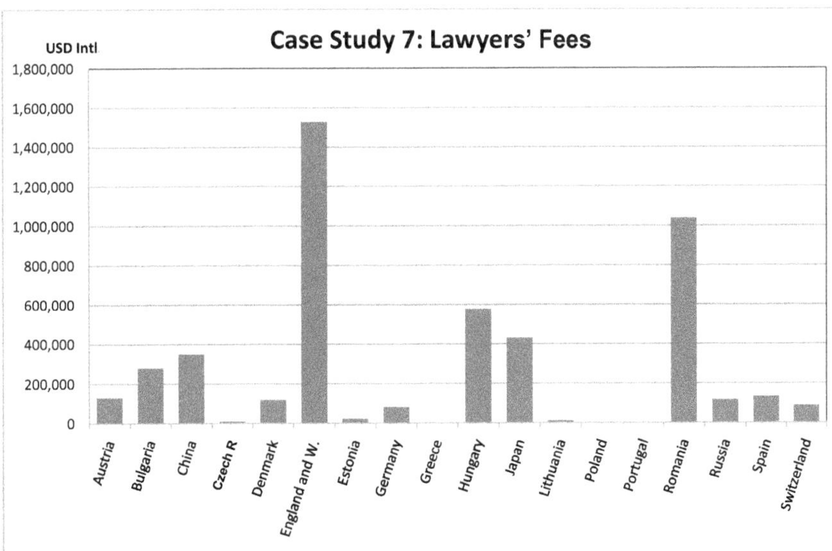

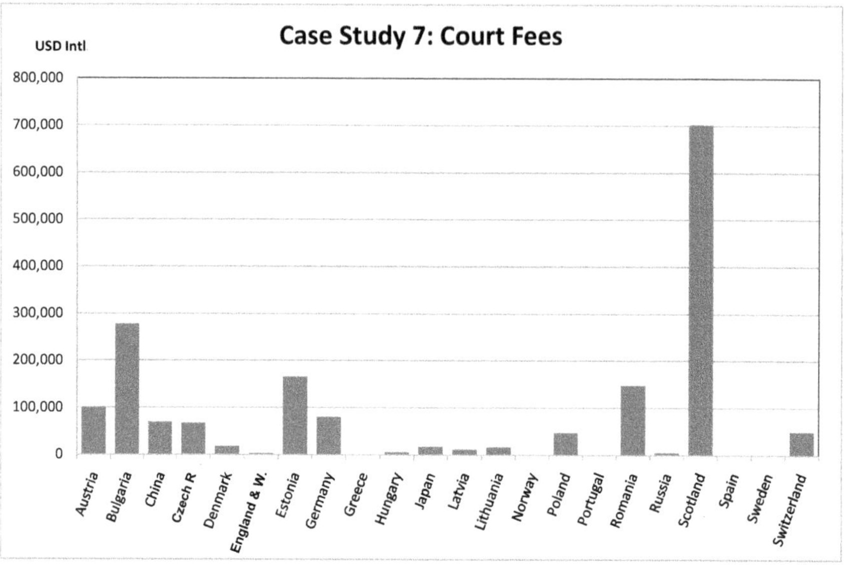
Case Study 7: Court Fees
USD Intl
800,000
700,000
600,000
500,000
400,000
300,000
200,000
100,000
0
Austria
Bulgaria
China
Czech R
Denmark
England & W.
Estonia
Germany
Greece
Hungary
Japan
Latvia
Lithuania
Norway
Poland
Portugal
Romania
Russia
Scotland
Spain
Sweden
Switzerland

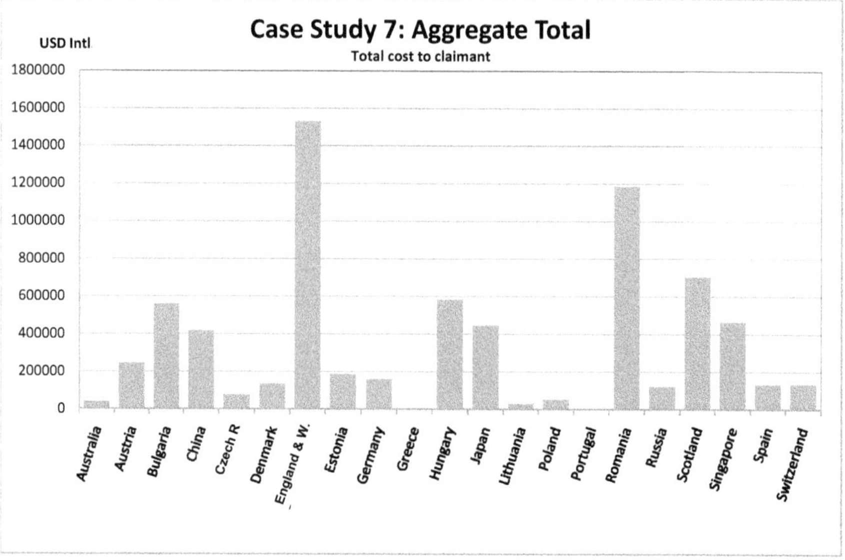
Case Study 7: Aggregate Total
Total cost to claimant
USD Intl
1800000
1600000
1400000
1200000
1000000
800000
600000
400000
200000
0
Australia
Austria
Bulgaria
China
Czech R
Denmark
England & W.
Estonia
Germany
Greece
Hungary
Japan
Lithuania
Poland
Portugal
Romania
Russia
Scotland
Singapore
Spain
Switzerland

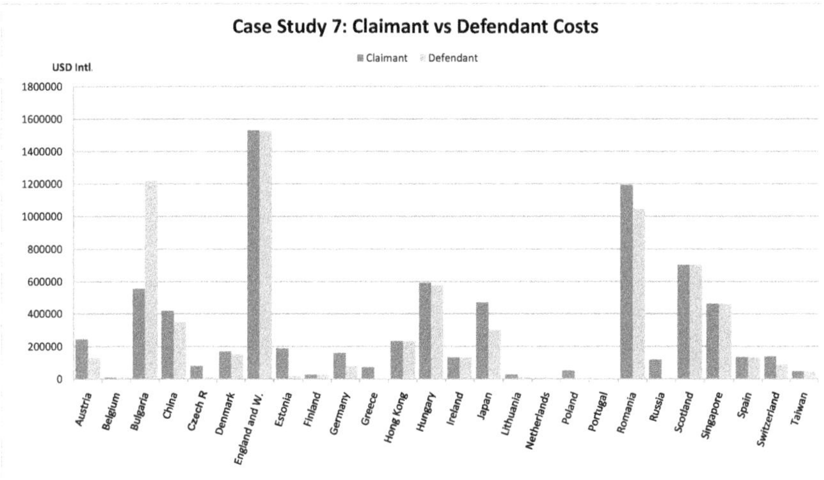

Findings

The scale of total costs is notably higher for this case study than for previous case studies, with total costs exceeding USD Intl 100,000 in a significant number of countries. Costs of this level of magnitude arise in those jurisdictions where lawyers undertake large amounts of work and/or are not subject to fee tariff controls. Thus, total costs and lawyers' fees are notably higher in China, Japan, Hungary, Romania, Canada (see note below) and especially England and Wales than they are in Greece, Portugal, Lithuania, the Czech Republic, Russia, Denmark, Spain, Switzerland and Germany. Court fees appear very high in Scotland and quite high in Bulgaria, Estonia and Romania.

In those jurisdictions in which lawyers' fees are not based on a tariff, it is difficult to predict the amount of work done and hence the lawyers' fees, so the potential range of such costs can vary hugely: see the comments below for Canada, France, Latvia and Norway.

Explanatory notes

Canada: costs could exceed C$1,000,000.

France: the lawyers' costs would depend on the hourly rate and amount of work done, and cannot be predicted. Experts' costs would depend on whether they were appointed by parties or the court. The costs shifted to the loser would probably be only €4,000.

Latvia: only court fees are quoted. Lawyers' costs depend on the amount of work involved.

Norway: lawyers' fees depend on the amount of work involved, and might amount to 2,000,000 NKK (219,082 USD Intl)

Portugal: an alternative pathway is that the parties can agree to submit the dispute to an arbitration centre, which will apply mediation, conciliation or arbitration. Both mediation and conciliation are free of charge; the arbitration would cost either €210,010 or €350,010, depending on whether it is a singular arbitrator or a collective tribunal.

Case study 8: Consumer injunction

Scenario

Injunction against neighbour to stop noise.

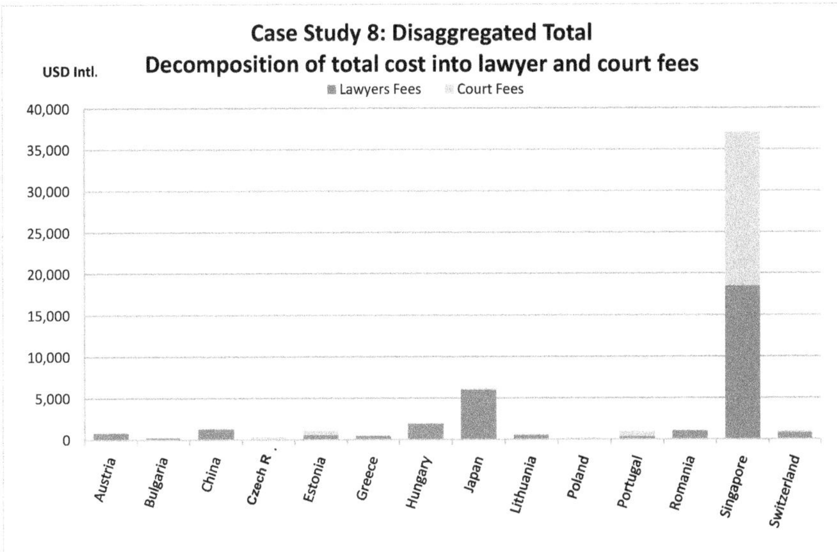

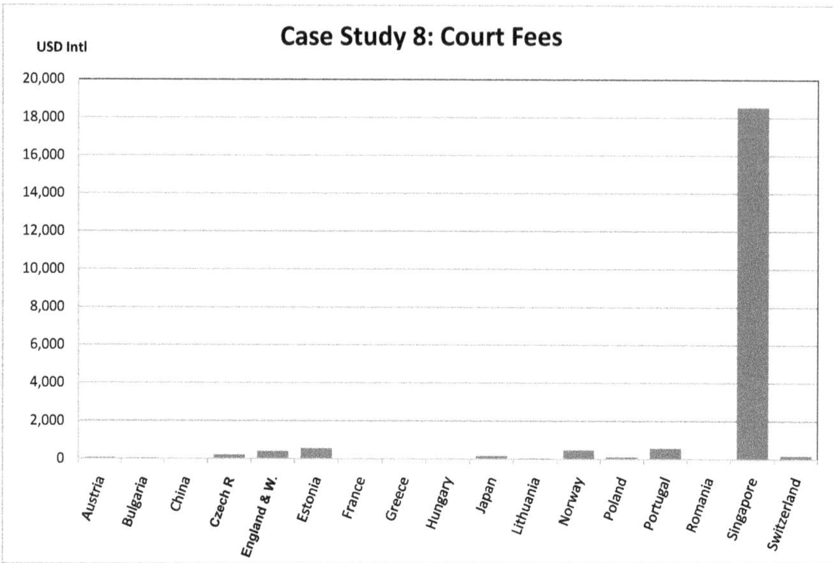
Case Study 8: Court Fees
USD Intl
20,000
18,000
16,000
14,000
12,000
10,000
8,000
6,000
4,000
2,000
0
Austria
Bulgaria
China
Czech R
England & W.
Estonia
France
Greece
Hungary
Japan
Lithuania
Norway
Poland
Portugal
Romania
Singapore
Switzerland

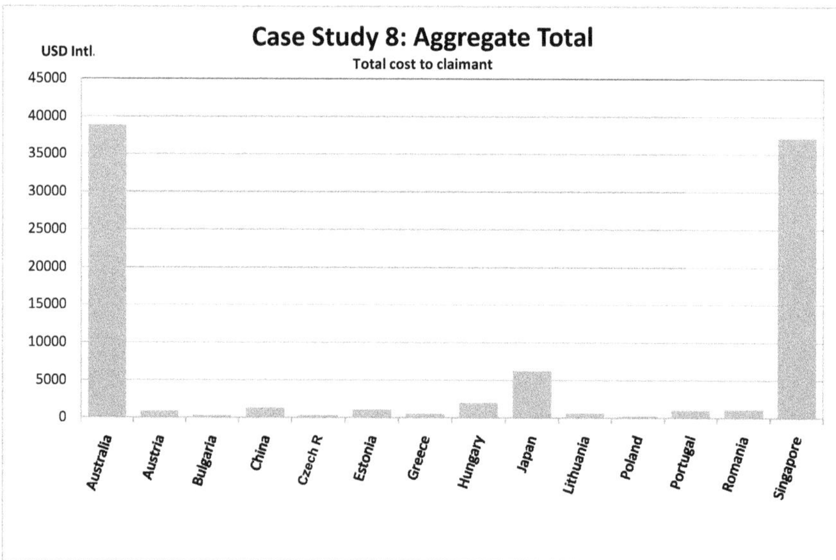
Case Study 8: Aggregate Total
Total cost to claimant
USD Intl.
45000
40000
35000
30000
25000
20000
15000
10000
5000
0
Australia
Austria
Bulgaria
China
Czech R
Estonia
Greece
Hungary
Japan
Lithuania
Poland
Portugal
Romania
Singapore

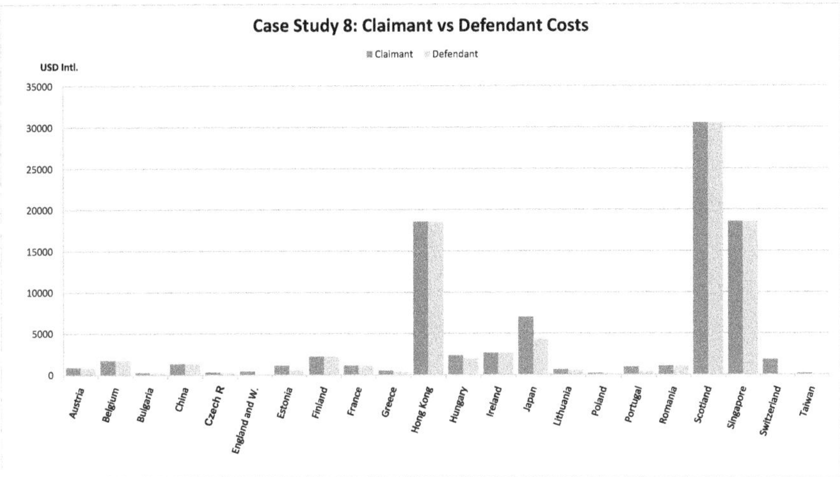

Findings

Whilst the charts indicate that total costs are low in many countries, reporters' comments indicate, first, that the scale of costs is very difficult to predict and could be much higher in those countries in which lawyers' costs are not regulated by tariff and, secondly, that a case such as this would not normally be pursued in the courts. Instead, the public authorities would become involved, or it would be impossible to pursue the dispute. If it were to be pursued through the courts, say in Singapore or Australia, the total costs could be very high indeed.

Explanatory notes

Denmark: a complaint would be made to the authorities; this would not be a civil matter.

England and Wales: it is not possible to estimate costs; a complaint to a regulator may produce results and would involve minimal costs to the initiator.

Germany: the costs would depend on the amount in dispute.

Latvia: an administrative procedure is used.

Netherlands: lawyers' costs would depend on the amount of work done.

New Zealand: this would not be pursued as a civil case. The only option would be to try to involve the local authorities.

Norway: lawyers' fees would depend on the amount of work involved; the total can often amount to 100,000 NKK.

Russia: this would not be brought as a civil case: the police would impose a fine on the neighbour of up to €20.

Spain: this would not be a civil case: a complaint might be made to the local authorities.

Sweden: this would not be a civil case: a complaint would be made to the local authority under the Environmental Code, and an appeal could be made to the

County Administrative Board. The claimant would be unlikely to use a lawyer, although a defendant might. Such claims would not be covered under Legal Expenses Insurance.

Switzerland: The total is uncertain. A very wide bracket of lawyers' fees was given (between CHF 280 and CHF 10,666). Where a case goes all through the court process to a first judgment (without settlement), the final fee will be approximately twice the base fee (ie between CHF 560 and CHF 21,332).

Case study 9: Commercial injunction

Scenario

Injunction to prevent illegal breach of intellectual property in commercial information between two substantial companies.

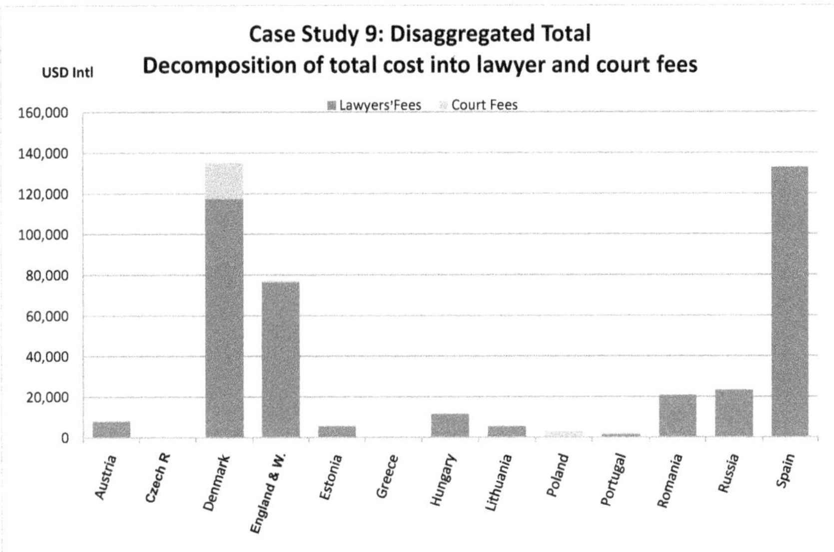

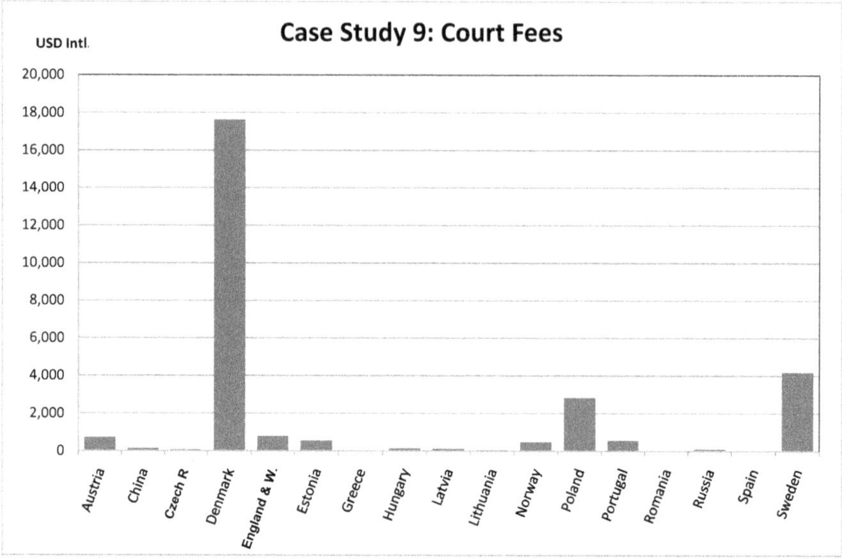
Case Study 9: Court Fees
USD Intl.
20,000
18,000
16,000
14,000
12,000
10,000
8,000
6,000
4,000
2,000
0
Austria
China
Czech R
Denmark
England & W.
Estonia
Greece
Hungary
Latvia
Lithuania
Norway
Poland
Portugal
Romania
Russia
Spain
Sweden

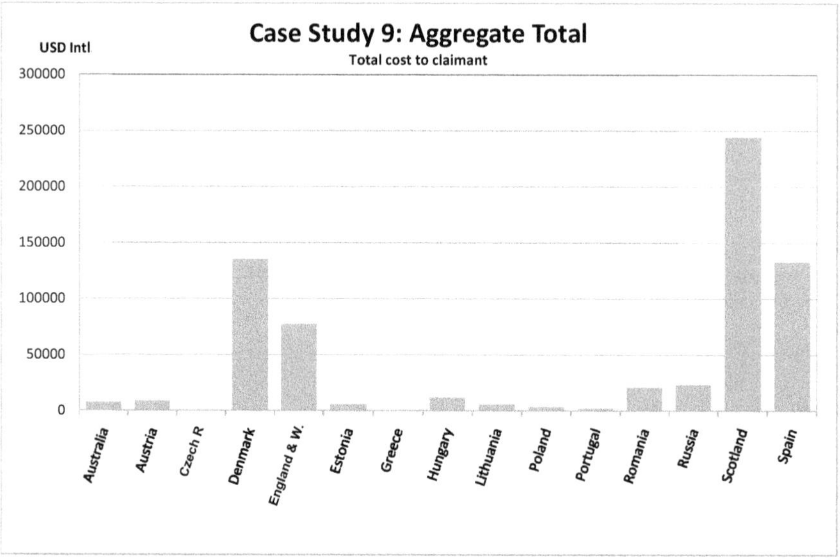
Case Study 9: Aggregate Total
Total cost to claimant
USD Intl
300000
250000
200000
150000
100000
50000
0
Australia
Austria
Czech R
Denmark
England & W.
Estonia
Greece
Hungary
Lithuania
Poland
Portugal
Romania
Russia
Scotland
Spain

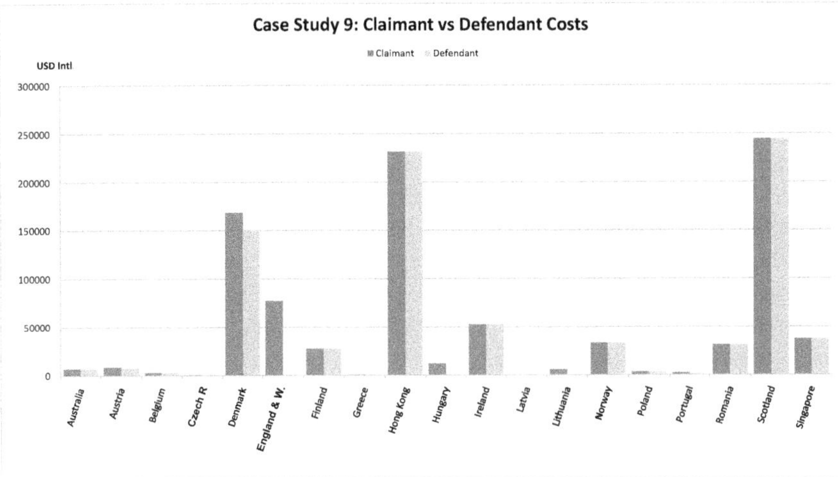

Findings

As with case study 7, in common law and non-tariff jurisdictions, the lawyers' costs would depend on the amount of work done, and could vary considerably. Accordingly, many national reporters felt unable to provide estimates, including those from Bulgaria, Canada, China, France, Latvia (lawyers' fees will depend on the billing arrangement and amount of work done or contingency or success fee: however, shiftable lawyers' fees cannot exceed 5 per cent of any sum awarded as damages), the Netherlands (full cost shifting would apply in this case), New Zealand, and Sweden (the court may combine a prohibition against use of the trade secret with a fine that would go to the state in case of infringement).

The costs are also unpredictable where court and lawyers' fees are based on a tariff unless the amount in dispute is identified or the claimant states a particular amount. This is the case in Germany, Japan, Switzerland and Taiwan (a special Intellectual Property court would be used).

It is the lawyers' fees that are usually far higher than the court costs. The lawyers' fees quoted for England and Wales, Denmark and Spain were notably higher than for other countries.

Explanatory notes

Latvia: only court fees are quoted. Lawyers' costs depend on the amount of work involved.

Norway: lawyers' fees depend on the amount of work involved; the total can often amount to 300,000 NKK.

IV. Levels of Court Costs and Lawyers' Fees

Table 5 (an Appendix to this study[57]) gives the range of costs charged as court fees, and the ranges of hourly rates quoted by national practitioner correspondents for the fees charged by lawyers in their countries. It should be noted that this data is preliminary and wider sampling needs to be undertaken. It is also difficult to compare these figures without the context of a comparable case, so we refrain from analysing these data in detail. However some general points can be made.

In relation to court charges, three points are important. First, there is a range in the percentages that are imposed under tariff-based systems. Not all the percentages are apparent, since some are 'hidden' within a layered approach to charges, where fixed costs or different percentages are applied for cases that involve different values. However, it will be seen that there is a range in the percentages that apply to court charges, from the small (Spain applies a small flat fee plus 0.50 per cent of the amount at stake, or 0.25 per cent for claims over €1 million) to the high (6 per cent in Hungary, 5 per cent in Poland).

Secondly, the court charges taper in many countries between low and high value cases. Good examples are Romania, which imposes percentages between 10 per cent in low value cases and one per cent in high value cases, and Russia (5 to 0.5 per cent respectively).

Thirdly, the overall level of court charges, whether based on flat fees or a tariff system, can lead to costs that can vary considerably, depending on the type of case involved.

In relation to lawyers' fees, the data in Table 5 indicates that countries in which the highest rates apply are (with highest figures at the top end of the ranges first) Hungary, Singapore, Japan, the Netherlands, China, England and Wales, Canada, Norway, France, Denmark. Countries in which the lowest rates apply are (with the lowest figures in the ranges first) Lithuania, Latvia, Poland, Hungary, Portugal, the Netherlands, Scotland and Singapore. It will be noted that national reporters for some countries found it impossible to quote reliable data on rates, so the data set is not complete.

Whatever the specific rates that may apply in different countries, a significant finding is that there is currently a wide variation in the hourly rates that lawyers charge, across countries and often within countries. This is apparent, for example, from the appearance of Hungary and the Netherlands at both the top and bottom of the above rankings of hourly rates. Many of the higher rates apply to commercial work undertaken for large corporations, which are repeat players and have some sophistication, understanding of the market and commercial leverage over rates and quantity of work done. The low rates apply to cases for individuals, which will differ in complexity and levels of cost from commercial cases.

[57] See pp 180–83 below.

Accordingly, those countries in which a large range of lawyers' costs is available may have a legal market that produces flexibility in the range of services that are available at different cost levels to different customers. The extent to which a national market in fact delivers a comprehensive supply to cover adequately a wide range of demand would, however, need to be considered in greater detail.[58]

V. Findings

The following findings emerge from the above data.

A. Variation in litigation costs

The total costs of litigation can vary widely among the jurisdictions included in this study. A frequent pattern is that costs (whether in total, or for court or lawyers' fees) may have a broadly similar level in the majority of jurisdictions (which some may interpret as being at a 'low' level) but some jurisdictions have costs that are considerably higher than the general level of the majority.

B. Lawyers' fees are the major component of total costs

Lawyers' fees are in almost all cases higher than court fees, and comprise the major element in total costs. This is generally the case irrespective of whether or not jurisdictions impose tariffs for lawyers' fees.

The highest lawyers' fees can be observed in Australia, England and Wales, and Denmark. Germany, Austria and Greece have relatively low lawyers' fees. Lawyers' fees in Central and Eastern Europe are comparatively modest overall.

Lawyers' fees are usually subject to VAT. VAT rates vary between countries (between no charge and 30 per cent), and can have significant impact.

C. Court costs are predictable

Court costs are predictable in almost all jurisdictions, and are based on published tariffs. Where the amount in dispute is certain, the court costs vary with the amount in dispute. Where the amount is unquantifiable, such as for a claim for injunctive relief, the tariff denotes a particular set fee. In some cases where the

[58] See, eg, GK Hadfield, 'The Price of Law: how the Market for Lawyers Distorts the Justice System' (2000) 98 *Michigan Law Review* 953 who argues that the ability and willingness of commercial clients to pay high prices for legal services results in legal resources being skewed towards the corporate sphere of the profession and away from the goal of achieving justice between individuals.

claim is for damages but is not quantifiable in advance, claimants may specify a particular amount claimed, which will usually be a modest sum, so as to avoid incurring unnecessarily large court fees.

In the majority of jurisdictions, court costs are relatively low compared with the amount in dispute, once that amount is over a certain size. The significant outlier is Singapore, which has notably higher court costs than other states for most of the case studies.

In France court fees are effectively nil. Court fees are generally low in Germany and Austria, as well as Greece. Beyond Europe, they are quite low in Taiwan and China.

Central and Eastern European states (such as Latvia, Estonia, Poland, Bulgaria, or the Czech Republic) have relatively high court fees proportionate to the value of the case, and proportionate to the level of lawyers' fees, but a different way of looking at this might be that lawyers' fees are low in those states and hence the court costs appear proportionately higher than in other jurisdictions. Hungary is a notable exception to this pattern, having relatively high lawyers' fees as well as relatively high court fees in many of the case studies.

Court costs also for some case studies tend to be high in England (and the available information indicates that the position is generally similar in Canada), Ireland, the Netherlands and Norway. However, these states often have another 'preferred dispute resolution route' for particular types of claims. Court costs appear high in comparison with total costs and lawyers' costs in Singapore (case studies 2, 3, 4, 8) and (on a far lower scale) in Poland (case studies 5, 7, 9).

Some court fees include VAT, while others do not. In some states VAT is not charged on court costs, in others it is. Also, VAT rates differ. Respondents' reports are not always precise about which rates do and which do not include VAT, and about the VAT rates.

D. Lawyers' costs are frequently unpredictable

The countries in which reporters stated that it was either straightforward or difficult to predict the total costs fell into a consistent pattern. The pattern depended upon whether lawyers' costs were or were not regulated by a tariff. Accordingly, where no tariff or ceiling applied, and lawyers' fees were based upon hours worked, this produced both unpredictable fees and levels of fees which, in low value claims, were high compared to the value at stake (cases 1, 3, 4, 6 and 8) and, in high value claims, could be potentially very high (cases 2, 5, 7 and 9).

E. High cost jurisdictions

The countries that have notably higher total costs than others for each case study are: Hungary and Australia (case 1); Hungary, Romania and Singapore (case 2); England and Wales, and Singapore (case 3); Singapore (case 4); England and

Wales, and Japan (case 5); Singapore and Hungary (case 6); England and Wales, Canada, Romania, Hungary, Japan and China (case 7); Singapore and Australia (case 8); and Denmark, Spain and England and Wales (case 9).

Overall, the countries that have the highest total costs in the largest number of case studies are Singapore (5 cases) and England and Wales (4 cases). It should be noted that the United States was not included in the data, and that data only for some of the case studies was available for Canada.

This does not mean that costs in the countries identified above are higher in all cases, but it does indicate that costs are very high in a number of specific types of case in those countries. However, several other countries would be included in that list if, first, claims were to be pursued through the courts rather than through alternative pathways and, secondly, if the amount of work done by lawyers in a given case were to be large and fees were based on hourly rates or where the lawyers' fees were to be based on a success fee and the amount recovered was to be significant.

The most important observation from consideration of the above names of countries is that they do not tend to include countries in which lawyers' costs are regulated by tariffs.

F. Costs to case value ratio: proportionality

In most states included in this study the costs of litigation are high in relation to the value of the case. Sometimes costs even exceed the value of the case. Here some Western European states (such as Denmark, England and Wales, Ireland) are particularly striking examples, but the problem also exists in Hungary and some other Central and Eastern European countries, as well as Singapore and Australia. China and Taiwan have more proportionate costs.

There is a clear link between the predictability and proportionality of lawyers' fees. Where lawyers' fees are predictable they tend to be more proportionate to the value at stake, and vice versa. In other words, the key factor is whether or not lawyers' fees are subject to a tariff.

However, in states where costs are sometimes high, not all cases are necessarily expensive or disproportionate. An example of this can be seen from the results for the nine case studies in Australia, New Zealand and England and Wales (and is confirmed in Chapter 4 below on Canada). There, the results for the small claim, divorce, employment, debt and consumer injunction case studies indicate comparatively low costs, whereas those for the road traffic, medical negligence, large commercial dispute and intellectual property injunction case studies are comparatively far higher. This may reflect the fact that different costs rules, or cost shifting rules, or alternative dispute resolution pathways, are available for some types of claims. Such a finding may indicate that future work on providing particular pathways, procedures and costs regimes for particular types of cases may be fruitful, in order to address those cases where costs are high.

G. Existence of a cost recoverability gap for winners

It is extremely rare for all lawyers' fees to be recoverable by the winning party. The recoverability gap clearly exists everywhere and applies in almost all types of case. The gap can be very high in some states and cases, requiring a winning party to have considerable financial resources.

H. Alternative solutions for low value cases

For those disputes that involve low amounts and where costs might be disproportionate (cases 1, 3, 4 and 6), reporters in many jurisdictions indicated that pursuing a claim through the civil court system was not the recommended or most popular route for obtaining redress in the given situation, and that alternative solutions are preferred. Thus, for low value claims that proceed in court, a number of jurisdictions have small claims procedures involving simplified procedures, or rules, such as excluding the involvement of lawyers (and hence the costs incurred by their involvement) and/or prohibiting cost shifting.

Sometimes extra-court procedures can be preferred, such as administrative (use of special tribunals, ombudsmen or regulatory officials) or insurance solutions, since they involve little or no cost to claimants and the state or business bears the cost of investigation. A tribunal or official may be able to exert some pressure to resolve issues more informally and quickly than the careful forensic approach of courts. Mediation or arbitration procedures were frequently mentioned (notably case 2 on divorce) in preference to court proceedings. Labour disputes are frequently brought in specialist tribunals (case 4).

However, such alternative approaches were mentioned less frequently in those jurisdictions where the court procedures are efficient and the costs predictable (such as those based on the German model).

VI. Conclusions

The above findings suggest the following conclusions. The cost of litigating a dispute is unpredictable unless all costs (court, process and lawyers) are specified in an *ex ante* tariff. Court costs are almost universally specified in such tariffs, whereas the costs of lawyers are subject to tariffs in some countries and not in others. Lawyers' costs are almost always the major element in the total costs (ie higher than court costs) in any case in which a lawyer is involved.

In low value claims, costs are frequently both high and disproportionate to the amount in dispute. This can be so irrespective of whether or not costs are controlled by a tariff. In other words, all court-based dispute resolution systems have an inherent level of costs that produces a threshold of cost proportionality: below the threshold, cases may not be worth pursuing and may either be dropped or pursued through alternative means.

In high value claims, costs can be very high where lawyers' fees are based on hourly rates. The same would be the case where amounts recovered are large and lawyers' fees are based on success fees or percentages of the sum recovered. In high value claims where costs are large, they do not exceed the sums at stake, unlike in small value claims, so are not disproportionate in that sense. However, where lawyers' fees comprise intrinsically very high sums, the issue arises of whether the cost is excessive.

Potential policy responses to these findings are discussed in the next Section.

SECTION 3

POLICY ISSUES AND RECOMMENDATIONS

This Section presents our views and conclusions on the policy issues that arise from the qualitative and quantitative findings of this study on costs and funding in relation to dispute resolution and access to justice generally. We include suggestions for future policy and further research.

I. The Need to Articulate a Policy on Costs and Funding: Maintenance of Access to Civil Justice

Issues of costs and funding seem to have received little critical or academic attention in many jurisdictions. Hence, the theories and policies underlying the rules have not always been clearly articulated or scrutinised. The rules seem to be based more on the pragmatic reality of the long-established tradition of litigation systems and the need to provide for the economic necessities of enabling litigation (and access to justice) based on broad principles of fairness. Thus, the general approach is merely that an instigator of litigation should have to provide funding for initiating the state's litigation machinery (use of the courts, a lawyer, witnesses of fact and expertise) and the loser should have the broad responsibility of reimbursing these sums. Few countries seem to state whether the user fees paid for the provision of their court systems in fact cover the cost or not, and whether the policy on court fees is at the 'free access' or 'full cost recovery' ends of the spectrum. Indeed, it appears that few countries know the answer to these questions.

However, the absence of more detailed thinking may provide an opportunity for governments to reassess how civil justice systems operate in the twenty-first century, and to reform their rules in accordance with modern principles, and even to produce a measure of alignment in them. Considerable scholarly and helpful work exists on some issues in some countries, for example on contingency fees in the United States of America, but some other areas are relatively unexplored. Our aim is to stimulate fresh consideration of policy issues based on a comparative and empirical viewpoint.

Funding and costs are fully inter-linked issues. If a litigant cannot afford to claim or defend a right or loss, access to justice is denied. Many legal systems are based on the 'loser pays' cost shifting rule. This is justified as a matter of fairness and compensation, but has the secondary functions of enabling the court to exercise some discretionary control over conduct during the litigation process and of encouraging reasonable behaviour and early settlement. Many systems differ in the extent to which costs are recoverable, and over whether the secondary objectives are achieved in practice.

The need to re-evaluate procedures and costs is particularly timely at present because of changes in sources of funding and policies on which sources are acceptable. Modern states that include emancipated consumers and extensive free market commercial arrangements give rise to considerable need for efficient and effective dispute resolution systems. Extensive public funding for vindication of individuals' rights is no longer an economically viable option. Viable sources of funding need to be found, and the 'privatised' options come either from independent parties (pooling arrangements through insurance or other sources of capital) or from intermediaries involved in dispute transactions. In the latter situation, private funding arrangements have arisen that facilitate claims by smaller companies. In the former situation, the options comprise lawyer funding through some form or combination of *pro bono*, success fees, uplift fees, or contingency fees. All of these potential sources of funding are subject to development and evaluation. Changes in the landscape of funding options may produce very significant consequences in dispute resolution processes and in the delivery of justice. Complex issues of ethics and public policy arise that need to be evaluated.

There is currently widespread unease about whether traditional costs regimes deliver best solutions. In particular, there remains debate over whether access to justice is being delivered for different sections of society, and for different types of cases. Some jurisdictions have embarked on cautious innovation. Real understanding on such issues is hampered by an absence of detailed analysis and reliable empirical data.

If procedures are too complex, then the whole process takes too long and is too expensive. There has been little attempt under any system to measure civil procedure systems against the parameters of duration and cost. This needs to be done.

II. Costs

A. Allocating costs between the state and the parties: the cost of accessing courts

Most countries levy a charge on litigants for use of courts in order to contribute to the expenses that fall on the public purse of maintaining a state court system. Although much of the cost, and hence the focus of the following discussion, lies with the costs of lawyers and experts, an important point remains to define what the basis of charging by a state should be for use of its courts. The general consensus (France and Sweden notably apart) is that individuals should pay a significant contribution for the dispute resolution services provided by the court. Such costs could, to a significant extent, then be passed on to the loser.

But there are arguments that the state has an interest in maintenance of the rule of law, in clarifying and applying the law, in providing affordable access to justice and in promoting dispute resolution through its approved processes. On that reasoning, the cost of the courts should, at least in part, be shared by society through general taxation. The result is perhaps influenced more by considerations of pragmatism than principle: it depends on how much the cost is. If the courts' budget is not particularly large, then access fees for individual litigants need not be large. But if court costs are high, and payable largely by individual parties, access to justice issues will tend to arise.

The problem with trying to identify a coherent national theory or policy on costs issues is that it inevitably involves a compromise between competing interests. The principle of 'free access' to the courts found in France and Sweden is an admirable approach, and emphasises social solidarity and cohesion. Since all citizens and businesses have strong reasons to support maintenance of the rule of law by which modern democratic and trading societies exist why should the cost of the ultimate binding mechanism for the resolution of disputes not be born from public funds? But is a constitutional guarantee of 'free access' effectively almost meaningless in the contemporary world?

The counter-argument is that everything has a price, and someone has to pay it. This is particularly significant where the cost is increasingly expensive. General economic policy may be (as it increasingly is in many countries) that users of any service should pay the price for use of that service. You may have access to justice but have to pay for it. Such a political policy is invoked to justify the clear trend towards privatisation of public services in many countries. The opposite extreme to 'free access' is 'full cost recovery'. The United Kingdom appears to be the only jurisdiction that espouses a full cost recovery policy, but it has been severely criticised for this reason.[59]

[59] Jackson LJ (n 2 above). The Report included data indicating that the state has recently over-recovered on court fees.

It is striking that several countries have had serious difficulties in balancing access, cost and level of use. Portugal attempted in 2008 to reduce what the government believed was excessive use of the courts, and introduced a series of measures including increasing the justice fee by 50 per cent for commercial companies. China introduced court fees in 1984, and its attempt in 2006 to reduce them for poorer people and their disputes caused increased use of the courts and a funding crisis for courts, which required injection of significant further state funds.

These examples illustrate some interesting points. Whilst in theory a right has either been broken or it has not, and if it has, justice is only served if a remedy is available and accessed so as to remedy the position, every litigation professional is aware that the rights and wrongs are rarely clear in most cases that occur in the real world. Hence, provision of a binary outcome (win or lose), which is the outcome delivered by a court, might not be appropriate in all, or even many, cases. This observation is supported by the empirical finding in many jurisdictions that the overwhelming number of claims are settled without a judicial ruling. Accordingly, a state might decide to leave litigation costs at a level that would encourage settlement, and make the court route comparatively more attractive than some possible alternative routes. If it fixes costs at a low level the incentive to settle is reduced. This can be seen in Germany, where the result is a high volume of litigation in the courts, little incentive to settle, and a high cost for the state to pay in providing a large number of courts and judicial staff. The interesting comparison here is with Italy, which has a civil procedure system that is similar to that of Germany, but where the courts are significantly under-funded and under-resourced, resulting in notoriously long delays.

The Chinese experience is also an example of the choices that states can make in the targeting of access to justice. Many countries remit or waive fees for the poor, or for particular types of cases, such as housing, employment and challenge to state administration. The rationale is not just that certain people may have insufficient resources to seek justice but also that certain types of justice are seen as priorities.

A further structural lever that a state may seek to use is to set costs at a level that encourages certain types of case to be resolved through extra-court means in priority to use of the courts. The rationale may be a recognition that courts are expensive both for individuals and the state. It may also be recognition that some types of disputes may be more appropriate—as well as cheaper—for resolution through procedures and institutions other than courts, such as mediated agreements in family or employment matters, where the concept of winning and losing may be unhelpful if ongoing relationships are needed and if legal merits are of lesser importance.

It can be seen that the question of whether a state should charge for accessing its justice system is not easy to answer. Principled answers (free access or full cost recovery) can clearly be defended, but our findings show that they are rarely adopted in the real world. If charges are to be levied, they can be set so as to prioritise certain types of dispute and to assist certain individuals. In practice it is very challenging to reconcile and balance these competing considerations.

It is clear that jurisdictions generally apply a cost tapering approach, that is, that court costs are low for low value claims, and/or negligible for needy people. Many states levy court costs that rise in accordance with the amount in dispute. The logic for such an approach is not clear: more expensive cases do not necessarily involve more court time or resources. There would seem to be much force in the principle that fees should be differentiated on the basis of the extent of use of resources. On the other hand, such an approach might be difficult and unduly complex to apply. There is also a point that some tapering of costs might be useful, since charges levied from higher cost cases might subsidize lower fees for smaller cases, thereby assisting access to justice. On the other hand, a more principled approach would be for fees to be set at a level that reflects actual costs, and if sums are to be reduced for low value cases on grounds of encouraging access to justice, the funding should come from general state funds and not be a hidden cross-subsidy from litigants in larger cases.

The rules on court costs in some jurisdictions include the imposition of many individual small charges, producing unnecessary complexity and increasing bureaucracy. It can, of course, be argued that if there are many particular circumstances or pathways that need to be considered, then charges should be clearly apportioned. However, there needs to be a balance between cost recovery and simplicity. Arguably there is scope for simplifying court charges in many countries. Court fees should be few in number and simple to apply.

If there is to be a charge for accessing the courts, there clearly needs to be an initial fee for accessing the system. Should there be further fees and, if so, how many and for what? One principle is that fees should tend to reimburse the use of public resources by litigants. On that basis, subsequent fees should apply to major subsequent steps, notably applications or hearings. However, as noted above, a proliferation of individual fees is inadvisable. Both civil law and common law systems charge fees for the major hearing: in the German system there is simply a fee for the first hearing (and a significant number of cases may only involve one hearing, or subsequent hearings may be short), whereas in England there is a significant fee for setting down a case for (the single) trial. Another approach would be that fees should tend to encourage particular behaviour, notably settlement. Hence, some systems return a proportion of court fees if a case settles before a specified event, such as delivery of judgment. That approach is attractive from the points of view of saving public resources and encouraging parties' resolution.

The conclusion is that a principle of free access to the courts is constitutionally and socially sound, but seemingly unsupportable in full in current economic and political conditions. In any event, many governments appear either unaware or indifferent to what their policy is on cost recovery for courts, so there is little transparency over exactly what national policies are and whether citizens regard them as acceptable. These areas deserve further scrutiny for two reasons. First, use of public funds should be a matter of transparency. Secondly, there might be a desire to review whether the funds are being spent on the appropriate dispute resolution options: this is an issue recently raised by Australian Attorneys-General, and is mentioned further below.

B. Allocating costs between the parties

(i) Cost shifting

Almost every legal system applies a cost shifting rule, and regards it as correct as a matter of principle, even where there are some exceptions for particular circumstances. The major country that exceptionally has a core no cost shifting rule is the United States of America, and the specific reasons why there is a different approach there are discussed below.

There is some evidence that a costs shift encourages settlement, or earlier settlement, but the strength of this effect obviously relates to the size of the expenditure and risk involved, and their predictability. Social circumstances can affect the approach to cost shifting: in China winners used not to collect reimbursement of lawyers' fees even though this was permitted; in Denmark almost all the population is covered by insurance or legal aid so shifting has a commercial rather than a social relevance, and should only affect the behaviour of the commercial parties involved.

The argument that a loser pays rule is justifiable as a matter of principle depends on the assumption that the axis of justice exists solely between the parties, namely that the question of the extent to which one side or the other has a just case (or: is right or wrong) is the only issue. But this assumes that the law is clear and the facts are known. However, is it right that parties should bear the expense of litigating in order to clarify the law or to contribute to its development? Is it right that one party should have to bear all the costs where the court or the parties were unable to identify the correct solution without extensive investigation of the facts, perhaps because the civil procedure rules required a particularly extensive and expensive investigation? Is the traditional Portuguese approach right in such circumstances, that costs should not be shifted if parties bring a dispute for resolution in good faith? Is the Spanish solution preferable that costs will not be shifted where the court holds that the case raised serious doubts of a factual or legal nature? There seems much to be said for such approaches.[60]

Most civil law systems adopt a tariff for shiftable costs. This approach gives claimants and defendants predictability of their financial exposure, and facilitates the availability of legal expenses insurance (LEI). It avoids the problem that parties to litigation can otherwise spend time before, during and after litigation in estimating their potential costs and trying to control them. Where shiftability is based on hourly fees and work done, the transactional cost of time recording and determination can be significant, and increases as more work is done.

Clearly, many jurisdictions have a problem with regard to the predictability of the costs that are shiftable in respect of lawyers' fees that are not tariff-based. It is to be recommended that recoverable costs be as fixed and predictable as possible,

[60] The Taiwanese rule that costs are not shifted *save* in the third instance court seems the wrong way round to us.

as early as possible. This provides transparency and predictability for all parties, and supports an equality of arms. The issue, therefore, is how to design a civil procedure system that enables costs to be predictable. Should the costs vary on a scale linked to the amount in dispute, or to the type of case? Which approach gives an accurate measure of the amount of work that needs to be done, and hence deserves to be paid for, whilst also providing the lowest acceptable cost?

The rule prevailing in the jurisdictions of the United States of America that 'each party pays their own lawyers' costs'[61] requires explanation. Whatever the origin of the 'American rule' of fee shifting, its persistence—in the face of repeated calls for changes to a loser pays system—is best explained by the critical role it plays in enabling the 'private enforcement' of law.[62] The 'private enforcement' theory gives civil litigation a distinctive role to play in the United States legal system, going beyond the award of compensation for loss and providing a mechanism for achieving wider public regulatory and behavioural observance goals. In most other jurisdictions, enforcement of public norms would be reserved for public agencies rather than private actors. The American 'private enforcement' policy encourages private actors to seek out, pursue and rectify corporate wrongdoing, with no risk but with distinct incentives for the 'private attorney general'.[63] Accordingly, the American rules impose no need for claimants to fund lawyers or to bear the risk of an adverse result, incentivise the legal intermediaries, and provide for extensive access to evidence and sanctions for wrongdoers. In addition, a significant number of individual statutes provide for 'one way' cost shifting against defendants, in accordance with facilitating the above policy of private law enforcement.

The primacy of the loser pays rule globally is itself supported by the finding that one way cost shifting is a rare exception. It occurs under certain statutes in the United States where the object is to further private enforcement and punishment of wrongdoing and under the limited legal aid regime in the United Kingdom in order to insulate public funds from the expenditure burden of liability for losers' costs where cases have been supported by legal aid (this is now a rare situation since the 1995–1999 reforms).

(ii) Imposition of costs as behavioural control?

We found that although the general rule is that the loser pays the costs, this rule is almost always subject to modification by the trial judge so as to be exercisable as a

[61] There is some cost shifting of court fees, but the amounts where this occurs are typically limited. The single exception where fees are shifted is Alaska, where a partial fee shifting rule is the norm under State law: see S Di Pietro and TW Cairns, 'Alaska's English Rule: Attorney's Fee Shifting in Civil Cases' (1996) 13 *Alaska Law Review* 33. A Texas statute provides for two-way fee shifting in contract cases.

[62] This key difference in enforcement policy and legal architecture between the United States and other jurisdictions has been recognized only recently. See F Cafaggi and H-W Micklitz (eds), *New Frontiers of Consumer Protection: The Interplay between Private and Public Enforcement* (Antwerp, Intersentia, 2009); S Issacharoff, 'Regulating after the Fact' (2007) 56 *DePaul Law Review* 375.

[63] Amongst a large quantity of literature see JC Coffee Jr, 'Rescuing the Private Attorney General: Why the Model of the Lawyer as Bounty Hunter is not Working' (1983) 42 *Maryland Law Review* 215, 217; RA Kagan, *Adversarial Legalism* (Boston/Mass, Harvard University Press, 2001).

sanction in response to unacceptable conduct during the litigation process. Hence, the justification for court discretion over the award of costs is to provide an incentive for the parties to behave reasonably during the procedure, and if they do not to act as a deterrent because costs may be awarded against them, even if they win. Unreasonable behaviour would include raising an unjustifiable claim, failing to disclose relevant evidence or acting in a timely fashion. Possible sanctions could include being denied an award of costs that would normally be made in a party's favour, or being ordered to pay more than would normally be the case.

References to the behavioural control justification seem to occur rarely in theoretical writing or in official policy statements (which are in any event rare themselves). This lever is simply not available where there is no cost shifting, or where costs are recovered on a tariff basis. It is unclear to what extent the behaviour sanction is in fact applied in practice, and how effective it is. Does it operate as a control on litigants' general behaviour, or on the amount of work done, or on the inclination to settle—and might there be other means of achieving those controls, if relevant?

A recoverability gap can provide a tool by which a lawyer may influence his client's conduct, such as in avoiding unnecessarily expensive inquiries or adopting a more reasonable approach to settlement. This is reported from Canada but may equally apply in other systems.

The cost sanction *could* be a useful judicial tool in controlling excessive costs. A number of countries effectively provide that only reasonable costs will be awarded to winners. But this case management tool appears to be rarely used in practice. It ought to act as a potentially important means of providing a level playing field between defendants who have significantly differing levels of resources, so as to avoid 'litigation bullying'. But it is not clear how often such a phenomenon occurs, and even less clear how often judges sanction it in their costs orders.

It may be questioned whether a costs sanction is relevant or not as a control on conduct during the litigation process. As yet there is no empirical evidence for assertions in either direction. Such a control does not apply under a civil law strict tariff system, but then the activities of parties and lawyers under that system are constrained by its architecture. The potential for bad behaviour to occur in litigation and carrying out excessive work, perhaps for tactical reasons, would seem to be greater under a common law system (with *ex post* control on costs) than under a civil law procedure system.

Further work could be done on proposing a coherent approach towards the circumstances in which costs should be awarded or not, or reduced. The Taiwanese codification offers an interesting and logical approach. There, a sequence of rules gives a general discretion to the court to award costs either in a certain proportion, or by one party alone, or by both without cost shifting.[64] There are some special rules, including: the claimant shall pay if the defendant immediately admits a

[64] Code of Civil Procedure, art 79.

claim (thereby encouraging pre-litigation bilateral negotiation and settlement),[65] parties shall pay for unnecessary acts during the litigation (to encourage proportionality and equality of arms),[66] and where a case is settled, the parties shall bear their own expenses unless otherwise agreed.[67]

C. Achieving predictability of costs

We found that court costs are always predictable, since they are published in official tariffs, whereas lawyers' costs are relatively predictable in those countries where tariffs exist but otherwise largely unpredictable. The civil procedure systems of jurisdictions where tariffs for lawyers' fees do not exist essentially require lawyers to undertake a significant amount of the effort in processing claims, and their costs will not be fully predictable since the amount of such effort can vary and fees are principally tied to hours worked. Three separate elements need to be addressed: the amount of work done and the cost that is payable per unit of time and in total. The first factor has two aspects: it relates first to the architecture of the civil process, which defines the general parameters of the work that needs to be done, and secondly to the amount of work actually done in an individual case by a given lawyer. The essential question is always the same, namely whether the amount of work is too big, and can be reduced. The latter factor gives rise to consideration of the available methods for funding and charging, for which every jurisdiction has a different set of options, albeit there are themes and similarities across many states.

A further feature of unpredictability follows from the loser pays principle. The exposure of a party to an opponent's costs can be entirely unpredictable in the absence of a tariff for shiftable costs. Again, the position is worse in those systems that revolve around hours worked and the unpredictable amount of work done. A party to litigation can therefore face the significant double risk of liability for his own costs and the risk of his opponent's costs, with little idea of how much the latter might be, and little means of controlling either figure.

Thus, lawyers' costs are only truly predictable where a straightforward tariff applies, irrespective of the amount of work done. Theoretically, of course, two tariffs are necessary, namely one for what a party has to pay his own lawyers and the second for the shiftable costs if he loses. The first aspect is important because a party may not be able to get a claim or a defence off the ground unless he has the resources to pay the process and legal costs. The second aspect is arguably more important than the first, since the party should be able to exercise some choice over instructing a lawyer that he might be able to afford, and to exert some degree of control over his own lawyer's costs if he wishes, even though that may be difficult in some circumstances, or he may not be paying because private insurance or

[65] ibid, art 80.
[66] ibid, art 81.
[67] ibid, art 84.

state funding may apply. An independent funder or insurer may also be able to exert some control over the party's lawyer's costs. But, in any event, the real unknown and uncontrollable aspect is the size of the opponent's costs, and if they are predictable through a tariff, that is an ideal solution. The existence of a tariff for shiftable liability may, in turn, set some benchmark or pressure in relation to the level of costs of a party's own lawyer.[68]

Such double predictability occurs in systems like Germany and many of the European civil law jurisdictions that follow its approach. In such systems, different tariffs apply to own-client and to shiftable costs, although the percentage shifted is dependent on the court's award over what percentage of the shiftable tariff costs each party should pay.

In contrast, in many common law jurisdictions (apart from the United States) the shiftable costs are linked to the time-and-hourly-rate basis of work actually done (what Americans would call a 'lodestar' rule) for own-client work for the winner. It is this situation that inevitably gives rise to the traditionally imponderable problem of how to control the amount of work done by an opponent, and how to reduce the shiftable costs *post facto*, which, as noted above, is always going to present a more difficult regulatory challenge. A party might not know whether she is going to win, and might be unable to know how much the other side is going to try to recharge, or how much the claimed bill is going to be able to be cut down by negotiation or, at further cost, by court assessment (taxation).

In common law countries, experienced lawyers might be able to predict both sorts of costs with some level of accuracy, but the level of accuracy may significantly depend on the type of case involved: for example, some cases (RTA, debt recovery) are straightforward and involve well known and predictable steps, so costs should be both predictable and relatively modest. Larger commercial cases, however, may involve a great deal of work (especially under the common law approach to civil procedure) and costs may be almost entirely unpredictable. This conclusion leads on to important consequences in relation to the design of the civil process, which are examined further below.

If a tariff merely for shiftable costs were applied more widely in a common law jurisdiction, it would deliver considerably increased certainty, offer the possibility of keeping such costs proportionate and low, and might have some consequential limiting effect on amounts charged for own-client costs. This route towards further use of fixed costs, on which England and Wales have made some progress and seem likely to extend, is an important and justifiable step. The approach depends on commodification of important types of claim that arise frequently and/or present cost problems, especially for those who have difficulty affording the level of costs that might be involved.

One way of looking at controls on costs is to analyse them into *ex ante* or *ex post facto* controls, in accordance with classic regulatory theory.[69] There should be a

[68] This was precisely the consideration that led the French Bar to defeat a proposal to introduce a tariff for shiftable costs.

[69] See A Ogus, *Regulation: Legal Form and Economic Theory* (Oxford, Clarendon Press, 1994).

strong expectation that *ex post facto* regulation (review and reduction by the court: common law 'taxation') will be less successful in delivering predictability. So *ex ante* controls such as tariffs and fixed costs should be far preferable in delivering predictability. That is borne out by the case studies: the tariffs of the civil law world are clearly preferable to the common law world (of free market rates and ineffective *ex post* optional costs assessment) in delivering predictable costs—where there is cost shifting.

Where there is no cost shifting, such as in the United States of America, a 'no win no fee' system is entirely predictable, since it delivers no cost to the claimant if he or she loses and no cost shift to the defendant if he or she wins. But there is still cost in the system: if the claimant wins, the contingency fee system reduces the claimant's damages by the amount of the (unrecoverable element of) success fee, and the defendant who settles often has to pay an element towards the winner's lawyer's costs. The American system of extensive discovery can clearly give rise to very high cost.

England has attempted to make lawyers' costs predictable in some types of cases, through introducing fixed costs.[70] This approach may potentially be extended as a result of the Jackson Review to all fast track cases (ie all under £25,000) and may be broadened further.[71] This development is to be welcomed. As noted above, one approach to the introduction of fixed costs depends on the ability to predict the amount of work that will be necessary in a particular type of case, the existence of a sufficient volume of individual cases of that type, and the fact that the amount of work done in the vast majority of cases of that type falls within an acceptably small range of cost. If this is so, then the question that arises is whether a system of civil procedure can identify individual case types that are susceptible to a standard procedural approach, since they involve a standard amount of evidence, pleading and work, and for which most individual cases do not diverge significantly from the standard model. It is inherent in such an approach that different case types need to be analysed individually, and might need to be processed differently.

It is not essential that every case should involve exactly the same amount of work, so that the fixed costs exactly cover the actual cost in each case. In order to make fixed recoverable costs work, assuming that no irrecoverable costs are to be paid by clients, the same approach is needed as has been found to apply in contingency fees in the United States, namely that lawyers may take on a portfolio of different cases, some of which involve higher or lower returns, but overall the portfolio balances out to be a sufficiently profitable business enterprise.[72] On this basis, there must be an acceptable range of risk and profit within the portfolio as a

[70] Fixed costs currently apply (with success) for (a) uncontested cases; (b) road traffic accidents: (i) predictable costs in low value RTA claims settled before issue, and (ii) predictable success fees in all other RTA claims; (c) success fees in employers' liability and employers' liability disease cases; (d) fast track (under £15,000) trials.

[71] See Jackson LJ (n 2 above) part 5.

[72] See HM Kritzer, *Risks, Reputations, and Rewards: Contingency Fee Legal Practice in the United States* (Stanford University Press, 2004).

whole. For example, it might be important that the cases should not deviate too far from a general standard amount of work or cost. However, if it is accepted that there is a recoverability gap that the client has to fund, for example out of damages if they are high enough, such considerations are ameliorated—unless the client loses.

A telling anecdotal comment made by practitioners who practise in European jurisdictions that do not have tariffs or fixed fees is that, unless a small claims procedure or other special process applies, cases for an individual under €10,000 or a company under €100,000 are not worth pursuing from the perspective of the prospective litigant, because costs are too high, ie not proportionate.

Courts almost everywhere have the power to award costs and to depart to some extent from any tariff that applies—at least in theory. Such an approach retains some control over behaviour by the parties and might encourage settlement, but the force of these discretionary rules in practice is unclear. The incentive to settle is clearly increased as higher costs apply, perhaps disproportionately. However, court discretion reduces predictability, at least if the discretion is exercised more than rarely. Further empirical research should examine how important court discretion is over costs, and the need to control party behaviour. The classic fixed tariff recoverable cost systems involve no discretion, so provide no such behavioural control, and seemingly have little need for it. Perhaps it would be better to develop a system with a strict tariff that allows for a number of limited and clearly circumscribed (and thus predictable) exceptions, rather than a conferral of vaguely defined 'discretion' on judges. Of course, such rigour will come at the expense of substantive justice in a (small) number of cases.

An argument against a fixed recoverable tariff is that it is arbitrary. Why should cost be based on an arbitrary percentage of the amount in dispute, since this does not take into account the amount of work that might be needed to be done in a case, especially in relation to different types of case? On the other hand, predictability has a number of benefits. Hence, certainty is traded for arbitrariness. If a tariff is to apply, should it be developed (on the approach outlined above) from consideration of the amount of work done in a standard case, or should it be linked (as under the German-style approach) to the amount at stake in a given case? The former approach might tend to be linked too closely to continuation of rent-seeking behaviour by intermediaries, whereas the latter approach is again largely arbitrary. Further consideration should be given to the extent to which either approach matters, or delivers proportionality. If a tariff is related to the value at stake, does this lead to enough work being done by a lawyer in a small case, or does the procedural framework of the legal system mean that such a consideration is not that important? Conversely, if the architecture of the legal system means that the amount of work that lawyers have to do does not vary significantly as the value at stake rises, does this not overpay them in higher value cases? Or, if that is so, are the amounts in the overall tariff set in such a way that lawyers can appropriately cross-subsidise taking on loss-making smaller value cases by dealing with a sufficient number of profit-making larger value cases?

Fixed costs are more difficult to apply to larger and more complex commercial cases, where the evidential and other issues involved vary between cases and are resistant to standardisation. In such cases, effective and strong case management by judges is of paramount importance, so as to define the issues, specify and limit the work done, manage costs as much *ex ante* as possible, and positively encourage settlement.

Where costs are based on a tariff or lump sum, the lawyer does not need to record individual units of time worked. Thus, if he is not working on an hourly rate, and costs are either not shiftable or are shifted on a basis that does not relate to time worked, there might be a saving in the costs and overhead of the time recording process.

D. Achieving proportionality of costs

Traditionally, few legal systems have included a principle that the total costs of access to justice be proportionate. However, this issue has recently been discussed in a number of jurisdictions. Such jurisdictions are primarily common law systems, in which lawyers' costs depend on the amount of work done in a case. Such work is inherently variable and hence the total bill is unpredictable. Further, costs are frequently disproportionate to the sums at stake in small cases, and in large cases they can be very high even if they amount to less than the sums at stake. Such issues arise to a far lesser extent in those (civil law) legal systems where the civil procedure rules require lawyers to perform less work than in common law systems and which are usually associated with tariffs for both lawyers' fees and shiftable costs.

How important is the principle of proportionality? It is suggested that the need for a dispute resolution mechanism that is provided by the state to operate on the basis of costs that are proportionate is of some relevance. Civil society and the state have an interest in ensuring that rights may be upheld, debts collected, government challenged, and the rule of law maintained. On this basis, the application of a principle of proportionality can be seen as a justifiable matter of public policy. Concern over proportionality has arisen precisely because costs have risen and access to justice is being threatened.

However, a principle of proportionality of costs can be difficult to apply in practice. It may vary from case to case, and between different types of case. The quantitative case studies in the previous Section of this study clearly show that not all types of cases or all countries' systems involve costs that are 'high' and/or 'disproportionate'.

(i) What should costs be proportionate to?

As the Jackson Review notes, there is an issue over what is meant by 'proportionate' costs. What should costs be proportionate to? What criteria should be applied to evaluate the proportionality of costs? Lawyers' principal concern is the amount of work done. A criterion of the amount of work done can clearly lead to problems, and justify an unacceptably high fee (especially if magnified also by a success fee). Most national rules provide that the factors that should be taken into account in setting a lawyer's fee include the amount of work done, the amount in dispute (where that is quantifiable, and some cases are not) and also the value of the case to the party. Proportionality to the sum in dispute might favour clients, since this might lead to a lower fee in smaller cases than if the importance of the case were taken into account: but it may equally favour lawyers in justifying an increase in fees for larger cases and where the 'value' of a dispute has non-monetary components that are of value to a particular litigant. In contrast, proportionality to the importance of the case to the client should favour the lawyer, by justifying a higher fee than would result from considering the sum in dispute. The value of a case might well justify a supplement in some other standard types of supply of services or goods, but the problem in relation to legal services in litigation is, again, the public policy interest in maintaining proportionality.

This study finds that few jurisdictions have any rule that costs, whether court costs or process or lawyers' costs, should be proportionate to the value of the case. Indeed, the rules consistently emphasise the 'value of work done' criterion. But issues of proportionality are increasingly arising, where what is meant is disproportionality between the costs and the value of the matters in dispute. This is so because, first, lawyers' costs, for some types of case at least, are too high (and this may be an inherent feature of the architecture of a civil justice system rather than an indictment of its intermediaries), secondly, a significant number of poor people cannot access justice (and, at the opposite extreme, the cost of large commercial litigation can be enormous) and, thirdly, state funding of justice through legal aid has at best a very restricted future, so the size of an access to justice gap is a matter of concern.

However, so far very few jurisdictions seem to have attempted to address the issue of whether lawyers' costs are proportionate. Where it has arisen, it is a significant issue, namely in England and Wales, New Zealand, Canada and Australia, ie in all major common law jurisdictions except from the United States of America.

The particular legal architecture of the United States means that proportionality is far less of an issue there: indeed, levels of remuneration can be very high in some cases, but are modest in many small cases, assisted by somewhat higher levels of general damages than in most other jurisdictions and by the fact that lawyers, rather than clients, bear the exclusive financial loss of unsuccessful cases. Proportionality is a fundamental constitutional principle in relation to action by the European Union and Member States,[73] although it does not apply under EU law in relation to private contracts, such as agreements with lawyers. However recent it may be as a concept, the principle of proportionality can be anticipated to have strong influence on future developments in EU legal systems.

[73] Art 5(4) Treaty on European Union.

Where proportionality has become an issue, it has lead to attempts to enshrine it as a fundamental value within the civil procedure system, specifically so as to try to control costs. The leading example of where this has been attempted is England and Wales from 1999, and Canada has introduced the concept of proportionality in 2007. But the English attempt is widely thought not to have succeeded, at least to date. In fact, success there has been partial: the fixed costs regimes have been successful; it is the larger types of cases (notably personal injury and larger commercial cases) where costs remain uncontrolled. The intention of Lord Woolf that case management by judges should control costs has not been sufficiently implemented in practice: whether such an approach might succeed remains unproven.

Proportionality is, of course, an inherent feature of a cost and cost shifting tariff system, such as the German model, where the prevailing level of fees is also not excessive. The proposals of the English Jackson Review are clearly moving towards increasing adoption within the English system of both predictable and proportionate costs. Lord Justice Jackson has signalled that it is time to reign in the unfettered principle of 'fair' remuneration for work done. He has set out an incremental programme of extending fixed and benchmark shiftable fees for different types of cases. His argument rests firmly on the argument that achieving access to justice, which he regards as the paramount principle, is consistent with ensuring that costs are proportionate: 'for the most part, achieving proportionate costs and promoting access to justice go hand in hand. If costs on both sides are proportionate, then (i) there is more access to justice and (ii) such funding as the parties possess is more likely to be sufficient.'[74] Accordingly, he seeks to trump the argument based on 'fair' remuneration by invoking the principle of access to justice. Under such a system, service providers whose bills are dramatically and perhaps arbitrarily reduced by a court *ex post facto* might have a strong case for unfair treatment. But the key to this issue lies in the architecture of the civil procedure system. If the system involves a clear and predictable amount of work, then a fair rate can be set and, even if it is a low rate, the market can be expected to generate some providers who are willing to accept it, having structured their overheads and profit expectations accordingly. Thus, there needs to be a satisfactory relationship between the amount of work that intermediaries have to do and their level of remuneration. This is achieved in the German system, and the combination of procedural pre-action protocols and guidelines coupled with fixed costs for lower value claims is the English common law equivalent.

The principle of proportionality of costs is still recent, and not yet widely adopted, but set to gain further recognition. The consistent impression from many national reports is that lawyers' fees are frequently too high, especially in common law jurisdictions, and governments may increasingly wish to regulate legal fees so as to reduce them. A debate has yet to occur over whether seemingly established 'rules of thumb' that fees, or success fees, payable to intermediaries (whether lawyers or other funders) of around 30 per cent (or any other percentage), whether

[74] Jackson LJ (n 2 above) ch 4, para 2.8.

of standard fees or of the amount recovered, represent fair value. Does a percentage approach include a proportionate result? English cases on CFA success fee uplifts in the past decade seem to set a far lower standard for acceptable uplifts, and there has been notable judicial consensus that some cases justify only small percentage uplifts.

In many common law jurisdictions it is possible to discern a major policy response to increasing costs, ie the adoption of case management techniques by courts. However, current concern over unpredictable and disproportionate costs represents, to a certain extent at least, failure of the case management policy as it has been applied in practice. This is a serious challenge to the reputation of courts and judges, and to the ability of a state and society to satisfy citizens' and businesses' legitimate expectations of delivery of justice. It is a fundamental threat to the rule of law. But is case management capable, as was thought, of solving the costs problem, since it itself involves cost through requiring work by both lawyers and judges? The Jackson Review in England and Wales, discussed in Chapters 7–9 below, highlights the need for courts to be aware of costs management in addition to case management.

In summary, there is a clear movement towards scrutinising the costs of litigation against a criterion of proportionality to the value of the dispute, and such a step raises questions over how lawyers' fees in particular can be controlled, whether the procedural steps in a civil procedure inherently involve unnecessary cost and can be reformed, and whether some non-court dispute resolution pathways are cheaper than court procedures.

(ii) Proportionality of lawyers' costs

This study has made several important findings in relation to lawyers' costs and how they are regulated. First, lawyers' costs constitute the principal element in the costs of accessing justice through litigation; secondly, lawyers' costs are lowest in countries where they are regulated by tariffs; thirdly, costs are frequently unpredictable unless lawyers' fees are specified in tariffs; fourthly, lawyers' costs, and costs generally, are frequently disproportionate to the sums at stake in small cases, and in large cases they can be very high even if they amount to less than the sums at stake.

These findings suggest that lawyers' fees should be regulated by tariffs in order to provide predictability, proportionality and acceptable levels of cost.

It was found in Section 1 of this study that current requirements on fees frequently list a series of factors that should be taken into account in deciding a fee for a given case. The existence of a multiplicity of factors that need to be taken into account can theoretically be used to justify either raising or lowering a fee in a given case. Concentration on any individual factor can, of course, be argued to have such a raising or lowering effect. But the purpose of providing a multiplicity of factors is ultimately to justify lowering a fee. There is evidence that lawyers waive or lower fees at their discretion in some countries depending on a client's ability to pay and in relation to the success of a case. So there is some flexibility in practice. But the system of regulation of fees, which is largely self-regulatory, is essentially designed to maintain fees at an acceptable level. The essential point is that fee levels and their regulation have not hitherto been subjected to assessment against a single over-riding objective of proportionality.

This raises the important point of how much lawyers should be paid? From a lawyer's perspective, there should be a fair fee for work done. That is the rule in, for example, Ireland, where the rules do not mention a requirement for proportionality between the level of fee and the value of the case. Most suppliers of goods and services would expect and be entitled to a fair fee for work done. In any civil procedure system, but especially in the common law systems, the amount of work that may have to be done varies from case to case, may well be unpredictable in many if not all cases, and may (validly or otherwise) end up constituting a significant amount of work. Should professional service providers not be paid fairly for effort? But a fair fee for the amount of work done might not necessarily be one that is proportionate to the sum in dispute. The Australian Victorian Law Reform Commission's recent 'Civil Justice Review'[75] questions whether it is appropriate to limit costs by reference to proportionality considerations. Should these principles of fairness and proportionality be reconciled, and how? Which principle should prevail?

A market-based structure for transparency of fees does, of course, widely exist. The essential element of such an approach involves publication of the criteria against which fees are assessed (which is widespread). However, does a mere requirement for lawyers to provide information on fees or, preferably, total costs, provide sufficient control over fees or costs? The theory is that market forces apply, but economists have pointed out that a proper market rarely applies in relation to most lawyers' services to clients.[76] The problem is exacerbated by the fact that price is not the most important factor in choosing a lawyer. Empirical evidence shows that private and business clients alike are much more concerned about the professional skills and reputation of their lawyers, as well as the personal relationship developed with them.[77] Individual customers do not have the expertise, commercial leverage or sophistication to differentiate between the quality or costs of different providers, or to negotiate lower or capped fees. Where high fees occur frequently, the issue is one of market capture by lawyers. However, in some societies, where clients' resources are limited, the lawyer may respond by having to restrict the amount of work done: the national correspondent in Japan pointed out that a client might tell the lawyer at the start how much money he had available to spend on a case and the lawyer would work within this budget, for example by

[75] Victorian Law Reform Commission, *Civil Justice Review Report* (2008) 656–658, available at http://www.lawreform.vic.gov.au/wps/wcm/connect/8137a400404a0bed9549fff5f2791d4a/VLRC+Civil+Justice+Review+-+Report.pdf?MOD=AJPERES.

[76] Hadfield (n 58 above) 963–999.

[77] Copenhagen Economics, *The Legal Profession: Competition and Liberalisation* (Copenhagen, January 2006). 11, 22-23, relying on surveys from Denmark and Norway. The study is available at http://www.ccbe.org/fileadmin/user_upload/NTCdocument/The_legal_profession1_1195120689.pdf.

deciding not to pursue certain witnesses or expert evidence if the cost were to exceed the budget.

In contrast, where clients are sophisticated and/or repeat players, negotiations may occur on a normal market basis. This should apply where clients are larger companies and insurance companies. Market forces operate more clearly in such circumstances (the report from the Netherlands noted that insurance companies had forced fixed rates on their lawyers, and this is anecdotally repeated widely elsewhere). For example, bargaining occurs in cases of commoditisation of legal services: lower rates will be negotiated in return for a volume of cases where the cases are similar in type and involve similar and predictable amounts of work. Road traffic accident (RTA) cases handled by insurance companies are a typical example. The insurers are able to instruct panels of lawyers at low rates. An issue that arises is whether the client or the insurer should make the choice of lawyer. From the perspective of the customer, there is a conflict between the right of selecting and controlling his own lawyer and permitting the insurer to choose a lawyer and thus obtaining lower insurance prices for simple, commoditisable work. In some cases, the freedom to choose one's own lawyer may be a false economy and worth surrendering.

However, it is argued that the legal services market does not operate on the basis of normal economic forces, and requires regulatory intervention, particularly in relation to small claims, since consumers and small companies might otherwise be denied access to justice.

E. Provision of dispute resolution pathways outside courts

Costs may be disproportionately high because of the complexities of the traditional mechanisms of civil litigation. In recent years, many countries have constructed pathways and procedures for the resolution of specific disputes that lie outside courts, because they are cheaper, quicker, offer greater expertise, greater confidentiality, a less aggressive forum, or perhaps greater flexibility in approach and in possible solutions. Arbitration, especially of commercial disputes, is a well-established example. Tribunals for family or employment disputes, and small claims procedures, are others. Yvon Desdesvises calls this trend 'de-litigation'.[78]

Specific examples in Canada include special administrative procedures, established as a response to an access to justice crisis, for employment matters, workplace injuries and motor vehicle accidents, and indemnity arrangements, such as under the Canadian Medical Practitioners Association, which assesses claims and decides either to pay out or defend. Other examples range across Denmark, the United Kingdom (a huge growth in non-court alternatives), Finland, Japan (especially since it has often been said that litigation runs contrary to the national culture), New Zealand (the Weathertight Claims Tribunal, the Disputes Tribunal

[78] See ch 10 below.

for small claims and the no fault accident compensation scheme), Norway (all claims under NOK 125,000 are required to start in the Conciliation Board before proceeding to court, and cases valued at over that amount may start at the Board or in court),[79] Portugal (2008 reforms), Sweden and consumer and business dispute fora throughout Spain, France and Nordic states. The Nordic states also have no fault compensation schemes for medical and medicinal product injuries.[80]

Concern over the economic aspects of litigation raises wider issues over national policy on dispute resolution, and the prioritization between different options. The costs rules provide a number of incentives and barriers to litigating parties, in relation to bringing, defending, settling or fighting disputes. Such rules also indicate governmental priorities as between different judicial or alternative dispute resolution pathways, or between the dispute resolution systems available in different jurisdictions. In this last respect, costs regimes are topical because they indicate the level of comparative efficiency between different court systems, and whether these systems involve procedures that are too costly or too slow.

Governments face choices in relation to establishing a coherent, just, efficient and co-ordinated national policy for the delivery of civil justice and dispute resolution. There appears to be little evidence from government publications in almost all states that serious attention has been given to what an integrated policy on these matters might look like. The task of drawing up such a policy may well, admittedly, be difficult for many advanced countries, since the spread of 'unofficial' dispute resolution mechanisms has not been planned or controlled, nor has it been mapped. But in some states, the spread of dispute resolution pathways that are an alternative to official court mechanisms has grown into being a considerable corpus of different techniques. This matrix of different mechanisms needs to be considered as a whole, if a national policy on dispute resolution and civil justice is to be valid and effective in a modern state.

Australia has recently realised this point. Given that 90 per cent of litigation disputes settle, the English approach of imposing a principle that costs must be proportionate and that the courts should be a 'last resort' dispute resolution technique are clearly exerting some influence in Australia. The 2009 Commonwealth 'Access to Justice' Report[81] signals a concern to take a holistic view of the various techniques and pathways that the state, citizens and businesses fund to enable dispute resolution. The Report makes clear that those who are responsible for the overall expenditure should be concerned that the money is spent effectively and efficiently. That means not only that litigation costs need to be proportionate, but also that a satisfactory range of dispute resolution pathways and techniques need to be available that collectively offer cost effective outcomes for resolving

[79] In 2004 in Norway, 218,157 cases were started in Conciliation Boards, of which 7,766 settled, 16,318 claims were accepted, and 3,791 cases were referred to the courts; 13,450 cases were filed in courts.

[80] CJS Hodges, 'Nordic Compensation Schemes for Drug Injuries' (2006) 29 *Journal of Consumer Policy* 143.

[81] Australian Government, Attorney-General's Department, *A Strategic Framework for Access to Justice in the Federal Civil Justice System* (September 2009).

problems. One simple illustration of a consequence of such an approach might be that instead of spending public funds on legal aid to support legal services for the resolution of disputes through courts, less money might be more effectively spent on other options, such as providing information and various types of mediation services. The same point is made by Pauline van der Grinten from the Dutch government's viewpoint.[82] Accordingly, the future of 'access to justice' may lie in an integrated policy of 'access to problem solving', and in integrated frameworks of techniques and pathways, rather than in traditional lawyer-led court pathways. The United Kingdom government has also noted the point about coordinating and prioritising pathways in its policies on collective redress.[83]

F. The difficulty of transplanting costs rules: costs and the architecture of civil procedure

It is tempting to argue that the optimal costs regime is one that combines the best features of the jurisdictions analysed in this study. Why not simply combine the rules that provide predictability in one legal system with those that lead to proportionate results in another? As usual, the transplantability of legal rules is limited because they cannot be sensibly divorced from their wider context. The context of costs rules is the architecture of civil procedure in a given legal system. It is helpful to consider three basic models of civil procedure: at the danger of overgeneralisation, these may broadly be described as the civil law model (typified by Germany, important features of which are shared by other civil law jurisdictions although significant differences exist) and the common law model, with the American model being a distinct further type.

a. The German civil procedure has admirable features of speed, and predictable and low costs. Much of the work is done by judges (hence a need for more judges than in some other systems) rather than lawyers (hence lower lawyers' costs than in some other systems). Judges focus on those issues that remain in dispute, and positively facilitate settlement. Evidence, expertise and narrowing of the issues occurs in a series of short hearings. The efficiency of the system and other factors have not encouraged the development of mediation or many other alternative settlement approaches.
b. In the common law system, much of the seeking out of evidence (witnesses of fact, documents, and expert assessment) is done by lawyers, which necessarily involves more people than if the work were done by a single judge, and the more work needed, the higher the costs. The objective is a final trial but many cases settle during the process through mediation and other ADR techniques. Recent innovations include attempts to restrict the extent of evidence and

[82] See ch 15 below.
[83] UK Government's Response to the Civil Justice Council's Report: 'Improving Access to Justice through Collective Actions', Ministry of Justice (July 2009), available at http://www.justice.gov.uk/about/docs/government-response-cjc-collective-actions.pdf.

experts, to have stronger directed case management through protocols and by judges, to identify streamlined approaches to different types of cases, and to encourage ADR.

c. An extreme and unique manifestation of the common law approach is the American civil procedure system. As noted above, the private enforcement function that is emphasized in the United States leads to the adoption of particular rules on no cost shifting, one way cost shifting under certain statutes, and no funding requirement for those individual claimants who agree contingency fees with their lawyers. Many cases may be resolved at proportionate cost to claimants, and successful claimants' recoveries fund their lawyers (but not opponents). In some cases, there will be a great deal of input by lawyers, so costs can be very high.

d. A further issue with some common law systems is that the involvement of both solicitors and barristers in a case may lead to an unnecessary increase in costs. The involvement of a team of different individuals who each have specialist functions (such as administration, collection of evidence, client relations and advocacy) might not necessarily lead to duplication of work or an overall increase in costs in a case of a certain size in a system in which all of those functions are required, but this is a factor that deserves further scrutiny. The underlying point seems to relate more to the procedural system than to maintenance of a split profession, but some questions remain over the latter. An issue is raised over the extent to which such a system should be reformed in order to reduce overall costs.

One conclusion from examining the above first two (civil law and common law) paradigms is that the models are fundamentally unlike each other in their basic architecture. Further, the American model of private enforcement is itself distinct from almost every other system, because its basic objectives are different. The German and English models, to take two European examples of the paradigms, are also quite different in their procedure, notably the division of workload between lawyers and judges, and many more detailed consequences follow. However, there are signs of some movement towards each other in relation to extending or limiting documentary evidence, use of single experts, and specification of activities through protocols that lead to fixed costs in certain types of cases.

A very important conclusion is that there is an inextricable connection between the architecture of the procedure and the cost rules. The rules were designed with the costs rules in mind, and vice versa. It may, therefore, be difficult to extract and transplant one feature, say predictable and low costs, into a foreign procedure that has a different architecture. For example, if the English system were to provide a German-style costs tariff for all cases, it would be inoperable without the aspects of German civil procedure that work together to produce low and predictable costs.

As noted above, a costs tariff only works where the amount of work is stable and predictable for the vast majority of cases of the particular type that it covers, with few outliers. The German model applies a costs tariff with a scale depending on the amount of money in dispute. That has the considerable benefit of simplicity, but the amount in dispute does not necessarily equate with either the complexity of a case or its importance to the parties, and takes no account of case types. In contrast, England has taken the approach of looking at some (not all) case types in order to define standard approaches and hence standard costs: the technique used has been the definition of pre-action protocols, which specify, to a greater or lesser extent, what each party has to do. Hence, both the traditional German and more recent English approaches in specifying predictable costs produce the similar outcome of predictability, although the mechanism by which they arrive at that result is different (one being based on a tariff dependent on the amount in dispute and the other defining a paradigm standard case and then costing the amount of work to be done). The German approach involves some level of proportionality (to the amount in dispute) whereas the English approach gives predictability but not necessarily proportionality. If the English fixed costs are to be proportionate, the review process needs to involve some reduction on either the amount of work done or the hourly rates on which the calculation is made to produce the final fixed amount.

The German model has predictable costs for virtually all cost items (court costs, lawyers' fees, and to a great extent for witness and expert costs).[84] It works particularly well for simple, lower value claims. It is, however, less effective for more complex cases, and it is notable that larger commercial cases tend to use arbitration, within which greater access to documentary evidence can apply or be ordered by the arbitrator.

In contrast, the basic common law or English model produces unpredictable lawyers' fees, but predictable court costs. This is because the amount of work done by the judges/courts is relatively predictable and so costable, whereas the amount of work done by lawyers is traditionally unpredictable. Indeed, the amount of work done by lawyers can vary widely between different type of cases, and in large cases can be huge (and far more than under the German system, where most of the work is done by the judge and not by the lawyers).

In recent years, however, the 'English model' has splintered into a number of separate tracks, each with different rules on evidence, lawyers and costs: small claims, fast track cases, multi-track cases, and specialist courts. This trend towards particularisation is capable of producing costs that are both more predictable and lower. The trend appears to deserve further attention.

The differing approaches towards settlement of cases is a good example for the link between the costs rules and the overall procedural architecture of a given jurisdiction. In some systems, such as in Spain, very few cases are settled between the parties, and the court is left to resolve the dispute by issuing a judgment: set-

[84] G Wagner, 'Litigation Costs and Their Recovery: The German Experience' [2009] *Civil Justice Quarterly* 368.

tlement rates quoted are Latvia 1–3 per cent, Italy 2 per cent (but 60 per cent in commercial cases), Lithuania 10 per cent, Estonia 11 per cent. In other systems, settlement rates before judgment are notably high: Canada (as reported), Norway 42 per cent, Switzerland 60–80 per cent in commercial cases, Australia 90 per cent, Ireland 90 per cent, England 90 per cent, and Scotland 93 per cent. Obviously there are other factors explaining these rates, notably citizens' prevailing expectations of the law (settlement of dispute by mutual compromise or by declaring one of the parties to be victorious). This, again, can be expected to be influenced by the overall level of costs of litigation in the respective country: if obtaining judgment is simply out of reach for most of the average citizens general expectations of the law will gradually change.

Under the common law system of proceeding towards a single final trial, the parties gain more information about the merits of the dispute and face a gradual increase in costs, which usually escalate in relation to a trial. So a successive increase in costs should encourage settlement. Under the civil law procedure, the process does not end in a single trial, but there is one or perhaps a succession of short hearings, and the overall costs are lower than in the common law system. Such a system would not tend to have such strong pressure on settlement. If a claimant has paid the fee at the start, and both parties can predict what their costs and their financial risk is, particularly if it is low, and if the process is the most speedy dispute resolution mechanism available, the balance of advantage may well lie in simply letting the court conclude the process and deliver a binding judgment. That attitude would avoid making the investment of effort, time and emotion in mediation or other settlement discussions.

The funding position and risk can clearly affect attitude to settlement. The Danish Report observes that almost all individuals have LEI or legal aid, hence they have no incentive to settle, and cases are usually not settled. On the other hand, businesses and individuals who self-fund have an incentive to settle, although in Denmark cases are often not settled once litigation commences.

However, the position is not always as simple as that. In some civil law systems, cases do settle during the process, and the court itself can facilitate this. Thus, judges in Germany and the Netherlands, for example, can indicate their view of the merits of a case from the first hearing, and even put pressure on parties to settle. This is done frequently. Judges in Switzerland may positively propose settlements. Such intervention has pragmatic force. But many systems would regard it as a breach of the principle that a case will be decided by an impartial tribunal. That consideration would be important in systems that emphasise final determination by a judge, who does not make her mind up before having heard all the evidence at a final trial.

In some states, emphasis is placed on settling cases before they reach court. One example is Norway, where cases must first be pursued through the Conciliation Board before going to court. Another example is the English pre-action protocol system and costs rules. Similarly, a recent German reform requires mandatory mediation in some cases before court proceedings can be triggered.

III. Funding

Mauro Cappelletti observed in 1978 that people had reinterpreted the traditional concept of 'justice' in the context of what a civil procedure was aiming to do, by expanding it to provide 'social justice'.[85] He argued for more 'access to justice', conceived in terms of more cases brought by those with fewer resources who would be funded by increased public finance. In retrospect, the idea of legal aid had peaked before the 1990s and significant provision of public funding for access to the judicial system is now no longer politically viewed as a sustainable economic choice. Levels of state funding are low and generally decreasing almost everywhere. The arguments for shared public support are similar to those raised above in relation to who pays for the courts. As a matter of principle, legal aid is a good idea, but it is increasingly viewed as largely unaffordable. Policy on this issue is highly unlikely to change in the foreseeable future. So governments and users seek cheaper alternatives for dispute resolution, whether within or outside courts. Privatised funding of litigation can come from two sources: intermediaries or externals.

A. Lawyer funding

Deferral of fees and waiver if a case is lost have long been practised by lawyers everywhere, whether permitted or not. The extent to which lawyers have performed this *pro bono* function deserves to be recognised. A typical approach may be a modest file opening fee, which might cover some overheads or litigation expenses, followed by a success fee in the event of a satisfactory outcome. In other words, payment of little in the event of failure is common.

The American model of contingency fees goes further and includes payment of a larger element in the event of success, explicitly linked to the size of the recovery. This is argued to align the incentives of the client and the lawyer in the same direction of recovery maximisation.[86] But it has also been criticised as reducing the maximisation incentive after a certain level of investment of time because of asymmetric incentives over settlement, although empirical evidence of such practice in the United States is difficult to find.[87] Kritzer has found that the type of fee arrangement is related to the type of client. A contingency fee is the arrangement of choice for individuals, whereas hourly rates or fixed fees are favoured by

[85] M Cappelletti, 'Introduction' in M Cappelletti and B Garth (eds), *Access to Justice: The Worldwide Movement to make Rights Effective—A General Report* (Alphen aan den Rijn and Milan, Sijthoff & Noordhoff and Giuffrè, 1978).

[86] Amongst numerous commentators see HM Kritzer, *The Justice Broker: Lawyers and Ordinary Litigation* (Oxford University Press, 1990).

[87] See A Tabarrok and E Helland, *Two Cheers for Contingent Fees* (Washington DC, AEI Press, 2005).

business clients.[88] A lawyer who works on a contingency fee case combines the roles of professional legal adviser, advocate, financier and insurance broker.[89] His effort is strongly influenced by how he is being paid,[90] and he will reject cases that do not satisfy his risk-to-return criteria.[91] The rejection rate of cases from potential clients appears to be around 50 per cent.[92] In the long run, compensation for professional services is dependent on performance.[93] Contingency fees are widely accepted in the United States, but there is considerable resistance to them elsewhere.

B. Independent funding

A significant level of lawyer funding has not been necessary in the civil law world where there are lower lawyer costs than in the common law world because of the architecture of civil procedure systems and the use of tariffs. This study clearly shows that predictable costs encourage the availability of insurance, and the low level of many national tariffs enhance the attractiveness of LEI through its low cost. So BTE insurance is the structural solution in civil law states whereas contingency fees are the American solution. The former may still have an access to justice problem for the poor, but that may be containable by some limited legal aid, public advice bureau, employee insurance, or lawyer *pro bono* work.

It is logical that there may be a demand for ATE insurance, but high and unpredictable costs make this largely uneconomic for providers. The English ATE experience during the 2000s, made possible by a rule on shifting the premium to defendants, has been signalled by Lord Justice Jackson as a wrong turning and ripe for constriction. It produces too much disproportion between the costs of claimant and defendant, and makes defendants and insurers fund those who need assistance instead of legal aid: as Jackson LJ pointed out, this is ironic because many defendants in England are state funded, and it is an expensive mechanism. The solutions lie elsewhere.

Access to litigation by larger companies does not encounter the same obstacles, since they have the resources to pay lawyers or buy insurance. There does, however, appear to be a gap in funding for SMEs. This gap is now being filled in some states by independent third party funders (Litigation Funding, or LF). LF is a recent and interesting development. The LF market has existed quietly in the United States for some years, seemingly on a restricted basis. It grew rapidly in Australia during the past decade and has spread to the United Kingdom. In some

88 See Kritzer (n 72 above).

89 HM Kritzer, 'The Wages of Risk: The Returns of Contingent Fee Legal Practice' (1997) 47 *De Paul Law Review* 267; Kritzer (n 72 above).

90 Kritzer (n 86 above) 126.

91 HM Kritzer, 'Seven Dogged Myths concerning Contingency Fees' (2002) 80 *Washington University Law Quarterly* 739.

92 Kritzer (n 72 above) ch 3.

93 WJ Lynk, 'The Courts and the Market' (1990) 19 *Journal of Legal Studies* 247.

other European states, LF is a natural extension of the business models of LEI insurers.

It would be useful to have more data on these issues. Just how much of an access to justice gap is there, for individuals or SMEs? It is also interesting to speculate whether a Jacksonian shift by non-American common law states towards tariff or fixed fees for low value claims will remove a need for contingency fees.

Because LF is such a recent phenomenon, the evidence from the jurisdictions studied is preliminary. It is clear that various issues arise in relation to LF, which need further research and wider debate. It is rather less clear how national systems will resolve them. At this stage, we merely raise a number of questions: we are engaged in ongoing research on these issues.

Are LFs any different to public funders or lawyer funders? What parameters do they need to operate under? What controls and regulation do they need? The long-enshrined principles of maintenance and champerty have swiftly crumbled under the pragmatic necessity of simply enabling the civil justice system to keep operating: what contemporary public policy issues apply?

Should LFs exercise control over litigation? How much, when, and how? The considerations to be balanced are, on the one hand, that the arrangement represents an investment decision by the funder and, on the other hand, the concern that there should not be undue interference in the collection or presentation of evidence or of a case or in relation to settlement, since this would undermine the fairness and objectivity of the legal process and decisions. So, who should have what risk? There is little objection that funders should be entitled to full information over the developing risk, in the same way that shareholders are entitled to disclosure of accurate and timely information on the value of their investments. But should funders be permitted closer access to the running of the enterprise, and be in a position to influence behaviour and decisions?

If LF is acceptable in principle, what is the difference between funding from independent parties and by lawyers engaged in the case? The simple difference is that where both the advice and funding functions are present in the same individual or entity, conflicts of interest inevitably arise. Are such conflicts of interest significant, acceptable or inappropriate? In what situations do they matter? Should particular arrangements be banned, or permitted, and if so, to what extent? How should arrangements be regulated: what elements of market forces, public regulation and/or self-regulation are required?

LF tends to apply only to high value cases, hence primarily commercial cases. If LF is not a solution to individual low value claims, and legal aid is limited or disappearing, what is the solution for funding small claims by needy individuals and companies, so as to provide effective access to justice? How many of such claims fall outside the 'small claims' track (typically not requiring lawyers and without cost shifting) that is spreading in some states, such that there remains a problem? How many such claims might be catered for through alternative pathways? How many remain? If a decision on merits and investment has to be made, is the simplest solution for this to remain that of an individual lawyer, who might decide whether to act on a CFA or contingency fee? If so, should the success fee be recoverable from the loser, or costs shifted only on a tariff fee basis?

IV. Responses to the High Cost of Litigation and the Funding Gap

This study confirms concern that the costs of some types of litigation in some jurisdictions are too high and that there is a gap in the availability of funding for individuals and business entities that have limited resources. However, it also reveals a range of responses to such problems, whether by reducing cost through procedural means or by change in funding sources and arrangements. The major mechanisms which we identified and which we recommend for further exploration are the following:

a. Encouraging settlement. This is policy in many countries, including Denmark, Japan, the Netherlands and the United States. Mediation has been widely encouraged, such as in England and Wales (1999), Portugal (2000), Poland (2005) and Belgium (2007). In China judicial mediation resolved 59 per cent of cases in 2008. Taiwan imposes lower fees for court mediation than for court litigation, and remission of court costs where settlement is reached.
b. Reducing cost in civil procedure. Case management has been adopted as a technique throughout common law jurisdictions, although with varying degrees of force and success. The experience in the United States and the Jackson Review in England and Wales show that if case management is to be effective it needs to be accompanied by education of judges and lawyers, and a change in culture, but may not deliver costs management. Costs management is emerging as a separate policy and discipline.
c. Establishing specialist courts for particular types of disputes, especially for small claims or in technical areas (intellectual property, construction, family, tax). Examples abound, such as in Australia, Canada, New Zealand, the Netherlands, the Nordic states, the United Kingdom, and the United States.
d. Encouraging *pro bono* advice, especially where there is a sufficient spread of affluent lawyers. Leading examples are Australia, Canada, England, Norway, Poland, Russia, and Singapore. These examples seem to include countries where either there are many rich lawyers, or there is a generally low standard of living, which often includes lawyers. On the other hand, *pro bono* is banned in Switzerland. This source of 'funding' may provide some assistance but it is questionable whether it is a structural solution.
e. Encouraging privatised funding through loosening the prohibitions against certain types of private funding, whether from lawyers or independent third parties. Examples of techniques include no win no fee, success fees, third party funders who take a percentage of the damages, and reforming recoverability of

costs. Notable examples occur in Australia, Germany (contingency fees permitted from 2008, although under restricted criteria and unlikely to be widely used) and England and Wales (conditional fee agreements (CFAs) since 1995, extended 1999 but possibly now to be replaced by contingency fees or other alternatives).

f. Providing alternative dispute resolution pathways that are cheaper (and quicker) than the courts, through some external pathway such as ombudsmen or compensation schemes, especially for certain types of disputes, such as small claims, debt, housing, and family issues.

In conclusion, it can be seen that issues of costs and funding of civil litigation necessarily lead to far wider policy questions than the price of lawyers and of courts, and how they are calculated. Important issues for governments and users of dispute resolution services relate to the comparative efficiency and appropriateness of different pathways, and the development of holistic frameworks for civil justice.

SECTION 4

SUMMARY OF FINDINGS

The final Section of this study summarises the findings of the comparative enquiry into the costs and methods of funding civil litigation in some 36 jurisdictions across the world, carried out in 2009. The jurisdictions are: Australia, Austria, Belgium, Bulgaria, Canada, China, the Czech Republic, Denmark, England and Wales, Estonia, Finland, France, Germany, Greece, Hong Kong, Hungary, Ireland, Italy, Japan, Latvia, Lithuania, the Netherlands, Norway, Poland, Portugal, Romania, Russia, Scotland, Singapore, Spain, Sweden, Switzerland, Taiwan, and the United States of America.

I. Costs

A. Overview of costs regimes

1. The litigation system in every jurisdiction studied gives rise to the same basic elements of costs: charges for use of the court and its personnel, evidential costs for witnesses and experts, and lawyers' fees. In other words, there are costs for the use of the litigation process and costs for the services of intermediaries.

2. Almost every country levies some charge for use of its courts. The charge is always based on fixed rules, involving a tariff system, so is fully predictable. The charge usually varies with the sum in dispute, which introduces an element of

proportionality, and tapers off as fees rise. The leading exception, where almost no cost is levied for access to the courts, is France.

3. Most countries do not seek to recover the full economic cost of the public justice system from user fees, but provide some funding from general taxation, although the proportion between user and general funding is rarely clear.
4. Witnesses of fact are reimbursed their expenses, but rarely otherwise paid. Expert witnesses are paid for their time, usually on an hourly rate basis regulated by the court.
5. Lawyers' fees to clients are almost always subject to open negotiation rather than regulation. Billing is frequently based on hourly rates. Some civil law jurisdictions have tariffs but they are rarely binding. Tariffs set by local Bars have been banned almost everywhere as anti-competitive.

B. Cost shifting

6. In almost all jurisdictions, the general position is that the loser pays the costs of the court, evidence and lawyer. However, the court often has discretion over awarding costs in cases where each side wins some points. Court discretion is also intended to maintain an ability to sanction poor behaviour during the litigation process. Some jurisdictions have rules on how costs are split when both sides have some success.
7. Some legal systems have exceptions to the general 'loser pays' rule in order to overcome funding barriers or encourage certain types of claims.
8. The United States of America are almost alone in maintaining a rule that each side pays their own costs, save where one way cost shifting has been expressly provided for under a range of statutes that encourage private enforcement.

C. Actual costs incurred: quantitative findings

9. The following are the empirical findings from data supplied by leading practitioners in the target jurisdictions to questions on the level of costs in nine case studies:

   a. Small claim: repayment to a consumer of €200 price paid for product not delivered.
   b. Family: divorce between husband on average income (say €50,000 pa), wife with no income, two children, living in an average home.
   c. RTA: road traffic accident collision, in which the rear of the claimant's car and the front of the defendant's car are moderately damaged (ie rear and front respectively require total replacement panels, but engine is undamaged); cost of repair and replacement car €6,000.

d. Employment: wrongful loss of employment by a middle-ranging manager (say salary €50,000 pa).
e. Medical negligence: doctor's error results in permanent (a) loss of ability to walk (b) paraplegia, for male claimant aged 25 on salary of €25,000 pa, no current dependents, but likelihood of marriage and two children.
f. SME: small company claim for unpaid debt of €8,000.
g. Large commercial case: substantial and complex breach of contract claim between two large companies over supply of defective machinery worth €2 million, with €5 million loss of profit.
h. Injunction—consumer: against neighbour to stop noise.
i. Injunction—commercial: prevent illegal breach of intellectual property in commercial information between two substantial companies.

(i) Variation in litigation costs

10. The total costs of litigation can vary widely among the jurisdictions included in this study. A frequent pattern is that costs (whether in total, or for court or lawyers' fees) may have a broadly similar level in the majority of jurisdictions (which some may interpret as being at a 'low' level) but some jurisdictions have costs that are considerably higher than the general level of the majority.

(ii) Lawyers' fees are the major component of total costs

11. Lawyers' fees are in almost all cases higher than court fees, and comprise the major element in total costs. This is generally the case irrespective of whether or not jurisdictions impose tariffs for lawyers' fees.

12. The highest lawyers' fees can be observed in Australia, England and Wales, and Denmark. Germany, Austria and Greece have relatively low lawyers' fees. Lawyers' fees in Central and Eastern Europe are comparatively modest overall.

13. Lawyers' fees are usually subject to VAT. VAT rates vary between countries (between no charge and 30 per cent), and can have significant impact.

(iii) Court costs are predictable

14. Court costs are predictable in almost all jurisdictions, and are based on published tariffs. Where the amount in dispute is certain, the court costs vary with the amount in dispute. Where the amount is unquantifiable, such as for a claim for injunctive relief, the tariff denotes a particular set fee. In some cases where the claim is for damages but is not quantifiable in advance, claimants may specify a particular amount claimed, which will usually be a modest sum, so as to avoid incurring unnecessarily large court fees.

15. In the majority of jurisdictions, court costs are relatively low compared with the amount in dispute, once that amount is over a certain size. The significant

outlier is Singapore, which has notably higher court costs than other states for most of the case studies.

16. In France court fees are effectively nil. Court fees are generally low in Germany and Austria, as well as Greece. Beyond Europe, they are quite low in Taiwan and China.

17. Central and Eastern European states (such as Latvia, Estonia, Poland, Bulgaria, or the Czech Republic) have relatively high court fees proportionate to the value of the case, and proportionate to the level of lawyers' fees, but a different way of looking at this might be that lawyers' fees are low in those states and hence the court costs appear proportionately higher than in other jurisdictions. Hungary is a notable exception to this pattern, having relatively high lawyers' fees as well as relatively high court fees in many of the case studies.

18. Court costs also for some case studies tend to be high in England (and the available information indicates that the position is generally similar in Canada), Ireland, the Netherlands and Norway. However, these states often have another 'preferred dispute resolution route' for particular types of claims. Court costs appear high in comparison with total costs and lawyers' costs in Singapore (case studies 2, 3, 4, 8) and (on a far lower scale) in Poland (case studies 5, 7, 9).

19. Some court fees include VAT, while others do not. In some states VAT is not charged on court costs, in others it is. Also, VAT rates differ. Respondents' reports are not always precise about which rates do and which do not include VAT, and about the VAT rates.

(iv) *Lawyers' costs are frequently unpredictable*

20. The countries in which reporters stated that it was either straightforward or difficult to predict the total costs fell into a consistent pattern. The pattern depended upon whether lawyers' costs were or were not regulated by a tariff. Accordingly, where no tariff or ceiling applied, and lawyers' fees were based upon hours worked, this produced both unpredictable fees and levels of fees which, in low value claims, were high compared to the value at stake (cases 1, 3, 4, 6 and 8) and, in high value claims, could be potentially very high (cases 2, 5, 7 and 9).

(v) *High cost jurisdictions*

21. The countries that have notably higher total costs than others for each case study are: Hungary and Australia (case 1); Hungary, Romania and Singapore (case 2); England and Wales, and Singapore (case 3); Singapore (case 4); England and Wales, and Japan (case 5); Singapore and Hungary (case 6); England and Wales, Canada, Romania, Hungary, Japan and China (case 7); Singapore and Australia (case 8); and Denmark, Spain and England and Wales (case 9).

22. Overall, the countries that have the highest total costs in the largest number of case studies are Singapore (5 cases) and England and Wales (4 cases). It should be noted that the United States was not included in the data, and that data only for some of the case studies was available for Canada.

23. This does not mean that costs in the countries identified above are higher in all cases, but it does indicate that costs are very high in a number of specific types of case in those countries. However, several other jurisdictions would be included in that list if, first, claims were to be pursued through the courts rather than through alternative pathways and, secondly, if the amount of work done by lawyers in a given case were to be large and fees were based on hourly rates or, where the lawyers' fee were to be based on a success fee and the amount recovered was to be significant.

24. The most important observation from consideration of the above names of countries is that they do not tend to include countries in which lawyers' costs are regulated by tariffs.

(vi) Costs to case value ratio: proportionality

25. In most states included in this study the costs of litigation are high in relation to the value of the case. Sometimes costs even exceed the value of the case. Here some Western European states (such as Denmark, England and Wales, Ireland) are particularly striking examples, but the problem also exists in Hungary and some other Central and Eastern European countries, as well as Singapore and Australia. China and Taiwan have more proportionate costs.

26. There is a clear link between the predictability and proportionality of lawyers' fees. Where lawyers' fees are predictable they tend to be more proportionate to the value at stake, and vice versa. In other words, the key factor is whether or not lawyers' fees are subject to a tariff.

27. However, in states where costs are sometimes high, not all cases are necessarily expensive or disproportionate. An example of this can be seen from the results for the nine case studies in Australia, New Zealand and England and Wales (and is confirmed in Chapter 4 below on Canada). There, the results for the small claim, divorce, employment, debt and consumer injunction case studies indicate comparatively low costs, whereas those for the road traffic, medical negligence, large commercial dispute and intellectual property injunction case studies are comparatively far higher. This may reflect the fact that different costs rules, or cost shifting rules, or alternative dispute resolution pathways, are available for some types of claims. Such a finding may indicate that future work on providing particular pathways, procedures and costs regimes for particular types of cases may be fruitful, in order to address those cases where costs are high.

(vii) Existence of a cost recoverability gap for winners

28. It is extremely rare for all lawyers' fees to be recoverable by the winning party. The recoverability gap exists everywhere and applies in almost all types of case. The gap can be very high in some states and cases, requiring a winning party to have considerable financial resources.

(viii) Alternative solutions for low value cases

29. For those disputes that involve low amounts and where the costs of litigation might be disproportionate (cases 1, 3, 4 and 6), reporters in many jurisdictions indicated that pursuing a claim through the civil court system was not the recommended or most popular route for obtaining redress in the given situation, and that alternative solutions are preferred.

30. Thus, for low value claims that proceed in court, a number of jurisdictions have small claims procedures involving simplified procedures or rules, such as excluding the involvement of lawyers (and hence the costs incurred by their involvement) and/or prohibiting cost shifting.

31. Sometimes extra-court procedures are preferred, such as administrative (use of special tribunals, ombudsmen or regulatory officials) or insurance solutions, since they involve little or no cost to claimants and the state or business bears the cost of investigation. A tribunal or official may be able to exert some pressure to resolve issues more informally and quickly than the careful forensic approach of courts. Mediation or arbitration procedures were frequently mentioned (notably case 2 on divorce) in preference to court proceedings. Labour disputes are frequently brought in specialist tribunals (case 4).

32. However, such alternative approaches were mentioned less frequently in those jurisdictions where the court procedures are efficient and the costs predictable (such as those based on the German model).

II. Funding

33. There are several potential sources of funding for litigation, although options in individual cases may be limited. The options can be categorized by the origin of the funding: personal resources of the litigant, funds provided by an independent source (insurance, bank, trade union or association, funder), or financing from the legal intermediary involved in the case (through *pro bono* waiver of fees, deferral until resolution, or charge dependent on outcome, ie waiver in the event of loss, perhaps with enhancement in the event of success, such as a success fee or uplift).

34. Legal Expenses Insurance (LEI) has developed widely as a principal source of litigation finance in many civil law states as a result of the lower cost of their civil procedures and the predictable cost based on tariffs.

35. Almost every jurisdiction has some form of independent support funding that is referred to as 'legal aid' but the modes of operation differ widely. Almost all state funding is subject to merits and means tests. Government funding for court and lawyers' fees is generally contracting, and this is placing greater emphasis on methods of funding by lawyers or others, especially in resolving low value disputes.

36. Success fees are widely permitted, but there is strong resistance to fees in which damages are reduced. American-style contingency fees form the established funding mechanism in the United States but are far more controversial and currently fairly rare from a global perspective. The reliance on contingency fees in the United States is one of a number of features of its almost unique policy of reliance on private enforcement of both private and (in particular) public law.

37. Independent commercial funders have emerged recently in some states, principally Australia, Canada, Germany, the United Kingdom and the United States of America. Historical objections to third party funding (maintenance and champerty) have crumbled in these jurisdictions in view of the perceived need to enable continued access to justice. Third party litigation funding raises a number of policy issues concerning practice and ethics that are still being debated, and further regulation is likely. It is unclear to what extent, if any, a funder should control or influence strategic decisions in the litigation of others. However, independent funding is currently only commercially viable for commercial claims of significant size, so largely restricted to litigation between companies, although some jurisdictions are experimenting with funding of class claims. A comparison of funding from independents and from lawyers suggests that conflicts of interest are more likely to arise in the latter case than the former, assuming the roles of client, funder and lawyer are separate and distinct.

38. Considerable developments are occurring in the mechanisms for funding litigation. This is a time of major change, that is unplanned, market-driven and where the future is uncertain.

III. Policy Issues and Recommendations

A. Costs and access to justice

39. The amount payable by litigants in costs is frequently high in relation to the amounts in dispute. Thus there is concern whether justice can be accessed,

and hence whether the rule of law can be maintained. The largest element of such costs is almost always lawyers' costs.

40. In low value claims, costs are frequently both high and disproportionate to the amount in dispute. This can be so, irrespective of whether or not costs are controlled by a tariff. In other words, all court-based dispute resolution systems have an inherent level of costs that produces a threshold of cost proportionality: below the threshold, cases may not be worth pursuing and must either be dropped or pursued through alternative means.

41. In high value claims, costs can be very high where lawyers' fees are based on hourly rates. The same would be the case where amounts recovered are large and lawyers' fees are based on success fees or percentages of the sum recovered. In high value claims where costs are large, they do not exceed the sums at stake, unlike in small value claims, so are not disproportionate in that sense. However, where lawyers' fees comprise intrinsically very high sums, it may be questioned whether the cost is excessive.

42. Costs are fully predictable only where *ex ante* tariffs exist for all costs (court, process and lawyers). Court costs are always predictable through tariffs, and such tariffs exist in almost every jurisdiction. Lawyers' costs are, as a general rule, regulated by tariffs in civil law jurisdictions. This is not the case in common law jurisdictions. Hence, costs are more predictable in civil law jurisdictions. This is because cases in common law systems can involve variable and unpredictable amounts of work by intermediaries: such systems have not yet found fully satisfactory ways through case management or other techniques of controlling costs or delivering predictability.

B. Causes of high costs: the architecture of systems of civil procedure

43. The existence of tariffs for lawyers' fees is related to the model of civil procedure in a given jurisdiction. The level of litigation costs is related to the amount of work done by the non-party actors in the litigation process, notably lawyers, judges and experts. Common law and civil law jurisdictions have distinct architectural features of civil procedure, which give rise to different roles for lawyers and judges, and hence typically to significantly different levels of cost between the two broad traditions.

44. In the civil law tradition, typified by Germany, judges have comparably more work to do than judges in common law jurisdictions, while in the common law tradition lawyers have a greater share of the workload than in civil law systems. Hence the balance between court fees and lawyers' costs is, as a general proposition, different between the two traditions: the percentage of total costs attributable to court fees is higher in most civil law jurisdictions, whereas lawyers' costs are usually clearly the more expensive element in common law systems.

45. Most civil law systems (notably except France) tend to shift costs to the unsuccessful litigant, according to a tariff based on the amount in dispute. This provides *ex ante* regulation of the level of costs and a relatively high level of predictability for all parties to litigation. This, in turn, facilitates the provision of legal expenses insurance (LEI), and LEI is common in Western European countries (it has yet to develop within the emerging new legal systems of Central and Eastern Europe).

46. By contrast, in common law jurisdictions, lawyers' fees will be variable, and hence often unpredictable, and can be high. In those jurisdictions (except those of the United States of America, apart from Alaska) the usual factor in such costs is the time spent on a case.

47. In many jurisdictions, lawyers' fees do not operate on normal market principles where individual claimants are involved. Market behaviour applies in setting the level of legal costs essentially only for large repeat players, such as insurance companies and major corporations.

48. There is an inherent conflict in civil procedure between providing a just result and providing a result at proportionate cost.[94] Resolving this conflict involves a level of compromise over the extent of access to appropriate evidence. The ways in which the civil procedure systems of, for example, Germany and England, deal with evidence constitute fundamentally different approaches. Shifting costs for obtaining evidence on a tariff basis provides predictability, albeit not necessarily proportionality, especially given the recoverability gap.

C. Meeting concerns about high costs

49. The high level of lawyers' costs, and the procedural architecture in some systems, produce significant challenges for delivery of access to justice at proportionate cost through courts.

50. In considering provision for systems of dispute resolution, especially through courts, governments have an overriding concern with ensuring justice. It is a fundamental feature of justice and a justice system that access to justice should be equal for all.

51. However, it is recognised that litigation and justice come at a price, and that some citizens and entities have greater resources than others. The problems of maintaining fair and equal access to justice for all, and of controlling cost and delay in courts, have long been recognised but remain unresolved in many jurisdictions.

[94] See GP Miller, 'The Legal-Economic Analysis of Comparative Civil Procedure' (1997) 45 *American Journal of Comparative Law* 905, 906–911.

52. Governments are set to impose significant cuts in public expenditure as a consequence of the financial environment, and civil justice is not a high priority for spending. Governments, businesses and citizens will be looking for ways of reducing costs.

(i) Adoption of a principle of proportionality

53. Few jurisdictions have historically applied a principle of proportionality to litigation costs, or to lawyers' costs, but such an approach is now gaining ground, especially in common law jurisdictions. The importance of such a principle has become particularly relevant where lawyers' costs have become too high, notably for small cases and very large cases. However, there is no consensus on what it is that costs should be proportionate to (the amount of work done, the value of the case to the party, or the amount at stake), and how proportionality should be achieved in practice.

(ii) Adoption of case management techniques

54. Special techniques are being created, such as procedure-light tracks (eg small claims or pre-action protocols), mediation or fixed cost regimes.

55. Those responsible for courts, including judges and lawyers, increasingly need to respond by lowering costs, streamlining procedures, simplifying unnecessary procedures, increasing predictability of costs, and delivering speedy services at costs that are proportionate to amounts in dispute. Questions arise over the duplication of functions, for example where lawyers work in a split profession. Applying case management techniques which attempt to ensure that procedural steps are minimised consistently with delivery of fair procedures and just results is an important approach for larger cases, but does not itself deliver cost management or proportionality of costs to the value of cases. There is not much evidence that many short-cuts in procedure are being taken that would threaten due process or delivery of justice through court procedures.

(iii) Adoption of alternative dispute resolution pathways

56. Outside courts, and sometimes in co-ordination with them, new pathways are being found for particular types of disputes and for lower value claims. Such pathways might not involve lawyers, or involve lawyers to a lesser extent. Many jurisdictions are encouraging settlement through mediation, other modes of ADR, small claims procedures or other streamlined approaches. Techniques involving ombudsmen, business complaint systems and involvement of regulators are also being more widely examined. There is evidence of continuing experimentation with a range of techniques, and diversification is far from complete.

57. A small number of governments are beginning to take an overview of all dispute resolution pathways, especially, but not limited to, those funded by public revenues, so as to evaluate all options and build an integrated framework of pathways for dispute resolution that are appropriately focussed on particular types of disputes.

D. Recommendations

58. If governments wish to deliver wider access to justice in those cases where proportionate cost is particularly important, they should introduce tariffs for lawyers' fees, introduce efficient case management techniques in the civil courts and devise alternative pathways for dispute resolution that deliver cheaper or more efficient solutions. This is not to say that justice will always come cheap. There will always be cases in which access to factual and/or expert evidence is viewed as important, and this necessarily involves a certain level of expenditure.

TABLES AND APPENDICES

Questionnaire on

FUNDING, COSTS AND PROPORTIONALITY IN CIVIL JUSTICE SYSTEMS

Please quote verbatim, or attach, all source documents.

1. What are the costs incurred in civil litigation?

What do the parties (claimants, defendants etc, or persons acting on their behalf) have to pay to the following persons and institutions, and at what stage of the proceedings do they have to make such payments?

1.1 Court charges.
1.2 Other official charges (VAT, translator, bailiff, service or process, enforcement of a judgment).
1.3 Lawyers' fees. Please cover all information on fee agreements, hourly rates, fixed fees, success fees, uplifts/contingency fees, pro bono, etc and say how extensive each method is in practice, and what the size (or range) of fees are in each case.
1.4 A witness of fact.
1.5 An expert.
1.6 Any other costs.
1.7 What other factors constitute a 'price' for bringing a claim, such as delays in the legal process, complex procedure, unpredictability of the outcome, opportunity cost, and other strains? How long do (different types of) cases usually take?

For each item, please:

(a) quote completely any law or guidance on the subject (general rules, reductions and exemptions),
(b) say what rules apply in special cases, such as small claims, special courts/ tribunals,
(c) give (or estimate) any relevant actual amounts of money involved, and
(d) say when the amount of money involved becomes clear to the payer.

2. Who bears the costs?

How are the costs ultimately divided between the parties and/or others (the state etc)? Who reimburses/indemnifies/pays which of the items listed in paragraphs 1.1–1.7 above?

Please identify:

(a) What law or guidance exists?
(b) What happens in practice? What percentage of costs ends up being paid by winner/loser/state/other?
(c) When must payment be made?
(d) When does an opponent receive information about the size of risk/actual amount of fees for which he might/does have to pay?

3. What are the sources of finance for bringing or defending a legal claim?

What funding is permitted from each of the following sources?

3.1 Personal funds.
3.2 Legal aid.
3.3 Legal Expenses Insurance (LEI, ie before-the-event), for individuals or companies.
3.4 After-the-event (ATE) insurance.
3.5 Loans or grants from banks, trade associations, etc.
3.6 Funding from a lawyer or other third party investor.

For each item, please

(a) quote completely any law or guidance on the subject.
(b) give or estimate any relevant actual amounts of money involved.
(c) say how extensively each source of funding is available and used in practice.

4. Further issues

4.1 How predictable are the amounts involved?
4.2 What strategies are used by the parties to lower costs (eg tactics in cases, or procedural options like budgets, cost capping orders, costs protection orders)?
4.3 How proportionate are the sums involved?
4.4 How long do the procedures take?
4.5 What proportion of cases is settled and how long do they take?
4.6 What figures (or estimates) are available on the numbers of civil litigation cases started, completed, or settled before judgment, for different available procedures, eg general courts, small claims, commercial or other special courts or tribunals, ombudsmen, special schemes, codes of business conduct, etc? Please give figures back to 2000 if available.
4.7 What restrictions apply to appeals? Are appeal courts bound by the findings of fact at first instance? What percentage of cases is appealed? How do the costs of an appeal compare to first instance?
4.8 What reforms can be recommended?

Case Studies

Please give figures for the costs of claimant and defendant in the following examples, identifying when sums are related to a tariff or are open to be freely agreed.

If a case would normally be resolved not by normal court process but by a different procedure (small claim, no fault compensation scheme, ombudsman, special court or tribunal, business scheme) please state or estimate the amount that such alternative procedure would cost.

Please assume the most normal fee arrangement would apply for the claimant and defendant in each case (as most appropriate for the type of case), but please give some alternatives if 'normal' and success/contingency fees might apply. Assume each case goes all through the court process to a first judgment, and is not settled.

In each case, state the total sum paid by claimant and defendant if (a) claimant wins and (b) defendant wins. If appropriate, give a range of costs where the case (a) is straightforward or (b) turns out to be more complex.

Please give a summary (not exhaustive if the detail would be complex) that shows the calculations and assumptions.

The objective is not to give definitive accuracy, but to give estimated 'bottom line' figures from which general comparisons between different costs systems in different countries can be made.

1. Small claim: repayment to a consumer of €200 price paid for product not delivered.
2. Family: divorce between husband on average income (say €50,000 pa), wife with no income, two children, living in an average home.
3. RTA: road traffic accident collision, in which the rear of the claimant's car and the front of the defendant's car are moderately damaged (ie rear and front respectively require total replacement panels, but engine is undamaged); cost of repair and replacement car €6,000.
4. Employment: wrongful loss of employment by a middle-ranging manager (say salary €50,000 pa).
5. Medical negligence: doctor's error results in permanent (a) loss of ability to walk (b) paraplegia, for male claimant aged 25 on salary of €25,000 pa, no current dependents, but likelihood of marriage and two children.
6. SME: small company claim for unpaid debt of €8,000.
7. Large commercial case: substantial and complex breach of contract claim between two large companies over supply of defective machinery worth €2 million, with €5 million loss of profit.
8. Injunction—consumer: against neighbour to stop noise.
9. Injunction—commercial: prevent illegal breach of intellectual property in commercial information between two substantial companies.

Questions for Scholars only

Please give the background and historical context to the rules on funding and costs. What principles and theory apply? How do the rules on civil procedure or substantive law affect the current situation on funding and costs?

Please give a critical review of the current position. Please identify general trends, unresolved or contentious issues, likely future reforms. Are the amounts of money involved predictable and proportionate? If not, how could the position be improved? Is settlement between the parties regarded as important, is settlement encouraged by the current system, and how might it be further promoted?

Thank you for completing this questionnaire.

Table 1: Basis of charges for court fees and lawyers' fees

Country	Court fees: additional remarks	Fees arranged between lawyer and client	Fees for cost-shifting purposes: tariffs[1]
Austria	TARIFF according to value of the case; tariff established by statute. Different tariff for appeal and third instance proceedings. Different tariff for execution proceedings. Loser pays rule applies.	These arrangements can detract from the tariff system, but in practice the Autonomous Fee Schedule, used as guidance for agreements, tends to use the Act.	Tariff system established by the Lawyers' Fees Act. The fees are dependent on the amount in dispute and the type of case. There are additional payments for hearings, also set by the Act. The tariff amounts range from 3.10 Euro to 181,000 Euro. When representing a client at a hearing the lawyer gets 50–60% of his tariff earnings, but no other costs are reimbursed.
Australia	FLAT FEE, depending on court; different for businesses (higher) and individuals (lower). Fees are regulated by statute on the Federal level and on the state level. The rules of the Federal Court of Australia provide rules on fees, so do the civil procedure rules regulating the Supreme Court, District Court and the Local Court of New South Wales. Additional fees for a hearing. Loser pays rule applies.	Fees are freely agreed between lawyer and client (conditional fee agreements are possible, also including an uplift up to 25% of base costs). The fees are subject to control by statutory requirements of costs disclosure and by cost assessment. There also are some statutory maximum caps on fees in some cases (such as workers compensation cases, and low value personal injury cases—$10,000 for the latter). Fees are based on time spent (six minute intervals or hourly rates), although fixed fees for specific tasks are also commonplace. Figures quoted in case studies are based on estimates of fees charged by lawyers, although the exact rate on law firm, position of lawyer, and will depend complexity of case.	There is a tariff system in the rules of Federal Court and state courts apart from New South Wales, where cost-shifting amounts are subject to cost-assessment. Fixed fees are item based.

[1] A tariff is a system of fixed fees, dependent on amount at stake and the type of case: either established by statute or by some other instrument regulating provision of legal services. The tariff can cover cost-shifting or lawyer-client arrangement.

Belgium	FLAT FEE, depending on type of court. Loser pays rule applies.	Hourly fees, or global fees with caps and success fees are common.	Tariff system, depending on value of the case—Royal Decree of 2007 introduced a tariff scale of between 75 and 30,000 Euro, depending on the value of claim. Same amounts for appeal. Before the Decree each party had to bear their own lawyers' fees. These amounts can be detracted from in exceptional circumstances (at the time when the court assesses costs).
Bulgaria	TARIFF established by statute, depending on the value of the claim; SOME FLAT FEES (for instance cases where value cannot be determined, divorce cases, or insolvency cases). Loser pays rule applies.	The Bar Act and Ordinance stipulate that lawyers' fees can be freely arranged with the client. It might be a lump sum or percentage of the value of the claim, also on a conditional basis. In practice the lawyers' fees are determined most often as percentage of the value of claim or on hourly fee basis. In the case of less complex trials, attorneys usually determine an initial lump sum for the whole process (usually between BGN 300 and BGN 800 per instance). The Ordinance stipulates the minimum fee levels that the lawyers must charge (based on value of claim), but in practice the lawyers charge more.	No tariff system. Court awards costs to the winning party based on the actual agreed fees, as long as they are reasonable.
Canada	No data.	Fee depends on location of firm and seniority of lawyers. It is, however, rare for lawyers to stipulate their total fee in advance (except in some large cases). Contingency fees are allowed.	No tariff system. Loser pays rule applies to lawyers' fees, and the reasonably incurred and proportionate fees will be recovered, subject to court's discretion (partial, substantial, or full indemnity, although the latter two are quite

Table 1: *cont.*

Country	Court fees: additional remarks	Fees arranged between lawyer and client	Fees for cost-shifting purposes: tariffs
Canada *cont.*			rare). Some courts provide guidelines as to maximum costs which can be awarded on a partial indemnity basis: Ontario Court Civil Rules Committee provided the rates of between CAD 60 and CAD 350 per hour depending on the lawyer's seniority. On a substantial indemnity basis this amount would be increased by 1.5.
China	TARIFF established by statute, depending on value of case; some FLAT FEES (for instance in IP, divorce, defamation, or labour cases).	Fees depend on value of the dispute. Usually: between 3% and 10%. Fee tariffs are established on a local level: for instance according to the *Shanghai Measures for the Charge of Legal Service*, lawyers' fees are paid per case or per hour. If the fees are paid per hour, the maximum charge rate is RMB 3,000 per hour. If per case, for a non-property dispute, the maximum fee is RMB 5,000, for a property dispute, it is between 2% and (for smaller claims) then progressively decreasing percentage for parts exceeding stated amounts (up to 0.25%).	No tariff system, and each party bears their own lawyers' fees, except in some patent, trademark, copyright or contract cases.

Czech Republic	TARIFF established by statute, depending on value of case and whether claim was brought online or not. Loser pays rule applies.	Lawyers are free to agree fees with clients, on an hourly basis or on a contingency fee (up to 25% of the claim) basis. If no agreed rates—law prescribes rates depending on value of the case (between 300 and 48,300 CZK for each 'act of legal representation'—such as participation in a hearing or drafting an appeal).	Tariff system. The Regulation 404/2000 Coll. Prescribes rates for cost-shifting purposes, depending on value of the case (rates per one instance in the proceedings range between 4,500 and 237,000 CZK). The limit does not cover court charges, witnesses and expert witnesses' costs, translation, travel costs or administrative costs (phone calls, letters). The court also has discretion to rule that each party bear its legal costs, but this is only available in 'unique circumstances'.
Denmark	TARIFF established by statute depending on value of the case. Loser pays rule applies.	Either a fixed fee or an hourly rate (specified here) can be applied in contractual arrangements, subject to the requirement of reasonability (Administration of Justice Act).	Tariff system. Rates for cost-shifting purposes are established by the Administration of Justice Act and are dependent on the value of the case: they range between 12,500 to 281,250 DKK. (If claims are worth more than 5,000,000 the fee is DKK 46,340 for the first DKK 1,000,000 and 3 % of the rest).
England and Wales	TARIFF established by statute, depending on value of case, payable for specific forms or activities. Amounts cited in the case studies—for lodging the case. Loser pays rule applies, subject to exceptions mentioned in the lawyers' fees section.	Hourly fees are most common. Fee depends on seniority of lawyer and location of law firm. They can be freely agreed with client, although they are subject to possible challenge by client and by the paying party and must be reasonable. Conditional Fee Agreements are quite common, with the uplift being a percentage of the hourly fee (up to 100%). They are accompanied by the	No tariff system. Loser pays rule is normally applied in practice, but it is subject to court discretion and the cost assessment rules are very complex. Normally the winner recovers up to 75% of costs.

Table 1: *cont.*

Country	Court fees: additional remarks	Fees arranged between lawyer and client	Fees for cost-shifting purposes: tariffs
England and Wales *cont.*		After-the-Event Insurance policies. The lawyers' fees, the uplift and the insurance premium are potentially recoverable from the loser.	
Estonia	TARIFF established by statute, depending on value of case. For example, the 'state fee' (key part of the court fee, although the latter also includes disbursements and some deposits) for submission of the claim in the value of 20,000 Estonian kroons (**1,282 Euro**) is 4,000 Estonian kroons (**255 Euro**). The maximum cap of state fee is 1,500,000 Estonian kroons (**95,867 Euro**). Loser pays rule applies.	The fees are not determined by law and vary greatly. The hourly fees are the most common (average amounts quoted in the case studies), however the arrangements fees are capped or a flat fee is used occur where hourly more often. Contingency fees are used very rarely.	No tariff system. Loser pays rule applies, and the court assesses costs to be awarded to the winner at the end of the proceedings. The loser can object to the amounts. No tariff for cost-shifting purposes, court assesses the reasonability of fees.
Finland	FLAT FEE established by statute. Amounts depend on the type of court: here for District Court (first instance). Court of Appeals and the Supreme Court have slightly higher rates (not more than 200 Euro). Payable at the end of the proceedings. Loser pays rule applies.	Normally hourly fees (average amounts are quoted in the case studies) are agreed with clients. Fixed fees or contingency fees are much less common.	No tariff system. The court awards reasonable fees to the winner. In special circumstances the court may also order that each party pay their own costs.

France	No charges to individual parties, some exceptions in commercial cases. On the other hand, parties must pay the costs of some third persons taking part in the proceedings (such as witnesses, experts, translators). These are recoverable from the loser.	Amounts depend on the area of law, urgency, and location of law firm. They can be freely agreed, and any attempt of Bar Associations to set fee tariffs would be considered anti-competitive. Hourly rates quoted in the case studies—average rates quoted by the reporter. Contingency fees are illegal, but an uplift for a particularly successful result could be agreed with the client.	No general tariff system. Loser pays rule applies (costs and disbursements are either fixed by a tariff or assessed by court), but in practice courts rarely order the loser to pay the total amount of lawyers' fees. Generally, the amount recovered is between 2,000 and 5,000 Euro. This amount may however be increased or decreased if one of the parties has acted in bad faith during the course of the trial and has therefore increased the legal costs of the other party.
Germany	TARIFF established by statute, depending on value of case (and varied in different instances). Amount quoted in the case studies—for a claim of 10,000 Euro in the first instance. Loser pays rule applies.	Agreements establishing a fee below the tariff set out by statute are not allowed. However, above this amount the lawyers can freely agree a fee with clients (such freely agreed additional fee would not be recoverable).	*Rechtsanwaltsvergütungsgesetz* (*RVG*)—Act on Lawyers' Fees of 2004) regulates fees for cost-shifting purposes. Fees depend on the value of the case (up to 30,000,000 Euro) and are charged for specific tasks or proceedings. There are a number of contents of the final fee: 1. Fee for proceedings: Example: value in dispute—10,000 Euro: the calculated lawyer's fee—486 Euro. The entire lawyer's fee for proceedings in the first instance—631,80 Euro (1.3 × 486 Euro). **2.** Fee for hearings: it is payable once-only, so irrespective of how many times the lawyer appears in court. Example: value in dispute—10,000 Euro: the calculated fee—486 Euro. The lawyer's fee for court hearings in the first instance—**583.20 Euro** (1.2 × 486 Euro).

Table 1: *cont.*

Country	Court fees: additional remarks	Fees arranged between lawyer and client	Fees for cost-shifting purposes: tariffs
Germany *cont.*			3. Fee for settlement: payable on top of the other two in case settlement in reached. 4. Freely agreed fee (subject to agreement with client, but not recoverable—see below). Following the 2006 judgment of the Constitutional Court, contingency fees can be agreed if the client could not pursue the case without such an arrangement.
Greece	TARIFF established by statute, depending on value of case. Percentage fee only payable if final decision is to include financial settlement of some kind. Loser pays rule applies.	Minimum fees for lawyers are established by statute. For instance, for filing of a civil claim before the Single-Member Court of First Instance, submission of pleadings and hearing of the case regarding an amount up to 12,000 Euro the fee would be 197 Euro (if the amount is up to 40,020 Euro then the minimum fee is 337 Euro). In practice, however, lawyers agree higher fees with clients, and there are no specific restrictions. Contingency fees are permitted, but up to the maximum of 20% of the amount awarded.	No tariff system. Loser pays rule applies, although in practice the true costs are rarely awarded. Courts rather tend to award small percentages of actual costs, and they also tend to detract from the loser pays principle if the case was partially won or if the winner behaved unreasonably.

Hong Kong	Data for District Court and High Court civil actions in the Hong Kong Special Administrative Region. FLAT FEE, depending on type of court. Loser pays rule applies.	Lawyers normally charge on an hourly basis, and it is extremely rare for them to charge fixed or capped fees. Contingency fees or uplifts are not allowed.	No tariff system. Loser pays rule applies, but the court may detract from this rule if certain conditions established by law apply: for instance the winner only won nominal damages, in some patent cases (where only a 'trifling infringement' has been committed), or if the winner behaved unreasonably during litigation. 100% recovery is rare. A costs order against a third party (such as a third party funder, is also possible).
Hungary	TARIFF established by statute; depending on value of case, and sometimes also FLAT FEE for certain cases (such as divorce cases or judicial review). Loser pays rule applies.	Freely established by agreement. Normally, hourly fees apply. Fixed fees are also used. Contingency fees and success fees are rarely used (success fee would be attached to the fixed fee agreement).	Decree no. 32/2003. (VIII.22.) of the Minister of Justice establishes a Tariff system for cost-shifting purposes: • 5% of value of the claim not exceeding 10,000,000 HUF (min 10,000 HUF) • the above amount + 3% of the remaining amount up to 10,000,000,000 (min 100,000) • the above amount + 1% of the remaining amount up to 10,000,000,000,000 (min 1,000,000) • 5,000 per hour (min 10,000) if value of claim cannot be determined. The tariff applies where the parties have not agreed on another amount for reimbursement. If there is an agreement, this will be applied. The court can also use its discretion to decide whether the actual fee agreed by the winning party with their lawyer can be awarded.

Table 1: *cont.*

Country	Court fees: additional remarks	Fees arranged between lawyer and client	Fees for cost-shifting purposes: tariffs
Ireland	No amounts in report. Loser pays rule applies to court fees.	Freely agreed hourly fees. The Rules (Rule 11(3)) specify that: '*all costs incurred with the express or implied approval of the client evidenced by writing shall be conclusively presumed to have been reasonably incurred, and where the amount thereof has been so expressly or impliedly approved by the client, to have been reasonable in amount*'. The District Court Rules (Schedule of Costs) S.I. No. 93, of 1997, specify a Tariff system of additional ('exclusive of and in addition to all actual and necessary outlay') solicitors' and attorneys' costs in various types of cases, which depend on amount in dispute and are normally quite low.	No tariff system. How much is actually awarded to the winner is subject to the discretion of the Court but in practice the winner would recover between 60 and 80% of the total fees. If there is any disagreement in relation to any party's costs they can be submitted to Taxation—the Taxation Master will assess the bill of costs at a level that he believes appropriate, based upon precedent and reasonableness. Under Order 99 rule 11(1)(2)(3) (Rules of the Superior Courts): '*On a taxation as between solicitor and client, all costs shall be allowed except in so far as they are of an unreasonable amount or have been unreasonably incurred*'.
Italy	TARIFF established by statute, depending on value of case and type of case. Payable at the outset by a purchase of a stamp. Loser pays rule applies.	Lawyers' fees are regulated by statute, which establishes minimum and maximum amounts that lawyers can charge. The amounts depend on value in dispute and on specific activity that the lawyer carries out. For example for a case worth up to 5,200 Euro, for drafting the summons, the levels are min. 70 Euro, max. 165 Euro. These amounts are added to by additional *diritti* dependent on the type of activity, and 12.5%	Fees agreed between lawyer and client (which are within the statutory limits) are awarded unless they are disproportionate.

		of general costs awarded by the court are due for general expenses. In anticipation of the December 2006 ECJ judgement in joined cases C-94/04 and C-202/04 concerning minimum lawyers' fees and the restrictive effect they have on freedom to provide services within the EU, the minimum levels were abolished in July 2006 by the Decreto Bersani. The maximum fee levels have also come under the ECJ's scrutiny. The Commission has brought an infringement action against Italy in 2008 (case C-586/08), claiming that the maximum caps on lawyers' fees contravene the EC Treaty's principles of freedom of establishment and freedom to provide services. This case is still pending. Contingency fees have been allowed since 2006.	
Japan	Tariff established by law. No amounts in report; case studies mention two payments: revenue stamp and prepaid stamp. Amounts quoted in the case studies: RTA case with 6,000 Euro cost of repair. Loser pays rule applies, albeit it is not often enforced by parties (see the lawyers' fees section).	Lawyers can freely agree fees with their clients. Hourly fees are less frequent than initial fixed fee + a success fee on winning the case. Contingency fees are also becoming popular.	Tokyo rates quoted in the case studies. Parties pay their own lawyers' fees, apart from tort law claims where the loser pays rule applies. The reporter indicated that even when the courts award costs to the winner, these awards are not often enforced. Parties do not consider this worth the extra trouble, unless the costs are quite high. The general tendency is for courts to avoid getting involved in cost shifting.

Table 1: *cont.*

Country	Court fees: additional remarks	Fees arranged between lawyer and client	Fees for cost-shifting purposes: tariffs
Latvia	TARIFF established by statute, depends on value of case; case studies describe that the percentage ranges from 15% for cases less than 1,423 Euro, through 2.5 % and 1.6% of larger value cases. Loser pays rule applies.	Lawyers freely agree their fees with their clients. These can be done on an hourly basis (average amounts quoted in the case studies), fixed fees or contingency fees (where no statutory limits are established, but normally the success fee is between 5% and 20%).	No tariff system. Lawyers' fees are potentially recoverable in full, subject to the statutory limit of 5% of amount of claim that was awarded.
Lithuania	TARIFF established by the Code of Civil Procedure, depends on the value of the case: between 3% and 1%. Lower percentage rates accompany higher value cases (more than 29,000 Euro), and there is also a lump sum (between 870 and 2,030 Euro) payable in such cases. No loser pays rule applies here.	Lawyers can freely agree the fee with their clients. The most common form of fee arrangement is an hourly fee (the average amounts are quoted in the case studies). Lawyers also sometimes agree a fixed 'per case' fee. Contingency fees are also allowed.	A regulated cost-shifting system (no tariff as such), established by the Order of the Minister of Justice of 2004: the maximum amount is either 'capped' (the maximum fee for preparation of a lawsuit or response to the lawsuit cannot constitute more than 434 Euro), or hourly rated (the maximum fee for representation of a person during the court hearings cannot be more than 22 Euro per hour). The exact amount must be calculated by the court; when doing this the court shall consider (i) the complexity of the case, (ii) specifics of legal knowledge to be used in the case, (iii) repeated participation in the examination of the case, (iv) necessity to render legal services in other place than established working place of the lawyer, (v) the amount of the claim, (vi) consistency of legal services, (vii) novelty of legal services provided, and (viii) other important circumstances.

Nether-lands	TARIFF established by statute. Court fees depend on the value of the claim. Loser pays rule applies.	Lawyers are free to agree fees with their clients. Contingency fees are not allowed, although it is possible to agree for a success fee, as long as the lawyer charges 'actual cost' and the success part is not excessive.	Tariff system established by an informal but national standard used by all Dutch courts. A plaintiff may ask the court to apply another method of calculation, 'but courts are extremely reluctant to apply any other set of standards.' Lawyers' fees awarded by the court depend on the value of the claim and on the number of legal actions. 'Each procedural act is worth a point (minor acts are worth 0.5 point). There are 8 levels. The levels are related to the value of the claim. At level 1, a point is worth 384 Euro (with a maximum of 5 points). At level 8 the points a point is worth 3211 Euro (no limit as to the amount of points). The court calculates the amount of points and cross indexes the amount of points against the applicable level.' In practice, winners do not recover a large percentage of the actual costs agreed with lawyers. IP cases are an exception. 'Based on the enforcement directive (Directive 2004/48/EC) art. 1019h of the Dutch Code on civil procedures was introduced. According to this regulation, the winning party has the right to recover all the costs made due to the civil procedure. However, since August 2008 the Dutch judiciary released guidelines on the application of this rule with regard to lawyers' fees in the judiciary. Depending on the kind of procedure, the losing party has to cover the lawyers' fees of the winning party with the maximum between 6,000 and 25,000 Euro.'

Table 1: *cont.*

Country	Court fees: additional remarks	Fees arranged between lawyer and client	Fees for cost-shifting purposes: tariffs
New Zealand	TARIFF system established by law, and the fees have been reported to be very high, in line with the 'user pays rule'. The example of a fee for a half-day hearing in High Court of 1,300 NZD has been given. The High Court Fees Regulations 2001 attached to the report indicate amounts payable. There are fees for most procedural activities, including filing the claim, filing the counterclaim, etc. Loser pays rule applies.	Lawyers can freely agree fees with clients. Hourly fees are most common, and fixed fees are quite rare. The average rates are quoted in the case studies. The exact rate depends on the area of the country, the seniority of the lawyer, the complexity of amount of work involved. Contingency fees the case and the are quite rare (not a preferred option for lawyers—considered too risky). Uplifts are also used, often to accompany contingency fee agreements.	No tariff system established by legislation, but courts started using daily recovery rates depending on complexity of the case. The High Court introduced such rates for three categories of cases (from simple to complex cases)—between 1,070 and 2,370 NZD. The exact recovery rates depend on the 'reasonable time' needed to proceed with the case. In practice, this leads to around 2/3 recovery. District Court also adopted similar rates. So did Appellate Courts. These rates are used very often, although in some cases a 'no costs order' can also be made. Total indemnity orders can also occur.
Norway	FLAT FEE established by statute. Conciliation Board is normally obligatory. Small claims: there is a cap of 20% of the value of the claim (max 25,000 NOK). Court fees are quite high. Fees are reduced if parties settle before hearing. Loser pays rule applies, although there are exceptions subject to court's discretion: for instance if case was only partially won, or if the winner behaved unreasonably during proceedings.	Lawyers are free to agree their fees with clients. Hourly fees are most common, but conditional or success fees also occur. Contingency fees are not allowed.	No tariff system. Court normally awards costs to the winner, and all costs are awarded.

Poland	TARIFF established by statute, and FLAT FEE for certain specified cases. Loser pays rule applies, although there are exceptions (subject to court's discretion). If the claim is only partially successful, the court fee will be proportionately divided or not shifted at all.	Lawyers are free to agree fees with their clients. Hourly fees are most common (average amounts of hourly fees quoted in the case studies). Success fees are also possible, and so are fixed fees. The Class Actions Law of 2009, in force since 2010, allows for contingency fee agreements in class actions (cap of 20% of damages awarded).	Tariff established by statute. The 'minimum amounts' set out by law depend on value of the case, and can be increased (maximum 6-fold) or decreased by court in the final cost assessment decision. These 'minimum amounts' range between 60 and 7,200 PLN.
Portugal	TARIFF established by statute, depending on value of case. IT system introduced in Portugal allows a reduction of between 25 and 50% on court fees. Loser pays rule applies.	Lawyers' fees, which can be freely agreed with client, depend on lawyer's experience and the specific issue at stake. Depending on the case, the lawyers' fees can be set on an hourly basis, or be fixed for the entire case or specific issue. The hourly rates may vary according to: '1. the lawyers' experience, 2. the Law Firm and 3. the clients' economic means.'	No tariff system. The winner recovers his lawyers' fees (determined according to equity). However, Portuguese law limits recovery to a 'sum equivalent to half of the value of the justice fees, intended to cover the lawyer's fees.'
Romania	TARIFF established by statute, and some FLAT FEES (for non-pecuniary claims). Loser pays rule applies.	Lawyers are free to agree fees with client on an hourly basis, cap them or agree a conditional fee, although not as a percentage of damages awarded (or a combination of the above).	Maximum amount quoted in the case studies can be lower. Loser pays rule applies, but there is no longer any tariff system. The previous tariff has been abolished, although courts may still use it. Courts can also decide that the recoverable fees ought to be higher or lower than the agreed fees. The reporter indicated that normally the fees awarded are lower than the actual agreed fees.

Table 1: *cont.*

Country	Court fees: additional remarks	Fees arranged between lawyer and client	Fees for cost-shifting purposes: tariffs
Russia	TARIFF established by statute, depending on type of court, type of case and value of the case. Loser pays rule applies.	Lawyers are free to conclude fee arrangements with clients on an hourly basis, or to agree a fixed fee or a success fee (often used by Russian law firms and barristers, normally 10% of amount of claim).	Case studies refer to a average amount for international law firm. Russian law firms and barristers charge less. Loser pays rule applies, although success fees are not enforceable or recoverable.
Scotland	FLAT FEE established by statute for each action, writ, etc. Loser pays rule applies.	Lawyers agree fees with their clients according to current market rates. Speculative fees are not the preferred option, according to the reporter. Contingency fees are not allowed, but solicitors may agree for a success fee (maximum 100% of the normal fee).	Figures in the case studies refer to the average hourly rate per the Law Society of Scotland data for 2008. Partial tariff system. Loser pays rule applies, although it is subject to the court's discretion. Courts follow precedents, although costs are always determined on a case-by-case basis. In Court of Session: When the costs are assessed, this is normally done on a party/party basis (which allows recovery of limited costs, based on Tables of Fees for the Court of Session). The Auditor who conducts the taxing of costs (this does not need to happen, and it is only necessary if the loser disputes the costs) follows the principle of reasonability. The costs can also be assessed on an agent/client basis, which allows recovery of a higher percentage of the actual costs (here, reasonable costs are allowed). While in a party/party situation the average fee recovery is between 40–60%, it can be higher in agent/client situation.

			In Sheriff Court the rules on recovery can be different, although they often follow the rules of the Court of Session.
Singapore	Court charges comprise: Court fees, electronic filing system fees (not specified in report), and hearing fees (if applicable). FLAT FEES are specified by statute for each action, writ, etc. There is a two-stage tariff (less than $1m and more than $1m). Loser pays rule applies.	Freely agreed fees, with hourly fees increasingly popular. Contingency fees are unlawful.	Fees are 'fixed by the court: if the application does not require more than an elaborate hearing spanning more than half a day in arguments, the court will usually substitute an assessment of costs with a fixed sum of money which may or may not include reasonable disbursements by parties. Where costs are assessed for establishing quantum, the recovery of costs from the opponent will generally be between 50% and 67% of the fees that the lawyer for the successful party will bill'.
Spain	TARIFF. If amount in dispute cannot be set, the amount is assumed as 18,000 Euro. Loser pays rule applies.	Freely agreed fees: often based on the Bar Council rates mentioned above; hourly or contingency fees are also popular.	Bar Council establishes rates for cost-shifting purposes (not binding, but in practice observed)—these depend on the value or type of case.
Sweden	FLAT FEE regulated by statute, depending on type of case. Loser pays rule applies, although it is subject to the court's discretion.	Freely agreed fees, hourly or fixed. Contingency fees are allowed only in certain cases: class actions, and where the party would not obtain access to justice in any other way. Success rates must be reasonable.	No tariff system, although only reasonably incurred costs will be awarded to the winner.
Switzerland	TARIFF established by statute; in cantonal courts—amounts quoted in the case studies for the canton of Zurich (amounts can be increased or decreased by court if case is especially complex or straight forward);	Fees can be freely agreed. Hourly fees are most common, although capped fees also occur. Success fees are allowed, provided they are not disproportionately high.	Rates quoted in the case studies are for major commercial firms in Zurich. Federal Supreme Court and each canton has its own fee schedule that sets forth what amount the losing party has to pay to the winning party for the latter's attorney's costs.

Table 1: *cont.*

Country	Court fees: additional remarks	Fees arranged between lawyer and client	Fees for cost-shifting purposes: tariffs
Switzerland *cont.*	In Federal Supreme Court: TARIFF established by statute, depending on value of case. Loser pays rule applies.		In most cantons as well as in federal proceedings, such compensation awarded by the court to the winning party is based on a tariff and is not equal to the actual costs. The attorney's fees awarded by the courts of the Canton of Zurich and the Federal Supreme Court based on the applicable fee schedule do in most cases not cover the actual costs—as the schedules foresee relatively modest compensations based on the amount of money in dispute. The base fees established for each court can be adjusted in particular cases if they were particularly complex, or if they were very straightforward.
Taiwan	TARIFF established by statute, depending on value of case; amounts quoted in the case studies: first instance costs. Loser pays rule applies, although there are exceptions: some are established by legislation and in other cases the court can apportion the fees in a different manner.	The lawyers can charge: hourly, fixed fees, or contingency fees (not in criminal or family cases). The fee in contingency arrangements can be as low as 2% of the proceeds, but it can also be as high as 50% in complex, risky cases. All bar associations in Taiwan are required by law to include provisions on lawyers' fees in their articles of incorporation. Taipei Bar Association, Taichung Bar Association and Kaohsiung Bar Association are the three major bar associations in	Amounts quoted in the case studies are maximum fees per hour specified in the Articles of Association of three major bar associations. No general tariff system. Each party bears their own lawyers' fees. There are two exceptions: when the court appoints a lawyer as a party's special representative, and when the court appoints a lawyer to represent a party in third instance proceedings (with regard to the latter—statute establishes a tariff system).

		Taiwan. They set out maximum hourly fees and maximum fixed fees for specific acts.	
USA	FLAT FEE established by statute; amounts quoted in the case studies—Federal Court only. No loser pays rule applies, although see the note in the lawyers' fees section.	Lawyers are free to agree fees with clients, and both hourly fees and contingency fees are common. Hourly fee arrangements can be accompanied by success fees. Contingency fees can range from 5 to just over 33%, and in non class actions up to 50%. They depend on the evaluation criteria established by courts.	Each party pays own costs, unless otherwise directed by court. There are also Fee-Shifting Statutes (such as the Clayton Act) that apply to specific cases.

Table 2: Success and contingency fees

'Contingency fee' is defined as a fee that is based on a proportion of the sum recovered (*pactum de quota litis*).

A 'conditional' or 'success fee' is payable only upon a successful conclusion of the case and may include an uplift over normal rates but does not include a proportion of the damages recovered.

Country	Success fee[95]	Contingency fee
Australia	Yes, capped in Federal Court at 25%	No
Austria	No: permitted for TPF	No
Belgium	Yes	No
Bulgaria	Yes	
Canada	–	Yes
China		Not for collective actions, criminal or administrative cases from 2006. Others capped at 30%
Cyprus	No	
Czech Republic	Yes, capped at 25%	No
Denmark	Yes	No
Estonia	–	Yes
Finland	–	Yes (rare)
France	Yes	No
Germany	No	Yes, 2008 on conditions (rare)
Greece	Yes, 20% cap	No
Hungary	–	Yes
Ireland	Yes: no win no fee common	No
Italy	–	Yes, from 2006 (agreement must be in writing)
Japan	Yes	Yes
Latvia	Yes	
Lithuania	–	Yes, but 50% uplift is illegal
Luxembourg	No	No

Country	Success fee[95]	Contingency fee
Malta	No	No
Netherlands	Yes	No. Bar lifted ban on contingency fees 2004, but Ministry not approved
Norway	Yes	No
Poland	Yes	Generally no (but occurs). From 2010 permitted for class actions, capped at 20%
Portugal	Yes	No
Romania	Yes	No
Russia	Unenforceable but used	Unenforceable but used
Singapore	No	No
Slovakia	–	Yes, up to 20%
Slovenia	–	Yes, up to 15%
Spain	–	Yes
Sweden	No	No. Yes for class action
Switzerland	Yes, 2005	No
Taiwan	–	Yes
UK: England and Wales	Yes (CFA 1995, 100% cap). Contingency fee in employment cases, capped at 35% of damages.	No
UK: Scotland	Yes, 100% cap	No
USA	–	Yes

Primary Sources: National Reports from the Oxford Study on Costs and Funding, 2009; National Reports in the Stanford-Oxford Global Class Actions Project 2008 (available at www.law.stanford.edu/classactionconf); and Reports in the IBA Task Force on International Procedures and Protocols for Collective Redress, 2007 (restricted copy).

[95] Where a contingency fee is permitted, this includes a success fee element.

Table 3: Total minimum cost to claimant[1] in the case studies

Showing itemized lawyers' fees and court fees, USD International (PPP)

Country		Case Study 1	Case Study 2	Case Study 3	Case Study 4	Case Study 5	Case Study 6	Case Study 7	Case Study 8	Case Study 9
Australia	Lawyers' fees:	3,500 AUD (2,381 USD Intl)	5,000 AUD (3,401 USD Intl)	5000 AUD (3,401USD Intl)	G[2]	G	2500 AUD (1,701 USD Intl)	G	G	G
	Court fees:	77 AUD (52 USD Intl)	835 AUD (568 USD Intl)	198 AUD (135 USD Intl)			77 AUD (52 USD Intl)			
	Total/ comments:	2,432 USD Intl	3,968 USD Intl	3,536 USD Intl	Costs of arbitrated hearing if Conciliation in Industrial Relations Committees fails (20,000 to 30,000 AUD) (Min 13,596 USD Intl)	100,000 AUD (67,981 USD Intl)	1,753 USD Intl	50,000 AUD (33,990 USD Intl) (Only typical hourly or daily rates for lawyers were quoted)	5,000 AUD 3,399 USD Intl)	10,000 AUD (6,798 USD Intl)
Austria	Lawyers' fees:	569.40 Euro (+ freely agreed fee (FAF)) (662 USD Intl)	1,363.10 Euro (+ FAF) (1,585 USD Intl)	1,702.80 Euro (+ FAF) (1,980 USD Intl)	U[3]	27,052 Euro (+ FAF) (31,456 USD Intl)	3,093.60 Euro (+ FAF) (3,597 USD Intl)	111,463.25 Euro (+ FAF) (129,608 USD Intl)	683.80 Euro (+ FAF) (795 USD Intl)	6,786.30 Euro (7,891 USD Intl)

[1] Amounts here do not include VAT, unless indicated. Conversion rates as per 20 July 2009, unless otherwise indicated. The total amount includes court fee and lawyers' fee, as well as, when applicable, other costs (mentioned in this chart if they were itemized by the reporter).

[2] G – only general costs given - unable to state itemized costs.

[3] U – unable to state total costs.

		37 Euro (44 USD Intl)								
	Court fees:	**706 USD Intl**	210 Euro (244 USD Intl)	257 Euro (299 USD Intl)		8,861 Euro (10,303 USD Intl)	607 Euro (706 USD Intl)	85,661 Euro (99,606 USD Intl)	52 Euro (60 USD Intl)	607 Euro (706 USD Intl)
	Total/ comments:		**1,829 USD Intl**	Total costs include an additional expert opinion of 172,000 Euro (2,331 USD Intl) **4,610 USD Intl**	Costs depend on the value of the case	**59,424 USD Intl** Total costs include an additional expert opinion of 15,000 Euro (17,483 USD Intl). Costs apply assuming the value is 600,000 Euro.	**4,303 USD Intl**	Total costs include and additional expert opinion of 12,000 Euro (13,986 USD Intl) **- 243,200 USD Intl**	**855 USD Intl**	**8,597 USD Intl**
Belgium	Lawyers' fees:	G	G	G	G	G	G	G	G	G
	Court fees:									
	Total/ comments:	1,000 Euro **– 1,143 USD Intl**	3,000 Euro **– 3,429 USD Intl**	500 Euro **– 571 USD Intl**	2,500 Euro **– 2,857 USD Intl**	12,500 Euro **– 14,286 USD Intl**	500 Euro **– 571 USD Intl**	7,500 Euro **– 8,571 USD Intl**	1,500 Euro **– 1,714 USD Intl**	2,500 Euro **– 2,857 USD Intl**

Table 3. *cont.*

Country		Case Study 1	Case Study 2	Case Study 3	Case Study 4	Case Study 5	Case Study 6	Case Study 7	Case Study 8	Case Study 9
Belgium *cont.*			(if straight-forward divorce case. Complex cases can cost as much as 50,000 Euro).							
Bulgaria	Lawyers' fees:	100 BGL (139 USD Intl)	300 BGL (417 USD Intl)	690 BGL (958 USD Intl)	2,450 BGL (3,403 USD Intl)	4,450 BGL (6,181 USD Intl)	770 BGL (1,069 USD Intl)	200,450 BGL (278,403 USD Intl)	Lawyers fees: 150 BGL (208 USD Intl)	N[4]
	Court fees:	50 BGL (69 USD Intl)	50 BGL (69 USD Intl)	480 BGL (667 USD Intl)	4,000 BGL (5,556 USD Intl)	8000 BGL (11,111 USD Intl)	640 BGL (889 USD Intl)	200,000 BGL (277,778 USD Intl)	30 BGL (42 USD Intl)	
	Total/ comments:	208 USD Intl	486 USD Intl	1,625 USD Intl	8,959 USD Intl (court fees only if manage-ment contract; if another type of contract – free)	17,292 USD Intl	1,958 USD Intl	557,012 USD Intl Total includes expert fee of 600 BGL (831 USD Intl)	250 USD Intl	
Canada	Lawyers' fees:	U	G	U	U	U	G	G	G	G
	Court fees:									

[4] N – No answer to the case study.

	Total/ comments:	Litigation is not the recom-mended route – although if it was pursued, the reporter suggested the possible cost as C$2,500	The range of possible costs might vary from C$2,000 to C$200,000.	Admini-strative insurance arrange-ments	Depend on value of case	Depend on value of case	If Small Claim – the costs would be between C$3,000–5,000. If in court under the Simpli-fied Rules – C$10,000–C$15,000 (results not included in charts)	The reporter indicated that the costs could exceed C$1,000,000 (not included in charts)	The reporter indicated that the costs would be about C$15,000 (not included in charts)	The reporter indicated that the costs could exceed C$1,000,000 (not included in charts)
China	Lawyers' fees:	180 CNY (**47 USD Intl**)		1,620 CNY (**419 USD Intl**)	1,500 Euro (14,957.21 CNY) **3,863 USD Intl**	U	2,160 CNY (**558 USD Intl**)	1,350,000 CNY (**348,837 USD Intl**)	5,000 CNY (**1,292 USD Intl**)	
	Court fees:	50 CNY (**13 USD Intl**)	50 CNY (**13 USD Intl**)	1,150 CNY (**297 USD Intl**)	10 CNY (**3 USD Intl**)		1,600 CNY (**413 USD Intl**)	266,800 CNY (**68,941 USD Intl**)	50 CNY (**13 USD Intl**)	500 CNY (**129 USD Intl**)
	Total/ comments:	**60 USD Intl**	Not able to specify – lawyers' costs and other expenses depend on value of case and complexity.	**716 USD Intl**	**3,866 USD Intl**	Depend on value of case	**971 USD Intl**	**417,778 USD Intl**	**1,305 USD Intl**	Not able to specify – lawyers' costs depend on value of case.

Table 3. *cont.*

Country		Case Study 1	Case Study 2	Case Study 3	Case Study 4	Case Study 5	Case Study 6	Case Study 7	Case Study 8	Case Study 9
Czech Republic	Lawyers' fees:	4,590.29 CZK (180 Euro) **(326 USD Intl)**	1,530.10 CZK (60 Euro) **(109 USD Intl)**	7,395.47 CZK (290 Euro) **(525 USD Intl)**	41,822.68 CZK (1640 Euro) **(2,968 USD Intl)**	63,754.08 CZK (2500 Euro) **(4,525 USD Intl)**	6,120.39 CZK (240 Euro) **(434 USD Intl)**	119,857.68 CZK (4,700 Euro) **(8,507 USD Intl)**	943.56 CZK (37 Euro) **(67 USD Intl)**	6,375.41 CZK (250 Euro) **(452 USD Intl)**
	Court fees:	586.54 CZK (23 Euro) **(42 USD Intl)**	586.54 CZK (23 Euro) **(42 USD Intl)**	6,120.39 CZK (240 Euro) **(434 USD Intl)**	12,750.82 CZK (500 Euro) **(905 USD Intl)**	132,608.49 CZK (5200 Euro) **(9,412 USD Intl)**	8,160.52 CZK (320 Euro) **(579 USD Intl)**	943,560.44 CZK (37,000 Euro) **(66,967 USD Intl)**	3,060.20 CZK (120 Euro) **(217 USD Intl)**	943.56 CZK (37 Euro) **(67 USD Intl)**
	Total/ comments:	**368 USD Intl**	**151 USD Intl**	**1,502 USD Intl** Total includes 300 Euro in expert fees	**3,873 USD Intl**	**14,479 USD Intl** Total includes 300 Euro in expert fees.	**1,014 USD Intl**	**80,904 USD Intl** Total includes trial expenses of 3,000 Euro.	**284 USD Intl**	**519 USD Intl** Total includes trial expenses of 100 Euro.
Denmark	Lawyers' fees:	10,000 DKK **(1,175 USD Intl)**	15,000 DKK **(1,763 USD Intl)**	12,000 DKK **(1,410 USD Intl)**	11,000 DKK **(1,293 USD Intl)**	27,500 DKK **(3,231 USD Intl)** In practice – 0	11,000 DKK **(1,293 USD Intl)**	1,000,000 DKK **(117,509 USD Intl)**	U	1,000,000 DKK **(117,509 USD Intl)**
	Court fees:	500 DKK **(59 USD Intl)**	**0**	1,000 DKK **(118 USD Intl)**	1,600 DKK **(188 USD Intl)**	22,400 DKK **(2,632 USD Intl).** In practice – 0	1,249 DKK **(147 USD Intl)**	150.000 DKK **(17,626 USD Intl)**		150,000 DKK **(17,626 USD Intl)**
	Total/ comments:	**1,235 USD Intl** (Comment of the reporter: the	**1,763 USD Intl**	**1,528 USD Intl**	**1,481 USD Intl** (Comment of the reporter:	claimant will not incur any costs irrespective	**1,440 USD Intl**	**168,136 USD Intl** Total includes min 80,000 DKK	Not a civil case.	**168,136 USD Intl** Total includes min 80,000 DKK

		consumer would likely have insurance and be out of pocket only DKK 0 – DKK 2,000 – up to 235 USD Intl)			because the claimant would be represented by Trade Union or have insurance, the costs to him/her would in practice not exceed 2,000 DKK – 235 **USD Intl)**	of case outcome. Defendant is the state.		in court appointed experts and witness costs).		in court appointed experts and witness costs).
England and Wales	Lawyers' fees:	50 GBP (**76 USD Intl**)	1,000 GBP (**1,526 USD Intl**)	14,500 GBP (**22,137 USD Intl**)	G	100,000 GBP (**152,671 USD Intl**)	0	1,000,000 GBP **1,526,717 USD Intl**	0	50,000 GBP (**76,336 USD Intl**)
	Court fees:	55 GBP (**83 USD Intl**)	340 GBP (**519 USD Intl**)	0		2,300 GBP (**4,320 USD Intl**)	925 GBP (**1,412 USD Intl**)	2,032.20 GBP (**3,102.06 USD Intl**)	265 GBP (**405 USD Intl**)	515 GBP (**783 USD Intl**)
	Total/ comments:	**160 USD Intl**	**2,046 USD Intl** Further costs possible if case is complex, also: different costs	**22,137 USD Intl**	Costs between 5,000 and 70,000 GBP (depending on work done) (not included in charts)	**156,992 USD Intl** (solicitors and barristers' fees, both acting on a CFA basis – otherwise	**1,412 USD Intl**	**1,529,820 USD Intl**	**405 USD Intl**	**77,122 USD Intl**

Table 3. *cont.*

Country		Case Study 1	Case Study 2	Case Study 3	Case Study 4	Case Study 5	Case Study 6	Case Study 7	Case Study 8	Case Study 9
England and Wales *cont.*			depending on whether parties agree or not.			half the amount. Includes 2,500 disburse-ments).				
Estonia	Lawyers' fees:	2,002.77 EEK (128 Euro) (221 USD Intl)	4,897.40 EEK (313 Euro) (539 USD Intl)	62,586.56 EEK (4,000 Euro) (6,893 USD Intl)	9,998.20 EEK (639 Euro) (1,101 USD Intl)	19,996.41 EEK (1,278 Euro) (2,202 USD Intl)	19,996.41 EEK (1,278 Euro) (2,202 USD Intl)	199,995.35 EEK (12,782 Euro) (22,026 USD Intl)	4,991.28 EEK (319 Euro) (550 USD Intl)	49,991.01 EEK (3,195 Euro) (5,506 USD Intl)
	Court fees:	1,001.38 EEK (64 Euro) (110 USD Intl)	5,006.92 EEK (320 Euro) (551 USD Intl)	9,998.20 EEK (639 Euro) (1,101 USD Intl)	0	0	15,005.13 EEK (959 Euro) (1,653 USD Intl)	1,499,996.44 EEK (95,867 Euro) (165,198 USD Intl)	4,991.28 EEK (319 Euro) (550 USD Intl)	4,991.28 EEK (319 Euro) (550 USD Intl)
	Total/ comments:	331 USD Intl Lawyers' fee quoted here, but lawyers are rarely used in such cases. Alternative: expedited procedure – payment order. In	1,090 USD Intl	7,994 USD Intl	1,101 USD Intl	2,202 USD Intl	3,855 USD Intl	187,224 USD Intl	1,100 USD Intl	6,055 USD Intl

		that case, the state fee would be 750 EEK (EUR 48).								
Finland	Lawyers' fees:	G		U	G	G	G	G	G	G
	Court fees:		79 Euro (**86 USD Intl**)							
	Total/ comments:	Claimant's costs are likely to be nil.	Unable to specify – dependent on complexity.	Cases settled by insurance. Payment by claimant (164 USD Intl) goes to insurance company.	Claimant's costs are likely to be nil	Wide bracket of costs was given by reporter – between 4,000 and 50,000 Euro. Not included in the charts.	Wide bracket of costs was given by reporter – between 2,000 and 20,000 Euro. Not included in the charts.	25,000 Euro (27, 352 **USD Intl**)	2,000 Euro (**2,188 USD Intl**)	25,000 Euro (**27,352 USD Intl**)
France	Lawyers' fees:	U	6,000 Euro (**6,565 USD Intl**)	1,000 (**1,094** USD Intl)	2,000 (2188 USD Intl)	30,000 Euro (32,967 **USD Intl**)	1,000 Euro (**1,094 USD** Intl)	U	1,000 Euro (**1,094 USD** Intl)	U
	Court fees:		0	0	0	0	0		0	
	Total/ comments:	No costs to parties: *juridiction de proximité*	**6,565 USD Intl** (if parties did not manage	**1,094 USD Intl**	**2,188 USD Intl**	**32,823 USD Intl**	**1,094 USD Intl**		**1,094 USD Intl**	

Table 3. *cont.*

Country		Case Study 1	Case Study 2	Case Study 3	Case Study 4	Case Study 5	Case Study 6	Case Study 7	Case Study 8	Case Study 9
France *cont.*			to settle the case before litigation). Amount includes fixed fee of 4,000 Euro. No court fee.							
Germany	Lawyers' fees:	89.25 Euro **(106 USD Intl)**	1,588.65 Euro **(1,891 USD Intl)**	1,029.35 Euro **(1,225 USD Intl)**	1,588.65 Euro **(1,891 USD Intl)**	4,086 Euro **(4,864 USD Intl)**	1,249.50 Euro **(1,488 USD Intl)**	66,949.40 Euro **(79,702 USD Intl)**	U	U
	Court fees:	75 Euro **(89 USD Intl)**	119 Euro **(142 USD Intl)**	408 Euro **(486 USD Intl)**	438 Euro **(521 USD Intl)**	2,568 Euro **(3,057 USD Intl)**	498 Euro **(593 USD Intl)**	67,368 Euro **(80,200 USD Intl)**		
	Total/ comments:	**195 USD Intl)**	**2147 USD Intl** (includes lawyers' fees for court hearing, a 1.2 % fee and expenses).	**1,711 USD Intl** (includes lawyers' fees for court hearing, a 1.2 % fee and expenses).	**2,412 USD Intl** (includes lawyers fees for court hearing, a 1.2 % fee and expenses).	**7,921 USD Intl** (includes lawyers fees for court hearing, a 1.2 % fee and expenses).	**2,081 USD Intl** (includes lawyers fees for court hearing, a 1.2 % fee and expenses).	**159,902 USD Intl** (includes lawyers fees for court hearing, a 1.2 % fee and expenses).	Depend on amount in dispute	Depend on amount in dispute

Greece	Lawyers' fees:	64 Euro (89 USD Intl)	321 Euro (446 USD Intl) + 343 Euro (second lawsuit)	170 Euro (236 USD Intl)	508 Euro (706 USD Intl)	508 Euro (706 USD Intl)	197 Euro (238 USD Intl)	2,466 Euro (3,426 USD Intl)	343 Euro (476 USD Intl)	343 Euro (476 USD Intl)
	Court fees:	5.50 Euro (8 USD Intl)	5 Euro (7 USD Intl) +5 Euro (second law suit)	46 Euro (64 USD Intl)	378 Euro (525 USD Intl)	700 Euro (972 USD Intl)	60 Euro (83 USD Intl)	48,655 Euro (67,389 USD Intl)	5 Euro (7 USD Intl)	5 Euro (7 USD Intl)
	Total/ comments:	97 USD Intl	934 USD Intl (amount includes court fees and lawyers fees for two separate lawsuits – one involving the divorce, one involving children arrange-ments).	300 USD Intl	1,231 USD Intl	1,678 USD Intl	321 USD Intl	70,805 USD Intl	483 USD Intl	483 USD Intl

Table 3. *cont.*

Country		Case Study 1	Case Study 2	Case Study 3	Case Study 4	Case Study 5	Case Study 6	Case Study 7	Case Study 8	Case Study 9
Hong Kong	Lawyers' fees:	U	G	G	U	G	0	G	G	G
	Court fees:						0			
	Total/ comments:	'minimal'	30,000 HKD (5,557 USD Intl)	50,000 HKD (9,261 USD Intl)	'minimal'	1,000,000 HKD (185,219 USD Intl)	No legal fees	1,250,000 HKD (231,524 USD Intl)	100,000 HKD (18,522 USD Intl)	1,250,000 HKD (231,524 USD Intl)
Hungary	Lawyers' fees:	589,438.42 HUF (2,200 Euro) (4,233 USD Intl)	1,232,462.15 HUF (4,600 Euro) (8,850 USD Intl)	803,779.66 HUF (3,000 Euro) (5,771.79 USD Intl)	4,000 Euro (7,696 USD Intl)	1,232,462.15 HUF (4,600 Euro) (8,850 USD Intl)	2,143,412.43 HUF (8,000 Euro) (15,391 USD Intl)	80,377,965.99 HUF (300,000 Euro) (577,179.13 USD Intl)	267,926.55 HUF (1,000 Euro) (1,923.93 USD Intl)	1,607,559.32 HUF (6,000 Euro) (11,544 USD Intl)
	Court fees:	6,162.31 HUF (23 Euro) (44 USD Intl)	10,717.06 HUF (40 Euro) (77 USD Intl)	96,453.56 HUF (360 Euro) (692.61 USD Intl) + expert fee of 2,000 Euro	0	10,717.06 HUF (40 Euro) (77 USD Intl)	128,604.75 HUF (480 Euro) (924 USD Intl)	803,779.66 HUF (3,000 Euro) + Expert fee of 4,000 Euro (5,771.79 USD Intl)	2,116.62 HUF (7.90 Euro) (15.19 USD Intl)	18,754.86 HUF (70 Euro) (135 USD Intl)
	Total/ comments:	4,277 USD Intl	8,927 USD Intl	10,316 USD Intl	7,696 USD Intl (state advances claimants costs).	8,927 USD Intl	16,315 USD Intl	582,951 USD Intl	2,324 USD Intl (includes 200 Euro for on-site survey).	11,679 USD Intl

Ireland	Lawyers' fees:	0	G	1100 Euro (1,155 USD Intl)	G	G	4,500 Euro (4,727 USD Intl)	G	G	G
	Court fees:	0		63.49 Euro (67 USD Intl)			500 Euro (526 USD Intl)			
	Total/ comments:	Small claims procedure used – free of charge	6,000 Euro (6,303 USD Intl) – minimum amount (could reach up to 25,000 Euro in complex cases).	1,222 USD Intl	12,500 Euro (13,130 USD Intl)	100,000 Euro (105,042 USD Intl)	5,253 USD Intl	125,000 Euro (131,303 USD Intl)	2,500 Euro (2,626 USD Intl)	50,000 Euro (52,521 USD Intl)
Japan	Lawyers' fees:	5,250 JPY (45 USD Intl)	400,000 JPY (3,431 USD Intl)	270,000 JPY (2,315 USD Intl)	1,100,000 JPY (9,434 USD Intl)	13,500,000 JPY + 6,800,000 = 20,300,000 JPY= 174,104 USD Intl	300,000 JPY (2,573 USD Intl)	50,000,000 JPY (428,816 USD Intl)	700,000 JPY (6,003 USD Intl)	U
	Court fees:	4,910 JPY (42 USD Intl)	19,400 JPY (166 USD Intl)	15,000 JPY (129 USD Intl)	21,400 JPY (184 USD Intl)	314,400 JPY + 230,400 JPY = 4673 USD Intl	17,400 JPY (149 USD Intl)	1,976,400 JPY (16,950 USD Intl) + 3,000,000 JPY for expert opinion	19,400 JPY (166 USD Intl) + 100,000 JPY for noise measure-ment	

Table 3. *cont.*

Country		Case Study 1	Case Study 2	Case Study 3	Case Study 4	Case Study 5	Case Study 6	Case Study 7	Case Study 8	Case Study 9
Japan *cont.*	Total/ comments:	**87 USD Intl**	**3,597 USD Intl**	**2,444 USD Intl**	**9,618 USD Intl**	**178,776 USD Intl** (costs include two separate claims: for loss of ability to work, and for paraplegia).	**2,722 USD Intl**	**471,508 USD Intl**	**7,028 USD Intl**	'Not possible to calculate costs'
Latvia	Lawyers' fees:				U	U			U	
	Court fees:	50.19 LVL (71 Euro) (**122 USD Intl**)	101.09 LVL (143 Euro) (**247 USD Intl**)	243.88 LVL (345 Euro) (**595 USD Intl**)			285.59 LVL (404 Euro) (**697 USD Intl**)	4,727.06 LVL (6.687 Euro) (**11,529 USD Intl**)		50.19 LVL (71 Euro) (**122 USD Intl**)
	Total/ comments:	Unable to establish. Lawyers' costs depend on amount of work involved. Alternative option is	Unable to establish. Lawyers' costs depend on amount of work involved.	Unable to establish. Lawyers' costs depend on amount of work involved.	Claimant is exempted from court fees. Unable to establish total costs. Lawyers' costs depend on amount	Claimant is exempted from court fees. Unable to establish total costs. Lawyers' costs depend on amount	Unable to establish. Lawyers' costs depend on amount of work involved.	Unable to establish. Lawyers' costs depend on amount of work involved.	Admini-strative procedure used	Unable to establish. Lawyers' costs depend on amount of work involved.

		Consumer Rights Protection Centre (free of charge).			of work involved.	of work involved.				
Lithuania	Lawyers' fees:	145 Euro (272 USD Intl)	232 – 869 Euro (min 435 USD Intl)	435 – 580 Euro (min 816 USD Intl)	580 – 870 Euros (min 1,088 USD Intl)	435 – 580 Euro (min 816 USD Intl)	435 – 580 Euro (min 816 USD Intl)	5,792 – 11,585 Euro (min 10,860 USD Intl)	290 Euros (544 USD Intl)	2,896 – 5,792 Euros (min 5,430 USD Intl)
	Court fees:	20.50 Euro (38 USD Intl)	14 Euro (26 USD Intl) (postage) + no need to pay if consent; otherwise 3% of estate	180 (Stamp duty) + 290 Euro (expert fee) (881 USD Intl)	0	0	240 Euros (450 USD Intl)	8,689 Euro (stamp duty) (16,296 USD Intl)	29 Euros (54 USD Intl)	29 Euros (54 USD Intl)
	Total/ comments:	165.50 Euro (571.44 LTL – 310 USD Intl)	min 246 Euro = 849.39 LTL (461 USD Intl)	min 3,124.78 LTL (1,697 USD Intl)	min 2,002.62 LTL (1,088 USD Intl)	min 1,501.97 LTL (816 USD Intl)	min 675 Euros = 2,330.64 LTL (1,266 USD Intl).	min 14,481 Euros; 50,000 LTL (27,152 USD Intl)	319 Euros (1,104.44 LTL = 599 USD Intl)	min 2,925 Euros (10,099.44 LTL = 5,484 USD Intl)
Netherlands	Lawyers' fees:	0	G	G	G	G	U	U	U	U
	Court fees:	100 Euro (229.88 USD Intl)								

Table 3. *cont.*

Country		Case Study 1	Case Study 2	Case Study 3	Case Study 4	Case Study 5	Case Study 6	Case Study 7	Case Study 8	Case Study 9
Netherlands *cont.*	Total/ comments:	230 USD Intl	Wide bracket of costs given: between 1,000 and tens of thousands Euro. Not included in charts.	Wide bracket of costs given: between 1,000 and tens of thousands Euro. Not included in charts.	Wide bracket of costs given: between 1,000 and tens of thousands Euro. Not included in charts.	Wide bracket of costs given: between 1,000 and tens of thousands Euro. Not included in charts.	Depend on amount claimed and complexity of litigation.	Depend on amount claimed and complexity of litigation.	Depend on amount claimed and complexity of litigation.	Depend on amount claimed and complexity of litigation.
New Zealand:	Lawyers' fees:	U	G	G	G	U	G	U	U	U
	Court fees:									
	Total/ comments:	Cases pursued in the Disputes Tribunal (only filing fee of between $30 and 100 (NZD)	A general costs bracket of between $30,000 and 60,000 given.	Cases can be pursued before the Disputes Tribunal (only filing fee of $100 (NZD). If in court – costs between $10,000 and $30,000	Cases dealt with by Employ-ment Mediation Service. Costs for cases which do not settle at early stage between $5,000 and 20,000	Cases dealt with by Accident Compensa-tion Scheme.	Costs between $1,000 and 2,000 ('simple matter')	Respondent indicated that the case 'could easily consume $500,000'.	Admini-strative path	Respondent indicated that the case 'could easily consume $500,000'.

Norway	Lawyers' fees:	360 NOK (39 USD Intl)	U	U	G	30,000 NOK (3,286 USD Intl)	up to 25,000 NOK (2,738 USD Intl)			
	Court fees:	3,010 NOK (330 USD Intl)				4,300 NOK (471 USD Intl)	3,010 NOK (330 USD Intl)	4,300 NOK (470.97 USD Intl)	4,300 NOK (470.97 USD Intl)	4,300 NOK (470.97 USD Intl)
	Total/ comments:	369 USD Intl	Admini-strative route	Insurance route	Total costs for claimant 75,000 NOK – 8,216 USD Intl	3,757 USD Intl	3,068 USD Intl Small Claims – Lawyers' fees depend on agreement with client. Amount here is the maximum for cost-shifting purposes. Alternative: direct enforcement – 1581 + 5000 NKK (722 USD Intl)	Lawyers' fees depend on amount of work involved. Total 'can amount to 2,000,000 NKKU' (219,082 USD Intl)	Lawyers' fees depend on amount of work involved. Total 'can often amount to 100,000 NKK' (5,477 USD Intl)	Lawyers' fees depend on amount of work involved. Total 'can often amount to 300,000 NKK' (32,862 USD Intl)

Table 3. *cont.*

Country		Case Study 1	Case Study 2	Case Study 3	Case Study 4	Case Study 5	Case Study 6	Case Study 7	Case Study 8	Case Study 9
Poland	Lawyers' fees:	min 40 Euro (85 USD Intl)	min 80 Euro (170 USD Intl)	min 550 Euro (1,171 USD Intl)	min 550 Euro (1,171 USD Intl)	min 1,600 Euro (3,407 USD Intl)	min 1,600 Euro (3,407 USD Intl)	min 1,600 Euro (3,407 USD Intl)	min 40 Euro (85 USD Intl)	min 130 Euro (277 USD Intl)
	Court fees:	10 Euro (21 USD Intl)	130 Euro (277 USD Intl)	300 + 70 Euro (expert) (788 USD Intl)	0	22,250 Euro + 1,200 Expert fee (51,638 USD Intl)	400 Euro (852 USD Intl)	22,250 Euro (47,379 USD Intl)	50 Euro (106 USD Intl)	130 Euro + 1,200 expert fee (2832 USD Intl)
	Total/ comments:	50 Euro 209.42 PLN[5] 106 USD Intl	210 Euro 881.08 PLN 447 USD Intl	920 Euro 3,857.54 PLN; 1,959 USD Intl	550 Euro 2,307.95 PLN; 1,171 USD Intl	25,050 Euro 105,121.89 PLN; 55,045 USD Intl	Min 2,000 Euro 8,393.62 PLN; 4,259 USD Intl	23,850 Euro 100,135.25 PLN; 50,786 USD Intl	90 Euro 377.95 PLN; 191 USD Intl	min 1,460 Euros; 6,126.17 PLN; 3,109 USD Intl
Portugal	Lawyers' fees:	0		500 – 1,000 Euro (min 715 USD Intl)	1,500 – 5,000 Euros (min 2,146 USD Intl)	2,000 – 5,000 Euros (min 2,861 USD Intl)	500 – 1,000 Euros (min 715 USD Intl)	0	250 – 1,500 Euros (min 357 USD Intl)	1,000 – 5,000 Euros (min 1,431 USD Intl)
	Court fees:	72 Euro (103 USD Intl)	396 Euro (565 USD Intl) + 250 Euro (357 USD Intl)	180 Euros (257 USD Intl)	504 Euro (721 USD Intl)	288 Euro (412 USD Intl)	206 Euro (295 USD Intl)	2.208 Euro (3,159 USD Intl)	396 Euro (566 USD Intl)	396 Euro (566 USD Intl)

[5] Rates per 23 Sep 2009.

	Total/ comments:	**103 USD Intl** (amount if claim brought electronically; if not – 96 Euro).	**min 972 USD Intl** Alternatives: mediation and conciliation – free of charge; or arbitration will cost 190 Euro or 310 Euro. Another alternative: magistrates' court – 70 Euro.	Unable to state total cost. Lawyers' fees were not quoted. Alternatives: mediation (50 Euro per party), and the registry procedure – 800 Euro total cost for both parties.	**min 2,867 USD Intl** Alternative: labour mediation, 50 Euro per party.	**min 3,273 USD Intl** Alternative: magistrates' court – 70 Euro.	**min 1,010 USD Intl** Alternative: magistrates' court – 70 Euro.	**3,159 USD Intl** Alternatives: mediation, conciliation or arbitration. Mediation and conciliation are free of charge; arbitration – €210,010 or €350,010.	**min 924 USD Intl**	**1,997 USD Intl**
Romania	Lawyers' fees:	210.57 RON (50 Euro) **(104 USD Intl)**	21,051.02 RON (5,000 Euro) **(10,370 USD Intl)**	4,252.26 RON (1,010 Euro) **(2,095 USD Intl)**	12,630.43 RON (3,000 Euro) **(6,221.88 USD Intl)**	12,630.43 RON (3,000 Euro) **(6,222 USD Intl)**	4,210.14 RON (1,000 Euro) **(2,074 USD Intl)**	2,105,070.82 RON (500,000 Euro) **(1,036,981 USD Intl)**	2,105.07 RON (500 Euro) **(1,037 USD Intl)**	42,101.42 RON (10,000 Euro) **(20,739.61 USD Intl)**
	Court fees:	71.58 RON (17 Euro) **(35 USD Intl)**	36.46 RON (8.66 Euro) **(18 USD Intl)**	1,321.99 RON (314 Euro) **(651 USD Intl)**	0	33,681.14 RON (8,000 Euro) **(16,592 USD Intl)**	42.10 RON (10 Euro) **(21 USD Intl)**	298,920.06 RON (71,000 Euro) **(147,251 USD Intl)**	8.42 RON (2 Euro) **(4 USD Intl)**	8.42 RON (2 Euro) **(4.14 USD Intl)**

Table 3. *cont.*

Country		Case Study 1	Case Study 2	Case Study 3	Case Study 4	Case Study 5	Case Study 6	Case Study 7	Case Study 8	Case Study 9
Romania *cont.*	Total/ comments:	139 USD Intl	11,392 USD Intl (amount includes 500 Euro for expert report).	3,214 USD Intl (amount includes 200 Euro for damage assessment report).	6,824 USD Intl (amount includes 300 Euro for damage assessment report).	22,814 USD Intl	2,095 USD Intl	1,191,137 USD Intl (amount includes 5,000 Euro for trial expenses).	1,041 USD Intl	31,023 USD Intl (amount includes 5,000 Euro for trial expenses).
Russia	Lawyers' fees:			U	219,625 RUB (max 5,000 Euro) (11,622 USD Intl)	219,625 RUB (5,000 Euro) (11,292 USD Intl)		2,196,248 RUB (50,000 Euro) (116,204 USD Intl)		439,249.68 RUB (10,000 Euro) (23,240.72 USD Intl)
	Court fees:	341.40 RUB (8 Euro) (18 USD Intl)	197.66 RUB (4.50 Euro) (10.45 USD Intl)		0	0	10,322.37 RUB (235 Euro) (546 USD Intl)	96,634.93 RUB (2,200 Euro) (5,113 USD Intl)		1,976.62 RUB (45 Euro) (104.58 USD Intl)
	Total/ comments:	Lawyers' fees have not been given, and the respondent indicated that a lawyer would be 'hard to get.'	The reporter indicated that the lawyers' fees would typically be as follows: 500 – 173,000 Euro for	No precisely itemized fees were quoted. The reporter indicated that the lawyers' case acceptance fee (if the	11,622 USD Intl	11,292 USD Intl	546 USD Intl	121,317 USD Intl. Reporter mentioned some other charges, but these were not itemized.	Police complaint route.	23,345 USD Intl

			acceptance of case, and 50 – 200 Euro for each court hearing (usually up to 10 hearings).	claim was between 3,000 and 6,000 Euro) is 300–500 Euro, and then the lawyer charges 100 Euro for each court hearing. An expert opinion costs 60–200 Euro.						
Scotland	Lawyers' fees: Court fees: Total/ comments:	G Min £500 **(763 USD Intl)**	G £35,000 **(53,435 USD Intl)** This is a typical amount, but costs could vary considerably.	G Estimated cost: £9,000 **(13,740 USD Intl)**	G Estimated cost: £26,500 **(40,458 USD Intl)**	G Estimated cost: £40,000 **(61,069 USD Intl)**	G Estimated cost: £6,000 **(9,160 USD Intl)**	G Estimated costs for both parties: £460,000; **702,290 USD Intl**		G For both parties: 186,763.99 Euro (£160,000) **244,275 USD Intl**

Table 3. *cont.*

Country		Case Study 1	Case Study 2	Case Study 3	Case Study 4	Case Study 5	Case Study 6	Case Study 7	Case Study 8	Case Study 9
Singapore	Lawyers' fees:	0	4,500 S$ (4,171 USD Intl)	5,000 S$ (4,634 USD Intl)	100,000 S$ (92,678 USD Intl)	G	10,000 S$ (9,268 USD Intl)	G		G
	Court fees:	10 S$	10,000 S$ (9,268 USD Intl)	min 15,000 S$ (13,902 USD Intl)	min 60,000 S$ (55,607 USD Intl)		min 15,000 S$ (13,902 USD Intl)			
	Total/ comments:	11 USD Intl	13,439 USD Intl	18,536 USD Intl	148,285 USD Intl	min 300,000 S$ 278,035 USD Intl	23,170 USD Intl	min 500,000 S$ (463,392 USD Intl)		min 40,000 S$ (43,160 USD Intl)
Spain	Lawyers' fees:	165 Euro (212 USD Intl)	1,041.81 Euro (1,336 USD Intl)	1,041.13 Euro (1,797 USD Intl)	1,421.13 Euro (1,822 USD Intl)	U	1,767.53 Euro (2,266 USD Intl)	103,567.13 Euro (132,778 USD Intl)		103,567.13 Euro (132,778 USD Intl)
	Court fees:	0	0	0	0		0	0		0
	Total/ comments:	212 USD Intl special procedure ('monitorio': small debts proceedings) for claims under 30,000 Euro.	1,336 USD Intl	1,797 USD Intl	1,822 USD Intl	Costs will depend on value in dispute.	2,266 USD Intl	132,778 USD Intl		132,778 USD Intl

Sweden	Lawyers' fees:	U								
	Court fees:		7,721.45 SEK (725 Euro) (832 USD Intl)		450 SEK (49 USD Intl)		450 SEK (49 USD Intl)	450 SEK (49 USD Intl)		450 SEK (49 USD Intl)
	Total/ comments:		Uncertain total. Lawyers' fees were not specified. They depend on amount of work done.	Compulsory insurance	Uncertain total. Lawyers' fees will depend on amount of work done.	Insurance route	Uncertain total. Lawyers' fees will depend on amount of work done.	Uncertain total. Lawyers' fees will depend on amount of work done.		Uncertain total. Lawyers' fees will depend on amount of work done.
Switzerland	Lawyers' fees:	0		1,600 CHF (936 USD Intl)		U	1,900 CHF (1,111 USD Intl)	148,500 CHF (86,842 USD Intl)		U
	Court fees:	65 CHF (38 USD Intl)	5,000 CHF (2,924 USD Intl)	1,165 CHF (682 USD Intl)	3,165 CHF (1,851 USD Intl)		1,445 CHF (845 USD Intl)	83,800 CHF (49,006 USD Intl)	300 CHF (175 USD Intl)	
	Total/ comments:	38.01 US Intl	Uncertain total. A wide bracket of lawyers' fees was given: 'between CHF 1,400 and CHF	1,618 USD Intl	Uncertain total. A wide bracket of lawyers' fees was given: 'between CHF 4,065 and CHF	Costs will depend on the amount in dispute.	1,956 USD Intl	135,848 USD Intl	Uncertain total. A very wide bracket of lawyers' fees given: 'CHF 280 up to CHF 10,666.	

Table 3. *cont.*

Country		Case Study 1	Case Study 2	Case Study 3	Case Study 4	Case Study 5	Case Study 6	Case Study 7	Case Study 8	Case Study 9
Switzerland *cont.*			16,000, in a case which goes all through the court process to a first judgment (without settlement), the final fee will be approximately twice the base fee, ie between CHF 2,800 and CHF 32,000.'		8,135 (§ 3 of the Zurich Tariff for Lawyers' Fees). Where a case goes all through the court process to a first judgment (without settlement), the final fee will be approximately twice the base fee, ie between CHF 8,130 and CHF 16,270.'				Where a case goes all through the court process to a first judgment (without settlement), the final fee will be approximately twice the base fee, ie between CHF 560 and CHF 21,332.'	
Taiwan	Lawyers' fees:		U	U	U	U	U	U		U
	Court fees:	863.14 TWD (18.50 Euro) (49 USD Intl)								
	Total/ comments:	Uncertain total.								

Table 4: Claimant and defendant costs in the case studies

Case Study 1: repayment to a consumer of €200 price paid for product not delivered

Country	**Claimant Costs** local currency[1]	**Claimant Costs** USD Intl	**Defendant Costs** local currency	**Defendant Costs** USD Intl	**Additional remarks**
Austria:	606.40 Euro	706	569.40 Euro	664	
Australia:	3,577 AUD	2,432	2,500 AUD	1,700	
Belgium:	1,000 Euro	1,143	1,000 Euro	1,143	Minimum costs[2]
Bulgaria:	150 BGL	208	200 BGL	277	
Canada:					No precise amounts in answer. Litigation is not the recommended route. If brought, costs could be 2,500 CAD
China:	230 CNY	60	180 CNY	46	Minimum costs
Czech Republic:	203 Euro	368	180 Euro	326	Minimum costs
Denmark:	10,500 DKK	1,235	10,000 DKK	1,176	Consumer would likely have insurance and be out of pocket only DKK 0 – DKK 2,000 (up to 235 USD Intl).
England and Wales:	105 GBP	160	75 GBP	115	
Estonia:	192 Euro	331	128 Euro	221	Alternative: administrative procedure: 48 Euro. Lawyers' fee quoted here, but lawyers are rarely used in such cases.
Finland:	0 Euro (could go up to 5000)		1,500 Euro	1,641	Minimum costs
France:	0 Euro		0 Euro	0	If lawyers used (not necessary): up to 1,500 Euro. Normally, however, no costs to parties: *juridiction de proximité.*
Germany:	164.25 Euro	195	89.25 Euro	106	
Greece:	69.50 Euro	97	68 Euro	94	
Hong Kong :					'Minimal amounts'

[1] If Euro amount was quoted instead of local currency, the Euro amount is quoted here – see for instance the Czech Republic.

[2] Meaning – can be higher.

Table 4. *cont.*

Country	**Claimant Costs** local currency	**Claimant Costs** USD Intl	**Defendant Costs** local currency	**Defendant Costs** USD Intl	**Additional remarks**
Hungary:	2,223 Euro	4,277	2,200 Euro	4,233	
Ireland:	0	0	0	0	Small claims – free; if district court – 100 Euro
Japan:	10,160 JPY	87	5,250 JPY	45	Minimum costs
Latvia:					Unable to establish total. Lawyers' costs depend on amount of work involved. Alternative option is Consumer Rights Protection Centre (free of charge).
Lithuania:	168 Euro	310	145 Euro	272	
Netherlands:	100 Euro	230	100 Euro	230	
New Zealand:					Cases pursued by the Disputes Tribunal (only filing fee of between $30 and 100 (NZD)
Norway:	3,370 NOK	369	360 NOK	39	Costs if small claims court (not recommended), Conciliation Board is cheaper, and Consumer Dispute Committee – free
Poland:	50 Euros	106	40 Euros	85	
Portugal:	72 Euros	103	0 Euros	0	Minimum costs (if claim brought electronically)
Romania:	67 Euros	139	50 Euros	103	
Russia:	8 Euros	18	0	0	Administrative enforcement recommended. Lawyers' fees have not been given, and the respondent indicated that a lawyer would be 'hard to get.'
Scotland:	500 GBP	736	0	0	

Country	Claimant Costs local currency	Claimant Costs USD Intl	Defendant Costs local currency	Defendant Costs USD Intl	Additional remarks
Singapore:	10 SGD	11	0	0	
Spain:	165 Euro	212	165 Euro	212	Costs as quoted: only if lawyers used (not very common). Special procedure ('monitorio': small debts proceedings) for claims under 30.000 Euro.
Sweden:					No amounts in answer
Switzerland:	65 CHF	38	0	0	Minimum costs
Taiwan:	18.50 Euro	49			Only part of the cost to the claimant, no other amounts in answer.

Case Study 2: Family: divorce between husband on average income (say 50,000 pa), wife with no income, two children, living in an average home

Country	Claimant Costs local currency[3]	Claimant Costs USD Intl	Defendant Costs local currency	Defendant Costs USD Intl	Additional remarks
Austria:	1,573.10	1,829	1,363.10 Euro	1,589	
Australia:	5,837 AUD	3,968	5,543 AUD	3,768	
Belgium:	3,000 Euro	3,429	3,000 Euro	3,429	Costs as quoted if straightforward divorce case. Complex cases can cost as much as 50,000 Euro.
Bulgaria:	350 BGL	486	400 BGL	554	Minimum costs
Canada:					Costs are not precisely itemised. They can range between $2,000 and $200,000

[3] If Euro amount was quoted instead of local currency, the Euro amount is quoted here – see for instance the Czech Republic.

Table 4. *cont.*

Country	Claimant Costs local currency	Claimant Costs USD Intl	Defendant Costs local currency	Defendant Costs USD Intl	Additional remarks
China:					Minimum costs. Not able to specify – lawyers' costs and other expenses depend on value of case and complexity.
Czech Republic:	83 Euros	151	60 Euros	109	
Denmark:	15,000 DKK	1,763	15,000 DKK	1,763	Minimum costs. Normally settled out of court (free)
England and Wales:	1,340 GBP	2,046	0	0	Further costs possible if case is complex, also: different costs depending on whether parties agree or not.
Estonia:	633 Euro	1,091	313 Euro	539	Minimum costs
Finland:	79 Euro	86	0	0	Minimum costs
France:	6,000 Euro	6,565	6,000 Euro	6,565	Costs quoted apply if parties did not manage to settle the case before litigation. Amount includes fixed fee of 4,000 Euro. No court fee.
Germany:	1,807.65 Euro	2,147	1,588,65 Euro	1,887	
Greece:	326+348 = 674 Euro	934	224+209 = 433 Euro	600	Amount includes court fees and lawyers' fees for two separate lawsuits – one involving the divorce, one involving children arrangements.
Hong Kong:	30,000 HKD	5,557	30,000 HKD	5,557	Minimum costs, if no trial.
Hungary:	4,640 Euro	8,927	4,640 Euro	8,927	
Ireland:	6,000 Euro	6,303	6,000	6,303	Minimum costs (could reach up to 25,000 Euro in complex cases).

Country	**Claimant Costs** local currency	**Claimant Costs** USD Intl	**Defendant Costs** local currency	**Defendant Costs** USD Intl	**Additional remarks**
Japan:	419,400 JPY	3,597	300,000 JPY	2,573	Minimum costs; Mandatory mediation (cheaper) is conducted before the start of litigation.
Latvia:	143 Euro	247	143 Euro	247	Minimum costs
Lithuania:	243 Euro	461	232 Euro	435	
New Zealand:					No precise amounts in answer
Netherlands:					Minimum costs 1,000 Euro – 1,144 USD Intl (can be much higher)
Norway:					Normally settled by administrative decision
Poland:	210 Euro	447	80 Euro	170	
Portugal:					Unable to state total cost. Lawyers' fees were not quoted. Alternatives: mediation (50 Euro per party), and the registry procedure – 800 Euro total cost for both parties.
Romania:	5,508.66 Euro	11,392	5,000 Euro	10,340	
Russia:					Only court fee quoted. The reporter indicated that the lawyers' fees would typically be as follows: 500 – 3000 Euro for acceptance of case, and 50 – 200 Euro for each court hearing (usually up to 10 hearings).
Scotland:	22,925 GBP	53,435	0	0	This is a typical amount, but costs could vary considerably.
Singapore:	7,750 SGD	13,439	7,750 SGD	13,439	

Table 4. *cont.*

Country	Claimant Costs local currency	Claimant Costs USD Intl	Defendant Costs local currency	Defendant Costs USD Intl	Additional remarks
Spain:	1,041.81 Euro	1,336	1,041.81 Euro	1,336	Costs if parties have separate lawyers and they agree, 1,735.97 Euro each if they disagree; but if income exceeds 7,582.05 Euro 'the fees will be proportionately increased'.
Sweden:					Uncertain total. Lawyers' fees were not specified. They depend on amount of work done.
Switzerland:					Uncertain total. A wide bracket of lawyers' fees was given: 'between CHF 1,400 and CHF 16,000, in a case which goes all through the court process to a first judgment (without settlement), the final fee will be approximately twice the base fee, ie between CHF 2,800 and CHF 32,000.'
Taiwan:					Uncertain total. Only court fees quoted: 49 USD Intl

Case Study 3: RTA: road traffic accident collision, in which the rear of the claimant's car and the front of the defendant's car are moderately damaged (ie rear and front respectively require total replacement panels, but engine is undamaged); cost of repair and replacement car €6,000.

Country	Claimant Costs local currency[4]	Claimant Costs USD Intl	Defendant Costs local currency	Defendant Costs USD Intl	Additional remarks
Austria:	3,959.80	4,610	1,702.80	1,985	Minimum costs
Australia:	5,198 AUD	3,536	0	0	
Belgium:	500 Euro	571	500 Euro	571	Minimum costs
Bulgaria:	1,170 BGL	486	1,170 BGL	486	Minimum costs
Canada:					Administrative insurance arrangements.
China:	2,770 CNY	716	1,620 CNY	418	Minimum costs
Czech Republic:	830 Euro	1,502	290 Euro	525	Minimum costs
Denmark:	13,000 DKK	1,528	12,000 DKK	1,411	Minimum costs, but such cases are normally settled by insurance
England and Wales:	14,500 GBP	22,137	14,500 GBP	22,137	
Estonia:	4,639 Euro	7,994	4,000 Euro	6,891	Minimum costs
Finland:	150	164	0	0	Cases settled by insurance – the payment quoted here goes to the insurance company.
France:	1,000 Euro	1,094	1,000	1,094	Minimum costs
Germany:	1,437.35 Euro	1,711	1,029.35 Euro	1,223	
Greece:	216 Euro	300	131 Euro	181	
Hong Kong:	50,000 HKD	9,261	50,000 HKD	9,261	Minimum costs
Hungary:	5,360 Euro	10,316	3,000 Euro	5,772	
Ireland:	1,163.49 Euro	1,222	1,103.38	1,159	
Japan:	285,000 JPY	2,444	250,000 JPY	2,144	Minimum costs

[4] If Euro amount was quoted instead of local currency, the Euro amount is quoted here – see for instance the Czech Republic.

Table 4. *cont.*

Country	Claimant Costs local currency	Claimant Costs USD Intl	Defendant Costs local currency	Defendant Costs USD Intl	Additional remarks
Latvia:	345 Euro	595	345 Euro	595	Minimum costs
Lithuania:	905 Euro	1,697	435 Euro	816	Minimum costs
Netherlands:					Wide bracket of costs given: between 1,000 and tens of thousands Euro.
New Zealand:					Cases can be pursued before the Disputes Tribunal (only filing fee of $100 (NZD)). If in court – costs between $10,000 and $30,000.
Norway:					Cases settled by compulsory insurance.
Poland:	920 Euro	1,959	550 Euro	1,171	
Portugal:	680 Euro	972	680 Euro	972	Minimum costs (if claim brought electronically).
Romania:	1,554 Euro	3,214	1,010 Euro	2,089	Minimum costs
Russia:					No precisely itemized fees were quoted. The reporter indicated that the lawyers' case acceptance fee is 300 - 500 Euro, and then 100 Euro for each court hearing. An expert opinion costs 60 - 200 Euro.
Scotland:	9,000 GBP	13,740	0	0	Estimated costs.
Singapore:	20,000 SGD	18,536	20,000 SGD	18,536	
Spain:	1,041.13 Euro	1,797	1,041.13 Euro	1,797	Figures according to Lawyers' Board Guidelines (no court fees).
Sweden:					Normally settled by compulsory insurance.
Switzerland:	2,765 CHF	1,618	1,600 CHF	936	Minimum costs
Taiwan:					Unable to state costs.

Case Study 4: Employment: wrongful loss of employment by a middle-ranging manager (salary €50,000 pa)

Country	**Claimant Costs** local currency[5]	**Claimant Costs** USD Intl	**Defendant Costs** local currency	**Defendant Costs** USD Intl	**Additional remarks**
Austria:					No amounts in answer, costs depend on amount in dispute.
Australia:	20,000 AUD	13,596	20,000 AUD	13,596	ADR-style mechanism (Conciliation).
Belgium:	2,500 Euro	2,857	2,500 Euro	2,857	Minimum costs
Bulgaria:	6,450 BGL	8,959	2,450 BGL	3,393	Costs for claimants in management contracts only, if employment contracts – no costs. Minimum costs.
Canada:					Costs will depend on value in dispute. Some experience with a previous case costing $25,000.
China:	14,967.21 CNY	3,866	14,957.21 CNY	3,863	First – mandatory arbitration; costs here – if arbitration fails.
Czech Republic:	2,140 Euro	3,873	1,640 Euro	2,968	Minimum costs
Denmark:	12,600 DKK	1,481	11,000 DKK	1,293	Minimum costs, but normally covered by insurance – cases normally settled by insurance
England and Wales:					Costs for both parties between 5,000 and 70,000 GBP, depending on work done, normally in the Employment Tribunal).
Estonia:	639 Euro	1,101	639 Euro	1,101	Minimum costs
Finland:	0		3,000 Euro	3,282	Minimum costs. Claimant's costs are likely to be nil.

[5] If Euro amount was quoted instead of local currency, the Euro amount is quoted here – see for instance the Czech Republic.

Table 4. *cont.*

Country	Claimant Costs local currency	Claimant Costs USD Intl	Defendant Costs local currency	Defendant Costs USD Intl	Additional remarks
France:	2,000 Euro	2,188	2,000 Euro	2,188	If lawyers used: 2000 – 6000 Euro; but many parties do not use lawyers.
Germany:	2,026.65 Euro	2,412	1,588.65	1,887	
Greece:	886 Euro	1,231	379 Euro	525	
Hong Kong:					'Minimal costs'
Hungary:	1,067.63 HUF	7,696	10,000 Euro	19,239	Employee exempted from costs – advanced by state.
Ireland:	12,500 Euro	13,130	12,500 Euro	13,130	Costs if lawyers used only (not necessary)
Japan:	1,121,400 JPY	9,618	1,500,000 JPY	12,865	Minimum costs
Latvia:					Claimant is exempted from court fees. Unable to establish total costs. Lawyers' costs depend on amount of work involved.
Lithuania:	2,002.62 Euro	1,088	2,002.62 Euro	1,088	Minimum costs
Netherlands:	500 Euro	572	500 Euro	572	Wide bracket of costs given: between 1,000 and tens of thousands Euro.
New Zealand:					Cases dealt with by Employment Mediation Service. Costs for cases which do not settle at early stage between $5,000 and 20,000.
Norway:	75,000 NOK	8,216	75,000 NOK	8,216	Maximum costs
Poland:	550 Euro	1,171	550 Euro	1,171	
Portugal:	2,004 Euro	2,867	1,500 Euro	2,146	Minimum costs (if claim brought electronically).

Country	Claimant Costs local currency	Claimant Costs USD Intl	Defendant Costs local currency	Defendant Costs USD Intl	Additional remarks
Romania:	3,300 Euro	6,824	5,000 Euro	10,340	
Russia:	10,000 Euro	11,622	0	0	Maximum cost
Scotland:	26,500 GBP	40,458	0	0	Estimated cost
Singapore:	160,000 SGD	148,285	160,000 SGD	148,285	
Spain:	1,421.13 Euro	1,822	1,421.13 Euro	1,822	Cost of legal fees in court case, but often these cases are settled through (obligatory) mediation, which costs the claimant 311.85 Euro and the defendant 138.60 Euro
Sweden:					Normally unions pay costs, ultimately born by employer. Uncertain total. Lawyers' fees will depend on amount of work done.
Switzerland:					Uncertain total. A wide bracket of lawyers' fees was given: 'between CHF 4,065 and CHF 8,135 (§ 3 of the Zurich Tariff for Lawyers' Fees). Where a case goes all through the court process to a first judgment (without settlement), the final fee will be approximately twice the base fee, ie between CHF 8,130 and CHF 16,270'.
Taiwan:					Unable to quote costs.

Case Study 5: Medical negligence: doctor's error results in permanent (a) loss of ability to walk (b) paraplegia, for male claimant aged 25 on salary of €25,000 pa, no current dependents, but likelihood of marriage and two children

Country	Claimant Costs local currency[6]	Claimant Costs USD Intl	Defendant Costs local currency	Defendant Costs USD Intl	Additional remarks
Austria:	50,913,70 Euro	59,434	27,052.70 Euro	31,530	Minimum amounts – depend on amounts claimed (here – assumption that amount is 600,000 Euro)
Australia:	100,000 AUD	67,981	100,000 AUD	67,981	Costs normally reimbursed by insurer
Belgium:	12,500 Euro	14,286	12,500 Euro	14,286	Minimum costs
Bulgaria:	12,950 BGL	17,292	4,450 BGL	6,163	Minimum costs
Canada:					No amounts in answer. Costs will depend on value of the case.
China:					No amounts in answer. Costs will depend on value of the case.
Czech Republic:	8,000 Euro	14,479	2,800 Euro	5,068	
Denmark:	27,500 DKK	3,233	27,500 DKK	3,233	State is the defendant, and the costs are as quoted if parties share lawyers' fees 50/50, normally funded by legal aid or insurance. In practice, however, claimant will not incur any costs irrespective of case outcome. Defendant is the state.
England and Wales:	102,830 GBP	156,992	50,000 GBP	76,336	
Estonia:	1,278 Euro	2,202	1,278 Euro	2,202	Minimum costs
Finland:					Wide bracket of costs was given by reporter – between 4,000 and 50,000 Euro.

[6] If Euro amount was quoted instead of local currency, the Euro amount is quoted here – see for instance the Czech Republic

Country	Claimant Costs local currency	Claimant Costs USD Intl	Defendant Costs local currency	Defendant Costs USD Intl	Additional remarks
France:	30,000 Euro	32,823	30,000 Euro	32,823	Minimum costs (+ expert costs if appointed by court).
Germany:	6,654 Euro	7,921	4,086 Euro	4,853	
Greece:	1,208 Euro	1,678	379 Euro	525	
Hong Kong:	1,000,000 HKD	185,219	1,000,000 HKD	185,219	
Hungary:	4,460 Euro	8,927	4,460 Euro	8,927	
Ireland:	100,000 Euro	185,042	75,000 Euro	78,782	Minimum costs, may be much higher in complex cases.
Japan:	17,644,800 JPY	178,776	13,000,000 JPY	111,495	Minimum costs for loss of ability to walk and paraplegia
Latvia:					Claimant is exempted from court fees. Unable to establish total costs. Lawyers' costs depend on amount of work involved.
Lithuania:	435 Euro	816	435 Euro	816	
Netherlands:					Wide bracket of costs given: between 1,000 and tens of thousands Euro.
New Zealand:					Cases settled through accident compensation scheme
Norway:	34,400 NOK	3,757	30,000 NOK	3,286	Minimum costs; Patient Injury Committee first; costs here if appeal to court
Poland:	25,050 Euro	55,045	2,800 Euro	5,962	
Portugal:	2,288 Euro	3,273	2,000 Euro	2,861	Minimum costs (if claim brought electronically).
Romania:	12,000 Euro	24,814	5,000 Euro	10,340	
Russia:	5,000 Euro	11,292	5,000 Euro	11,292	Minimum costs
Scotland:	40,000 GBP	61,069	0	0	

Table 4. *cont.*

Country	**Claimant Costs** local currency	**Claimant Costs** USD Intl	**Defendant Costs** local currency	**Defendant Costs** USD Intl	**Additional remarks**
Singapore:	300,000 SGD	278,035	300,000 SGD	278,035	Minimum costs
Spain:					Costs will depend on value in dispute.
Sweden:					Insurance route.
Taiwan:					No precise amounts.

Case Study 6: SME: small company claim for unpaid debt of €8,000

Country	**Claimant Costs** local currency	**Claimant Costs** USD Intl	**Defendant Costs** local currency	**Defendant Costs** USD Intl	**Additional remarks**
Austria:	3,700.60 Euro	4,303	3,093.60 Euro	3,606	
Australia:	1,577 AUD	1,753	1,577 AUD	1,753	Minimum costs
Belgium:	500 Euro	571	500 Euro	571	Minimum costs
Bulgaria:	1,410 BGL	1,958	770 BGL	1,066	Minimum costs
Canada:					If Small Claim – the costs would be between C$3,000-5,000. If in court under the Simplified Rules – C$10,000-C$15,000.
China:	3,760 CNY	971	2,160 CNY	558	Minimum costs
Czech Republic:	560 Euro	1,014	240 Euro	434	Minimum costs
Denmark:	12,249 DKK	1,440	11,000 DKK	1,293	Minimum costs
England and Wales:	925 GBP	1,412	225 GBP	344	
Estonia:	2,237 Euro	3,855	1,278 Euro	2,202	Minimum costs
Finland:					Wide bracket of costs was given by reporter – between 2,000 and 20,000 Euro.

Country	Claimant Costs local currency	Claimant Costs USD Intl	Defendant Costs local currency	Defendant Costs USD Intl	Additional remarks
France:	1,000 Euro	1,094	1,000 Euro	1,094	If lawyer appointed: 2000 – 3000 Euro between parties, but often lawyers are not used
Germany:	1,747.50 Euro	2,081	1,249.50 Euro	1,484	
Greece:	257 Euro	321	132 Euro	183	
Hong Kong:					'No legal fees', small claims court.
Hungary:	8,480 Euro	16,315	8,000 Euro	15,391	
Ireland:	5,000 Euro	5,253	4,000 Euro	4,202	If use of ADR – 2,500 Euro for each party.
Japan:	317,400 JPY	2,722	200,000 JPY	1,715	Minimum costs
Latvia:					Only court fees for claimant quoted: 404 Euro. No other amounts in answer.
Lithuania:	1,266 Euro	633	1,154.32 Euro	627	
Netherlands:					Depend on amount claimed and complexity of litigation.
New Zealand:					Costs between $1,000 and 2,000 ('simple matter').
Norway:	28,010 NOK	3,068	0	0	Direct enforcement cost, include legal assistance. Small Claims - Lawyers' fees depend on agreement with client. Amount here is the maximum for cost-shifting purposes. Alternative: direct enforcement – 1581 + 5000 NKK (722 **USD Intl**)

Table 4. *cont.*

Country	Claimant Costs local currency	Claimant Costs USD Intl	Defendant Costs local currency	Defendant Costs USD Intl	Additional remarks
Poland:	2,000 Euro	4,259	1,600 Euro	3,407	Minimum costs
Portugal:	706 Euro	1,010	500 Euro	715	Minimum costs (if claim brought electronically)
Romania:	1,010 Euro	2,095	1,000 Euro	2,068	
Russia:	235 Euros	546			No other amounts in answer – only court fees were quoted here.
Singapore:	10,000 SGD	9,268	10,000 SGD	9,268	Minimum costs; Costs if lawyers involved
Scotland:	6,000 GBP	9,160	6,000 GBP	9,160	
Spain:	1767.53 Euro	2,266	1,767.53 Euro	2,266	If court procedure used (normally settled through simplified procedure which costs each party 165 Euros)
Sweden:					Uncertain total. Lawyers' fees will depend on amount of work done.
Switzerland:	3,345 CHF	1,957	0	0	Minimum costs
Taiwan:					Costs will depend on stage at which the case concluded and the work involved.

Case Study 7: Large commercial case: substantial and complex breach of contract claim between two large companies over supply of defective machinery worth €2 million, with €5 million loss of profit

Country	Claimant Costs local currency[7]	Claimant Costs USD Intl	Defendant Costs local currency	Defendant Costs USD Intl	Additional remarks
Austria:	222,124.25 Euro	243,200	112,463.25 Euro	131,076	Minimum costs

[7] If Euro amount was quoted instead of local currency, the Euro amount is quoted here – see for instance the Czech Republic.

Country	Claimant Costs local currency	Claimant Costs USD Intl	Defendant Costs local currency	Defendant Costs USD Intl	Additional remarks
Australia:	50,000 AUD	33,990	50,000 AUD	33,990	Minimum costs
Belgium:	7,500 Euro	8,571	7,500 Euro	8,571	Minimum costs
Bulgaria:	401,281 BGL	557,012	881,050 BGL	1,220,291	Minimum costs
Canada:					The reporter indicated that the costs could exceed C$1,000,000.
China:	1,616,800 CNY	417,778	1,350,000 CNY	348,657	Minimum costs
Czech Republic:	44,700 Euro	80,904	6,200 Euro	11,222	
Denmark:	1,430,000 DKK	168,136	1,280,000 DKK	150,500	Minimum costs
England and Wales:	2,032.20 +1,000,000 (maximum – lawyers' fee) = 1,002,032.20 GBP	1,529,820	1,797.26 +1,000,000 (maximum – lawyers' fee) = 1,001,797.26 GBP	1,529,461	Lawyers' fees can be lower
Estonia:	108,649 Euro	187,224	12,702 Euros	18,438	Minimum costs
Finland:	25,000 Euro	27,352	25,000 Euro	27,352	Minimum costs (up to 200,000 Euro), arbitration is an alternative here, but the costs are not lower.
France:					No amounts in answer
Germany:	134,317.40 Euro	159,902	66,949.40 Euro	78,512	
Greece:	51,121 Euro	70,805	1,649 Euro	2,284	
Hong Kong:	1,250,000 HKD	231,524	1,250,000 HKD	231,524	Minimum costs
Hungary:	307,000 Euro	590,591	300,000 Euro	577,179	
Ireland:	125,000 Euro	131,303	125,000 Euro	131,303	Minimum costs (up to 2,000,000 Euro in complex cases)

Table 4. *cont.*

Country	Claimant Costs local currency	Claimant Costs USD Intl	Defendant Costs local currency	Defendant Costs USD Intl	Additional remarks
Japan:	54,976,400 JPY	471,508	35,000,000 JPY	300,179	Minimum costs
Latvia:	6,687 Euro	11,529			No other amounts in answer. Lawyers' costs depend on amount of work involved.
Lithuania:	14,481 Euro	27,152	5,792 Euro	10,860	
Netherlands:					Costs will depend on amount of work involved.
New Zealand:					Respondent indicated that the case 'could easily consume $500,000'.
Norway:	2,000,000 NKK	219,082	2,000,000 NKK	219,082	Lawyers' fees depend on amount of work involved. Total 'can amount to 2,000,000 NKK' (219,082 USD Intl)
Poland:	23,850 Euro	50,786	1,600 Euro	3,407	
Portugal:	2,208 Euro	3,159	2,208	3,159	Minimum costs (if claim brought electronically).
Romania:	576,000 Euro	1,191,137	505,000 Euro	1,044,313	
Russia:	52,200 Euro	121,317	0	0	Minimum costs; No other amounts in answer.
Scotland:	230,000 GBP	351,145	230,000 GBP	351,145	Estimated costs.
Singapore:	500,000 SGD	463,392	500,000 SGD	463,392	
Spain:	103,567.13 Euro	132,778	103,567.13 Euro	132,778	

Country	Claimant Costs local currency	Claimant Costs USD Intl	Defendant Costs local currency	Defendant Costs USD Intl	Additional remarks
Sweden:					Uncertain total. Lawyers' fees will depend on amount of work done.
Switzerland:	232,300 CHF	135,927	148,500 CHF	86,893	Minimum costs
Taiwan:					Unable to give amounts.

Case Study 8: Injunction – consumer: against neighbour to stop noise

Country	Claimant Costs local currency[8]	Claimant Costs USD Intl	Defendant Costs local currency	Defendant Costs USD Intl	Additional remarks
Austria:	735.80 Euro	855	683.80 Euro	797	Minimum costs
Australia:	5,000 AUD	3,399	5,000 AUD	3,399	Minimum costs
Belgium:	1,500 Euro	1,714	1,500 Euro	1,714	Minimum costs
Bulgaria:	180 BGL	250	150 BGL	208	Minimum costs
Canada:					The reporter indicated that the costs would be about C$15,000.
China:	5,050 CNY	1,305	5,000 CNY	1,291	
Czech Republic:	157 Euro	284	120 Euro	217	
Denmark:					Administrative complaint.
England and Wales:	265 GBP	405			No lawyer fees quoted, so answer incomplete; administrative path can be used.
Estonia:	638 Euro	1,100	319 Euro	550	
Finland:	2,000 Euro	2,188	2,000 Euro	2,188	Minimum costs (up to 10,000).

[8] If Euro amount was quoted instead of local currency, the Euro amount is quoted here – see for instance the Czech Republic.

Table 4. *cont.*

Country	Claimant Costs local currency	Claimant Costs USD Intl	Defendant Costs local currency	Defendant Costs USD Intl	Additional remarks
France:	1,000 Euro	1,094	1,000 Euro	1,094	Minimum costs; costs only if lawyers used, and this does not happen always
Germany:					Costs will depend on amount in dispute.
Greece:	348 Euro	483	241 Euro	334	
Hong Kong:	100,000 HKD	18,522	100,000 HKD	18,522	Minimum costs
Hungary:	1,207.90 Euro	2,324	1,000 Euro	1,924	
Ireland:	2,500 Euro	2,626	2,500 Euro	2,626	Minimum costs (up to 20.000 Euro in complex cases).
Japan:	819,400 JPY	7,028	500,000 JPY	4,288	Minimum costs
Latvia:					Administrative procedure
Lithuania:	319 Euro	599	290 Euro	544	
Netherlands:					Depends on amount claimed and complexity of litigation.
New Zealand:					Administrative path
Norway:	50,000 NOK	5,477	50,000 NOK	5,477	
Poland:	90 Euro	191	50 Euro	106	
Portugal:	646 Euro	924	0		Minimum costs (if claim brought electronically); administrative complaint recommended
Romania:	502 Euro	1,041	500 Euro	1,034	
Russia:					Complaint to the police should be made
Scotland:					No response.

Country	Claimant Costs local currency	Claimant Costs USD Intl	Defendant Costs local currency	Defendant Costs USD Intl	Additional remarks
Singapore:	20,000 SGD	37,071	20,000 SGD	37,071	Minimum costs; if lawyers used (otherwise 10.000 SGD each).
Spain:					Administrative path
Sweden:					Administrative path
Switzerland:	3,100 CHF	1,814	0	0	Uncertain total. A very wide bracket of lawyers' fees given: 'CHF 280 up to CHF 10,666. Where a case goes all through the court process to a first judgment (without settlement), the final fee will be approximately twice the base fee, ie between CHF 560 and CHF 21,332.'
Taiwan:					No total can be calculated.

Case Study 9: Injunction – commercial: prevent illegal breach of intellectual property in commercial information between two substantial companies

Country	Claimant Costs local currency	Claimant Costs USD Intl	Defendant Costs local currency	Defendant Costs USD Intl	Additional remarks
Austria:	7,393.30 Euro	8,597	6,387 Euro	7,444	Minimum costs
Australia:	10,000 AUD	6,798	10,000 AUD	6,798	
Belgium:	2,500 Euro	2,857	2,500 Euro	2,857	Minimum costs
Bulgaria:					No answer to the case study

[9] If Euro amount was quoted instead of local currency, the Euro amount is quoted here – see for instance the Czech Republic.

Table 4. *cont.*

Country	**Claimant Costs** local currency	**Claimant Costs** USD Intl	**Defendant Costs** local currency	**Defendant Costs** USD Intl	**Additional remarks**
Canada:					The reporter indicated that the costs could exceed C$1,000,000.
China:	129 CNY				Only court fees quoted. Lawyers' fees will depend on amount of work.
Czech Republic:	287 Euro	519	250 Euro	453	
Denmark:	1,430,000 DKK	168,136	1,280,000 DKK	150,000	Minimum costs
England and Wales:	50,515 GBP	77,122	0	0	
Estonia:	3,514 Euro	6,055	0	0	Minimum costs
Finland:	25,000 Euro	27,352	25,000 Euro	27,352	Minimum costs (up to 100.000 Euro)
France:					No costs in answer
Germany:					Costs will depend on amount of work.
Greece:	348 Euro	483	241 Euro	334	
Hong Kong:	1,250,000 HKD	231,524	1,250,000 HKD	231,524	Minimum costs
Hungary:	6,070 Euro	11,678	0	0	
Ireland:	50,000 Euro	52,521	50,000 Euro	52,521	Minimum costs (up to 2,000,000 Euro in complex cases)
Japan:					Not possible to calculate costs
Latvia:					Unable to establish total. Lawyers' costs depend on amount of work involved.
Lithuania:	2.925 Euro	5,484	0	0	
Netherlands:					Costs will depend on amount claimed and complexity of litigation.

Country	Claimant Costs local currency	Claimant Costs USD Intl	Defendant Costs local currency	Defendant Costs USD Intl	Additional remarks
New Zealand:					Respondent indicated that the case 'could easily consume $500,000'.
Norway:	300,000 NKK	32,862	300,000 NKK	32,862	
Poland:	1,460 Euro	3,109	1,330 Euro	2,832	
Portugal:	1,396 Euro	1,997	0	0	Minimum costs (if clam brought electronically)
Romania:	15,002 Euro	31,023	15,000 Euro	31,019	
Russia:	10,045 Euro	23,345	0	0	Minimum costs
Scotland:	80,000 GBP	122,135	80,000 GBP	122,135	Minimum costs
Singapore:	40,000 SGD	43,160	40,000 SGD	43,160	Minimum costs
Spain:	103,576,13 Euro	132,778	0	0	
Sweden:					No amounts in answer
Switzerland:					No amounts in answer
Taiwan:					IP court

Table 5: Ranges of court fees and lawyers' hourly rates

Country	**Court fees** (Originals were given in local currency and Euro[1], and have been converted into *USD Intl*)	**Lawyers' hourly fees in local currency,** (Originals were given in local currency and Euro[2], and have been converted into *USD Intl*)
Austria	Scale for cases between 150 and 363,360 Euro (*175 – **423,497 USD Intl***): between 19 and 5,962 Euro (*22 – **6949 USD Intl***)	
Australia	Flat fee: for instance, in the Supreme Court of New South Wales: $1,453 (***988 USD Intl***) (company) $606 (*412 **USD Intl***) (individual) to lodge a case and the same amount for filing a cross-claim.	150 – 600AUD: ***102 – 408 USD Intl***
Belgium	Flat fee: 35 Euro (***40 USD Intl)*** in lower court, 186Euro (*213 **USD Intl)** in* appeal court), 325 Euro (*371 **USD Intl)** in* Supreme Court.	No data
Bulgaria	4% of value of claim, min 50 BGN (*69 **USD Intl***). If this value cannot be evaluated, the fee is determined by the court between BGN 30 and BGN 80 (*42 **and** 111 **USD Intl***)	No data
Canada	No data	CAD 125 – CAD 900: ***104 – 749 USD Intl***
China	Minimum amount – 50 RMB (*13 **USD Intl***), tariff varies from 2.5% in low value cases to 0.6% in high value cases	3,000 RMB: *775 **USD Intl***
Czech Republic	4% of value of the case: fees range between 600 CZK (*43 **USD Intl***) and 1,000,000 CZK (*70,977 **USD Intl***). If claim brought online (and not worth more than 1,000,000) fees are 2%, they range from min 300 (*22 **USD Intl***).	Hourly rates are not common.
Denmark	500 DKK (*59 **USD Intl***) for non-pecuniary claims and pecuniary claims up to 50,000 DKK; For pecuniary claims exceeding 50,000 DKK in value: 500 + 250 (*88 **USD Intl***) + 1.2% of value of case (maximum 75,000 DKK: **8,818 USD Intl**).	1.000 – 3,750 DKK: ***118 – 441 USD Intl***

[1] Conversion rates as per 16 July 2009 at: http://www.xe.com/ucc/.
[2] Conversion rates as per 30 June 2009 at: http://www.xe.com/ucc/convert.cgi.

England and Wales	Between £30 (***45 USD Intl***) (for a claim of less than £300) and £1,530 (***2,318 USD Intl***) (for a claim of £300,000 or of unlimited value).	109 – 402 GBP: ***165 – 609 USD Intl***
Estonia	Tariff system depending on value of the case, for instance: for case worth 20 000 EEK (1,282 Euro) the fee is 4,000 EEK – ***438 USD Intl***; the maximum cap of ***164,841 USD Intl***	64 – 128 Euro: ***110 – 220 USD Intl***
Finland	Cases decided: • in writing: 70 Euro: ***77 USD Intl*** • orally: 100 Euro: ***109 USD Intl*** • in one-judge hearing: 130 Euro: ***142 USD Intl*** • in 'full court': 160 Euro: ***175 USD Intl***	150 – 400 Euro: ***164 – 438 USD Intl***
France	0	220 – 500 Euro: ***241 – 547 USD Intl***
Germany	Tariff depending on value of case and specific instance. For example, for a claim worth 10,000 Euro in the first instance: 3 x 196 Euro = 588 Euro: ***698 USD Intl***	Hourly rates vary. Tariffs for costs and shiftable costs.
Greece	Court fee consists of: (1) judicial stamp duty: 4 – 5 Euro: ***7 USD Intl*** (first instance), 7 – 8 Euro: ***10 – 11 USD Intl*** (appeal), or 18 Euro: ***25 USD Intl*** (Supreme Court), and (2) duty to the state (6.95% of the value of the case).	No data.
Hong Kong	Flat fee depending on type of court: High Court: for issuing writ of summons: HK$1,045 (***194 USD Intl***); For setting case down for trial: same amount. District Court: HK$630 (***117 USD Intl***)	No data.
Hungary	6% of value of case: min 7,000 HUF (25.52 Euro: ***50 USD Intl***), max 900,000 HUF (***6,475 USD Intl***)	35 – 500 Euro: ***67 – 964 USD Intl***
Italy	Between 30 and 1,100 Euro: ***35 and 1,269 USD Intl***; if non-pecuniary claim: flat fee of 340 Euro: ***392 USD Intl*** for civil cases	No data.
Japan	Revenue stamp: 9,000 Yen (68.84 Euro: ***77 USD Intl***) + Prepaid stamp: 6,000 Yen (***51 USD Intl***)	20,000 – 100,000 Yen: ***172 – 858 USD Intl***

Table 5 *cont.*

Country	**Court fees** (Originals were given in local currency and Euro, and have been converted into *USD Intl*)	**Lawyers' hourly fees in local currency,** (Originals were given in local currency and Euro, and have been converted into *USD Intl*)
Latvia	Tariff: Case studies describe that the percentage ranges from 15% for cases less than 1,423 Euro, through 2.5 % and 1.6% of larger value cases.	20 – 300 LVL: ***49 – 730 USD Intl***
Lithuania	Tariff, depends on the value of the case: between 3% and 1%. Lower percentage rates accompany higher value cases (more than 29,000 Euro), and there is also a lump sum (between **870 and 2,030 Euro**) payable in such cases.	51 – 831 LTL: ***28 – 452 USD Intl***
Netherlands	Tariff: 36 – 1,184 Euro (***41 – 1,355 USD Intl***) for individuals; up to 6,174 Euro (***7,064 USD Intl***) for companies	75 – 700 Euro: ***86 – 801 USD Intl***
New Zealand	Tariff: fees payable for specific procedural activities. 1,100 NZD (***708 USD Intl***) for filing a claim, and same for filing a counterclaim in High Court.	270 – 800 NZD: ***174 – 515 USD Intl***
Norway	Flat fees: Conciliation Board: 860 NOK (95.55 Euro: ***94 USD Intl***); District Court: 5 x 860 NOK = 4,300 NOK = 477.69 Euro: ***471 USD Intl***; but small claims: 3,010 NOK (334.26 Euro: ***330 USD Intl***)	1,000 – 4,000 NOK + VAT (25%) = 1,250 – 5000 NOK: 138.49 – 553.95 Euro: ***137 – 548 USD Intl***
Poland	5% of value of case (30 – 1,000 PLN in civil cases (***15 – 509 USD Intl***), 50 – 3,000 PLN (***25 – 1,528 USD Intl***) in commercial cases);	100 – 400 PLN: ***51 – 204 USD Intl***
Portugal	Tariff depending on value of the case: 96 – 2,340 Euro: ***137 – 3,348 USD Intl*** (+ additional 480 Euro: ***687 USD Intl*** for each amount of 25,000 Euro in high value cases)	60 – 300 Euro: ***86 – 429 USD Intl***
Romania	Between 1% (high value cases) and 10% (low value cases) of value of case.	350 Euro: ***172 USD Intl***
Russia	Between 0.5% (high value cases) and 5% (low value cases) of value of case, maximum 440 Euro	300 Euro: ***683 USD Intl***
Scotland	Flat fee: Court of session (ordinary civil cases): 170 GBP (***258 USD Intl***) Sheriff Court (initial writ): 120 GBP (***182 USD Intl***)	69 – 169 (average 149) Euro: ***90 – 220 USD Intl***

Singapore	500 SGD (***460 USD Intl***) (if claim less than 1,000,000 SGD) and 1000 (***930 USD Intl***) (if claim more than 1,000,000 SGD) – initial writ fee.	100 – 1000 SGD: ***93 – 930 USD Intl***
Spain	90 Euro: ***115 USD Intl*** (oral proceedings); 300 Euro: ***385 USD Intl*** (appeal); amount established by statute + 0.50% of amount at stake (if up to 1,000,000 Euro), and above that 0.25% (max 6,000 Euro)	94.50 – 252 Euro: ***121 – 323 USD Intl***
Sweden	Flat fee: 450 SEK (40.83 Euro: ***48 USD Intl***) (application for summons)	1.104 SEK: ***119 USD Intl***
Switzerland	Tariff: Canton court: 150 CHF (98.73 Euro: ***88 USD Intl***) to 120,750 CHF (79,469.51 Euro: ***70,655 USD Intl***) + 0.5% of the value of case above 10,000,000 CHF; for non-pecuniary claims: 300 (197.44 Euro: ***176 USD Intl***) to 13,000 CHF (8,554.76 Euro: ***7,607 USD Intl***); In Federal Supreme Court: 200 CHF (131.63 Euro: ***117 USD Intl***) to 100,000 CHF (65,814.21 Euro: ***58,514 USD Intl***)	350 – 600 CHF: ***205 – 351 USD Intl***
Taiwan	Different fees apply at different levels, ranging from a flat fee of NTD 1,000 (***57 USD Intl***) for cases worth below NTD 100,000 (***5,733 USD Intl***) to NTD 66 for each 10,000 in cases worth over NTD 1,000,000,000 (***57,189 USD Intl***). In non-pecuniary claims: 3,000 NTD (64.60 Euro: ***172 USD Intl***). Below are examples of case values and fees payable in first instance: *Value of claim* — *Fee* Below NTD 10,000 — NTD 1,000 NTD 100,000 — NTD 1,000 NTD 1,000,000 — NTD 10,900 NTD 10,000,000 — NTD 100,000 NTD 100,000,000 — NTD 892,000 NTD 1,000,000,000 — NTD 7,822,000 Above 1,000,000,000 — NTD 66 for each NTD 10,000	5,000 – 8,000 NTD for consultation, 10,000 NTD for hearing attendance: ***286 – 458 USD Intl***
USA	Flat fee: $350 (***350 USD Intl***) (Federal Court)	No data.

Table 6: PPP Currency conversion rates used in the case studies
PPP: number of local currency units per international USD (2009 prices).

Source: IMF, *World Economic Outlook* Database April 2009 available at http://www.imf.org/external/pubs/ft/weo/2009/01/weodata/index.aspx

Country	Conversion Rate
Australia	1.471
Austria	0.858
Belgium	0.875
Bulgaria	0.722
Canada	1.201
China	3.872
Czech Rep.	14.089
Denmark	8.505
Estonia	9.082
Finland	0.914
France	0.914
Germany	0.842
Greece	0.722
Hong Kong	5.399
Hungary	139.260
Ireland	0.952
Italy	0.867

Country	Conversion Rate
Japan	116.597
Latvia	0.411
Lithuania	1.840
Netherlands	0.874
Norway	9.129
Poland	1.963
Portugal	0.699
Romania	2.031
Russia	18.897
Singapore	1.079
Spain	0.780
Sweden	9.282
Switzerland	1.709
Taiwan	17.486
UK	0.655
USA	1.000

Part II

National Reports

1

An Introduction to the Range of National Approaches

CHRISTOPHER HODGES

The following chapters comprise descriptions of the rules and situation on funding and costs in a series of jurisdictions. This chapter provides a summary of the major features that emerge from the countries that are covered. It is not intended to give a complete picture of each legal system, but to highlight some particularly striking aspects of differing national costs regimes and to illustrate the range of different approaches that exist. The aim is to assist readers by providing a convenient short overview. The facts set out in this chapter are drawn from the national chapters save where otherwise stated, although citations have not been included in order to avoid repetition: reference should be made to the succeeding chapters.

There are two striking comparative features about the system of litigation costs in France. First, almost no court costs are payable by litigants. Accordingly, although such costs as may be paid (*dépenses*) can be shifted at the end to the loser, the amounts will be small. Secondly, the amount that the courts will generally order a loser to reimburse in respect of lawyers' fees is also notably low. Anne-Laure Villedieu notes the codified rules on costs, which have some complexities, but indicates that shiftable lawyers' costs are not based on a formal tariff, save for the limited category of postulation acts solely in the Tribunal de grande instance.

Yvon Desdevises explains the rationale for these rules in his illuminating exposé of the application of the (revolutionary) principle of liberty to concepts of justice and freedom, hence producing (almost) free access to justice. He notes that lawyers themselves resisted attempts to introduce a tariff of shiftable fees, since that might have influenced the level of fees that were in fact charged. He also notes more recent political debates between guardians of the public purse (government) and the legal professions over what might be required, and at what cost, for delivering justice in a modern, industrial and mass society. It appears that traditional reliance on free access to lawyers and courts cannot be taken for granted. A proposal that lawyers and notaries public should extend their *pro bono* work in order to finance legal aid through a tax was met, perhaps unsurprisingly, with strong opposition.

Belgium has a codified system of costs rules, historically based largely on the French system. However, several major changes in policy were enacted in 2007. Formerly, lawyers' fees were not shiftable under the court costs rules, and each party had to pay their own experts during the investigation of a case, such costs not being shiftable either. Since the reforms, both lawyers' costs (on a tariff basis) and expert's costs are payable by the losing party, and experts are no longer paid on a longer retention fee claimed from a party. However, payment is supervised by the court, so as to avoid bias and to speed up the delivery of the expert's service. In these reforms, Vincent Sagaert and Ilse Samoy highlight the linkage that the Belgian government was seeking to make with other issues of policy on civil justice and procedure: a need to reduce lengthy arrears in judicial caseload, to accelerate expert investigations, and to facilitate mediation so as to encourage more cases to settle, and settle earlier and hence more cheaply.

The reasons for the shift in policy on adoption of a loser pays rule in Belgium are particularly interesting. There were no rules on the recoverability of the costs of enforcement of a debt through the courts. This led to extensive contractual provisions being imposed for recovery of enforcement costs, but it was felt that such provisions were too often abusive and punitive. By way of response, the government effectively introduced regulation of such amounts by shifting recovery costs from the contractual arena to court rules under a statutory scheme with a fixed tariff. This is an interesting example of an exercise in market regulation. A further factor was the impact of the European Late Payment Directive (2000/35), which requires provision for reimbursement of enforcement costs. Having made that change for commercial cases, Belgium then saw a need to ensure a degree of consistency between commercial and other claims, so introduced a standard approach for all cases. These reforms in turn caused revision of the previous orthodoxy as to the irrevocability of lawyers' fees: it had been considered, first, that lawyers' costs were not part of damages, and secondly, that a claimant's decision to involve a lawyer was a personal and autonomous one. Both those tenets collapsed in the face of the pragmatic need to permit recovery of enforcement costs and to regulate such costs.

Germany is widely regarded as the classic fully regulated system of both court costs and costs payable by losers. The levels set in the tariffs for both sets of costs are based on a policy of cross-subsidisation so as to facilitate access to justice for smaller claims. Burkhard Hess and Rudolf Hübner maintain that this is not 'fee shifting', because the full fee is not shifted. One may debate the terminology but, elsewhere in this book, a broader definition of fee shifting has been adopted. Germany has recently moved away from a system where the level of fees that lawyers were allowed to charge their clients in litigation was fully regulated. Nowadays the level of fees that a loser has to pay to a winner is still fixed, but this may be only partial reimbursement of the cost that the winner has in fact agreed to pay his lawyer. The legal market in Germany is still such that a potential litigant may always be able to find a lawyer who will agree to charge him or her only the fee stated in the reimbursement tariff, and this situation may be expected to have some effect in limiting the demand for legal aid expenditure. However, it may be wondered whether the growth in the number of law firms that charge commercial rates that are increasingly above the reimbursement tariff rates will lead to an increase in the number of impecunious claimants who cannot afford a lawyer.

The German costs system is a clear example of the close link between the system of civil procedure and the costs regime. Taken together, these features produce several important outcomes. First, they tend to impose pressure on claimants to claim only reasonable provable amounts, and induce strategies for reducing the sum claimed. Secondly, the existence of the tariffs provides a notably high degree of predictability of costs, both for claimants and defendants in evaluating their respective exposures. The existence of quantified and certain outcomes, especially at relatively low rates, in turn facilitates the existence of legal expenses insurance. LEI, therefore, has long been a notable feature of the German legal scene, but there is no need for ATE insurance. This feature in turn facilitates a higher level of litigation than occurs in many other similar countries. Further, the efficiency and low cost of the court system, plus the maintenance of a monopoly on legal advice for lawyers, has tended to limit pressure for mediation and ADR services in Germany. Nevertheless, despite a high degree of predictability, the cost system does include some elements aimed at deterring and sanctioning party misbehaviour.

Japan borrowed much from German law in the late-nineteenth century, so the civil procedure systems and costs regimes are similar, save with one exception. As Ikuo Sugawara and Eri Osaka explain, until very recently there were very few lawyers in Japan, so no rule was introduced requiring legal representation in court. Accordingly, no rule was introduced for shifting of lawyers' fees in litigation. The result is that a loser pays the court costs, but not lawyers' costs. Partly for this reason and partly, no doubt, for cultural reasons, Japan has a strong emphasis on settlement and on non-court dispute resolution pathways: there is wide use of the court-annexed conciliation procedure, the labour dispute determination procedure and the less formalised (and cheaper) demand for payment procedure. Yet there has been extensive debate over whether to introduce shifting of lawyers' fees, over the level of lawyers' fees and their transparency, and over other possible sources of insurance or legal aid. The legal aid budget has expanded dramatically in the past few years.

Similarly, Taiwan also adopted a German-inspired Code of Civil Procedure but, as Kuan-Ling Shen and Helena Chen note, the loser pays rule does not apply to lawyers' costs, save in the court of third instance. Taiwan permits contingency fees.

The same model of a loser pays rule applying to court charges but not lawyers' fees is found in Russia. Dimitri Maleshin outlines that impecunious parties who are granted 'legal aid' are exempt from court charges but must pay a lawyer or find one who will act for free, possibly on a success fee basis.

The overview of funding and costs in Latin American jurisdictions by Manuel Gómez illustrates the concerns of those civil law jurisdictions to expand access to justice. Eight of the countries waive court fees for all, but are left with underfunded courts and litigants having to pay for legal services. Not surprisingly, experiments with legal aid, *pro bono* work, contingency fees and class action procedures are amongst the innovations being assessed.

Poland, like its fellow post-socialist states, is experiencing considerable reform in civil procedure and costs rules, as part of the process of adopting market-based substantive law. The release of market forces is also affecting private forms of litigation funding: although contingency fees have been technically banned, Magdalena Tulibacka notes that they have unofficially filled a gap so as to deliver some access to justice. The 2009 Class Actions Act makes contingency fees permissible in a collective action, but capped at 20 per cent of the damages recovered. Nevertheless, it is unclear whether the loser pays rule will make contingency fees an attractive funding option. The loser pays rule (both for lawyers' costs and court costs) also applies to any person who receives legal aid (in the form of a free lawyer): such a person is relieved of the burden of funding his case but remains liable for opponents' costs. This situation clearly imposes a disincentive to litigate.

Reforms in 2008 in Portugal have raised serious controversy over what is meant by access to justice. In reviewing what was considered to be an unacceptably high case load for the courts, the Portuguese government identified that about half of the workload constituted debt claims that were brought by financial institutions or collection agencies. One possible response might have been to increase state funding for the courts, so as to enable them to process more cases more quickly, but this did not occur. The actual response was to attempt to cut the supply side, by increasing the filing fee by 50 per cent, and permitting judges to impose exceptional sanctioning fees or fines, so as to encourage use of ADR solutions. Henrique Antunes reports on the severe scholarly and other criticism of the government's policy towards restricting access to the courts in this fashion. On the other hand, Portugal has a rich corpus of alternative dispute resolution means, including Magistrates' Courts, an employment mediation system, a family mediation system, an automotive arbitration centre and several consumers' arbitration centres. The 2008 reforms also simplified matters, in providing for payment of a single justice (court) fee, rather than as previously in two installments.

Portugal has a loser pays rule, based on outcome, but its nineteenth century history includes an interesting precedent that the obligation to pay costs was related to the good of bad faith of the parties in the dispute, regardless of success or failure, and this can be seen today in the survival of a rule that fault in the proceedings (such as lack of procedural interest or misuse of the procedure) can justify imposition of a costs liability.

Spain also has a loser pays rule. It is provided that the rule will not apply where the court considers that the case 'presented serious doubts of a factual or legal nature'. However, that exception is applied very rarely in practice. In addition to the situations where a party has to pay a lawyer as adviser, every party is required to appoint a court agent as a procedural liaison for court proceedings, whose fees typically amount to 20 per cent of a lawyer's fees. It remains to be established whether this bifurcation gives overall value for money. In Spain, a person whose lawyer is paid by the regional government's legal aid system is not liable to pay anything if he loses his case. Aránzazu Calzadilla Medina, Carlos Trujillo Cabrera and Alejandro Ferreres Comella note the very low rate of settlement of litigation in Spain, and also the existence of efficient alternatives to courts, such as consumer mediation and arbitration bodies.

In Switzerland, the problems of integrating 26 cantonal jurisdictions and a single federal jurisdiction are the origin of major reform that aims to introduce (from 2011) a new Federal Code of Civil Procedure (FCCP). Walter Stoffel and James Reardon note that this development has given rise to unresolved issues of exclusivity or overlap of jurisdiction between the different levels. Although the FCCP applies a loser pays rule, there are a series of interesting exceptions, including where a party went to trial in good faith. Out-of-court settlements are encouraged, but for the reason that they can be more flexible than court judgments, and may therefore be more likely to be observed. The FCCP supports use of the conciliation authority and also, more tentatively, of mediation. Social law cases are dealt with in a separate procedure within which no costs apply.

The civil law model of civil procedure and tariff-based cost shifting has largely remained intact in the Netherlands, but Mark Yuil identifies a significant cost irrecoverability gap produced by the low figures in the lawyers' fees' shifting tariff, which leads to the system being described as 'mitigated loser pays'. There is an unresolved debate over the introduction of contingency fees. Finally, the Dutch system is also notable for its long standing tradition of non-court dispute resolution, through dispute resolution boards and ombudsman-like institutions, and incentives for use of ADR in preference to courts.

Nordic states are well known for their reliance on a high level of social protection through various state or private insurance mechanisms. Consistent with this approach, the Danish state pays for individuals' legal assistance through a legal aid scheme, but only up to 75 per cent of cost for basic advice (capped at a low figure) or 50 per cent (again capped) for negotiations. The picture of the litigation costs system revealed by Kristine Svenningsen, Jan-Erik Svensson, and Anders Ørgaard is one of balancing the competing principles and goals that we referred to earlier in this chapter. On the one hand, the legal system should be available to all so as to vindicate rights and maintain confidence in the rule of law and, on the other hand, costs should not be so high as to deter genuine claims whilst, again, they should be high enough to protect against frivolous claims and against inflation of claims, but also encourage settlement. Settlement rates have risen during the past decade, considerably assisted by the introduction of compulsory judicial mediation from 2005. The loser pays principle is applied to both court costs and lawyers' fees, but in mediated fashion. Thus, a tariff sets the level of reimbursable lawyers' fees. Court costs are notably simple: there is merely a filing charge and, if appropriate, a hearing charge. These rules are influenced by the context of social reality in Denmark, whereby 80 per cent of the population is covered by legal expenses insurance through membership of a trade union, and perhaps more have personal insurance. As the authors note, the existence of legal aid or insurance removes an individual litigant's incentive to settle, although there may still be some pressure on insurers.

A series of major reforms has recently occurred in China in relation to costs, all designed to increase access to justice. First, a simplified structure of court fees has been introduced in 2006, with the objectives of reducing the cost of litigation and making costs more predictable. Particularly low court fees have been specified for targeted types of claims, notably matrimonial, labour and administrative claims, so as to take account of the social importance that these types of claims are facilitated and of the limited resources of the typical claimants. The local investigations of Michael Palmer and Chao Xi have identified that the introduction of reduced court costs caused a significant shortfall in local courts' finances, which has had to be at least partially filled by a large injection from central funds.

Secondly, a specific policy of encouraging mediation has been introduced in China, through use of fee levers. One such lever allows the courts to take into account a party's behaviour and attitude towards mediation in awarding costs to winners. A second lever is the rules on splitting costs awards between winners and losers, which has the objective of encouraging claimants to be realistic in quantifying their claims and not exaggerating them.

This is linked to the third reform, which alters the mechanism by which the loser pays the court costs. The change is not in the 'loser pays' rule itself, but in the procedure by which it operates, in order to remedy the situation that in practice losing parties were not ending up paying the court costs. Instead of a defendant reimbursing the winning claimant for the court fees that the latter had initially paid, the court now reimburses the claimant and itself collects the sum from the defendant. This change in practice reflects sociological reality in China, which some other societies might overlook. However, a summary of the Chinese position would be incomplete without noting the traditional rule that each party pays his own lawyer and cannot be reimbursed for this (ie no 'loser pays' applies for lawyers' costs), save under a small number of exceptions, which include intellectual property claims and where the claimant has legal aid. Palmer and Xi note that legal aid is provided in a number of forms in China, and these appear to be developing but generally only apply to those on very low incomes.

Turning now to the common law world, the legal system of England and Wales has been noted for its vigorous and wide-ranging reform of civil procedure (led by Lord Woolf) and for the simultaneous replacement of legal aid by conditional fee agreements plus, in order to accommodate the 'English rule' of loser pays, ATE insurance. As John Peysner comments, however, these reforms failed to stem ever-rising litigation costs for many types of claim. The Jackson Costs Review, reporting in 2010, attempts to grasp the various multiple problems. The dispute resolution scene in England and Wales is particularly complicated. There are many possible methods of funding litigation, including the new arrival of commercial litigation funding. There are also many different pathways for resolving different types of disputes.

'Traditional' common law approaches to 'loser pays' also apply in Australia, Canada and New Zealand, but differing approaches have emerged towards funding. New Zealand, with a population of only 3 million, an established no fault accident compensation scheme and various tribunals including the Disputes Tribunal for small claims, is one of the few countries that seem to be increasing their legal aid budget. Certainly, as Kim Economides and Graham Taylor record, New Zealand has devoted extensive efforts into reforming its legal aid scheme. At the same time, there is concern in the country that litigation costs are too high, and the 'irrecoverability gap' for a successful plaintiff can be up to 80 per cent.

By contrast, Australia, with a population of 23 million, has significantly reduced legal aid (a reduction in expenditure since 1995–96 of 78 per cent has driven a third of legal aid providers from the market) and instead has removed the traditional common law ban on contingency fees (capped at 25 per cent) in 2006, as well as permitting third party commercial litigation funders to flourish. Perhaps surprisingly, there is a strong *pro bono* commitment by lawyers. Litigation has a high settlement rate (90 per cent) and the government has instigated an extremely interesting holistic review of dispute resolution pathways and expenditures.

Canada attempts to combine American-style contingency fees for consumer plaintiffs with a cost-shifting regime, and this seems to produce a predictably lower rate of litigation. It is widely felt in Canada that litigation is too expensive, and Erik Knutsen and Janet Walker identify several responsive strategies, including small claims procedures, aggregation through class actions, *pro bono* schemes (but including eligibility for cost-shifting), legal assistance centres, and a clear policy of taking litigation out of the courts and into administrative solutions, such as schemes for health and safety in the workplace injuries, employment disputes and road traffic accidents. A concept of cost proportionality has only recently been introduced into court rules, although it applies to the 'importance and complexity of the issues, and to the amount involved', so it will be interesting to see how effective it turns out to be in reducing cost.

Finally, the United States of America have their unique costs and funding system. Although there is widespread use of contingency fees, Deborah Hensler points out that hourly rates or fixed fees are both permissible and used. The general American rule on costs is that each side bears their own costs (apart from in Alaska), but a significant number of statutes impose one-way cost shifting in favour of winning plaintiffs in civil rights, public law or some consumer protection suits. The American systems have considerable simplicity and score highly on access to justice criteria. Third party litigation funding appears to be emerging.

2

Australia

CAMILLE CAMERON*

Introduction

Australia is a federation. It consists of six States and two self-governing Territories. It is a common law system and operates according to rules of civil procedure and practice similar to those used in England. The Australian Constitution divides responsibility for matters related to civil courts and the administration of civil justice among the Commonwealth and the State and Territory governments. In addition to civil courts, there are numerous tribunals at the Commonwealth and State/Territory levels. This chapter will focus primarily on the Commonwealth Federal Court and the Supreme Courts in the States of Victoria and New South Wales.

Understanding litigation costs and funding in Australia is hampered by a lack of empirical information. These issues have not attracted much attention from researchers, most likely because of the obstacles that are encountered in getting enough information from sufficiently wide samples. This is exacerbated by the fact that there is limited statistical information gathered by individual courts, tribunals and other service providers. A recurring theme in policy and law reform reports is the need for more empirical information, comparative analyses across various State, Territory and Commonwealth jurisdictions, and a more systematic approach by courts and tribunals to gathering statistics about costs.[1] The lack of such information imposes limits on any attempt to answer costs-related questions about proportionality, predictability and efficiency.

* Professor, Melbourne Law School, Victoria, Australia.

[1] See, eg the Victorian Law Reform Commission (VLRC) Report, *Civil Justice Review: Report,* May 2008 ('VLRC Civil Justice Review 2008'), ch 11 and Recommendation 141, and Australian Government, Attorney-General's Department, *A Strategic Framework for Access to Justice in the Federal Civil Justice System,* Sept 2009, ('Commonwealth Access to Justice Report 2009'), ch 9.

General Overview And Trends

Principles

One of the threshold questions that this Comparative Project asks is whether the funding and costs rules in the countries being studied fit within a broader national theory and practice of civil litigation and dispute resolution. Variations between the Australian Federal and State systems, and among States, make it difficult to identify any overall national theory. A frank and somewhat bleak assessment was offered in the recent *Commonwealth Access to Justice Report 2009*:

> 'Decisions about designing and funding the federal civil justice system are not currently based on any overarching conceptual framework . . . The design and funding of most aspects of the system may be better seen as an accident of history and prevailing politics rather than a deliberate system-wide approach to avoiding disputes and resolving disputes better.'[2]

It is possible, however, to identify recurring and common themes across Australian jurisdictions. The first of these is access to justice. This theme is identified as a priority by many community organisations, judges and academics, and in Commonwealth and State policy and law reform documents. A recent example is the *Commonwealth Access to Justice Report 2009*.[3] That report uses the term 'access to justice' to mean access not only to courts and legal advice but also to information and a range of appropriate dispute resolution options.[4] Another common theme is proportionality, used in a variety of contexts. One is the concern about the expense of civil litigation and the need to ensure that the cost of pursuing a claim in court is proportionate to the amount and issues involved. The term also arises, especially but not exclusively at the Commonwealth level, as a reason to justify 'directing resources to early and less formal dispute resolution services before issues escalate and impose greater costs on the system.'[5] Finally, a related and recurring theme is efficiency. This term is also used in various ways, often to mean directing a matter to the least expensive option that can produce a fair outcome.[6]

[2] *Commonwealth Access to Justice Report 2009* (n 1) ch 3, 4.

[3] *Commonwealth Access to Justice Report 2009* (n 1).

[4] *Commonwealth Access to Justice Report 2009* (n 1) ch 1, especially 3–7. There are conflicting views about what can and should be done in the name of access to justice. One recent and robustly critical view of how the term is used—especially to endorse commercial litigation funding—was expressed by Keane JA, Judge of the Queensland Court of Appeal, in *Access to Justice and Other Shibboleths*, speech delivered on 10 Oct 2009, available at www.jca.asn.au/attachments/2009AccesstoJustice.pdf.

[5] *Commonwealth Access to Justice Report 2009* (n 1) ch 9, 121.

[6] See eg *Commonwealth Access to Justice Report 2009* (n 1) ch 3, 34.

Settlement and Alternative Dispute Resolution (ADR)

Introduction

The principles and practice of settlement of civil cases in Australia are broadly consistent with those in other common law jurisdictions. While estimates vary, it is safe to say that at least 90 per cent of civil disputes settle without a court hearing.[7]

Procedural rules in Australia do not reflect the 'litigation as a last resort' philosophy that is such a central feature of the English Civil Procedure Rules (CPR). Australia has not yet, for example, explicitly incorporated pre-action protocols into its procedural rules.[8] The English CPR pre-action protocols, and explanations of their purposes, are unequivocal in their preference for settlement over litigation.[9] Reform initiatives in Australia have proposed such protocols[10] and it is likely that they will soon become a feature of procedural rules and practices. In other settlement-related areas, notably ADR, Australian procedures reflect a stronger settlement sentiment than their English counterparts.[11]

Civil Procedure Rules: Offers of Compromise

Australian procedural rules contain provisions for offers of compromise. While there are variations across jurisdictions, the following general description indicates how the rules work. These formal offers can be made by any party. They are 'without prejudice' offers, which means that they do not come to the attention of the court until there has been a final adjudication on the merits of the dispute. If a party rejects a reasonable settlement offer and receives a final judgment that is not more favourable than the rejected offer, adverse costs consequences may follow. These adverse costs consequences can vary depending on the type of case and who made the offer. In the State of Victoria, for example, if a plaintiff in a personal injury case makes an offer of compromise which is rejected by a defendant, and if that case proceeds to judgement and the plaintiff gets at least as much as the amount of the offer, the usual costs consequences will be that the plaintiff will

[7] See eg the Law Society of New South Wales estimates, reported in the Practitioner Report for Australia submitted as part of this Comparative Litigation Funding and Costs Project ('Practitioner Report'), available at www.csls.ox.ac.uk/COSTOFLITIGATIONDOCUMENTSANDREPORTS.php.

[8] In the State of Victoria, the Civil Procedure Bill 2010, awaiting Royal assent, will make such protocols a requirement in most civil disputes.

[9] See, eg the comments of Sir Anthony Clarke, Master of the Rolls, in *The Future of Mediation*, 8 May 2008, Speech delivered at The Second Mediation Council National Conference.

[10] Victorian Law Reform Commission, *Civil Justice Review 2008* (n 1) ch 2, especially 142–146 and *Commonwealth Access to Justice Report 2009* (n 1) ch 8, 103–104 are examples.

[11] See the discussion of ADR below, this Part. The use of ADR referrals as a settlement tool has been criticised, most recently by Professor Hazel Genn in her Hamlyn Lectures, delivered in London and Edinburgh in Nov and Dec, 2008. See H Genn, *Judging Civil Justice* (Cambridge, Cambridge University Press, 2009).

receive an order for indemnity costs from the commencement of the proceeding.[12] If this rejected offer had been made in a breach of contract case rather than a personal injury case, then the plaintiff would have received costs on a party and party basis to the date of the offer, and costs on an indemnity basis from that point to judgment. As with most decisions about costs orders, this is a matter for judicial discretion. However, the tenor of Australian case law is that there is a presumption in favour of the adverse costs consequences unless the party who rejected the offer can point to good reasons for doing so. A good reason might be, for example, that the terms of the offer were too vague to enable the offeree to determine whether the offer was reasonable.

It is possible for litigants to make other types of offers in addition to those made pursuant to specific procedural rules. These include *Calderbank* offers,[13] which are made in a letter headed 'without prejudice save as to costs'. Such offers enjoy the usual protection afforded to without prejudice communication, except on the matter of costs. A party wishing to get a costs benefit from such an offer would ask the judge, after issues of liability have been determined, to make an unusual costs order because the offeror has done at least as well at trial as the terms of her (rejected) *Calderbank* letter.

These are direct examples of procedural rules that encourage settlement in civil litigation. Other rules do so in a less direct way. There are, for example, rules that provide for costs penalties if a party fails to admit a matter that should reasonably have been admitted, thus requiring an opponent to prove it. This refusal to admit may add to the duration and the cost of the case. While rules such as this are not focused on settlement of an entire case, they are aimed at resolving some of the less contentious issues in dispute. Other relevant rules are those regarding judicial case management and the use of alternative dispute resolution.

Judicial Attitudes Toward Settlement

Australia shares with other common law jurisdictions a robust judicial preference for settlement over litigation. This is evident in the presumption that the usual adverse consequences should and will flow from rejection of a reasonable settlement offer, the robust use of ADR orders, and occasional comments in cases about the advantages of settlement over litigation.[14] Such comments often appear in discussions of the relative merits of litigation and ADR.[15]

[12] *Supreme Court (General) Civil Procedure Rules 2006*, Order 26, 'Offers of Compromise'. In Victoria indemnity costs are almost a complete recovery of all costs expended, whereas party and party (ordinary) costs amount to approximately 60% of actual costs. This is discussed below.

[13] *Calderbank v Calderbank* [1976] FM 73.

[14] In *Mercantile Mutual Custodians Pty Ltd v Village Nine Network and Bars Pty Ltd Restaurants and Bars* [1999] QCA 276, Byrne J stated that while 'as a means of resolution of civil contention litigation is certainly preferable to personal violence it is not intrinsically a desirable activity'. He was quoting Lord Simon of Glaisdale in *The Ampthill Peerage* [1997] AC 547 (HL). Lord Simon was, however, referring to the kind of protracted *Jarndyce v Jarndyce* litigation that Charles Dickens described in *Bleak House*. Lord Simon's theme was that there must at some point be an end to litigation.

[15] See for example Lord Clarke, the Master of the Rolls, in a speech endorsing the use of ADR in civil litigation: 'We all know that a cast iron case is a very rare bird indeed; so that for the most part only a

Alternative Dispute Resolution

The Federal Court of Australia and the State and Territory courts have the power to order litigants to participate in ADR. Such orders can be made even if litigants are unwilling to participate. Anecdotal evidence indicates that judges use this referral power robustly, although there are different levels of commitment and use across jurisdictions and across courts and judges in the same jurisdiction.[16] While the preferred ADR method is mediation, there are additional options in the relevant legislation in some jurisdictions.[17] The proximity of these processes to the courts making the orders varies. The Federal Court encourages parties to use that court's own mediators.[18] Until recently, most court-ordered mediations in the Supreme Court of Victoria were referred to external mediators, but that court has begun to make in-house mediators available. The mediators in mediations done outside the court are usually barristers, solicitors and former judges. The cost is generally shared by the parties, subject to any final order that may be made regarding the costs of the proceeding.

While there is some reliable empirical evidence to shed light on the impact of ADR on the cost of litigation, many of the claims that are made about the cost-saving benefits of ADR, and mediation in particular, are based on anecdote,[19] limited samples[20] or participants' impressions about costs saved rather than costs actually saved.[21] Notwithstanding this information deficit, some general statements relevant to costs can be made.

—If parties participate in a mediation or some other form of ADR which is unsuccessful, they will still have to prepare for trial but will also have had to incur the cost of participating in the mediation. This will increase rather than decrease litigation costs.

madman does not want to settle' (above n 9). In some Australian jurisdictions, however, adherence to a now discredited interpretation of 'justice on the merits' has impaired robust management of cases and arguably belies this judicial preference for settlement. This is explored below.

[16] In an Issues Paper published in Mar, 2009 by NADRAC (the National Alternative Dispute Resolution Advisory Council), *Alternative Dispute Resolution in the Civil Justice System*, NADRAC states that 'annual reports from the federal courts indicate that only a small percentage of matters are referred to ADR processes' (34 [6.22]). The statistics to support this statement were not included, but taken at face value it contradicts conventional wisdom about the use of mediation orders by judges. One explanation may be that the practices differ across States. There is some anecdotal information to support this suggestion. This report is referred to below as 'NADRAC Issues Paper 2009'.

[17] See for example Parts 4 and 5 of the *Civil Procedure Act 2005* (NSW) and Part 20, Divisions 1 and 2 of the *Uniform Civil Procedure Rules* (NSW). In Victoria, the Supreme Court has begun to use early neutral evaluation, in addition to mediation.

[18] See *ACCC v Cadbury Schweppes*, (Gray J, Federal Court of Australia Transcripts, 22 Apr 2002).

[19] There is also insufficient empirical evidence regarding the degree of satisfaction amongst participants in Australia's mandatory court-ordered mediations.

[20] See, eg Professor Tania Sourdin, *Mediation in the Supreme and County Courts of Victoria*, Department of Justice Victoria, Mar2009, available at www.justice.vic.gov.au/. This report consisted of a quantitative and qualitative analysis of civil disputes finalised in 2 courts in a 3-month period. It was based on 98 disputant surveys and 34 mediator surveys. (Interviews of litigants and mediators were also conducted).

[21] ibid.

—If the case settles at mediation or as a result of some other ADR process, however, then time and money will have been saved. Critics might respond that this is so only if the case would not have settled but for the mediation. The contribution of early mediation/ADR, however, is that it may result in settlements at an earlier stage than would otherwise have happened. It may also resolve individual issues, thus reducing the time and cost required to litigate the remaining issues.
—If mandatory orders are made as a matter of course and without adequate attempts to distinguish between cases that might benefit from ADR and cases that will not, litigants might treat the order as a step that must be taken on the path to trial, rather than as a dispute resolution prospect that offers a real opportunity of early settlement. This would tend to increase overall litigation costs.
—Finally, there are very many non-court dispute resolution entities in Australia that use ADR processes to resolve a wide variety of disputes. Any attempt to understand the 'big picture' of the cost of dispute resolution in Australia must take the processes and contributions of these entities into account. It is beyond the scope of this chapter to describe or analyse them in detail, but there is some further consideration of their role below in Part III.

In *Alternative Dispute Resolution in the Civil Justice System*,[22] NADRAC proposed various costs incentives to encourage greater use of ADR in litigation.[23] NADRAC's costs-specific suggestions were:

—weighted filing fees so that commencing litigation would be more expensive for those who do not attempt ADR
—refunding filing fees when cases settle in ADR
—judicial discretion to take participation in ADR into account when making costs orders
—full recovery by the court of court hearing fees (a user pays approach)
—making the costs of ADR tax deductible for individuals
—removing or limiting the tax deductibility of litigation costs for corporations
—finding ways to reward lawyers for resolving disputes without litigation.[24]

In its final report, however, NADRAC concluded that it was 'unable to develop a formula that would achieve the desired encouragement and at the same time avoid injustice in those cases where ADR is inappropriate and court proceedings are necessary.'[25] The specific recommendations in its final report regarding costs incentives are limited to giving courts and some tribunals the power to make

[22] NADRAC Issues Paper 2009 (n 16).
[23] These suggestions were made in response to a request from the Commonwealth Attorney-General to consider ways to encourage greater use of ADR in civil proceedings.
[24] NADRAC Issues Paper 2009 (n 16) 31–32.
[25] *The Resolve to Resolve, Embracing ADR to Improve Access to Justice in the Federal Civil Justice System*, National Alternative Dispute Resolution Advisory Council, September 2009 ('NADRAC Report 2009'), [2.24].

adverse costs orders against parties that do not take appropriate steps to try and resolve matters, either before or during proceedings.[26]

Cost Shifting And Costs Orders

General

The costs-shifting rule applies in Australia.[27] Successful parties are as a general rule entitled to their costs of the proceeding. The usual order will be for costs on a party and party (ordinary) basis.[28] Such an order is not a complete indemnity. Successful litigants who receive an order for costs will not be able to shift to the paying party all of their costs of the proceeding. Estimates of the extent of this irrecoverable portion of costs vary considerably. The usual range of these estimates is 30 per cent to 50 per cent. The Victorian Law Reform Commission recently considered this issue in its review of the civil litigation system in Victoria.[29] A small empirical survey conducted as part of this review led the Commission to conclude that 'in many instances only about half or less of the costs between lawyers and their clients are recovered on a party-party basis following taxation of costs.'[30] If the order is for indemnity costs, recovery is much closer to 100 per cent of the successful party's expenditure, but indemnity costs orders are rarely made.

There is some anecdotal evidence to suggest that the gap between actual costs and recoverable costs is smaller in New South Wales, where there are no prescribed scales of costs. It is estimated that on an assessment of costs in New South Wales the receiving party will recover 65 per cent to 85 per cent of their actual costs.[31]

One consequence of the gap between actual and recoverable costs is that people considering litigation must include in their risk assessment the fact that even if they have a strong case and are likely to succeed, they will be unable to recover a substantial portion of their costs of the litigation.[32]

[26] NADRAC Report 2009 (n 25), [2.24]–[2.25].

[27] For a recent analysis of the origins and present state of the rule, see G Cazalet, 'Unresolved Issues—Costs in Public Interest Litigation in Australia', [2010] 29 *Civil Justice Quarterly* 108.

[28] See *Practitioner Report* (n 7) 20–22 for additional information on the types of costs orders made in civil proceedings. Judicial discretion includes the power to apportion costs if parties succeed on some issues and fail on others. There are various tribunals and small claims courts in Australia in which the general costs rule is that the parties will bear their own costs. See below and Lord Justice Jackson, *Review of Civil Litigation Costs, Preliminary Report*, May 2009 ('Lord Justice Jackson, Preliminary Report 2009'), vol 2, ch 58, 584–85.

[29] VLRC Civil Justice Review 2008 (n 1) 681, 693.

[30] VLRC Civil Justice Review 2008 (n 1) 681, 693.

[31] Lord Justice Jackson, Preliminary Report 2009 (n 28) ch 58, 583, n 147 and related text.

[32] Different considerations apply where the litigation is being funded by a commercial litigation funder. The role of commercial litigation funders is considered below in Part V.

If parties do not agree on costs, the costs are taxed (formally assessed). Taxation of costs usually occurs after final determination of a case. This includes interlocutory costs.[33] Interlocutory procedural disputes are a feature of common law civil litigation. These typically include requests for particulars of a pleading and disagreements about whether one party has given to another proper discovery of documents that complies with the rules and that does not, for example, make unjustifiable privilege claims. While practices vary across jurisdictions in Australia, interlocutory costs will not usually be taxed and paid until the matter is finally resolved. In Victoria, however, such costs can be taxed and paid immediately.[34]

It is possible in an unusual case for a litigant to receive an order for costs on an indemnity basis. If such an order is obtained, the receiving party will recover almost all of the costs incurred. Such orders are rare. Typical cases include those in which the conduct of the paying party has been unreasonable and has significantly exacerbated the cost and duration of the case. Indemnity costs orders may also be made if a defendant has refused a reasonable settlement offer.

In all State and Federal jurisdictions in Australia, there are tribunals in which cost shifting is the exception rather than the norm. Many of these tribunals also encourage self-representation. The Victorian Civil and Administrative Tribunal (VCAT) in the State of Victoria is one example. It can make costs orders against a party in cases of unusual complexity or where justified by the misconduct of that party, but the norm is that the parties bear their own costs.[35] The VCAT also encourages parties to represent themselves, in keeping with its aim to avoid complexity and delay and to provide access to justice for ordinary citizens. It has received strong endorsements from consumer action groups for removing what one of those groups has described as 'one of the most significant barriers to a person pursuing their legal rights through legal action'—the risk of an adverse costs order.[36] While these tribunals make a significant contribution to providing access to justice, they do not always and in all respects achieve their aims of avoiding complexity and promoting informality. The VCAT, again, is illustrative. Recurring themes in a major review of its role are that lawyers and experts are too dominant, that ordinary citizens find the processes intimidating and feel disempowered in the face of its complex processes, and that proceedings are expensive.[37]

[33] See Practitioner Report (n 7) 20–22.

[34] See the discussion in VLRC Civil Justice Review 2008 (n 1) 633. One of the VLRC recommendations is that there should be a presumptive rule in Victoria, similar to the practice in the Federal Court and New South Wales, that interlocutory costs orders will not be taxed and assessed until final determination of the case: 692. An advantage of such an approach may be efficiency. A contrary argument is that awarding costs at an interlocutory stage might deter unnecessary interlocutory applications.

[35] Information about the kinds of claims which VCAT hears, and its rules about costs, is available in various locations on the VCAT website. See for example 'Civil Disputes—Small Claims', at www.vcat.vic.gov.au/CA256DBB0022825D/page/Civil+Disputes-Small+Claims/. See also Consumer Action Law Centre, 'Submission to VCAT President's Review, 12 June 2009', available at www. consumeraction. org.au/downloads/VCATreviewsubmission120609.pdf.

[36] Consumer Action Law Centre, 'Submission to VCAT President's Review' (n 35).

[37] See Australia Broadcasting Corporation, Stateline Victoria, 'Criticism prompts overhaul of disputes body', Oct 23, 2009, at www.abc.net.au/news/video/2009/10/23/2722910.htm. There are many

In addition to the many tribunals and industry dispute resolution schemes, there are also Magistrates, Local and other small claims courts. Procedures and subject-matter jurisdiction vary considerably amongst these courts, but they all generally aim to use expedited and simple procedures. They hear claims with values in the range of $50,000 to $100,000.

Scales of Costs

Scales of costs apply in the Federal Court and in all State Supreme Courts except New South Wales.[38] They prescribe the amounts that can be recovered by the successful party when the costs are taxed. The scales are increased periodically.

It has been suggested that the absence of the constraints imposed by scale costs in New South Wales is one reason for the higher recovery range in that State.[39] (One of the reasons for the gap between actual costs incurred and costs recovered is that most lawyers charge for their time based on hourly rates rather than the amounts set in the scales). It is hard to find a consensus about the desirability of scale costs. Some people think they increase predictability while others criticise them for being too rigid, failing to reflect the true market price for legal services and preventing successful litigants from obtaining an indemnity for their actual costs.[40] Various reforms have been proposed, from retaining scales but setting them at a more realistic (and generous) level to abolishing them. There is no empirical evidence, and very little anecdotal evidence, that can be used to evaluate these claims and inform policy choices. If we value predictability, then fixed fees are attractive. If the fixed fees do not represent the fair market value of the services provided, however, then lawyers will pass on the difference to their clients, thus increasing the gap between actual costs and recoverable costs. This suggests that if the scale fees are retained, then the amounts should be adjusted to a more realistic level. It also suggests that we cannot consider the scale fees question without also exploring alternative funding and billing models, including contingency fees, capped fees and perhaps even whether the costs shifting rule ought to be retained.

other formal dispute resolution processes in Australia that offer alternatives to adversarial litigation. One example is the investigation and mediation services offered by the Offie of the Victorian Small Business Commissioner. This Office reports on its website that from 1 May 2003 to 24 Sept 2009, over 6000 matters had been referred to the VSBC for resolution and that it 'has maintained a dispute resolution success rate of over 80 per cent'. (It did not include the factors it used to define success, for example, settlement and/or user satisfaction).

[38] See, eg *Federal Court of Australia Regulations 2004* (Cth), Schedule 2 to the *Federal Rules of Court.* New South Wales has abolished scale fees in all but a limited number of cases, including low value personal injury actions, proving a will, and workers compensation cases. See Practitioner Report (n 7) 9 for additional information and references.

[39] Lord Justice Jackson, Preliminary Report 2009 (n 28) ch 58, n 147–48.

[40] These conflicting views were considered by Lord Justice Jackson, Preliminary Report 2009 (n 28) ch 58, 583–84.

Court Fees and Cost Recovery

All courts in Australia charge fees prescribed by statute.[41] Examples of typical fees are fees for filing documents with the court, issuing a subpoena, using the mediation services provided by a court, daily charges for court hearings and enforcement of court judgments. There are exemption and waiver provisions for various categories of persons, including those who have received legal aid and who are financially disadvantaged. This is subject to a means test.[42]

There is no 'user pays' system in Australia. The court fees charged fall well below the actual cost of Government expenditure on courts. While there has been no comprehensive study of the gap between court fees and actual court costs in Australian State and Federal courts, the *Commonwealth Access to Justice Report 2009* contains some instructive statistics.[43] In 2007–8, fees paid in the Federal Court of Australia amounted to 9.3 per cent of the Federal Government's expenditure on that Court.[44] Costs recovery for the Federal Magistrates Court was higher, at 22.4 per cent and much lower in the Family Court, at 0.9 per cent.[45]

The *Commonwealth Access to Justice Report 2009* recommends that full cost recovery be considered and incorporated when appropriate. One of the principles on which it relies to justify that recommendation is that much civil litigation has at least some element of private gain. Other principles explicitly relied on in the *Report* to justify this recommendation are proportionality and improved access. One that is implicitly relied on is encouraging and rewarding early resolution and identification of the real issues in dispute. This is clear from Recommendation 9.2, which states that 'full cost pricing for long hearings is generally appropriate' because (1) the public costs of court hearings are significant; (2) parties have opportunities to resolve matters without a hearing; and (3) they also have opportunities to minimise the length of hearings by identifying and limiting the issues in dispute.[46]

The *Report*'s authors also suggest that full cost recovery might effect a necessary change in culture, by sending a message to litigants that court services are a finite, valuable, public resource.[47] They cite as an example a case from Western Australia in which the full cost of the matter to the State Government was $6.19 million and the amount recovered from fees was $0.9 million.[48] While concerns about

[41] See, eg *Federal Court of Australia Act 1976 (Cth)*, s 60 and *Federal Court of Australia Regulations 2004 (Cth)*, Sch 1.

[42] Commonwealth Access to Justice Report 2009 (n 1) ch 3, 42.

[43] See especially Commonwealth Access to Justice Report 2009 (n 1) chs 3 and 9.

[44] Productivity Commission, *Report on Government Services*, 2009, quoted in Commonwealth Access to Justice Report 2009 (n 1) ch 3, 45.

[45] ibid. Lower recovery is to be expected in the Family Court, where fewer fees are charged. The reason advanced in the Report for the higher recovery in the Federal Magistrates Court is that while the fees in that court are lower than in the other courts, 'the matters are also simpler and quicker, leading to a greater proportion of costs being recovered.' (ch 3, 45)

[46] See Commonwealth Access to Justice Report 2009 (n 1) ch 8, Recommendation 9.2.

[47] ibid, ch 8.

[48] ibid, ch 8, n 302 and the related discussion.

'mega-litigation' in Australia are at least partially responsible for the growing interest in increased or full costs recovery from litigants, the *Report* states that it is not just these mega-cases that might be appropriate for full, or at least fuller, cost recovery.[49]

The federal nature of Australia's court system is one potential barrier to implementation of full costs recovery. Commonwealth and State courts are competing courts, and the implementation of fuller costs recovery at one level might mean that parties who have a choice (where there is concurrent jurisdiction) would choose the court without costs recovery. There is some evidence to substantiate this concern.[50]

Costs Estimates and Litigation Budgets

The Australian legal profession is regulated by State and Territory laws. Those laws require law firms to provide their clients with estimates of the costs of a case, including estimates of the costs payable if successful or unsuccessful.[51] There is not yet any requirement, however, for the exchange of litigation budgets. One exception is the requirement in the Federal Court for parties to exchange their best estimates of discovery costs.[52]

The *Commonwealth Access to Justice Report 2009* recommends that lawyers prepare litigation budgets and that these be given to the other parties and to the court.[53] The *Report* identifies the following potential benefits of such a practice: forcing parties to give early consideration to how best to resolve their dispute, encouraging them to consider other options, providing greater certainty generally about costs, and allowing the judge to consider whether the proposed costs are proportionate to the issues in dispute.[54] The authors of the *Report* suggest that any additional costs incurred in preparing the budgets would be offset by an overall reduction in litigation costs. They also recommend a pilot scheme to test this hypothesis.[55]

Lawyers' Costs

The costs between lawyers and their clients consist of the lawyers' fees and disbursements. The primary method of charging clients is by time billing based on an

[49] ibid, ch 9, 123.

[50] ibid, 50.

[51] ibid, ch 9, n 306 and related text. For an example of a standard costs disclosure agreement between lawyer and client, refer to the Practitioner Report (n 7) 6 and Attachment 9.

[52] Federal Court of Australia, Practice Note 17, *Pre-Discovery Conference Checklist.* Lord Justice Jackson reports that there is a clear message of support from a majority of practitioners for the restricted approach to discovery adopted by some federal court judges: Lord Justice Jackson, Preliminary Report 2009 (n 28) 586. Both requirements—for the exchange of budgets and for limited discovery—are attempts to control the most expensive element of civil cases: discovery of documents.

[53] Commonwealth Access to Justice Report 2009 (n 1) ch 9, 125–126.

[54] ibid.

[55] ibid, 126.

hourly rate. There are some exceptions to the hourly rate approach, however, and these may be increasing. Some law firms have moved away from this method of billing to one or more of those discussed below. Fixed fee agreements for specific services or discrete tasks, such as preparing a will or a contract, are common. Some commercial clients use their market power to demand alternatives to hourly billing, and law firms have responded to this market demand by bidding for legal services. This can be in the form of an agreed amount for a project or for parts of (or events within) a project. The *Commonwealth Access to Justice Report 2009* notes the market power of the government as a consumer of legal services (in 2007–8 Commonwealth agencies reported an expenditure for legal services of over $500 million[56]) and recommends that the Government use that power to require lawyers to bill on an event basis.[57] This recommendation, which is generally consistent with complaints that time billing encourages inefficiency, is not a giant leap. It is consistent with the trend among some commercial entities to demand alternative billing models.

Another common billing arrangement is the conditional fee (also called 'no win-no fee'). Lawyers using this model agree not to bill the client until the case is resolved. If the client is successful, then the lawyer will be paid his fees, either calculated on an hourly basis or at an amount agreed in advance between the lawyer and the client (but not as a percentage of the damages awarded). If the client is unsuccessful, the lawyer will not be paid. The risk of an adverse costs order, always a factor in a system with costs shifting, remains with the client. These conditional fee agreements often include a term that the lawyer will in the event of a successful outcome charge a premium, also known as an uplift (success fee). This fee is a matter between the lawyer and her own client; it is not recoverable from the opposing party. The maximum uplift fee permitted in Victoria and New South Wales is 25 per cent.[58] There is some evidence to indicate that in personal injury cases in Victoria, claimants receive 80–85 per cent of their damages, after deduction of the success fee.[59]

These conditional fee agreements are to be distinguished from a contingency fee arrangement whereby a lawyer takes a percentage of the amount recovered. Lawyers in Australia are prohibited from charging on this basis. (Commercial litigation funders have emerged as an exception. They can fund cases in exchange for an agreement that they will receive a percentage of the amount recovered. This is discussed below).

[56] ibid, ch 9, 120.

[57] ibid, ch 9, 127–28.

[58] State practice varies. Recovering a success fee under a conditional fee arrangement is more common in Victoria than in New South Wales.

[59] Lord Justice Jackson, Preliminary Report 2009 (n 28) ch 58, 588.

Departing From the Cost-Shifting Rule: Public Interest Litigation

Introduction

While one of the first rules of costs is that costs orders are discretionary, that discretion operates within predictable boundaries. Australian judges are disinclined to depart from the usual rule that costs follow the event (loser pays winner). Subject to the few exceptions described below, all major reviews of civil justice in Australia have favoured retention of cost shifting.

One area in which the issue has arisen is public interest litigation. An argument advanced by losing plaintiffs in such cases is that they should not be called on to pay the costs of the winning defendant. While this argument has succeeded in some cases the High Court has affirmed the primacy of the cost shifting rule in public interest cases.[60]

Protective Costs Orders

There is a high degree of unpredictability in costs matters in public interest cases. One source of unpredictability is uncertainty about whether the case is a public interest case. Another source of unpredictability is how the costs discretion will be exercised if a public interest case reaches final judgment. A litigant making a decision whether to bring such a case must live with this unpredictability and financial risk for the duration of the case. The Environmental Defenders Office (EDO) has described the threat of an adverse costs order as 'a crude exclusion device the burden of which falls disproportionately on individuals and community groups which do not have the same deep pockets as governments and corporations.'[61] In its 1995 report on cost shifting the Australian Law Reform Commission (ALRC) stated that submissions made during the consultation process indicated that the costs shifting rule is most likely to deter 'people who may suffer substantial hardship, such as the loss of their home, car or livelihood, if required to pay the other party's costs, and people or organisations involved in public interest litigation who have little or no personal interest in the matter.'[62]

One reform option is the protective costs order.[63] In *Civil Justice Review 2008*, the Victorian Law Reform Commission considered the availability and nature of such orders in England and Canada and recommended that they be considered for

[60] *Southwest Forest Defence Foundation Inc v Department of Conservation and Land Management (No 2)* [1998] HCA 35. See also *Ruddock and Others v Vadarlis and Others* [2001] FCA 1865, where the full Federal Court reviewed academic commentary criticising the application of the cost shifting rule in public interest cases and stated: 'These criticisms will not justify a global modification, in public interest cases, of the usual rule that costs follow the event. They do, however, indicate the desirability of avoiding calcification of the discretion with rigid rules governing its exercise.' (Black CJ and French J).

[61] Quoted in VLRC Civil Justice Review 2008 (n 1) 675, n 18.

[62] Australian Law Reform Commission, 'Cost Shifting—Who Pays for Litigation in Australia?' (1995) ('Cost Shifting 1995'), [4.14].

[63] The English CPR protective costs order is one example.

adoption in Australia. The VLRC discussed and relied on similar recommendations made by the ALRC in *Cost Shifting 1995*, in which the ALRC proposed various costs orders options for public interest cases, including: an order that the parties would bear their own costs, that a plaintiff's liability for another party's costs would be capped, or that a third party might be liable for costs.[64] The ALRC recommended that a public interest costs order should be possible at any stage of the litigation, including at the outset.[65] Similar recommendations were made in the *Commonwealth Access to Justice Report 2009*.[66] These recommendations have generated debate, including suggestions from some members of the business community that such reforms would give activists special treatment, tip the balance in favour of plaintiffs, deprive defendants of their costs and lead to frivolous litigation.[67]

Courts have acknowledged that they have the discretion to make protective costs orders.[68] The power to do so is expressly set out in Order 62A of the *Federal Court Rules*. The intention of Order 62A, rule 1 was that it would be used mainly in commercial litigation at the low end of the scale in terms of value and complexity. It is, therefore, a tool aimed at achieving proportionality.[69] Notwithstanding that the power to make such orders exists in common law and explicitly in procedural rules, there have been very few protective costs orders in Australia. A recent exception is a case in the Land and Environment Court of New South Wales, *Blue Mountain Conservation Society Inc v Delta Electricity*.[70] The evidence was that the defendant would incur costs in the range of $332,000 to defend the proceeding and that it would be able to recover costs in the range of $232,000–266,000 in the event of success. The plaintiff received an order limiting

[64] Cost Shifting 1995 (n 62) [13.22].

[65] ibid, [13.27].

[66] Commonwealth Access to Justice Report 2009 (n 1) ch 8, Recommendation 8.10 and accompanying text.

[67] See C Merritt, 'Business uproar over litigation' *The Australian* (Sydney 9 Oct 2009) available at www.theaustralian.com.au/business/legal-affairs/business-uproar-over-litigation/story-e6frg97x-1225784569661. Others have suggested that if litigation is truly 'in the public interest', then the costs should be publicly funded rather than shifted to defendants. One response of public interest advocates to this suggestion has been that if the costs become a public expense, then corporations will have to give up their present entitlement to tax deductibility of legal fees (a deduction not allowed to individual citizens). These issues are canvassed in *Business warned of tax break loss*, The Australian, Business, 12 Oct 2009, available at www.theaustralian.com.au/BusinessNews/pg/0/fi13372.htm.

[68] See the decision of Black CJ and French J in *Ruddock v Vadarlis* (No 2) (2001) 115 FCR 229, considered in *Corcoran v Virgin Blue Airlines Pty Ltd* [2008] FCA 864 (Bennett J). The decision of Bennett J in *Corcoran* is one of the few cases in which an Australian judge has made such an order.

[69] The origins and rationale of the rule are discussed by Bennett J in *Corcoran v Virgin Blue Airlines*, above n 68 at [51]. See also section 49(1)(c) of the *Judicial Review Act* (Qld), which provides '(d) that another party to the review application indemnify the relevant applicant in relation to the costs properly incurred in the review application by the relevant applicant, on a party and party basis, from the time the costs application was made; or (e) that a party to the review application is to bear only that party's own costs of the proceeding, regardless of the outcome of the proceeding.' An order under (e) of this provision was made by Jones J of the Supreme Court of Queensland in *Alliance to Save Hinchinbrook Inc v. Cook and Others* [2005] QSC 355. See also Rule 42.4 of the *Uniform Civil Procedure Rules 2005 (UCPR) of New South Wales*, which provides for protective costs orders.

[70] [2009] NSWLEC 150 (Pain J), 9 Sept 2009.

to $20,000 the maximum amount of costs that either party would have to pay to the other.

While the 1995 ALRC Report on cost shifting endorsed retention of the loser pays rule, and has generally been referred to since 1995 as having done so, it did identify some exceptions. One of these is the protective costs order, discussed above. The ALRC also recommended that 'a court should be able to vary the rule that costs follow the event where it is satisfied that a party's ability to present his or her case properly or to negotiate a fair settlement is materially and adversely affected by the risk of an adverse costs order.'[71] This recommendation is based on principles of proportionality and equality, and recognises the impact that unequal resources can have on access to justice, especially in a costs shifting environment. It has not been adopted and it is more far-reaching than any major reform proposal that has been made since then about exceptions to the loser pays rule.

Judicial Case Management

Active judicial case management is a feature of civil litigation in Australia, although it is more robust in some jurisdictions (and across courts within jurisdictions) than others. One of the aims of judicial case management is to provide a costs control mechanism by, for example, making orders for ADR in an appropriate case, ensuring that the parties and their lawyers adhere to agreed schedules, keeping the scope of discovery of documents within reasonable bounds, and generally requiring parties to focus on case preparation at an early stage, with a view to settling the case or narrowing the issues in dispute. It has obvious potential to control costs,[72] although of course it can also result in added expense by requiring investment of more lawyer time in the early stages of a case.

Principles of judicial case management have gradually been included in civil procedure rules and practice directions in Australia. A more recent trend, however, has been to put case management provisions in legislation. When the State of New South Wales reformed its civil procedure rules in 2005, it put judicial case management, proportionality and related provisions in the *Civil Procedure Act*[73] instead of in civil procedure rules or practice directions. In his Second Reading Speech,[74] the Attorney-General of New South Wales stated that this had been done to emphasise the importance of these provisions and to counteract the effects of *Queensland v JL Holdings.*[75]

[71] Cost Shifting 1995 (n 62) [12.40].
[72] The Australian Law Reform Commission has identified case management as one way of controlling costs in a system that adheres to the cost shifting rule: see Costs Shifting 1995 (n 62) [2.20]–[2.23].
[73] *Civil Procedure Act 2005* (NSW).
[74] New South Wales Legislative Assembly Hansard, Second Reading Speech, 6 Apr 2005.
[75] *Queensland v JL Holdings Pty Ltd* (1997) 189 CLR 146.

A similar approach is evident in the *Access to Justice (Civil Litigation Reforms) Amendment Act 2009*, most provisions of which came into effect in January 2010.[76] The Explanatory Memorandum states that one of the main purposes of the proposed legislation is to overcome the restrictive interpretation by courts of what is in the interests of justice, as a result of *JL Holdings*.[77] In *JL Holdings*, the High Court of Australia reversed a case management decision of a trial judge who had refused, for case management reasons, to allow a late amendment. The High Court described case management as 'an important and useful tool for ensuring the prompt and efficient disposal of litigation'[78] but added that 'the ultimate aim of a court is the attainment of justice and no principle of case management can be allowed to supplant that aim.'[79] This decision has been criticised as inconsistent with modern principles of active judicial case management.[80] In August 2009, in *ANU v AON*,[81] the High Court departed from *JL Holdings* and stressed the importance of considering not only the interests of the parties before the court but also the interests of the court, other litigants and the community. A review of decisions since *AON v ANU* suggests that it has empowered judges to use their judicial case management powers more robustly.[82]

One recent case management initiative is the use of a fast track procedure in the Federal Court in Melbourne. The fast track (also referred to as the 'rocket docket') uses expedited procedures such as streamlined pleadings, abbreviated discovery and an early trial date. The rocket docket has received favourable comments from lawyers and their clients. Anecdotal evidence suggests that its benefits include considerable cost savings. One solicitor interviewed by Lord Justice Jackson estimated a 50 per cent cost saving.[83]

[76] *Access to Justice (Civil Litigation Reforms) Amendment Act 2009* (Cth).

[77] The Explanatory Memorandum is available at www.aph.gov.au/Library/Pubs/BD/2009-10/10bd014. pdf.

[78] *Queensland v JL Holdings* (n 75), 154.

[79] ibid.

[80] In *Black and Decker Australasia v GMCA* [2007] FCA 623, for example, Finkelstein J opined that *JL Holdings* has had a chilling effect on the development of judicial case management.

[81] *AON Risk Services Limited v Australian National University* [2009] HCA 27.

[82] These issues are explored in more detail by Camille Cameron in *New Directions for Judicial Case Management in Australia* ([2010] 29 Civil Justice Quarterly 337 *AON v ANU* will have a negligible impact in New South Wales, which had already enacted legislation to counteract the effects of *JL Holdings*.

[83] See Lord Justice Jackson, Preliminary Report 2009 (n 28) ch 58, 592. This fast track is available for commercial cases with a trial length of 8 days or less.

Other Funding Arrangements

Pro Bono

The Australian Bureau of Statistics (ABS) has estimated that Australian private law practitioners annually contribute 692,000 hours of *pro bono* legal services.[84] The ABS translated this to mean an average of 23 hours per year for each solicitor. At least four States have pro bono 'clearing houses' whose activities include referring *pro bono* cases to law firms. *Pro bono* services are also provided by barristers, community legal advice centres and consumer advocacy organisations.

Legal Aid[85]

The *Commonwealth Access to Justice Report 2009* estimates that there has been a reduction of 78 per cent since 1995–6 in the amount of legal aid funding available for civil matters. Almost all of the available legal aid funding in Australia is used in family and criminal law matters. The Commonwealth has relied on the private sector to deliver services for approximately half of all grants of legal aid. However, a 2006 study reports that about one third of private providers had ceased to provide legal aid services because the fees paid were about 50 per cent less than fees available in the private sector.[86] An examination of fee waivers in the Federal Court in 2007–8 revealed that most litigants who probably met the socio-economic criteria for legal aid were not legally aided.[87]

The *Commonwealth Access to Justice Report 2009* thus conveys a grim picture, describing 'a significant and continuing shortfall in legal aid for civil law matters'.[88] It does not, however, appear to recommend an increase in government funding for civil legal aid as a solution. Its preferred strategies seem to be to reapportion existing resources in a way that responds to citizens' needs for basic information and for non-litigation dispute resolution options.[89]

[84] Australia Bureau of Statistics, *Legal Practices, Australia*, 2001–2, 8667.0, 25 June 2003, quoted in Practitioner Report (n 7) n 41.

[85] The information in this section is derived entirely from statistics reported in the Commonwealth Access to Justice Report 2009 (n 1) ch 3, 42–44.

[86] TNS Social Research, 'Legal Aid Remuneration Review: Final Report 2007', quoted in Commonwealth Access to Justice Report 2009 (n 1) fn 125.

[87] Commonwealth Access to Justice Report 2009 (n 1) ch 3, 42–44.

[88] ibid, 43.

[89] See especially Commonwealth Access to Justice Report 2009 (n 1) chs 8 and 9.

Institutional Litigation Funding

Institutional litigation funders have a significant presence in commercial litigation in Australia. There are at least five litigation funding companies (LFCs)[90] and the largest of these, IMF, is a public listed company. Canadian, American and European funders have also begun to show an interest in the Australian market. Commercial litigation funding has grown out of insolvency practice but LFCs in Australia now also fund large class actions, especially securities class actions. They generally do not fund claims for personal injury or those with a relatively small value because of the risks and costs relative to potential return.[91]

The role of LFCs in cases other than insolvency cases was, until recently, uncertain. Their legitimacy was challenged on the basis of maintenance (improperly encouraging litigation), champerty (funding a third party's litigation for profit) and abuse of process, and there were conflicting judicial decisions.[92] In 2006 the High Court of Australia resolved the conflict by endorsing the role of institutional litigation funders.[93] The trial judge had accepted arguments that the litigation funding agreement was invalid because it amounted to 'trafficking in litigation'. The Court of Appeal reversed this finding and described a need for a change in the attitude towards litigation funding.

> 'These changes in attitude to funders have been influenced by concerns about access to justice and heightened awareness of the costs of litigation. Governments have promoted the legislative changes in response to the spiralling costs of legal aid. Courts have recognised these trends and the matters driving them. 'Ambulance chasing' still has negative connotations in many quarters, but it is now widely recognised that there are some types of claims that will simply never get off the ground unless traditional attitudes are modified. These include cases involving complex scientific and legal issues. The largely factual account in the book and film *A Civil Action* has demonstrated the social utility of funded proceedings, the financial risks assumed by funders, and the potential conflicts of interest as between group members in mass tort claims propounding difficult actions against deep-pocketed and determined defendants.'[94]

Other judges have endorsed commercial litigation funding for its potential to foster the aims of Australian class action legislation[95], 'inject a welcome element of commercial objectivity into the way in which [litigation] budgets are framed'[96] and increase the efficiency with which litigation is conducted.[97] Support for

[90] *Litigation Funding in Australia*, Discussion Paper, Standing Committee of Attorneys General, May 2006 ('SCAG Report 2006').

[91] ibid, p 4.

[92] The key cases are discussed in *Fostif v Campbells Cash and Carry Pty Ltd* [2005] NSWCA 83.

[93] *Campbells Cash and Carry v Fostif* [2006] HCA 41.

[94] *Fostif v Campbells Cash and Carry* [2005] 63 NSWLR 203. (The appeal to the High Court failed on this ground but was successful for other reasons). For a different perspective on litigation funding see Keane, 'Access to Justice and Other Shibboleths' (n 4).

[95] *Kirby v Centro* [2008] FCA 1505.

[96] *QPSX Limited v Ericsson Australia Pty Ltd* [2005] FCA 933, at [54].

[97] *QPSX Limited v Ericsson Australia Pty Ltd* [2005] FCA 933, at [54].

commercial litigation funding has also come from the Law Council of Australia and the Law Institute of Victoria.[98]

Commercial litigation funders exist and thrive in Australia primarily because of the costs shifting rule and the prohibition against lawyers charging contingency fees.[99] They have grown in an ad hoc way and in the absence of any regulatory framework tailored to their particular nature and role. In *Brookfield Multiplex*[100] the Full Court of the Federal Court ruled (2-1) that the arrangement between the commercial litigation funder, the law firm representing the class, and the members of the class was a managed investment scheme as defined in the *Corporations Act*.[101] One result of this decision is that the funding arrangement should have been registered under the relevant provisions of the *Corporations Act*. Another result is that other class actions underway at the time were also affected. The Australian Securities and Investments Commission intervened to grant an exemption (limited in time to 30 June 2010) to ongoing class actions affected by the decision.

The Commonwealth Government responded to the *Brookfield Multiplex* case by changing the relevant regulations to exclude funded class actions from the definition of 'managed investment scheme'. While this removed the uncertainty created by the decision, the case reignited discussions about how best to regulate the commercial litigation funding market in Australia.[102] That market is no longer nascent.[103] The number of funders is growing and overseas funders are showing

[98] See Law Council of Australia, 'Submission to Standing Committee of Attorneys-General', 14 September 2006; John North, 'Litigation Funding: Much to be Achieved with the Right Approach' (2005) 43 *Law Society Journal* 66, 69. For a recent robust criticism of the role of litigation funders and litigation funding, see Keane, 'Access to Justice and Other Shibboleths' (n 4). A recent challenge to the participation of a LFC indicates that the High Court decision in *Fostif* is not the last word on the issue. In *Brookfield Multiplex Limited v International Litigation Funding Partners* [2009] 147 FCFCA (a class action), Multiplex argued that the aggregate of the arrangements between the class lawyers and the litigation funders established a managed investment scheme which should have been, but was not, registered under the *Corporations Act*. Finkelstein J had rejected this argument at first instance but on appeal the Full Court disagreed. This case reminds us that the role of litigation funders is not yet settled and that the regulatory framework in which they do and should operate is evolving.

[99] It may be that Federal Court judges have the power under s 33ZJ of the *Federal Court Act* to make an order for costs on a contingent fee basis in a class action, but thus far in the life of that legislation no such application has been made. (Section 33ZJ(2) states: 'If, on an application under this section, the Court is satisfied that the costs reasonably incurred in relation to the representative proceeding by the person making the application are likely to exceed the costs recoverable by the person from the respondent, the Court may order that an amount equal to the whole or a part of the excess be paid to that person out of the damages awarded.')

[100] *Brookfield Multiplex Limited v. International Litigation Funding Partners Pte Ltd (No 2)* [2009] FCAFC. This was a representative proceeding (i.e., a class action) by shareholders against Brookfield Multiplex for damages for losses allegedly caused by the company's belated disclosure of cost problems related to the construction of the Wembley Stadium.

[101] *Corporations Act 2001* (Cth). The first instance judge, Finkelstein J, had ruled that the funded class action was not a managed investment scheme.

[102] This issue was considered by the Standing Committee of Attorneys General in 2006, without any concrete regulatory outcomes.

[103] The nascent nature of commercial litigation funding in England was one of the reasons why Lord Justice Jackson opted, for the time being, for a voluntary code of conduct rather than full statutory regulation: see *Review of Civil Litigation Costs: Final Report*, Dec 2009, ch 11.

an interest in competing in the market. Most of the funded cases are securities class actions with large numbers of class members. Some of these class members are sophisticated institutional investors and some are not. The regulation of funders that has occurred thus far has been in the form of judicial decisions and funder self-regulation.

While a full statutory scheme would increase certainty and transparency, it was possible to address the problem created by *Brookfield Multiplex* with a minor change in the law to exempt funders from the definition of a managed investment scheme. Some observers consider this to be the most proportionate and appropriate response. They argue that commercial litigation funders have behaved responsibly and have paid adverse costs orders when required to do so, and that there is no evidence of any serious risk to consumers. In such circumstances, the costs associated with developing, implementing and enforcing a statutory regulatory scheme may not be justified . . . at least, not yet.

Insurance for Legal Expenses

There is no developed market in Australia for After the Event (ATE) insurance or for other legal expenses insurance as a distinct product. It is common, however, for insurance policies issued for other purposes (homeowners' or Directors and Officers, for example) to provide for a defence at the insurer's expense and for the payment of any costs an insured person is ordered to pay.

Conclusion

Notwithstanding the lack of reliable empirical information about litigation costs and funding issues in Australia, it is possible to draw some tentative conclusions about the Comparative Project's key themes of predictability and proportionality. First, predictability of legal costs must receive relatively low marks. Various attempts have been made to address this problem. These include requiring lawyers to disclose billing practices and to give clients costs estimates, and exchanging budgets for discovery costs. However, these disclosures and estimates are given in a system with hourly billing and without costs capping, in which the duration of most cases has no upper limit that can be identified in advance and where, notwithstanding increasingly robust judicial case management, interlocutory procedural disputes can add considerably to the duration and cost of litigation. Predicting overall cost is an easier task for cases that have a relatively small value, are not complex and can be dealt with in tribunals and small claims courts that offer expedited procedures.

Proportionality is even harder to assess. Most Australian jurisdictions have embraced a modern view of proportionality and have incorporated it into their procedural rules. Asking whether legal costs are proportionate, however, requires an analysis of various factors in samples of cases sufficiently large to produce valid results, including the amounts involved, the amounts recovered, the fees charged by lawyers and the gap between costs incurred and costs recovered by the successful parties. If we interpret 'proportionality' broadly, our analysis would also have to include court time and resources used, the cost to the public of the tax deductibility of legal fees as a business expense, the costs to a business entity of the time and resources directed to the litigation effort (thus diverted from other efforts) and (arguably) the less tangible but real emotional and psychological costs often associated with litigation. We do not yet have this information. One risk is that large, complex cases and a relatively small number of high profile 'mega-litigation' cases have become our data source. The substantial demands which those cases place on the civil justice system has to be addressed, but they are not sufficiently representative of all of the work that courts and tribunals do to become the justification for broad-ranging policy decisions.

3

Belgium

VINCENT SAGAERT* AND ILSE SAMOY**

Introduction

The issue of judicial expenses and costs is, in Belgian law, situated in a field of tension between two conflicting starting points. On the one hand, litigation in Belgian is free, in the sense that litigating parties do not have to pay the wages of the judges or their affiliates.[1] On the other hand, parties exercising their right of access to justice have the obligation to pay expenses in order to obtain a final judgment. The way in which the Belgian legislator has balanced these two starting points has been subject to a number of recent developments.

The statutory provisions on judicial expenses and costs and their recoverability in civil proceedings[2] are laid down in the Judicial Code (JC), in particular in the fourth Part on civil procedure, Book II on legal proceedings, Title IV on expenses and costs, Articles 1017–1024. Article 1017 JC contains the basic principle that each final judgment specifies the costs to be borne by the party found to be in error (the losing party). Articles 1018–1019 and 1022 JC give an overview of the recoverable costs. Articles 1020–1021 JC concern the payment of and the decision upon the costs. Article 1023 JC introduces a prohibition of 'increasing clauses'. Article 1024 JC, finally, deals with the costs of enforcement. These provisions will be explained below.

* Professor of private law KULeuven and Professor of property law University of Antwerp, lawyer at the Brussels Bar.

** Professor of private law KULeuven, Institute of the law of obligations.

[1] See L van Bauwel, *Handboek voor het burgerlijk procesrecht* vol I (Antwerp, Standaard, 1934) 425, no 761.

[2] The rules discussed here only apply in civil litigation. A specific provision applies to proceedings before the Belgian Supreme Court (see below) and the Administrative Court (*Conseil d'Etat/Raad van State*). The rules do not apply to arbitration proceedings. Criminal proceedings are subject to specific provisions under the Criminal Code: Belgian Supreme Court 29 Nov 1983, *Arresten Cassatie* 1983–84, 366; D Maes, 'Artikel 1017 Ger W', in X, *Artikelsgewijze commentaar: Gerechtelijk recht* (Mechelen, Kluwer)('D Maes') 3, no 3.

General Overview And Legal Developments

The rules on funding and costs of judicial proceedings have been the subject of major debate lasting several years, which led to four important statutory amendments between 2005 and 2007. The detail of the current rules is described in the main part of this chapter, but this introduction explains the reasons for change and the nature of the main changes.

The Act of 21 April 2007: the Recoverability of Lawyers' Fees

Before the 2007 amendment, article 1022 JC merely allowed the recovery of the costs of 'material acts' accomplished by a lawyer. The sums recoverable under article 1022 were fixed in the Royal Decree of 30 November 1970,[3] but did not refer to the lawyers' fees.[4] Each party (the losing as well as the winning party) had to pay his own lawyers' fees, which were irrecoverable. The amount of the expenses varied depending upon (1) the court or tribunal before which the case was brought and (2) the value of the claim, but were generally rather limited. Additional expenses of judicial proceedings could be awarded for additional judicial acts, for instance personal appearance, reopening of debates, expert investigation, witness interrogation, and so on.[5]

The lawyer's fees were not part of the expenses of judicial proceedings, nor were lawyers' fees regulated in the chapter of the Judicial Code on expenses and costs, so that they could not be charged to the other party to the litigation. The initial draft of the Judicial Code, as it was proposed by the Royal Commissioner in the middle of the 1960s, provided for the possibility of the judge to 'award to a party a compensation for the charges of its defence'.[6] The rationale for this provision was revealing:

> 'In the current status of judicial proceedings, the introduction of a judicial action entails expenses which burden the disputed claim, but which can according to the law not be recovered. Therefore, numerous sales agreements stipulate that the amount of the debt will be increased if the debt has to be enforced before courts or tribunals. This increase aims to enable the creditor to recover the expenses that he would make if he has to enforce payment in judicial proceedings. Practice has demonstrated abuses of such clauses, which often ultimately came down to penalty clauses. The current proposal proclaims on the one hand the invalidity of clauses containing an increase of a claim in case it has to be enforced in judicial proceedings (article 1022 JC), but on the other hand the possibility of recovering the expenses of defense to a reasonable extent (article 1023 JC).'

[3] Royal Decree 30 November 1970, *Belgian Official Gazette* 3 Dec 1970, erratum 12 Feb 1971.

[4] G de Leval, *Eléments de procédure civile* (Brussels, Larcier, 2003) 431; B de Temmerman, 'De verhaalbaarheid van kosten van juridische of technische bijstand' (2003), *Tijdschrift voor Privaatrecht* ('B de Temmerman') 1016, no 2.

[5] Art 4 Decree of 30 Sept 1975.

[6] See B de Temmerman (n 4) no 3.

Further, parties could not contractually agree that the need to initiate judicial proceedings in order to get payment would increase the amount of the claim. Such a clause would be an indirect way of being compensated for the attorney fees, but was prohibited. The Belgian Supreme Court even held that this prohibition was part of the Belgian public order. In other words, such a contractual clause was absolutely void.[7]

However, this proposal to allow the recoverability of lawyer's fees did not reach the final text of the Judicial Code in 1967. During the parliamentary debate, different Members of Parliament opposed the proposal on the basis that this would result in a tarification of lawyers' fees.[8] Although this observation was totally incorrect, this criticism became the majority opinion. This resulted in the exclusion of lawyers' fees from the expenses of judicial procedure, which were limited to 'material acts' of the lawyer. The result was that in the Judicial Code of 1967 both the legal possibility of recovering (a part of) the lawyers' fees and a contractual basis of recovering lawyers' fees were excluded.

This situation has drastically changed as a result of several different factors. First of all, the Directive 2000/35/EC of the European Parliament and of the Council of 29 June 2000 on combating late payment in commercial transactions (Late Payment Directive)[9] has amended the general framework of the Belgian legal rules in the field. Article 5.1 of the Directive provides that

> 'unless the debtor is not responsible for the delay, the creditor shall be entitled to claim reasonable compensation from the debtor for all relevant recovery costs incurred through the latter's late payment. Such recovery costs shall respect the principles of transparency and proportionality as regards the debt in question. Member States may, while respecting the principles referred to above, fix maximum amounts as regards the recovery costs for different levels of debt.'

This provision was incorporated into Belgian law through article 6 of the Act of 2 August 2002 on the combating of late payment in commercial transactions.[10] According to this provision, unless parties have agreed otherwise, the creditor is entitled, in case of late payment by his debtor and without prejudice to the provisions of the Judicial Code, to fair compensation to be paid by the debtor for all relevant expenses of recovery of the claim that have been made because of the late payment. This payment excludes the payment of 'expenses of judicial procedure'. This compensation must be in line with the principle of transparency and proportionate to the debt at stake. The King will determine the maximum amount of compensation in relation to the different levels of debt.

The break-through in the ability of the winning party to recover his lawyer's fees occurred through the law of contractual and extra-contractual liability. For two centuries, lawyers' fees could not be recovered by the victim of a contractual or

[7] Supreme Court 7 April 1995, *Rechtskundig Weekblad* 1995–96, 188, note A van Oevelen.
[8] B de Temmerman (n 4) 1017–1018, no 4.
[9] *Pb L* 8 Aug 2000, no 200.
[10] *Belgian Official Gazette* 7 August 2002.

extra-contractual fault on the basis of liability law. Two underlying reasons were stated for this position. Firstly, the fees of a lawyer were not considered to be costs of the victim in determining the amount of damages and, therefore, could not give rise to compensation on the basis of contractual or extra-contractual liability. In other words, the lawyer's fees would not be part of the damage that needed to be compensated. It was said that where a victim of a fault has to use a lawyer, this only assists the victim's claim for damages, but is not itself a component of the damages.[11] A second explanation was found in the theory of breach of causation. According to this approach, the lawyer's costs and fees were indeed part of the recoverable damages, but the causal connection between the fault and the damages was breached by the autonomous decision of the victim to appeal to a lawyer.[12] The causal connection between expenses and the fact causing damages could be breached if the contractual obligation leading to the expenses (*in casu* the contract concluded by the processing party and the lawyer in order to assist and to represent said party in court) has the purpose of permanently leaving the costs as an expense of the contracting party.[13]

This position of the Belgian Supreme Court dramatically changed in a judgment of 2 September 2004. According to this judgment, 'the fees of an attorney or technical expert which have been paid by the victim of a contractual non-compliance can be part of the damage to be compensated, as far as they are a necessary effect of the non-compliance.'[14] This case law was transposed two years later from the contractual to the extra-contractual situation. Hence, the victim of a wrongful act is now entitled to the 'necessary fees of an attorney'.[15]

Finally, the Constitutional Court contributed to the need for reform when it ruled in 2007 that the distinction between creditors of commercial transactions (governed by article 6 of the Act implementing the Late Payment Directive) and other creditors was contrary to the principles of equality and non-discrimination as laid down in articles 10 and 11 of the Belgian Constitution. According to the Court 'the discrimination was not based in the Late Payment Act, but in the absence of a general solution which must be provided by the legislator in line with articles 10 and 11 of the Constitution'.[16] Hence, the Constitutional Court obliged

[11] Supreme Court 18 Jun 1964, *Pasicrisie* 1964, I, 1121 and *Rechtskundig Weekblad* 1964–65, 1303; Supreme Court 11 Jun 1956, *Pasicrisie* 1956, I, 1098 and *Rechtskundig Weekblad* 1956–57, 1935; Supreme Court 11 Apr 1956, *Arresten Cassatie* 1956, 656, *Pasicrisie* 1956, I, 841 and *Rechtskundig Weekblad* 1956–57, 1355.

[12] Supreme Court 19 Feb 2001, *Arresten Cassatie* 2001, 324 and *Rechtskundig Weekblad* 2001–02, 238.

[13] Supreme Court 5 May 1999, *Arresten Cassatie* 1999, 612 and *Rechtskundig Weekblad* 2001–02, 1171, note.

[14] Belgian Supreme Court 2 Sept 2004, *Rechtskundig Weekblad* 2004–05, 535, concl. Adv. Gen. A Henkes and note B Wilms and K Christiaens, *Journal des Tribunaux* 2004, 684, note B de Connick.

[15] 'Les frais et honoraires d'avocat exposés par la victime d'une faute extra-contractuelle peuvent constituer un élément du dommage donnant lieu à indemnisation dans la mesure où ils sont nécessaires pour permettre à la victime de faire valoir ses droits à l'indemnisation de son dommage' (Cass 16 Nov 2006, *Journal des Tribunaux* 2007, 14, *Rechtskundig Weekblad* 2006–07, 1128).

[16] Constitutional Court n° 16/2007, 17 Jan 2007, *Belgian Official Gazette* 9 Mar 2007 (2nd eds) (extract), 12396, *Revue Générale des Assurances et des Responsabilités* 2007, n° 14.222, note F Glansdorff.

the Belgian legislator to introduce general rules with regard to the recovery of lawyers' fees. This gave rise to the Act of 21 April 2007.

The Act of 15 May 2007: the Recoverability of Technical Experts' Fees

The rules in the Judicial Code governing expert investigation were changed by the Act of 15 May 2007. The main reasons for this amendment concerned the high level of experts' costs, made worse by the lack of transparency and delay in expert investigations. The previous practice was that an expert, immediately after his nomination by the court, requested an advance payment from the party who was 'most interested', namely the party who had asked for the expert. This request was difficult to refuse, and led to delay in starting the investigation until the payment had been made.

The objectives of the 2007 reform were to accelerate expert investigations, to limit the expenses and to guarantee their transparency, and to stimulate experts to finish their job within fixed time limits. During the investigation, the expert is no longer allowed to receive any direct payment from the parties, thereby guaranteeing the expert's impartiality and also putting pressure on the expert to finish his investigation within the fixed time limits.[17] He is now only paid at the end of the investigation, and is paid through the court, which has a more active role in determining the initial retaining fee, the total amount to be paid at the end (called 'taxation'),[18] and the final settlement.[19]

Some scholars take the view that these measures will have a positive influence on costs.[20] Others are more reticent and emphasise that the key to success is dependent upon specifying a clear description of the expert's mission and making a deliberate choice of an adequate expert, taking into account the value and the nature of the proceedings.[21] Under the previous legislation, the value of the proceedings was a criterion for evaluation of the expert's fee (taxation), but this criterion has now been abolished. However, this does not mean that the expert does not have to take into account the principle of proportionality: he has to take care that the value of the proceedings is proportionate to his costs.

[17] D Mougenot, 'La rémunération de l'expert dans la loi du 15 mai 2007 modifiant les règles relatives à l'expertise' in H Boularbah (ed), *Le nouveau droit de l'expertise judiciaire en pratique: commentaires de la loi du 15 mai 2007* (Ghent, Larcier, 2008), 109–110; T Lysens and L Naudts, 'Kosten en ereloon' in D de Buyst (ed), *Bestendig handboek deskundigenonderzoek* (Mechelen, Kluwer, 2008) ('Lysens/Naudts') 2.

[18] It has been argued that more transparency would be guaranteed if more details were prescribed for taxation in article 990 JC: Lysens/Naudts (n 17) 2.

[19] These three stages are specified in articles 987–991*bis* JC.

[20] X Malengrau, 'Les frais et honoraires des experts: le point de vue d'un juge' in H Boularbah (ed), *Le nouveau droit de l'expertise judiciaire en pratique: commentaires de la loi du 15 mai 2007* (Ghent, Larcier, 2008) 133.

[21] M Binard and F de Geradon, 'Les frais et honoraires de l'expert: le point de vue de l'expert', in H Boularbah (ed), *Le nouveau droit de l'expertise judiciaire en pratique: commentaires de la loi du 15 mai 2007* (Ghent, Larcier, 2008) 154–155.

A final important amendment concerns the availability of legal aid. Under the earlier legislation, the rules on legal aid did not cover the assistance of an expert. In its judgment of 26 October 2005, the Constitutional Court came to the conclusion that parties who could not afford a technical expert were discriminated against, since an expert's report can have a decisive influence on the outcome of a case.[22] This judgment caused the law to be amended: since 1 January 2007, a party can ask for legal aid to cover the assistance of a technical expert.[23]

The Supreme Court also changed its position as to the recoverability of the costs of an extrajudicial expert as for lawyer's fees. Originally, the victim of a wrongful act could not include expert's fees in his damage. In its judgment of 28 February 2002,[24] the Supreme Court abandoned its previously-held opinion and considered that the duty to compensate damages can extend to the costs of a technical expert that a victim had to pay in order to determine the amount of damages. The judgment concerned the costs of an extrajudicial expert investigation and recognised that reimbursement of these costs can be claimed from the losing party on the basis of contractual or extra-contractual liability law. Since the Act of 21 April 2007 concerns only lawyers' costs and fees, this jurisprudence of the Supreme Court is still relevant for technical experts' costs and fees.

The Act of 21 February 2005 on Mediation and the Act of 26 April 2007: Combating Judicial Arrears

For some decades, the Belgian legal system has struggled with long delays in the resolution of legal claims by the courts. Such delays can have an effect on judicial costs and expenses. Two new laws have addressed this problem. First, settlement was encouraged through the Act of 21 February 2005 on mediation. Secondly, although the title is said to be misleading, the Act of 26 April 2007 amended the Judicial Code in order to combat the arrears of the juridiciary.[25] After a first attempt in amending the Judicial Code by the Act of 3 August 1992, the Parliamentary documents of the Act of 26 April 2007 enumerate eight goals: to simplify and to generalise the rules on preparing a case and to time the deposition and the submission of the statements to the clerk's service; to stimulate the active role of the judge during the meeting; to improve the possibilities for clearing up procedural defects; to encourage short debates; to abolish Articles 751 and 753 JC; to encourage the use of summary statements; to shorten deliberations and the judgment; and to enforce the remedies for abuse of legal proceedings.

[22] Constitutional Court 26 Oct 2005, n° 2005/160, *Nieuw Juridisch Weekblad* 2006, 503.

[23] Arts 664, 665, 671 and 692*bis* JC. The amendment was made by arts 10, 11, 12, 13 and 14 Act 20 Jul 2006 containing various provisions, *Belgian Official Gazette* 28 Jul 2006.

[24] Supreme Court 28 Feb 2002, *Arresten Cassatie* 2002, 642, *Rechtskundig Weekblad* 2002–03, 19, note S Mosselmans, *Nieuw Juridisch Weekblad* 2002, 351, note I Boone, *De Verzekering* 2002, 701, note P Graulus and *Revue générale des assurances et des responsabilités* 2003, no 13754, note F Glansdorff.

[25] Act 26 Apr 2007, *Belgian Official Gazette* 12 Jun 2007.

Although the reform has been the target of criticism, the Act could at least result in new dynamics and in the acceleration of judicial proceedings. From the beginning of the process, the parties will have more certainty about the starting date, the time schedule for deposing statements, the dates of the hearing, deliberation and judgment. It remains to be seen whether the judicial administration will provide sufficient resources to realise these reforms.

Funding Claims

Legal Aid

The Belgian Constitution guarantees each Belgian citizen 'a right to judicial aid'.[26] Judicial aid contains two aspects: exemption from paying judicial costs (legal aid)[27] and provision for payment of lawyers' fees (known as a *pro Deo* lawyer and judicial assistance).[28] The term legal aid can also be used to cover both aspects.

Judicial costs for specified judicial or extra-judicial proceedings and acts may be fully or partially waived for persons who do not have enough income to cover them.[29] This exemption can apply to payment of registration duties, courts fees, the price of an authenticated copy of the judgment, the enforcement of judgments, judicial and extrajudicial mediation, and other expenses that arise from the litigation.[30] It is also possible to be awarded free assistance by a technical expert. Legal aid is restricted to Belgian citizens whose claim seems legitimate and who can prove that their income is insufficient.[31] Persons not having Belgian nationality can be awarded legal aid under the same conditions if they fall within the categories enumerated in article 668 JC. A request for legal aid must be submitted to the office of the court or tribunal before which a judicial proceeding would be initiated or of the place where the act has to be performed.[32] In urgent cases, the judge of the pending litigation can grant legal aid for the acts specified.

The rules on judicial assistance guarantee a free lawyer. Since 31 December 1999, the rules are integrated in a broad system of 'judicial assistance'.[33] A distinction is made between first line judicial assistance[34] and second line judicial assistance (article 508/7-13 JC).[35] First line judicial assistance is delivered as practical

[26] Art 23, para 3.2 of the Constitutional Act.
[27] Arts 664–669 JC.
[28] B Allemeersch, M Boes and P van Orshoven, *Beginselen van gerechtelijk recht* (Leuven, Acco, 2008) 349.
[29] Art 664 JC.
[30] Art 665 JC.
[31] Art 667 JC.
[32] Art 670 JC.
[33] Arts 446*bis* and art 508/1-23 JC.
[34] Art 508/1-6 JC.
[35] Art 508/7-13 JC.

information, legal information, a first legal advice or the referring of the person to a specialised body or organisation, such as legal shops, tenants' organisations, syndicates, health services, and so on. Second line judicial assistance is delivered to a natural person as an elaborate legal advice, legal assistance and representation in a law suit (by a so called *pro Deo* lawyer). A request to obtain a free lawyer has to be submitted to the Office of Judicial Assistance (*Bureau voor juridische bijstand*). The lawyer receives a payment from the State, which is determined according to the acts he has performed, each act being awarded a certain number of points. There is a list of lawyers who are prepared to act as *pro Deo* Lawyers. All trainees, in other words lawyers in their first three years of professional experience, are automatically included in the list.

Legal Expenses Insurances

It is possible, and in certain situations normal practice, to cover the risk of litigation through an insurance agreement. The Belgian legislator has recently chosen to promote access to justice through granting a tax advantage for use of legal expenses insurance. A Royal Decree of 15 January 2007[36] specifies the conditions that are to be met in the insurance policy, in order for it to be exempt from the annual tax of 9.25 per cent imposed to insurance policies under Article 173 of the Code of various duties and taxes. The purpose of the Royal Decree is not to fix the contents of a legal expenses insurance policy, nor to prescribe minimal conditions, but to encourage people to take out such insurance and hence indirectly assist access to justice.

The Act of 21 April 2007 on recoverability of lawyers' fees and the Royal Decree of 16 October 2007 are expected to have important effects on the practice of legal expenses insurances. On the one hand, possibilities are opened up for insurers to reclaim some or all of their payments. On the other hand, it is expected that legal expenses insurance policies will become available to cover the new risk that a losing party has to pay the lawyer's fees of the other party.[37]

[36] *Belgian Official Gazette* 27 Feb 2007.

[37] See on this expected development: E Jacques and R D'Hondt, 'Actualités en matière d'assurance protection juridique: évolutions normatives'(2007) *Droit de la Consommation/Consumentenrecht* 3–27.

Court And Process Costs

Article 1018 JC specifies the judicial expenses and costs that are payable:

1. the various court fees (*griffierechten/droit de greffe*) and registration duties (*registratierechten/droit de régistration*), as well as the stamp duties (*zegelrechten*) paid before the abolition of the Code on Stamp Duties;[38]
2. the price and the emoluments and wages for the judicial deeds;
3. the price for the authenticated copy (*uitgifte/expédition*) of the judgment;
4. the expenses concerning all investigation measures, including the expenses of witnesses and experts;
5. the expenses for travelling and acommodation of judges, clerks of the court and the parties, when their trip has been imposed by the judge, and the expense of deeds which have been drafted with regard to the legal proceedings;
6. the expenses of judicial procedure (*rechtsplegingsvergoeding/indemnité de procédure*), as stated in article 1022 JC;
7. the fees, the emoluments and the costs of the mediator, nominated according to article 1734 JC.

Some of these items are described in more detail below. The list in article 1018 JC is not exhaustive.[39] Parliamentary documents confirm that the judge has some discretion with regard to expenses that are not included in the list.[40] Additional expenses and costs can be, for instance, expenses made to obtain a certificate of the defendant's domicile or a copy of a criminal file (for example if needed to sustain a divorce claim).

The amount of judicial expenses and costs can give rise to cases being delayed, because the decision on allocation of expenses and costs is only made in the final judgment, so payment and interest are only due thereafter, after proof of default.[41]

Court Charges

Article 1018 JC starts with the court fees, that is, fees for the following acts carried out by the judicial services:

a. The inscription of the case on the role of the court or tribunal (*rolrecht/droit de rôle*). In principle, this 'role fee' differs depending upon the court or tribunal before which the case is introduced and upon the way the case is introduced (by citation, request or summary proceedings).[42]

[38] The Code on Stamp Duties has been abolished by an Act of 19 Dec 2006, *Belgian Official Gazette* 29 Dec 2006, date of entry into force: 1 Jan 2007.

[39] J Kerkhofs, 'Uitgaven en kosten' in G van Mellaert (ed), *Praktijkboek gerechtelijk recht* (Bruges, Vanden Broele, 2006) ('J Kerkhofs') 22; J Laenens and others, *Handboek gerechtelijk recht* (Antwerp, Intersentia, 2008) ('Laenens et al') 484.

[40] F Meersschaut, 'Draaglast van de gedingkosten' (1986–87) *Jura Falconis* 277.

[41] Supreme Court 30 Mar 2001, *Arresten Cassatie* 2001, 547 and *Pasicrisie* 2001, I, 541.

[42] Art 269 of the Code of Registration Duties.

	Justice of the peace	Tribunal of first instance	Industrial Tribunal	Commercial Tribunal	Court of Appeal	Industrial Court of Appeal	Supreme Court
General role fee	€35	€82	–	€82	€186	–	€325
Request	€27	€52	–	€52	–	–	–
Summary proceedings	–	€69.50	–	€69.50	€139	–	

b. The writing by the clerks of the deeds that have been passed before them or certain deeds of judges and officers of the prosecutor (*opstelrecht/droit de rédaction*). These expenses give rise to a lump sum of €30 (same amount for each court or tribunal).
c. The handing over of an authenticated copy of a deed or judgment and of other copies that are kept at the clerk's service (*expeditierecht/droit d'expédition*).[43]

	Justice of the peace	Tribunal of first instance	Industrial Tribunal	Commercial Tribunal	Court of Appeal	Industrial Court of	Supreme Court
Expedition duties	1.50 / page	2.85 / page	0.75 / page	2.85 / page	2.85 / page	0.75 / page	4.83 / page

Other Official Charges

Registration duties include the general fixed rate, specific fixed rates, and rates owed on judgments leading to a condemnation, a taxation or a transfer of amounts or movables values.[44] These charges are due pursuant to each final, provisional, subsidiary or principal or conditional condemnation with regard to movable amounts or values (ie money debt). The tax charge rises to 3 per cent of the amount of the money debt that is declared by the court or tribunal.[45] But if the amount of the condemnation does not exceed €12,500, no tax charge is levied.

The price and emoluments and wages for the judicial deeds are, in general, the expenses of the bailiff. The terms 'wages and emoluments' are dated, but they are nevertheless retained in the Judicial Code of 1967. 'Wages' means fees, and 'emoluments' means expenses. The amounts payable are fixed in a Royal Decree of 12 September 1969,[46] and cover, for instance, costs made in obtaining information or in searching the defendant's domicile and moving expenses.[47]

[43] Arts 270 and 271 of the Code of Registration Duties.
[44] Art 1019 JC.
[45] Art 142 of the Code of Registration Duties.
[46] Laenens et al (n 39) 485.
[47] D Maes (n 2) 53, no 5.

Witness of Fact

The expense of investigation measures, including expenses of witnesses and experts, are included as recoverable costs.[48] Persons who give evidence before a court or tribunal are entitled to compensation,[49] which is to be paid in advance by the party who calls the witness, although the sum will be settled after the judgment. The compensation amounts to approximately €5, plus travel expenses (at €0.0868 per kilometre).[50] Distances up to 10 kilometres are not compensated.

Expert

There are three stages in the payment of an expert: the initial retaining fee, the total amount to be paid at the end (called 'taxation'),[51] and final settlement.[52] The expert is now only paid after the end of the investigation.

The purpose of the retaining fee, which has to be paid to the clerk's service, is to secure payment so as to protect the expert against the parties' insolvency. The amount of the retaining fee is fixed during the meeting in which the expert investigation is launched.[53] It is for the judge to decide on the apportionment between the parties of payment of the retaining fee,[54] taking into account the sole restriction that if under article 1017 JC a party cannot be charged to pay the judicial expenses and costs (for example in social security proceedings), he also cannot be made to pay the expert's retaining fee, and the State will have to pay the expert's retaining fee.

The expert is, as a general rule, required to draw up a detailed account (the taxation), listing his hours worked, hourly rate, travelling expenses, general expenses, amounts paid to third parties and prepayments.[55] There are no fixed legal scales for the expert's expenses. The taxation must be based on three elements: the diligence with which the work has been carried out, the compliance with the planned deadlines, and the quality of the investigation.[56] The amount at stake is not an element.

The judge attributes responsibility to pay the expert's costs in his decision upon the judicial expenses and costs in the final judgment,[57] at which point interest

[48] Art 1018, para 4 JC.

[49] Art 953, para 1 JC.

[50] Art 953 JC and Royal Decree 27 Jul 1972, *Belgian Official Gazette* 31 Aug 1972.

[51] It has been argued that more transparency would be guaranteed if more detail were prescribed for taxation in article 990 JC: Lysens and Naudts (n 17) 2.

[52] These three stages are specified in articles 987–991*bis* JC.

[53] Art 972, second para JC.

[54] Art 987 JC.

[55] Art 990 JC.

[56] Art 991, second para JC.

[57] Art 1018 JC.

starts to run. The winning party who has paid a part of the retaining fee cannot claim interest on such sum for the period preceding the judgment.[58]

Mediation Costs

The Act of 21 February 2005 has introduced a new chapter on mediation in the Judicial Code, regulating judicial and extrajudicial mediation,[59] in order to encourage mediation. A mediator tries to settle the dispute by agreement. The costs of *judicial* mediation (contrary to the costs of *extrajudicial* mediation) are now made part of the judicial expenses and costs enumerated in article 1018 JC, and are to be borne by the losing party (but see further below).

Lawyers' Costs

Article 446ter JC specifies a general rule with regard to the fee that applies in the contractual relationship between a lawyer and his client: namely, lawyers calculate their fees with the modesty that can be expected from their profession. A contractual clause that makes the fees exclusively dependent upon the result of the litigation, is forbidden. There are no fixed rates given by the legislator or professional Bar Associations. Hence, lawyer's fees are based on individual decisions by every party, subject to the restrictions, firstly, of the obligation to calculate in modesty and, secondly, not to connect the fee exclusively to the result of the litigation. This party-by-party decision covers both the legal acts and intellectual performances.

If the fees are not modestly calculated, the Bar Association can mitigate the fee, taking into account the importance of the litigation and the nature of the performances accomplished. Parties have the right to bring this litigation before arbitration courts or judicial courts. From a legal point of view, the Bar Association does not have jurisdiction to decide upon the civil rights and obligations of the parties, nor is the decision of the Bar Association to be considered as an advice. It is legally to be considered as a third party decision that is binding upon parties. Tribunals/courts and arbitral courts only have the right to judge whether a party's decision, or a third party decision by the Bar Association, infringed the obligation of parties to act in good faith.[60]

An inquiry by the Bar Associations in 2006 demonstrated that one can distinguish in legal practice different ways in which fees are calculated, notably:

[58] Supreme Court 30 Mar 2001, *Rechtskundig Weekblad* 2001–02, 699; Supreme Court 24 Sept1953, *Pasicrisie* 1954, I, 36.

[59] Arts 1724–1737 JC.

[60] Orde van Vlaamse Balies, *Advocatenerelonen*, Bruges, 2006, 14.

—an hourly rate fee. This is the most common way of calculating fees (40 per cent of the cases in the inquiry): 33 per cent of lawyers worked for an hourly fee of €75–99 and 27 per cent estimated their fees as €100–149. Only a minority of lawyers deviated from these ranges.

—a fee based on the value of the litigation. The fee is often calculated at 15 per cent where the value of the case is from €0–6,200, 10 per cent from €6,201–50,000, 8 per cent from €50,001–125,000, 6 per cent from €125,001–250,000 and 4 per cent from €250,000 upwards. This basis of calculation only represents about 15 per cent of cases.

There are two Professional Bar Associations: a Flemish association and a French-speaking and Germanic Association. The French-speaking and Germanic Association decreed rules in 2004 with regard to the information duties that a lawyer has in relation to his client. The duties which the lawyer is charged with are (1) the obligation to inform his client that he has the possibility of taking recourse to a third party, (2) the details of the manner in which the lawyer will calculate his fees and costs, (3) the details of the result of the calculation of fees, (4) provisional information with regard to intermediate fees at regular points in the litigation and (5) the manner in which costs and expenses are recovered on behalf of the client.[61]

These fees are independent of the amounts that are the basis for cost shifting in the light of the result of the litigation (see below).

Cost Shifting: Lawyers' Fees

Article 1018 JC enumerates 'the expenses of judicial procedure, as stated in article 1022 JC'. Article 1022 JC was been drastically amended by the Act of 21 April 2007,[62] under which it has become possible to recover fixed rates for lawyers' fees.

General Rule

Article 1022 JC defines the expenses of judicial procedure as 'a fixed compensation for the expenses and fees of the lawyer of the winning party'. The term 'fixed' shows that the actual fees are not recoverable, but only a fixed amount, related to the amount of the claim. The word 'lawyer' shows that the winning party is only entitled to expenses of judicial procedure if he is assisted and/or represented by a lawyer. Thus, a party who defends himself or who is assisted by another

[61] Règlement relatif à l'information à fournir par l'avocat à ses clients en matière d'honoraires, de frais et débours of 26 Nov 2004 of the French-speaking and Germanic Bar Association.

[62] Act of 21 Apr 2007 concerning the recoverability of fees and costs related to a lawyer's assistance, *Belgian Official Gazette* 31 May 2007.

non-lawyer (eg a trade union representative in the industrial courts, or a public servant in tax matters) is not entitled to these expenses. The Constitutional Court has held several times that this distinction is not contrary to the Constitution non-discrimination provision.[63] A lawyer acting *qualitate qua* as tutor *ad hoc*, provisional administrator, or trustee in bankruptcy is not entitled to expenses of judicial procedure, unless he is represented by another lawyer.[64]

The amount of the judicial expenses is now essentially determined by the King. A basic amount, a maximum amount, and a minimum amount, depending on the value of the litigation, have been prescribed in a Royal Decree of 26 October 2007. The legislator has provided that, where specific reasons exist, the judge can increase or diminish the basic amount at the request of one of the parties, without exceeding the fixed minimum and maximum amounts. If he does so, the judge has to take into account specified factors: the financial abilities of the forfeiting parties (in order to diminish the amount); the complexity of the litigation; the contractually agreed compensation for the winning party; and whether the situation is manifestly unreasonable.

Value of the litigation	**Basic amount**	**Minimum amount**	**Maximum amount**
Up to €250.00	€150.00	€75.00	€300.00
From €250.01 up to €750,00	€200.00	€125.00	€500.00
From €750.01 up to €2,500.00	€400.00	€200.00	€1,000.00
From €2,500.01 up to €5,000.00	€650.00	€375.00	€1,500.00
From €5,000.01 up to €10,000.00	€900.00	€500.00	€2,000.00
From €10.000,01 up to €20.000,00	€1,100.00	€625.00	€2,500.00
From €20,000.01 up to €40,000.00	€2,000.00	€1,000.00	€4,000.00
From €40,000.01 up to €60,000.00	€2,500.00	€1,000.00	€5,000.00
From €60,000.01 up to €100,000.00	€3,000.00	€1.000,00	€6,000.00
From €100,000.01 up to €250,000.00	€5,000.00	€1,000.00	€10,000.00
From €250,000.01 up to €500,000.00	€7,000.00	€1,000.00	€14,000.00
From €500,000.01 up to €1,000,000.00	€10,000.00	€1,000.00	€20,000.00
More than €1,000,000.01	€15,000.00	1,000.00	30,000.00

[63] Constitutional Court 5 May 2009, n° 73/2009, www.grondwettelijkhof.be, r.o. B.4.3; Constitutional Court 18 Dec 2008, n° 182/2008, *Belgian Official Gazette* 22 Jan 2009, *Rechtskundig Weekblad* 2008–09, 1217 and www.grondwettelijkhof.be.

[64] Laenens et al (n 39) 488.

No party can be required to pay additional compensation for a lawyer's intervention above the amount of the expenses of judicial procedure, on whatever basis, such as under the rules on contractual or extra-contractual liability.[65]

It remains questionable whether the tariffs can be cumulated with damages for vexatious, manifestly inadmissible, disallowed or redundant proceedings. A proceeding is not only vexatious if a party has the intention of harming the other party, but also if the procedural behaviour contravenes that of a prudent and careful person.[66] The victim of vexatious or foolhardy proceedings can not only claim damage on the basis of liability for a wrongful act, but article 780*bis* JC[67] also allows the judge to award a civil penalty. Although many legal scholars have argued that these damages and penalty cannot be accumulated with the judicial expenses,[68] the Constitutional Court has suggested a different view.[69]

Exceptions to the General Rule

Article 1022 JC and the Royal Decree provide some exceptions to the general rule:

—If the forfeiting party qualifies for free legal aid, the recoverable lawyers' fees are automatically reduced to the minimum amount, unless the case results in a manifestly unreasonable situation.

—No lawyers' fees are due for acts made before a court from which the case has been withdrawn by decision of the district court.

—If the defendant pays a debt that is the object of the claim before submission of the claim on the list of cases in the court or tribunal, no judicial procedure expenses are due. If payment intervenes after submission on the list, only ¼ of the basis amount, with a maximum of €1,000.00, is due.

—Where there is a default of appearance (ie a party was not present in court), the amount of expenses of judicial procedure is automatically the minimum amount: this is because the legislator deems that these cases do not have any complexity.

Last but not least, an exception to the general rule applies to 'commercial transactions' regulated by the Act of 2 August 2002 on the combating of late payment in

[65] Art 1022 *in fine* JC.

[66] Supreme Court 31 Oct 2003, *Arresten Cassatie* 2003, 2011, *Journal des Tribunaux* 2004, 135, note JF van Drooghenbroeck.

[67] This provision has been introduced in the Judicial Code by Act 26 Apr 2007: 'The party who manifestly uses judicial proceedings with delaying or illegal purposes can be condemned to pay a pecuniary offence from €15 up to €2500, without prejudice to claimed damages . . .'.

[68] *Report of the Senate, Parliamenty Documents* 2006–07, n° 3-1686/5, p 27; P Lefranc and F Evers, 'Leidt de verhaalbaarheid van de advocatenkosten tot een meer toegankelijke justitie?' (2007) *Tijdschrift voor Mensenrechten* 9; JF van Drooghenbroeck and B de Coninck, 'La loi du 21 avril 2007 sur la répétibilité des frais et honoraires d'avocat' (2008) *Journal des tribunaux* 37, no 5.

[69] Constitutional Court 18 Dec 2008, *Belgian Official Gazette*, 22 Jan 2009, 3343 and www.grondwettelijkhof.be, B.10.2.

commercial transactions.[70] This Act covers all payment obligations due to the delivery of goods or accomplishment of services between professionals, or between a professional and a public authority. According to article 6 of this Act, unless the parties have agreed otherwise, the creditor is entitled, in case of late payment by his debtor, and without prejudice to the provisions of the Judicial Code, to 'fair compensation' to be paid by the debtor for all relevant expenses of recovery of the claim which have been made because of the late payment, including lawyer's costs and fees. The compensation must be transparent and proportionate to the debt at stake. Thus, in commercial transactions, the creditor is not bound by the fixed amounts of the expenses of judicial procedure: he can ask for a fair compensation for his lawyer's fees. However, a creditor who obtains such compensation cannot claim expenses of the judicial procedure.

Article 6 of the Late Payment Act transposed European Directive 2000/35 of 29 June 2000 into Belgian law, at a moment at which no general rule provided for the recoverability of lawyers' fees in the Judicial Code. When the general rule in the Act of 21 April 2007 was introduced, the legislator did not take the opportunity to abolish the *lex specialis* on commercial transactions. Since then, and pending any correction of this situation, judges seem to take the fixed amounts of the expenses of judicial procedure as guidelines for sums awarded under Article 6 of the Act of 2 August 2002.[71]

Cost Shifting: Judicial Expenses

General Rule

According to article 1017 JC, each final judgment specifies the expenses to be paid by the party found to be in error by the judgment (the forfeiting party). In other words, the forfeiting party has to pay or reimburse the specified costs to the winning party. Since referring to the costs is a legal consequence of the basic judgment, the court or tribunal should not give a specific reason for the inclusion of this charge, unless a party has expressly argued this point, in which case the arguments must be answered.[72] The reference to the costs is not based on a liability,[73] but is based on the principles of procedural risk and policy: each party starting legal

[70] *Belgian Official Gazette*, 7 Aug 2002.

[71] An amendment to the Act Project of 7 Dec 2009 (*Parl Doc* 2009–2010, no 2313/001) proposes to abolish article 6. The amended Project has been adopted by the Commission of Justice in Jan 2010.

[72] Supreme Court 11 May 1989, *Arresten van het Hof van Cassatie* 1988–89, 1059; Supreme Court 18 Oct 1985, *Arresten van het Hof van Cassatie* 1985–86, 228; Laenens et al (n 39) 490; D Maes (n 2) 103, no 2.

[73] Supreme Court 15 May 1941, *Pasicrisie* 1941, I, 192; G de Leval, *Eléments de procédure civile* (Ghent, Larcier, 2005) 453.

proceedings bears the risk that his claim or defence will be dismissed.[74] If the Public Prosecutor, acting as principal party in civil matters, is the losing party, the judicial costs and expenses are to be borne by the State.[75]

Two conditions have to be met in order that expenses may be allocated to the forfeiting party: there has to be a *final* judgment and there has to be a *forfeiting* party. A *final* judgment is each judgment in which a court or tribunal depletes its power to decide on a litigated aspect, except the means to appeal against this decision.[76] An intermediate judgment will adjourn the issue of expenses until the final judgment. The *forfeiting* party is the party which has been condemned as against the other party.[77]

There is legal debate on the indictment of the expenses in *summary proceedings*, which only aim to obtain provisional injunctions. The traditional view is that summary proceedings may not cause any harm to the situation of the parties, but this has been challenged during parliamentary debate preceding the Judicial Code,[78] and the position contested by leading scholars and practitioners.[79] The Belgian Supreme Court has ruled that if the claim is dismissed in summary proceedings, the court or tribunal has to condemn the claimant to those expenses.[80] However, a majority of legal scholars continue to argue that the judge has the freedom in summary proceedings over whether or not to charge the expenses to the losing party.[81]

Article 1021 JC deals with the taxation and payment of the expenses and costs. Parties can hand in a detailed specification of their costs, including the expenses of the judicial procedure, in which case the costs are settled in the judgment. If the costs are not settled in the judgment, fully or partly, the decision on the costs is considered to be adjourned.

Exceptions

The general rule of Article 1017 JC is subject to several exceptions.

Specific Rules

The general rule applies unless specific laws state otherwise.[82] There are numerous examples of *leges speciales*, including the following:

[74] B de Temmerman, 'Rechtsvergelijkende variaties op een heikel thema' in F Evers and P Lefranc (eds), *De verhaalbaarheid van de kosten van verdediging: en wat met de toegang tot de rechter?* (Bruges, Die Keure, 2005) 25 and 29.

[75] Supreme Court 11 May 1922, *Pasicrisie* 1922, I, 285.

[76] Art 19, para 1 JC.

[77] Belgian Supreme Court 26 Sept 1983, *Arresten Cassatie* 1983–84, 72; Laenens et al (n 39) 490.

[78] C van Reephingen, *Verslag over de gerechtelijke hervorming*, Belgian Official Gazette, 1964, 393.

[79] D Lindemans, *Het kort geding* (Antwerp, Kluwer, 1985) 144–146; D Maes (n 2) 4, no 7.

[80] Supreme Court 29 Apr 1982, *Arresten Cassatie* 1981–82, 1058; Supreme Court 9 Feb 1984, *Arresten Cassatie* 1983–84, 703.

[81] Art 1017, first para JC.

[82] D Maes, 'Ger. W. art 1017' in *Commentar Gerechtelijk recht* 1997, afl 37, 110–15, nr 23–36.

—The most important *lex specialis* is that of the general rule on tort law,[83] under which a party can be charged to pay the expenses, if these are caused by his wrongful act, even if he is the winning party.[84] The principle is that expenses for redundant acts or useless expenses have to be borne by the party who has accomplished the act, irrespective of whether that party is later followed in his arguments.

—The expenses of proceedings successfully intended to correct a purely material mistake or interpretation of a judgment are always at the charge of the Belgian State.[85]

—When a party renounces a judicial action after it has been initiated, that party will have to pay the judicial expenses.[86]

—An interesting exception applies in the case of divorce as a result of the permanent breakdown of marriage. Article 1285 JC states that the costs are divided between the parties, unless the judge or the parties state otherwise, if the divorce is claimed by both parties together. If only one party claims the divorce as a result of the permanent breakdown of the marriage, the costs have to be borne by the claimant. However, the Constitutional Court has held that this distinction is discriminatory, on the basis that since the legislator considers both ways of divorcing to be faultless, imposing a financial sanction where there is a unilateral request cannot be considered to be correct.[87] More fundamentally, it may be questioned whether the condition of article 1017 JC that there must be a 'losing party' is met in case of faultless divorce.[88]

—As outlined above, new provisions on judicial and extrajudicial mediation were introduced in 2005. The costs of *judicial* mediation (contrary to the costs of *extrajudicial* mediation) are included in the judiciary expenses and costs enumerated in article 1018 JC, and are to be borne by the losing party. However, article 1736 in conjunction with article 1731 JC seem to be considered a *lex specialis* to article 1017 JC. Article 1736 JC on judicial mediation refers to and declares applicable article 1731 JC on extrajudicial mediation, stating that both of the parties have to bear together the costs of the mediation, unless they agreed otherwise. Therefore, the costs of (an unsuccessful) mediation have to be borne exclusively by the forfeiting party if the parties have agreed so. Article 1731 JC states further on that the mediation protocol must clearly state the manner of taxation of the mediator's fees, the rates, and the payment conditions. The rules on legal aid are extended to judicial and extrajudicial mediation.

[83] Art 1382 of the Civil Code.

[84] Supreme Court 14 May 2001, *Pasicrisie* 2001, 852; Supreme Court 24 Apr 1978, *Pasicrisie* 1978, I, 955.

[85] Art 801 JC.

[86] Art 827 JC.

[87] Constitutional Court 21 Oct 2008, *Rechtskundig Weekblad* 2008–09, 1341, note F Swennen and S Eggermont.

[88] See also F Swennen and S Eggermont, 'Kosten en rechtsplegingsvergoeding bij de echtscheiding op grond van onherstelbare ontwrichting op basis van art. 229, § 3, B.W.' (2008–09) *Rechtskundig Weekblad* 1343–1344.

Agreement between the Parties

Parties may enter into a different agreement upon the bearing of the judicial expenses and costs, which will be ratified by the judge.[89] Parties can agree to waive any claim for judicial expenses and costs, to waive any derogation from the basic amount of the expenses of judicial procedure, or that some optional costs are to be borne by the losing party (eg costs of a reminder, moving expenses).

However, article 1017, first para JC has to be read together with article 1023 JC. According to the latter provision, all contractual stipulations requiring that the amount of the claim will increase if the claim should be enforced in a lawsuit, are void. According to the Belgian Supreme Court, this provision is one of public order.[90] Any contractual derogation is hence absolutely void, and this point can be argued at any stage of the law suit and should even be raised *ex officio* by the court or tribunal. The underlying justification is to be found in the preservation of the right of each party to defend itself. The possibility of contractually increasing the amount of compensation would tend to make the defendant waive his right of defence, in order to gain that reward.[91]

Historically, article 1023 JC was inserted in the draft of the Judicial Code, together with a possibility of recovering attorney fees. Although this latter possibility was dropped during the ensuing parliamentary debate, the prohibition of increasing clauses of article 1023 JC was maintained. Accordingly, this provision is often interpreted such that contractual clauses that aim to change the legal rules with regard to judicial expenses *before* a legal proceeding has been initiated are deemed to be absolutely void, but once a legal proceeding has been initiated such a clause is considered valid under article 1017, first paragraph JC. The High Council of Justice has also advised in favour of the possibility of contractually derogating from to the statutory rules.[92]

Proceedings with regard to Social Security Law

A major exception applies to certain judicial proceedings with regard to social security.[93] In those proceedings, irrespective of who is claimant or defendant and irrespective of the result, the judicial expenses and costs (including costs of enforcement) have to be paid by the Belgian State, save for 'vexatious and foolhardy proceedings' (see above). The legislator found it advisable to provide more cost-efficient proceedings than normal for socially secured persons. This rule does not provide an exception to the general rule of article 1382 Civil Code and from the duty of the victim to take all reasonable measures in order to limit his damage.

[89] Art 1017, first para JC.

[90] Supreme Court 7 Apr 1995, *Pasicrisie* 1995, I, 403.

[91] A van Oevelen, 'De ongeldigheid van het beding tot verhoging van de schuldvordering ingeval deze in rechte wordt opgeëist en de toepassing ervan op de invordering van advocatenhonoraria', (case note of Supreme Court 7 Apr 1995), (1995–96) *Rechtskundig Weekblad* 190; E Wymeersch, 'Toetsing van verhogingsbedingen' (1976–77) *Rechtskundig Weekblad* 137–38.

[92] Hoge Raad voor de Justitie, www.hrj.be, 24.

[93] Art 1017, second para JC.

If a person receiving social security causes expenses for redundant acts, he can be condemned to pay damages, in the form of having to bear the judicial expenses and costs. Such condemnations are rare however.

Apportionment of the Costs (*omslaan van de kosten/répartition des coûts*)

A judge can, even *ex officio*, apportion (*divide*) judicial expenses and costs in two situations: if both parties are to be considered as 'partly losing parties', or if the parties are spouses, family members in the ascending line, brothers or sisters or family members in the same degree.[94] In the latter case, the apportionment of the costs is optional, not obligatory.[95]

Plurality of Parties

Where there are several losing parties, article 1020 JC states that the costs are legally divided 'per head', unless the judgment indicates otherwise. If the main judgment leads to several liability (*hoofdelijkheid/solidarité*), the parties will also be severally liable to bear the costs.

Where there are several winning parties and one losing party, the amount of expenses of the judicial procedure is limited. The total amount is twice the maximum amount that can be claimed by the winning party with the highest claim. The judge divides the final amount between the winning parties. An example can illustrate this rule. Party X is a losing party towards three winning parties A, B and C. Each of them has been assisted by a lawyer. A can claim the basic amount of €900 (the maximum amount would have been €2,000); B and C both can claim the basic amount of €2,000 (maximum amount: €4,000). The limit is the double of the maximum amount of the highest expenses of judicial procedure (€4,000), thus €8,000. This limit is not exceeded. The total amount of expenses of judicial procedure is €4,900 (900 + 2000 + 2000). If this limit would otherwise have been exceeded, the three expenses of judicial procedure would be proportionally reduced.

Where there are several successful parties, different parties with the same interest who are represented by the same attorney have to divide the judicial proceeding expenses amongst them.[96]

[94] Art 1017, third para JC.

[95] Supreme Court 17 Mar 1966, *Pasicrisie* 1966, I, 920.

[96] This was governed by the Royal Decree of 30 Sept 1975.

Appeal Proceedings

It is possible to appeal against the award of expenses. However, this possibility is only open to parties that have the right to appeal against the substance of the litigated object itself.[97] The general rule of article 1017 JC applies in relation to both the costs at first instance and of the appeal. If a first instance judgment is amended or annulled on appeal, the party who is in the wrong will be charged with the judicial expenses of both instances. If a first instance judgment is confirmed on appeal, the appellant will be charged with the judicial expenses of the appeal.[98]

Supreme Court

Special rules apply to proceedings before the Belgian Supreme Court.[99] The Supreme Court settles in its judgment the judicial expenses and costs, and states the party to which the costs have to be compensated. If the Supreme Court dismisses the claimant, he will be obliged to pay the expenses. If the Supreme Court reverses the decision of an appeal court, it will normally not take a final decision itself, but refer the case to another appeal court, in which case the expenses are adjourned until this latter court has rendered its final judgment. However, the Supreme Court can decide to settle the costs if it partly reverses the decision, or if the circumstances of the case justify it. The Supreme Court has confirmed that the new rules with regard to shifting of lawyers' fees do not apply to its proceedings.[100]

Unilateral Proceedings

It is generally acknowledged that no expenses can be transferred in case of *unilateral proceedings*. The claimant always has to pay his own expenses, irrespective of the outcome of the proceedings.[101]

[97] J Kerkhofs, 'Uitgaven en kosten' in G van Mellaert (ed), *Praktijkboek gerechtelijk recht* (Bruges, Vanden Broele) 15; J Laenens, 'Appellabiliteit van een vonnis over de kosten' (1981–82) *Rechtskundig Weekblad* 1683; D Maes (n 2) 6, no 10.

[98] Laenens et al (n 39) 490; D Maes (n 2) 6, no 11.

[99] Art 1111 JC.

[100] Supreme Court 27 Jun 2008, *Rechtskundig Weekblad* 2008–2009, 45.

[101] *cf* Court of Appeal Brussels 9 June 2008, *Rechtskundig weekblad* 2008–2009, 872, note B Allemeersch; Tribunal of First Instance Brussels 19 Jan 2009, *Journal des Tribunaux* 2009, 217, note. Opposed to this opinion: Court of Appeal Liège 29 Apr 2008, *Journal des Tribunaux* 2008, afl 6313, 366, note H Boularbah; J Kerkhofs (n 39) 18.

Arbitration

The rules of articles 1017–1024 JC, in particular the new Act of 21 April 2007 on recoverability of lawyer's fees, do not apply to arbitration proceedings.[102] Arbitration costs are the arbiters' fees, the costs of the arbitral institution, the lawyer's fees. According to pre-2007 Belgian law, a distinction is made between international and national arbitrations. In international arbitrations, lawyers' fees were considered to be recoverable towards the losing party. In national arbitrations however, lawyers' fees were considered not to be recoverable, due to the traditional view in Belgian law. An arbitrator decided upon the expenses in the light of the arbitration agreement that had been entered into between parties. However, public order prohibited contractual clauses on recoverability of lawyers' fees. The question rises whether the 2007 reforms, described above, have brought any change in arbitration costs.

[102] O Caprasse and F Henry, 'Répétibilité des frais de conseils dans l'arbitrage national et international' (2008) *Journal des Tribunaux* 561–86.

4

Canada

ERIK S KNUTSEN* AND JANET WALKER**

Introduction: What is the Cost of Litigating in Canada?

In Canada,[1] as in most countries with an adversary system, the primary cost of litigating comes from the expense of obtaining legal advice and representation and, where necessary, expert evidence[2] and other disbursements.[3] Together, legal fees and disbursements comprise the 'costs' of litigating in the Canadian legal system. The courthouses, the court staff and the adjudicators are publicly funded, and the filing fees are modest.[4]

In Canada, the costs of litigation are usually borne in the first instance by the parties, but they are subject to redistribution by the court at the end of the litigation through costs awards. The expense of litigating disputes is such that the economic framework for the costs system has a significant impact on the decisions of potential litigants about whether to sue and how to frame the litigation. The economic framework also has a significant impact on the decisions that litigants make once they have become engaged in the process. It affects their decisions about whether and when to settle and, if they do not, how they prepare for trial and how they conduct themselves at trial.

* Assistant Professor, Faculty of Law, Queen's University, Kingston, Ontario, Canada (LLM, Harvard), of the Ontario Bar.

** Professor, Osgoode Hall Law School, York University, Toronto, Ontario, Canada (DPhil, Oxon), of the Ontario Bar.

[1] Most of the references in this paper are made to Ontario statutes and rules, which are generally representative of the statutes and rules in other provinces. Differences in the practices in other parts of Canada are indicated where applicable.

[2] In most cases, experts are retained by the parties. While some courts in Canada are authorized to appoint their own experts, this is rarely done because under the principle of party prosecution, the parties have carriage of the matter and the court is not in a good position to anticipate in detail the issues that will be raised and the kind of evidence that will be needed. Concern that this approach has hindered the impartiality of experts and increased the expense has given rise to changes in the procedure in a number of courts in Canada, including the Federal Court: www.gazette.gc.ca/rp-pr/p1/2009/2009-10-17/html/reg1-eng.html, and Ontario's new Rule 4.1, outlining the duty of an expert.

[3] These would include not only the expenses of expert witnesses, but also of fact witnesses presented by the party, together with the myriad administrative expenses of managing the file and the filing fees which, in the aggregate, can be significant.

[4] And there is no practice of informal payments to officials for the processing of claims or defences.

This economic framework or 'costs system' consists of three main aspects: first, the way in which legal fees are calculated and charged; second, the way in which legal fees and disbursements are financed through the course of the litigation; and, third, the way in which costs are ultimately allocated between the parties through costs awards, or 'fee-shifting'. This chapter considers each of these aspects of the Canadian costs system and assesses the incentives and deterrents created by current features of the system as a means of calibrating access to justice and encouraging a sound approach to the conduct of litigation once commenced.

Before embarking on the analysis, however, it is important to mention one significant contextual factor. A large portion of the matters in which individuals might otherwise have sought compensation for loss through litigation in Canada are dealt with through administrative schemes. For example, regulatory regimes have been established for claims in respect of workplace health and safety complaints, employment matters, and some traffic accidents in which individuals might wish to bring claims for compensation. These regimes are generally beyond the scope of the discussion here. However, it is worth bearing in mind that the social implications of litigation funding and costs in Canada relate primarily to litigious matters in areas other than those covered by administrative regimes.

How Are Legal Fees Calculated and Charged?

The financial dealings between lawyer and client are governed by a contractual relationship called a 'retainer'. The term 'retainer' is used to describe three things: the general arrangements for legal services between lawyer and client; the actual contract for legal services, if one is concluded; and a deposit for legal fees and disbursements that may be requested and held in trust by the lawyer, if this is part of the arrangement.

The client is initially and ultimately responsible for the costs of the litigation. In the adversary system in Canada, this appears to be an important means of ensuring that the matter is conducted in accordance with the principle of party prosecution. Accordingly, any adverse impacts that this might have on access to justice or on the manner in which litigation is conducted have not served to draw this basic approach into question. Rather, various mechanisms that are discussed below, such as fee-shifting, have been developed to ameliorate the adverse impacts of the basic responsibility of the parties for the expenses of litigating.

In many cases, when a client chooses a lawyer and he or she enters into a retainer relationship, this relationship does not involve a formal written agreement. By requesting and receiving legal services, the client impliedly agrees to pay for them and the lawyer agrees to charge only a reasonable fee. On the one hand, even in the absence of a written retainer, a lawyer's fee is secured, in part, by the operation of the solicitor's lien on the file. A lien could impede a client's ability to transfer the matter to another lawyer without first resolving any outstanding issues over fees owing to the lawyer. The lawyer's fee is also secured by the ability of the lawyer to seek an order for payment following a formal assessment or 'taxation' of the account. It is rare for either of these means of securing or obtaining payment to be invoked. On the other hand, the client is protected from being overcharged by the lawyer even in the absence of a written retainer by the rules of professional conduct. These rules require the lawyer to ensure that the nature of the economic relationship with the client is fair and reasonable.[5]

In situations where there is a written agreement setting out the terms of the retainer, it is relatively uncommon for it to specify in any detail the actual amount that a client will ultimately pay his or her lawyer for legal services in respect of the matter for which the lawyer has been retained. In part, this is because it is often not entirely clear at the outset of a matter precisely what the lawyer will do for the client in the course of the matter. In Canada, where lawyers are permitted to practice both as barristers and solicitors, they may be retained to serve a client in a variety of capacities in respect of a particular matter—giving advice, representing the client at a mediation or negotiation, and appearing on behalf of the client in court. As a result, a retainer agreement will often specify the nature of the matter for which legal services are to be provided, but it will speak in more general terms about the nature of the advice and representation to be provided and about the financial aspects of the retainer. Retainer agreements will often specify only the lawyer's hourly rate and the client's promise to pay.

Whether or not there is a written retainer, lawyers are often reluctant to provide written estimates at the outset as to the total fees likely to be payable for their services. However, they may give their clients verbal estimates, based on the anticipated course of the litigation and its degree of complexity. This is not necessarily a disadvantage to the client. If a lawyer were to charge fixed rates in matters where it was not clear what services might need to be provided, this could create an incentive for the lawyer to dispose of the matter in the least labour-intensive way regardless of whether this was in the best interests of the client.

Where the retainer agreement does cover the subject of the lawyer's remuneration, it may provide for the fees to be payable through periodic billings or at specified points in the litigation. Often, clients will be billed monthly. Alternatively, where the lawyer is retained on a contingency fee basis, under which the lawyer may take as a fee a percentage of the final proceeds in the matter (as is discussed further below), the retainer agreement may provide for the client to be billed for services only at the end of the matter. The agreement will also explain whether or not the client is responsible for paying disbursements when they are paid by the lawyer during the course of the litigation, or only when the matter has been concluded. Disbursements include the out-of-pocket expenses the lawyer pays on the client's behalf, such as fees for experts and other witnesses, photocopying, postage, and court fees.

[5] Ontario Rules of Professional Conduct, available at www.lsuc.on.ca/regulation/, Rules 2 and 3 (rules respecting reasonableness of fees).

The retainer agreement may also require the client to pay a deposit, also referred to as a 'retainer', to be held by the lawyer in trust, and used to fund the disbursements and fees as services are rendered. In some cases, where a retainer is taken, the agreement may provide for the periodic replenishment of the retainer as the matter progresses and as the legal fees are earned and the other expenses are incurred.

A high proportion of litigation is conducted without formal written retainers or with written retainers that specify only an hourly rate or a contingency fee formula. However, complex matters involving litigation over large sums between sophisticated parties may proceed on a very different footing. In those cases, the parties may seek bids from several firms for their 'litigation business.' These proposals may relate to individual matters, or to all that party's matters on an ongoing basis or for a fixed period of time. These requests for tender or 'beauty pageants' can involve highly detailed specifications for the full range of legal services, including the staffing of files, the rates to be charged, the principles governing charges for disbursements, the obligation to obtain instructions for steps to be taken, and when and how invoices will be rendered. Although interesting issues arise for the profession in this context, many aspects of these dealings are driven by and responsive to market conditions. Accordingly, the costs of litigation between sophisticated parties in large matters will not be the primary focus of this discussion.

A lawyer's hourly fee varies, depending upon the lawyer's experience and geographical market. For example, a lawyer's hourly fee in a smaller, rural setting could be $125 an hour. In a larger urban setting, an experienced lawyer at a large firm could charge between $300 to $900 or more per hour. Where a large firm is involved and the hourly fees among lawyers vary greatly, there will exist formal or informal practices and policies for the staffing of files to ensure that the work is done efficiently and the client is billed appropriately.

In all lawyer-client relationships, including those involving institutional clients and individual clients, and those with written retainers and without them, as a matter of law, a Canadian lawyer's fees must be 'fair and reasonable.'[6] Provincial rules of professional conduct such as Ontario's Rules of Professional Conduct[7] list the factors that are used to determine whether a fee is 'fair and reasonable':

(a) the time and effort required and spent,
(b) the difficulty and importance of the matter,
(c) whether special skill or service has been required and provided,
(d) the amount involved or the value of the subject-matter,
(e) the results obtained,
(f) fees authorised by statute or regulation,
(g) special circumstances, such as the loss of other retainers, postponement of payment, uncertainty of reward, or urgency.

[6] *Boucher v Public Accountants Council (Ontario)* (2004), 71 OR (3d) 291 (Ont CA) ('*Boucher*').
[7] Ontario Rules of Professional Conduct (n 5) Rule 2.08.

If either a client or a lawyer has a dispute regarding payment of the fee, the courts can review the arrangement through a process called an assessment (or 'taxation' in some Canadian jurisdictions). A court assessment officer examines the lawyer's account and determines if the fee is 'fair and reasonable.' The assessment officer's findings are enforceable as a judgment of the court, and the lawyer and client may rely on it as such. Typical criteria for assessing a lawyer's bill, like those found in Ontario's Rules of Civil Procedure,[8] include the following factors, which closely parallel those found in the rules of professional conduct:

(a) the amount involved in the proceeding;
(b) the complexity of the proceeding;
(c) the importance of the issues;
(d) the duration of the hearing;
(e) the conduct of any party that tended to shorten or to lengthen unnecessarily the duration of the proceeding;
(f) whether any step in the proceeding was,
   (i) improper, vexatious or unnecessary, or
   (ii) taken through negligence, mistake or excessive caution;
(g) a party's denial of or refusal to admit anything that should have been admitted; and
(h) any other matter relevant to the assessment of costs.

The assessment process is not frequently used either by clients or by lawyers in resolving disputes over fees. In fact, it is even less likely to be used by litigants who have large claims or who are large corporate clients.[9]

Despite the relatively infrequent occurrence of formal disputes over billings, some have criticised the legal profession's practice of billing on an hourly basis as inefficient and unfair because it creates an incentive for work that is not tied to results but instead to the time the lawyer spends on the case.[10] This may be of particular concern in a legal community that has only recently relaxed the historical restrictions on advertising and competition, and in which the practice of openly soliciting clients is far from the norm. Under such circumstances, restraint in the legal work performed and billed depends primarily upon the lawyer's desire to maintain a good relationship with the client, and to comply with the lawyer's professional obligations.

[8] Ontario Rules of Civil Procedure, R.R.O. 1990, Reg 194 ('Ontario Rules of Civil Procedure') Rule 58.06(1).

[9] HM Kritzer, 'Fee Arrangements and Fee Shifting: Lessons from the Experience in Ontario' (1984) 47 *Law and Contemp Probs* 125, 126 (noting that the nature of the relationship between large corporations and lawyers is not affected by the taxation process; also noting that taxation is often for the 'little guy').

[10] A Woolley, 'Time for Change: Unethical Hourly Billing in the Canadian Profession and What Should be Done about It' (2004) 83 *Can Bar Rev* 859 (Canadian law firms are just as affected as American law firms by the temptations to practice unethical and over-inflated billing due to the unique nature of hourly billing).

How is the Litigation Financed?

Direct Client Billing

The traditional method for financing most Canadian litigation is to bill the client directly on the basis of an hourly rate multiplied by the number of hours spent on the client's matter. This is still the norm in business litigation, as well as most defence litigation for institutional defendants, such as insurance companies or banks. In other words, clients pay for increments of a lawyer's time, and they are billed periodically, often monthly, for the lawyers' time plus any disbursements expended on the client's behalf.

Large institutional clients who are often defendants (for example railways and banks) sometimes contract with large law firms for a negotiated bulk hourly rate or a block rate for a certain set of hours of legal work. In this fashion, institutional clients expecting to have regular litigation work benefit from being repeat players with a particular law firm. These institutional clients negotiate preferential or block rates of the law firm's hourly time in exchange for exclusive guaranteed legal work from the institution.

Alternatives to Litigation for Individuals

The expense of ordinary litigation is such that few persons other than large institutional clients can afford to finance it on a current basis by paying a lawyer's regular billings as the case proceeds. This has given rise to a range of responses. Some of these responses have altered the way in which some claims are resolved so as to remove them from the ordinary litigation process.

For example, one response to the widespread crisis of access to justice for individual claimants that would inevitably result from the high cost of litigation has been the establishment of specialised administrative procedures for compensation for harm. The federal and provincial governments in Canada have created administrative regimes for claims relating to employment matters, workplace injuries and some motor vehicle accidents.[11] In some of these regimes the right to sue is abrogated entirely. In others, the right to sue is restricted to claims above a specified level of harm or quantum of damages.

[11] For example, a number of Canadian provinces, such as Manitoba, Saskatchewan, and Quebec, have no-fault automobile insurance regimes, where the right to sue in tort for automobile accident-related injuries is eliminated altogether in exchange for first-party insurance benefits from the driver's own insurance company. Ontario operates a hybrid tort—no-fault auto insurance system where access to the tort system for auto accident-related injuries is reserved for very serious cases. The inability to sue in tort for auto-related injuries in some Canadian provinces has shifted the civil litigation landscape with respect to automobile accidents and the necessity of lawyers in the process. Claims in those jurisdictions are focused more on issues between the injured victim and his or her insurance company.

In addition, although there is no meaningful 'litigation insurance' market in Canada for the costs of bringing a lawsuit, most private law tort and insurance lawsuits in Canada are actually brought by liability insurance companies. These suits are brought in the names of insured parties on a subrogated basis by the insurers.[12] Tort and insurance litigation makes up a large component of civil litigation in Canada.

Further, most liability insurance policies in Canada provide for the funding of the cost of a defence in the event the insured is sued.[13] In addition, these insurance contracts usually stipulate that the insurer will choose and instruct the lawyer in defending the insured. Insurers generally negotiate preferential rates with particular law firms because of the high volume of defence-side legal work created in the liability insurance industry. Unlike their policyholders, insurers are able to pay for defence litigation work on an hourly basis through regular payments during the course of the litigation.

Specialised Forms of Litigation for Smaller Claims

It has long been clear that the litigation of smaller claims is not economically viable in the ordinary courts. As a result, 'Small Claims Courts' exist in Canada for cases whose claims fall under specified amounts, usually ranging from $10–25,000. These courts have simplified procedures that were designed to enable parties to appear without legal representatives. In theory, therefore, under these circumstances, there would be no need for litigants to incur expenses for legal fees. Although the procedures have become somewhat more detailed over the years, and parties are sometimes represented by legal counsel, the costs awards that are now available cannot ordinarily exceed 15 per cent of the amount claimed, or the value of the property sought to be recovered.

For slightly larger cases, simplified procedures have been developed to limit the steps that may be taken before the matter comes to trial and to limit the length of the trial.[14]

The aggregation of economically non-viable claims in class actions is a further well-established means of enhancing access to justice in Canada. All class action legal fees are subject to the approval of the court, in the best interests of the class members.[15] There are many challenging issues currently being addressed in connection with the funding of class actions, such as third party financing, and in

[12] Canadian insurance policies provide that the insurance company has the right to sue the wrongdoer in the insured's name, to recoup the company's losses. The injured insured person is paid directly by his or her insurer, which then sues the alleged wrongdoer to recoup its losses from the one at fault: G Hilliker, *Liability Insurance Law in Canada*, 4th edn (Canada, LexisNexis Canada, 2006).

[13] Physician's liability insurance is provided by the Canadian Medical Protective Association, which represents and defends Canadian physicians.

[14] Ontario Rules of Civil Procedure (n 8) Rule 76—Simplified Procedure, which, as of 2010, applies to cases up to $100,000.

[15] Class Proceedings Act, SO 1992, c 6; *Western Canadian Shopping Centres v Dutton*, [2001] 2 SCR 534.

connection with costs, such as whether fee-shifting is appropriate. However, these are beyond the scope of this chapter.

Contingency Fees

Where the claims of individuals are not covered by insurance or an administrative regime and are above the monetary limit for small claims courts or special procedures, it has been necessary for the legal system in Canada to respond in other ways to enable parties to finance the litigation.

One such response has been for lawyers themselves to provide financing for the litigation through deferred payment schemes. Until recently, Ontario's laws proscribing champerty and maintenance precluded lawyers from entering into formal contingency fee arrangements. However, the need for legal services for persons who were unable to finance them on a current basis, particularly in personal injury cases, led to an informal practice of deferring the billings in such cases until after the matters were concluded, with the understanding that no fee would be charged unless the party was successful in obtaining an award. It was prohibited by the Solicitor's Act to charge a premium for success, and a retainer that purported to provide for this would be unenforceable. However, there was nothing to prohibit a lawyer from providing legal services for free, and so the practice emerged in such cases of charging a fee only in the event of success.

Every jurisdiction in Canada now permits lawyers, either by statute, regulation, case law, or as a matter of practice, to be paid by a contingency fee.[16] A contingency fee arrangement is an agreement between the lawyer and client whereby the lawyer's fee is tied to the success of the client's matter. With these recent changes in the law, if the client is successful in the litigation, the lawyer may take a fee either on the basis of an hourly rate with a risk-premium or in the form of a percentage of the proceeds of the litigation. This percentage is typically between one-fifth and one-third of the client's net proceeds of the litigation. Although there was initial resistance to the assessment of fees on the basis of a percentage of the award, in most cases, the method of calculation has not proved to be significant in affecting the reasonableness of the fees sought.

Factors that may affect the agreed fee proportion include: the expense and risk that will be undertaken by the lawyer; the complexity and type of matter; the likelihood of success; and the amount the client and lawyer expect to recover. Clients generally do not shop around among lawyers for preferable contingent fee rates.

Costs awards in cases in which a party has a contingency fee arrangement are provided for in the Solicitors Act, as follows:

> 20.1(1) In calculating the amount of costs for the purposes of making an award of costs, a court shall not reduce the amount of costs only because the client's solicitor is being compensated in accordance with a contingency fee agreement.

[16] Ontario's Rules of Professional Conduct (n 5) Rule 2.08 and Ontario's Solicitor's Act, RSO 1990, c S-15, as amended by SO 2002, c 24, Sch A.

(2) Despite subsection 20 (2), even if an order for the payment of costs is more than the amount payable by the client to the client's own solicitor under a contingency fee agreement, a client may recover the full amount under an order for the payment of costs if the client is to use the payment of costs to pay his, her or its solicitor.

(3) If the client recovers the full amount under an order for the payment of costs under subsection (2), the client is only required to pay costs to his, her or its solicitor and not the amount payable under the contingency fee agreement, unless the contingency fee agreement is one that has been approved by a court under subsection 28.1 (8) and provides otherwise.

Contingency fees have increased access to justice for clients who are unable, or unwilling, to pay for a lawyer on an hourly basis.[17] It has been argued that permitting lawyers to provide legal services on a contingency fee basis with a fee based on a percentage of the result would address the potential for hourly rates to provide an incentive to inefficient or ineffective legal services. By aligning the lawyer's interests with the client's interest in an expeditious resolution of the matter with the maximum recovery, the introduction of contingency fees was heralded as improving access to justice and the quality of legal services. While there is no doubt that contingency fees have become a regular feature of personal injury litigation, there do not appear to have been any studies confirming a salutary effect on previous inefficiencies or ineffectiveness in the legal services provided.

One aspect of contingency fees that has recently been at issue is the practice of Ontario courts ordering a risk 'premium' as part of a successful plaintiff's costs award when the plaintiff's lawyer took the case on a contingency fee basis.[18] The concept of a risk premium was introduced to encourage lawyers to risk their time and money on behalf of indigent clients by taking on meritorious cases that have a high risk element. The risk premium was designed as a sort of bonus, on top of the usual costs award, to reward a lawyer for gambling his or her time and money for the good of the client's interests.

Risk premiums became something of a feature in successful Ontario contingency fee cases until the Supreme Court of Canada sought to limit the practice in 2006.[19] The Supreme Court held that risk of non-payment was not an enumerated factor in the costs analysis applicable in Ontario's costs rule,[20] and as a result courts could not award a 'bonus' to plaintiffs' counsel. In addition, the Court held that the fee arrangement was a matter between the plaintiff and her counsel, and a defendant could not reliably predict the costs exposure if premiums were to exist in the costs regime. Curiously, the Court rejected access to justice as a justification for risk premiums, which encourage plaintiffs' counsel to take on meritorious, risky cases. Instead, the Court suggested that a litigant could find counsel willing to take the case *pro bono*, a litigant could use publicly funded legal aid, or a litigant

[17] *McIntyre Estate v Ontario (Attorney General)* (2002) 61 OR (3d) 257 (CA).
[18] *Desmoulin v Blair* (1994) 21 OR (3d) 217 (CA).
[19] *Walker v Ritchie* [2006] 2 SCR 428.
[20] Rule 57.01.

could apply to a court for interim cost funding for public interest cases. The Court of Appeal for Ontario has since accepted this precedent[21] and reversed a risk premium originally granted at trial, again citing the inability of the current costs rules to accommodate costs premiums and bonuses based on risk.

Despite these rulings, courts continue to award a kind of risk premium to lawyers who take on meritorious, risky cases. They do so by reference to the enumerated factors for discretionary costs awards contained in the rules. In one 2008 decision,[22] the Court of Appeal for Ontario reversed a $350,000 risk premium awarded at trial as a reward for a lawyer undertaking the risk of non-payment but increased the free-shifted costs award by $50,000. It did so on the basis of enumerated factors in the rules, namely that the case was complex and lengthy, the issues were important, and the result achieved was outstanding. In another case,[23] while acknowledging that risk premiums had been formally eliminated, the trial judge nevertheless awarded a $50,000 'cost premium' because the case was complex and important. These results suggest that the courts are persuaded of the value of providing financial incentives to counsel to take on meritorious but risky cases.

Despite the similarities with personal injury litigation in the United States that the introduction of contingency fees might have appeared likely to produce, there remain marked differences. Plaintiff personal injury litigation is far less lucrative for lawyers in Canada than in the United States. As a result, despite the existence of contingency fees, the Canadian personal injury bar is not as large, as entrepreneurial, or as well-compensated as its American counterpart.[24] Personal injury litigation is not 'big business' because the recoveries are smaller. Universal health coverage in Canada tends to keep the extent and urgency of tort recovery small in comparison with that in the United States. Furthermore, the practice of fee-shifting makes it unnecessary to take into account legal fees when determining the quantum of compensatory awards. Finally, most civil cases are litigated without a jury and by a judge alone, and punitive and exemplary damages awards are uncommon and small by comparison with those granted in the United States.

Pro Bono Legal Services

In addition to deferring payment for legal services, the profession in Canada has played a role in the financing of legal services through a strong tradition of pro-

[21] *Ward v Manufacturers Life Insurance Co*, [2007] ONCA 881 (CA).

[22] *Sandhu v Wellington Place Apartments* [2008] ONCA 215 (CA).

[23] *Berendsen v Ontario* [2008] CarswellOnt 4142 (SCJ).

[24] For example, non-pecuniary damages ('pain and suffering') are capped by law at a maximum of $321,000 for the worst kinds of injury imaginable, or $100,000 in 1978 dollars for a 21 year old quadriplegic: *Andrews v Grand & Toy* [1978] 2 SCR 229. Punitive damages are exceedingly rare, reserved for only malicious and high-handed conduct: *Whiten v Pilot Insurance* [2002] 1 SCR 595; and *McIntyre v Griegg* (2006) 83 OR (3d) 161 (CA).

viding litigation advice and representation on a *pro bono* basis. Many lawyers and law firms regularly take cases for indigent clients and for clients whose matters have a strong social justice component. These clients pay no fees for the legal services they receive. This *pro bono* work is seen as part of the professional duty of a Canadian lawyer to promote access to justice. It is not mandatory and is up to the individual lawyer whether or not to take a case on a *pro bono* basis. However, many large firms have established substantial *pro bono* programmes.

Even *pro bono* work is subject to Canada's fee shifting scheme, which is discussed below. If a lawyer acting *pro bono* for a client is successful on a client's behalf, that client remains eligible under the fee-shifting scheme to recover from the losing party the legal costs that would have been payable had the client been paying for the legal services.[25]

Third-Party Financing

Third-party financing of civil litigation, other than for class proceedings, is relatively new in Canada.[26] Since 2004, two or three firms have been making loans to plaintiffs on the basis of pending awards. Generally, these firms charge interest on the loans and they do not take a portion of the award because of the concerns of champerty and maintenance. They rely upon an assignment of the proceeds to secure the loan and, in some cases, they operate on the basis that "nothing is owed if the case is lost".[27]

Public Financing

Beyond providing the courthouses, the court staff and the judges,[28] the governments in Canada contribute relatively little to the funding of civil litigation. The provinces in Canada each have schemes called 'legal aid', which provide public funding for legal assistance for those who cannot afford a lawyer. However, this once robust institution has been subject to cutbacks for such a long time that the assistance is now almost entirely directed to criminal defence work. Only those who are truly indigent are eligible to receive it for civil matters, and only in a small

[25] *1465778 Ontario Inc v 1122077 Ontario Ltd.* (2006) 82 OR (3d) 757 (CA) (successful *pro bono* counsel are entitled to fee-shifted costs) ('*1465778 Ontario Inc*').

[26] P Puri, 'Financing Litigation by Third Party Investors: A Share of Justice' (1998) 36 *Osgoode Hall LJ* 515 (arguing that, in the interests of access to justice, the Canadian legal market should allow greater participation of third party investor financing in litigation).

[27] A Ceballos, 'Third party litigation funding: will it increase access to justice in Canada?' *The Lawyer's Weekly* (Ottawa/Toronto, 7 Mar 2008).

[28] CM Hanycz, 'More Access to Less Justice: Efficiency, Proportionality and Costs in Canadian Civil Justice Reform' (2008) 27 *Civil Justice Quarterly* 98, 108 (noting the contributions of the state to the administrative costs of the public justice system in Canada).

range of cases.[29] In addition, for those who do qualify for legal aid, it is necessary to find a lawyer who is willing to provide services for the modest rates that are paid.[30]

In most provinces in major centres there are, however, legal aid clinics, that are specialised government-funded law centres where those with modest economic means can go for legal assistance. The centres are staffed with salaried lawyers as employees, and in some cases, with law students who assist the lawyers for a period of time as part of their course of study. The focus of these centres is on poverty law issues (immigration, landlord and tenant issues, family matters, and elder law). Only lower-income persons are eligible to receive legal advice and assistance.

In principle, there also exists a method by which a court may order interim funding of public interest cases from government funding sources, but the eligibility requirements are very restrictive.[31] To date, only a handful of cases have met the strict test for interim funding of litigation, which provides that it is to be made available only in 'rare and exceptional circumstances':

1. the litigant must be genuinely not able to afford to pay and have no other option for payment of interim litigation expenses;
2. the claim must be meritorious, such that it is against the interests of justice to preclude it from being heard; and,
3. the issues in the case must transcend the individual litigant and be of public importance and not previously decided by another court.[32]

Most of these cases have been in the area of aboriginal law. Thus, the test is of little practical assistance to the broader range of cases that are sought to be litigated.

[29] Parties generally have to demonstrate that they are incapable of funding any aspect of the litigation. This typically requires that the potential applicant for legal aid be qualified as having severe economic limitations. For more on Canada's publicly funded legal aid system, *see* Report of the Ontario Legal Aid Review, 'A Blueprint for Publicly Funded Legal Services' (Toronto, Queen's Printer, 1997); F Zemans and P Monahan, 'From Crisis to Reform: A New Legal Aid Plan for Ontario' (Toronto, Osgoode Hall Law School, 1996); M Trebilcock, 'Report of the Legal Aid Review' (Toronto, Ontario Ministry of Attorney General, 2008) ('Trebilcock'); and M Fenrick, 'Habermas, Legal Legitimacy, and Creative Cost Awards in Recent Canadian Jurisprudence' (2007) 30 *Dalhousie LJ* 165, 168 (reliance on either *pro bono* counsel or legal aid funding as a method of funding for Canadian legal services is less than optimal).

[30] Trebilcock (n 29) noting that the rates paid by the legal aid programme are often far lower than the lowest market rates for the legal service.

[31] *British Columbia (Minister of Forests) v Okanagan Indian Band* [2003] 3 SCR 371 and *Little Sisters Book & Art Emporium v Canada (Commissioner of Customs & Revenue)* [2007] 1 SCR 38 (interim costs not awarded in case where bookstore challenged customs seizure of gay and lesbian material). A number of commentators have noted that the substantive law test to meet for interim funding of public interest cases is too difficult and impedes the evolution of public interest law: C Tollefson, 'Costs and the Public Interest Litigant: Okanagan Indian Band and Beyond' (2006) 19 *Can J Admin L & Prac* 39; L Friedlander, 'Costs and the Public Interest Litigant' (1995) 40 *McGill LJ* 55; B McLaughlin, C Tobias and C Cameron, 'Interim Costs: The Impact of Okanagan Indian Band' (2005) 54 *UNBLJ* 126; C Tollefson, D Gilliland and J DeMarco, 'Towards a Costs Jurisprudence in Public Interest Litigation' (2004) 83 *Can Bar Rev* 473; F Bhabha, 'Institutionalizing Access-to-Justice: Judicial, Legislative and Grassroots Dimensions' (2007) 33 *Queen's LJ* 139; and C Tollefson, 'When the "Public Interest" Loses: The Liability of Public Interest Litigants for Adverse Costs Awards' (1995) 29 *UBCL Rev* 303.

[32] ibid.

Who Funds the Litigation?

Fee Shifting in Canada

Despite the various ways in which legal fees and disbursements may be financed through the course of the litigation, in most cases, a large part of the costs of litigating are ultimately ordered to be paid by the unsuccessful party through a 'costs award.' Accordingly, in general, in addition to any award in damages, the unsuccessful party will pay a portion of the successful party's legal fees and disbursements. This is called 'fee shifting.'

In an environment in which the expense of litigating is otherwise often prohibitive, the chance of recovering one's own costs or being required to pay the opposing party's costs can have a significant influence on the decision to commence litigation or to continue it. As a result, the fee shifting regime has given rise to a large body of law regarding the amount of costs that should be recovered in litigation and the process through which such orders should be made. In addition, considerable commentary has been devoted to the way in which costs awards can facilitate access to justice, discourage frivolous litigation and encourage the parties to conduct the litigation in a way that will 'secure the just, most expeditious and least expensive determination of . . . (the) proceeding on its merits.'[33]

The underlying reasoning for fee shifting is to compensate a successful party in civil litigation for some of the expense incurred in exercising a legal right.[34] Had the unsuccessful defendant satisfied the plaintiff's claim rather than resisting it, the plaintiff would have been spared the expense of litigating, and should be indemnified for this expense. Similarly, had the unsuccessful plaintiff not brought the claim, the defendant would have been spared the expense of defending against it, and should be indemnified for this expense.

Costs are included in the prayer for relief in the parties' pleadings and they are akin to a damage award consistent with the principle that it is the losing party's fault that the successful party was put to the cost of hiring a lawyer and prosecuting or defending the claim. As the Court of Appeal for Ontario explained in a 2006 decision:[35]

> 'Traditionally the purpose of an award of costs within our 'loser pay' system was to partially or, in some limited circumstances, wholly indemnify the winning party for the legal costs it incurred. However, costs have more recently come to be recognized as an important tool in the hands of the court to influence the way the parties conduct themselves and to prevent abuse of the court's process. Specifically, the three other recognized

[33] Ontario Rules of Civil Procedure (n 8) Rule 1.04.

[34] J Robert and S Prichard, 'A Systematic Approach to Comparative Law: The Effect of Cost, Fee, and Financing Rules on the Development of the Substantive Law' (1988) 17 *J Legal Studies* 451, 456 and MM Orkin, *The Law of Costs*, 4th edn (looseleaf), s 1 ('Orkin').

[35] *1465778 Ontario Inc* (n 25).

purposes of costs awards are to encourage settlement, to deter frivolous actions and defences, and to discourage unnecessary steps that unduly prolong the litigation.'

The Court also mentioned a fifth purpose: access to justice.

Judicial Discretion

Costs awards are assessed either by the judge or by an officer of the court appointed for that purpose, either at the end of a step in the proceeding, or at the end of the hearing of the matter, or in a separate hearing for that purpose. The courts have considerable discretion in making a costs award. As the Courts of Justice Act in Ontario provides:

> 'Subject to the provisions of an Act or rules of court, the costs of and incidental to a proceeding or a step in a proceeding are in the discretion of the court, and the court may determine by whom and to what extent the costs shall be paid.'[36]

The courts exercise this discretion pursuant to a range of factors. For example the Ontario Rules of Civil Procedure provide:

> 57.01(1) In exercising its discretion under section 131 of the Courts of Justice Act to award costs, the court may consider, in addition to the result in the proceeding and any offer to settle or to contribute made in writing,
>
> (0.a) the principle of indemnity, including, where applicable, the experience of the lawyer for the party entitled to the costs as well as the rates charged and the hours spent by that lawyer;
> (0.b) the amount of costs that an unsuccessful party could reasonably expect to pay in relation to the step in the proceeding for which costs are being fixed;
> (a) the amount claimed and the amount recovered in the proceeding;
> (b) the apportionment of liability;
> (c) the complexity of the proceeding;
> (d) the importance of the issues;
> (e) the conduct of any party that tended to shorten or to lengthen unnecessarily the duration of the proceeding;
> (f) whether any step in the proceeding was,
>
> (i) improper, vexatious or unnecessary, or
> (ii) taken through negligence, mistake or excessive caution;
>
> (g) a party's denial of or refusal to admit anything that should have been admitted;
> (h) whether it is appropriate to award any costs or more than one set of costs where a party,
>
> (i) commenced separate proceedings for claims that should have been made in one proceeding, or
> (ii) in defending a proceeding separated unnecessarily from another party in the same interest or defended by a different lawyer; and
> (i) any other matter relevant to the question of costs.[37]

[36] Courts of Justice Act, RSO 1990, c C 43, s 131(1).
[37] Ontario Rules of Civil Procedure (n 8) Rule 57.01(1).

In all cases, a court will assess an unsuccessful party's cost awards based on what is 'fair and reasonable' for that party to pay.[38] A party is free to take a 'money is no object'[39] approach to the presentation of its claim or defence but, if successful, it is entitled to recover only 'the amount of costs that an unsuccessful party could reasonably expect to pay in relation to the step in the proceeding for which costs are being fixed.'[40]

In most cases, counsel's submissions on costs at the end of the hearing of a motion or a short trial, will be relatively brief. It is understood that 'it is not the role of the judge to minutely examine and dissect docket entries or to second guess the utilization of personnel and resources by counsel.'[41] This means that the court will generally rely on counsel's submissions, and counsel will be concerned to maintain a reputation for trustworthiness so that the court will continue to have confidence in doing so. The court will also assess counsel's submissions with an eye to the costs incurred by both parties. For example, in one case where the successful plaintiff had spent more than four times on its case than the defendants had spent on the defence, the Court observed, 'the comparison of the fees charged to the Defendants and the cost being claimed by the Plaintiffs is persuasive in determining the reasonable expectations of the losing party.'[42]

Finally, the concept of proportionality[43] has recently been introduced into the Rules of Civil Procedure as follows:

> 1.04 (1.1) In applying these rules, the court shall make orders and give directions that are proportionate to the importance and complexity of the issues, and to the amount involved, in the proceeding.

The amount of the claim, the amount of the judgment at the end of the matter, the complexity, and the importance of the dispute are all considerations in assessing proportionality of the costs award. For example, if a successful party's actual costs to litigate the matter were $80,000 and the amount at stake was $100,000, those costs are likely not proportional in relation to the amount at stake. In small to medium-sized matters it is increasingly difficult to prevent the legal costs from eclipsing the amounts at stake in the litigation.

[38] *Boucher* (n 6). *See also Celanese Canada Inc. v Canadian National Railway Co* [2005] CarswellOnt 1124 (C.A.) (costs fixed by a court must be fair and reasonable).

[39] *Canadian National Railway Co v Royal and Sun Alliance Insurance Co of Canada* (2005) 77 OR (3d) 612 (SCJ) ('*Canadian National Railway Co*').

[40] Ontario Rules of Civil Procedure (n 8) Rule 57.01(1) (0.b).

[41] *Canadian National Railway Co* (n 39).

[42] ibid; and *Smith v Mardana* (2005) 45 CCEL (3d) 140 (Ont SCJ) (the court must account for the reasonable expectations of the losing party); *Westlake v Westlake* [2006] CarswellOnt 3022 (SCJ) (court must account for reasonable expectations of the losing party).

[43] CM Osborne QC, 'Civil Justice Reform Project' (Ontario, Ministry of Attorney General, 2007) (calling for increased attention to proportionality to the matter at stake and the step in the legal proceedings in awarding costs in litigation).

Standard Costs Awards—Partial Indemnity

There are, in principle, three scales upon which a court may order an unsuccessful party to pay a successful party's costs: partial indemnity,[44] substantial indemnity,[45] and full indemnity.[46]

Ordinarily, costs are awarded on a partial indemnity basis. In other words, the award will only partially indemnify the successful party for the expense of bringing the claim or defending against it. The award will provide some contribution toward the successful party's legal costs without putting the award out of reach of the unsuccessful defendant to pay.[47] The Courts have not defined with precision what portion of the actual expense incurred is appropriate for a partial indemnity award.[48] Partial indemnity costs generally range from 40 per cent to 75 per cent of the actual, reasonable legal fees and disbursements of the successful party, with 60 per cent frequently being cited as representative.[49] Because costs awards depend upon so many factors in a case and are based on an assessment of what is 'fair and reasonable', it is not possible to describe the quantum of costs recovered with greater precision.

Costs Sanctions—Substantial and Full Indemnity

Exceptionally, a court will award costs payable on a substantial indemnity basis and, in very rare circumstances, on a full indemnity basis. These scales of costs awards are reserved for circumstances involving sanctionable behaviour in the manner in which the litigation was conducted, or the failure to accept a reasonable offer of settlement. A substantial indemnity costs award is closer to dollar-for-dollar indemnity of the expenses incurred to bring or defend the claim, yet is still mediated by fairness and reasonableness. Substantial indemnity awards are typically 90 per cent of a successful litigant's actual legal costs.[50] In Ontario, sub-

[44] Called 'ordinary costs' in British Columbia, and 'party and party' costs in most other provinces.

[45] Called 'special costs' in British Columbia, and 'solicitor and client costs' in other provinces.

[46] Once called 'solicitor and his own client' costs.

[47] *Buchanan v Geotel Communications Corp* [2002] CarswellOnt 1720 (SCJ) (courts must avoid awarding excessively high costs for fear of putting litigation out of reach of most litigants); *Stratton Electric Ltd. v Guarantee Co. of North America* [2007] CarswellOnt 599 (SCJ) (costs must be proportionate in order to avoid chilling effect on modest claims); *Leggat Estate v Leggat* (2003) 64 OR (3d) 347 (CA) (financial means of losing party taken into account in fixing reasonable costs).

[48] Orkin (n 34) s 2–3, 2–34 (noting that Canadian courts have not attempted to define with any precision the various scales of costs); *Wasserman, Arsenault Ltd. v Sone* [2002] CarswellOnt 3230 (CA) at para 5 (partial indemnity costs have "never been defined").

[49] Orkin (n 34) 2–36; *Riddell v Conservative Party of Canada* [2007] CarswellOnt 4202 (SCJ) (partial indemnity costs are 60%); *Canadian National Railway Co* (n 39) (partial indemnity costs were 65%); *Computerized Security Systems Inc v Eco Tech Cleaning Systems* [2006] CarswellOnt 4368 (substantial indemnity costs reduced by one-third to arrive at partial indemnity costs).

[50] *Venture Refractories Inc v Technical Strategies Inc* [2007] CarswellOnt 3392 (SCJ) (substantial indemnity costs are 90% of actual legal fees); *Li v Huang* [2007] CarswellBC 2986 (BCSC) (special costs in British Columbia are 90% of actual legal fees); *but see College of Optometrists v SHS Optical* [2007] CarswellOnt 624 (SCJ) (substantial indemnity costs are 80% of actual legal fees).

stantial indemnity is roughly 1.5 times the costs awarded on a partial indemnity basis.[51] Awards for full indemnity, or dollar-for-dollar indemnity for legal services, are rare; and this is the ceiling for Canadian costs awards.[52] Successful parties cannot profit from cost awards.

If an unsuccessful party has conducted itself in a manner that unnecessarily increased the time and expense of the litigation, the court may order that party to pay substantial indemnity costs as a punishment for such behaviour. In this way, adverse cost awards can be used to discourage frivolous or vexatious behaviour[53] or to punish the failure to respond to requests to admit information and thereby unnecessarily lengthen proceedings.[54] Certain other instances also attract sanctions of substantial indemnity costs. If a party brings a motion for summary judgment, advocating there is no genuine issue requiring a trial, and loses such a motion, the losing party is often subject to substantial indemnity costs.[55] There are similar sanctions for maintaining unfounded allegations of, for example, fraud, that attack the integrity of the opposing party, or for improperly seeking punitive damages, and failing to prove the basis for them.[56]

These examples would suggest that costs awards depart from the norm only to increase the sanction for unsuccessful parties. However, the court also enjoys broad discretion to limit the recovery of costs for successful parties who have been inefficient in their conduct of the litigation, and to apportion the costs recovered in cases in which the success has been divided. In this way, counsel are vigilant throughout the litigation about the way in which their handling of the case will affect the award of costs.

In addition, it is not uncommon for costs to be awarded and made payable forthwith at the end of interlocutory motions. This encourages counsel on both sides to develop the case in preparation for trial in a way that will not unduly give rise to the need for motions, especially where such motions might create unnecessary expense and delay for the parties.

In truly extraordinary circumstances, the court also has the power to award costs against a lawyer personally as sanction for improper conduct in the course of

[51] Ontario Rules of Civil Procedure, above note 8, Rule 1.03(1). So, if a partial indemnity award is 60% of a party's actual legal costs, substantial indemnity is 90% of that party's actual legal costs.

[52] *Stellarbridge Management Inv v Magna International (Canada) Inc* (2004) 71 OR (3d) 263 (CA) (parties cannot recover in costs more than is actually spent on the litigation, so the actual amounts billed and paid for are relevant considerations).

[53] *Lanty v Ontario (Ministry of Natural Resources)* (2007) 61 RPR (4th) 161 (Ont CA) (the plaintiff's unreasonable and uncooperative behaviour warranted a higher costs award).

[54] *Tricontinental Investments Co v Guarantee Co of North America* (1988) 29 CPC (2d) 99 (Ont HC) (costs denied to successful defendant for six out of nine days of trial because defendant refused to admin a fact which plaintiff proved at great expense).

[55] Ontario Rules of Civil Procedure (n 8), Rule 20.06 (failing to prove a motion for summary judgment typically attracts substantial indemnity costs against failing party).

[56] *DiBattista v Wawanesa Mutual Insurance Co* (2005) 78 OR (3d) 445 (CA) (substantial indemnity costs when unfounded allegations made and not proven with respect to party being fraudulent or dishonest or when other seriously prejudicial character allegations are made).

the litigation,[57] or against a third party where it emerges that that party has had an interest in the litigation and acted as a driving force.[58]

Encouraging Settlement

Cost-shifting mechanisms are also used to encourage early settlement of lawsuits. For example, in Ontario, special rules for costs provide a strong incentive to both parties to settle that goes beyond the ordinary practice of fee-shifting.[59]

On the one hand, if a plaintiff makes an offer to settle at least seven days before trial and the offer remains open until the trial, and the plaintiff obtains a judgment at trial that is at least as favourable as the terms of its offer, then the plaintiff receives costs on a partial indemnity basis up to the date of the offer, and costs on a substantial indemnity basis from the date of the offer onward. The theory is that the offer was reasonable and should have been accepted by the defendant; and the expenses incurred after that time were unnecessary and should be recoverable on a substantial indemnity basis.

On the other hand, if a defendant makes an offer to settle at least seven days before trial that remains open until the trial, and the plaintiff obtains a judgment at trial that is no more favourable than the terms of the defendant's offer, then the plaintiff receives costs on a partial indemnity basis up to the date of the offer, and the *defendant* receives costs on a partial indemnity basis from the date of the offer onward. The theory is that the offer was reasonable and should have been accepted by the plaintiff; and only the expenses incurred by the plaintiff before that time were necessary, and the expenses incurred by the defendant after that time should be partially recoverable.

In most cases, where the costs are significant in relation to the amount in dispute, this mechanism provides a powerful incentive to make reasonable offers to compromise, to resolve the matter early on in the process, and to consider seriously any offers received. Moreover, it provides an incentive that operates throughout the pre-trial process, giving the parties good reason to re-evaluate the benefits of settling at each stage of the litigation.

Calculating Costs

At the end of the hearing of a matter, or at the end of the hearing of an interlocutory step, the parties make submissions to the court with respect to costs. Where possible, the parties may agree on costs. If the parties do not agree, each submits a costs outline which details the years of experience of each lawyer involved, the

[57] *Standard Life Assurance Co v Elliott* (2007) 86 OR (3d) 221 (SCJ) (court awarded costs payable jointly and severally by both lawyer and client due to sharp conduct in litigation) and Ontario Rules of Civil Procedure (n 8), Rule 57.07(1) (liability of lawyer for costs).

[58] *Smith v Canadian Tire Acceptance Ltd.* [1995] O.J. No. 3380, 26 OR (3d) 94 (Gen Div).

[59] Ontario Rules of Civil Procedure (n 8), Rule 49.

partial indemnity and the actual hourly rate of each lawyer, a detailed description of the time spent on the matter, and all disbursements spent on the client's behalf.[60] The court hears submissions and then determines the costs. If the matter has ended in a trial, the trial judge will determine the total cost award for the matter, including any interlocutory motions, discovery, and other steps in the litigation (although these will have been made before other adjudicators). Costs generally follow the event in Canada, such that the losing party pays the cost of prosecuting the entire claim.

If the matter is an interlocutory motion, the amount of the costs for that step in the proceeding will be set by the judge who heard the motion but those costs may be borne by the party that is ultimately unsuccessful, unless the motions judge wishes to sanction with costs a party's behaviour on the motion. If there are multiple parties in complex litigation, courts may make costs orders directing certain unsuccessful parties to pay the costs of certain successful parties. For example, a Bullock order directs an unsuccessful defendant to reimburse a successful plaintiff for the costs that the plaintiff had to pay to another defendant in the litigation who was successful.[61] A Sanderson order directs an unsuccessful defendant to pay directly the costs of a successful defendant in multi-party litigation. For appeals, costs are set at the conclusion of the appeal. In some instances, if an appeal reverses a trial judgment, the cost order for the prior trial below may also be set aside.[62]

Costs submissions by counsel can be lengthy if the matter was complicated and involved many parties, many lawyers, and many days at trial. They may involve a separate hearing and the documentation required to support a party's claim may be substantial. Occasionally the submissions involve criticism of opposing counsel's hourly rate or the way in which the time or resources were spent.

The court's process in arriving at the end result costs award is not strictly mathematical, where the judge takes the hours spent and multiplies that by the lawyer's hourly rate.[63] In addition to the actual cost of the litigation, a court will be

[60] Ontario Rules of Civil Procedure (n 8) Rule 57.01(6) (requirement for costs outlines).

[61] *Rooney v Graham* (2001) 53 OR (3d) 685 (CA) (details when a court can order a Bullock or Sanderson order) and *Moore v Weinecke* (2008) 90 OR (3d) 263 (CA) (outlining factors for overturning a Sanderson order).

[62] The discretion of the trial judge to award costs at trial attracts great deference by appellate courts. Before a party can appeal a costs award from a lower court, it must seek leave from the applicable court. See Ontario *Courts of Justice Act*, RSO 1990, c C 43, s 133(b). A costs award in a lower court will only be set aside by a higher court if the lower court judge abused his or her discretion in setting the costs award, or if the lower court misapplied applicable costs law. This system of reversing costs awards on appeal has met some criticism, because the reversal on appeal is typically not the fault of the parties but the fault of the trial judge who arrived at an incorrect legal conclusion: GD Watson and P Lantz, 'Bringing Fairness to the Costs System—An Indemnity Scheme for the Costs of Successful Appeals and Other Proceedings' (1981) 19 *Osgoode Hall LJ* 447 (arguing that the loser on appeal should perhaps not have to pay the costs of the entire proceeding, even though the error at trial resulted from a trial judge's incorrect application of the law).

[63] *West v Workplace Safety and Insurance Board* (2005) 78 OR (3d) 270 (Div Ct) (court refused to apply a simple mathematical approach of hours worked multiplied by hourly rate); *Trapeze Software Inc v Bryans*, [2007] CarswellOnt 1229 (SCJ) (costs does not 'begin and end with a calculation of hours times rates').

concerned to ensure that the cost award to the unsuccessful party is not putting litigation out of reach of litigants, in a more general way. The amount must be what a losing party would reasonably expect to pay. In arriving at such an amount, some Canadian jurisdictions provide guidance as to reasonable lawyers' hourly rates. For example, in Ontario, the Civil Rules Committee in 2005 produced the following guidelines for courts and lawyers alike to use in setting the maximum hourly rates on a partial indemnity basis:

Law Clerks	Maximum of $80.00 per hour
Student-at-law	Maximum of $60.00 per hour
Lawyer (less than 10 years)	Maximum of $225.00 per hour
Lawyer (10 or more but less than 20 years)	Maximum of $300.00 per hour
Lawyer (20 years and over)	Maximum of $350.00 per hour

Substantial indemnity rates in Ontario would thus be 1.5 times the above rates. These are suggested guideline maximums only. While unsuccessful litigants would not be forced to pay costs of a 'Cadillac variety',[64] courts also do not expect that successful litigants would have shopped around for a less expensive alternative to their counsel of choice. Courts also expect that the lawyers take responsibility for keeping costs proportional to the matter at stake.[65] As one court put it:

> 'Judges and assessment officers have a duty to fix or assess costs at reasonable amounts and, in this process, they have a duty to make sure that the hours spent can be reasonably justified. The losing party is not to be treated as a money tree to be plucked, willy nilly, by the winner of the contest.'[66]

Despite the fact that Canada is a common law jurisdiction, where the principle of *stare decisis*—comparing like cases to like cases—is strongly held, the courts appear to make a special exception for costs cases. Courts do not often look to other cases when calculating the value of costs,[67] though some cannot resist in doing so.[68] There is no consistent percentage for partial or substantial indemnity costs.[69] Litigants in Ontario have the maximum partial indemnity guidelines from the Rules Committee in 2005 but there is no strict requirement to adhere to the guidelines and no guidance on when to use the maximum rate. Litigants and courts are left with the simple notion that adverse costs awards are to be 'fair and

[64] *Liu v Sung* (1995) 37 CPC (3d) 44 (BCSC).

[65] *Roach v Saito* [2004] CarswellOnt 4825 (SCJ) (counsel has a duty to limit time spent so it bears 'some passing resemblance' to what is at issue in the case); *Volchuk v Kotsis* [2007] CarswellOnt 8027 (SCJ) (proportionality important in assessing costs).

[66] *Pagnotta v Brown* [2002] CarswellOnt 2666 (SCJ).

[67] *Andersen v St. Jude Medical Inc.* (2006) 264 DLR (4th) 557 (Ont Div Ct) at para 42 (difficult to make comparisons that will 'provide firm guidance' on costs issues); *Mandeville v Manufacturers Life Insurance Co.*, [2002] OJ No 5388 (Ont SCJ) at para 28 ('comparisons are probably not very useful').

[68] *See Toronto Transit Commission v Gottardo Construction Ltd* (2005) 77 OR (3d) 269 (CA) (costs award reduced when bills of costs of one party were twice as high as those of the other party); Orkin (n 34) 2–32 ('the concept of comparing the costs of opposing parties appears to have taken hold').

[69] *Lawyers Professional Indemnity Co v Geto* [2002] CarswellOnt 769 (SCJ).

reasonable.' Indeed, as the Court of Appeal in *Boucher* put it, in deciding what is 'fair and reasonable:'

> 'I refrain from attempting to articulate a more detailed or formulaic approach. The notions of fairness and reasonableness are embedded in the common law. Judges have been applying these notions for centuries to the factual matrix of particular cases.'[70]

Conclusion

It is difficult to predict the final dollar amount of a costs award in Canadian civil litigation. Guided by the principle that costs borne by an unsuccessful litigant in Canada's fee shifting regime are to be 'fair and reasonable,' courts fix cost awards on a contextual, case-by-case method.[71] Courts must account not only for the market rates the successful party would expect to pay her own lawyer, but also for the behaviour of the parties throughout the litigation, the proportionality of the costs award to the amount at stake in the matter, and whether or not there were any offers to settle that attract settlement cost consequences. The result is a multi-factoral, fact-specific analysis.

It appears that costs awards are effective in regulating the conduct of litigation, but the amounts of the awards are difficult to predict at the outset of the litigation. Costs sanctions in Canada are used as behavioural modification devices—to punish litigants who waste court time, party resources, take frivolous and vexatious actions,[72] and refuse to accept reasonable settlement offers. There are indications that this achieves a measure of the desired results in Canada, because costs sanctions for litigation behaviour are not reserved for exceptional circumstances and there are often reasons in the judgment to guide litigants and counsel in future cases.

However, as a means of making sound decisions about whether to commence litigation, the lack of predictability of the ultimate expense of litigating can be a deterrent.[73] In this way, costs may be disproportionately driving the decision-making concerning whether to commence a claim and whether to continue the claim. The current high price of litigation keeps the risk of adverse cost awards foremost in the minds of litigants and their lawyers. This may have the effect of

[70] *Boucher* (n 6) para 38 (per Armstrong JA).

[71] *Boucher* (n 6). *See also Celanese Canada Inc. v Canadian National Railway Co* [2005] CarswellOnt 1124 (CA) (costs fixed by a court must be fair and reasonable); *Coldmatic Refrigeration of Canada Ltd v Leveltek Processing LLC* (2005) 75 OR (3d) 638 (CA) (overriding principle of reasonableness should drive cost awards); *Ellis v MacPherson* (2005) 15 CPC (6th) 253 (PEICA) (reasonableness important in awarding costs); *Yendrowich v Yendrowich* (2004) 50 CPC (5th) 167 (Man QB).

[72] *Standard Life Assurance Co. v Elliott* (2007) 86 OR (3d) 221 (SCJ) (court sanctioned both lawyer and client for frivolous conduct in litigation).

[73] P Lantz, 'Costs as a Regulatory Device' (1979) 2 *Advocates Quarterly* 396 (examining 468 cases in 1979 and concluding that the 'most disturbing' aspect of costs was the 'apparent lack of consistency' for regulatory cost orders in the form of sanctions for behaviour).

supplanting the concern about vindicating the substantive rights being asserted in the litigation with a concern about the risk of considerable expense in doing so. Litigants cannot *ex ante* predict the twists and turns of their case and they cannot predict the costs that might be awarded at the end. There are too many factors involved to make an informed, reliable risk calculus. The fee shifting costs system has resulted in the creation of a large body of complex substantive law, all measured by discretion and amorphous "reasonableness." This flexibility may itself have a cost in the loss of predictability.

5

The People's Republic of China

MICHAEL PALMER* AND CHAO XI**

General Overview and Trends

In 2006, as part of the overall judicial reform programme, the People's Republic of China ('China') revamped its litigation costs regime. In December, China's central government—the State Council—issued the Measures on the Payment of Litigation Fees ('2006 Measures').[1] In April 2006, the National Development and Reform Commission and the Ministry of Justice jointly promulgated the Administrative Measures on Lawyers' Service Fees ('2006 Measures on Lawyers' Fees').[2] These two documents lay down the framework for the current litigation costs system in China. The general aim of the 2006 reforms is to afford Chinese citizens greater, easier and less expensive access to civil and administrative justice.

At the same time, there has been a significantly greater emphasis on using judicial mediation to resolve civil and administrative disputes in recent years.[3] This is reflected, inter alia, in the promulgation by the Supreme People's Court ('SPC')—China's highest level court—in March 2007 of a normative document,[4] which encourages and, indeed, requires courts in China to mediate. In addition, in 2009 the SPC issued a document that encourages a wider use of mediation both within

* Professor of Law & Associate Dean for Research and Global Development, and Director, Cheung Kong Centre for Negotiation and Dispute Resolution, STU Law School, China; Research Professor (SOAS & IALS, London University), Joint Editor, *Journal of Comparative Law*; Barrister (England and Wales), Serle Court Chambers, Lincoln's Inn.

** Assistant Professor, Faculty of Law, The Chinese University of Hong Kong; Adjunct Professor, School of Law, Jilin University, China.

1 *Susong Feiyong Jiaona Banfa*, promulgated by the State Council on 19 Dec 2006, and in effect on 1 Apr 2007.

2 *Lüshi Fuwu Shoufei Guanli Banfa*, promulgated on 13 Apr 2006, and in effect on 1 Dec 2006.

3 M Palmer, 'Controlling the State? Mediation in Administrative Litigation in the People's Republic of China,' (2006) 16 *Transnational Law & Contemporary Problems* 165.

4 *Guanyu Jinyibu Fahui Susong Tiaojie zai Goujian Shehui Zhuyi Hexie Shehui zhong Jiji Zuoyong de Ruogan Yijian* [Several Opinions Regarding Further Improving the Positive Roles Judicial Mediation Plays in the Construction of Socialist Harmonious Society], promulgated on 1 Mar 2007.

court proceedings and also extra-judicially.[5] Official statistics show that, in 2008, 58.86 per cent of civil cases in China were resolved by mediation.[6]

Funding Claims

Personal Funding

Subject to some exceptions noted below, litigants meet their own litigation costs, paying court fees and lawyer's fees from their own pockets.

Legal Aid

Partly in response to this burden, since the mid-1990s China has developed a nationwide formal legal aid system, providing free legal assistance to economically disadvantaged citizens who would otherwise have no access to the relevant legal services.[7] Most legal aid programmes have been established by the Ministry of Justice ('MOJ') and local justice bureaux, and are funded mainly by the government. Some legal aid centres are based at government-funded universities and sponsored by, in a few cases, the Ford Foundation or other external funders. These centres see themselves as non-governmental legal aid providers.

Under the 2003 Regulations on Legal Aid,[8] plaintiffs on low or modest incomes may apply for legal aid under six circumstances.[9] In addition, the 2003 Regulations on Legal Aid authorise provincial governments to make local rules expanding the

[5] *Guanyu Jianli Jianquan Susong yu Fei Susong Xiang Xianjie de Maodun Jiufen Jiejue Jizhi de Ruogan Yijian* [Several Opinions Regarding the Establishment and Reinforcement of Conflict and Dispute Resolution Mechanisms that Connect Litigation and Non-Litigation], promulgated on 24 Jul 2009.

[6] 2009 *Zuigao Renmin Fayuan Gongzuo Baogao* [2009 SPC Work Report], available at news.xinhuanet.com/newscenter/2009-03/17/content_11024682_2.htm.

[7] See generally BL Liebman, 'Legal Aid and Public Interest Law in China,' (1999) 34 *Texas International Law Journal* 211; BL Liebman, 'Lawyers, Legal Aid, and Legitimacy in China' in WP Alford (ed) *Raising the Bar: The Emerging Legal Profession in East Asia* (Cambridge MA, Harvard University Press, 2006) 311. Legal aid is delivered in a number of ways in China, and is subject to considerable regional variation (despite the existence of a national legal aid centre in the Ministry of Justice in Beijing, and a national-level legal aid foundation: see, for example, www.chinalegalaid.gov.cn:8080/english/index.asp). Three of the most important types of delivery are: first, a full time legal aid lawyer scheme; secondly, an arrangement that allocates work to lawyers (for example, by requiring a law firm to offer various legal services annually); and thirdly, a system of legal aid centres staffed by lawyers from law firms and legal aid workers. Legal aid typically involves either the provision of free legal advice or the allocation of a lawyer or an employee (who may or may not be a lawyer) working in a legal aid provider or one of China's nascent NGOs, and who acts on a pro bono basis. Arts 2, 21 & 25, 2003 Regulations on Legal Aid, see n 8.

[8] *Falü Yuanzhu Tiaoli*, issued by the State Council on 21 Jul 2003, and in effect on 1 Sept 2003.

[9] Art 10. These circumstances include claims for: (a) state compensation; (b) social insurance and minimum living standards guarantees; (c) survivor's pension and relief funds, (d) several kinds of family maintenance and support; (e) employment remuneration; and (f) certain other kinds of civil rights and interests.

circumstances under which litigants may apply for legal aid (article 10). Liaoning Province, for example, permits those who have a right to claim damages arising from environmental pollution, public health, and production incidents, among other things, to apply for legal aid.[10] Rules on legal aid in Guangdong Province place so few restrictions on the standing of individuals to apply for legal aid that virtually anyone who is unable to afford a lawyer is entitled to make an application.[11]

Despite the growth of legal aid programmes in China, there are significant barriers to greater use of legal aid in civil actions. For one thing, many provinces set a very low maximum income eligibility level for legal aid, and only a small fraction of the population (ie those living in extreme poverty) is therefore eligible for legal aid. This creates a serious impediment to access to justice for a large number of people who are not eligible for legal aid but also cannot afford to pay for their own lawyer.

In addition, legal aid providers tend to lack independence. Decisions as to whether to provide legal aid are made by government-funded aid centres and subject merely to administrative review by local justice bureaux.[12] In civil actions that involve, for example, a powerful local state-owned enterprise, intervention from the local government may result in a decision that favours the defendant.

Judicial Aid

China has also developed a so-called 'judicial aid' (*sifa jiuzhu*) system, which operates alongside the legal aid system. Under the judicial aid system, Chinese courts provide financial aid—in the form of full or partial remission, or postponement of payment, of court fees—to those who cannot afford to undertake litigation.[13]

Thus, articles 45 and 46 of the 2006 Measures specify the kinds of situation in which the court should remit fees in whole or in part, respectively. Article 47 of the 2006 Measures provides for the circumstances under which the postponement of payment of court fees is permissible. There are reports, for example, of collective suits in China in which local courts has exercised this discretion and exempted plaintiffs from paying the court fees—in one recent case, a group of 73 claimants who were victims in a chemical explosion incident thus benefited.[14] All three

[10] Art 7(8), *Liaoning Sheng Falü Yuanzhu Shishi Banfa* [Liaoning Provincial Implementing Rules on Legal Aid], issued the Liaoning Provincial People's Government on 4 Nov 2004, and in effect on 1 Dec 2004.

[11] *Guangdongsheng Falü Yuanzhu Tiaoli* [Guangdong Provincial Rules on Legal Aid], issued by the Guangdong Provincial People's Government on 29 Sept 2006, and in effect on 1 Jan 2007.

[12] *Guanyu Minshi Susong Falü Yuanzhu Gongzuo de Guiding* [Rules on Legal Aid Work in Civil Litigation], issued by the SPC and the Ministry of Justice on 22 Septr 2005, and in effect on 1 Dec 2005.

[13] Arts 4 and 44, 2006 Measures.

[14] See Chen Anqun et al, 'Huangling Baojian Renshen Sunhai Jituan Susong Chenggong Tiaojie' [Collective Action Arising from the Incident of Explosion of Yellow Phosphorus Successfully Mediated], *Zhongguo Fayuan Wang* [China Court Net], available at www.chinacourt.org/public/detail.php?id=194236. In this case, a car carrying yellow phosphorus exploded, resulting in injuries to 73 persons. These victims initiated a group action suit, claiming over RMB 8 million in compensation. The local court resolved the case by mediation, and the victims accepted a compensation of RMB 4 million in settlement. In addition, the local court exempted the victims from payment of court fees.

Articles contain, however, catch-all provisions[15] that in effect give the court the discretion to determine the remission or postponement of court fees as it sees fit.

Contingency Fees

Prior to 2006, contingency fee arrangements had operated unofficially in China for many years. Chinese lawyers charged clients on a 'speculative' basis in a growing variety of cases, ranging from industrial injury compensation to recovery of non-performing bank loans. The contingency fee charged typically ranged from 10 per cent to 40 per cent of the recovery.[16] Lawyers, when facing substantial risk of non-recovery, might charge a fee as high as 50 per cent.[17] Some lawyers, on the other hand, took a fee that was significantly smaller than the fee that they would have taken under the terms of the retainer agreement.[18]

Entrepreneurially-minded Chinese lawyers have brought securities' collective actions on a contingency fee basis. In one high profile securities fraud case,[19] for example, a group of lawyers headed by a prominent shareholder activist, Professor Guo Feng, represented a large number of injured investors on a 'no win, no fee' basis. The lawyers eventually walked away with a contingency fee of 20 per cent of the net recovery, that is, the awarded damages minus, first, case acceptance fees, secondly, application fees (for enforcement of judgments) and, thirdly, other costs such as lawyers' expenditure (on such items as air tickets, accommodation, meals, and so on).[20]

Unfortunately, this option of using contingency fee arrangements to fund collective actions is no longer available under Chinese law. The 2006 Measures on Lawyers' Fees now expressly prohibit contingency fees in collective actions, criminal cases, administrative litigation cases, and state compensation cases.[21] And in other kinds of case the contingency fee is now capped at 30 per cent of the recovery (article 13, 2006 Measures).

Court Costs

For more than three decades after the establishment of the People's Republic in 1949, China imposed no charges on litigants for their use of the courts. Since 1984,

[15] Arts 45(5) and 46(4), 2006 Measures.
[16] Yao Ying, 'Legal "Saviour" Fighting for His Fees', *China Daily*, 5 Jul 2004 (Legal Saviour).
[17] Interviews with PRC lawyers.
[18] Legal Saviour.
[19] For more details of the case, see C Xi, 'Private Enforcement of Securities Law in China: *Daqing Lianyi Co v ZHONG Weida and Others* (2004) Heilongjiang High Court' (2006) 1 *Journal of Comparative Law* 492.
[20] Announcement available at feng-guo.blog.sohu.com/28354620.html.
[21] Art 12, 2006 Measures.

however, the Chinese courts have charged court fees.[22] The rationale behind this change in policy was, according to senior Chinese government officials, that the litigant's costs in safeguarding her or his legitimate interests through the process of litigation should not be born in full by taxpayers. Parties to an action are under an obligation to contribute to the expense of maintaining the state court system.[23] Until 2006, the SPC dominated administration of the court fee regime. That regime came to be widely criticised as serving the courts' own interests rather than benefiting needy litigants. It was robustly characterised as overly arbitrary, expensive, unreasonable, unpredictable, and in need of significant modification.[24] This Chapter offers below an overview of the three types of court fee now permissible under the 2006 Measures, and then discusses the implications of the 2006 reform for both litigants and courts in China.

Permissible Types of Court Fee

Under Art 6 of the 2006 Measures, court fees are divided into three types, namely, case acceptance fees, application fees, and expenses. These are examined in turn below.

Case Acceptance Fees

Where a dispute is accepted for adjudication by the court,[25] a single case acceptance fee must be paid in advance (article 20, 2006 Measures), except in respect of claims for unpaid labour remuneration, where the case acceptance fee may be paid ex post.

In general, the case acceptance fee must be prepaid for case acceptance by the court of first instance, for cases accepted by the court of second instance, and for certain types of retrial proceedings prescribed by the 2006 Measures (article 7, 2006 Measures). The fee is to be prepaid by the plaintiff, a third party with an independent claim, or the appellant (article 20, 2006 Measures).

More specifically, for cases of first instance, the court will serve a notice on the claimant—and the defendant where a counterclaim is filed—requiring payment of the case acceptance fee. Upon receipt of the notice, the fee is payable within seven days. In appeal cases, payment for the fee needs to be made by the appellant when submitting the petition of appeal, or, at the latest, within seven days when the period of appeal has elapsed. Non-payment of the case acceptance fee

[22] Y Wang, *Shehui Biange zhong de Minshi Susong* [Civil Litigation in Social Transformations] (Beijing, China Legal Publishing House, 2001) 181.

[23] Legislative Affairs Office of the State Council, 'Why the Measures on the Payment of Litigations Fees was Enacted by Us' [Susong Feiyong Jiaona Nanfa Weishenme you Women Zhiding], *Fazhi Ribao* [China Legal Daily], 8 Jan 2007.

[24] L Fang, 'Minshi Susong Shoufei Kao' [Textual Research on Civil Litigation Fees] (1999) 20 *Social Sciences in China* 130.

[25] Chinese courts have reportedly refused to take on some types of civil action on grounds of political sensitivity. See M Palmer and C Xi, 'Collective and Representative Actions in China' www.law.stanford.edu/library/globalclassaction/PDF/China_National_Report.pdf.

will result in the case being struck out, unless a fee remission is granted under the judicial aid system (article 22, 2006 Measures).

For disputes over property, the case acceptance fees are payable based on the monetary value of the property in dispute. The fees are calculated on an incremental basis, with the percentage rates reducing as disputed amount increases. Table 1 shows the rates schedule for case acceptance fees in property disputes.

Paragraphs 2 to 6 of article 13 of the 2006 Measures spell out the case acceptance fee to be prepaid in non-property disputes (divorce cases, disputes over rights to name, rights to business name, rights to portrait, rights to honour, and so on),[26] intellectual property disputes, labour disputes, administrative litigation cases, and disputes over the court's jurisdiction. Although there are some exceptions, the case acceptance fee payable in these types of case is set at a fixed amount, ranging from as little as RMB 10 in labour disputes to RMB 1,000 in intellectual property cases.

The case acceptance fee is charged at half the above rates in summary proceedings (article 16, 2006 Measures). The half rate rule also applies where the claimants or appellants withdraw the lawsuit, or where the case is settled through mediation

Table 1: Case Acceptance Fees Rates Schedule

Over (RMB)	But not over (RMB)	Rate	of the amount over (RMB)
0	10,000	Fixed fee of RMB 50	
10,000	100,000	RMB 50 + 2.5%	10,000
100,000	200,000	RMB 2,300 + 2%	100,000
200,000	500,000	RMB 4,300 + 1.5%	200,000
500,000	1,000,000	RMB 8,800 + 1%	500,000
1,000,000	2,000,000	RMB 13,800 + 0.9%	1,000,000
2,000,000	5,000,000	RMB 22,800 + 0.8%	2,000,000
5,000,000	10,000,000	RMB 46,800 + 0.7%	5,000,000
10,000,000	20,000,000	RMB 81,800 + 0.6%	10,000,000
20,000,000	–	RMB 141,800 + 0.5%	20,000,000

Source: Art 13(1), 2006 Measures.

[26] These rights are the 'personal rights' provided for by the *Minfa Tongze* [General Principle of Civil Law] (promulgated by the National People's Congress on 12 Apr 12, 1986 and in effect on 1 Jan 1987). Rights to name refer to a citizen's rights to determine, use and change her or his personal name, and the rights to prevent others from misusing her or his name. Rights to business name refer to legal person's rights to use and assign its business name (art 99). Rights to portrait refer to one's rights to prevent any third parties from using her or his image for profit without consent (art 100). Rights to honour refer to a citizen's rights to prevent third parties from depriving her or him of honorary titles (art 102).

(article 15, 2006 Measures). These provisions reflect the Chinese Party-state's renewed emphasis on the use of the mediation to resolve disputes in its attempt to create a 'harmonious society' (*hexie shehui*).

Application Fees

Under article 10 of the 2006 Measures, a litigant must pay an application fee where he applies for any of the following: (a) enforcement by the people's court of a legally effective judgment or ruling, enforceable deed, or arbitral award; (b) preservation measures; (c) a payment warrant; (d) a public summons;[27] (e) revocation of an arbitral award or affirmation of the effectiveness of an arbitration agreement; (f) bankruptcy proceedings; (g) certain types of application under the 1999 PRC Special Maritime Procedure Law; or (h) recognition and enforcement of a foreign judgment or foreign arbitral award.

The rates of these application fees vary in accordance with the nature of the application, and are provided for under article 14 of the 2006 Measures. Application fees payable for the enforcement of court judgments or arbitral awards, preservation measures, payment warrants, and insolvency proceedings are calculated according to the monetary value of the claim. Nevertheless, the application fees for preservation measures and for insolvency proceedings are capped at RMB 5,000 and RMB 300,000, respectively. The application fees with respect to public summons, revocation of arbitral awards, confirmation of effectiveness of arbitral awards, and certain types of applications under the 1999 PRC Special Maritime Procedure Law are fixed, ranging from RMB 100 to RMB 10,000.

The 2006 Measures contain a special provision for representative group litigation under article 55 of the 1991 Civil Procedure Law, which governs representative action suits where the number of claimants or defendants with similar claims is 'large' (namely, ten or more people) but *not* fixed at the time the case is filed.[28] The court handling the suit may issue a notice, specifying the circumstances of the suit and instructing all persons whose interests are similarly affected to come forward and register with the court within a specific period (normally, less than 30 days). The court's decision is binding on all those who register with the court, and on those who do not register with court but bring similar claims within 'the limitation period of the action' (generally two years under Chinese law). In the latter situation, the litigants are required only to pay the application fee, and the case acceptance fee is waived (article 14(1)(3), 2006 Measures).

In general, the application fee must be paid in advance when the litigant makes the application or within the time limit prescribed by the court.[29] Non-payment

[27] Under art 193(1) of the 1991 Civil Procedure Law, the holder of transferable negotiable instruments may apply for a public summons where such negotiable instruments are stolen, lost or destroyed. The effect of a public summons is to nullify such negotiable instruments.

[28] M Palmer and C Xi, 'The Globalization of Class Actions: China' (2009) 622 *The Annals of the American Academy of Political and Social Sciences* 270, 274.

[29] There are two exceptions, ie, application for the enforcement of judgments or arbitral awards and application for insolvency proceedings, in which case the application fee is paid after the judgments or arbitral awards are enforced or the insolvency proceeding is concluded, respectively.

of the application fee will result in the application being struck out, unless a fee remission is granted under the judicial aid system (article 22, 2006 Measures).

Expenses and Subsidies

According to articles 6 and 11 of the 2006 Measures, the litigant may be liable for travel expenses, accommodation costs, living expenses and subsidies for missed work incurred by witnesses, authenticators, interpreters, and loss adjustment assessor for their appearing before the court at designated dates. Fee schedules vary according to the local living standards and the seniority of the authenticator, interpreter or adjustment makers.

Payment for such expenses and subsidies is made after they have been incurred (article 20(3), 2006 Measures).

Implications for Both Litigants and Courts

From the perspective of the litigating parties, the reform of the court fee regime in 2006 brings two major benefits: reduction in costs and increased costs predictability. First, the 2006 Measures reduce litigation expenditure for socially or economically disadvantaged groups so as to provide them with easier and less expensive access to justice. Thus, the plaintiff in a matrimonial case needs only to pay a small fixed case acceptance fee (RMB 50-300) as long as the matrimonial property involved does not reach a certain threshold, which under the 2006 Measures has been increased significantly from RMB 10,000 to RMB 200,000. One of the main goals of the amendment is to drive down the costs for peasants living in economically less developed regions in China, where the household property typically has a value of less than RMB 200,000.[30] In addition, there is an especially low case acceptance fee for labour disputes: a mere RMB 10. Presumably, this act of state generosity is designed to help to remove the economic barriers to justice for claimants in employment disputes, many of whom are financially strapped and laid-off, or industrially disabled workers. Another important example is the case acceptance fee payable in administrative litigation cases, in which aggrieved citizens challenge illegal administrative conduct.[31] The fee was in the past linked to the amount in dispute, the ironic effect of which was the greater the wrong, in economic terms, done to the aggrieved citizen, the larger the court fee the citizen had to pay in order to gain access to administrative justice. The 2006 Measures overcome this weakness by setting the case acceptance fee at a low fixed rate for administrative litigation: RMB 100 for cases involving patents, trademark and maritime disputes, and RMB 50 for all other types of administrative disputes.

[30] See Legislative Affairs Office of the State Council, n 23.

[31] See M Palmer, 'Controlling the State?: Mediation in Administrative Litigation in the People's Republic of China' (2006) 16 *Transnational Law & Contemporary Problems* 160; M Palmer, 'Compromising Courts and Harmonizing Ideologies: Mediation in the Administrative Chambers of the People's Courts in the People's Republic of China' in A Harding and P Nicholson (eds) *New Courts in Asia* (London, Routledge, 2009) 194–214 and 375–82.

The second benefit for litigants is the greater certainty and predictability that the 2006 Measures afford. The pre-2006 regime allowed courts to charge the litigants 'any additional court fees that the court thinks fit' and 'any expenses occurred by the court'. Such provisions gave the courts unfettered discretion, which in practice they used to charge the plaintiff additional fees. The insecurity this created in respect of the plaintiff's potential exposure on costs became a significant source of public discontent. The 2006 Measures reformed the pre-existing regime by removing altogether the discretionary powers of the court to charge court fees. The rates for court fees are now unalterably fixed, and any additional charges beyond the three types of court fee prescribed by the 2006 Measures are strictly prohibited. The 2006 reforms thus give litigants, especially plaintiffs, much needed costs certainty and predictability.

Official statistics show that as a result, at least in part, of the 2006 reforms, the number of first instance civil and commercial cases rose remarkably in China in 2007, suggesting that citizens are again increasingly willing to resolve their disputes through the court system.[32] The reforms benefiting the litigants have come, however, at the cost of inadequate funding for local courts. In general, court funding in China has two components: the budgetary funds provided by the local government at the same administrative level and extra-budgetary funds derived mainly from court fees. Although the income structure of Chinese local courts varies significantly from region to region, both at national level and in less developed hinterland areas, the major source of court income is court fees.[33] The 2006 Measures, by lowering significantly the rates for court fees and prohibiting local courts from levying extra charges, is thought to have had a negative impact on the income of local courts. For example, courts in China had charged, under the pre-reform court fee regime, altogether some RMB 12.6 billion in court fees in 2005. The figure would have been reduced to only RMB 5.2 billion under the rates introduced by the 2006 Measures, representing a drop in court income of more than one-half.[34]

This problem emerged very soon after the implementation of the 2006 Measures in April 2007. The income of some local courts was reduced swiftly to such a level that the courts' normal functioning was significantly impaired. It is the basic level courts in economically less developed areas—which already had long-standing financial problems—that the 2006 reforms hit most hard.[35] The financial

[32] Y Wang, 'Susong Feiyong yu Sifa Gaige: Susong Feiyong Jiaona Banfa Shixing hou de Yige Zhongqi Kaocha' [Litigation Costs and Judicial Reform: An Interim Assessment after the Implementation of the Measures on the Payment of Litigation Fees'] (2008) 267 *Falü Shiyong* [Journal of the Application of Law] 2. The 2009 SPC Work Report suggests that, for example, the number of labour dispute cases increased by 93.93% year-to-year: available at news.xinhuanet.com/newscenter/2009-03/17/content_11024682_2.htm.

[33] See generally, X He, 'Court Finance and Court Responses to Judicial Reforms: A Tale of Two Chinese Courts' (2009) 31 *Law and Policy* 463, 465–8.

[34] S Gao, 'Susong Feiyong Jiaona Banfa Shishi hou de Wenti yu Duice' [Problems Arising from the Implementation of the Measures on the Payment of Litigation Fees and Countermeasures] (2007) *Zhongguo Shenpan* [China Trial] 8, 9.

[35] Y Wang, see n 32.

well-being of many courts was deteriorating to such a degree that the Chinese authorities, at the request of the SPC, allocated in September 2007 an extra RMB 3 billion from the central government budget to subsidise the financially hard-pressed courts.[36] Our interviews with a number of court presidents suggest that the financial standing of local courts in economically less developed regions has been improved as a consequence.

Lawyers' Costs

Generally there are four different bases on which Chinese lawyers charge fees: First, a fixed fee per case, which is normally applicable in non-property cases; secondly, the monetary value of the claims, which can only be used in property cases; thirdly, an hourly rate, which may be applicable in all types of cases;[37] and lastly, on a contingency basis, subject now to the various limitations discussed above.[38] Lawyers participating in litigation must work at fee rates prescribed by the guidance issued by provincial governments. Non-compliance with the prescribed 'guidance rates' is meant to result in administrative sanctions being imposed on the deviant lawyer, under the 1997 PRC Price Law and 1999 Regulations on Administrative Penalty Against Price-Related Illegal Practices.[39]

The guidance rates vary from one province to another. In Guangdong Province, China's wealthiest province in terms of GDP (gross domestic product), for example, if the lawyers' fees are paid on an hourly basis, the hourly rate ranges enormously from RMB 200 to RMB 3,000. Where a lawyer's fees are calculated according to the monetary value of the claims, the rates are as shown in Table 2. A flexibility of up to twenty percent in the rates is allowed.[40]

In Shanghai, the 'guidance rates' are set at a similar level, suggesting that this level is the norm for the wealthier, eastern seaboard parts of China. The hourly rate range is also large, varying from RMB 200 to RMB 3,000. For property disputes, the fee is charged at 8–12 per cent for the part not more than RMB 100,000 (with a minimum rate of RMB 3,000 per case), 5–7 per cent where the value of the property in dispute is between RMB 100,000 and RMB 1,000,000, 3–5 per cent for value is between RMB 1,000,000 and RMB 10,000,000, 1–3 per cent for between

[36] 'Zhongyang Caizheng Jianli Buzhu Fayuan Ban'an Zhuankuan Zhidu' [Central Finance Establishes a Dedicated Fund to Subsidize the Courts' Handling of Cases], *Renmin Ribao* [People's Daily] 9 Sept2007.

[37] Art 10, *Lüshi Fuwu Shoufei Guanli Banfa* [Measures on the Administration of Lawyers' Service Fees], issued by the National Development and Reform Commission and the Ministry of Justice on 13 Apr 2006 and in effect on 1 Dec 2006.

[38] ibid, art 11.

[39] ibid, art 26.

[40] Appendix, *Lüshi Fuwu Shoufei Guanli Shishi Banfa* [Implementing Measures on the Administration of Lawyers' Service Fees], issued jointly by the Bureau of Price and the Bureau of Justice of Guangdong Province on 25 Dec 2006, and in effect on 10 Jan 2007.

Table 2: Fee Schedule (Based on the Value of the Claims) in Guangdong Province, China

Over (RMB)	But not over (RMB)	Rate	of the amount over (RMB)
0	50,000	Base rate (RMB 1,000–8,000)	
50,000	100,000	Base rate + 8%	50,000
100,000	500,000	Base rate + RMB 4,000 + 5%	100,000
500,000	1,000,000	Base rate + RMB 24,000 + 4%	500,000
1,000,000	5,000,000	Base rate + RMB 44,000 + 3%	1,000,000
5,000,000	10,000,000	Base rate + RMB 164,000 + 2%	5,000,000
10,000,000	50,000,000	Base rate + RM B264,000 + 1%	2,000,000
50,000,000	–	Base rate + RMB 664,000 + 0.5%	20,000,000

RMB 10,000,000 and RMB 100,000,000, and 0.5–1 per cent for a value exceeding RMB 100,000,000. Deviation from the above-mentioned standard rates is, however, permissible: thus, lawyers may, charge up to five times the standard rates in 'important, difficult or complicated' litigation cases.[41] The rates are generally lower in economically less developed regions. The hourly rate in Sichuan Province, for example, is normally capped at RMB 500,[42] and that in Ningxia Hui Autonomous Region ranges between RMB 50 and RMB 1,000.[43]

Cost Shifting

Court Fees

As a general principle, the successful party is entitled to recover his court fees from the unsuccessful party (article 29, 2006 Measures). Traditionally, Chinese courts would order the losing party to pay directly to the winning party the latter's prepaid court fees, if any such payments had been made. Given the general difficulty in enforcing court judgments and rulings in China, however, there was a substantial risk of non-payment on the part of the unsuccessful party. The SPC issued a

[41] *Shanghai Shi Lüshi Fuwu Shoufei Zhenfu Zhidaojia Biaozhun* [Standards of Government Guidance Rates for Lawyers' Service Fees in Shanghai Municipality], issued by the Bureau of Price and the Bureau of Justice of Shanghai Municipality on 13 May 2009, and in effect on 1 Jul 2009.

[42] *Sichuan Sheng Lüshi Shoufei Xiangmu ji Biaozhun* [Items and Standards of Lawyers' Fees in Sichuan Province], issued jointly by the Bureau of Price and the Bureau of Justice of Sichuan Province on 15 Dec 2008, and in effect, retroactively, on 1 Dec 2008.

[43] *Ningxia Huizu* Zizhiqu *Lüshi Fuwu Shoufei Biaozhun* [Standards of Lawyers Fees in Ningxia Hui Autonomous Region], issued jointly by the Bureau of Price and the Bureau of Justice of Ningxia Hui Autonomous Region on 16 May 2007, and in effect on 1 Jun 2007.

Notice in 2007,[44] which orders a change from the traditional court practice. Now, where the claimant wins her or his lawsuit, the initial payment made to the court will be refunded to the claimant first, and then the court will recover the fees from the losing party (article 3). The right of the successful plaintiff to be indemnified for her or his court fees is thus better protected.

If, however, the claimant wins only a limited victory then the court has discretion to determine the allocation of court fees as between the winning and losing parties. Our interviews with Chinese judges suggest that the court fees are normally apportioned between the parties according to the degree to which they succeeded in recovering the amount claimed. For example, a claimant who brings an action for RMB 1,000,000 but recovers only half that amount would be ordered to pay for one-half of the case acceptance fee. This practice is intended to encourage claimants to put a more realistic monetary value on their claims. Other factors, such as the successful party's reasonableness and the parties' attitude towards mediation and other forms of ADR, are not normally taken into consideration when Chinese courts decide on the apportionment of court fees.

Unsuccessful plaintiffs are to bear the cost of the court fees should they lose, and in these circumstances, the court has discretion to decide, in a collective suit, the manner in which court fees will be shared among the claimants (article 29, 2006 Measures).

Since the court's decisions on court fees are discretionary, appellate interference with such decisions is limited under Chinese law. The 2006 Measures provide that the parties may not appeal solely on the basis of the court's decision on the court fees (article 43, 2006 Measures). That is to say, procedurally, an appeal court would not be in a position to exercise its powers to review, if the issue in dispute is about the court fees, alone. However, the parties may request the court to reconsider its decision on fees, and the court's decision is final (article 43, 2006 Measures).

Lawyers' Fees

With respect to lawyers' fees, however, the 'loser-pays' rule that requires the losing party to pay some or all of the winning party's legal expenses does not exist in China. Chinese courts, in general, leave each side responsible for its own lawyers' fees, regardless of who wins. In other words, lawyers' fees are generally irrecoverable. In a high-profile securities fraud case, for example, claimants sought to recover their attorneys' fees from the losing defendant company. The SPC rejected the claim, indicating that such recovery was 'groundless in law'.[45]

[44] *Guanyu Shiyong Susong Feiyong Jiaona Banfa de Tongzhi* [Notice Concerning the Implementation of the Measures on the Payment of Litigation Fees], issued by the SPC on 20 Apr 2007.

[45] 'Chen Lihua Deng 23 Ming Touziren Su Daqing Lianyi Gongsi, Shenyin Zhengquan Gongsi Xujia Chenshu Qinquan Peichang Jiufen An' [Chen Lihua and Others v Daqing Lianyi Co and Shenqing Securities Company for Damages Arising from False Statements], (2005) *Zuigao Renmin Fayuan Gonggao* [Gazette of the Supreme People's Court] 30.

There are, however, one or two exceptional circumstances under which the court may order the unsuccessful party to pay, to a reasonable extent, the successful party's lawyers' fees. These circumstances include:

(1) A creditor sues successfully to exercise her or his right to revoke a contract between the debtor and a third party that unfairly undermines the debtor's ability to repay his debts;[46]
(2) A copyright owner wins a lawsuit to prevent the defendant from copyright infringement;[47]
(3) A trademark owner wins a lawsuit to prevent the defendant from trademark infringement;[48]
(4) A patent owner wins a lawsuit to prevent the defendant from patent infringement;[49]
(5) The party receiving legal aid wins the case.[50]

Our interviews with PRC lawyers suggest that even in the above-stated circumstances, Chinese courts in practice do not usually allow recovery of lawyers' fees, either in full or in part.

Reflections

Developments in the fee regime on civil litigation in the PRC reflect, *inter alia*, the Chinese leadership's increasing emphasis on enhancing access to justice—including access through the courts—in the face of growing social inequality and social unrest. We see parallel, simultaneous policies of promoting greater use of the courts as well as increased reliance on mediated outcomes, reflecting a more nuanced approach to civil and administrative justice than has existed in the past, as an important aspect of the Party-state's efforts to deal with the increasingly pressing issue of social injustice. The reforms to the fee system have also thrown into sharp relief the continuing issue of how best to finance the people's courts in

[46] Art 26, *Guanyu Shiyong Zhonghua Renmin Gongheguo Hetong Fa Ruogan Wenti de Jieshi (Yi)* [Interpretations on Several Issues Regarding the Application of the PRC Contract Law (I)], issued by the SPC on 19 Dec 1999, and in effect on 29 Dec 1999.

[47] Art 26, *Guanyu Shenli Zhuzuoquan Minshi Jiufen Anjian Shiyong Falü Ruogan Wenti de Jieshi* [Interpretations on Several Issues Regarding the Application of Law in Adjudicating Civil Disputes Involving Copyrights], issued by the SPC on 12 Oct 2002, and in effect on 15 Oct 2002.

[48] Art 17, *Guanyu Shenli Shangbiao Minshi Jiufen Anjian Shiyong Falü Ruogan Wenti de Jieshi* [Interpretations on Several Issues Regarding the Application of Law in Adjudicating Civil Disputes Involving Trademarks], issued by the SPC on 12 Oct 2002, and in effect on 16 Oct 2002.

[49] Art 22, *Guanyu Shenli Zhuanli Minshi Jiufen Anjian Shiyong Falü Ruogan Wenti de Jieshi* [Interpretations on Several Issues Regarding the Application of Law in Adjudicating Civil Disputes Involving Patents], issued by the SPC on 22 Jun 2001, and in effect on 1 Jul 2001.

[50] Art 7, *Guanyu Minshi Falü Yuanzhu Gongzuo Ruogan Wenti de Lianhe Tongzhi* [Joint Notice on Several Issues Regarding Civil Legal Aid Work], issued by the SPC and the Ministry of Justice on 12 Apr 1999.

China, an issue that continues to be of considerable importance as the current system of local government part-funding undermines the ability of the courts to be properly independent. At the present time, the fee regime contains some encouragement for the parties to mediate, and it may well be that this encouragement will be strengthened in future reforms given the continuing and growing emphasis in China on securing outcomes in civil and administrative case through mediation.

6

Denmark

KRISTINE SVENNINGSEN*, JAN-ERIK SVENSSON†
AND ANDERS ØRGAARD‡

General Overview And Trends

The Danish rules on court fees and court costs are based on the fact that the legal apparatus must be available to the public. This ensures citizens the opportunity to have their disputes decided in accordance with thorough procedural rules and highly qualified judges.

The idea of user fees, where the people who use the legal system in preference to other systems provide some payment for it, plays a significant role. Legal fees help to ensure a judicious use of the system, and this view has been of vital importance to the legislation on legal fees and court costs. One the one hand, the fee must protect against the bringing of frivolous proceedings and inflation of the subject matter. On the other hand, the fee must not be so high that it prevents substantiated claims.[1] The Danish Administration of Justice Act was extensively revised in 2005. Denmark thus now has a very modern act.

Principles

The rules on imposition of costs follow the principle that the losing party must compensate the counterparty for its costs.[2] The losing party is thus liable to compensate the successful party for the costs inflicted by the litigation. This is a question of responsibility without guilt. The fact that the case is lost is crucial to the ascription of litigation costs. The main rule is that the losing party pays the costs, but if there are special circumstances, the court may decide that the losing party

* Cand merc jur.
† Partner, Gorrissen Federspiel.
‡ Professor, Aalborg University.

1 cf B Gomard and M Kistrup, *Civilprocessen* 6th edn (Forlaget Thomson, 2007) 52.

2 s 312 of the Danish Administration of Justice Act.

need not compensate the counterpart for some or all of the costs incurred.[3] Examples of this are cases where disputes are caused by ambiguities in the parties' contract for which both parties are responsible. It was intended that the rule was to be ameliorated by the change in the Administration of Justice Act in 2005, so that the losing party does not have to pay the full cost if the litigation is a leading case, but this is a very narrow exception.

Court fees are directly related to the size of the claim and counterclaim with respect to both minimum and maximum levels.[4] Litigation costs frequently exceed the amount first estimated or budgeted. This is frequently seen in cases of a complex technical nature, where each party hires expert advisers and the court has its own expert. Such cases, and cases which involve a significant volume of documents, are notoriously hard to budget. Consumer claims and tort claims are easier to budget. The costs in such cases are usually tempered by the fact that the costs and fees are covered by insurance.

Is Settlement Encouraged By The Rules On Costs?

Litigation fees and costs to some extent contribute to the desire to settle disputes, but individuals with either legal aid or insurance have no incentive to settle, and such cases are frequently not settled. Individuals and businesses that fund litigation themselves have a strong incentive to settle, but such cases are often not settled once litigation commences.

As shown in Figure 1 below, 15 per cent of cases in the municipal courts in 2008 were settled before the hearing. This is due to the rules on mediation. Following these rules, the courts are actively trying to encourage the parties to settle their disputes. The rules on mediation became effective in 2004 and are found in chapter 26 of the Administration of Justice Act. Court mediation in the first court is compulsory, while in the higher court it is optional. Mediation can occur at any time after proceedings are instituted and where the court deems it appropriate, but encouragement is given to considering the matter as early as possible. If mediation results in settlement, the parties pay their own costs of mediation.

The figure shows the percentages of all civil cases that were settled by conciliation either after litigation or through other avenues. The Danish Administration of Justice Act was amended in 2005 with a consequent decrease in the total number of cases. This explains the substantial difference as of 2005.

The possibility of settlement must also be investigated before litigation. It follows from section 3.7.1 of the Code of Conduct that lawyers should '. . . advise the client, when appropriate, as to the desirability of attempting a settlement and/or a reference to alternative dispute resolution'.[5] Settlement is thus encouraged both

[3] ibid, s 312(2).
[4] ch 1 of the Danish Court Fees Act.
[5] The Code of Conduct for the Danish Bar and Law Society, April 2008, s 3.7.1.

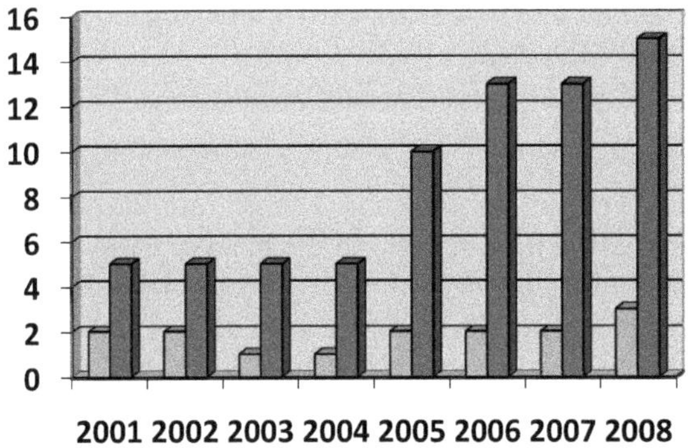

Light: per cent of settlement after litigation
Dark: per cent other settlement

Figure 1—The Emergence of Mediation[6]

before and after litigation is instituted. This is further encouraged by the fact that the fee for assigning the trial lapses if the court receives notification of the case's withdrawal not later than six weeks before the trial (section 2(4) second sentence of the Danish Court Fees Act).

Funding Claims

Personal Funds

Personal funding takes place to the extent to which the individual is not covered by the right to legal aid or has insurance for legal costs as described below. For individuals, this is probably not very widespread. As will be seen, the vast majority of Danes are covered by insurance for legal costs. Those citizens who do not have such insurance are often the economically vulnerable citizens who qualify for legal aid.

Benefits of Membership of an Organisation

In Denmark, approximately 80 per cent of the workforce is organised in trade unions.[7] The Danish labour market is mainly regulated by the collective agreements between both sides, and legal regulation thus does not play a decisive role. The unions provide legal assistance to their members if disputes between employees and employers arise. If the dispute is to be settled by litigation, the union assists in either providing financial assistance to the member's lawyer or by the union's making a lawyer available. The unions themselves also conduct cases on behalf of

[6] Source: www.domstol.dk.
[7] www.lo.dk.

their members, so that it is the union that becomes a party to the litigation, thus incurring the costs if the union loses the case.

Legal Aid

Any party is entitled to legal assistance from lawyers in the form of basic verbal advice (section 323(2) of the Administration of Justice Act). Additional assistance is provided to individuals who meet specific economic conditions. Additional assistance is provided to individuals with an income below DKK 264,000 (2009). If you are married or living with a partner, the aggregate income must be less than DKK 336,000 (2009). The amounts are increased by DKK 46,000 per child under the age of 18 living in the household. If you meet these conditions, the State pays 75 per cent assistance up to DKK 900 (2009) for advice beyond very basic verbal advice. For advice in connection with settlement negotiations, the state pays 50 per cent up to DKK 2,050 (2009).[8] A further condition for this assistance is that the case is not covered by insurance.

In addition to this legal assistance, free legal aid may be granted in specific cases under section 327 of the Administration of Justice Act when the applicant is deemed to have reasonable grounds on which to take legal action (section 328) or a leading case is involved (section 329). The effect of one party being granted free legal aid follows from section 331 of the Administration of Justice Act, which states that the party will have all costs covered and a lawyer appointed to him or her. In addition, free legal aid means that the party will not be required to pay the counterparty's costs in cases where the party with free legal aid is unsuccessful. The grant of legal aid is made under the same rules as the above rules on additional assistance. This means that an individual must meet the specified economic conditions and not possess insurance to cover legal costs.

Legal aid and public assistance are financed by the state. Legal assistance may be provided by the lawyers who are engaged to carry out legal aid matters, or by voluntary lawyers.

Legal Expenses Insurance

Insurance for legal costs is incorporated into many types of insurance for individuals, and most households will have LEI. This does not cover disputes in the area of family law, marriages, adoption and estates. Where the costs are covered by insurance, the party must be represented by a lawyer (section 11 of the Conditions of Insurance).[9] The lawyers' fees will generally be fixed in accordance with the

[8] This amount is indexed annually under s 326 of the Administration of Justice Act. The amount quoted in the section above is for 2009 at www.advokatsamfundet.dk/Default.aspx?ID=11762.

[9] 'Conditions of Insurance for Legal Aid' ('Forsikringsbetingelser for Retshjælp'), valid from 1 Jan 2007.

High Court guidelines for a reasonable fee (see below). Under section 2 of the Conditions of Insurance, the insurance covers private disputes. The insurance covers the costs of the proceedings subject to the conditions in section 4, ie the party's own costs and those of the counterparty when the court decides that the party must compensate the counterparty for its costs, and also costs of expert reports. These insurances do not cover disputes in connection with professional activities (section 3.1.1 of the Conditions of Insurance). LEI is available for businesses, but is less frequently used.

After-the-Event (ATE) Insurance

As noted above, most Danes are covered by insurance that provides legal aid. There is thus no great need in Denmark for ATE insurance.

Loans or Grants from Banks, Trade Associations, etc.

Litigation funding is not common Denmark, and loans are thus rarely given for a particular case. Trade associations provide legal aid for their members. Trade associations will frequently represent a member using their own in-house or external lawyers. Free legal representation in labour disputes is a major selling point for trade associations and labour unions in Denmark. This ensures that such cases are conducted even if the individual does not have the means to do so.

Funding from a Lawyer or Other Third Party Investor

As noted above, litigation funding is not common in Denmark. Lawyers are permitted to agree to represent clients on a no win, no fee basis, a flat fee basis, and a cost plus success fee basis. Lawyers are not permitted to agree on a fee based on a percentage of the amount recovered (*pactum de quota litis*—Code of Conduct for the Danish Bar and Law Society section 3.3.1).

Court Or Process Costs

The fee has two components. The filing charge is paid at the time of filing. The hearing charge is payable three months in advance of the hearing, but some courts set the payment date at six weeks before the hearing. Both charges are politically determined in chapter 1 of the Danish Court Fees Act and are based on a balance between user fees and free access to justice. As noted above, the intention of the fee structure is that fees both protect against frivolous proceedings and inflation of the subject matter, while not being so high as to discourage the pursuit of an otherwise well-founded claim. The fee is not based on actual costs of a trial, but is politically determined. The fee depends in part on the subject matter. The value of the action is determined on the basis of the claim in the writ or, if this is not possible, the plaintiff must make an estimate as accurately as possible (section 3 of the Court Fees Act).

As a rule, the filing charge is DKK 500. In actions concerning money or a value in excess of DKK 50,000, the fee payable is DKK 750 plus 1.2 per cent of that part of the value that exceeds DKK 50,000. However, the total payment cannot exceed DKK 75,000 (section 1 of the Court Fees Act). The hearing charge follows from section 2 of the Court Fees Act. This provision states that the fee is DKK 750 plus 1.2 per cent of that part of the value that exceeds DKK 50,000. The hearing fee may only be imposed in matters relating to money or value, where the value exceeds DKK 50,000. These fees must be paid in advance and they follow the above statutory formula. This means that these costs are clear to the parties before the trial begins.

Other Official Charges

In Denmark there is no VAT on court fees. For services such as translations, the party requesting the service pays. However, such costs are very rare. When documents need translation, the parties presenting the document will arrange the translation at their expense. Translators are usually paid for their services at an hourly rate agreed between the party and the translator. Rates of DKK 500 to DKK 1,000 per hour are normal. If a party or a witness does not understand or speak Danish, an interpreter is provided.[10] Fees for a state-authorised translator are around DKK 550 per hour.[11]

For execution and attachment of goods, a basic fee of DKK 300 is payable. In the event that the claim exceeds DKK 3,000, an additional ½ per cent basic fee is payable on the excess. Among other things this fee covers the execution and attachment of goods[12] as well as proceedings for the enforcement of a non-monetary judgment.[13] As these charges follow from the Court Fees Act, they are known in advance. The fees become payable once the first application for the claim is filed with the enforcement court.[14] A number of enforcement proceedings under section 20 the Court Fees Act are free of charge, for example concerning claims under a party's eligibility for court fee exemption.[15] Enforcements are subject to a charge in accordance with chapter II of the Court Fees Act and are DKK

[10] s 147 of the Administration of Justice Act.

[11] Circular letter on the guidelines for remuneration of interpreters within the area of the Minister of Justice ('*Cirkulæreskrivelsen om vejledende retslinjer for honorering af tolke inden for Justitsministeriets område*').

[12] s 16 of the Court Fees Act.

[13] ibid, s 17.

[14] ibid, s 18.

[15] s 331(1) of the Administration of Justice Act.

400. For court-assisted taking of evidence, for example in aid of arbitration, the court charge is DKK 400.

Witness of Fact

With few exceptions, witnesses are obliged to testify in court. Witnesses must be reimbursed for travel expenses and any loss of income they suffer due to their appearance in court. The amounts are determined by the Danish Court Administration.[16] The starting point is that the witness is entitled to reimbursement of DKK 40 for each newly commenced period of two hours, but at least DKK 80. If the witness can prove that this does not cover his or her actual loss, the court may award greater compensation. This is, for example, the case if the witness has a statement from his or her employer of the number of hours and the amount that will be deducted from the salary. The typical reimbursement of lost income is equivalent to a day's wage.

The reimbursement of travel costs is DKK 3.35 per kilometre travelled in own vehicle, or refund for public transport tickets. The amounts are usually not clear before the day of the trial. The reimbursements are at the discretion of the court.

Expert

Expertise may be required in some court cases to illustrate the issues on which this expert has a particular expertise and on which the parties disagree, such as whether an object or process is fair or proper. An expert's report is an expert's visual inspection combined with his expert assessment. If there is no visual inspection, it is an abstract assessment. Both cases fall under the Administration of Justice Act's provisions on experts' reports.

Typical fees include fees of DKK 2,000 to 5,000 to appointing bodies plus remuneration to the expert for his time. The experts are usually remunerated according to a fee agreement between the party hiring the expert and the expert himself. Typical rates are DKK 1,000 to DKK 2,000 plus VAT. In several cases the High Courts have reduced the fee proposed by the expert himself on the ground of its not being in accordance with the issues listed by the parties for the expert to answer. Remuneration is often calculated as an hourly rate regardless of the amount in dispute, thereby making small claims disproportionate in comparison with larger cases.

The fee for the expert's report is paid by the requesting party, but with the possibility of refund by the counterparty if the latter loses the case. The amount will frequently not become clear until the bill is received or the day of the trial, where the fee for court-appointed experts will be fixed.

[16] ibid, s 188.

Lawyers' Costs

General

The main rule is that the lawyer himself determines his fee. Fee agreements between lawyer and client are valid unless they fall under the ordinary rules of invalidity. This is governed by section 126(2) of the Administration of Justice Act, which states that a lawyer may not demand higher payment for his work than what may be considered reasonable. This provision thus sets the upper limit for legal fees. This is to ensure that the lawyer does not place his or her own profit ahead of the client's interests. In determining what is considered reasonable, the following matters must be taken into account: the nature and extent of the work, the responsibility related to the case, the size of the case, the importance to the client, the time spent and the result obtained. It is not enough to operate with a fixed hourly rate that is simply multiplied by the number of hours spent. However, it is permissible to use the time spent as a basis, as is done by many law firms. The hourly rate for a lawyer varies depending on, among other things, his seniority and whether the task is within his area of specialisation. Whether the lawyer is a partner, a general attorney or an assistant attorney is also a factor. For partners, the hourly rate approaches DKK 4,000, while for an assistant attorney it may be around DKK 1,000.

The result obtained is also included in what must be taken into account when calculating the lawyer's fee. This might occur in rare instances when the lawyer only accepts a fee if the case is won, the so-called no-win-no-fee-principle. In such cases fees can exceed what would normally be payable to the lawyer without such an agreement, and can still be considered reasonable under section 126(2) of the Administration of Justice Act. It is not permissible in Denmark to agree that payment will be a share of the profit that may be gained in the trial: in other words, *pactum de quota litis* is not permitted.

As noted above, the losing party pays the winning party for its expenses. This also applies to costs of legal representation. Costs of legal representation are paid only at an amount determined by a court as appropriate under section 316 of the Administration of Justice Act, for which purpose the Court uses the standard rates in Table 1.[17]

If the value of the case exceeds DKK 5,000,000, the costs of legal representation are determined under a concrete assessment.

In so-called small claims, which are considered according to a special process, standard rates are also used to calculate lawyers' costs. In this case the fee is calculated on the basis of the duration of the main hearing. If, for example, this lasts for two hours, the lawyer is awarded DKK 4,300. If the main hearing lasts three hours,

[17] Guiding rates in DKK for determining the appropriate amount to cover the costs of legal counsel in procedural matters, valid from 1 Jan 2009. Source: www.domstol.dk.

Table 1: Rates for legal representation

Value of the case:	Fee (excluding VAT)	Fee (including VAT)
0–50,000	10,000–18,000	12,500–22,500
50,001–200,000	11,000–37,500	13,750–46,875
200,001–500,000	22,000–55,000	27,500–68,750
500,001–1,000,000	37,500–82,500	46,875–103,125
1,000,001–2,000,000	55,000–115,000	68,750–143,750
2,000,001–5,000,000	87,500–225,000	109,375–281,250

the amount is DKK 6,500. Lawyers may and sometimes do enter into fixed fee arrangements. This is especially so where a client has a high volume of small claims.

The winning party must itself bear that portion of the lawyer's fee that is not covered by the compensation awarded by the court according to the above chart. These standard rates are also applied in assessing the lawyer's fee for the attorney appointed in legal aid cases.

How Are Fee Arrangements Regulated?

The lawyer must, if requested, provide the client with information on the most important elements of the calculated fee and the size of the fee that the lawyer intends to charge. Where it is not possible to give a fixed fee, the lawyer must either state the way in which the fee will be calculated, or provide and explain an estimate.[18] If the client is a consumer, the lawyer must give the client the information provided above in writing.[19] Hidden fees are inadmissible under section 3.4.3 of the Code of Conduct. The lawyer must inform the client as far as possible of the fees to be expected so that this is clear to the client.

Official or Unofficial Tariff for Payment

Previously standard rates for calculation of attorneys' fees were applied. Although these were merely indicative and could be adjusted both up and down depending on the case, they were considered sufficiently fixed for the competition authorities to find that they restricted competition. They were thus abolished in 1996.[20] Indicative tariffs are thus no longer used for setting reasonable fees. Fees are instead set in light of the above principles concerning the nature and extent of the work, the responsibility related to the case, the size of the case, the importance to

[18] s 3.4.2 of the Code of Conduct.
[19] ibid, s 3.4.2(5).
[20] L Lindencrone and E Werlauff, *Dansk Retspleje* 4th edn (Forlaget Thomson, 2007) 152.

the client, the time spent and the result obtained. These principles all contribute to the pricing of legal counsel. If specific information on legal costs in a given case is required, the lawyer must be contacted and asked for an estimate.

Cost Shifting

As noted above, the main rule is that the losing party bears the cost of litigation. This therefore means that the losing party must pay the counterparty's costs. The main rule follows from section 312 of the Administration of Justice Act. This provision is declaratory and specifies that it may be waived by the parties by agreement. Such an agreement complies with the general rules in the Contracts Act. In consumer affairs, an agreement that each party must bear its own costs of a trial will be invalid if it is made before the dispute occurs.

In cases where the losing party has been granted free legal aid, the legal costs are paid by the state.[21] If the losing party has insurance for legal costs, it is this insurance which covers the costs of the counterparty. If there are multiple parties who are jointly the losing party, these parties are jointly and severally liable for these costs.

Section 312(2) of the Administration of Justice Act provides an option for the court to 'decide that the losing party will not, or will only partly, compensate the counterparty for the costs incurred if special reasons so dictate'. This applies mainly in leading cases, or if the counterparty is a public authority, a large corporation or a professional organisation. In several trials the courts have exempted the losing party from payment of legal costs as above. There are also examples where the losing party has been exempted from payment if the winning party has given conflicting, contradictory or incomplete information, and is thus held to be partly responsible for the process. In cases concerning marriage, child custody, guardianship etc, the main rule is that no party pays legal costs to the other party unless special reasons so dictate.[22]

If one party has been responsible for wasted meetings, unnecessary delays, futile production of evidence or other unnecessary procedural steps, this party must compensate the counterparty for the costs involved regardless of which party wins the case.[23] Whether the successful party is awarded costs in this way is determined on grounds of *culpa*. The application of this provision thus presupposes that the party that launched the redundant processes knew, or should have known, that they were redundant.

[21] s 332(1) of the Administration of Justice Act.
[22] ibid, s 312(6).
[23] ibid, s 318.

Partial Success

If a party wins only partially or both parties are partially successful, the question of who should pay the costs is determined by section 313 of the Administration of Justice Act. This provision states that the court will order one of the parties to pay partial legal costs to the counterparty, or decide that neither party is to pay legal costs to the counterparty. The decision whether one party is to pay partial costs is based on which of the parties has been more successful in terms of their principal claims in the case.

Where both sides' cases are substantially upheld, neither is considered the losing party, and they must themselves bear their own costs of legal representation. The costs of necessary procedural steps, fees, presentation of evidence etc. are divided equally between the parties. The above normal principle may be altered if one party has imposed costs of redundant procedural steps on the other party.[24] Section 313(2) of the Administration of Justice Act deals with cases where one party's claim differs only slightly from the outcome of the case, that is, this party has been almost entirely successful. If so, the court may require the counterparty to pay full costs to the former party.

The line between whether one party has been more successful than the other and whether the parties have been more or less equally successful is vague. Decisions on costs between these two extremes are therefore determined in a flexible and nuanced way.

How Much Does A Successful Party Have To Fund?

Under section 316 of the Administration of Justice Act, the costs of legal representation as described above are only awarded at 'an appropriate amount.' It may therefore happen that the standard rates shown above do not cover the actual cost of the lawyer. If this is the case, the otherwise winning party must itself pay the remainder of the cost, as long as the total fees to the lawyer comply with the rules of section 126 on reasonable fees. It may, on the other hand, also happen that the winning party did not incur the cost of a lawyer because it used an in-house lawyer, but it is still awarded damages in accordance with the standard rates.[25] As described above, the successful party must also pay such costs to the counterparty as are incurred by the party via redundant procedural steps.

[24] ibid, s 318.
[25] L Lindencrone and E Werlauff, *Dansk Retspleje*' 4th edn (Forlaget Thomson, 2007) 151.

General Cost Issues

As previously noted, there are special rules for small claims, that is, cases with a value below DKK 50,000. Among other things, court fees are lower, and costs payable to lawyers assigned by the court are smaller. Especially for private parties, there are several options other than the court system. If there is a dispute between a private and public authority, there are complaint systems within the administration. If an authority's decision is tested in court, court fees may not exceed DKK 2,000. In addition, a complaint to the parliamentary ombudsman does not incur any charge.

There are various boards that act in disputes between consumers and business-people. These boards are specific to each area. Examples include the Consumer Complaints Board and the Insurance Appeals Tribunal. It costs approximately DKK 200 to appeal to these boards. If the consumer loses such a case, the consumer is not required to pay the businessman's costs.

Strategies To Lower Costs

The best option for the parties to minimise their costs is to have an insurance policy which covers these costs. As noted above, most Danes have such insurance. The possibility that the winning party may be ordered to pay costs if this party has introduced an unnecessary procedural step may induce the parties to consider what steps are actually necessary. This can ensure that the parties gain a faster trial because they do not have to go through unnecessary procedural steps, while also reducing the cost to those steps which are actually needed for the case.

As noted above, mediation became compulsory in 2004. This is the court's option to endeavour to limit costs. Lawyers are also obliged to limit their clients' expenses. This is specified in the Code of Conduct, by the rule that the lawyer must safeguard the client's interests and advise on the possibility of settlement as early as possible.

The length of a trial depends to a great extent on the individual character of the case. The more complex the matter, the more items are disputed by the parties, the longer it will probably take to decide the case. As indicated in Table 2 below,[26] many cases were decided within a year, and the average number of months is a little over a year.

The length of the litigation may also affect costs indirectly. It can be costly for a businessman to have a case pending. Customers and suppliers can lose confidence in him regardless of whether he is subsequently found to be in the right. The time spent on litigation could be spent on other things, such as doing business.

[26] The length of litigation for civil cases decided by court ruling or settled after litigation. Source: www.domstol.dk.

Table 2: Case statistics

	Total number of cases	Average number of months	Cases decided within one year
2009	2,352	18.1	34%
2008	5,243	15.7	46.4 %
2007	4,719	14.2	55.5 %
2006	5,249	13.5	60.3 %
2005	5,859	13.6	59.6 %

7

England and Wales

JOHN PEYSNER*

Introduction: General Overview

'We will proceed with the hearing on Wednesday fortnight' says the Chancellor. For, the question at issue is only a question of costs, a mere bud on the forest tree of the parent suit . . .'[1]

This volume of comparative studies now reaches the cost and associated financing environment in England and Wales. Whilst it is an over used phrase it can be fairly said that in comparison with the litigation cost systems in other developed countries it is simply 'not fit for purpose'. Whilst, avoiding too close a detailed examination of the ghastly complexities of the English system it should be noted that it is in a state of transition. The system *will* be changed in the next few years. The extent of reform is at the time of writing uncertain and is likely to remain so for some time.

Following the Money

Money is often the key to the door marked access to justice. Its importance is in three areas.

1. *Court costs.* A fee for using state power to adjudicate disputes. This will include the formal processing of the claim; the 'hire' of the judge and courtroom and the enforcement of judgments. What the litigant's money buys will vary from jurisdiction to jurisdiction. In civil law systems the court will conduct an inquisition, examine witnesses and instruct experts. In common law system these steps are under the control of the court (case management) but the cost of the work initially falls on the litigant.

* Professor of Civil Justice, Lincoln Law School, University of Lincoln.

[1] C Dickens, *Bleak House* (London, Penguin Classics, 1995) 18.

2. *Lawyer's costs.* This includes the lawyer's time charged hourly, as a fixed fee or wholly or partly determined by a scale. In addition, as described above, in common law systems the out-payments of the lawyer (disbursements) including court fees and expert fees fall to be paid by the litigant client. However, in most jurisdictions, excluding state courts in the USA but not federal courts, the full blown or modified 'English Rule' will apply so that the 'winner' recovers some or all of this outlay from the 'loser'. In England under the Civil Procedural Rules the *intention* is that costs should be predictable and proportionate. The various tools to accomplish these objectives are outlined below. In fact these methods are ineffective and are subject to a current review by Lord Justice Jackson whose reform proposals are discussed in a separate chapter.

3. *Financing.* The implication of court costs and lawyers' costs are universally a matter of concern to clients in any dispute of substance or, in cost benefit terms, in minor matters. In fact it is only in 'super' litigation between hulking corporate giants that the legal costs will be regarded as insignificant compared with the sums in dispute and here the parties will often shuffle off to the confidentiality of arbitration. For most litigants self-funding is deeply unattractive and, increasingly, state support through legal aid is not available. This conundrum can be solved in a number of ways that are described in detail below but can be summed up as private funding for most commercial cases, usually on an hourly paid basis and conditional fees for individual claims.

The inter-relationship between the three elements above exists in all jurisdictions and is rarely without some difficulty. The court fees may be too low and central state support insufficient to generate enough judges to ensure efficient and timely disposal. The funding of cases through contingency fees is generally not a cause of controversy but in the USA it is alleged to be the engine behind 'clientless' or lawyer lead litigation: cases brought for the benefit of the lawyers not 'real' cases. Contrariwise without legal aid or insurance contingency fees may be the only means of bringing cases. However, it is fair to say that in most jurisdictions the balance between the elements and the whole subject of litigation costs ranks fairly well down the list of concerns. Issues such as judicial corruption, procedural complexity or delay are of greater concern. Litigation costs are merely the dessert following the main course. Except, in England . . .

Despite the comments quoted above from Bleak House costs in England have grown from a 'mere bud' into a hideous excrescence. The infamous case of *Jarndyce v Jarndyce* was fictional but based according to Dickens, writing in 1853, on a case that had started at the close of the previous century and was not yet decided. The central problem was delay, complexity and unpredictability of procedure. The costs were vast but this was inevitable considering the huge labour expended on such marathon cases: the cost issue was simply a symptom of a procedural disease. In the period up to the present the complexity of Chancery and the less high profile but equally obscure problems of High Court procedure have been slowly ameliorated until Lord Woolf in his epic Access to Justice Enquiry finally identified and resolved procedural problems and brought them to heel. Woolf wanted to go further and change the cost system to introduce elements of predictability but opposition from practitioners—and insufficient interest from government—baulked him. Perhaps in resignation, but certainly in hope, Woolf took the view that case management and rationing of procedure would strangle the cost monster. It didn't and since then, partly fuelled by conditional fees, costs have continued to be a serious problem for access to justice.[2]

The issue of cost reform was first raised in the modern era in the Civil Justice Review 1988 followed by the Small Personal Injury Claims consultation in 1993;[3] the Hodge/Heilbron Report in1993;[4] the Woolf Interim Report in 1995 and his Final Report in 1996;[5] the Middleton report in 1997;[6] reviews by the government on Personal Injury costs[7] and now the review by Lord Justice Jackson whose interim report was published in mid 2009[8] and whose final report was published in January 2010.[9] This sequence of major reviews and interventions is significant in public policy for failing to produce a sustainable and long lasting solution to a problem which is widely recognised and which has been largely tamed in other jurisdictions. It is reflected in the creation of a cadre of senior lawyers, solicitors and barristers including Queen's Counsel, who practice mainly in cost litigation once the preserve of non-legally qualified cost clerks.

The following chapter outlines the reform proposals made by Lord Justice Jackson and considers their prospects. This chapter now offers a snapshot of the current funding and cost position in England and Wales with the proviso that it will change to a greater or lesser extent according to the success of the Jackson initiatives.

Settlement and Alternative Dispute Resolution

Before moving to describe the current picture, the importance of settlement and ADR must be addressed. The litigation process in England and Wales is dominated not by trials but by settlement. The statistics in Table 1 are for the County Court, which is the most important jurisdiction, the High Court being for a limited number of high value claims.

[2] For a similar academic analysis see AAS Zuckerman, 'Lord Justice Jackson's Review of Civil Litigation Costs—Preliminary Report' (2009) 28 *CJQ*. 435–47.

[3] Lord Chancellor's Department.

[4] H Hodge & H Heilbron, 'Civil Justice on Trial—Joint Report of the General Council of the Bar and the Law Society' (1993) *Joint Report of The Bar Council and The Law Society.*

[5] Lord Woolf 'Access to Justice: Interim Report to the Lord Chancellor on the Civil Justice System in England and Wales', HMSO (Final Report).

[6] www.dca.gov.uk/middleton/report.doc.

[7] 'Low Value Personal Injury Costs in Road Traffic Accidents', www.justice.gov.uk/publications/docs/personal-injury-claims.

[8] www.judiciary.gov.uk/about-judiciary/costs-review/index-htm.

[9] Lord Justice Jackson, *Review of Civil Litigation Costs, Final Report,* Jan 2010.

Table 1: County Court statistics

Year	Number of Defences	Number of claims allocated to a track	Difference
2000	250,442	155,208	95,234
2001	255,035	142,781	112,254
2002	266,625	142,031	124,594
2003	268,042	157,175	110,867
2004	261,666	152,913	108,753
2005	278,019	155,541	122,478
2006	295,372	157,192	138,180
2007	341,956	176,210	165,746

The statistics for civil litigation undertaken in the County Court between 2000 and 2007 demonstrates the volume of claims that never reach the court process, by comparing the number of claims on which a declaration of an intention to defend was entered against the number of claims allocated to a case management track, ie the fast track for lower value cases or the multi-track for higher value and more complex cases. (The same cost regime applies in both of these tracks. The essential difference is procedural—in the fast track the process is broadly proscribed, in the multi-track it will mostly be tailor made to the case.) The difference between these figures demonstrates cases that were settled between these two stages.

This winnowing of cases away from a litigation process towards resolution by withdrawal or settlement is mirrored at each stage in the system so that fewer than two per cent of cases reach a substantive trial.

The winnowing down of the numbers of cases is necessary to sustain the system. If cases had a propensity to reach trial at the German rate the system, which is short of resources, would collapse. The model adopted is based on the fact that litigation costs are high *and* unpredictable; settlement introduced predictability *and saves costs.* The system has two main parts that can apply before and during the currency of litigation:

1. CPR part 36. This is described in more detail below but essentially it is a form of spread betting. A party makes a calculation as to whether he will win his case and by how much and makes, accepts or refuses an offer to settle according to this view with cost consequences that can be penal.

2. Increasingly, cases that are not zero sum games settle by use of ADR, normally mediation. This is enhanced by the threat of a cost penalty if parties do not enter mediation when it is reasonable to do so.[10]

[10] *Halsey v Milton Keynes GH* [2004] EWCA (Civ) 576

In a sense this can be seen as a counsel of despair and antithetical to access to justice and the development of common law precedents.[11] Cases settle without adjudication in some instances because parties can come to a genuine agreement and down swords, resuming a relationship. This is the theoretical basis of mediation in, say, family matters and commercial disputes between members of the same supply chain. However, in England the majority of cases settle simply because of the fear of costs with a pragmatic but hardly rigorous resolution.

Funding Claims

No fewer than eight major possible sources of finance for litigation must be considered.

1. **Personal Funding.** It follows from the discussion above that the costs of litigation are daunting to most individuals and SMEs. Pooling of this risk is possible with individuals, friends, family and others who *bona fide* fund litigation, provided they are without a personal interest in the outcome (other than the recovery of the funding) and without attempting to control it. Such are permitted to fund litigation without restriction or liability for costs.[12] This type of assistance has largely been phased out by the development of conditional fees, discussed below.

2. **Civil Legal Aid.** The Legal Services Commission manages the civil legal aid fund. Different levels of legal help are granted on the basis of a demonstration of merit and proof of financial eligibility.[13] The Civil Legal Aid fund is means tested and restrictive in nature. Cases where costs are expected to exceed £ 25,000 are unusual in this method of funding and largely relate to areas of law such as clinical negligence and judicial review. Essentially government policy is that citizens should litigate using conditional fees, described below.

3. **Legal Expense (before the event) Insurance.** While available in England, 'BTE' insurance is rarely bought directly but is bundled into another product, such as house or car insurance, at low cost or no cost. How can this be when the insured risk—the cost of paying legal fees if the litigation is unsuccessfully brought or defended—is so high? The answer is that this type of insurance is normally just a system for referring cases to lawyers who finance cases either through speculation (recovering basic fees from the other side and standing the loss if the case is lost)[14] or through the more lucrative conditional fee route discussed below.

[11] OM Fiss, 'Against Settlement', (1984) 93 *Yale LJ* 1073.

[12] *Hamilton v Al Fayed* [2002] EWCA Civ 665.

[13] The eligibility criteria and procedures are set out in The Funding Code and Decision Making Guidance, made under the Access to Justice Act 1999, available at www.legalservices.gov.uk/civil/guidance/funding_code.asp.

[14] Speculation is theoretically unlawful as it breaches the indemnity principle but it is common and was endemic in this field of practice before CFAs.

4. **A Contingency Fee**, that is a sharing of recovered damages between the client and lawyer, is not legal in civil litigation in England. It is, however, possible (although rare) in pre-litigation settlement, and is common in employment tribunals, which for arcane reasons fall outside the ambit of civil litigation.

5. **A Contingency Fee Fund** (a pooled state or voluntary fund that supports cases in return for a cut of damages). Whilst, this is a perennial interest to the Bar in England it is unlikely ever to be a practical prospect.

6. **A Conditional Fee** system: basic fees plus a reward.[15] This form is most developed in England and Wales and incorporates recovery from the 'loser' of a reward (the success fee) which can double the successful lawyer's hourly fee. In addition disbursements can be recovered, including the premium for Litigation (After the Event) Insurance, which has held the litigant harmless against an adverse cost order. Whilst seeming to be a mere gloss on the normal 'English' rule of cost recovery, it has in fact become the prime mechanism for financing much commodity litigation, such as personal injury cases, as well as esoteric litigation, such as defamation. The lawyer's caseload finances the operation of the litigation business: winning cases produce sufficient surplus to cover 'lost' hours involved in fighting losing cases (The Warchest). Invariably, the client pays little or nothing, win or lose, and this includes the Litigation Insurance premium. In practice most personal injury cases that proceed beyond initial enquiries recover because they are either 'good' cases or it is not worth defending them and defendants take an 'economic' view.

7. The most recent development in funding is **Third Party Funding**. Here an external investor will fund the whole of the client's lawyer's costs and disbursement and the risk of paying adverse costs in return for a cut of any damages recovered. This system, which is well developed in Australia and in some parts of Europe, is making inroads into England spearheaded by merchant banks and insurers looking for higher rates of return post credit crunch. The concomitant risk is rewarded by high returns in winning cases, anything up to 40 per cent. The risk/reward balance and the need for due diligence imposes a heavy cost if the funder backs a losing case and it follows that they are highly risk averse and will only back cases where the prospects are for substantial damages. However, they do represent a new stakeholder in the contested area of litigation costs. Unlike conditional fee lawyers they have no interest in maintaining high levels of costs as this is not the way they make their money. They make money from recovery of damages and whilst they will understand that litigation effort with associated costs may give

[15] The concept of a conditional fee agreement (CFA) was introduced by the Courts and Legal Services Act 1990, s 58, and opened up by the Access to Justice Act 1999, s 27. A CFA may include a success fee to be payable in specified circumstances (usually if the client wins the case), and a success fee must be expressed as a percentage uplift on the amount which would be payable if there was no CFA. Under the Conditional Fee Agreements Order 2000, the maximum uplift may be 100% of the basic fee. Save as permitted under the CFA legislation, other types of damage-based fee agreements remain prohibited under the traditional rules on maintenance and champerty.

a higher chance of success they will always be conscious of their potential liability as payer.[16] In so far as Third Party Funding becomes less exotic the voice of funders will be one calling for more predictable and moderated costs.

8. Historically a **Trade Union** (and some trade associations) supported a member's litigation by paying the member's own solicitor's costs and any costs awarded to the member's opponent. Many trade unions now insist on their members taking out legal expenses insurance to cover any liability for party and party costs, but some do not and continue to pay such costs from their own funds. Section 30 of the Access to Justice Act 1999 not only recognises this practice but also encourages it by enabling the union to recover from an unsuccessful opponent a contribution to the union's costs in other cases where the member loses.

Court Fees and Disbursements

Most court charges are payable on issue of the relevant form.[17] By way of example, court fees on issue of the originating process vary between £30 (for a claim of less than £300) to £1,530 (for a claim of £300,000 or of unlimited value). There are fees for most stages of the litigation. Contrary to all other civil justice systems in the developed world, the system in England is not intended to be a service provided by the state out of general taxation to support civil society: it is intended to be self supporting through the fees levied. This applies even in the small claims track: applying for a hearing in such a case can involve fees, for example the fee for a £3000 claim is £300. That is a considerable sum for what was intended to be a means of access to justice without the need for lawyers at modest cost in small cases. In fact this self funding objective is limited by two factors: the availability of fee remission on a means tested basis or for the diminishing numbers of those parties who qualify for legal aid and the fact that whilst fees are high there is some taking into account of what the traffic will bear. This policy is highly contested but it appears to be a central plank of Treasury policy.

With respect to disbursements, the fees paid to expert witnesses and for other forensic assistance are recoverable. The cost of after the event insurance (although not before the event insurance) and notional insurance premiums levied by trade unions or other organisations as the price of their support is recoverable. Counsel's fees may be levied on a conditional fee basis but they are normally payable by the client irrespective of winning or losing the case. If the case is won they are recoverable as a disbursement.

[16] *Arkin v Borchard* [2005] EWCA Civ 655: litigation funders' liability for costs increases the more they contribute to their own side, such that potential liability for opponents' costs arise up to the same amount.

[17] See SI 2008/1053 at www.opsi.gov.uk/si/si2008/uksi_20081053_en_1 and amendments in SI 2009/1498 at www.opsi.gov.uk/si/si2009/uksi_20091498_en_1. VAT is payable on such costs.

How the Cost System Works

The technical position is that no party has a right to have its costs paid by the other party, and that costs are in the discretion of the court. However, the normal outcome is that costs follow the event, ie the successful party recovers from the loser or losers any court fee paid, disbursements and most (say 75 per cent) of the party's own lawyer's costs.

The court system is divided into three tracks: the small claims track, the fast track (a procedurally rationed track for most cases) and the multi-track (for higher value, more complex cases). Cost shifting applies in a broadly similar way to the fast track and multi-track but in the small claims track only in respect of court fees and disbursements not lawyer's fees.

The Costs Systems in Greater Detail

The costs regime is outstandingly complex, varies between different types of cases, and its tangles are not relevant to this discussion. The detailed rules and practice for the costs regime are complex, and. The main provisions dealing with costs are CPR 43–48 and the Costs Practice Direction.[18] Under CPR 44.3, the court will take into account the following factors when making costs orders:

1. The conduct of the parties, including:
   a. conduct before and during the proceedings, including the observance of any pre-action protocol;
   b. whether it was reasonable to raise issues or allegations. The court is prepared to make issue based costs orders to reflect the level of success achieved by any party;[19]
   c. the manner in which a party has pursued or defended its case;
   d. whether its case was exaggerated.
2. Whether a party succeeded on part, if not all of his case.
3. Any offers to settle the case[20] or payments made during the course of the case.

There is a bewildering range of possible costs orders that a court may make.[21] Relevant factors the court will take into account in determining whether to deal with costs on an issue basis include the:

1. reasonableness of taking the point;
2. extra time taken up prior to trial/the hearing in preparing to argue the point;

[18] See especially CPR 44.3 at www.justice.gov.uk/civil/procrules_fin/contents/parts/part44.htm.
[19] *AEI Rediffusion Music Ltd v Phonographic Performance Ltd* [1999] 1 WLR 1507, CA.
[20] See www.justice.gov.uk/civil/procrules_fin/contents/parts/part36.htm.
[21] See Costs Practice Direction 44PD, s 8 para 8.5, at www.justice.gov.uk/civil/procrules_fin/contents/practice_directions/pd_parts43-48.htm.

3. extra time taken up in court to argue the point;
4. extent to which it is just in all the circumstances to deprive the successful party of its costs;
5. extent to which the unsuccessful point was related to any successful point.

The court may at any stage require a party file an estimate of costs and serve copies of the estimate on all other parties.[22]

The English Rule states that the losing party or parties pay the winning party or party's costs. These costs may be on a fixed fee basis but more typically nowadays they are made up of an hourly rate for the relevant fee earner or fee earners multiplied by the number of hours of work (calculated in minimum six minute units ie an acknowledgment letter equals six minutes; longer letters are costed as to how long they took to the nearest six minutes. This bears resemblance to the lodestar model in the USA in the context of a cost shifting statute). Between client and lawyer the contract will determine the hourly rates and the contractual charge forms the *maximum* of what *can be* recovered from the other side if the party is successful (the so called indemnity rule).

As well as 'normal' costs ((hourly rate x hours spent) + disbursements) a successful case conducted on a conditional fee (normally but not inevitably a claim or counterclaim where there are damages to bite on rather than a defence) will also have as an additional element of costs a further fee called the 'success fee' of up to 100 per cent of basic fees. This is not subject to court discretion in most cases, although in some classes of cases, road traffic and industrial disease the success fee is capped at a lower level. As stated above, this system is available to the Bar but is unusual, probably because barristers do not have a sufficiently wide caseloads to spread their risk of losing some cases and they have less influence than their instructing solicitor on the decision to settle which can crucially affect the decision whether or not to fight a less than open and shut case to trial.

Proportionality

The golden thread running through the discretion on cost shifting set out above is Lord Woolf's concept of proportionality ie that access to justice predicates that legal costs and, in particular, costs shifted to the loser should bear some reasonable proportion to the claim broadly described and including its value, complexity, importance etc. The rules state:[23]

[22] CPR Part 43, note, para 6.3 at www.justice.gov.uk/civil/procrules_fin/contents/practice_directions/pd_parts43-48.htm—id3585917.

[23] CPR, 44.4.

'(2) Where the amount of costs is to be assessed on the standard basis, the court will—

(a) *Only allow costs which are proportionate to the matters in issue*; and
(b) resolve any doubt which it may have as to whether costs were reasonably incurred or reasonable and proportionate in amount in favour of the paying party.'

Section 11 of the Costs Practice Direction adds some further detail:

'11.1 In applying the test of proportionality the . . . relationship between the total of the costs incurred and the financial value of the claim may not be a reliable guide. A fixed percentage cannot be applied in all cases to the value of the claim in order to ascertain whether or not the costs are proportionate.

11.2 In any proceedings there will be costs which will inevitably be incurred and which are necessary for the successful conduct of the case. Solicitors are not required to conduct litigation at rates which are uneconomic. Thus in a modest claim the proportion of costs is likely to be higher than in a large claim, and may even equal or possibly exceed the amount in dispute.'

The combination of the discretions outlined above and the attempt to introduce a concept of proportionality has not been successful. The rules do not explain what proportionality means in practice and although the case of *Lownds v The Home Office*[24] gives some help there is room for considerable argument. As explained below, argument over costs means more costs. The predictability of a system such as that used in Germany seems very attractive compared to this arrangement. Short of the introduction of such a scheme, which Lord Woolf proposed in his initial report and Lord Justice Jackson is clearly interested in, we must search for elements of predictability in the thicket of English cost uncertainty.

How Predictable is the Cost System?

Predictability is important in civil litigation system based on transferring costs from loser to winner:

1. Predictability makes underwriting decisions by After the Event insurers easier. It makes Before the Event insurance cheaper.

2. It reassures the paying client as to one quantum element of the risk of litigation. Factored into the risk of failure it would make it easier to make decisions. This might not be wholly welcome to all constituencies. Historically the judges have long fretted about the risk of floods of litigation overwhelming the courts and imposing excessive liability on, for example, local authorities. Against a background of fear of the emergence of a 'compensation culture' the Compensation Act 2006 brought statutory force to these concerns. It might seem that insurers

[24] [2002] EWCA Civ 365.

would take the same view but equally the threat of litigation is a potent reason to insure. Ultimately, litigation should be primarily about access to justice and predictability adds to a clients' ability to obtain it.

Elements of Predictability

The current system in England whilst essentially unpredictable compared with other jurisdictions has elements of predictability:

1. Between lawyer and client the system of enforceable estimates and conditional fees, if utilised together with disbursements (eg expert fees) agreed in advance makes the system reasonably predictable on a unilateral basis. If the outturn bill is 20 per cent more than estimated then the lawyer will have difficulties in recovering it from his own client.[25]

2. In a successful case this bill then falls to be recoverable from the loser. As stated above the general rule is that the unsuccessful party will be ordered to pay most of the costs of the successful party—a very approximate guide is 75 per cent. A figure of between 66 per cent and 75 per cent recovery seems hard wired into the brains of cost judges and has survived a number of changes in the procedural 'theory' of cost calculation. It is a regulatory compromise between holding the successful client harmless and ensuring that the client retains some interest in the costs as he will have to pay a proportion. One of the difficulties of the conditional fee system is that this link between client and payer is broken in most cases, such as personal injury or road traffic litigation, as market forces dictate that clients are offered a guarantee that they will have nothing to pay, win or loss. This forms a sharp contrast with contingency fee litigation where there are no transferred costs. Here is no incentive to keep costs high (which in conditional fees benefits the lawyer and normally does not affect the winning client), rather the reverse: the contingency fee lawyer who wins a case with minimum effort takes home more profit from his share of the damages.

3. The system of summary assessment of costs under CPR 43.3 and Sections 3 and 13 of the Costs Practice Direction is to provide some degree of prior warning regarding costs and to prevent them from becoming unmanageably high. The court will normally conduct a summary assessment of the costs at the conclusion of the trial of a fast track case (which must be no more than one day), where it will assess the costs of the whole case or at the conclusion of any other hearing which has lasted not more than one day. However, the court has discretion. If summary assessment is not conducted, the court must order that the costs be dealt with by way of a detailed assessment. This tends to happen if the trial or hearing has dragged on and time is short at the end of the day.

[25] *Wong v Vizard (a firm)* [1997] 2 Cost LR 46.

4. Cost capping. CPR rule 44.18 allows a judge to limit the amount of future legal costs and disbursements that are recoverable from a losing party (although the winning party will remain liable for the balance). The effect would be to produce a flexible cost structure up to a cap. Thus, recoverable costs might be less but cannot be more than a certain figure. In the context of, for example, multi-track cases with tailor-made case management directions this would be as close to a predictable regime as could be obtained without moving to scale costs on the German model.

> '(5) The court may at any stage of proceedings make a costs capping order against all or any of the parties, if –
>
> (a) it is in the interests of justice to do so;
> (b) there is a substantial risk that without such an order costs will be disproportionately incurred; and
> (c) it is not satisfied that the risk in sub-paragraph (b) can be adequately controlled by –
>
> (i) case management directions or orders made under Part 3; and
> (ii) detailed assessment of costs.
>
> (6) In considering whether to exercise its discretion under this rule, the court will consider all the circumstances of the case, including –
>
> (a) whether there is a substantial imbalance between the financial position of the parties;
> (b) whether the costs of determining the amount of the cap are likely to be proportionate to the overall costs of the litigation;
> (c) the stage which the proceedings have reached; and
> (d) the costs which have been incurred to date and the future costs.
>
> (7) A costs capping order, once made, will limit the costs recoverable by the party subject to the order unless a party successfully applies to vary the order. No such variation will be made unless –
>
> (a) there has been a material and substantial change of circumstances since the date when the order was made; or
> (b) there is some other compelling reason why a variation should be made.'

This offers, in theory, a strong argument for obtaining a cost capping order if applied for at an early stage in proceedings. However, the application has to show that absent the order costs will be disproportionality incurred *and* case management *and/or* post case detailed assessment cannot control the risk. The relevant Practice Direction (guidance to the cost judge) states that cost capping orders should only be made in 'exceptional circumstances'. Added to the perceived reluctance of the lawyers to apply for such orders it is not surprising that they are rare beasts.

A Paradigm of Unpredictability

If costs are not summarily assessed or settled by negotiation they are subject to a process of detailed assessment, a trial of the costs. A detailed assessment of costs (in effect a trial to determine the reasonableness of the costs incurred) will be decided by a costs judge. Generally, detailed assessments are not conducted until the conclusion of the proceedings.

This is an adversarial process and the 'winner' of this parasitic trial can recover a further tranche of costs, sometimes as much or more than the costs of the substantive litigation. It is hardly surprising then that this has become a new practice area for lawyers!

Tactical Means of Reducing Cost Liability

Against this background a plethora of procedural means have developed to curtail the level of cost liability. In general these measures are patches on the hull of a leaky boat; they do not cure the essential problem of high and unpredictable costs. A primary objective of the CPR was to restrict the costs of litigation through case management, with the court controlling the work to be done by the parties to ensure that it was proportionate to the issues. Other cost limiting mechanisms encouraged by the CPR are early stage case management conferences, ADR mechanisms and allocation to a management track to suit the scale of the case. None of these measures have proved to be very effective.

Potentially more effective are two measures:

1. The rules require the use of costs estimates and requires these to be available to the court (and clients) at stages throughout the life of the case. The system which was fairly recently introduced is modelled on the estimate regime between client and his own lawyer. If the final bill produced for payment by a loser is 20 per cent or more higher than the estimate, then it may be more difficult to recover, although in practice, this rule seldom bites.

2. The defendant may make a Part 36 offer to settle the case prior to it going to court. (The consequence of making a Part 36 offer and finding that the court awards a greater sum by way of damages than the amount contained in the offer is set out below, as is the consequence of a party rejecting an offer only to find that the court make a greater award on judgment.)

If a claimant fails to 'beat' a defendant's offer when the judgment is handed down the claimant will be ordered to pay the defendant's costs plus interest from 21 days after the offer was made, unless the court considers it unjust to do so If a claimant does better than the offer when the judgment is handed down the court may order interest on the whole or part of any sums awarded to the claimant at a rate of up to 10 per cent above base rate from 21 days after the offer was made, unless the court considers it unjust to do so. A similar process of offers can be used in the detailed assessment process.

Conclusion

There is little doubt that compared with many jurisdictions the English jurisdiction remains highly unpredictable. In Germany the client in commercial litigation may increasingly be asked to pay over and above the scale costs but at least the client can have confidence that the recovery might be set against the final bill. In England whilst a defendant under the case management system knows how many experts the opponent can field he doesn't know what their fee is; he doesn't know what time has been spent on searching for abortive experts. He knows the limits of the disclosure (discovery) exercise but he doesn't know how much time the opposing lawyer spends on the exercise. The effect of this uncertainty is that in complex cases the shock of receiving an opponent's bill and the need to recover one's own bill to its maximum converts what should be a quiet epilogue to the litigation into what can be a vicious battle: often more bitterly fought than the litigation itself. Given the persistence of this problem in English civil procedure whilst problems such as delay and complexity have been successfully tackled, optimism for an early resolution to the problem may be foolhardy.

8

England and Wales: Summary of the Jackson Costs Review

CHRISTOPHER HODGES

The reason why the Jackson Costs Review was instigated was a belief by the senior judiciary that litigation costs in *some*—but important—types of cases in England and Wales were far too high and uncontrolled. Lord Justice Jackson was asked to investigate and to propose solutions. He produced two huge, detailed and carefully reasoned documents: a Preliminary Report in May 2009[1] and a Final Report in January 2010.[2]

Various general observations can be made. Firstly, Lord Justice Jackson was immensely diligent in leaving no stone within his remit unturned or unexamined. Secondly, he held extensive public consultations and made himself available to all. He carefully noted all points of view. He also involved many people and interested groups in producing information and examining options. His inclusive methodology clearly paid dividends in that everyone felt that they were consulted, even if they did not like some of the judge's conclusions.[3] Thirdly, the judge was at pains to identify and rely on relevant empirical data and research. Leading examples are the detailed calculations made by economist Professor Paul Fenn (which underpinned various decisions, such as raising damages by 10 per cent) and the comparative project carried out at the University of Oxford by the editors of this book (which showed that the loser pays rule is applied almost universally (apart from USA) and that only in England and Wales were conditional fee agreement (CFA) success fees and ATE insurance premiums recoverable from defendants).

Fourthly, he recognised that the issues of funding and costs are entirely interlinked, and individually extensive in range and deep in complexity. Solutions had to be found that would work within the holistic context. Fifthly, many separate aspects needed to be considered, and the maxim 'one size does not fit all' is frequently repeated in his Final Report. Cases that were reviewed include small claims, personal injury, clinical negligence, road traffic, housing, judicial review,

[1] R Jackson, *Review of Civil Litigation Costs: Preliminary Report* (The Stationery Office, 2009), ('Preliminary Report'), at http://www.judiciary.gov.uk/about_judiciary/cost-review/jan2010/vol1-low.pdf.

[2] R Jackson, *Review of Civil Litigation Costs: Final Report* (The Stationery Office, 2010), ('Final Report'), at http://www.judiciary.gov.uk/about_judiciary/cost-review/jan2010/final-report-140110.pdf.

[3] 'The stakeholders are deeply divided on all major issues': Final Report, ch 1, para 6.4,

intellectual property, construction and technology, large commercial cases. All these situations, and many more, raise particular considerations, and call for distinct answers. The lesson is that it is almost impossible to specify a single approach for funding, procedure and costs that can apply equally to cases. Nevertheless, fifthly, certain general principles are applied, mostly ones that are well-familiar both historically and from Woolf: maintaining access to justice and the rule of law, ensuring that cases are dealt with justly, and that costs should be proportionate.

Sixthly, the need for review is a constant requirement, and part of an ongoing process of continuous development. This review took place ten years after two major reforms, the extensive Woolf reforms of civil procedure and the extension of CFAs so as to replace legal aid. Lord Justice Jackson recommended significant changes in relation to both those aspects, plus many more. He made clear that periodic review is essential and ongoing: several issues that he considered were identified for further investigation and future review. Indeed, he refrained from recommending that some reforms that he would like to see should be implemented too soon, in view of not wishing to impose too much major change at any one time, and so enable people to concentrate on successfully embedding what he regards as the major aspects.

The major changes that Lord Justice Jackson focussed on can be categorised as reforming funding mechanisms and many individual improvements in case management designed to improve procedures and manage costs so that they are proportionate. Overall, he made 109 individual recommendations. Questions arise over whether and when they might be implemented. Some require primary legislation, and the 2010 UK Parliamentary elections mean that it is entirely unclear whether any legislation may be brought forward. Some aspects can be introduced through rules changes or Court of Appeal decisions, and these can be expected, but individual changes are dependent on what the legislative framework looks like. Further, since the stakeholders are deeply divided on all major issues, further lobbying cannot be discounted.

The Situation Before and After the 1999 Reforms

The historical background is important in order to understand the conclusions that Lord Justice Jackson came to. From 1947, the costs of litigation by individuals were in many cases paid by the state through legal aid. Legal aid operated as a loan by the state to an individual who satisfied both merits and means tests, in other words the individual's level of disposable income and capital had to fall below specified limits and the case had to have reasonable prospects of success. If legal aid was granted, public funds paid for legal advice and representation. If the case was won, the defendant would reimburse the legal aid fund its costs under the loser pays rule. If the case was lost, however, the winner was not entitled to enforce an order for costs against either the legal aid fund or against the assisted party, unless that party then or later turned out to have more money. Thus, there was one-way qualified cost shifting. Defendants described their position as subject to 'legal aid blackmail',[4] since they had to pay costs if they settled but could not recover them if they lost, and although they were typically powerful defendants, the power of legally aided claimants to force settlements was significant.

Legal aid initially covered 80 per cent of households, but the level of expenditure was uncontrollable and uncapped. By the 1980s and 1990s, successive governments had reduced the financial eligibility limits so that the middle classes were both ineligible for legal aid and unable to afford to pay lawyers themselves: 36 per cent of households were eligible by 2009. Further, the legal aid budget was controlled by decisions of its service providers and escalating. Inevitably, the government decided to restrict civil legal aid very severely, control the expenditure within a finite budget, and make an administrative authority responsible for allocation decisions within specified priorities of types of cases and subject to availability of funds.

In order to maintain access to justice for the poor, and re-open it for the middle class, the government privatised funding. Whilst not wishing to completely deregulate funding or overturn centuries of prohibitions on independent parties being able to profit from or control others' litigation, expressed through the mediaeval concepts of maintenance and champerty, the government introduced a legal exception for specified arrangements called conditional fee agreements (CFAs). A CFA combined a 'no win no fee' concept (which had widely existed in practice even if prohibited) with the concept of a basic fee (based on traditional hourly rates times work done) with a success fee (a proportionate uplift of the basic fee). The proportion of the success fee in a given case would represent an appropriate uplift depending on the size of the risk, but subject to capping the uplift at 100 per cent, which created a framework for proportionality. This system was intended to maintain stability by enabling lawyers to cross-subsidise winning and losing cases through the success fee element.

The normal loser pays rule has always applied to claimants, whereas it has been suspended for those supported under the legal aid system. In order to provide cover for that risk, insurance policies were encouraged. At that time, legal expenses insurance (LEI) was growing in the UK but was not extensive. New after-the-event (ATE) policies were created, distinguished from the normal LEI type of before-the-event (BTE). From 1995 to 1999, the cost of success fees and ATE premiums was born by successful claimants out of their damages. However, there was a 'big bang' in 1999 with the simultaneous introduction of the new Woolf-inspired Civil Procedure Rules and the removal of much civil legal aid. In order to provide stability for the new system, the government provided that success fees and ATE premiums should be recoverable from defendants in addition to 'normal' costs.

[4] For an explanation of how Legal Aid Act 1988, s 18(4) worked see C Hodges, *Multi-Party Actions* (Oxford, Oxford University Press, 2001) 308.

This change increased defendants' bills (especially liability insurers') and was justified on grounds of enabling full recovery by claimants and of pragmatism in ensuring that access to justice was maintained.

> '. . . the burden of financing a huge swathe of litigation was transferred from taxpayers to opposing litigants. Ironically, those opposing litigants are, in many cases, funded by taxpayers or council taxpayers: for example, the NHS Litigation Authority, local authorities, police authorities, etc.'[5]

Over the following decade, insurers forced a series of gruelling 'costs wars' to try to limit their exposure, whilst costs rose. The key battlegrounds were personal injury and defamation cases, where usually modest amounts of damages were accompanied by large and disproportionate costs to be paid by defendants, and large commercial, construction, technical and intellectual property cases, where the amount of work done by both sides could be considerable and costs were uncontrollable through Woolfian case management techniques.

A further issue was that Woolfian pre-action protocols, under which parties were encouraged to voluntarily exchange allegations and evidence with a view to enabling early settlement, front-loaded the costs and sometimes made the work unnecessary and the costs disproportionately high.[6] Various amendments were made, with a proliferation of protocols or approaches for different types of case in order to try to fine tune the balance between promoting settlement and enabling litigation to proceed, both at minimal and proportionate cost. This mixture of issues comprised the situation for Lord Justice Jackson to grapple with.

Jackson's Analysis of the Causes of High Costs

Lord Justice Jackson viewed his project as 'essentially a matter of building on Lord Woolf's work and proposing reforms where (after ten years experience) these appear to be appropriate'.[7] He identified 16 general causes that give rise to excessive costs:[8]

(i) The rules of court require parties to carry out time-consuming procedures involving professional skill.
(ii) In some areas of litigation, the complexity of the law causes parties to incur substantial costs.[9]
(iii) The costs rules are such as to generate satellite litigation.
(iv) Too few solicitors, barristers and judges have a sufficient understanding of the law of costs or how costs may be controlled.

[5] Final Report, ch 10, para 4.3.
[6] See D Dwyer, *The Civil Procedure Rules Ten Years On* (Oxford, Oxford University Press, 2010).
[7] Final Report, ch 1, para 6.2.
[8] Final Report, ch 4, para 3.1.
[9] A particular example of this complicating complexity is the law on housing, for which he recommended that three Reports of the Law Commission should be implemented: Final Report, ch 26.

(v) Lawyers are generally paid by reference to time spent, rather than work product.
(vi) The recoverable hourly rates of lawyers are not satisfactorily controlled.
(vii) The preparation of witness statements and expert reports can generate excessive costs.
(viii) The costs shifting rule creates perverse incentives.
(ix) The CFA regime has had unfortunate unintended consequences, namely (a) litigants with CFAs have little interest in controlling the costs which are being incurred on their behalf and (b) opposing litigants face a massively increased costs liability.
(x) The advent of emails and electronic databases means that, in substantial cases, the process of standard disclosure may be prohibitively expensive.
(xi) There is no effective control over pre-issue costs; certain pre-action protocols lead to magnification of these costs and duplication of effort.
(xii) In some instances there is ineffective case management, both by the parties and by the court.
(xiii) Some cases which ought to settle early settle too late or not at all.
(xiv) The procedures for detailed assessment are unduly cumbersome, with the result that (a) they are unduly expensive to operate and (b) they frequently discourage litigants from securing a proper assessment.
(xv) The current level of court fees is too high and the current policy of full cost pricing is wrong in principle.[10]
(xvi) Despite the growth of court fees in recent years, the civil courts remain under-resourced in terms of both staff and IT.

Further work is outlined in the Final Report on a large number of detailed issues for specific courts and types of case. One example is establishment of a uniform calibration for all software systems used to assess damages for pain and suffering and loss of amenity.

The Principle of Proportionality of Costs

Lord Justice Jackson's package of solutions was soundly based on the principle of enabling access to justice. He defined the concept as follows:

> 'Access to justice entails that those with meritorious claims (whether or not ultimately successful) are able to bring those claims before the courts for judicial resolution or post-issue settlement, as the case may be. It also entails that those with meritorious defences (whether or not ultimately successful) are able to put those defences before the courts for judicial resolution or, alternatively, settlement based upon the merits of the case.'[11]

He went on to assert that

> '[a]ccess to justice is only possible if both parties have adequate funding . . . Access to justice is only practicable if the costs of litigation are proportionate. If costs are

[10] Jackson LJ made clear his opposition to the government's policy of setting court fees on the basis of full cost recovery: Final Report, ch 4, para 3.35 *et seq*.
[11] Final Report,ch 4, para 2.3.

disproportionate, then even a well-resourced party may hesitate before pursuing a valid claim or maintaining a valid defence. That party may simply drop a good claim or capitulate to a weak claim, as the case may be.'[12]

Whilst accepting that there may be some antithesis between controlling costs and promoting access to justice, 'for the most part, achieving proportionate costs and promoting access to justice go hand in hand. If costs on both sides are proportionate, then (i) there is more access to justice and (ii) such funding as the parties possess is more likely to be sufficient.'[13]

Although a test of proportionality of costs was introduced under the Woolf reforms,[14] and underlay the whole concept of the fast track for smaller cases, interpretation of the rules led to the re-introduction of the concept of necessity into assessing work done.[15] The current rule is that, in applying the (normal) standard basis award of costs, the court will not allow costs that have been unreasonably incurred or are unreasonable in amount,[16] and will only allow costs that are 'proportionate to the matters in issue'.[17]

Lord Justice Jackson recommended that the concept of proportionality should prevail on a global basis over the test of reasonableness by enabling disproportionate costs to be disallowed in an assessment of costs on the standard basis. 'Proportionate costs' should be defined by reference to sums in issue, value of non-monetary relief, complexity of litigation, conduct and any wider factors, such as reputation or public importance.[18]

Funding

Data obtained by Lord Justice Jackson from numerous sources showed that the financial impact of shifting CFA success fees and ATE premiums was significant. In a survey of 699 personal injury cases, for every £1 paid as damages by liability insurers, £1.80 was also paid in claimants' costs. In a survey of 128 cases dealt with by district judges, the total costs paid to claimants were on average 203 per cent of

[12] Final Report, ch 4, paras 2.4 and 2.5.
[13] Final Report, ch 4, para 2.8.
[14] The 'overriding objective' requires: 'Dealing with a case justly includes, so far as practicable . . .

(c) dealing with the case in ways which are proportionate –

(i) to the amount of money involved;
(ii) to the importance of the case;
(iii) to the complexity of the issues; and
(iv) to the financial position of each party . . .': CPR rule 1.1(2).

[15] *Lownds v Home Office* [2002] EWCA Civ 365; [2002] 1 WLR 2450; *Willis v Nicolson* [2007] EWCA Civ 199.
[16] CPR rule 44.4(1).
[17] CPR rule 44.4(2).
[18] Final Report, ch 3, para 6.1.

the damages paid in CFA cases, but on average 55 per cent in non-CFA cases. Other surveys produced similar differentials, the evidence overall showing that claimant costs ranged between 158 and 203 percent in CFA cases and between 47 and 55 per cent in non-CFA cases. The implicit conclusion was clearly that the disparity between the two types was unacceptably large.

Lord Justice Jackson considered that the recoverability regime possessed four significant flaws: it was not targeted on persons who merited financial support with their litigation; it did not require an assisted person to make a contribution towards costs if they were able to do so (in both cases, unlike the legal aid regime); it placed a burden on opposing parties that was simply too great; and it presented an opportunity for some lawyers to make excessive profits, through cherry picking and thereby demeaning the profession in the eyes of the public.[19]

The major structural proposal made by Lord Justice Jackson was that CFA success fees and ATE premiums should no longer be recoverable from defendants. The cost shifting rule would revert to its pre-1999 status.[20] ATE insurance would not be banned but the sector would be expected to shrink, and expand into BTE or private funding products.

Nevertheless, Lord Justice Jackson recognised that a one way cost shifting regime needs to contain elements that deter against bringing frivolous claims or applications, and incentives for claimants to accept reasonable offers of settlement.[21]

Contemporaneously, the government implemented a further restriction on funding arrangements. Any fees based on a percentage of damages in employment cases (which are almost the only area where contingency fees are permitted) must not exceed 35 per cent of the damages.[22] Requirements to inform clients were strengthened in such employment cases. A proposal to cap success fees under CFAs in defamation cases at 10 per cent was dropped just before the general election.[23]

In order to give effect to the social policy that certain types of claimants should be protected against the risk of adverse costs,[24] there should be a qualified one way cost shifting rule for them,[25] instead of the normal two way rule. The 'one way' aspect means that if a member of a privileged class of claimant succeeds, she will recover her costs, but if she fails she will not have to pay costs. The 'qualified' aspect means that if she is wealthy, or subsequently becomes wealthy, she could be ordered to pay all or part.[26] The qualified approach enables targeting of the protection on those who need it, and gives them a stake in the outcome so as to exert

[19] Final Report, ch 10, paras 4.5 *et seq.*

[20] Final Report, ch 10.

[21] Final Report, ch 19, para 4.5.

[22] The Damages-Based Agreement Regulations 2010/1206 at http://www.opsi.gov.uk/si/si2010/pdf/uksi_20101206_en.pdf. See Practice Note at http://www.lawsociety.org.uk/productsandservices/practicenotes/damagesbasedagreements.

[23] C Baksi, 'Government abandons libel fee cut bid' (*Law Society Gazette*, 9 Apr 2010), 2. The prior consultation was at http://www.opsi.gov.uk/si/si2010/draft/pdf/ukdsi_9780111496510_en.pdf.

[24] And in the light of data that suggests that most personal injury claims are valid.

[25] Final Report, chs 9 and 10.

[26] Final Report, ch 19.

some control on costs. This was the approach operated successfully under the legal aid regime.[27] The protection should apply to cases where there is an asymmetric relationship between the parties, so it should apply in personal injury cases and defamation cases,[28] and there should be further consultation[29] on application to housing disrepair, actions against the police, claimants seeking judicial review, and individuals claiming defamation or breach of privacy.

Personal injury claimants would in future have to meet success fees out of their damages.[30] In order to assist this, there would be three responses. Firstly, the level of general damages for pain and suffering and loss of amenity would be increased by 10 per cent. It was calculated that that figure would leave the great majority of claimants no worse off. Secondly, the amount of success fees that lawyers may deduct would be capped at 25 per cent. For similar reasons, the general level of damages would be raised by 10 per cent for defamation and breach of privacy cases.[31] Thirdly, the reward for making a successful claimant's offer to settle, which the defendant fails to beat at trial, would be enhanced. This would also address a generic problem of late settlements: earlier settlements would be promoted through greater certainty about the effect of offers to settle [Part 36 offers], so that claimant offers have more 'teeth'.

Lord Justice Jackson made clear that he wished to maximise alternative options for funding litigation.[32] He favoured increasing the legal aid budget and eligibility, but accepted that these were political matters outside his control and that change was unlikely in the prevailing economic conditions.[33] He favoured the encouragement of BTE insurance by both householders and SME businesses as a low cost source of finance ('the many pay for the few').[34] He also approved of the recent availability of third party commercial funders, subject to suitable practice in relation to aspects such as capital adequacy.[35] He agreed with criticism of a decision[36] that such funders should be liable for the costs of opposing parties only to the extent of the funding provided, and favoured such liability to be a matter for the discretion of the judge in the individual case, without limit. He would not repeal the statutory restrictions of maintenance and champerty, but permit third party funders who comply with regulatory requirements, which may be self-regulatory requirement in the first instance. However, he came down strongly against the payment of referral fees by lawyers.[37]

[27] Still enshrined in the Access to Justice Act 1999, s 11(1): 'Costs ordered against an individual . . . shall not exceed the amount (if any) which is a reasonable one for him to pay having regard to all the circumstances including—(a) the financial resources of all parties to the proceedings and (b) their conduct in connection with the dispute . . .'

[28] Final Report, ch 32.

[29] Final Report, ch 30.

[30] Final Report, ch 10.

[31] Final Report, ch 32.

[32] Final Report, ch 12, para 4.2.

[33] Final Report, ch 7, para 4.1.

[34] Final Report, ch 8, para 4.1.

[35] Final Report, ch 11.

[36] *Arkin v Borchard Lines Ltd* [2005] EWCA Civ 655.

[37] Final Report, ch 20. It has been suggested that such fees may simply go underground.

He also favoured both solicitors and counsel being permitted to enter into contingency fee agreements, on the Ontario model of generally maintaining the loser pays rule.[38] However, he considered that various safeguards were necessary against the potential for abuse. No contingency fee deducted from damages should exceed 25 per cent of the damages, excluding damages referable to future costs or losses. There should be agreement at the outset of a case on who would be responsible for any adverse costs order and for disbursements. No contingency fee agreement should be valid unless it was countersigned by an independent solicitor who certified that he had advised the client on the terms of the agreement. (Responses to the last restriction include that it may either cool the spread of contingency fees, or be itself abused). He favours a Contingency Legal Aid Fund (CLAF) or a Supplementary Legal Aid Fund (SLAS) financed by a levy on damages of 10 per cent or so, but has difficulty seeking how one would be established, and suggests further modelling.[39]

Extending Fixed Costs

Both certainty and proportionality can be enhanced where costs are fixed in advance. Woolf intended costs of smaller claims to be fixed, and some fixed costs regimes were introduced for some individual types of claims by agreement during the following decade. Lord Justice Jackson concluded that this was the right approach and it should be extended. He noted that this approach should reduce the need for documentation and produce internal efficiencies. It is quietly modelled on the German-style system of tariffs for legal costs and shiftable costs. His proposed next steps were that all costs for personal injuries claims in the fast track should be fixed, and there should be an upper limit of £12,000 (12.5 per cent higher for London) on pre-trial costs for any non-personal injury fast track case.[40]

Lord Justice Jackson stated that the goal is that all lower value cases will be subject to fixed costs, but this will take time to introduce. Work had been done during the Review on evaluating a fixed costs regime for multi-track cases, and this would be continued but no proposals were made for the present.[41] Whilst clearly favouring raising the limit of £1,000 for personal injury claims in the small claims track, a recommendation for implementation was deferred until the other changes in the Review had been established.[42] Benchmark costs for bankruptcy petitions and winding up petitions would be implemented.[43]

[38] Final Report, ch 12.
[39] Final Report, ch 13.
[40] Final Report, ch 15.
[41] Final Report, ch 16.
[42] Final Report, ch 18.
[43] Final Report, ch 28.

The Comparative Relevance of Courts and Other Dispute Resolution Mechanisms: Need for Overarching Policy

Finally, a somewhat broader perspective of the Jackson Review might be taken. The focus of the Jackson Review is the court system. Obviously important as that is, it is equally important to take a wider view of dispute resolution, which encompasses all the available optional pathways. This is the point made by the Australian Standing Committee of Attorneys-General in their 2009 Report on Access to Justice.[44] The real world of dispute resolution, and the viewpoints of users and governments, in fact has that wider focus. A recent study has shown that many alternative dispute resolution mechanisms exist in England and Wales,[45] and many of them are unfamiliar to judges, practitioners, and potential users. A debate is necessary on what overarching policy should be on the relative prioritisation of alternative pathways for different types of claim and different litigants, encompassing both court and extra-court routes.

For example, it may be that a judicial procedure is a relatively unimportant long-stop for certain types of claim (such as family, inheritance, labour and housing disputes, and collective redress), in which case it may be good public policy to discourage court claims of that type unless and until other pathways have been reasonably attempted. It may, therefore, be that there may be positive reasons why costs or delay are relatively unimportant issues to solve for certain types of court cases. Alternatively, if court mechanisms are made cheaper, but are less appropriate for certain types of case, the opportunity for effective and cheapest dispute resolutions may be lost. Apart from a suggestion that housing disrepair claims might be better dealt with under an ombudsman system,[46] few of these issues are, for understandable reasons, raised in Lord Justice Jackson's extensive Review, but they now deserve serious further consideration.

[44] *A Strategic Framework for Access to Justice in the Federal Civil Justice System,* Report by the Access to Justice Taskforce, Australian Government, Attorney-General's Department, 2009.

[45] C Hodges and M Tulibacka, *Alternative Dispute Resolution Procedures in England and Wales*, research paper, 2009.

[46] Final Report, ch 15, para 6.17.

9

England and Wales: Woolf for Slow Learners[1]

JOHN PEYSNER

Introduction

This chapter deals with the background to and prospects for Lord Justice Jackson's Cost Review, which is a comprehensive plan to reform recoverable costs in England and Wales. The complexities and unpredictability of the costs rules were described in chapter 11 and a wider summary of the Jackson Report is at chapter 12. This chapter argues that Jackson reproduces to a great extent the proposals made by Lord Woolf in his Interim Report into Access to Justice,[2] which did not survive into the Final Report.[3] In the meantime, much 'blood and treasure' has been spent on the continuing problem of costs in both large complex cases and lower value commodity cases, particularly personal injury cases.

The Woolf Proposals

To understand the Jackson review it is necessary to go back to the earlier attempt by Lord Woolf to reform civil procedure *and* its attendant recoverable costs. The Woolf report was in two parts: a discursive preliminary Interim Report, which floated a number of ideas, and the Final Report, which offered a new regime for case management, in particular the introduction of two cost bearing tracks, the Fast Track with broadly proscribed case management and the Multi Track for

[1] Seamus Mallon, the Deputy Leader of the Social Democratic and Labour Party, described the Good Friday Agreement 1998 that finally resolved the Northern Ireland 'Troubles' as 'Sunningdale for slow learners'. This was a reference to the 1973 Sunningdale Agreement, a similar cross-community political settlement that lasted only five months, before being brought down by the Loyalist Workers Strike.

[2] Lord Woolf, *Access to Justice: Interim Report* (HMSO, 1995).

[3] Lord Woolf, *Access to Justice: Final Report* (HMSO, 1996).

more weighty cases with tailor made directions. Case management was a major step forward, since historically the pace and resources employed in English litigation were largely the preserve of the parties, with the judge acting as a neutral observer. It was only after the conclusion of the case, in the process of taxation (now assessment), that excessive litigation effort and excessive costs by the winning lawyer would be tested by the payer and the cost judge. The Interim Report had proposed a number of cost initiatives, of which two were groundbreaking: fixed costs on a German inspired matrix model for the Fast Track and budgets at pre trial review in the Multi Track. Before the Final Report these proposals were amplified by an issues paper which included proposals for budgets filed in the court and exchanged. These budgets would have provided the information by which the new case managing judges could have controlled recoverable costs, possibly by capping recoverable costs. Both of these initiatives were intended to make recoverable costs more predictable and proportionate.

It is not an exaggeration to say that these ideas were met with a storm of protest by the legal profession, through a range of arguments that alleged that the proposals were inequitable (limiting costs would allow richer parties, for example insurance companies, to outspend poorer parties, especially claimant personal injury victims on recoverable fixed costs, who could not recover all their costs) or that budgeting and project management were inherently impossible in litigation (as opposed to virtually all other business activities). Lord Woolf responded by dropping these proposals from his Final Report taking the view that control of the litigation process by judicial case management would exercise sufficient discipline on costs.[4] In so far as there was an evidence base[5] that outcome seemed unlikely, and events rapidly demonstrated the limits of case management when faced with the incentives for lawyers to be paid more by doing more, and the introduction of the deeply flawed Access to Justice Act.

A Fatal Combination

The Access to Justice Act introduced the machinery that was necessary for the Government to accomplish its objective of removing legal aid for most civil cases, in particular the large number of personal injury cases. The prime objective was to ensure that litigants in these cases, who, broadly speaking, had been held harmless against the danger of costs if their case was lost, should not be disadvantaged. The method was to alter the existing conditional fee machinery so that the additional liabilities (the success fee and the premium for after the event insurance) never

[4] A later consultation on the introduction of budgeting mounted by the Civil Justice Council met considerable opposition and the proposal was shelved.

[5] JS Kakalik, T Dunworth, LA Hill, T McCaffrey, M Oshiro, N Pace and ME Vaiana, *Just, Speedy, and Inexpensive? An Evaluation of Judicial Case Management Under the Civil Justice Reform Act* (Santa Monica, CA, RAND Institute for Civil Justice, 1996).

troubled the personal injury client. If the case was won in court or settled (which most were) the defendant paid these additions on top of ordinary recoverable costs. If the case was lost, then the insurance protected the client against adverse costs and disbursements and the client's own lawyer made no charge (on a no win no fee basis). Having introduced this momentous change, the government stood aside and the blue touch paper was lit. The result was an explosion of costs as lawyers were incentivised by a reward of up to double their ordinary costs to increase their litigation effort and their reward. Since most cases in this area were against liability insurers and self-insuring bodies (such as local authorities), the effect was a huge transfer of risk and the recycling of additional liabilities into increased premiums and local taxation. The "Cost War" was born. Thrown into the battle was cost control by case management, which, as described above, was a largely post hoc exercise. It became very clear that the method was wanting and costs were running out of control

Could It Have Been Different?[6]

The writer has consistently taken the view that the Woolf reforms 'worked'. In other words, the creation of managed tracks and the focus of tailored case management for more weighty, and possibly complex, cases was an appropriate response. Essentially, the reforms, which were introduced against an unusual chorus of approval and even enthusiasm from the legal community, arose from a broad consensus that the pre-Woolf system was broken and had to be fixed, and that the reforms through the Civil Procedure Rules were the answer. Indeed, it appeared that, at a fairly early stage, litigators accepted that case management was a fact of life and responded by 'conspiring' to accept or create case management directions that went with the grain of the response by case managing judges.[7] Broadly speaking, it remains the case that the reforms have bedded in and represent the new reality.

This consensus has always had one intransigent and dogged opponent Professor Michael Zander. In a recent chapter,[8] he has reiterated his long-standing opposition to the reforms and takes the view that history has proved him right: he maintains that the objectives of Woolf were to reform the problems of cost, delay, complexity and excessive adversarialism and they have not worked. The current

[6] In Scotland, the Gill Review into Civil Justice has deliberately not proposed cost changes whilst introducing procedural changes and a new first level civil jurisdiction. The Scottish cost system incorporates no win no fee but without success fees (speculation), with legal aid retained and has generally not been problematic. *Report of the Scottish Civil Courts Review*, 2009 at http://www.scotcourts.gov.uk/civilcourtsreview.

[7] J Peysner and M Seneviratne, *The Management of Civil Cases: the Courts and the Post-Woolf Landscape* (Research Department, Department of Constitutional Affairs, 2005) 1–84

[8] M Zander, 'The Woolf Reforms: What's the Verdict?' in D Dwyer (ed), *The Civil Procedural Rules Ten Years On*, (Oxford, Oxford University Press, 2009) 417.

book is focused on costs, so it is that part of Zander's analysis that needs to be examined. He states correctly 'There seems to be more or less universal agreement that, far from costs being reduced by the Woolf Reforms, they have increased.'[9] He quotes the writer: 'It is quite apparent in the current discussion on costs that virtually all commentators agree that Lord Woolf's vision of the new litigation landscape has been largely successful except in relation to costs.'[10] So while there may be a difference of opinion on the reforms in relation to delay, complexity, and excessive adversarialism, there is none in relation to costs. It is not surprising that highly complex litigation with huge sum sums at stake produces massive legal bills. Very often the parties can afford them. Much more worrying is that in small cases the toxic combination of forward loading and recoverability produced recoverable legal costs which are almost invariably more, and sometimes much more, than the value of the claim. This challenges access to justice for any party not protected by a CFA or ATE insurance.

This argument invites a thought experiment. *What would have happened to costs if the proposals in Woolf's Interim Report had been adopted, particularly fixed costs in the fast track and budgeting with cost capping in the multi-track?* This exercise in virtual reality or a counter-factual[11] might seem to be of academic interest only but as explained below it is an exercise that has practical relevance.
The question suggests two possible answers:

a) The reforms, by their combination of front loading (through pre-action protocols and so forth) and case management, would have generated more work and, under the English system of hourly rates, more expense. In other words, the Zander position.

b) The introduction of effective cost control measures (fixed costs and budgeting) would have produced a more predictable and economical cost regime. Any contrary tensions in the system (for example forward loading through pre-action

[9] ibid, 424.

[10] ibid, 417.

[11] Counter-factuals are a recognised if controversial method of analysing history by making changes in the historical record and then speculating on what might have happened rather than what did happen. They can be divided into 'plausible' or 'miracle' scenarios. If Hitler had stood a foot to the side when von Staufenberg's bomb went off he would have been assassinated—a plausible scenario. If nuclear weapons had not been invented suggests a 'miracle' scenario. Whether 'plausible' or miracle', there must be some thing or things that would realistically have altered the course of history: if Hitler had substituted coffee for tea on the morning of the attempted assassination this would have had no effect on the stream of history.

Speculating on law reform proposals that were not initiated seems to belong to the 'plausible' category. They may be a zero sum game: the death penalty was not abolished. They may be more complex and multi-factorial: crucial amendments in legislation or the pace of introduction of a statute were altered. In any event, whether the reform effort failed entirely or in part, speculating on what might have happened if these 'defects' were cured is susceptible to the law of unintended consequences—something to which cost and financing reforms (for example, conditional fee agreements) seem to have been particularly prone. For counter-factual theory generally see RN Lebow, 'Counterfactual Thought Experiments: A Necessary Teaching Tool' (2007) 40.4 *The History Teacher* 153, and also http://www.historycooperative.org/journalsd/ht/40.2/lebow.html and the bibliography thereto.

protocols and the demands of case managing judges to do extra work) would not have overwhelmed this effect. So, for example, litigators might be tempted to do more work than was necessary in a multi track case. If this exceeded a budget signed off by the court that restrained future recoverable costs, they would either have to return to court for permission to have a higher cap on the budget, which might well be difficult, or come to an agreement with their own client to bear these additional costs.

It is apparent that the writer considers that the latter is more likely. The CPR would have written through them, like a stick of rock: 'limit costs and make them more economical'.

The Impact of Recoverability

It does not require an overly cynical view of lawyers to assume that rational economic actors, paid by the hour, will, if unrestrained, tend to increase the number of hours they devote to a job. If the actors are paid by a stranger (as in successful litigation), rather than by their own client, they have none of the emotional pressure that often comes with a professional relationship with a client (possibly someone who may instruct you again). If they act under a conditional fee, when each recoverable hour may be doubled, the result is predictable. The result of additional litigation effort by the lawyer acting under a CFA will be met to an extent by additional work by the opponent. As these costs have to be insured against, the incentive on the CFA lawyer operates through a transmission belt to the ATE and increases the premium.

As stated above, it was hardly surprising that liability insurers were reluctant to accept the steep increase in costs that recoverability introduced. They resisted it with a variety of technical challenges that were particularly toxic, as it was a zero sum game. Payers found that ex post facto assessment of costs had a limited effect and, in any event, any costs that survived this process were subject to the success fee multiplier. The advantage of a technical challenge was that, as well as creating huge delays in payment, a successful challenge could prevent the successful party recovering *any* costs.[12] Caught between these opposing incentives it has taken ten years of negotiations through the Civil Justice Council and re-jigging of the system by the Ministry of Justice to produce changes, particularly in personal injury and defamation cases, which have trimmed success fees and made procedures simpler. There have also been some moves to introduce limited fixed costs (in road traffic cases). However, these changes, while welcome, are far from comprehensive

[12] Because of the effect of the indemnity rule. In English cost law costs are only recoverable up to, but no more than, the amount due to the lawyer from the successful client. The technical challenges were to the nature of that contract, so as to demonstrate it to be unenforceable and thus no costs could be recovered.

and have not really grasped the central problems of unpredictability and excessive cost.

Counter-factually, an early introduction of fixed costs in the fast track (where the vast majority of all litigation proceeds) would have produced a much more predictable system. In particular this would have had a benign impact on personal injury litigation, which, whilst not the largest proportion of cases in the fast track (debt cases constitute the largest class), are the most contested and most likely to be conducted on a CFA agreement with a success fee generating the most disproportionate costs. (Small business contractual claims are not as attractive to solicitors to take on a CFA as they are less predictable.) Recoverable costs would have been fixed by a system that was proportionate to the value of the claim. They may have exceeded the value of relatively small claims because of the need to pay for an irreducible minimum of work, but they would form a lower proportion as values rose. In turn, the success fee would be less and, as opposition costs would in turn be lower (on the assumption that they would reflect more limited litigation effort by the opponent), ATE premiums would also have faced downward pressure. No doubt liability insurers would not have been happy about any increase in costs consequent on recoverability, but the financial pressure would have been much less and the 'Cost War' may never have happened. There would have been a more seamless development from the withdrawal of legal aid: CFAs would have simply become an established part of the scene as speculation is in Scotland. However, that was not to be, and the effect was a continuing tension about financing and costs, which led to the setting up of the Jackson Review.

The Jackson Review

The broader context of the Jackson review and a summary of its proposals are described in chapter 12 above. This chapter focuses on its potential impact of the proposals on the fast track, particularly in relation to personal injury cases, and budgeting, but the proposals go wider to include changes to defamation procedure and intellectual property litigation. Jackson gives a clean bill of health to procedures in the Commercial Court and Technology and Construction Court (TCC). The terms of reference were to review the rules and principles governing the costs of civil litigation and to make recommendations in order to promote access to justice at proportionate cost. The Woolf review had three aims:

a) to improve access to justice and reduce the costs of litigation;
b) to reduce the complexity of the rules and modernise terminology;
c) to reduce unnecessary distinctions of practice and procedure.[13]

[13] Introduction to Woolf, *Interim Report* (n 2 above).

Focusing on (a), the issue of costs reappears in CPR rule 1(1)(1) as the overriding objective, namely including statements that expense should be saved and *dealing with cases in ways which are proportionate* to the amount of money involved; the importance of the case; the complexity of the issues and the financial position of each party.

The objectives set for Jackson move the debate on. Case management (*dealing with cases in ways which are proportionate*) has not produced a cost regime that promotes access to justice at proportionate cost. In some, possibly most, areas, costs are excessive and disproportionate.[14] Jackson's mantra of proportionality focuses on reducing costs (making them more reasonable) but crucially making them more proportionate. To the question 'what resources does this case justify', Woolf answers in various *procedural* ways, for instance by creating tracks to allocate resources. Jackson goes further by tying costs *and* financing models to values and types of cases.

The headline proposals that focus on the fast track and personal injury are:

(a) Recoverability of success fees and ATE premiums should be abrogated in all civil litigation. These elements can be recovered in a CFA from the client, not the opponent, as was the position before the Access to Justice Act.
(b) To protect personal injury claimants, the English rule of costs should be disapplied: only the claimant's costs should be recoverable (one way cost shifting). This immediately reduces the need for ATE insurance. While the claimant is held harmless from his own lawyer's fees in unsuccessful cases by the CFA this does leave the question of who pays for the disbursements in unsuccessful cases and can these be insured (particularly if the ATE market collapses as its main market disappears). The claimant will be liable for the success fee but will be protected to some extent by increasing general damages by 10 per cent.[15]
(c) The final link in this chain of mandating proportionality is that fast track costs will be fixed, which in turn will, in most litigated cases, reduce the success fee.[16] This will initially be applied for personal injury cases with a view to covering other types of cases in due course.
(d) Contingency fees should be introduced on the Ontario model, namely that costs can be recovered (unlike in most US litigation) and those costs are set off against the lawyer's 'cut' of damages.
(e) For cases outside the fixed cost jurisdiction, case management should incorporate *cost management*. The key element of this is the introduction of budgets disclosed to the court and the opponent, which form the evidence on

[14] Paraphrasing the Executive Summary to Woolf, *Final Report* (n 3 above) para 1.3.

[15] The Jackson Final Report suggests that, based on economist's modeling, a 10% increase in general damages will be broadly neutral for payers and claimants when set against the ending of the English rule in personal injury cases. At the Civil Justice Council Cost Forum 2010 an insurer suggested that his company's modeling suggested that the effect would be to *increase* their outlay. Clearly, further work will be needed in this area to reach the policy objective.

[16] In any event reduced in elements of personal injury by industry agreement.

which case management orders (possibly including cost capping) can be introduced.

A number of important issues are explored that run alongside this overall scheme:

(a) Abolition of the indemnity principle. This is the rule that caps any recoverable costs (not covered by a specific exemption such as the CFA success fee) to the amount agreed between the party that is recovering costs and the client's lawyer. As explained above, arguments about the indemnity rule underpinned most of the technical challenges in the 'Cost War'. It has been argued that it has a regulatory purpose, under which a client puts downward pressure on his own lawyer, which in turn reduces the bill of the other side if these costs become recoverable. This has turned out to be a very roundabout and ineffective way of reducing costs and certainly does not make them predictable. Abolishing the rule focuses attention on direct ways of limiting costs.

(b) Referral fees. Lord Justice Jackson, like most judges, has a visceral dislike of referral fees, that is, the price that a solicitor pays to a referrer for a case (usually but not invariably a case involving personal injury or damage done to vehicles in an accident). Clearly, buying work constitutes a different model of professional services from the traditional roles of the legal professions, but it has long been the position that volume (commodity) personal injury cases have been acquired for value, whether by giving free work to a BTE insurer, free advice to trade union members, the cost of advertisements or for cash. The complexities of the modern system of acquisition have been discussed elsewhere[17] but it is highly unlikely that referral fees can be done away with by rule. They are likely to be a feature of any future system albeit possibly reduced by a cap.[18]

(c) A segmented approach to the cost reform. Although, Lord Justice Jackson has described his proposed reforms as a package, it would be more accurate to say they are a series of linked packages. For example, specific proposals are made for intellectual property cases, small business disputes, housing cases and so on. In essence, rather than produce a 'Big Bang' that uniformly impacts on all aspects of litigation, the report identifies areas where costs are a serious problem (for example personal injury cases) and areas where they are less so (for example the TCC). In some areas, such as defamation, the changes go with the grain of existing promoted reforms promoted by the Civil Justice Council.

[17] J Peysner, 'Referring to Justice' (2008) 19 *European Business Law Review* 1105.

[18] Jackson LJ suggests that if referral fees cannot be done away with they should be capped at £200 per case. This begs the question, which has plagued this area, as to what exactly is a referral fee. For example, a properly regulated claims management company referring cases to a solicitor may charge a fee which includes their cost in acquiring the case by advertising, giving it an initial risk assessment, and in a disease case carrying out a screening medical test. Will they be able to charge separately for these items *plus* £200? If not, £200 may not be enough to allow them a profit for their (legal) activity and appears to be anti-competitive.

Need for Primary Legislation

Civil justice is regulated in three ways: primary legislation, delegated legislation (court rules) and precedent. Only the latter two areas are in the 'control' of the judiciary. Court rules are decided by the Civil Procedure Rules Committee, which is chaired by the Master of the Rolls, the senior civil judge. Leading precedents in civil litigation are primarily decided in the Court of Appeal, again under the presidency of the Master of the Rolls. While, common law precedent is often seen as an unplanned accretion of new law, depending on the accidental fact pattern of a dispute or the wealth (or stubbornness) of parties, this is not the whole picture. Controversies over procedure may emerge in related groups as new rules, procedures or financing packages emerge. The staff of the Court of Appeal and the judiciary will then marshal these cases to ensure that appropriate issues are placed before the court for decision.

These approaches cannot annul or substantially amend existing primary legislation or create substantive new law in areas that are seen to be within the purview of Parliament. Early on in the 'Cost War', the indemnity principle was seen as a barrier to a more logical approach to cost recovery. Although the rule originates in the common law,[19] it has been both extended by statute and, while latterly much trimmed by exceptions,[20] it still underpins the English rule of cost recovery. However, it was generally accepted that primary legislation is required and Lord Justice Jackson sums up the situation with, perhaps, a degree of understatement: 'The technical details of how, as a matter of mechanics, to achieve abrogation are complex and lie beyond the scope of this review'.[21]

Will Jackson be Implemented?

There is a curious symmetry between the Woolf Inquiry and the Jackson Inquiry. Both reported in the run up to a General Election. In the case of Woolf, the incoming Labour government initiated the Middleton Report[22] to see if the reforms could be given a clean bill of health, which it did. The key difference is that Woolf reported to the Lord Chancellor (Minister of Justice), while Jackson reported to the Master of the Rolls (Head of Civil Justice). In the intervening period, the judiciary have acquired much of the trappings of a department of state—a web site, a

[19] See *Harold v Smith* (1860) 5 H 7 N 381.

[20] Particularly the CFA regime.

[21] Jackson, *Final Report* p 53. Cost anoraks will enjoy the discussion on how to go about abolishing the principle in *Cook on Costs*, (London, Lexis Nexis, 2006) 220.

[22] Sir P Middleton, *Report to the Lord Chancellor* (HMSO, 1997) at http://www.dca.gov.uk/civil/reportfr.htm.

spokesperson—but they would be unlikely to initiate any necessary legislation even through 'friends' in the House of Lords. Again, the attitude of any incoming government would be vital. At a time of major economic difficulties, it is unlikely that civil justice reform would have a high priority in the legislative timetable.[23]

In any event, large swathes of the Jackson reforms can be implemented by rule changes. If the introduction of Fast Track fixed costs follow the model of fixed costs for pre-issue road traffic cases, then a model will be developed based on historical bills paid in litigated cases together with the levels of damages achieved by settlement or judgment.[24]

Cost management in the multi track poses a more difficult problem. The CPR can be altered to build on the rules relating to estimates to allow the case managing judge to require budgets to be prepared and disclosed to the other parties and the court. Changes in the procedural nature of the case (an expert witness dies, a new tranche of disclosure documents comes to light) will require new case management orders and changes in the budgets. None of this poses intractable difficulties. The problem lies in the willingness of the actors. Solicitors have been reluctant to disclose their budgets but will do so if ordered and, generally, do not appeal such orders.[25] The problem will lie with the judges who have to oversee the scheme. While District Judges (usually former litigation solicitors) have experience in costs, this is not often matched by Circuit or High Court judges, who will usually be barristers. This lack of experience (and lack of interest in some quarters) has led to the creation of a cadre of specialised cost judges based in the Supreme Court Cost Office in London or in the regions. The difficulty is that these judges generally deal with ex post facto cost assessment. They will not normally be involved in the case management of cases, particularly more complex cases. The Jackson report suggests that training for the judiciary will be offered and, certainly, cost judges will be able to offer advice in particular cases. However, a major cultural change will be required in the judiciary if this part of the proposals is to be successful.

Conclusion: Who Will Benefit?

If, as suggested, budgeting and cost control in the Multi Track is a more uncertain prospect, the changes outlined above will, if implemented, have the greatest effect in the area of personal injury and accident work. The government of England and

[23] Except if 2010 produces a minority (hung) administration or a coalition when non-contentious and non-party measures might jump the queue.

[24] These figures cannot be readily obtained from the courts themselves and would need access to payers (insurance companies and large self-insuring organisations, such as local authorities and the NHS) for the initial roll-out for personal injury cases.

[25] This is the experience of the handful of District Judges who routinely order budgeting and cost capping in the County Court.

Wales broke new ground internationally when it created a funding model for litigation based on the CFA with recoverability. While this was available for all civil litigation, it has been primarily used in personal injury cases. If the Jackson proposals to abolish recoverability for personal injury CFAs are introduced, the experiment can be largely consigned to the dustbin of history as a piece of English exotica, not copied in any other jurisdiction. It may limp on in other areas of civil litigation, but ATE insurance, which is an essential part of its operation, will become more expensive or less available as its core business in personal injury disappears.

Undaunted by the torrid history of recoverability, the New Labour government did not lose its interest in novel solutions to issues of access for and competition in legal services. By 2011 the provisions of the Legal Services Act 2007 relating to Alternative Business Structures ('ABS') will come into force. Ever since the Clementi Review,[26] which followed the Office of Fair Trading (OFT) report into competition in the professions,[27] there has been a belief in government that there needs to be more competition in the legal profession and one way to do this was to introduce a series of new structures. Initial interest was centred on transactional work, such as domestic conveyancing, with the introduction of multi-disciplinary partnerships in which groups of professionals operate a 'one stop shop', which was believed to be more competitive. More recently, as the housing market has declined in importance, two areas for restructuring have come to the fore.

The first was in the area of City firms and the global market. In this area, the perceived need was to allow firms to introduce external capital rather than relying solely on partners' capital or bank finance. It is likely that these firms will retain the same 'look and feel'. Theoretically, in the area of dispute resolution, they might benefit from a reform that allows them a share in contingency fees but this is unlikely to be as attractive as high hourly fees.

The greater changes in dispute resolution will take place in the broader consumer or commodity market. The prospects are as yet unclear, particularly in relation to the eventual regulatory regime. For example, it is currently proposed that certain types of legal activity—including litigation[28]—should be 'reserved' and only carried out by lawyers.

The model that will emerge to deal with commodity dispute resolution will be quite different from the City law firms on their global stage. Instead of investing *in* law firms, external capital will *become* legal players. Some law firms will be acquired by insurers or venture capitalists. Perhaps more likely (and possibly to the chagrin of partners in law firms that do not have strong brands), external capital may decide to create a different model. Already, insurance companies and

[26] Sir D Clementi, *Review of the Regulatory Framework for Legal Services In England and Wales*, (2004), at http://webarchive.nationalarchives.gov.uk/+/http://www.legal-services-review.org.uk/content/report/report-chap.pdf.

[27] *Competition in Professions*, (Office of Fair Trading, 2001), at http://www.oft.gov.uk/shared_oft/reports/professional_bodies/oft328.pdf.

[28] Defining litigation is not an exact science. Employment cases do not constitute litigation; neither do most road traffic cases, which are settled before court issue.

other intermediaries that provide non-litigation advice through before-the-event insurance employ lawyers, sometimes in teams numbering hundreds, to deal directly with clients rather than to farm the work out to panel firms in return for referral fees. A future step would allow these operations to conduct litigation. Into this new environment new players will also emerge. Since the Access to Justice Act, a new breed of intermediaries—claims management or accident management companies—have carried out dispute resolution and recovery work, which was traditionally seen as law firm activity and in most jurisdictions could only be carried out by law firms. This market place was originally not regulated and produced the chaos of the rise and fall of Claims Direct and the Accident Group (TAG). Now regulated by the Compensation Act 2006 these companies are likely to enter the market to provide a broader range of dispute resolution services. Rather than just acquiring and farming out cases to law firms, again for a referral fee, they will acquire cases and then carry out the work themselves. While, this would initially have to be done under the supervision of an externally regulated lawyer, it would allow, as it does now, a range of different models, employing high levels of gearing with a small qualified legal staff running a large operation of paralegals tied in to an all-pervasive and powerful case management system.[29]

These new models will not replace the traditional arrangement of law firms providing services in partnership with others. Even in the highly competitive sector of personal injury and accident work, firms will continue in partnership with trade unions and niche firms will attract complex cases from a national or international market. Federations of law firms will advertise to attract work. What will drive the changes suggested is not just the ability to attract capital on corporate-based models but the changing patterns of referral fees. As indicated above, these are likely to continue in some form but, perhaps, at a reduced level. At this stage, there will be a strong incentive to change the business model for commodity work from a referral-based arrangement to a vertically integrated arrangement. For example, at present a liability insurer may acquire cases by capturing them when the insured seeks first party recovery, leaving the excess and personal injury payments (uninsured losses) to be pursued by a law firm that has paid for the case. That payment is financed out of the recoverable costs and success fee currently available. Under a fixed cost regime and an ABS environment it might make more business sense for the insurer to retain the case, referring it internally to a subsidiary legal service operation geared up to do mass volume work, with shared IT systems, whose income comes largely from fixed fees and who makes payments up the chain by way of transfer prices rather than referral fees. Large law firms will continue to compete directly or to service insurers through arbitrage (including benchmarking internal law firms) but this market will be led by the corporates and not the lawyers.

Many lawyers in private practice will see this as an unattractive prospect. Certainly, it is a model that would not be recognised by the independent legal

[29] Jackson suggests the de-skilling of calculations of personal injury by moving to a system of agreed software to calculate general damages, which would fit well into this system.

professions of Europe or North America. It will be limited to certain areas of practice only but, taken with the decline in legal aid, it seems to suggest that the current reduction in the numbers of small and medium sized solicitors firms in this sector will increase rapidly.

It may be that, in retrospect, firms with a largely individual and claimant base may regret their opposition to fixed costs in the interim Woolf Report. If the concept of fixed costs had been accepted at an earlier stage and attention had been focused on the level of those costs and making procedure simpler to match those fees then the 'Cost War' might never have broken out. Referral fees would have been a minor issue and the legal profession would have been in a stronger position to meet any competitive challenge from corporates—indeed the market would be both solicitor led *and* competitive and the OFT might not have entered the picture. The opposition to fixed fees turned into a decade-long strategic retreat, as fixed elements were introduced bit by bit to various elements of the commodity market. While the 'claimant lobby' still opposes the introduction of fixed fees, their position has been weakened and it is likely that, in some form or another, they will be introduced. Woolf for slow learners?

10

France

A. Theoretical Perspectives

YVON DESDEVISES*

The purpose of this academic contribution is to place the principles and rules mentioned in Part B below by Maître Villedieu within a historic and evolutionary framework and to summarise the recurring debates about justice reform that take place within French society as well as in the legal and judicial communities.

Principle of 'Free Access to Justice'

One of the first points mentioned in every pedagogical and scientific work on the subject relates to Free Access to Justice. All, or nearly all of these works, address the issue of Free Access to Justice as a *grand principe* that the French so often flaunt. Thus technical developments are exposed within the concept that justice is a public service, and like all other public services, but *a fortiori* those whose mission is to render justice must illustrate our fine republican motto: Liberty, Equality, Fraternity. All in all, French authors favour quite naturally 'justice' as an administrative service, as opposed to other senses of the word 'Justice'[1] (equity versus administration, where ambivalence allows the legal-media debate much room to play), considering that a well-organised judicial public service, taking into account specific rules, can only render good judgments in all aspects relevant to the word 'justice'. In this sense, it is perfectly logical that Part B below starts with a reference to the French Revolution. The majority of authors see in the Revolution the source of the principles that gave birth to a theory, particularly sophisticated, of the public service *à la française* governed notably by the principle of Free Access to Justice. One of the foremost writers about litigation considers that the whole subject, including its most technical aspects, may be studied under the triple standard of

* Professor, Nantes University.

[1] R Perrot, *Institutions judiciaires*, 13th edn (Paris, Montchrestien, 2008) no 21, p 21.

liberty, legality and fraternity, which represent the three parts of one of his major works.[2]

Freedom of Access to Justice

Free Access is presented as the guarantee of freedom of access to justice[3] (equally here understood as an ambivalent notion for some, as an ambiguous one for others: ie access to an equitable system of justice and access to the judicial administration) like any other public service. One can also speak of the 'right to a judge.'

Financing of the Public Services: Taxpayers or Users?

This evidently gratifying presentation of the democratic and republican state's role, in the end accountable for public services, sends it back to its responsibilities. To claim that justice is free cannot obscure the fact that there are costs that require financing. In the logic of some basic public services (roads, but not toll roads) or naturally requiring state regulation (army, police), the public collectivity (in practice using taxes levied on the taxpayers) is supposed to provide for the entirety of their requirements. In other cases, the theorists, and above all the public service practitioners, naturally acknowledge that the users can bear a part of the costs. The financing of the public services by the taxpayers and/or the users is in any case one of the most recurring debates with which French political life delights itself, wherein one can ascertain the traditional right-left split on the dividing line.

Particularities of Justice as a Public Service

With respect to the justice system, the above-mentioned assessment is specific for a number of reasons: the notion of Justice as a state public service, complicates, on the theoretical as well as on the practical side, the preservation of the independence—considered necessary by all—of magistrates, the main public servants

[2] S Guinchard, F Ferrand, C Chainais, *Procédure civile, Droit interne et communautaire*, 29th edn (Paris, Dalloz, 2008).

[3] L Cadiet and E Jeuland, *Droit judiciaire privé*, 6th edn (Paris, LexisNexis, Litec, 2009) 38 *et seq*, 45 *et seq*.

within this public service. One has also to take into account the existence of those members of the legal professional community (notably the members of the bar) who claim rightly the title of *auxiliaires de la justice* and not only the one of representation of their clients before the courts: must the links, often essential between the litigant and his judge, be considered as components of the public service for which they contribute indisputably? If so, what must one conclude as to their condition and the nature of their retribution? Should they, on the contrary, be considered professionals exercising a fundamentally liberal profession who, in the interest of their clients, cannot submit themselves to the logic of a public service? The French lawyers who are most involved in this debate answer in varying ways depending on their professional practice.

Justice Within the State Budget

The principles which govern the financing of the French justice system and thus of the trials that take place within it are described in Part B below: the state budget, supplied by all taxpayers—thus including the taxes of the great majority of the French population who do not litigate—bears the cost of professional judges and magistrates as well as the indemnities some lay judges benefit from; the state budget equally bears the cost of the public servants of the courts, more specifically the clerks of the court. The state also finances the infrastructure, buildings and furniture, essential for the proper functioning of the service (courts, equipment, maintenance and so forth). Even if this principle is not challenged and represents the reality and the limits of 'Free Access to Justice', it is in practice exposed to the current political views on public budget restrictions. Free Access to Justice has, however, been sensibly reinforced by the state giving up the tax levied at each trial, this tax in the end being borne by the 'usual' litigants before the courts. This renunciation results generally from the law of 30 December 1997; but the tax reappears nonetheless from time to time, sometimes in a temporary manner in order to finance a judicial reform in lieu of increasing the general tax, at other times on a longer term basis, re-establishing a tax on specific judicial acts.

Payment of Legal Advisers

The intervention of the members of the legal community has never been submitted to the principle of Free Access to Justice, which might arguably lead them to be considered public servants suspected of protecting the interests of their own administration rather than those of the parties they are charged with assisting or representing. The most ancient interpretation is to consider that every party is free to protect its own interest as it sees fit, and can decide freely to choose its own legal advisers, negotiating with them the financial conditions of their intervention. In this approach, the legal expenses are normally borne by those who assumed them. Such a concept seriously hampers the principle of Free Access to Justice; it has thus always been conditioned by various processes.

Legal Assistance

The legal profession has considered for a very long time that it was its moral duty to ensure the defence of litigants of limited means by assisting them, if necessary, free of charge (legal aid system). Without diminishing such generosity, one has to admit that legal aid did not represent an excessive burden at a time when civil justice dealt with the issues of wealthy litigants assisted by legal advisers having themselves at their disposal some personal wealth which would enable them to help the litigant of limited means, either plaintiff or defendant, in the rare event of a trial involving such litigants. This commendable attitude has lived on and it is evident that the public authorities do not hesitate, even nowadays, to have recourse to such a contribution in order to relieve the state budget (see below). It is however less common at times when many legal professionals earn their living by working as legal advisers.

Legal Aid

The significant increase in litigation before the courts by litigants of modest means, most notably in family affairs, was perceived in France as a call to satisfy this 'demand of justice' by a corresponding increase in the number of judicial officers. This development presupposed that public finances would adapt themselves by bearing the costs of legal advisers from the middle class. The very flexible interpretation of Article 6 § 1 of the European Convention on Human Rights as to the entitlement of 'everyone' to a fair hearing has rather encouraged the increase in litigation by persons unable to cover their own legal expenses. In 1972, an important change resulted from a new law establishing a system of legal aid that was supposed to purge the previous system of any remnants of charity. For the first time, crucially, it was accepted that the professionals acting within the legal aid framework must earn a certain income. This system continued in 1991 without major amendments. But the question of the financing of the system has become all the more pressing with respect to the 'right to a judge' and thus to competent legal advisers, all things which would involve increasing resources. One idea recently debated involves levying a tax on all the legal and judicial regulated professions: this idea was hotly contested by the notaries public, who are not directly concerned with litigation. The lawyers equally opposed this proposal due to the fact that their work already represented a contribution to the financing of the system and that the modest income available under the legal aid system did not even cover the costs of their own engagement.

Payment of the Representatives of the Law With Respect to Legal Aid

The part of the legal profession most affected is the bar. It was confronted by the embarrassing issue of the amount of public funds paid to lawyers working within the legal aid system. To admit on the one hand that this amount is a proper payment would enable public authorities to enjoy some say in the notion of 'normal' fees, in cases within the legal aid system; the bar can only fear such a normalisation of fees, which runs counter to the freedom of contract generally applicable to such issues. On the other hand, if one sees the payment as merely an 'indemnity' without any real purpose, but to pay the lawyer for his *peines et diligences*, one returns to the traditional view according to which the bar must fulfil some duty towards needy litigants; but it also acknowledges the increasing hardship amongst members of the bar, and consequently reflecting on the bar as a whole, once it is known that nowadays a significant number of lawyers live mainly on revenue from legal aid cases.

Payment of Legal Fees and Costs

A similar problem is posed with respect to the burden of legal fees and costs. The former principle according to which each party pays its own fees has developed in a quite foreseeable way put simply in the following manner: in general the loser pays the legal fees and costs of the victor. The amount of legal costs that the victor may recuperate should not be difficult to account for, at least when they are fixed by law and by the judge (the legal costs); with respect to other expenses—in practice the lawyer's fees—the law states that the judge determines 'an amount' in favour of the victor without indicating any detail as to the the nature or the effective amount. The legal community supported this lack of clarity, fearing above all else that the court or tribunal might, at the end of the trial, determine the fees that the lawyer would 'normally' have received. In the end, and for this reason, the victor bears, despite his success, a share of his lawyer's fees (except when the litigant benefits from legal aid). One may consider that winning the trial is reason enough to bear some sacrifices!

Justice Budget and State Budget

Our contemporary culture asks tough questions of the legal community and society at large about the place they consider giving to Justice. In concrete terms, this questioning impacts on the financing of the Ministry of Justice. It is quite usual to emphasise the fact that the budget for the justice ministry is one of the smallest within the French ministries (at around 2.50 per cent), and in comparison with other European countries.[4] Comparisons are, however, very difficult to make, especially when the observations are so superficial, without entering very complex comparative analysis of budgetary resources (taxes paid by all the taxpayers or levied on all users) and of their use. A rehabilitation of some sort of taxes, rights or financial contribution by the users of the justice public service finds its roots within the law of 1977 that was supposed to abolish those taxes, rights or financial contributions. Who does what with respect to justice? The ministerial departments concerned in the areas of criminal, civil or administrative justice are diverse and not always the same as in other countries that one might use as a comparative basis. Thus, the comparison of global budgets is not very enlightening.

Spending Limitations on the Public Service and Offer of State Justice

A serious trend, reinforced by the economic crisis, seems inescapable: the reduction in (and in any case the limitation of) public spending will put pressure on the Ministry of Justice's budget, as with other Ministries. Such a trend will modify the availability of justice to the public and for some it will be altered. Numerous reforms or projects of reform have taken place aimed at making the justice service profitable, even though the logic behind profitability seems foreign to many with respect to the 'aims' of public service. These include reform of the *carte judiciaire* (in concrete terms: suppression of jurisdictions functioning at a reduced level), 'de-litigation' of issues which will treated outside of the courts and beyond the reach of judges (for example: excessive household debt, modification of matrimonial regimes), recourse to a single judge, in spite of another French legal *grand principe*, namely collegiality, repeated attempts to create alternative dispute resolutions mechanisms (thus contractual and out of court settlements) and so forth. The list of planned or recent reforms is even longer, sometimes effected with difficulty, and which confuse the legal community even though such reforms correspond to practical and natural solutions in other legal systems. The impact on the legal community of such reforms is equally notable.

[4] S Guinchard et al, *Institutions juridictionnelles*, 10th edn (Paris, Dalloz, 2009) no 247, 314.

Monopolies and Regulated Legal Professions

The legal and judicial trades, very compartmentalised in France, must face the general trend for high quality of work and profitability in order to succeed in the European and globalised law markets. Legal monopolies—supposedly maintaining these high standards—are now considered potential impediments not only to the European common market but also to the healthy management of every public and private undertaking. Reports commissioned by public authorities gave signals pointing in that direction: the most well-known report results from a commission *pour la liberation de la croissance française* (a commission with the aim of increasing French influence)presided over by Jacques Attali (a close adviser to the former French president, François Mitterrand); in 2009, this report was superseded, and on occasions toned down, by other reports (most notably the report by a commission presided over by Maître Darrois, business lawyer and member of the Attali commission). In practice, one of the results is the disappearance of the barrister (*l'avoué*) before the Courts of Appeal, professionals who enjoyed a monopoly of representation before the Courts of Appeal. These reports have opened the debate about the creation of a 'unified legal profession' that would regroup notaries public (whose *de lege* involvement is practically required in every sale of property) and lawyers whose monopolistic activities are limited compared to their other practices. Even though this debate has been taken out of the political and legislative agenda, one has to assume that it will be put forward in the medium term. Its importance for the financing and the costs of justice is indeed essential.

Monopolies, Competition, and the Costs of Justice

The logical compensation for those persons who are obliged, because of a monopoly in supply of a service, to have recourse to professionals is the rate fixed by law and by regulation of their services when their intervention is performed within the monopolistic market. These fixed rates are applicable, for example, to many acts undertaken by notaries public, bailiffs, barristers (before the disappearance of their monopoly), clerks of the Commercial Courts who, contrary to the clerks of the Civil Courts, are not considered as public servants, and so forth. The fixed rates were supposed to limit expenditure on mandatory legal acts and guarantee a moderate income to those professionals. In reality, the various fixed fees afforded a decent remuneration for those professionals; the acts to which the fixed rates apply also include some non-monopolistic areas enabling those professionals to earn fees free of regulatory oversight, thereby compensating for the relatively limited income of the fixed rate acts. Rather strangely, these professionals, who are basically liberals, staunchly defend the current system, thus arguing against inappropriate deregulation of these legal markets. They readily describe their function as a public service that should not be inappropriately put into an open market. The current public authorities appear to disagree and believe that reasonable competition guarantees a 'more effective judicial system,' an improvement of 'the performance of the legal professionals,' having 'an impact organising economic growth,' and source of 'a better integration in international trade' (all phrases taken from the Attali Report). In the end, the belief that competition better regulates the costs of justice and of civil trials than public authorities seems to have a considerable impact on relevant judicial policy.

Legal Insurance

Futher evidence of the above-mentioned trends can be found in the growth of the *Assurance de Protection Juridique.* This mechanism, purely private, rests on the ability to subscribe to an insurance policy that would cover legal fees arising from any proceedings in which policyholder, either as plaintiff or as defendant might become involved. This guarantee is frequently included in general liability insurance policies, at a relatively low cost (between €50 and €100 per year, although holders often overlook the legal fees element). The insurance company indicates the conditions upon which the insurance will apply: the nature of the litigation, the maximum amount of fees, the freedom of the policyholder to conduct the trial as he sees fit, the choice of legal advisers and so forth. In economic terms, this mechanism gives considerable influence to insurance companies which are already major economic actors, in the minimisation of the costs of justice. Legal advisers, notably lawyers, agree to intervene on behalf of the policyholder and receive a pre-agreed fixed fee. The bar has recently tried to limit this dependence on insurance companies. Public authorities see in such insurance a possible substitute for legal aid: indeed, a litigant who is a policyholder cannot qualify for legal aid. Legal insurance is a privatisation of the basic legal protection, paid for by the policyholder, or more exactly by all policyholders. However, subscription to such insurance is not mandatory.

B. The Rules On Funding And Costs

ANNE-LAURE VILLEDIEU*

General Overview and Trends

The French justice system dates back to the 1789 Revolution and is based on written law derived from a corpus of texts comprising Acts of Parliament, the Constitution of the fifth Republic (4 October 1958), international conventions and treaties, Community and European law, case law and custom. Justice in France is a state monopoly and is a public service. French judges, in the civil law tradition, do not create law. Thus, there is no proper case law in France. The courts interpret legislation and the decisions of the highest court (Cour de Cassation) are of great importance and may establish long-lasting doctrine known as *jurisprudence constante*. While there is no *stare decisis* rule forcing the lower courts to decide according to precedent, they tend to do so in practice with respect to *jurisprudence constante*. The judges must substantiate their decisions, explain the grounds of fact and law on which they base their decision, and are subject to the overseeing of application of the law by the Cour de Cassation.

Civil litigation in France is managed by a judge, who leads and controls the proceedings. The Courts exercise control over proceedings but do not conduct a full inquiry. The judge directs the steps that the parties must take during the proceedings, and calls upon the parties to produce evidence that the judge considers relevant.

The oral part of the proceedings is far less important, in comparison with common-law jurisdictions, than the exchange of written submissions prior to the trial *per se*. In contrast to common-law proceedings, civil matters do not involve cross-examination of witnesses and there are no juries in civil matters.

The basic structure of the Civil Courts in France is shown in Table 1.

EC Regulation no 861/2007 establishing the European Small Claims Procedure came into force 1 January 2009 (concerning claims up to €2,000). The Decree No 2008-1346 of 17 December 2008 incorporates the Regulation within the Code of Civil Procedure (CPC) under Articles 1382 to 1390.[5]

When the designation of a lawyer or an *avoué* is not mandatory, the latter is not entitled to a regulated remuneration. This is the case of the procedures

* Avocat à la Cour, CMS Bureau Francis Lefebvre, Paris.

[5] Decree No 2008-1346 of 17 Dec 2008, JORF No 0295 of 19 Dec 2008.

Table 1: Structure of Civil Courts

Court	Function	Jurisdiction	No. of claims in 2005[6]
Juridiction de proximité[7]	Deals with the claims 'of ordinary life'[8]	Claims up to €4,000	52,679
Tribunal d'Instance (Lower District Court)[9]	Claims 'of ordinary life', disputes between neighbours, claims of 'rural life'[10]	Claims up to €10,000	596,390
Tribunal de Grande Instance (Higher District Court)	General jurisdiction in first instance for civil proceedings	N/A	947,657
Tribunal de Commerce (Commercial Court)[11]	Matters relating to trade and commerce disputes	N/A	208,867
Conseil de Prud'homme[12]	Matters relating to labour law	N/A	202,827
Cour d'Appel (Court of Appeal)	Appeal of the decisions of the Civil Courts, the Commercial Court and the Conseil de Prud'homme	N/A	21,8216

[6] Annuaire Statistique de la Justice 2007.

[7] This court was created by Act No 2002-1138 of 9 Sept 2002. A single judge, who is not a professional, is in charge of claims of less than €4,000 commonly called claims 'of ordinary life'. It is not mandatory to be represented by a lawyer before the Court and the proceedings are conducted orally. Even if written evidence is given to the judge during the hearing, the judge will not take it into account if the other party has not been informed of this evidence prior to the hearing and given an opportunity to answer or explain. The decisions of the Judge de Proximité cannot be appealed, but they can be taken to the Supreme Court (Cour de Cassation).

[8] V Fortier and M Fabre, *Le Juge de proximité, une nouvelle offre de justice*, Mission de Recherche Droit et Justice, UMR 5818-IRETIJ—Faculté de droit, Université de Montpellier, Apr 2007.

[9] Trials are dealt with by a single professional judge. The proceedings are conducted orally and it is not mandatory to be represented by a lawyer. Decisions are usually issued within four or five months and these courts are regarded as being efficient in delivering justice.

[10] Art R 321 of the Code of judicial organisation.

[11] Arts L 721-1 to L 721-6 of the Commercial Code define the Commercial Courts' jurisdiction (Act No 2001-420 of 15 May 2001), and these Courts specialise in trade and commercial disputes. Decisions by the Commercial Court are final (unappealable) regarding claims up to €4,000 (Art R 721-6 Commercial Code). Above this amount, the Courts' decisions can be appealed. The judges are French and specialist in commercial law. Three judges (non-professional, elected by their peers) conduct the hearings and examine the evidence brought by the parties. Commercial usages apply. The court hearings are conducted orally.

[12] Art L 1442-3 of the Labour Code provides that the judges of the Conseil des Prud'hommes are elected for 5 years. The quorum in the Conseil is six: half of the Prud'hommes are employers and half are employees, each side electing its own representatives. The Prud'hommes, and to a lesser extent those who elect them, must possess certain qualifications as to ability, experience, age, residence and character. The Prud'hommes hold office for six years and, together with the officers, are re-eligible. They serve without pay. The Conseil does not have any specific cost rules.

Court	Function	Jurisdiction	No. of claims in 2005
Cour de Cassation (Supreme Court)[13]	Responsible for ensuring compliance with the rules of law applied by lower Courts. It judges the form and not the merits, unlike the Courts of first instance and the Court of Appeal, which judge the facts.	N/A	24,776

without mandatory representation before the Court of Appeal,[14] the Conseil des Prud'hommes,[15] the Juridiction de Proximité, and the Tribunal d'Instance.

Funding Claims

Personal funding is the most common source of finance for bringing or defending a legal claim. Whilst individuals may be entitled to legal aid, corporations can very rarely obtain such legal aid.

Legal aid is governed by Act No 91-647 of 10 July 1991. People with low incomes are eligible for legal aid. The state therefore pays, totally or partly, the costs of justice in order to enter into a settlement agreement, the costs of procedure or the costs involved in having a decision executed. These costs are essentially lawyers' fees, costs of procedure, of *avoués*, of bailiffs, of notaries, of mediation and of expertise.

The conditions for being entitled to legal aid are the following:

—The applicant must be a French citizen, or a citizen of a Member State of the EU, or a citizen of a state having entered into an international Agreement with the French state, or a person legally residing in France. Legal aid is rarely granted to a legal entity. However, non-profit legal entities having their corporate seat in France and having no sufficient resources may benefit from legal aid. This residence condition of living is not required for children under the age of 18.

—The applicant's income must not exceed €911 per month for the complete legal aid and €1,367 per month for partial legal aid (in 2009—the amounts are

[13] This court does not give a decision on the facts, but only on questions of law. If it finds that the lower Court's decision cannot stand it sends the matter back to a (different) Court of Appeal for a rehearing. It has been known for matters to take between 22 months and three years to be heard before the Court of Cassation.

[14] Decree No 80-608, 30 Jul 1980, arts 2 and 3.

[15] Cass Soc, 14 Nov 1985: Bull civ V, No 537.

revised every year and are higher when the requesting person has persons in charge).
—The applicant must not have entered into any legal insurance agreements covering the proceeding or settlement.

An application for legal aid can be filed before or during the course of the procedure. A file is obtained in a special office within the Tribunal de Grande Instance. If legal aid is allocated, the procedure for which the aid is given needs to be introduced within one year from the date when the decision has been sent to the beneficiary, otherwise the beneficiary loses the benefit of the aid and needs to reapply. The decision to grant legal aid does not depend on the merits of the applicant's case.

The applicant for legal aid can choose his lawyer. If he does not choose a lawyer, a lawyer will be designated by the special office. If legal aid is total, the lawyer is not allowed to ask for any further fee. If the legal aid is partial, the lawyer is entitled to further fees, which amount is freely negotiated.

Legal expense insurance (before-the-event) is increasingly popular in France for individuals and companies. It used to be attached to liability insurance but has become more autonomous, covering all kind of proceedings.[16] It is defined by article L 127-1 of the Insurance Code[17] as

> 'Any transactions that consist, in consideration of the payment of a previously agreed premium or a contribution, in covering the costs of proceedings or in providing services arising from the insurance cover in the event of a dispute or litigation between the insured and a third party, with a view, in particular, of defending or representing the insured as a claimant in civil, criminal, administrative or other proceedings or against a claim brought against him or to obtain out of court compensation for the loss sustained shall be deemed to be a legal expense insurance transaction'.

The insurance contract shall respect the conditions mentioned in article L 127-3[18]:

—'All legal expense insurance contracts must explicitly stipulate that, when a lawyer or any other person qualified under current law or regulations is called on to defend, represent or serve the insured's interests in the circumstances provided for in Article L 127-1, the insured shall be free to choose such person';
—'The contract shall also stipulate that the insured shall be free to choose a lawyer or, if he prefers, a qualified person to assist him whenever a conflict of interests arises between him and the insurer';
—'No contract clause shall interfere with the insured's freedom of choice, within the cover limit, under the previous two paragraphs'.

[16] Mémento F Lefebvre, *Vos Droits, Votre Argent*, 2009, 39450.

[17] Inserted by Act No 89-1014 of 31 Dec 1989, Article 5, Official Journal of 3 Jan 1990 in force on 1 Jul 1990.

[18] Inserted by Act No 89-1014 of 31 Dec 1989, Article 5, Official Journal of 3 Jan 1990 in force on 1 Jul 1990.

In consideration of the payment of the insurance premium, the insurer must pay, in the event of a proceeding with a third party, the experts' costs and the costs of proceeding (lawyers' fees and bailiffs' fees) and/or will provide assistance and advice. The insurance can be operated during a proceeding, regardless of whether the insurer is the plaintiff or the defendant, or to settle a claim outside the Courts. Legal expense insurance is regulated by the Act of 31 December 1989[19] which provides that the client shall freely choose his lawyer and the insurer may propose a lawyer to the client only if the client so requests. Article 3 of the Act (now article L 126-3-1 of the Code of Insurance) states that 'the legal fees are agreed between the lawyer and the client, and cannot be agreed with the insurer'. However, all agreements provide that the warranty is capped, so if the client appoints a lawyer whose fees exceed this limit, he has to pay the excess. Thus the fact that cover is only partial influences the client's choice of lawyer.

Article L 127-8 of the Insurance Code provides that any sum obtained as reimbursement for the costs and fees paid during the procedings shall be paid as a priority to the client to reimburse the excess amount he had to pay; and any remaining amount shall pay the insurance within the limits of the sums spent. The indemnity of Article 700 (see above), which can exceed the insurance limit, can be paid to the client. However, legal aid is not granted when the costs covered by this legal assistance are covered by an insurance contract (article 5 of the Act). French policy is to encourage the replacement of legal aid with insurance. Some authors emphasise, however, that the practical results of this trend may be disappointing, since those eligible for legal aid will rarely obtain insurance as they may be unable to pay the insurance premium.[20]

Finally, the insurance code provides for the event of a disagreement between the insurer and the insured. According to article L 127-4,

> 'The contract shall stipulate that in the event of disagreement between the insurer and the insured concerning the measures to be taken to settle a dispute, such difficulty may be referred to the assessment of a third party appointed by mutual agreement of the parties or, for want of such agreement, by the presiding judge of the Tribunal de Grande Instance ruling in summary proceedings. The insurer shall bear the costs incurred to implement such right. However, the presiding judge of the Tribunal de Grande Instance, ruling in summary proceedings, may decide otherwise if the insured implemented such right in abusive conditions.
>
> If the insured brought contentious proceedings at his expense and obtains a more favourable solution than that proposed by the insurer or the third party mentioned in the previous paragraph, the insurer shall indemnify the insured for the costs incurred in bringing such legal action, within the limit of the cover amount.
>
> When the proceedings referred to in the first paragraph of this Article are implemented, the time limit for the contentious proceedings shall be suspended for all courts covered by the insurance cover and the insured is liable to bring as a claimant until the third party in charge of proposing a solution has notified the purport thereof.'

[19] Modified by Act 2007-210 of 19 Feb 2007.

[20] R Martin, *Déontologie de l'avocat*, 10th edn (Paris, Litec, 2008) 26.

After-the-event (ATE) **insurance** is not used in France. The concept is generally unknown to the public and practitioners. This may be due to the fact that the main principle in French insurance law is that the customer must not be aware of the damage he wishes to insure before the insurance agreement is entered into. The insurance contract, according to article 1964 of the Civil Code, is a random contract, ie 'a reciprocal agreement whose effects, as to advantages and losses, either for all the parties, or for one or several of them, depend upon an uncertain event'. If the damage occurs before the parties enter into the agreement, the insurance contract is regarded null and void and the insurance company will not have to pay for the damage suffered by the customer.

Funding from a lawyer or other third party investor. Loans or grants from banks, trade associations or other persons or entities would theoretically be allowed under French law but are not used in practice. This may be due to (i) major third-party funders not having established significant businesses in France; and (ii) the widespread availability of legal aid.

Court or Process Costs

Court charges

Under French law, the parties do not have to pay court charges. Law No 77-1468 of 30 December 1977 upholds the principle of free access to justice, having brought to an end certain costs, traditionally referred to as the *frais de greffe,* although some court charges remain. The costs of transport, accommodation for the judges and the court clerks, the stamp duties, the registration rights, the postal costs and the royalties paid to the court clerks shall no longer be paid by the parties.

This gratuity, however, does not apply in commercial matters where the clerks still receive royalties for the registration of liens, the provision of commercial information and the *mises au role* (act by which a case is put on the Court's docket).

Each time the trial needs a person who is not a judge or a person attached to the Registry (*greffe*) of the Court, the state will not pay remuneration to such person (except when legal aid is given) but, instead, one of the parties must pay. These costs are therefore born by the losing party, as stated by the Code of Civil Procedure (CPC) as explained below.

Other official charges (VAT, translator, bailiff, service or process, enforcement of a judgment)

Most of the official charges constitute the *dépens,* as defined and listed by Article 695 of the CPC. In principle, the party who paid the *dépens* in advance may fully recover these costs from the losing party. These costs are called 'recoverable costs' (*frais répétibles*). The judge may, under article 700 CPC, order the losing party to payup to a certain amount fixed by the judge, other costs that are not listed under Article 695 CPC, which are usually referred to as 'irrevocable costs' (*frais irrepétibles*).

Article 695 of the CPC provides an exhaustive list of the *dépens*. In certain areas of law, however, the *dépens* do not have to be paid and, even when listed under article 695 CPC, will not be regarded as procedural *dépens*.

Article 695 CPC provides a list of costs that shall be regarded as *dépens* when they 'are related to instances, acts and procedures of execution':

> '[T]he fees, taxes, royalties or emoluments levied by the clerk's offices of courts or by the tax administration with the exception of fees, taxes and penalties which may be due on documents and titles produced in support of the claims of the parties, the costs of translation of the documents when such translation is requested by law or by an international commitment; the indemnities of the witnesses, the fees of the experts, the fees of the bailiffs, the emoluments of the law officials and public officers, the fees of the lawyers for the part of them which are regulated (legal aid or postulation before the Tribunal de Grande Instance), the costs of notification of the documents in a foreign country'.[21]

Fees, taxes, royalties or emoluments levied by the clerk's offices of courts or by the tax administration

This category is becoming residual since the law, dated 30 December 1977 that stated free access to justice before the civil Courts. Nowadays, the only claims that give rise to the payment of fees are those brought before the commercial courts and decisions giving rise to a proportional or progressive registration right;[22] such decisions tend to relate to the transfer of real estate, goodwill (*fonds de commerce*) or a similar right, the transfer of shares or the sharing (*partage*), unless the exception of article 695-1 CPC applies.

The fees, taxes and penalties that may be due regarding the acts and titles provided to support the parties' demands are not included in the *dépens*. These acts and titles, indeed, are not linked directly to the case. They are provided for evidence purposes, are outside the procedure and pre-exist the proceeding.

[21] Art 695 CPC. This provision requires the parties to pay most court costs. However, the principle remains that justice in France is free, even if this principle is restricted to the fact that the judge and other court officials are paid by the State and not by the parties, as reflected in Act No 77-1468 of 30 Dec 1977. The principle of free justice has existed since the time of the French Revolution.

[22] Art 6 of the law of 30 Dec 1977.

Regulated disbursements (*débours tarifés*)

These are the disbursements provided by the tariffs of the lawyers[23] and ministerial officers (*avoués*[24] and bailiffs[25]), and the disbursements of the parties. The disbursements are the sums paid for the proceedings.

The regulated disbursements include the costs of the acts of the bailiffs; experts fees; translation costs; witness indemnities; the costs paid by the Court in case a hearing is held at a specific place ; the costs of transport when the presence of the *avoué* is requested by law or demanded by a party; and certain copying costs. Regarding bailiffs, the regulated disbursements include tax stamps (*droits fiscaux*), transport costs, stamps of the letters designated by law as mandatory procedure formalities (signification by report of search of premises under article 659 CPC).

The regulated disbursements of lawyers cover the case management steps involved in the process (*postulation* payments), which exist solely before the Tribunal de Grande Instance. Decree No 72-784 of 25 August 1972 applies and refers to Decree No 60-323 of 2 April 1960, which provides that the following costs are regarded as disbursements:

'The copies or extracts of pieces to be notified, unless these pieces are established or drafted by the *avoué*; transports costs; costs of paper, printing and correspondence; and costs of publication of the sales in court (*ventes judiciaries*).'

Finally, the public officers or ministerial officers, namely the receivers, the *avoués*, the auctioneers, the *greffiers de commerce*, bailiffs, liquidators and notaries, are entitled to a remuneration called *émoluments*. Provided their action is linked to the proceeding, these *émoluments* can be included in the *dépens*, even if they have been assigned by a decision taken before the proceeding by one of the parties. In contrast, in the context of experts, the *émoluments* are regulated and the part of the remuneration of these persons that is not regulated (fees) cannot be included in the *dépens*.

Lawyers' Costs

Law No 71-1130 dated 31 December 1971 regulates lawyers' fees.[26] Lawyers' fees are regulated, as far as the *postulation* is concerned, and free for any other act or representation. Lawyers receive regulated fees, as provided by the Decree No 60-323 of 2 April 1960 and Decree No 72.784 of 25 August 1972, when they perform '*postulation works*' (representation before the Tribunal de Grande Instance). The postulation fees consist in (i) a fixed fee that varies depending on the nature of the

[23] Art 2 of Decree No 60-323 of 2 Apr 1960.
[24] Art 21 of Decree No 80-608 of 30 Jul 1980.
[25] Art 3 of Decree No 96-1080 of 12 Dec 1996.
[26] Art 10, as modified by the Law No 91-647 of 10 Jul 1991 and by the Decree of 27 Nov 1991.

case; and (ii) a variable fee depending on the actual amount of the case. This regulated compensation can be included in the *dépens*. When a lawyer is simply a '*postulant*', which means that he represents the case before the Court because the lawyer in charge of the case is not a member of the Bar Association attached to that specific court, the postulant is only entitled to *postulation fees*, which are regulated and are very low. However, the *postulant* can also receive free fees if he has done more than simple postulation; these fees must not be included in the *dépens*.

For other acts or representation, fees are freely agreed between the lawyer and his client. Article 10 of Law No 71-1130 of 31 December 1971 states:

> 'Fees for consulting, assistance, advice, drafting of private legal acts and pleadings are agreed with the client.
>
> If no agreement has been entered into, the fees shall be determined following the usages, taking into account the financial situation of the client, the difficulty of the case, the lawyers' expenses, his awareness and his work.
>
> Any determination of fee that would solely depend on the result of the case is forbidden. Is lawful the agreement which provides, over the payment of the work done, a complementary fee depending on the result obtained or the service rendered.'

The fees can be agreed in advance (*convention d'honoraires*). This agreement is mandatory when the client is entitled to partial legal aid and the lawyer asks for a complementary fee. In that case, the agreement is controlled by the representative of the Bar (the '*bâtonnier*'). Otherwise the agreement is not mandatory. However, clients are becoming more willing to enter into an agreement with their lawyer.[27] This agreement can state that the fees will consist of a lump sum or a *fourk* of fees depending on the risks of the claim.

Contingency fees (*pacte de quota litis*) are strictly forbidden by statute[28] and a French attorney may be disbarred if he were to conclude a solely contingency fee agreement with his client.

However, a written fee agreement with a client that is subject to an uplift in the event of a particularly positive outcome and of which the calculation is set out in advance is permitted. The relatively few law firms dealing with non-contentious corporate and international matters but who are able to handle litigation tend to bill according to time spent and the identity of the fee earner. The notional hourly rate depends on several factors including, the specialist area, urgency of the work and location of the law practice: figures tend to be between €220 and €500.

However, litigators, in contrast with those who are used to dealing with an international clientele, tend to bill according to slightly different criteria, including the nature of the work performed, the amount of the claim, the reputation of the attorney dealing with the matter and the result obtained.

Indeed, lawyers are entitled to different items of remuneration. Article 695-7 CPC also includes within the *dépens* the costs of pleading (*frais de plaidoirie*). Fees

[27] J-J Taisne 'Avocat', 2009 *Répértoire de procédure civile* (Paris, Dalloz).

[28] Art 10 of the Act dated 31 Dec 1971.

are for each pleading and finance the *Caisse de retraite des barreaux francais*, which deals with the lawyers' retirement insurance.

Fees to be charged by a lawyer to his clients are freely determined between the lawyer and his client. The Bar Association of Nice in 1990 and 1994 published a document called 'recommendations as to lawyers' fees' where recommendations as to the fees were provided, aiming at fixing a break-even point for files with no particular difficulties in order to allow the lawyer, on first meeting with the client, to agree with him the bases of a decent remuneration. The Conseil de la Concurrence (council in charge of competition matters), in a decision 00-D-52 of 15 January 2001, ruled that if a Bar Association conveys information to its members, 'this help must not exercise any direct or indirect influence on the structure of competition in the profession'. The Conseil decided that the indicative list regarding lawyers' fees issued by the Bar Association exercised such an influence, and was therefore a cartel. The Bar Association was ordered to stop the publication of the indicative recommendations and to pay a fine.[29]

The fees can consist of:

—A fixed fee agreed in advance (usually for simple proceedings such as referee or divorce agreed by the parties);
—Hourly rates;
—A fixed fee or an hourly rate completed in consideration of the result of the proceeding. These fees are generally agreed when the result of the proceeding is financial. It is therefore a percentage of the sums obtained in Court.

The lawyer must inform his client of the fees he shall eventually be charged.[30] The client shall not be surprised at the conclusion of the claim by the amount of the invoice.[31]

The client can refuse to pay the fee invoiced by his lawyer. The claim must be brought before the *bâtonnier* (the representative of the Bar). The *bâtonnier* collects the observations of the lawyer and of the client and issues a decision within four months (eight months max). The decision of the *bâtonnier* can be challenged before the first president of the Court of Appeal within the months following the decision.

[29] Cons Conc 3 Dec 1996, Gaz Pal 1997.1.310.

[30] The Memento Francis Lefebvre 2009 provides examples of fees to be paid for certain proceedings:

—€500 to €1,000 for a referee proceeding;
—€1,000 to €3,000 plus complementary fees for a proceeding before the Conseil des Prud'hommes;
—€1,500 to €3,000 for a divorce agreed by both parties;
—€3500 or more for a claim linked to construction defects.

[31] Cass 2e civ 10 Mar 2004, decisions No 02-18-241 and 02-21-318, D 2004, IR 921 and IR 994.

Witness Of Fact

Article 221 of the CPC allows the judge to give the witnesses heard during an inquiry, on demand, some indemnities. The evaluation of these indemnities is made by reference to Decree of 27 December 1920 revising the travel costs of the parties, of the experts of the Tribunaux de Grande Instance, *dépositaires de pièces* and witnesses. An indemnity can be paid for the examination of the witness, for his journey and for his accommodation. The costs are paid in advance by the party that requires the hearing of the witness, and may be eventually refunded by the other party as *dépens.*

Expert

According to the CPC, an expert is a person designated by the judge to 'enlighten by her findings, through a written advice or an expertise those facts requiring the views of an expert.' (article 332 CPC). Beside the court experts as defined by article 332 CPC, this category includes persons whose mission consists in undertaking a social inquiry in matters of divorce or separation (*séparation de corps*). Article 3 of Decree No 76-998 of 4 November 1976, as amended by Decree No 88-600 of 6 May 1988 expressly provides that the remuneration of the person having made the inquiry is included within the *dépens.* Generally, every time one party, unilaterally and without a decision of a judge, uses an expert, the payment of this expert is not included within the *dépens.* Article 700 CPC may then apply to these costs. The remuneration of the court expert (*expert judiciaire*) is regulated and fixed by the judge following a specific procedure stated by articles 248, 262, 269, 724 and 725 CPC. The judge who has ordered an inquiry in the meantime sets a consignation of an advanced payment of the expert and designates the party in charge of this consignation. Once the inquiry is over, the expert asks the judge to fix his fees and is paid by *prélèvement* on the consignation and possibly through a complementary payment by the party in charge of the advanced payment of the expert's fees. The fees paid in advance shall thereafter be reimbursed as *dépens.*

In relation to social inquiries, the fees are always paid in advance by the state, but the final amount of fee to be paid to the expert is still determined by the judge having ordered the inquiry.

Cost Shifting

In litigation in France, as a matter of law and practice, full costs do not habitually follow the action and thus the losing party rarely has to pay a substantial amount to the other side in regard to costs. The judge who determines the case decides the costs recoverable by the parties. The judge determines the amount of the *dépens* following the list mentioned in article 695 of the CPC. He also determines the costs he considers shall be paid by either party depending on the merits of each party's case.

The Courts generally apply the 'loser pays' rule. Article 696 CPC states 'The legal cost will be borne by the losing party, unless the judge, by a reasoned decision, imposes the whole or part of it on another party.' The rules concerning the *dépens* are self-explanatory and the list of costs provided by article 695 CPC is comprehensive.[32] These costs are all fixed by a tariff or by a taxation procedure. There is therefore no arbitrary of either party for the fixation of their amount.

However, pursuant to Article 697 CPC, lawyers, *avoués* and bailiffs 'may be personally liable for the legal cost pertaining to the proceeding, process and enforcement procedures instituted outside the scope of their agency.'

Article 698 CPC states that 'The legal cost pertaining to unjustified proceeding, process and enforcement procedures will be borne by the representatives of the law who undertook them, without prejudice to the damages that might be claimed. The same will apply to legal costs relating to proceeding, process and enforcement procedures that are null due to the fault of those representatives of the law.'

The Courts rarely order the losing party to pay the total amount of fees that have been paid to the lawyer for the winning party. Generally, the amount that can be recovered is between €2,000 and €5,000. This amount may, however, be increased or decreased if one of the parties has acted in bad faith during the course of the trial and has therefore increased the legal costs of the other party.

The payment of the costs as ordered by the judge has to be made once the judgment is published, and in the case of a judgment in first instance if it is not appealed, except if the judge has ordered the provisional execution of his judgment. From the date of the notification of the judgment to the losing party by a bailiff, the winning party will have the right to sue for payment.

General Costs Issues

How predictable are the amounts involved?

For small cases or proceedings before courts where the appointment of a lawyer is not mandatory, the amounts involved are reasonably predictable, as the state will bear most of the costs (costs of the judges and the courts). In small cases and proceedings before the Juridiction de Proximité, as well as before the Tribunal d'Instance and Conseil de Prud'hommes, when the parties represent themselves, the case usually does not require an expert. Therefore the costs of small cases are small and reasonably predictable, subject to exceptions when the case reveals more

[32] Cass 2e civ, 6 May 1987.

complexities than expected. In contrast, in the courts where a lawyer needs to be appointed, the amounts involved are unpredictable at the stage when the first writ of summons has been sent.

The lawyers' *postulation* fees are predictable since they are regulated and depend on the nature of the case and the amount of the claim. A tariff is published[33] which enables their calculation. Other legal fees are not predictable unless their amount is determined and agreed in advance between the lawyer and his client. However, article 10 of Decree No 2005-790, dated 12 July 2005, provides that the lawyer must inform the client, as soon as appointed and regularly thereafter, of the methods of calculation of the fees and of any foreseeable variation of this amount.[34]

An agreement is mandatory when:

1. the client has obtained partial legal aid and the lawyer wishes to be paid fees exceeding the amount of legal aid; and/or
2. the lawyer's fee are paid, partly or completely, through a legal insurance.[35]

The lawyer can also ask his client for retainer fees, which will eventually be deducted from the fees actually due. These retainer fees shall not exceed a reasonable estimate likely to be generated in the case at issue.[36] In case of dispute between the lawyer and his client regarding the fees, the *bâtonnier* adjudicates the dispute.[37] If an agreement is entered into, information regarding fees shall be within the agreement. Fixed fees can be agreed.

The lawyer can receive periodic fees from a client, including fixed periodic fees. Article 12 of Decree 2005-790 provides that 'before any complete payment, the lawyer shall provide his client with a detailed account. This account clearly underlines the costs and *débours*, the regulated emoluments and the fees. It mentions the retainer fees already paid and any other sum already paid.'

How Long Do The Procedures Take?

In 2006 the average lengths of proceedings were as follows (in months):[38]

Court of Appeal: 13.3
Tribunaux de Grande Instance: 6.6
Tribunaux d'instance et Juges de Proximité: 4.7

[33] Decree no 72-784 dated 25 Aug 1972 modified by Decree no 75-785 dated 21 Aug 1975 and Decree dated 2 Apr 1960.

[34] This text has been reproduced under Article 11.2 of the *Règlement Intérieur National* (RIN) of the lawyers' Bars.

[35] Act No 2007-210 of 19 Feb 2007 and Decree No 2007-932 dated 15 May 2007.

[36] Art 11 of the Decree 2005-790.

[37] Art 175 of Decree No 91-1197 dated 27 Nov 1991.

[38] Les chiffres-clés de la Justice, Oct 2007, Secrétariat Général Direction de l'Administration Générale et de l'Equipement, Sous-Direction de la Statistique, des Etudes et de la Documentation.

Commercial Courts: 6
Conseils de Prud'hommes: 9.9

Court proceedings in France can take a long time to reach a conclusion. In one egregious case decided in 2008,[39] the Cour de Cassation ordered the French government to pay damages to an individual because of the length of the proceedings. The plaintiff, who was claiming compensation after suffering an industrial accident, had had to wait 14 years before the Court issued a final decision concerning his indemnity. The Cour de Cassation ruled that this delay revealed a malfunctioning of the justice system.[40] On the other hand, some courts like the Tribunal d'Instance, which has jurisdiction for claims up to €10,000, will commonly pronounce a judgment in a case within four to five months of proceedings being commenced.

The Courts of Appeal are not bound by the findings of fact at first instance.

According to a study published in 2007[41] by the Ministry of Justice, the percentage of cases appealed in 2005 are the following:

Tribunaux d'instance	4.4%
Tribunaux de Grande Instance	12.4%
Conseil de Prud'hommes	62.5%
Tribunaux de commerce	14.4%

The costs of an appeal are similar to first instance, except for the costs of *avoués,* which only occur on appeal.

[39] Cass 1re Civ, 20 Feb 2008, No 06-20.384.
[40] A similar case was *Malve v France* (No 46051/99 [2001] ECHR).
[41] Les chiffres-clés de la Justice, 2007.

11

Germany

BURKHARD HESS* AND RUDOLF HÜBNER**

General Overview and Trends in the German Civil Litigation Cost System

Background and Context to the Rules on Funding and Costs

The German civil litigation cost system—implementing a liberal nineteenth-century agenda[1]—has always placed its emphasis on the equal availability of civil justice for all regardless of social status.[2] It is thus intended to promote the rule of law in order to facilitate economic activity for everybody. Therefore, some integral parts of the cost system have been remarkably constant ever since their introduction together with Germany's most important civil procedure laws[3] on 1 October 1877.[4] The provisions on the allocation of costs among parties in contentious civil litigation, in particular, have almost entirely kept their original wording.[5] Also, from the very beginning, there have been provisions on legal aid (originally known as *Armenhilfe*—pauper relief)[6] and the remuneration of attorneys. Other than those relating to legal aid, there are few rules relating to litigation funding since it is traditionally perceived to be an obligation of the parties to obtain the necessary funds unless they are eligible for legal aid.

Perhaps the most contentious and most visibly changing part of the original system is the regulation of remuneration of attorneys. The relevant law (RVG) was completely remodelled and renamed twice. However, the provisions have always

* Professor, Institute for Private International and Comparative Law, University of Heidelberg.
** Institute for Private International and Comparative Law, University of Heidelberg.

1 cf P Murray and R Stürner, *German Civil Justice* (Durham, Carolina Academic Press, 2004) 30.

2 cf O Kissel, '125 Jahre Reichsjustizgesetze' (2004) *NJW* 2872.

3 While cost laws themselves are procedural laws, for purposes of easier distinction between the proceedings and their costs they shall be excluded from that term hereinafter.

4 cf P Hartmann, *Kostengesetze* 20th edn (München, Beck, 1981) Einl I, 1 (including the Civil Procedure Code (*Zivilprozessordnung (ZPO)*) and the Court Organisation Law (*Gerichtsverfassungsgesetz—GVG*).

5 cf Reichsgesetzblatt (RGBl) 1877, 98—ss 87 ZPO) as well as the first major reform, RGBl 1898, 256 (259 *et seq*) and compare them to the current wording of ss 91 ZPO.

6 cf ss 106 ZPO of 1877, RGBl 1877, 101.

reflected the policy that attorneys are traditionally perceived to be a public institution that is not only devoted to the interests of its clients but also to the promotion of the administration of justice.

Taken as a whole, rules relating to civil litigation costs correspond well to the general procedural objective[7] of protecting and implementing substantive private rights. They also have considerable significance in practice, since extra-court dispute resolution alternatives are so far—with the exception of arbitration—of little relevance in Germany.

Abbreviations and translations

Principles and Theory

Abbreviation	Full Term (German)	Translation
AktG	Aktiengesetz	Stock Corporation Act
BGB	Bürgerliches Gesetzbuch	Civil Code
BGH	Bundesgerichtshof	Federal Court of Justice
BRAO	Bundesrechtsanwaltsordnung	Federal Attorneys Code
BVerfG	Bundesverfassungsgericht	Federal Constitutional Court
FamFG	Gesetz über das Verfahren in Familiensachen und den Angelegenheiten der freiwilligen Gerichtsbarkeit	Code of Family Proceedings and Non-Contentious Proceedings
FamGKG	Gesetz über Gerichtskosten in Familiensachen	Family Matters Court Charges Act
GG	Grundgesetz	Federal Consitution (Basic Law)
GKG	Gerichtskostengesetz	Court Charges Act
JVEG	Justizvergütungs- und Entschädigungsgesetz	Judicial Remuneration and Compensation Act
RDG	Rechtsdienstleistungsgesetz	Legal Services Act
RVG	Rechtsanwaltsvergütungsgesetz	Attorney Remuneration Act
ZPO	Zivilprozessordnung	Civil Procedure Code

The German civil litigation cost system is designed to provide equal access to a high standard of justice at costs such that no claimant shall refrain from pursuing his right simply because of the costs of litigation. This approach is not merely a consequence of substantive private law, which would be largely ineffective without the general availability of either private or public enforcement. It is also a consequence of the constitutional guarantee[8] of free access to justice, as set out in articles 2(1),

[7] cf P Hartmann in A Baumbach et al (eds), ZPO 66th edn (München, Beck, 2008), Einl III, 9 (9).

[8] cf BVerfG, 12 Dec 2006—1 BvR 2576/04, BVerfGE 117, 163, 186; also cf W Brehm in F Stein and M Jonas, ZPO 22nd edn (Tübingen, Mohr Siebeck, 2003) ss 1, 287–288, 103.

20, 3 GG.[9] That guarantee prohibits any unnecessary and disproportionate costs in civil litigation—although leaving much discretion to the legislator when elaborating a cost system.

The relevant costs laws try to achieve that aim by adhering to the following basic principles.

Predictability—High Level of Regulation

A high level of regulation[10] of all types of costs incurred in civil litigation is supposed to deliver a greater predictability of costs of any proceeding. As a rule, parties are fully informed as to the amount of costs to be incurred. This information (which means that the precise amount of the costs can be calculated) is intended to enable them to take a reasoned decision as to the prospects of the case when they consider initiating court proceedings.

Court Charges and Statutory Lawyer Fees Are Calculated on the Amount in Controversy (hereinafter: Amount in Controversy Based Costs)

Tying court charges and statutory lawyers' fees to the amount of a claim is supposed to set the costs in proportion to the economic value of the claim, rather than the actual costs of the work performed by courts and attorneys. This legal technique is intended to promote both the predictability of costs and the pursuit of small claims.[11]

Fee Shifting

German procedural law does not allow any fee shifting at the discretion of the court. According to section 91(1) ZPO, the losing party must bear all statutory costs of the litigation in civil and commercial matters, including the costs incurred by the opponent, (*loser pays* rule[12] and indemnity principle). If each party is successful in part and fails in part, costs are mutually cancelled or proportionally divided (section 92(1) ZPO). The rule is supposed to allow a claimant to base his or her decision on initiating court proceedings primarily on the probability of a positive result. The claimant shall not fear costs of achieving vindication of a valid claim. Altogether, the rule corresponds to the general procedural objective[13] of protecting and implementing substantive private rights: Parties shall be encouraged to bring forward valid claims and discouraged from pursuing unmeritorious claims. Thus, it also promotes the efficient use of the judiciary (see below).

[9] cf P Hartmann (n 7) para 128, 14, 619.

[10] See above General Introduction for the numerous laws on all aspects of civil litigation costs.

[11] Via cross financing: the (higher) remuneration of claims of high value shall cross-finance the representation of small claims which may involve an (even) greater workload than the pursuit of claims of a higher amount, see C Wolf, 'Recht durch Rechtsanwälte' in *BRAK, 4. Zivilprozessrechtssymposium* (München, Beck, 2008) 14–16.

[12] P Murray and R Stürner (n 1) 341.

[13] cf P Hartmann (n 7) Einl III, 9 (9).

Proportionality of Costs

The cost reimbursement provisions in section 91 et seq ZPO provide that only necessary, rather than proportional, costs are reimbursed. The necessary costs are fixed by the specific statutes on costs (see below). Disproportionalities may therefore arise only from extensive evidence gathering—which is a rare exception.

The advantage of the German system is its considerable predictability. However, for lawyers representing small claims, the system may have considerable disadvantages. If a lawyer is unable to represent both large and small claims, his income, based on the fixed levels of remuneration may be insufficient. At present, the growing specialisation of the German bar may lead to imbalances among specialist law firms representing professional clients and the traditional attorney representing clients of all kinds.[14]

It remains to be seen whether, and to what extent, claimants in Germany may prefer national proceedings to the European Small Claims Procedure, which provides for the allocation of proportional cost on an individual basis (cf article 16 of Regulation (EC) No 861/2007).[15]

Costs in Contentious Cases are to Subsidise the Pursuit of Small Claims and Claims Brought Forward with Legal Aid—Cross-Subsidisation

The costs of pursuing small claims would often be considerably higher if costs were calculated on the actual work performed by courts and attorneys. In order to avoid this major obstacle to the pursuit of small claims, costs based on the amount in dispute are designed to subsidise small claims proceedings.[16] Whereas costs for small claims proceedings may not cover the actual costs, costs for proceedings concerning larger claims are designed to over-compensate both courts and attorneys for the work they actually perform in these cases.[17] This principle of cross-subsidisation has been characteristic of both German court charges and attorney remuneration since the nineteenth-century.[18]

In addition, costs in proceedings on larger claims are not only to subsidise smaller claims but also legal aid cases. In legal aid cases, which attorneys are

[14] cf C Wolf (n 11) 17.

[15] cf I Jahn, 'Das Europäische Verfahren für geringfügige Forderungen' (2007) *NJW* 2890, 2892 et seq; G Volkommer and S Huber, 'Neues Europäisches Zivilverfahrensrecht in Deutschland—Das Gesetz zur Verbesserung der grenzüberschreitenden Forderungsdurchsetzung und Zustellung' (2009) *NJW* 1105, 1109.

[16] C Hommerich et al, 'Quersubventionierung im RVG: Fiktion oder Wirklichkeit?' (2006) *Anwaltsblatt* 406.

[17] While small claims are usually less complex and thus also require less work, the work required for the pursuit of larger claims usually does not increase proportionally to the amount in dispute. Rather, the workload usually increases more slowly proportionate to the amount in dispute—within the German system leading to different remuneration for an identical workload. This finding is also the reason for the reducing levels in dispute-based cost structure, cf s 34 GKG, 13 RVG. Hence the subsidies result from—on average—a lower than adequate reduction in the costs in comparison to the (typical) actual workload of arising increasing amount in dispute: cf C Hommerich et al (n 16) 406.

[18] C Hommerich et al (n 16) 406.

obliged to accept (section 48 BRAO—Federal Attorney Code), attorney remuneration is reduced in comparison to other cases (section 49 RVG).

Minimum Attorneys' Fees in Judicial Proceedings

In civil litigation, attorneys are not allowed to work for less than the statutory fee (sections 49b(1) BRAO, 4(1) RVG).[19] This regulation is to protect the system of cross-subsidisation and is based on the traditional German perception of lawyers being bound to promote the administration of justice. It is perceived that 'quality has a certain price tag'.

Settlement and General Trends

Importance of Settlement—Statistical Data

The statistical data in Table 1 shows the proportion of disputes resolved in German courts by settlement in comparison to all disputes resolved (2007 data)

Table 1: Case and Settlement Statistics

Court	Statistics
Local Courts—first instance (*Amtsgerichte*):[20]	
—Total No of resolved disputes:	1,276,426
—Disputes resolved by settlement:	181,762
—Settlement share:	14.2 %
District Courts—first instance (*Landgerichte*):[21]	
—Total No of resolved disputes:	377,779
—Disputes resolved by settlement:	90,102
—Settlement share:	23.9 %
District Courts—second instance (*Landgerichte*):[22]	
—Total No of resolved disputes:	61,357
—Disputes resolved by settlement:	7,442
—Settlement share:	12.1 %
Higher Regional Courts (*Oberlandesgerichte*):[23]	
—Total No of resolved disputes:	54,184
—Disputes resolved by settlement:	9,187
—Settlement share:	17.0 %

[19] Also cf P Hartmann, *Kostengesetze* 38th edn (München, Beck, 2008), § 4 RVG, 3, 54 *et seq.*

[20] Federal Statistics Agency, Report on the Civil Judiciary 2007—Statistisches Bundesamt, Statistik Rechtspflege (Zivilgerichte) für 2007, Fachserie 10, Reihe 2.1, 18, 22.

[21] Federal Statistics Agency, Report on the Civil Judiciary 2007—Statistisches Bundesamt, Statistik Rechtspflege (Zivilgerichte) für 2007, Fachserie 10, Reihe 2.1, 42, 46.

[22] Federal Statistics Agency, Report on the Civil Judiciary 2007—Statistisches Bundesamt, Statistik Rechtspflege (Zivilgerichte) für 2007, Fachserie 10, Reihe 2.1, 58, 62.

[23] Federal Statistics Agency, Report on the Civil Judiciary 2007—Statistisches Bundesamt, Statistik Rechtspflege (Zivilgerichte) für 2007, Fachserie 10, Reihe 2.1, 80, 84.

The proportion of disputes resolved by settlement has continually risen over recent years. At the same time, judges have extended the use of mediation techniques.[24] It should be noted that these figures do not mirror the factual situation entirely, since the concluding of litigation by settlement is only one way of concluding litigation by consent. It is common practice for German judges to advise parties at the hearing to withdraw or to acknowledge the claim (according to the prospects of success). In addition, the statistics do not include those claims where parts of the claim are voluntarily terminated.

Settlement Incentives in the Current German Cost Structure

There are two major incentives for settlement in the German litigation cost provisions: First, consensual dispositions—among them settlement—lead to considerably smaller court charges (appendix 1 to sections 3(2) GKG, KV 1211, KV 1222, 1232). Second, in the case of settlement, lawyers receive an additional (legal) settlement fee (cf. appendix 1 to sections 2(2) RVG, VV 1000, 1003, 1004), giving them a very strong incentive to push their clients toward settlement. Both incentives are available at every stage of the litigation, including appeal proceedings (appendix 1 to sections 3(2) GKG, KV 1222, 1232).

General Trends in the German Civil Litigation Cost System

At present, deregulation can be perceived as a general trend in the regulation of attorney remuneration.[25] As yet, it is unclear whether there is any economic advantage, since German civil litigation costs are relatively low even in comparison with less regulated or unregulated markets.[26] In addition, deregulation efforts have to take into account that deregulation may have disadvantages related to the transparency of litigation costs.[27]

Despite the trend of deregulating the legal profession (including the remuneration of lawyers), there is strong political trend towards leaving the basic statutory system untouched, based as it is on the *loser pays* principle, which does not permit the court any discretion in fee shifting.

Unresolved or Contentious Issues

For many years, contingency fees have been debated intensely in Germany. Traditionally, they were not permitted under German lawyers' remuneration laws.

[24] B Hess, *Gutachten Mediation für den 67. Deutschen Juristentag* (München, Beck, 2008) 19 *et seq.*

[25] C Wolf (n 11) 1.

[26] J von Seltmann, 'Rechtsanwaltsvergütung in Europa' (2008) *BRAK-Mitteilungen*, 118, 119; Litigation costs on average account for only 14.4 % (11.8 % in 2008) of the amount in controversy leaving Germany among the most cost efficient countries in Europe, cf. the *Doing Business 2008 Report*, 49, 50 and 105, published by the World Bank and available on www.doingbusiness.org/.

[27] J von Seltmann (n 26) 119.

However, in 2006, the Federal Constitutional Court (BVerfG) ruled that the ban on contingency fees was not wholly in accordance with the German Constitution (GG).[28] According to this decision, the constitutional guarantee of access to justice requires allowing for exceptions in cases in which parties might be deterred from pursuing their rights unless they had the possibility of negotiating a contingency fee. With reluctantly introduced changes to the RVG, effective since 1 July 2008, the legislation sought to implement the standards demanded by the BVerfG. It remains the case that the regulation of contingency fees is criticised both for its consequences[29] and its reach.[30] Some critics fear contingency fees as an further step towards an Americanisation[31] of German (and or continental European) law.[32]

Since the principle of cross subsidisation—with regard to attorney remuneration—is losing its factual basis and justification through lawyers' specialisation (see below), pressure to change the system may eventually evolve. The major challenge will be the elaboration of adequate remuneration structures for small claims, which still provides a quality service for clients in these situations.

Likely Future Reforms

The German legislator is considering various changes to the cost system in an process that began in 2003 with the call by Germany's then[33] Federal Minister of Justice, Brigitte Zypries, for a 'structural cost reform'.[34] The legislative process has already produced two new statutes: the RVG and the FamGKG. At present various proposals are being discussed; two of them may be worth presenting here.

Firstly, some Federal states wished to reduce their spending on legal aid because of budgetary constraints. They finally introduced federal legislation in 2006 that would have overhauled the system of spending on legal aid.[35] However, in a 2007 parliamentary discussion the proposal faced considerable resistance.[36] At present, the process appears to be stalled.[37] According to its critics, the proposal did not adequately observe constitutional rights guaranteeing equal access to justice[38] and

[28] BVerfG, 12 Dec 2006—1 BvR 2576/04, BVerfGE 117, 163.

[29] cf eg H-J Mayer, 'Die Vereinbarung eines Erfolgshonorars nach §4 a RVG n F' (2008) *Anwaltsblatt* 473, 477 criticising changes on the consequences of a lack of form in remuneration agreements.

[30] cf eg M Hartung, 'Wer schützt wen vor wem?—oder: Muss der Mandant vor Erfolg geschützt werden?' (2008) *Anwaltsblatt* 396.

[31] cf M Hartung (n 30) 398 on what is understood as Americanisation in Germany.

[32] cf eg B Stüer, 'Erfolgshonorar: Fällt die letzte Bastion des anwaltlichen Standesrechts?' (2007) *Anwaltsblatt* 431 et seq.

[33] Mrs Zypries was in office from Oct 2002 until Oct 2009.

[34] B Zypries, (2003) *Anwaltsblatt* 381, 382.

[35] Materials of the German Federal Parliament (*Bundestag*), BT Drs 16/1994.

[36] Plenary protocols of the German Federal Parliament (*Plenarprotokoll*) 16/97 9966; also cf R von König, *Zivilprozess- und Kostenrecht*, 2nd edn (Bielefeld, Gieseking, 2008) 320 *et seq.*

[37] cf dip.bundestag.de/extrakt/16/019/16019184.htm documenting the legislation process.

[38] For European aspects of the access to justice topic cf B Hess, in A Uzelac and CH van Rhee (eds), *Public and Private Justice: Dispute Resolution in Modern Societies* (Antwerp/Oxford/Portland, Intersentia, 2007).

article 47 (3) of the Charter of Fundamental Rights of the European Union.[39] Additionally, the mere aim of reducing costs appears questionable, since Germany—despite considerable spending increases[40]—is already spending comparatively little on legal aid compared to other European States.[41] However, it would be too easy to explain this finding simply by referring to the comparatively low average of litigation costs in Germany.[42] Yet, the broad availability of LEI may also offer part of an explanation. Also, legal aid work offers only reduced remuneration for attorneys, giving them a strong incentive to look for every possible way to advise clients on the basis of a different funding source. Thus, the reduced rates should themselves be an effective means of limiting legal aid spending. In conclusion, the current discussion is mainly triggered by budgetary constraints, but it has not yet sufficiently focussed on the constitutional guarantee of access to justice.[43]

Secondly, a proposal for legislation was introduced in the Bundesrat aimed at extending the advancement of court costs in appellate proceedings.[44] Obviously, the Federal States have to write off significant amounts of court charges that are not reimbursed by court users and they incur high costs for the enforcement of such receivables.[45] Since the requirement of advance payments at first instance is not commonly perceived to be a restriction on the constitutional guarantee of access to justice, there seems to be no serious argument against the extension of advancing the costs in appellate proceedings. In fact, the proposal seems to aim at a reasonable protection of state fiscal interests. Legal aid recipients are not adversely affected because they do not have to make advance payments (section 14.1 GKG).

Although there is currently no new legislation proposed with regard to contingency fees, the topic may eventually re-emerge when the current regulation is applied by the courts. Further, in pursuit of their aim to reduce expenditure on legal aid, legislators may be inclined to use contingency fees as a facilitator for commercial financing, thus allowing for the reduction of legal aid in some cases.[46] However, since most legal aid cases involve small amounts in dispute or concern family matters,[47] they hardly qualify for commercial financing. Accordingly, such

[39] [2000] OJ C 364/1, 20.

[40] cf C Hommerich, M Kilian and R Dreske, *Statistical Yearbook of the Lawyers Profession 2007/ 2008* (Bonn, Deutscher Anwaltverlag Gm, 2007) 152 et seq.

[41] German states spent an overall of € 490 million on legal aid in 2006, cf C Hommerich, M Kilian and R Dreske (n 40) 154; That leaves Germany in 11th place out of 12 industrialised nations, cf C Hommerich, M Kilian and R Dreske (n 40) 155.

[42] cf M Kilian, 'Zugang zum Recht' (2008) *Anwaltsblatt* 236, 240; for average costs of litigation in Germany in comparison to the EU average cf. K Hartmann, 'Der Zugang zum Recht und seine Kosten' (2008) *Anwaltsblatt* 592.

[43] cf M Kilian (n 42) 236.

[44] Materials of the German Federal Parliament (*Bundestag*), BT Drs 16/5335.

[45] ibid, 6.

[46] cf M Kilian (n 42) 239.

[47] cf C Hommerich and M Kilian, 'Die Finanzierung von Rechtsverfolgungskosten durch die Bevölkerung' (2007) *Anwaltsblatt* 523, 525.

a fundamental change to the costs system would hardly lead to a significant reduction in expenditure on legal aid.

Funding Claims

Funding Mechanisms and Their Relevance in Practice

In Germany, 90 per cent of funds for civil procedure costs emanate from three sources:

(1) Personal funds of the party/client (47%),
(2) Legal Expenses Insurance (LEI) (35%)—approximately 43 % of the German population holds a LEI policy,[48]
(3) Legal aid (8%).[49]

Consequently, other sources of financing, such as lawyers, commercial lenders or other professional investors, account for approximately 10 per cent of the financing sources and are—in comparison—of minor relevance.[50] However, with the loosening of the strict ban on contingency fees, including *quota litis*, the relevance of such funding instruments may increase.[51]

The following paragraphs will introduce the several funding sources, roughly describe how they work, and assess some of their economic advantages or risks.

Personal Funds of the Party/Client

Interest payments incurred by the prevailing party, for example in financing advance payments in the litigation, cannot be claimed from the losing party under section 91 (1) ZPO, and section 5 (4) GKG.[52] Compensation for these costs may, however, be included in a substantive law claim of the winning party.[53] Other than that, neither substantive law nor civil procedure law contains any provisions that have a particularly negative effect on self-financing.

Benefits of Membership of an Organisation, eg Trade Union

There are several organisations that provide legal and funding assistance to their members, in accordance with their articles of association. Among them, trade and labour unions probably hold the most prominent position.

[48] cf C Hommerich et al, 'Anwaltschaft und Rechtsschutzversicherungen' (2006) *Anwaltsblatt* 200.
[49] cf C Hommerich, M Kilian and R Dreske (n 40) 139.
[50] It is estimated that commercial financing accounts for less than 1% of the funding portfolio, cf C Hommerich and M Kilian, 'Die Finanzierung von Rechtsverfolgungskosten durch die Bevölkerung' (2007) *Anwaltsblatt* 523, 524.
[51] cf M Kilian, 'Zugang zum Recht' (2008) *Anwaltsblatt* 236, 239.
[52] K Herget in R Zöller, ZPO 27th edn (Köln, O Schmidt, 2009), s 91, 13, 395.
[53] cf K Herget (n 52) vor s 91, 11, 365.

Legal Aid

Section 114-127a ZPO and section 76–78 FamFG provide for general and publicly funded legal aid. Legal aid is available to individuals who are unable to pay for part or all of the procedural costs, at all or at once (section 114 ZPO; section 76 FamFG). As a second condition, the applicant's claim or defence against the claim must have adequate prospects of success. If these conditions are met, legal aid is granted, either as an interest-free loan[54] (sections 114, 115 and 120(1) ZPO) or as a full grant without any repayment obligation (section 127(III) 1 ZPO)[55], depending on the ability of the applicant to financially contribute to the litigation. Interest-free loan legal aid has to be repaid in monthly instalments (section 120(1) and 115 ZPO).

Applications for legal aid must be filed with the same court that is to decide on the merits of the case, section 117(1) ZPO. Legal aid is granted or denied without a hearing, but the opposite party is heard, section 127(1) ZPO. The decision can be appealed (section 127(2) and (3) ZPO). Legal aid is granted independently in every instance of the proceedings (section 119(1) ZPO).

Legal aid does not remove the cost risk of the litigation from the recipient. If the recipient of legal aid loses the litigation, he must reimburse the necessary costs of the prevailing party (cf sections 91(1), 123 ZPO; section 76(1) FamFG). However, since the granting of legal aid depends on the (rough) prospects of success, the risk of losing the litigation is reduced considerably (it mainly applies to the—disputed—facts of the case).

For lawyers, working on the basis of legal aid is less attractive, as their statutory compensation is significantly reduced (section 49 RVG).[56] As cross-subsidisation is losing its effectiveness, lawyers may be inclined not to put enough effort into legal aid cases, despite their obligation to accept them (section 48 BRAO).

Legal Expenses Insurance

Germany can be considered to be a stronghold of Legal Expenses Insurance. During the two last decades, legal expense insurance policies have become widespread in Germany.[57] These policies usually cover specific risks, such as legal costs arising out of motor accidents. The main advantage of such insurance, compared with legal aid, is that the insurance covers the risk of losing the lawsuit: The typical legal cost insurance reimburses the whole litigation costs, which include representation by a lawyer and the obligation to pay the opponent's cost should the lawsuit be lost. The growth of legal cost insurance has been criticised by judges:

[54] Note: The applicant never receives any payment; instead the state pays the costs on behalf of the applicant.

[55] cf P Philippi in R Zöller, ZPO 27th edn (Köln, O Schmidt, 2009) s 120, 7, 565; s 127, 14, 605.

[56] The amount of the fee in a claim for €3,500 is reduced from €317 to €297; in a claim for €30,000 it is reduced from €758 to €354 and there is a ceiling starting at an amount of value at €30,000.01, which provides for a fee of €391—the normal ceiling is €30,000,000 (section 22 RVG).

[57] In 2002, German insurance companies earned approximately €2.8 billion in LEI premiums from issuing about 25 million policies (the total amount of the German population is about 80 million people).

They complain about a 'litigation explosion' in Germany and the bringing of lawsuits without serious chances of success.[58]

Insurers are not legally bound to offer only specific types of LEI. The freedom of contract leaves them many options for designing their policies. However, insurers offering LEI usually use the uniform conditions on legal expenses insurance (*Allgemeine Bedingungen für die Rechtsschutzversicherung—ARB 2000*).[59]

Legal expenses insurance can also be included in various types of liability insurance policies. However, liability insurance policies usually offer only passive protection. This means that the insurer will only pay for the costs of a defence against claims that the insurer believes to be invalid.

Because statutorily defined litigation costs keep cost risks computable, they are a precondition to the good pricing and attractiveness of policies. Additionally, it is important that the coverage matches the actual expenses of the insured, where possible. Despite Germany's traditionally predictable costs, the latest large reform of statutory attorney remuneration has apparently toppled many insurers' calculations and thus unsettled the market.[60]

After-The-Event Insurance

After the event insurance is untypical in Germany. There are no regulations known to the authors governing the issue.

Loans or Grants

Since section 91(1) ZPO does not cover any interest for advance payments etc.,[61] interest paid for commercial financing of proceedings is also not necessary under that provision and thus not recoverable from the losing party.[62] However, loan financing is facilitated by the *loser pays* rule, since the reimbursement of the winning party's necessary costs decreases financial risks and correspondingly eases the burden of repayment.

Funding from Lawyer or Investor without a Repayment Obligation in the Case of a Loss

Because of the nature of investor funding and the typical content of such contracts,[63] the scope of claims which can be financed by an investor is limited.[64] Thus, only monetary claims exceeding a certain face value and having a creditworthy debtor tend to meet investors' conditions.

[58] Statistics did not confirm these critics, P Murray and R Stürner (n 1) 124.

[59] www.gdv.de/Downloads/allg_Bedingungen_pSV/ARB_2000_06_Juni.pdf.

[60] cf H Schons, 'Beziehungskrise ohne Happy—End?' (2008) *Anwaltsblatt* 523.

[61] K Herget (n 52) s 91, 13, 395.

[62] OLG Koblenz, 4 Jan 2006—14 W 810/05, NJW-RR 2006, 502.

[63] cf H Buschbell, 'Prozessfinanzierung als Instrument der Anspruchsverfolgung' (2006) *Anwaltsblatt* 825, 829.

[64] cf H Buschbell (n 63) 827; A Siebert and S Nagata, 'Prozessfinanzierung—Etabliertes Institut auf dem Rechtsmarkt?' (2007) *BRAK-Mitt* 49, 50 *et seq*.

In Germany, claims can be *sold and transferred* for purposes of litigation within the limits of substantive law. Section 398 BGB determines that all claims can be subrogated unless a special provision prohibits the cession of the claim. The two most important of these limiting provisions are as follows. Section 399 BGB excludes claims from transfer if the parties agreed to a prohibition of any transfer, or if the claim cannot be ceded without a change of its content. Section 400 BGB specifies that a claim cannot be transferred to the extent that it is not subject to pledge.

However, if claims are (collectively) collected for the account of a third party, such business is restricted by section 2(2) and 3 RDG. Under these provisions, only persons who have a license to offer legal services, and some exempt organisations such as consumer protection agencies (section 8(1) no 4 RDG)[65] may engage in such business. At the litigation stage, section 79(1) and (2) ZPO reflects these restrictions. Otherwise, the transfer of the claim is considered as void (cf section 134 BGB).

One of the most prominent cases currently in court concerns a claim of at least €114 million[66] against an alleged cartel of cement producers. A Belgian stock company specialised in cartel litigation bought the claims from several large German cement buyers that had been victims of the cartel. The defendant relied on section 8(1) no 4 RDG and argued that the assignment of the claim to the plaintiff was null and void. The BGH, ruling only on the admissibility of the action, did not directly decide the issue but held that the lawsuit was admissible. This judgment demonstrates a growing willingness to permit innovative forms of litigation financing.

In Germany the *loser pays* rule negatively affects investor funding, since it heightens the financial risk for the investor who has to cover all the costs of the litigation. Simultaneously, the limited recoverability of the prevailing party's costs renders these risks at least fairly calculable. The limited permissibility of negotiating contingency fees (cf section 4a RVG) considerably limits the ability of lawyers to offer funding to their clients. However, investor funding may be attractive to some commercial claimants, who seek to avoid the impact of advance payments on their solvency and or balance sheet.[67] The positive effect on the balance sheet is a consequence of the investor taking the full cost risk of the litigation.

[65] Also cf B Hess in H-P Mansel, B Dauner-Lieb and M Henssler (eds), *Zugang zum Recht: Europäische und US-Amerikanische Wege der Privaten Rechtsdurhsettzung* (Baden-Baden, Nomos, 2008) 67. Note that at the time the RDG was not yet in force. The RDG replaced the RBG, which covered the same topic.

[66] The exact amount of the claim was not specified by the claimant. The admissibility of the lawsuit was most recently confirmed by the BGH: cf BGH, 7 April 2009—KZR 42/08 and press release 80/2009, both available on www.bundesgerichtshof.de/ (in German), second instance ruling: OLG Düsseldorf, 15 May 2008—VI-U (Kart) 14/07, WUW/E DE-R 2311.

[67] cf H Buschbell (n 63) 827.

Court or Process Costs

Court Charges

Policies

Rules on court charges are—as with all German cost laws—designed to promote free access to justice (see above). On the other hand, litigating parties utilise public resources (the court system) for the resolution of their individual disputes. Accordingly, the court fees are designed to charge the parties for the use of a public institution. Therefore, the structure of court charges generally covers most of the state expenses on the civil judiciary.[68] Technically, court charges are not based on the actual costs incurred. Instead, general and abstract criteria are applied to cover the typical cost and cross-subsidise the pursuit of small claims (see below 0).[69]

Description

Court charges are generally lump-sum payments and calculated on the basis of the amount in controversy (section 3(1) GKG and section 3(1) FamGKG; 18(1) KostO).

Since the court fees are solely based on the amount in controversy, they do not depend on the work efforts undertaken by the Court. Both the length and complexity of the proceedings are not taken into account. However, appellate proceedings regularly entail additional workload and are, therefore, charged with higher costs. Court fees rise with the amount in controversy, on a diminishing scale. The diminution is based on the consideration that the workload of the court does not usually increase proportionally to the amount in controversy. Therefore, in comparison to the workload, court charges are comparatively low for small claims and raise strongly enough to constitute a system of cross-subsidisation in which large claims financially subsidise the pursuit of small claims.[70]

The following is an overview of how costs are calculated. They also include some general aspects of German cost laws that apply to other types of litigation-related costs as well. Cost laws generally have to answer five basic questions: (1) Who has to pay (a) initially and (b) ultimately? (2) When? (3) For what? (4) How much?

[68] cf P Hartmann, *Kostengesetze* 38th edn (München, Beck, 2008) GKG, Grundzüge 10.

[69] Official statistics on the expenses of the state for providing court services are available at: Federal Statistics Agency, Report on budgets and taxes (2008–2006 data)—Statistisches Bundesamt, Statistik Finanzen und Steuern für 2006, Fachserie 14, Reihe 3.1, 35.

[70] While usually small claims are less complex and require less workload, the work required for the pursuit of larger claims on average does not increase proportionally to the amount in controversy. Rather, the workload usually increases slower than the amount in controversy. This finding is also the reason for the declining design of the amount in controversy based cost structure, cf ss 34 GKG, 13 RVG. Hence the subsidies result from a—on average—lower than adequate decline of the costs in comparison to the (typical) actual workload of a rising amount in controversy. cf C Hommerich et al (n 16) 406.

(5) And what if a party is unable to afford any procedural costs? These points are discussed below.

(1) Cost debtors are determined by sections 22–33 GKG (court charges and expenses, remuneration of experts and translators[71]) or contractual obligation (extrajudicial costs).

(1a) The initial debtor is the person (plaintiff) that initiated the proceeding by filing the lawsuit or motion (section 22(1) GKG—court and other official charges).

(1b) The ultimate cost burden is imposed on the losing party to the extent it has lost (sections 91(1) and 788 (1)[72] ZPO, 113 FamFG) (see below for details).

(2) There are maturity provisions in all major cost laws (section 6 GKG, section 8 RVG). However, it is necessary to pay most costs in advance (court charges (first instance only) and expenses[73], (sections 12, 17 GKG)[74]) or admissible (attorney remuneration, cf section 9 RVG), if necessary upon request of the court (witnesses of fact and court appointed experts, cf sections 379, 402 ZPO). Costs for the taking of evidence by the court may have to be advanced according to which party has the burden of proof of the point to which the evidence relates. Reimbursement will only take place after independent proceedings have taken place on the taxation of costs.

(3) Cost items are regulated in appendix 1 to section 3(2) GKG (court charges and expenses), appendix 1 to section 2(2) RVG (attorney remuneration and expenses), appendix 1 to section 3(2) FamGKG (court charges in family matters), the KostO (non contentious proceedings) and the JVEG (remuneration and expenses of experts and translators, compensation of witnesses of fact).

(4) The amount due is mainly calculated with reference to the amount in controversy as far as court charges (cf section 3 GKG, 3 FamGKG) and attorney remuneration (cf section 2 RVG) are concerned. The overall calculation consists of three steps:

—Assessment of the amount in controversy, according to the relevant provisions,
—Allocation of the amount in controversy to the corresponding tariff (section 34 GKG, section 28 FamGKG, section 32 KostO, section 13 RVG),
—Application of multipliers for incurred cost items, as stated in relevant provisions.

The most important provisions on the amount in controversy are sections 39–65 GKG (subsidiary, sections 3–9 ZPO apply, cf section 48 GKG), 33–56

[71] Appendix 1 GKG KV 9005.

[72] The latter for enforcement proceedings.

[73] Court charges include the remuneration of court appointed translators and experts; cf KV 9005 of appendix 1 to the GKG.

[74] In case of the initiation of proceedings s 12(1) GKG does not technically demand an advance payment as payment of the costs is also due under s 6(1) GKG.

FamGKG and 18–31 KostO. In addition, the pertinent provisions on the remuneration of attorneys also refer to the GKG, sections 23, 32, 33 RVG. Since 2002, the amount in controversy is capped at a maximum of €30 million, sections 39(2) GKG, 33(2) FamGKG[75], 22(2) RVG.[76] There are also lower caps on the amount in controversy for some special types of proceedings. Expenses are usually rated as fixed amounts for certain items. Provisions on expenses of courts and attorneys are detailed in the GKG, FamGKG and the RVG, especially in their respective appendices. Experts and translators are paid on an hourly basis (section 8(1), 9 JVEG) and receive reimbursement of their expenses (section 8(1), 5, 6, 7, 12 JVEG). Witnesses of fact are compensated pursuant to sec. 19 JVEG.

(5) Legal Aid is available pursuant to sections 114-127a ZPO and sections 76–78 FamFG (see above).

Other Official Charges

There is no VAT on court charges. The costs of a bailiff etc. and the enforcement of a judgment are governed by a partially separate and complex system of interacting laws. Since separate authorities are responsible for enforcement in, for example, movable property cases (costs are mostly governed by the *Gerichtsvollzieherkostengesetz*—GvKostG—bailiff charges act) and immovable property cases (costs are mostly governed by the GKG, cf appendix 1 to section 3(2) GKG, KV 2210 et seq), there is no single structure that can be described comprehensively within the scope of this chapter.

Experts, Translators and Witnesses of Fact

The remuneration of court-appointed experts and translators, as well as the compensation of witnesses of fact, is governed by the JVEG (*Justizvergütungs-und Entschädigungsgesetz*—Judicial Remuneration and Compensation Act). Court appointed experts and translators are remunerated according to their workload on an hourly basis and receive compensation for their expenses (sections 8–14 JVEG). The lowest hourly rate is €50, the highest €85 (section 9 JVEG). Recoverable expenses are defined by section 5–7 JVEG.

The service of experts and translators will in many cases be subject to VAT, according to their personal responsibility to levy this tax on behalf of the state (cf especially section 1 (1), 19 UStG).

Witnesses of fact receive compensation for their expenses and their time (sections 19–22 JVEG). The minimum compensation for time loss is €3 per hour

[75] This legislative change immediately increased the number of high value litigation in Germany.

[76] It should be noted that the cap has triggered a considerable raise of high value litigation in the German civil courts since 2002.

(section 20 JVEG). Witnesses of fact who would otherwise have worked during the time they devoted to their witness duty receive compensation for loss of earnings capped at €17 per hour (section 22 JVEG).

Court Decisions on Costs

In contentious proceedings, a court decides on the allocation of costs among the parties at the same time as making its decision on the material claim, cf section 308(2) ZPO, 63 GKG (*Kostengrundentscheidung*[77]). The taxation of costs is, however, determined by a court officer (*Rechtspfleger*) in separate proceedings, section 103–107 ZPO (*Kostenfestsetzungsverfahren*). The decision fixing the amount due is an enforceable title.

To What Extent Can Costs Be Identified In Advance (Before Or During Litigation)? When Must They Be Paid?

Costs can usually be identified as soon as the amount in controversy is known. If a claim has a face value, costs can consequently easily be assessed in advance (sections 61 and 63 GKG). In more complex cases the amount in controversy may itself be contested. However, in such cases, the court will usually issue a preliminary ruling on the amount in controversy at the very beginning of the proceedings (section 63(1) GKG). At the latest, the court will decide on the amount in controversy together with issuing its decision on the material claim, but in a separate court order (sections 308(2) ZPO; 63(2) GKG).

Lawyers' Costs

Available Options

With regard to attorney remuneration for court-related work in Germany, one has to distinguish between what parties can negotiate with their lawyer and what can be recovered by the party who wins the litigation.

[77] Usually the last part of the decision. An exemplary decision dividing the costs is: *Von den Kosten des Rechtsstreits trägt der Beklagte 4/5 und die Klägerin 1/5.* (On litigation costs, the respondent bears 4/5 and the claimant 1/5.)

Available Options for Court related Attorney Work

Statutory Amount in Controversy Based Remuneration

Lawyers' fees are regulated by statute. Pursuant to the Attorney Remuneration Act (RVG) the remuneration of lawyers is regularly fixed according to the amount in controversy (section 2 RVG). The calculation of the amount in controversy is defined by sections 22–33 RVG which largely refer to the GKG and ZPO. Section 13 RVG contains the tariff. There is a cap of €30 million on the amount in controversy here as well (section 22(2) RVG).

For court-related work, lawyers receive a so-called proceedings fee once in every instance (cf appendix 1 to sections 2(2) RVG, VV 3100, 3200, 3206, 3208) and, when court hearings take place, a court hearing's fee is established once in every instance (cf appendix 1 to sections 2(2) RVG, VV 3104, 3202, 3210). Statutory lawyers' fees are calculated in a similar way to court charges, cf above for further details.

Possibilities for Differing Negotiated Remuneration

Lawyers are permitted to negotiate higher fees, section 2, 3a RVG on any basis (such as hourly or fixed), provided it is not success related. Indeed, a negotiated decrease is not permitted for court-related attorney work (sections 49b(1) BRAO, 4(1) RVG). Section 4a RVG, a provision enacted in 2008, permits success fees under specific and very restricted circumstances (see above). However, as a rule, German law does not permit contingency fees (section 49b(2) BRAO).

Recoverability of Negotiated Remuneration

According to section 91 (1) ZPO, only the 'necessary costs' are reimbursable. The term 'necessary' directly refers to the statutory provision on the remuneration of lawyers. Consequently, any negotiated excess remuneration cannot be recovered from the losing party (also see below).[78]

Cost Shifting

Rules on Cost Shifting

As a rule, German law does not provide for any fee shifting. The most important provisions dealing with the final allocation of costs among the parties are sections 91-101 ZPO. According to sections 91(1), 788 ZPO, 113 FamFG, the losing party

[78] cf M Giebel in *MünchKomm-ZPO* 3rd edn (München, Beck, 2008) s 91, para 49.

must bear all statutory costs of the litigation in civil and commercial matters, including the necessary costs incurred by the opponent (*loser pays* rule[79] and indemnity principle). Accordingly, section 91(1) ZPO excludes any discretionary fee shifting by the court. The few exceptional rules allowing for (limited) discretion are explained below.

If the case is litigated in several instances, the party losing at the highest instance must bear the litigation costs of all instances, regardless of whether it prevailed at a lower level or not. If a party prevails on appeal by presenting new facts—which by negligence were not presented at the first instance—the court may (at its discretion) order the prevailing party to carry fully or partly the cost of the appeal (section 97(2) ZPO).[80]

If a party fails to observe a time limit and the hearing is adjourned, the negligent party must bear the additional costs irrespective of the outcome of the litigation (section 95 ZPO). Additional costs for unsuccessful or unnecessary motions (section 96 ZPO) can also be allocated to the responsible party. As far as the allocation of (additional or unnecessary) costs is concerned, German law provides for a limited discretion of the court. However, the court is not permitted to completely deviate from the general rule in section 91 ZPO—its discretion is limited to the allocation of additional costs. In this context, the principle guiding the discretion is that the party who caused additional costs (cf section 96 ZPO) must compensate these costs.

At first sight, section 81 FamFG—a provision that entered into force on 1 September 2009—contains a wide-ranging exception allowing for full discretion of the court in some family proceedings and non-contentious proceedings. However, the most important family proceedings (marital matters and contentious family matters) are still governed by the general rules of the ZPO as described above (cf sections 112 and 113 FamFG). The scope of section 81 FamFG is limited to non-contentious proceedings. The most prominent of these comprise matters concerning the supervision of natural persons and the confinement of supervised persons and the mentally ill, (*Betreuungs- und Unterbringungssachen*), bequest and bequest-division matters (*Nachlass- und Teilungssachen*), matters concerning public registers, and specific company law matters (*Registersachen und unternehmensrechtliche Sachen*). In these non-contentious proceedings, section 81 FamFG gives the court wide discretion when allocating the costs among the parties.[81] The court may even decide that no one shall be charged for the proceedings. However, limiting the court's discretion, section 81(2) FamFG enumerates several situations where the court shall allocate the costs to a specific party.

[79] P Murray and R Stürner (n 1) 341.

[80] Additionally, the costs of unsuccessful appeals are borne by the party that initiated the appellate proceedings (s 97(1) ZPO).

[81] Also see the materials of the German Federal Parliament (*Bundestags Drucksache*) BT Drs 16/6308, 215.

Partial Success and Partial Failure

If each party is successful in part and fails in part, costs are mutually cancelled or proportionally divided (section 92(1) ZPO). The court will decide on the issue together with its decision on the material claim, see above.

Irrecoverability Gaps

Only the necessary costs of the litigation are recoverable, section 91(1) ZPO. The term 'necessary' refers, where applicable, to the statutory costs.[82] Consequently, a winning party that, for example, agreed to pay more fees to its attorney than provided for by the Attorneys Remuneration Act (RVG) is only reimbursed the legally fixed fees, not the additional agreed costs.[83] It can be highly contested which additional costs are necessary (especially for the gathering of evidence) under section 91(1) ZPO. Typical issues are the necessity of party experts or the hiring of (additional) foreign lawyers in cases that involve foreign law.

However, this limited recoverability renders the system fairly calculable and thus reduces the financial risk of civil litigation. The losing party, in particular, is protected by limiting the recovery to necessary costs.

General Costs Issues

Rules for Special Cases

There are no special rules on small claims in German cost laws. However, claimants may pursue their claims within the European small claims procedure under Regulation (EC) No 861/2007. With some minor exceptions, the same rules describes above also apply to special courts.

Strategies to Lower Costs

Claimants can reduce the amount in controversy by claiming only a certain portion of the full amount of their claim (*Teilklage*). Respondents may, however, defend against such behaviour by asking the court to declare that they owe nothing beyond the amount claimed. Thus, the respondent can increase the cost pressure on the claimant.

[82] For details see M Giebel (n 78) s 91, paras 38–77.
[83] cf M Giebel (n 78) s 91, para 49.

In addition, parties can significantly lower the court charges if they reach a consensual disposition such as settlement or the abandonment of the action (cf. appendix 1 to section 3(2) GKG, KV 1211, KV 1222, 1232).

Length of Proceedings

The statistical data in Table 2 show the average length of civil proceedings (2007 data).

Table 2: Duration of proceedings

Court	Duration
Local Courts—first instance (*Amtsgerichte*):[84]	
—Average length of all proceedings:	4.5 months
—Average length of proceedings finalised by contentious judgment:	7.0 months
District Courts—first instance (*Landgerichte*):[85]	
—Average length of all proceedings:	7.9 months
—Average length of proceedings finalised by contentious judgment:	12.8 months
District Courts—second instance (overall length of both instances) (*Landgerichte*):[86]	
—Average length of all proceedings:	16.5 months
—Average length of proceedings finalised by contentious judgment:	19.3 months
Higher Regional Courts (overall length of all instances) (*Oberlandesgerichte*):[87]	
—Average length of all proceedings:	24.1 months
—Average length of proceedings finalised by contentious judgment:	28.1 months

[84] Federal Statistics Agency, Report on the Civil Judiciary 2007—Statistisches Bundesamt, Statistik Rechtspflege (Zivilgerichte) für 2007, Fachserie 10, Reihe 2.1, 26.
[85] ibid, 50.
[86] ibid, 66.
[87] ibid, 80 and 84.

Critical Review

Critical Review of the Basic Objectives of the German Civil Litigation Cost System

In general, the German civil litigation cost system provides for comparatively economic yet effective high quality justice. Litigation costs on average account for only 14.4 per cent (11.8 per cent in 2008)[88] of the amount in controversy, making Germany one of the most cost efficient countries in Europe.[89]

High Level of Regulation

The high level of regulation in the German litigation cost system renders cost risks fairly calculable. Only the costs of presenting evidence—although they are also regulated—cannot be calculated easily in cases involving complex factual questions. However, statutory costs may sometimes not be sufficient for adequately rewarding the sophisticated advice of a lawyer. In such circumstances, parties may negotiate a higher remuneration at their own expense, but such higher remuneration is not recoverable.

Fee Shifting

The fundamental decision of the German legislator not to provide for any discretionary fee shifting must be seen in connection with the basic decision for a 'loser pays' system. It leaves almost no discretion for the court and constitutes an effective deterrent for lawsuits with a low or no probability of success. Abusive litigation, which is initiated in order to put pressure on the opponent, will be sanctioned by section 91 ZPO. It also promotes access to justice for valid claims, since the plaintiff does not incur any costs for their vindication. In conclusion, the renunciation of any discretionary fee shifting is a very valuable component of the German litigation cost structure, which should be maintained.

Amount in Controversy-Based Statutory Costs

The amount allowable under controversy-based statutory costs may in some cases constitute little or no incentive to put adequate efforts into a case. If you earn the same no matter how much you work on the case, you will be less inclined to do more, even if the merits of the case require more efforts. Yet, if the lawyer expects or hopes for a lasting relationship with a client, this lack of monetary incentive will

[88] cf the *Doing Business 2008 Report*, 50, published by the World Bank and available at www.doingbusiness.org.

[89] cf the *Doing Business 2009 Report*, 49, 50 and 105; however, the statistical basis of the World Bank accounting for the 2.8% change in just one year remains unclear. Also cf K Hartmann (n 42) 592; J von Seltmann (n 26) 119.

be mitigated. For consumers, the system seems to be more disadvantageous than for businessmen.

On the other hand there are several positive effects that should be mentioned. The amounts in controversy-based costs deter parties from claiming too much, as long as the €30 million threshold (sections 39(2) GKG, 22(2) RVG) is not crossed.[90] Where too much is claimed, one would be held liable for the costs of the litigation to the extent one loses, ie claimed too much. Additionally, with the remuneration being irrespective of the actual workload, there is no incentive for lawyers to accumulate (unjustified) billable hours.

Cross-Subsidisation

The specialisation of attorneys and law firms has proved to be a considerable strain on the principle of cross-subsidisation with regard to attorney remuneration. Still, according to a review conducted among 1,000 lawyers, around 45 per cent were of the opinion that cross-subsidisation works in their practice, whereas 49 per cent indicated it does not. Smaller and less specialised law firms with fewer commercial matters are paying a 'toll' for larger specialised firms that handle more commercial matters in their portfolio.[91] This imbalance is exacerbated for the smaller firms by the fact that they usually cannot compensate for their loss by higher negotiated fees, as their clients are usually unable or unwilling to afford such higher fees.[92] In conclusion, the principle of cross-subsidisation has not become entirely obsolete but has considerably lost momentum through the development of much stronger specialisation among lawyers. As this development will most probably continue, so will its effect on cross-subsidisation.

Still, with regard to court charges, the principle of cross-subsidisation remains intact since the state is the beneficiary of all such revenues.

Minimum Attorney Fees

The purpose of protecting cross-subsidisation via minimum fees is losing its credibility as the actual practice of lawyers and law firms is less diversified than it used to be (see above). Therefore, it is estimated that, despite the interdiction, some attorneys offer their advice in civil litigation for less than the statutory fees in order to gain competitive advantage. If such a practice should prove to be widespread, it will add to the pressure on minimum fees. Minimum fees are also considered as an impediment to free competition by the European Commission.[93]

[90] However, once the threshold is exceeded, it presents Germany as a very attractive jurisdiction for limiting cost risks, for example in patent proceedings cf 25 of 'Law–Made in Germany' a booklet published by several organisations of legal professionals and available at www.lawmadeingermany.de/. Accordingly, several very large claims have been filed in German courts in recent years, eg '*Kirch Media*', cf BGH 24 Jan 2006–XI ZR 384/03, BGHZ 166, 84 and '*Zementkartell*', BGH, 7 Apr 2009–KZR 42/08 and press release 80/2009, both available at www.bundesgerichtshof.de (in German) also see (n 66).

[91] see C Wolf (n 11) 14–16.

[92] cf C Hommerich et al (n 16) 407.

[93] J von Seltmann (n 26) 119.

Predictability

As already indicated, because of the high level of regulation, Germany has a comparatively high predictability of civil litigation costs, which is perceived and marketed as a strong advantage of the German litigation structure.[94] Nevertheless, there are two factors that may considerably lower the predictability in certain cases. Firstly, for very complex or sophisticated cases, it may be hard to find a lawyer who is prepared to accept the workload based merely on the level of statutory remuneration. Secondly, such cases may also require extensive gathering of evidence, including the use of expensive (court appointed and or party) experts. Although the remuneration of court-appointed experts is also regulated, costs are hardly predictable, as experts are paid on an hourly basis according to their actual workload.

[94] cf 'Law–Made in Germany', 29, also see (n 90) the booklet is available at www.lawmadeingermany.de.

12

Japan

IKUO SUGAWARA* AND ERI OSAKA†

Costs of Litigation in Japan

General Overview of Current Situation

Costs of Litigation

In Japan, the costs required for filing a civil suit can roughly be divided into two types: litigation costs and other costs.

The former refers to costs stipulated in Article 2 of the Act on Costs of Civil Procedure,[1] including the filing fees and expenses required for investigation of evidence and delivery of documents (hereinafter referred to as 'litigation costs'), while other costs refer to expenses other than those specified by the Act, which should be paid by the litigant to parties other than the court, including the fees required for attorneys (hereinafter referred to as 'attorneys' fees'), as well as expenses for evidence collection conducted by the litigants, travel expenses to/from the court, and so on.

The basic structure of Japan's civil litigation system is the same as in Germany, since it was originally introduced from that country. However, regarding the costs required for litigation, especially attorneys' fees, a big difference exists between Japan and Germany. In the German system, where employment of an attorney is compulsory in district courts or higher court cases, attorneys' fees are considered necessary expenses and must be borne by the losing party much as the litigation fees that are paid to the court; therefore the amount of attorneys' fees is determined by the court. In Japan, however, due to the smaller number of attorneys at the time the litigation system was imported, the compulsory attorney system was not adopted and therefore the *loser pays* principle was not introduced either. As a result, in Japan the *loser pays* principle is applied to the litigation costs described above while attorneys' fees are borne by both litigants whether they win or lose the

* Nagoya University.
† Toyo University.
[1] Act No 40 of 6 Apr 1971.

case (the so-called 'American rule'.) However, there are some exceptions to this principle. For example, in tort litigation, an exceptional case law has been established that stipulates, in view of the practical need to employ attorneys, that attorneys' fees should be included in the damage award and borne by the losing party according to the court judgment. Other examples are claims by local residents against local government (taxpayer's suit) and shareholder claims. For these types of claim, the winning plaintiffs may charge their reasonable attorneys' fees against the defendants under Article 242-2, paragraph 12 of the Local Autonomy Law[2] and Article 852 of the Commercial Code.[3] The nature of this charge is not the recovery of damages but the reimbursement of expenses in the public interest in a broad sense, because the plaintiffs in these claims take action in the interest of the local community as a whole or of all shareholders. Therefore, even when a plaintiff loses the case, they do not need to bear the defendants attorneys' fees.

Costs for Dispute Resolutions Other Than Litigation

There are several dispute resolution systems other than litigation in Japan. The most popular one is the court-annexed conciliation. Parties to a dispute can reach a settlement through the intervention of a conciliation panel generally composed of one judge and two conciliation commissioners appointed from members of the public. There are two types of court-annexed conciliation: civil conciliation which deals with general civil cases and domestic conciliation which deals with domestic relations cases. Since their filing fees are fixed and less expensive than those for litigation, both conciliation systems have been widely used, especially since in domestic relations cases, when a party seeks judicial divorce, judicial confirmation of existence or non-existence of family relations, etc, he or she must first commence conciliation proceedings in the family court before filing litigation (Domestic Determination Act,[4] Article 18).

Also, the labour dispute determination procedure has been increasingly used for labour dispute cases between employers and workers since its establishment in 2006.[5] A labour dispute determination panel is composed of one judge and two impartial labour dispute determination commissioners appointed from people who are specialised in labour relations. As a general rule, the panel makes a recommendation of a settlement for the parties by the third date. If the recommendation is not accepted by either party, the panel will make a determination based on the actual state of the case. If there are no objections to the determination, it will be final and will have the same effect as a final judgment in litigation. If either party raises an objection, the case will follow the ordinary litigation procedure. The filing fee for the labour dispute determination procedure is based on the

[2] Act No 67 of 17 Apr 1947.

[3] Act No 48 of 9 Mar 1899.

[4] Act No 152 of 6 Dec 1947. It should be noted that married couples can divorce by mutual agreement in Japan.

[5] Labour Dispute Determination Act, Act No 45 of 12 May 2004.

amount claimed, in the same way as the filing fee for general litigation described below. The amount of the former is, however, half the amount of the latter.

In addition, one more cost-free way to resolve a dispute is the demand for payment procedure. This is a special procedure in summary courts. Upon a creditor' s motion, the procedure starts with an assumption that there is no dispute as to rights and duties between parties but the debtor will not pay. Based on this assumption, the court will issue the demand for payment to the debtor without hearing his or her allegation. If the debtor makes an objection to the demand within two weeks from the date of its service, the case will proceed through the ordinary procedure of litigation. If there is no objection within two weeks, the demand will have attached to it a tentative power of enforcement; and if there is no objection within two more weeks, the demand will be final and will have the same effect as a final judgment in litigation. Though this procedure can be used for collection of consumable goods (eg stock), it is widely used for collecting money. A large number of credit companies use this procedure because the filing fee is only half of that for litigation. In 2008, 388,230 cases used this procedure.[6]

Litigation Costs and Attorneys' Fees

In practice, litigation costs and attorneys' fees are calculated and paid as follows:

Litigation Costs

The filing fee, constituting the main part of the litigation costs, is based on the amount claimed. As the amount claimed increases, the ratio of filing fee to claimed amount decreases while the amount of the fee itself becomes higher. For example, in cases claiming 20 million yen, 50 million yen and 100 million yen, the filing fee would be 97,600 yen, 217,600 yen and 417,600 yen, respectively.[7]

Other expenses that are payable to the court include postage on complaints and other documents mailed by the court, daily allowances paid for witnesses who are summoned and fees for expert opinions. All of these expenses should, in principle, be paid in advance. As for the postage costs, the plaintiff pays in advance the expected amount when filing a suit in the form of postage stamps and later pays any additional amount that may be necessary. Costs for witnesses or expert opinions are required to be paid in advance by the parties who call them when the court accepts an application to summon them. In Japan, under the principle that witnesses or expert witnesses shall be called in the name of the court, these costs must be formally paid into court; therefore, the court basically asks the applicant parties to pay in advance any costs to be paid by the court. Since, however, the amounts of travel and per diem allowances for a witness are usually not very large and the

[6] General Secretariat of the Supreme Court, *Annual Report of Judicial Statistics for 2008 Volume 1 Civil Cases* 7 (Tokyo, Hosokai, 2009) (in Japanese).

[7] The complete schedule of filing fees can be available at www.courts.go.jp/saiban/tetuzuki/pdf/beppyo.pdf (in Japanese).

witness often has a close relationship with the party who calls him or her, it is often the case that the witness declines to receive payment of such allowances partly to avoid the cumbersome payment collection procedures. In contrast, the fee for expert opinions is considerably higher than the witness's daily allowance and therefore receipt of such fee is rarely waived.

As described above, litigation costs are in principle paid in advance by the applicant party, while the law requires that these costs should eventually be collected from the party that loses the case and that a decision regarding payment of the litigation costs shall be included in the court ruling (Code of Civil Procedure,[8] Article 67). However, due to the practical complexity of calculating the costs based on such a decision and the relatively small amount of these costs compared to attorneys' fees, collection of these payments is rarely carried out. Regarding payment of the fee for expert opinions as mentioned above, however, some criticisms of the current situation have arisen, where the fee is virtually borne by the applicant party. In recent discussions some have argued for system reform so that the fee for expert opinions is calculated separately to make collection from the losing party easier, though this has yet to result in specific reform.

If a case concludes in a court settlement, the parties shall bear their own litigation costs except as otherwise agreed by the parties (Code of Civil Procedure, Article 68).

Attorneys' Fees

Attorneys' fees are usually paid in two parts; the first payment is the retainer fee, which is paid to the attorney regardless of the outcome of the litigation, and the second payment is the success fee, which is paid upon completion of the case on the basis of the profit obtained or loss avoided as a result. In the past, the amounts of the retainer and success fees were determined according to the standards established by bar associations based on the amount claimed, as in the calculation of litigation costs. The greater the amount claimed, the higher the amount received by the attorney. For example, in a case claiming three million yen, if the attorney recovers the entire three million yen claimed he/she receives a retainer fee of eight per cent, or 240,000 yen, and a success fee of 16 per cent, or 480,000 yen (if only two million yen was won, then the success fee would be 16 per cent of that amount, or 320,000 yen).

In 2004, however, partly due to a claim by the Fair Trade Commission that the bar associations' establishment of a standard for attorneys' fees may constitute a cartel hindering fair competition regarding such fees, provisions concerning the standard for attorneys' fees were deleted from the bar rules. Today, bar rules regarding attorneys' fees only provide such statements as 'An attorney's fee shall be determined reasonably and adequately according to the economic benefit, difficulty of the case, and time and labour spent' (Rules Concerning Attorney's Fees

[8] Act No 109 of 26 Jun 1996. Its unofficial English translation is available at www.japaneselawtranslation.go.jp/law/detail/?id=90&vm=02&re=01.

of the Japan Federation of Bar Associations,[9] Article 2), and 'An attorney must establish a standard concerning fees and keep it in his/her office' (Article 3, paragraph 1 of the Rules.) The lack of a consistent standard, however, could confuse users, therefore the bar associations show the prevailing rates of attorneys' fees gathered from a survey of actual attorneys' fees. Since most attorneys decide the amount of their fees in accordance with past standards, there appears to be little difference between fees today and in the past. For example, for a case claiming three million yen as repayment from a debtor, the result of the JFBA survey shows that 43.9 per cent of attorneys who responded receive 200,000 yen and 26.2 per cent receive 150,000 yen as the retainer fee, while 50.2 per cent receive 300,000 yen as the success fee.[10] These figures indicate that a variation has arisen in the calculation of attorneys' fees since 2004 though most attorneys still adopt the conventional method. Examples of new calculation methods include setting a fixed retainer fee (eg 200,000 yen) regardless of the amount claimed with the total amount adjusted by the success fee. Also, the number of lawyers who introduce an hourly-based fee system is increasing.

Shiho-Shoshi Lawyer's Fees

In Japan, a *Shiho-Shoshi* lawyer (judicial scrivener) can represent a party in summary court which has jurisdiction for cases under 1.4 million yen. Generally speaking, fees for a *Shiho-Shoshi* lawyer are less expensive than those of a regular attorney, even though there is no uniform standard as with attorneys. Although there used to be a standard, the Japan Federation of Shiho-Shoshi Lawyer's Associations abolished it after the Fair Trade Commission's adverse opinion on the illegality of fee standards. In 2008, the JFSLA conducted a survey on fees. According to the survey, the retainer fee for a case in which one million yen is claimed is between 40,000 and 60,000 yen, and the success fee for such cases is something between 60,000 and a 101,000 yen.[11]

Costs and Settlements

In civil litigation, except for default judgment cases in which defendants do not appear in court, many cases end in settlement (38 per cent in 2008). Though it is easy to assume that one of the reasons why parties choose settlement is the cost of litigation, there is no strict evidence to support such an assumption.[12] Before the

[9] Its unofficial and tentative English translation is available at www.nichibenren.or.jp/en/about/pdf/rcsaf_2004.pdf.

[10] Japan Federation of Bar Associations, *Citizen's Rough Guide of Attorneys' Fees Based on Survey Result (2008 Survey Result)* (Tokyo, Japan Federation of Bar Associations, 2009) (in Japanese). Attorneys must register with the Japan Federation of Bar Associations.

[11] See Japan Federation of Shiho-Shoshi Lawyer's Associations, Questionnaire Survey on Fees, available at www.shiho-shoshi.or.jp/about_shiho_shoshi/remuneration/data/questionnaire.pdf (in Japanese).

[12] A survey on judicial settlements conducted in 1998 shows that many respondents specified economic reason for choosing settlement. See M Ito et al, 'Round-table Discussion: Settlement from the Parties' Viewpoint (1999) 1008 *Hanrei Times* 4, 17 (in Japanese).

reform of the Code of Civil Procedure in 1998, many cases reached a settlement in the early stage of the procedure; however, as issue-finding procedure and concentrated-examination procedure became widely used, the number of settlements reached in the later stage of the procedure is increasing.[13]

Controversy over Calculation and Payment of Litigation Costs

As explained above, the amount of the filing fee, the main part of litigation costs, is proportional to the claimed amount. There is some controversy as to the adequacy of this method of calculation. Because the amount of the fee increases according to the amount claimed, the possibility that people will be reluctant to file litigation claiming a large amount increases accordingly. Therefore, the reasons for charging larger filing fees for litigation claiming larger amounts should be clarified. Conventionally, the reasons given have been the beneficiaries-pay principle (which requires that the party pursuing benefits from the suit (ie plaintiff) bears the costs according to the value of the benefits), and the advantages of the sliding scale fee system (which helps inhibit vexatious litigation such as thoughtless filing and extortionate claims). However, there are criticisms of these reasons; considering that litigation costs are eventually borne by the losing party as explained above, it is unrealistic to see the losing party as the beneficiary. Regarding prevention of vexatious litigation, since it is impossible to determine whether or not a suit is vexatious when filed, the sliding scale fee system seems to equally inhibit all litigation to a certain extent. Thus, in recent years there have been opinions insisting that the filing fee should be considered part of the judicial costs that should be borne by the party causing the cost to the system according to the amount of cost caused, and that the fee does not need to be increased on a sliding scale based on the claimed amount but should be fixed.

A similarly important point to the issue of how costs are calculated is the question of who should be the final bearer of the costs, over which there has also been controversy. As explained previously, litigation costs should, in principle, be paid in advance by each litigant and finally collected from the losing party, while attorneys' fees are basically paid by each party. In most cases, parties pay the retainer fee at the time an attorney is hired, with the winning party additionally paying the success fee upon completion of the case. In relation to these fees, a problem has been noted that despite the *loser pays* principle, the litigation costs paid in advance are in fact rarely collected from the losing party due to the complexity of the collection procedure, and therefore the rightful claimant must often bear considerable costs in addition to attorneys' fees which should be borne by each party even though the claim has been successful in court. This situation has drawn criticism in that it is unreasonable that the value of the entitlement supposedly achieved at no cost outside the court is virtually reduced as a result of the use of an attorney in

[13] See Study Group on Field Survey of Civil Litigation (ed), *Quantitative Analyses of Civil Litigation (Sequel)* 487 (Tokyo, Shoji Homu, 2008) (in Japanese).

litigation. There have also been long-held opinions that a system based on the loser-pays principle should be introduced for all costs required for litigation, including attorneys' fees.

However, one conventional opinion against the idea of introducing the *loser pays* principle for attorneys' fees insists that since employing an attorney is not compulsory in Japan it is unreasonable to require one party to bear the cost of an attorney's contract concluded personally by the other party, even as a result of losing the case. Moreover, in recent years other strong counter-opinions from different viewpoints have emerged. Examples include: (i) Considering that a decision by the court in a civil case is made not simply through confirmation of existing rights but as a result of comprehensive, unbiased evaluation of evidence submitted by both parties by the court and finally based on the principle of burden of proof, it seems unfair that the losing party bears all of the litigation costs based on the results of the court's decision. (ii) The cost of litigation is not directly related to the actual right claimed and should instead be considered as the cost of dispute resolutions related to such right. Thus, in terms of dispute resolution, both the winning and losing parties equally benefit and therefore it is fair that both parties bear their own costs of the litigation. It is also pointed out that the risk of bearing the other party's attorneys' fees may lead to a tendency to avoid filing a suit involving consumers' rights or relating to policy formation, where predicting the court judgment is often difficult due to undeveloped legal systems. Meanwhile, in cases involving moneylenders or consumer credit loan companies in which the court judgments are clearly predictable, the risk of abusing the *loser pays* principle may arise, such as forcing the other party to pay for an excessive amount of attorneys' fees.

As described above, there have been several conflicting opinions regarding payment of the costs of litigation. The justice system reform launched in 1999 has attempted to achieve legislative solutions to this issue. Discussions were held on various points, including the possibility of separating the calculation of the cost of expert opinions, which accounts for a large portion of the costs of litigation. The main focus of the discussions, however, was whether the *loser pays* principle should be adopted for attorneys' fees. The conflict over this issue could not be settled due to strong opposition by bar associations to the *loser pays* principle. Consequently, a compromise bill was submitted to the Diet that allows the *loser pays* principle to be adopted for attorneys' fees when both parties employ attorneys and when such adoption is requested jointly by both parties, though in the end the bill did not pass the Diet. In the discussions at the Justice System Reform Council, bar associations presented an opinion regarding cases whose results would bring public benefits to the effect that a 'one-sided *loser pays* system' should be adopted where the defendant must pay the plaintiff's attorneys' fees only when the plaintiff wins the case.

Other Problems Regarding Costs for Litigation

Method for Calculating Litigation Costs

An important issue relevant to the costs of litigation is the calculation of those costs. The Act on Costs of Civil Procedure states that filing fees shall be determined based on the value of the subject matter (claimed amount) of litigation, but if it is difficult to calculate this value, then payment of the fee would be difficult too, which could hinder the filing of such procedings. Meanwhile, if the amount claimed increases depending on the method of calculation, then the filing fee would rise accordingly, which might also hinder the filing of proceedings.

In order to solve these problems, several revisions were made to the Code of Civil Procedure of 1996. Article 8, paragraph 2 of the Code of Civil Procedure stipulates that the value of the subject matter of proceedings shall be deemed to exceed 900,000 yen (now 1,400,000 yen) even 'if it is extremely difficult to calculate the value [of the subject matter of the suit]', a revision of Article 22 of the former Code that stated that when it is impossible to calculate the value of the subject matter, the value shall be deemed to exceed 900,000 yen (upper limit of the subject matter jurisdiction of a summary court at that time.) As a result, this revised provision could be directly applied to lawsuits by local residents against local authorities under Article 242-2, paragraph 1, item 4 of the Local Autonomy Act, for which Article 22 of the former Code had been applied by analogy. This revision also made it easier to determine the value of claims in proceedings seeking an injunction based on personal rights or an injunction to prevent illegal acts by board members based on the Companies Act,[14] etc, as well as in litigation seeking reversal of dismissal or securing of employee status, etc. Moreover, the proviso of Article 9, paragraph 1 of the Code of Civil Procedure stipulates that when the interest alleged in an action is common to two or more claims, the value of those claims shall not be added together. Before this proviso was established, the main provision of Article 9 stipulating 'where two or more claims are to be made by a single action, the sum of those claims shall be the value of the subject matter of the suit' had been strictly applied. For example, when several hundred citizens jointly filed a suit seeking an injunction for the purpose of conserving the environment of a region, the value of the subject matter was calculated by adding together the value of each individual party's claim, which resulted in a considerably large amount. But due to this added provision, the value of a single claim (by an individual) could be considered the basis for calculating the filing fee of the litigation.

Jurisdiction

Rules regarding jurisdiction also influence the amount of costs related to litigation. Litigation outside the area of residence naturally involves greater costs due to

[14] Act No 86 of 26 Jul 2005. Its unofficial translation is available at www.japaneselawtranslation.go.jp/law/detail/?id=177&vm=02&re=01.

transportat requirements and other expenses. The further away the court, the greater the costs.

For this point, the effect of agreement jurisdiction between the parties is particularly important. In cases involving a contract between companies and general citizens, an agreement disadvantageous to the citizens on exclusive jurisdiction is often concluded due to the difference in power between the parties. To remedy such cases, Article 17 of the Code of Civil Procedure of 1996 allows the court to transfer the suit to another court 'when it finds it necessary in order to . . . ensure equity between the parties' and Article 20 ensures that this provision will not be hindered even when there is agreement on exclusive jurisdiction between the parties.

Duration of Trials

In Japan, extending the duration of a trial does not directly cause an increase in litigation costs, though it sometimes does lead to a partial increase in attorneys' fees. However, prolonged trial duration may increase the psychological burden as well as indirect economic burden such as the impact on the litigants' working hours. Thus, the prolonged duration of trials could be a significant factor hindering litigation.

In Japan, the harm caused by prolonged trials is widely recognised. In the Code of Civil Procedure of 1996, with the aim of expediting the court processes, a system for intensively investigating evidence was established by organising the procedures for etermining issues and enhancing the means of collecting evidence. In 2003, the Act on the Expediting of Trials[15] was established. Article 2 of this Act presents the objective of concluding proceedings in the first instance within two years in principle, while Article 8, to achieve this objective, states

> '[i]n order to clarify the matters required for promoting the expediting of trials, the Supreme Court shall conduct a comprehensive, objective, and multilateral review of the expediting of trials through investigation and analysis of the conditions of the length of time required for the proceedings at the court, the causes for prolonged proceedings and other necessary matters, and shall disclose the results every two years to make them clear to the people.'

Under this provision, efforts for improvement and review have been made to promote the expediting of trials. As a result, in 2008 the average trial duration was 6.5 months (versus 7.8 months in 2006 and 8.2 months in 2004) and cases whose trial duration exceeded two years accounted for 3.6 per cent (versus 5.5 per cent in 2006 and 6 per cent in 2004) of the total.[16]

[15] Act No 107 of 16 Jul 2003. The unofficial English translation is available at www.japaneselawtranslation.go.jp/law/detail/?id=133&vm=02&re=01.

[16] See General Secretariat of the Supreme Court, *Review Report of the Expediting of Trials* 3rd edn (Tokyo, Shiho Kyokai, 2009) (in Japanese); General Secretariat of the Supreme Court, *Review Report of the Expediting of Trials* 2nd edn (Tokyo, Shiho Kyokai, 2006) (in Japanese); and General Secretariat of the Supreme Court, *Review Report of the Expediting of Trials* 1st edn (Tokyo, Shiho Kyokai, 2004) (in Japanese).

Costs Shifting

As mentioned above, while the general rule in Japan is that the losing party has to pay the entire litigation fee, each party has to pay their own attorney's fee even if he/she has won. There is only one exception to this principle, namely case law that allows courts discretion to include a plaintiff's attorney's fee as part of an award of damages. Recently, as stated above, the Japanese government has been trying to introduce the English rule but has not yet succeeded. In the process of this debate, though the JFBA proposed to introduce one side loser-pay principal, it has not yet happened.

Other approaches to reduce costs are to reduce the amount of the claim in order to save the litigation fee, and to make joint multiple claims, considering that the ratio of the fee will reduce when the amount of claim increases. However, these strategies are not always effective for cost reduction.

Support For Costs Associated With Litigation

Current Status of Judicial Aid

The above section discusses who should finally bear the burden of expenses associated with litigation. Regardless of how the matter is concluded, there is no dispute that a person who brings a suit to court must have a certain amount of money available for expenses. Even if this amount is kept as low as possible, there will always be people who cannot afford the expenses. Unless appropriate aid is provided, such people cannot enjoy the constitutionally guaranteed right of access to courts. Two aid systems are in place for such people: a judicial aid system, which is designed to defer payment of litigation costs, and a legal aid system, which is designed to such people lend money for attorneys' fees.

As provided in the Code of Civil Procedure, the judicial aid system permits a period of grace for payment of litigation costs subject to certain requirements. Part of the provisions for this system was amended in 1996 to ease the requirements, thereby expanding the scope of those eligible for aid; while the target for aid prior to the amendment was 'a person who lacks the financial resources to pay the litigation costs and is not considered to be unlikely to win the case', after the amendment is now 'a person who lacks the financial resources to pay the expenses necessary for preparing for and conducting a suit or person who will suffer substantial detriment in his/her standard of living by paying such expenses.' (Code of Civil Procedure, Article 82)

Current Status of Legal Aid

Attorneys' fees are paid for each litigant in advance, subject to certain requirements, by the Japan Legal Aid Association, which was established with contributions from bar associations. Until 1952, this advance payment had been sourced only from bar associations' contributions. Due to financial difficulty, however, the payment has shifted to also rely on the subsidy received from the Ministry of Justice since 1958. In most Western countries, laws supporting legal aid systems has been enforced, and abundant aid is provided at national expense. In Japan, on the other hand, the legal aid system had long been outside the support of national law and has therefore had an extremely weak financial base. This situation changed in 2000 when the Civil Legal Aid Act[17] was enacted and put into effect. This Act clearly stipulated governmental responsibility for legal aid, and helped expand the legal aid provision service thereafter. In 2004, the Comprehensive Legal Support Act[18] was enacted, expansively taking over the provisions of the Civil Legal Aid Act. An organisation called the Japan Legal Support Centre as known as *Houterasu* (legal terrace), has been set up under the Comprehensive Legal Support Act to provide legal aid services and legal information for anyone who needs it at anytime and anywhere.

Current Status of Legal Expenses Insurance

Legal expenses insurance (LEI) is available in order to alleviate the economic burden on citizens of attorney' fees, along with the legal aid system. In Japan, this kind of insurance is called 'insurance for protecting rights' or 'attorney insurance', and it is sold as a policy option added to the main insurance policy, such as motor insurance, fire insurance and accident insurance. An LEI policyholder can claim for legal counselling fees, attorneys' fees, and/or litigation costs incurred as a result of legal counselling or a damages lawsuit. Though this is BTE insurance, which means that policyholder must buy it before the event, he or she can claim one to five million yen for attorneys' fees and/or about 100,000 yen for a legal counselling fees, if he or she pays an LEI premium of about 1,000 to 3,000 yen per year. LEI therefore plays a significant role in providing financial assistance for a citizen's access to justice. In 2000, the JFBA entered into an agreement with eight major insurance companies to hold discussions with them on the operation of the LEI system. Since then, it has been promoting the LEI system by providing an attorney referral service, and other services. The Justice System Reform Council stated in its 2001 recommendations that the development and spread of legal expenses

[17] Act No 55 of 28 Apr 2000.

[18] Act No 74 of 2 Jun 2004. The unofficial English translation is available at www.japaneselawtranslation.go.jp/law/detail/?id=1832&vm=02&re=01.

insurance was expected to be a way to facilitate citizens' access to justice.[19] The number of LEI policyholders has been increasing annually since its release in 2000; however, the number in 2008 was 6.5 million, which means that only 13 per cent of households were insured. Therefore, in order to improve the LEI system, the JFBA has been considering expanding LEI coverage to individual labour relations cases, and it has also been trying to reinforce the structure so as to encourage the spread of LEI.[20]

Critical Review

Expenses Necessary for Litigation

The expenses necessary for litigation in Japan today involve two problems: transparency and reasonableness. The former problem concerns whether the expenses are predictable. The latter problem concerns whether the expenses actually incurred from litigation are adequate. The latter problem can further be divided into a total-cost problem and a cost-sharing problem. These problems are discussed below.

Transparency of Expenses Necessary for Litigation

The amount of expenses necessary for litigation is one of the greatest concerns for a person who intends to bring a suit to court. It is essential to keep this amount as reasonably low as possible. Also important is that the amount of these expenses should be predictable before the court process begins. The Justice System Reform Council conducted a survey targeted at parties to civil litigation.[21] The result reveals that only 49 per cent of respondents could predict the amount of necessary expenses before the court process began. The remaining 51 per cent answered that they could not predict the amount at all. Almost the same result was obtained by a similar survey of civil litigants conducted by the Japan Law Foundation in 2006: 48.4 per cent of respondents answered that they could not predict the amount at all.[22] A nationwide field survey was also conducted in 2003 targeted at ordinary

[19] Justice System Reform Council, *Recommendations of the Justice System Reform Council: For a Justice System to Support Japan in the 21st Century* (12 Jun 2001). The English translation is available at www.kantei.go.jp/foreign/policy/sihou/singikai/990612_e.html.

[20] For the change in the number of LEI policyholders and the JFBA's efforts in recent years, see JFBA Centre for Promotion of Legal Practice, *Report on Citizens' Legal Needs* 113-116 (Tokyo, Japan Federation of Bar Associations, 2008) (in Japanese), available at www.nichibenren.or.jp/ja/committee/list/data/shimin_needs.pdf.

[21] Judicial System Reform Council, *Report of Field Survey on Civil Litigators* (2000) (in Japanese). See also I Sugawara & I-Ching Tseng, 'Field Survey on Users of Civil Litigation' (2006) 212 *Nagoya University Journal of Law and Politics* 1.

[22] Study Group on Civil Procedure System (ed), *2006 Field Survey on Civil Litigators* (Tokyo, Shoji Homu, 2007).

citizens with no experience in litigation. This survey contained the question, 'Supposing you are going to file a lawsuit, do you have any idea of how much money the suit would cost?' To this question, 93 per cent of respondents answered 'No idea at all.'[23]

In Japan, where only few people use their litigation right, most people have a stereotyped image that using litigation or an attorney is costly and time-consuming. Against this background, there is no doubt that the uncertainty of cost predictions significantly obstructs the use of litigation. Discussion of the costs associated with litigation generally tend to focus on the amount of the costs itself. To promote the use of litigation, due consideration should also be given to provision of cost-related information. As attorneys' fees account for the majority of expenses of litigation, further discussion should continue to ensure fair competition for attorneys' fees and proper price formation. Efforts should also be made to keep potential litigants informed of the proper price.

Reasonableness of Expenses Necessary for Litigation

Before discussing the reasonableness of the total expenses necessary for litigation, a review must be made of the reasonableness of the current method of calculating court and attorneys' fees. As discussed above the basis for calculating the litigation costs to be paid to the court, the current system cannot be said to be very reasonable. However, the current system in which the litigation costs are linked with the amount claimed does not, at present, receive heavy criticism. Considering the access of financially distressed people to the court system, the litigation costs should be reduced since they can directly prevent such people from going to court. At least for the present, however, this obstacle can be avoided by using the judicial aid the scope of application of which has been expanded. Although the problem of litigation costs is important, it is economically absorbed by the problem of attorneys' fees, which are far higher than litigation costs.

The reasonableness of attorneys' fees has significant influence on potential litigants. However, determining the reasonableness of attorneys' fees is not easy since it is virtually impossible to set up objective criteria on which the reasonableness of the price of intellectual labour is based. In this sense, the recent practice of leaving this problem to fair and open competition is reasonable. As pointed out above regarding transparency, however, it is extremely difficult for potential litigants to attain a true figure of attorneys' fees. Fair and open competition is not likely to be realised simply by eliminating the ongoing criteria. Use of a single standard for attorneys' fees would be detrimental to open competition and must be avoided. Nevertheless, we think it necessary that some form of information disclosure system that enables potential litigants to compare attorneys' fees be implemented.

In reviewing the reasonableness of attorneys' fees, it is also necessary to consider the reasonableness of the method of paying such fees. At present, the traditional

[23] See I Sugawara, 'Consciousness Survey on Civil Procedure System' Project-Completion Report of 2003–2004 Grant-in-Aid for Scientific Research (C)(2) (15530061) (in Japanese).

practice is to pay the fee in two stages (ie, initial retainer fee and success fee). It is not the case that this method is absolutely reasonable. Diverse payment methods should be prepared to meet various working patterns of attorneys and various client needs. In this regard, there is a certain trend towards diversification, including a uniformly low initial retainer fee and increased adoption of a time-charge system. The reasonableness of any such options should also be determined under fair competition and with reference to sufficient information disclosed. In any case, since a complex payment method could cause misunderstanding among potential litigants, a simple and clear payment method is desirable.

What needs discussion more than these general issues, however, is whether adoption of the contingency fee system is adequate. In the past, the dominant opinion in this regard was that the contingency fee system was undesirable from the attorney's moral perspective since it might promote vexatious litigations. However, this system has become accepted as one payment method option, against the background of the recent trend toward diversification of payment methods. For those with the right to bring a lawsuit but who have limited financial resources, the contingency fee system is certainly useful and should not be abandoned. In Japan, where there is no damages system that combines punitive and compensatory damages, however, the contingency fee system, which involves extremely high rates of pay for attorneys, can not only incite attorneys' fondness for speculation but can also ruin the substance of the damages system. In this sense, a specific upper limit should be placed on the rate of pay for attorneys.

The discussion is now turned to who should bear the burden of paying attorneys' fees. As previously noted, whether the burden should be borne by each litigant (current system) or solely by the losing party has been the focus of heated arguments. A system of imposing the burden on the losing party is surely advantageous in that the right to bring a suit can be completely realised. However, there are many suits for which the contents of the right itself remain uncertain until the end of the court process. In such lawsuits, it is not reasonable to impose an absolute liability on the losing party and to make the litigant bear the burden of paying attorneys' fees for the winning party. The problem of who should bear the burden of paying attorneys' fees should be addressed case-by-case while the current system (where the burden is borne by each litigant) is applied as a general rule. For example, a one-sided system that burdens the losing party with attorneys' fees could be applied in cases where promotion of litigation is politically desirable, such as antitrust and environmental litigation. For litigants who have suffered significant infringement of rights, attorneys' fees may be included in the total damages as is presently practiced in tort litigations.

Aid for Costs Associated with Litigation

As described earlier, various measures have been taken to promote the use of the judicial aid system and legal aid system in Japan. The current status of using the judicial aid system is not clear since recent statistical data have not been published. The requirements for receiving judicial aid have been eased as has already been mentioned.

The scale of legal aid provision has expanded dramatically compared with what had been provided in the past. In 1996, it totalled about 1.31 billion yen, of which the government funded 271 million yen, when the Japan Legal Aid Association was the only source of aid.[24] Today the budget for legal aid exceeds 10 billion yen.[25] However, many problems remain to be solved. Among them is the small number of applications for aid due to poor knowledge of the system. According to the survey conducted by the Japan Legal Support Centre in 2008, only 36 per cent of respondents know about the free legal counselling service provided under the system, and only 23 per cent of respondents know of the service of lending money for attorneys' fees.[26] Present criteria for legal aid provision target 20 per cent of the Japanese population on low incomes. However, those of low income are not well informed of the legal aid system. It is likely that considerable needs remain unmet. In fact, most users of the legal aid system are litigants in personal bankruptcy cases, indicating that widespread use of the system has not been achieved.

Another problem is that attorneys' fees lent under the present system must in principle eventually be repaid. In other words, the aid is not provided as a benefit. Though there are many cases where repayment is waived under certain conditions, the degree of recognition and therefore use of the exemption system remains very low. According to the survey above, many of the respondents who have never used the loan service believe that hiring an attorney is ultimately costly. To promote the use of the legal aid system, therefore, it is vital to either expand the scope of repayment exemptions or change the loan service to a benefit service.

[24] See Study Group on Legal Aid, *Report of Study Group on Legal Aid* (1998) (in Japanese).

[25] See Japan Legal Support Centre, 2009 Annual Plan (2009) (in Japanese).

[26] The Cabinet Office also conducted the opinion survey on the visibility of the Japan Legal Support Centre. The result shows that only 1.4 % of respondents received its support. 8% know both its name and its service contents; 18.6 % know its name only; and 67.5 % know neither its name nor its service contents. See Cabinet Office, *Report of Opinion Survey on Comprehensive Legal Support* (2009) (in Japanese).

13

Latin America: A Regional Report

MANUEL A GÓMEZ*

Introduction

The judicial reform agendas sponsored throughout Latin America by the World Bank, the Inter American Development Bank and other multilateral and foreign aid organisations during the 1990s sparked the interest of many Latin American governments in the economic consequences of litigation as part of their task to facilitate access to justice. Court and attorney fees, as well as cost shifting regimes had been traditionally regulated throughout the region, but no interest had been paid to comparing how the various systems worked within each jurisdiction, or what regional trends could be identified. A relatively recent surge in the use of aggregate procedures and the growth of public interest litigation in several jurisdictions has motivated a revision of the traditional principles involving litigation costs, such as contingency fee arrangements, and also the expansion of funding schemes, such as legal aid regimes and third party funding in general.[1]

This chapter seeks to provide an overview of the main issues dealing with litigation costs and funding throughout Latin America. Mindful of the critical differences that exist among the twenty jurisdictions that form the region,[2] the complexity of each national legal system, and the lack of systematic research on litigation costs and funding regimes;[3] this chapter modestly aspires to at least

* Associate Professor. Florida International University College of Law, Miami, USA. I express my gratitude to the Latin American practitioners that accepted to participate in this research, for taking the time to respond the questionnaire, and for agreeing to be interviewed for this project.

[1] MA Gomez, *Class actions, group litigation and other aggregative procedures in Latin America: A general overview*, The Globalization of Class Actions Conference Proceedings, Dec, 2007. Available at: www.law.stanford.edu/library/globalclassaction/reports.html#latinamerica.

[2] These countries are: Argentina, Bolivia, Brazil, Chile, Colombia, Costa Rica, Cuba, Dominican Republic, Ecuador, El Salvador, Guatemala, Honduras, Mexico, Nicaragua, Panama, Paraguay, Peru, Puerto Rico, Uruguay and Venezuela. In spite of its common historical and cultural roots with the rest of the region, I have excluded Puerto Rico from this study in light of its inclusion as part of the legal system of the United States.

[3] Only a few published studies have focused on costs and funding issues related to litigation in Latin America. The most comprehensive one was conducted in 2004 by the Justice Studies Center of the Americas (CEJA) under the auspices of the Presidents of the Supreme Courts of Central American countries, the Caribbean and Mexico. See V Viancos and J Enrique, 'Financiamiento Privado de la

provide a general overview that highlights the most salient commonalities and differences that exist with regards to the economic consequences of litigation, including court-related and procedural costs, attorney fee regimes, cost shifting rules, and the different schemes of civil litigation funding.

The discussion presented in this chapter is based on an empirical investigation conducted during 2009. In addition to relying on a number of secondary sources, which include scholarly research on costs and funding issues, national legislation, and administrative data dealing with litigation costs and funding in Latin America; my analysis is also based on data obtained from an especially designed questionnaire responded to by legal practitioners with litigation experience in several Latin American jurisdictions.[4] My observations are also based on a series of semi-structured interviews conducted with legal actors (judges and lawyers alike) to gain a deeper understanding of the nuances and complexities associated with the different cost and funding regimes that prevail in the region.

Litigation Costs

Constitutional Framework and Access to Justice

The issue of litigation costs in Latin America has generally been approached from an access to justice standpoint. Based on the idea that court costs can pose a barrier to ordinary citizens and despite the fact that the judiciary is generally underfunded, in at least eight countries of the region court fees and other related costs are waived for all users regardless of their ability to pay, type of claim, and amount in dispute. The fact that this has generally been established as a fundamental right in the Constitution reveals the importance of this policy.

Most countries in this group have adopted a broad constitutional provision establishing that all activities related to 'the administration of justice shall be free of charge',[5] including but not limited to filing fees, court taxes, and other procedural expenses. None of these provisions, however, indicates whether the exemption also includes court-appointed experts or costs associated with the taking of evidence, but the general interpretation in most countries has been that while court-appointed experts might be included, party-appointed experts, attorney fees, and evidence taking activities are not.

This is certainly the scope of article 303 of the Honduran Constitution of 1982,[6] article 181 of the El Salvadorian Constitution of 1983, article 165 of the Nicaraguan

Justicia: Las Tasas Judiciales', 2004 Centro de Estudios de Justicia de las Americas. Available at: www.cejamericas.org/doc/ informes/jev-tasas-judiciales.pdf.

[4] The questionnaire devised for this research was largely based on the one previously designed and administered by Dr Christopher Hodges and Professor Stefan Vogenauer as part of the Oxford Comparative Survey on Funding and Costs.

[5] pdba.georgetown.edu/Constitutions/ElSal/constitucion2003.pdf.

[6] pdba.georgetown.edu/Constitutions/Honduras/hond05.html.

Constitution (1987),[7] and article 26 of the Venezuelan Constitution of 1999, which provides that the use of the justice system shall be completely free of charge to all users.[8] Similar provisions are contained in article 201 of the Panamanian Constitution (2004),[9] article 17 of the Mexican Constitution of 2009,[10] article 115, 2 of the recently approved Bolivian Constitution (2009),[11] as well as in article 168, 4 of the Ecuadorean Constitution of 2008.[12]

The Peruvian Constitution of 1993, on the other hand, has explicitly limited the principle to cases involving indigent parties and has established it as an exclusive right of those eligible to litigate in *forma pauperis* (articles 139, 16).[13] Article 254 of the Uruguayan Constitution of 1997[14] follows a similar principle, but, in order to deter the abusive exercise of this benefit and to counteract potential power imbalances, it also extends the privilege to the non-indigent defendant in a litigation initiated by the indigent party.

In the rest of the countries, there is no specific constitutional language about judicial costs, and the different systems generally operate on a fee-basis scheme regulated by special statute, which I now turn to describe.

Legal Systems, Procedural Principles and the Role of Latin American Judges

The array of institutions, processes and rules that define most Latin American civil justice systems can be traced back to their common history as former colonies of Spain and Portugal, and their characterisation as members of the 'civil law tradition'.[15] Despite the important political, social and institutional changes that have taken place in the region during the last century, most of the prevailing procedural principles are still very similar, which obviously has a direct effect on the way cost and litigation finance regimes are established.

The recent years have witnessed a rise in the enactment of special legislation geared to govern important aspects of litigation costs, namely court fee collection and administration regimes.[16] As mentioned above, recently enacted constitutions have also embraced the notion of a 'cost-free' justice as a way to facilitate access to

[7] www.asamblea.gob.ni/index.php?option=com_content&task=view&id=228&Itemid=156.

[8] www.constitucion.ve/constitucion_view_en/view/ver_arbol.pag. Moreover, in an advisory opinion issued on 20 Jun 2001, the Attorney General of Venezuela interpreted the constitutional provision to be sufficiently broad to include any cost or expenses associated with the use of the courts, at www.pgr.gob.ve/PDF/Dictamenes/CONSTITUCIONAL2.pdf.

[9] www.asamblea.gob.pa/asamblea/constitucion/.

[10] www.diputados.gob.mx/LeyesBiblio/pdf/1.pdf.

[11] www.presidencia.gob.bo/download/constitucion.pdf.

[12] www.asambleanacional.gov.ec/documentos/constitucion_de_bolsillo.pdf.

[13] pdba.georgetown.edu/Constitutions/Peru/per93reforms05.html#titIcapI.

[14] www.rau.edu.uy/uruguay/const97-1.6.htm.

[15] J H Merryman, and R Perez-Perdomo, *The Civil Law Tradition: An introduction to the legal systems of Europe and Latin America* (Stanford, Stanford University Press, 2007).

[16] For example, Argentina, Ley N° 23.898, Ley de Tasas Judiciales / 1990; Brazil, Lei 9.289, 4 Jul 1996. 'Tabela de Custas Judiciais'; Ecuador, 'Reglamento de Tasas Judiciales', publicado en el Registro Oficial No 298, 3 Apr 2001; Venezuela, Ley de Arancel Judicial, at: www.tsj.gov.ve/legislacion/dfrlaj.htm;

the official courts. However, most principles regarding attorney fees, cost shifting rules, and the handling of evidence are still included in the codes of civil procedure which continue to be the centrepiece in most jurisdictions. The fact that the majority of the codes are similar in terms of structure and scope facilitates their comparison and enables us to make some generalisations.

Based on a historically-rooted inquisitorial approach to judging,[17] most Latin American codes of civil procedure assign judges a preeminent and active role in leading the proceedings and acting as true gatekeepers. This is clearly different from the image of a judge as a mere 'umpire' that is stereotypical of adversarial jurisdictions where litigation is more party-driven and less judge-controlled. In Latin America, as in many other civil law jurisdictions, judges are given a broad discretion to control what type of evidence is admitted, how is the evidence presented and examined, and what weight, if any, can be given to the evidentiary means brought into the litigation.

More importantly, Latin American judges are generally given the power to gather evidence *sua sponte*, to appoint experts, and lead the deposition of witnesses.[18] All this has an obvious impact on litigation costs, among other reasons because the evidence-gathering activities conducted by judges on their own volition are paid for by the state without creating any burden on private litigants.

Pre-trial discovery or any similar system to elicit general information or obtain evidence possessed by the other side or by a third party is clearly absent from all Latin American jurisdictions. The only way to obtain documents from the opponent or from a third party against their will is through a special mechanism commonly known as exhibition of documents (*exhibición de documentos*),[19] which entails a very difficult standard to meet,[20]and is also largely controlled by judges.

Court Usage Fees

Court fees are generally assessed on the parties as a way to offset some of the costs associated with the handling of their claims, and the overall operation of the court

Colombia. Acuerdo Nro 576 de 1999 por el cual se regula el Arancel Judicial en materia civil. Available at: www.ramajudicial.gov.co/csj_portal/acuerdos/576-99.HTM.

[17] Several codes of civil procedure specifically refer to the civil judge as 'the conductor of the proceedings' (*director del proceso*).

[18] See, for example, Argentina, Code of Civil Procedure, arts 36(b) and 452; Bolivia, Code of Civil Procedure, art 4, 4; Colombia, Code of Civil Procedure, arts 207, 233, and 244.

[19] See, for example, Colombia, Code of Civil Procedure, article 283; Peru, Code of Civil Procedure, arts 300-04; Venezuela, Code of Civil Procedure, art 436. This usually requires the submission of a request to produce that shall include a detailed description of the requested documents, a description of how the documents are relevant to the outcome, and a statement indicating why the requesting party believes that said documents are in possession of the opponent or a third party.

[20] Interestingly, some of our informants mentioned the possibility of relying upon a statutory device included in section 1782 of the United States Judicial Code that allows anyone (including foreign nationals) involved in litigation or arbitration before a foreign or an international tribunal to obtain US style discovery from a US party. It was not clear, however, how often Latin American parties use this mechanism, if at all.

system. However, as we will see below, not all countries allow the collected funds to go back to the judiciary, but instead use them for other purposes.

Court fee regimes can be compared from at least five different angles, depending on what types of claims court fees are charged for, when court fees are paid, who is responsible for paying court fees, what the criteria are for calculating court fees, and how court fees are allocated within the state apparatus.

Regarding the types of claims, the general trend is to assess court fees in civil and commercial cases, and to waive them for criminal, family (non-patrimonial), and labour claims. Some countries such as Argentina,[21] Brazil, Paraguay,[22] Colombia,[23] and Peru,[24] also exempt claims dealing with constitutional rights, and establish some sort of benefit for indigent litigants that have been formally authorised by the court to litigate in *forma pauperis*, and therefore exempted to pay all fees. Brazil has also a specific provision that exempts parties involved in small claim proceedings and consumer claims from paying court fees.[25]

In Argentina, the recently adopted Consumer Protection Act of 2008 has extended the benefit to all fees and court-related expenses associated with collective claims filed on behalf of consumer groups. The exemption is broad enough to include witness and expert fees.[26] In addition, plaintiffs in consumer cases are exempt from liability regarding the recovery of attorney fees, but defendants are not, thus making litigation high-risk for the latter, and significantly inexpensive and low-risk for the former. Even though the rationale behind this benefit has been to facilitate consumer access to the court system, this mechanism has also been criticised for encouraging abusive filing of claims and for creating imbalance among the parties.[27] Finally, in Peru, the law has established blanket exemptions to benefit inhabitants of remote rural areas from having to pay court fees.[28]

In terms of the opportunity when court fees are due, the general trend is to require the payment of a single fee at the outset, upon the filing of the initial claim. In Brazil, however, the posting of a bond is required every time an appeal is filed, even in labour cases.[29] Peru, has adopted a system that requires a series of fees

[21] Argentina, Law No. 23,898.

[22] Paraguay, Law 284 of 1971; Law 669 of 1995.

[23] Colombia, Popular and Group Litigation Statute (Law 472), art 19.

[24] Peru, Law 26,846; Law 27,231.

[25] Brazil, Consumer Defense Code, art 87.

[26] Argentina Consumer Protection Act, Law 26,361 B.O. 7 Apr 2008, at www.mr.gov.ar/Documentos/varios/leydefensa.PDF.

[27] HA Mairal, *Collective and Class Actions in Argentina, National Report*, The Globalization of Class Actions Conference Proceedings, 2007, at globalclassactions.stanford.edu/PDF/Argentina_National_Report.pdf.

[28] V Viancos and J Enrique, 'Financiamiento Privado de la Justicia: Las Tasas Judiciales', 2004 Centro de Estudios de Justicia de las Americas, 35, at: www.cejamericas.org/doc/informes/jev-tasas-judiciales.pdf.

[29] In labor claims, cases are filed irrespectively of costs being paid. The amount of court costs is then set at the end of the case and paid by the party who loses the case. When filing an appeal to the appellate (second instance) courts, the parties are required to post a bond of R$4.993,78 and a bond of R$9.987,56 for appeals to the third instance courts. In small claim courts, such amount varies from State to State.

throughout different procedural steps instead of the one-time fee system adopted in the rest of the jurisdictions.[30]

In jurisdictions where a single fee is established, these charges are levied on the claimant or on the requesting party in the case of court charges that are due at different stages. Court fees are also recoverable by the prevailing party at the end of the proceedings or, in any case, are subject to compensation depending on the number of times that each party has been defeated or has prevailed throughout the various procedural stages. The only exception to court fee shifting seems to be in the case of Argentine collective consumer claims, as noted earlier.

Regarding the method for calculating court fees, at least Argentina, Ecuador, Paraguay, Peru and Uruguay follow a system that takes into account the amount of the claim (*estimación de la demanda*), as expressed by the plaintiff at the time of filing her complaint. Filing fees, in these cases, are a percentage that ranges between 0.60 per cent in the case of Paraguay, to one per cent in the case of Ecuador, and three percent in the case of Argentina. The plaintiff's own estimation of the value of the claim also determines the jurisdiction of the court,[31] the eligibility for judicial review, and in some jurisdictions such as Venezuela, it also determines the maximum amount of recoverable fees and costs.[32]

Peru establishes a sliding scale with fixed amounts ranging between €8 and €800 for the enforcement of conservatory measures.[33] In the majority of the cases, court fees are paid through a bank deposit, with the exception of Paraguay where fees are paid through a special excise stamp that is affixed to the initial court filing.[34]

Finally, a comment about the allocation of court fees is in order. Even though we are not aware of any express policy statements outlining the principles and objectives for establishing court charges in any jurisdiction, the general rule has been to allocate a percentage of the total amount of court fees collected every year, to help financing the judiciary. In Argentina, for example, all fees go directly to a National Justice Fund managed by the Supreme Court, and the same occurs in Peru, where at least 80 per cent goes to cover the salaries of judges, and the remainder 20 per cent is invested in modernisation and judicial infrastructure projects.[35] In Brazil (at the Federal level) and Uruguay, a significant percentage of the collected funds go to financing the modernisation and maintenance of the prison system, and at least in the case of Brazil, the remainder goes to the National Treasury for its further allocation to other projects.

[30] V Viancos, and J Enrique, 'Financiamiento Privado de la Justicia: Las Tasas Judiciales', 2004 Centro de Estudios de Justicia de las Americas, 35, at: www.cejamericas.org/doc/informes/jev-tasas-judiciales.pdf.

[31] See, for example, Argentina, Federal Procedural and Civil Code of the Nation (Law 25,488 of 2001), art 321; Colombia, Code of Civil Procedure, articles 19 and 20 (Decrees 522 of 1988 and 2282 of 1989); Venezuela, Supreme Tribunal of Justice, Resolution 2009-006; Ecuador, Code of Civil Procedure, art 65 (1987).

[32] See Venezuela, art 286 of the Code of Civil Procedure.

[33] See Peru, Administrative Resolution No. 111-2009-CE-PJ.

[34] V Viancos and J Enrique, 'Financiamiento Privado de la Justicia: Las Tasas Judiciales', 2004 Centro de Estudios de Justicia de las Americas, 35, at www.cejamericas.org/doc/informes/jev-tasas-judiciales.pdf.

[35] ibid.

Other Procedural Costs

The taking of evidence is generally the stage that requires the most important investment of resources from the parties to a civil court case. To prove their assertions, litigants often rely on court and party-appointed experts, witnesses, and other evidentiary means that often require an important disbursement of funds. As noted earlier, even in those jurisdictions where the administration of justice is conceived as a free service, the parties are generally responsible for advancing the costs of their own experts and expenditures incurred in the handling of witnesses.[36] In these jurisdictions, even though the judiciary is supposed to absorb the cost of any experts independently appointed by the court and of any witnesses summoned by the judge when exercising her inquisitorial powers, this hardly ever happens as the budget allocated to the judiciary does not contemplate the use of funds for such purpose.[37] The same occurs in the case of indigent parties authorised to litigate *in forma pauperis* by the court, as none of the existing legal aid schemes appears to cover expert fees or the use of other evidentiary means by the indigent party, thus putting them at a significant disadvantage.

The reality is that the parties are the ones who generally request the appointment of experts and the calling of witnesses, therefore advancing the necessary expenses.[38] The determination of the amount of expert fees is generally done by the judge, pre-established by statute,[39] or based on tariffs established by professional associations, so there is little or no room for negotiation with the court or for the adoption of market prices. The same occurs in connection with other expenses related to the taking or preservation of evidence, such as court-led inspections *in loco*, or the analysis of highly technical evidence that requires the use of special equipment and the assistance of experts.

Finally, expert fees and other procedural costs incurred by the parties are generally recoverable at the end of the proceedings,[40] except when the parties have incurred in payments beyond the parameters established by the judge or provided for by statute (eg by retaining their own private experts), or when the losing party is the state proper or a public agency, which are generally exempted from paying court costs and fees altogether.[41]

[36] Interview with Latin American counsel (interview #12); Interview with Latin American counsel (interview #3).

[37] ibid.

[38] Brazil, Code of Civil Procedure, art 33. Pursuant to this provision, the party who requested the expert examination shall initially bear the cost, but if the expert has been requested by both parties, then the cost shall be borne by the plaintiff, who will obviously be able to recover it in case her case prevails.

[39] Ecuador, Code of Civil Procedure, art 288 (1987), Bar Federation of Ecuador Act ('*Ley de Federacion de Abogados del Ecuador*') arts 12 and 45; Argentina, Federal Procedural and Civil Code of the Nation (Law 25,488 of 2001), art 227; Argentina, Civil Code, article 505.

[40] See, for example, Peru, Judicial Code, art 412.

[41] Ecuador, Code of Civil Procedure, art 289 (1987)

Lawyer Fees and Recoverability

As is the case in other jurisdictions around the world,[42] lawyer fees are the single biggest cost for the parties to a civil litigation in Latin America. Except in the case of legal aid systems that establish a cap for lawyer fees,[43] or when Bar Associations establish a tariff,[44] fees are generally negotiated between the client and the lawyer based on market forces. Different statutes and Bar Associations' Ethics Codes, however, require lawyers to consider several parameters when establishing their professional fees, and judges also take these into account when assessing the reasonableness of fees to be recovered by the prevailing party at the end of the proceedings. Some of these parameters are related to the importance of the case, its novelty or difficulty, the experience and expertise of the lawyer, time commitment on the lawyer's part, and the impact on its overall professional practice.[45]

A percentage of the claim is sometimes used in lieu of a pre-fixed lawyer fee, or in addition to the regular compensation as a bonus or success fee, but success fees are never the sole element in the remuneration of lawyers. Fixed fees or a variation thereof is broadly used in small and mid-sized litigation, even though there seems to be a trend among plaintiff lawyers who handle labour, tax, and consumer cases, towards adopting contingency fee agreements.

Similar to what has occurred in other civil law jurisdictions, contingency fee agreements have been traditionally banned or heavily discouraged throughout Latin America as a way of deterring lawyers from having a personal interest in their clients' causes. However, recent legal reform efforts have recognised their potential in helping claimants who otherwise would not be able to finance their litigation expenses to attain adequate legal representation. As a result, contingency fee agreements are now allowed in areas where power imbalances tend to be salient, such as labour and consumer disputes.

In these instances, contingency fee arrangements usually require the client to pay a small fee at the beginning of the litigation just to cover a fraction of administrative expenses and the preparation of the case, and the remainder is paid after a favourable judgment is handed down by the court or at the time of settlement. Under this method, the lawyer is usually entitled to a compensation that ranges between 35 per cent and 40 per cent of the value of the claim, that is, between five

[42] H M Kritzer, 'Fee Regimes and the Cost of Civil Justice', (2009) 28 *Civil Justice Quarterly* 345.

[43] Peru, Judicial Code, arts 179 and 562.

[44] Venezuela. Regulation of Minimum Lawyer Fees of the Federation of Bar Associations (*Reglamento de Honorarios Minimos de Abogado*), arts 15–24; Laywer's Act (*Ley de Abogados*), art 46.5; and Lawyer's Code of Ethics (*Código de Etica*), art 40.

[45] See, for example, Venezuela, Regulation of Minimum Lawyer Fees of the Federation of Bar Associations (*Reglamento de Honorarios Minimos de Abogado*), art 3. The Brazilian Bar Ethics Code, determines that the minimum amount for each type of claim/area is set forth in the Lawyer Fees Chart (*Tabela de Honorários*), but this chart varies from State to State. The maximum amount, although not established by law, is limited by some criteria ser forth in the Brazilian Bar Ethics Code such as the quality of the attorney's work and the complexity of the case.

and ten percent in excess of the average recovery amount ordered by a judge as a result of cost shifting rules.[46]

Even though the calculation of lawyer fees based on a percentage of monies recovered through litigation has been historically banned as a *pactum de quota litis*, lawyers have frequently circumvented this prohibition by entering into private—though non-enforceable—agreements with their clients.[47] The rise of collective litigation in the region has been a key factor in the increasing popularity of these and other similar fee arrangements, and a few statutes, such as the Colombian Popular and Group Actions Act (*Ley 472*) have now created other incentives like the possibility of a risk premium for prevailing plaintiff lawyers in collective cases.[48]

A less widespread, but increasingly common, method of calculating lawyer fees is the hourly rate, which has become broadly accepted in large cities throughout Latin America due to the growing presence of US firms. This method is mostly used in large and complex commercial cases involving multinational corporations or large corporate clients, but very rarely in litigation.[49] The alleged delay of court proceedings throughout the region seems to be an important factor in the scarce use of hourly fees among litigators, whose clients tend to favour pre-established fees instead.

Hourly rates vary greatly depending on each local legal market, the type of client, the type of lawyer, and the nature of the claim. The most expensive markets seem to be in large cities where the presence of foreign law firms is common, such as Mexico City, Sao Paulo, or Buenos Aires, and with important caveats, the average hourly fee in the region ranges between €30 for a junior associate to €300 for a firm partner.[50] Lawyers tend to prefer establishing their hourly fees in US Dollars as a way to protect themselves from domestic inflation rates and financial instability in their home countries.[51] Whenever hourly fees are charged in local currency, the US Dollar is almost always used as a reference.

In spite of the perceived advantage of hourly rates for enabling clients to condition their lawyers' compensation to the amount of time invested in handling their case, hourly fees pose at least one significant obstacle when it comes to recoverability. Since in most jurisdictions the amount of recoverable fees is capped at a

[46] See DR Hensler, 'The Globalization of Class Actions: An Overview' (2009) 7 *Annals of the American Academy of Political and Social Sciences* 13. See also, HA Mairal, 'Collective and Class Actions in Argentina' (2009) 7 *Annals of the American Academy of Political and Social Sciences.* (discussing the scope of art 4 of Law 21,839, which caps contingency fee arrangements to 40%).

[47] See MA Gomez, 'Like Migratory Birds: Latin American Plaintiffs in US Courts and the Ford-Firestone Rollover Litigation', (2005) XI *Southwestern Journal of Law and Trade in the Americas* 2.

[48] Colombia, Popular and Group Actions Statute (Ley 472), art 46, 4.

[49] Peruvian lawyers report the use of hourly rates in handling family cases. See, Peruvian Report (2009) How much does it cost to litigate in Latin America? [Unpublished survey, on file with author].

[50] See Peruvian Report (2009); Brazilian Report (2009) How much does it cost to litigate in Latin America? [Unpublished surveys, on file with author].

[51] See MA Gomez, 'Like Migratory Birds: Latin American Plaintiffs in U.S. Courts and the Ford-Firestone Rollover Litigation', (2005) XI *Southwestern Journal of Law and Trade in the Americas* 2.

fixed percentage of the claim (usually between 10 per cent and 30 per cent)[52], when the total number of hours invested by the lawyer exceeds the official cap, the tendency has been for judges never to override this limit, thus forcing the winning party to absorb the differential.[53]

Most Codes of Civil Procedure in the region contain a specific provision that requires the judge to include a reference about cost shifting in all her interim and final decisions.[54] The general rule is that the losing party will bear her own and her opponent's total costs, including attorney fees, expert fees, and most authorised procedural expenses, but there is also room for judicial discretion in allowing or excluding certain items, or in imposing a cap on the total amount.[55] The judge's ruling on the costs usually triggers a separate proceeding, by which the party responsible for bearing the costs requests the revision of each expenditure, and a further assessment by experts of the total amount subject to recovery.[56] Based on the experts' reports, the judge issues another ruling by which the final amount to be shifted is established.

There is an important variation in the cost shifting rules across Latin American jurisdictions. While the general principle in most legal systems is to impose the obligation to bear all costs on the losing party,[57] some statutes go even further by also requiring that the loser be found to have acted in bad faith or that litigation was promoted unnecessarily.[58] In other instances, the judge is given discretion to exempt a losing party from cost liability if is concluded that such party had reasonable cause to litigate.[59] Finally, indigent parties are obviously exempt from bearing the costs in case they lose, but are given the possibility to recover if they prevail.

Funding Issues

No Latin American jurisdiction seems to impose a particular obstacle to the development of different litigation funding regimes. With the exception of the modest limitations imposed on Legal Expense Insurance (LEI) mechanisms, as part of the overall regulation of the insurance industry in some jurisdictions, and the para-

[52] See, for example, Brazil, Code of Civil Procedure, article 20, 3. Venezuela, Code of Civil Procedure, art 286.

[53] The recoverability gap varies greatly across jurisdictions and type of claim, making it very difficult to assess its real dimension at a regional level.

[54] See, for example, Venezuela, Code of Civil Procedure, article 274; Ecuador, Code of Civil Procedure, art 287.

[55] See, Chile, Code of Civil Procedure, art 140.

[56] This process is known in some jurisdictions as '*retasa*'. See, for example, Venezuela, Lawyers' Act (*Ley de Abogados*) art 27; Chile, Code of Civil Procedure, art 138.

[57] See, for example, Peru, Code of Civil Procedure, art 412; Colombia, Code of Civil Procedure, art 304; Argentina, *Ley* 11,330, article 24.

[58] See, for example, Ecuador, Code of Civil Procedure, art 287.

[59] Chile, Code of Civil Procedure, art 144.

meters established for the few existing legal aid regimes, most funding methods are largely unregulated.

Self-financing is by far the most common litigation-funding scheme in the region. The parties are usually required to advance the litigation costs, which poses a significant obstacle to disputants of modest means. Interestingly, parties to large and complex business transactions seem to be the ones that most commonly seek to obtain Legal Expense Insurance or third party litigation funding, but the prohibitive transaction costs limit considerably the use of these methods.[60] In a more general fashion, the intervention of third parties is usually limited to posting bonds in order to secure injunctions or other interim or conservative measures, but not necessarily to provide an advancement of costs to private parties.

With the advent of collective litigation and the resulting legal developments geared to facilitate the filing and processing of aggregative claims in jurisdictions such as Argentina, Brazil and Colombia, new conditional funding systems have emerged. In Colombia, for example, the Popular and Group Litigation Statute (*Ley 472*) created a special Fund for the Defence of the Collective Rights and Interests, which goal is to provide funding for actions filed to protect collective rights.[61]A similar system exists in Argentina under the General Environmental Act, which established the creation of a Fund for Environmental Compensation geared to help finance private litigation.[62]

The increased interest of Latin American governments in regulating and protecting the rights of socially identifiable groups of citizens[63] and the comprehensive criminal justice reform movement in which some governments have embarked during the last decade, have played an important role in the expansion of publicly funded legal aid regimes. Argentina and Colombia are good examples of this trend with the enactment of consumer protection statutes or legislation dealing with group litigation.[64]

Legal aid remains a benefit generally awarded to indigent litigants, or to certain categories of plaintiffs, such as individuals or groups of consumers pursuant to article 55 of the Argentine Consumer Defence Act, or to plaintiffs in labour cases. As a consequence, legal aid beneficiaries are also exempted from paying court charges and from bearing litigation costs in case the other party prevails.

An important component of most legal aid schemes is the provision of legal representation, which in most countries is channelled through a state-sponsored public defender programme. Public defenders are usually government employees that work closely with the courts in ensuring that needy litigants are able to obtain

[60] Interview with Latin American counsel (interview #1); Interview with Latin American counsel (interview #4); Peruvian Report (2009); Brazilian Report (2009) How much does it cost to litigate in Latin America? [Unpublished surveys, on file with author].

[61] Colombia, Popular and Group Litigation Statute, art 70.

[62] Argentina, General Environmental Act, art 34.

[63] L Perez-Luño, *La Tercera Generación de Derechos Humanos* (Navarra, Thomson-Aranzadi, 2006).

[64] See Colombia, Popular and Group Litigation Statute; Argentina, Consumer Protection Act of 2008.

adequate representation.[65] The main problem, however, is that most public defender offices are underfunded and understaffed.[66] In other instances, the law mandates the appointment of a public attorney on behalf of indigent litigants, but does not establish the mechanism to pay for it.[67]

Finally, a few words on *pro bono* practice. In spite of being historically absent from most Latin American jurisdictions, *pro bono* advice has been gaining importance in the region during the last eight years. Starting in 2001, several law firms from Argentina, Brazil, Chile, Colombia, Mexico and Peru began working together with the support from the Cyrus Vance Center for International Justice of the New York Bar Association,[68] in order to provide *pro bono* services to different categories of clients, and "to work on behalf of NGOs and public interest organisations that are engaged in access to justice, human rights, and related activities and are in need of *pro bono* legal support".[69] This network is currently formed by more than 400 lawyers in the region who have committed themselves to provide at least 20 hours of *pro bono* work per year in their areas of expertise.[70] In spite of the enormous benefits that arise from these privately funded initiatives, *pro bono* practice is still very limited and has not yet reached the large number of litigants that are underserved by state sponsored legal aid schemes.

[65] This legal assistance system is known as the 'public salaried model'. See M Cappelletti, B Garth and N Trocker, 'Access to justice: variations and continuity of a world-wide movement', (1985) 54 *Revista Jurídica de la Universidad de Puerto Rico*, 221.

[66] See M Dakolias, 'The judicial sector in Latin America and the Caribbean: Elements of reform', (1996) *World Bank Technical Paper No. 319* (The World Bank, Washington, DC, 1996), 45.

[67] This is the case of Venezuela as indicated by Dakolias (n 67).

[68] See, www.nycbar.org/citybarjusticecenter/pdf/Declaracion%20Pro%20Bono_poster09.pdf.

[69] www.nycbar.org/citybarjusticecenter/vancecenter-projects/.

[70] ibid.

14

The Netherlands

MARK L TUIL*

General Overview And Trends

The issue of litigation costs is a contentious one in the Netherlands. The general opinion is that litigation costs are too high and are an obstacle to giving effect to claims. This general opinion has however not caused much change in the actual rules governing litigation costs. The last PhD thesis on this topic dates back to just after the Second World War and can still be considered the seminal work in this field.[1] Of course since then the topic has continued to attract attention in the form of articles in legal journals or as the topic of meetings of professional legal societies such as the association for procedural law (*Nederlandse Vereniging voor Procesrecht*)[2], but as a whole the law remains much the same as it was in 1945, or even 1838, the year the Dutch replaced the laws stemming from the Napoleonic occupation for their own.

The rules on litigation costs may be summarised as follows. Litigation is not free. During the course of litigation, parties pay their own lawyer. In addition to these lawyer's costs parties have to pay a variety of charges such as court charges, bailiff's costs, witness' costs etc. Court charges are levied at the start of the procedure from both parties; the other costs are paid by the party in whose interest the costs are made at the moment these costs are made. For example, the party that requests that a witness be heard is responsible for reimbursing the witness for his costs. At the end of the procedure, the general rule is that the loser pays and the losing party is required to reimburse the winning party for her costs. The lawyer's costs of the prevailing party make up a large part of the total costs, and for the purpose of cost shifting these lawyer's costs are calculated on a tariff that falls far short of full compensation. Therefore the prevailing party is only partially compensated.

* Postdoctoral researcher at the Erasmus University School of Law.

[1] WL Haardt, *De veroordeling in de kosten van het burgerlijk geding* ('s-Gravenhage, Martinus Nijhof, 1945) ('Haardt').

[2] *De kosten van de procedure* (Deventer, Kluwer, 1993) and *De prijs van het gelijk* (Den Haag, Boom Juridische Uitgevers, 2007).

Developments

Although legal doctrine concerning litigation costs has to a large degree remained the same since 1945, in recent decades two issues have attracted scholarly attention. First of all in 1987 the *Hoge Raad* (the Dutch Supreme court in civil matters) ruled that the so called extra-judicial costs (*buitengerechtelijke kosten*), that is the costs that are the result of assessing damages and establishing liability and the costs of receiving payment outside of litigation, should be regarded as damages and should therefore be fully reimbursed, providing these costs are reasonable.[3] In this ruling the *Hoge Raad* in effect introduced the rules that were proposed as part of the new Civil Code that was introduced in 1992 (art 6:96 (2 sub b and c) Civil Code). In line with the proposed rules, the *Hoge Raad* ruled that extra-judicial costs do not include the costs that the winning party is normally reimbursed on the basis of the 'normal' costs shifting rules, which are known as the judicial costs. This distinction between judicial and extra-judicial costs is far from clear and remains contentious.

The second item that received attention in legal writing is the ban on some result-based fee arrangements for lawyers. The rules of conduct for lawyers forbid no-win-no-fee arrangements (arrangements where the lawyer will receive no payment if the case is lost), and *quotum pars litis* arrangements (arrangements where the lawyer will receive a percentage of the claim). These prohibitions came under scrutiny at the end of the 1990s as they were considered to be in breach of competition law.[4] Indeed, in 2002, the Dutch competition authority (*NMA*) ruled that these prohibitions were indeed in breach of competition law, but the *NMA* also ruled that they would not breach completion law if they were reintroduced in the form of a regulation.[5] The bar association introduced the regulation in 2002. Initially, the bar association proposed an experiment allowing no-win-no-fee and *quotum pars litis* arrangements in some cases, but the Minister for Justice quashed the regulation containing this proposal, since he was of the opinion that the special role of a lawyer would be compromised if a lawyer were to be allowed to use no-win-no-fee or *quotum pars litis* arrangements. The minister cited conflict of interest issues as his main concern, but also expressed the opinion that the experiment might contribute to a claim culture.[6] In a 2009 press release, the Ministry for Justice announced that legislation would be introduced allowing a lawyer to agree to so-called arrangements where the lawyer will charge a higher fee on success and no fee on losing a case. The legislation would prohibit arrangements whereby the lawyer is rewarded as a percentage of the claim.[7]

[3] HR 3 Apr 1987, *NJ* 1988, 275 (*London and Lancashire/Drenth*).

[4] PJM von Schmidt auf Altenstadt, 'Zeg eens NMA' (1999) *Advocatenblad* 195.

[5] Decision by the director general of the NMA dated 21 Feb 2002 in case 560 (*Engelgeer*), available at www.nmanet.nl.

[6] Royal Decree of 9 Mar 2005, *Stb* 123.

[7] Press release by the Ministry for Justice dated 10 Nov 2009, available at www.justitie.nl.

Role of Alternative Dispute Resolution

The Netherlands have a long standing tradition of non-governmental dispute resolution. Two main methods are used, dispute resolution boards and ombudsman-like institutions. In addition, other methods such as arbitration are used.

Of these two methods, dispute resolution boards function most like courts. These boards are set up to resolve disputes between a consumer and a professional.[8] They are principally paid for by industry. The consumer has to pay only a nominal fee, usually ranging from €25 to €125. This fee is reimbursed by the professional party if the consumer wins his case. No other cost shifting rules are applied. The dispute resolution board normally issues its ruling within a few months.[9] These boards do not replace traditional courts. The ruling of a dispute resolution board is regarded as a settlement agreement. If the parties refuse to honour the ruling, it may be enforced with the assistance of the traditional courts. In such an event, the courts will limit themselves to checking to see whether the basic rules of a fair trial were applied by the dispute resolution board.[10] If this is the case, the courts will issue a ruling enabling the prevailing party to enforce the decision of the dispute resolution board. In most cases, this will not be necessary, since the professional organisation that sponsors the dispute resolution board will monitor the compliance of its members with the rulings of the dispute resolution board. Furthermore, in most cases the professional organisation will guarantee the compliance of its members with a ruling.

In addition to dispute resolution boards, the Netherlands also boast a system of ombudsman-like institutions. As with dispute resolution boards, these institutions are funded by industry. They are usually free to the consumer. They do not have the power to issue binding rulings but rather mediate between the parties, set out guidelines in order to establish the norm that professional parties should adhere to, or verify and report whether professional parties have complied with the given norm in a specific case.

It is not easy to gauge the importance, or otherwise, of these alternative dispute resolution methods. In 2009, 11,064 new cases where brought before the dispute resolution boards[11] and an additional 10,266 cases were brought before the lease dispute resolution board.[12] No combined figures exist that give an indication of the use of ombudsman-like institutions, but it seems quite possible that the relative importance of ombudsmen exceeds the importance of dispute resolution

[8] For an overview of dispute resolution boards in the Netherlands see www.degeschillen commissie.nl. On this site 44 dispute resolution boards advertise the possibility of settling claims without judicial intervention.

[9] In their annual report the associated dispute resolution boards report an average of 5.2 month; *Jaarverslag* 2008 (Stichting Geschillencommissies voor Consumentenzaken, Hasselt (Belgium), 2008) ('Jaarverslag Geschillencommisses') 21.

[10] AS Rueb, *Compendium van het Burgerlijk Procesrecht* (Deventer, Kluwer, 2009) 328.

[11] Jaarverslag Geschillencommisses (n 9) 21.

[12] Excluding subsidy related cases.

boards. This may be illustrated by the figures from the financial services industry. That sector operates both an ombudsman and a dispute resolution board. In 2008, 6,411 complaints were filed with the ombudsman, while only 347 cases were started with their dispute resolution board.[13] In the same period, the courts of first instance had an influx of 522,400 cases that started with a summons (the traditional way of starting a case concerning a normal monetary dispute).[14] Of course, this figure includes a very large number of cases that fall outside the scope of alternative dispute resolution as described above. For example, the figure includes cases of professionals versus consumers and B2B cases. All in all, the conclusion is probably that alternative dispute resolution still only plays a complementary role, while the traditional courts continue to handle the bulk of disputes.

Principles Governing Litigation Costs in the Netherlands

In Dutch legal doctrine, four principles may be discerned that apply to litigation costs. The first principle is that litigation should not be free.[15] This principle ties in with the idea that litigation should be an *ultimum remedium*.[16] In this respect, litigation costs serve as an incentive to parties only to use litigation after all other options have been exhausted. The next principle is the principle of access to justice. The idea is that high litigation costs may unduly impede access to justice. To these two principles may be added the principle of predictability. As will become apparent, most litigation costs are calculated on the basis of a tariff, greatly enhancing their predictability. A final principle governing litigation costs is the loser pays principle. However, this principle must be regarded as rather weak, as it has no firm underpinning in substantive Dutch law. Starting litigation to give effect to perceived rights, or forcing another party to start litigation to give effect to his right, is not considered to be tortious behaviour.[17] The basis for the loser pays rule is found in the concept of *billijkheid*, a concept that may best be translated as 'fairness'.[18] According to the legislator, policy objectives also play a role in applying the concept of *billijkheid* with regard to cost shifting. The policy objective that is being served is the objective of access to justice. In serving this objective, the

[13] *Jaarverslag 2008* (Amsterdam, Klachteninstituut Financiële Dienstverlening, 2008) 10.

[14] Based on the figures reported on the website of the Dutch Central Statistic Bureau (*Centraal Bureau voor de Statistiek*) under 'Kerncijfers' on their website www.cbs.nl. These figures include small claims.

[15] HJ Snijders, CJM Klaassen and GJ Meijer, *Nederlands burgerlijk procesrecht* (Deventer, Kluwer, 2007) no 28.

[16] ibid, no 56.

[17] HR 27 Jun 1997, *NJ* 1997, 651 (*Vaston/Smith*), HR 18 Feb 2005, *NJ* 2005, 216 (*Allesbrander*) and HR 8 Sept 2006, *NJ* 2006, 492 (*Benetton/G-Star*).

[18] Haardt 18 and EM Wesseling-van Gent, 'Proceskostenveroordeling' in NVv Procesrecht (ed) *De kosten van de procedure* (Deventer, Kluwer, 1993) 2–3.

interests of two parties are weighed against each other, on the one hand, the interest of a party that has prevailed in litigation and wants to recover his or her costs, on the other hand, the interest of a party with an arguable claim who should not be deterred from instigating his claim.[19]

Proportionality is not a principle that is expressly recognised as a principle governing litigation costs in general, but it may be said to be integrated into some of the tariffs employed to calculate litigation costs. The most important tariff that incorporates proportionality as a guiding principle is the tariff on which lawyer's costs are calculated for the purpose of costs shifting.[20] This tariff employs higher rates in higher value cases. Proportionality is also of importance for extra-judicial costs (*buitengerechtelijke kosten*). These costs are, in principle, fully shiftable and no tariff applies. They are, however, governed by the 'double reasonableness test', meaning that the costs themselves have to be reasonable and it has to be reasonable to incur these costs.

Encouragement of Settlement

Dutch legal policy encourages settlements in a number of ways. As stated above, in Dutch legal culture alternative dispute resolution is encouraged. Should the parties still chose to bring their case to court, a number of other ways to encourage settlements are employed.

First of all, the rules of conduct for lawyers stipulate that a lawyer should realise that a settlement is often preferable to a litigated outcome.[21] This rule places a duty on lawyers to try to effect a settlement. If a case is still brought before the court, the court will, after the parties have stated their case in their initial briefs, order the parties and their representatives to appear for a meeting (*comparitie* or *mondelinge behandeling)*. Such a meeting has multiple purposes. Among those purposes is the exploration of the possibility of a settlement.[22] The judge may facilitate the settlement by giving a preliminary view of the case.[23] Parties are also encouraged to settle their disputes by way of mediation. For this purpose, the Netherlands have a system of court-annexed mediation. The first 2.5 hours of mediation are provided free of charge.[24] Any subsequent hours are billed to the parties, who have to decide how to divide these costs. A mediator will cost approximately €150 per hour.[25] Mediation is also covered by legal aid. Settlement is further facilitated by the possibility of the provisional examination of witnesses or a provisional report by an

[19] cf Wesseling-van Gent 3.

[20] Liquidatietarief rechtbanken en gerechtshoven to be found on www.rechtspraak.nl under 'landelijke regelingen'.

[21] Rules of conduct for lawyers 1990 ('Gedragsregels 1990') Rule 3, at www.advocatenorde.nl.

[22] For procedures that start with a summons this objective can be found in art 87 Rv. For procedures that start with a request, an explicit rule is absent; however this does not mean to say that the judge is not allowed to try to affect a settlement.

[23] HR 24 Sept 1999, *NJ* (*Bleij/Stegeman*).

[24] Policy Resolution 'Stimuleringsbijdrage conflictbemiddeling' (2009) *Stcr* 63.

[25] Acording to the website of the Dutch Judiciary, www.rechtspraak.nl.

expert.[26] These measures aim to reduce uncertainty, thereby facilitating a settlement. In some (rare) instances the law obligates parties to negotiate before they are allowed to start their suit.[27]

Funding Claims

In the Netherlands, personal funds remain the default option to fund litigation. However a great variety of alternative ways of funding litigation are available.

Benefits of Membership

Some organisations offer legal aid to their members. For example, the Road Users Association (*ANWB*) (approx four million members) and the Consumer Association (*Consumentenbond*) (approx half a million members) offer legal advice. Other organisations, most importantly the trade unions, will also assist in handling the actual litigation. The two major trade unions in the Netherlands (*FNV* and *CNV*) have about 1.75 million members. Of course, each of these organisations operates within its own area of expertise.

Legal Aid

Legal aid is relatively widely available in the Netherlands. The right to government-sponsored legal aid is enshrined in the Dutch Constitution. Article 18 paragraph 2 places the onus on the government to provide legal aid to persons with limited financial means (*minderdraagkrachtigen*). The Legal aid Act[28] is based on this constitutional provision. It stipulates that legal aid is available to both natural and legal persons. Legal aid is provided for all legal disputes.[29] As a consequence, legal aid is also available for 'normal' civil cases, such as the sale of goods, rent disputes and so on. To be eligible for legal aid, the applicant has to pass means and merit tests. Legal aid is not available for cases without apparent grounds, cases where the costs of legal aid are not in proportion to the interest at stake, and cases where the applicant can reasonably be left to manage his own interest.[30] As a rule, legal aid is also not provided in cases where the applicant is involved in a profes-

[26] Arts 186 *et seq* and 202 *et seq* Rv. See Snijders, Klaassen and Meijer 247.

[27] The division of co-owned property (art 3:185 Civil Code); see ML Tuil, *Verdelingsbeslagen* (Den Haag, Boom Juridische uitgevers, 2009) 191–193, in collective actions (art 3:305a Civil Code) and in separation cases concerning children (art 815 Rv).

[28] Law of 23 Dec 1993, houdende regelen omtrent de door de overheid gefinancierde rechtsbijstand, *Stb* 1993, 775 ('Wrb').

[29] Art 12 Wrb.

[30] Art 12 (2) Wrb.

sional capacity. To pass the means test, the applicant has to have a taxable income of less than €33,600 for couples or €23,800 for single persons.[31] Additionally, people applying for legal aid may not have taxable assets worth more than €20,315 or €40,615 for couples. Persons who are eligible for legal aid may be required to pay a contribution towards the costs of the legal aid. The contribution is dependent on the income of the applicant. Couples with an income of €23,400, or less or single persons with an income of €16,800 or less, will be required to pay €98. This contribution rises to €732 at the maximum income threshold. Legal aid does not cover the recovery of costs by the winning party.[32]

Legal Expense Insurance

Before the event legal expense insurance (BTE) has penetrated the Dutch insurance market to a large degree. The Dutch Association of Insurers (*Verbond van Verzekeraars*) reports that in 2008 at least 2,212,000 households held a BTE policy.[33] This is an increase of 22 per cent since 2004. The penetration of BTE is obviously correlated with income. 19.1 per cent of all households with a monthly income after tax of less than €1,000 held BTE policies in 2008, for households with an income of over €3,000 this figure rises to 61.1 per cent. On average 47.8 per cent of households have BTE. Between 2004 and 2008, the claim rate has dropped slightly from 13 to 12 claims per 100 policies. In 2008 on average €872 was claimed by households per claim (2004: €1,080).

In contrast to BTE, the after-the-event legal expense insurance (ATE) market has not developed in the Netherlands. It is not impossible for ATE to be offered, but none of the big insurance companies in the Netherlands advertise this product on their websites. The absence of ATE cannot be explained by any legal prohibition. Insurance law, nor any other part of Dutch law, forbids ATE. The absence of ATE in the Dutch market is most likely explained by the mitigated loser pays rule.

Funding by Lawyers

The rules of conduct for lawyers restrict lawyers' ability to offer funding. These rules forbid no-win-no-fee and *quotum pars litis* arrangements. As explained below, these prohibitions are narrowly construed by the bar association's disciplinary authorities. Nevertheless, these prohibitions are broad enough to obstruct a lawyer from funding a case. However, legal assistance on the basis of such result-based fee arrangements is offered by claims agencies. In this arrangement, the client does not deal directly with the lawyer but only through the claims agency.

[31] Art 34 Wrb.

[32] Art 38 Wrb.

[33] *Verzekerd van cijfers 2009* (The Hague, Verbond van verzekeraars, 2009) 94. In addition 1,444,000 BTE policies covering motor vehicle related claims were sold.

The client commissions the claims agency to instigate the claim on the basis of a no-win-no-fee or *quotum par litis* basis. The claims agency then commissions the lawyer on the basis of a traditional fee arrangement. The legality of these arrangements has not (yet) been tested by the bar association's disciplinary authorities.

Third Party Funding

Third party investors are not subject to the rules of conduct for lawyers and are therefore not inhibited in their ability to fund claims. However, although the phenomenon of third party funding is known in the Netherlands, it does not seem to have taken off on any wide scale. The Netherlands do, however, boast a spectacular instance of third party funding. In 1997, a claim was funded by means of securitisation, with the stocks being publicly traded. The claim concerned an accusation and subsequent prosecution of a Dutch businessman and his company for insider trading and related offences. After being acquitted the businessman and his company claimed compensation from the state for the damage cause to their reputations. They securitised their claim and the claim was traded on the Amsterdam Stock Exchange.[34] After unfavourable court rulings by the *Hoge Raad*, the claim was dropped and the stock listing ended.[35] At no point in the procedure was the legality of this funding method raised.

Collective Action

An interesting new development is the use of collective actions as a way of addressing funding problems. The last few years have seen a marked increase in collective actions. The Dutch approach to collective actions is twofold. First of all, since 1994, associations and foundations (*verenigingen* and *stichtingen*) are allowed to bring a claim that concerns the interests of a group of people with similar interests, provided the association or foundation's articles of incorporation task the association or foundation with promoting the interests at stake.[36] This collective claim is in a legal sense not identical to the sum of the claims of the people whose interests are at stake, but rather has a parallel existence. Most importantly the association or foundation does not require a power of attorney to instigate a claim on behalf of the 'class members'. If the collective claim is denied, individuals may still bring their claims. An important limitation to the possibility of bringing collective action is the fact that a collective claim may not be a claim for damages.[37] This ties

[34] *Volkskrant* 2 Oct1997, 'Flitsende start van Begaclaim op Amsterdamse effectenbeurs'. Apparently 77.5 % of the claim was securitised with 5.1 million stocks traded. The first trading day investors valued the claim of about €550 million at about €18 million.

[35] See for the ruling of the *Hoge Raad* HR 13 Oct 2006, *LJN* AV6956, *NJ* 2007. For the District Court ruling and the ruling of the Court of Appeal see Rb Den Haag, 4 Apr 2001, *LJN* AB0850 and Hof Den Haag, 14 Oct 2004, *JOR* 2004, 318.

[36] Art 3:305a (3) Civil Code.

[37] Art 3:305a Civil Code.

in with the fact that a collective claim cannot be a claim that can only be decided after assessing the situation of each individual concerned. In theory, this means that in order to receive damages or other individual redress the group members must still instigate individual litigation. In this litigation, the group members may benefit from the ruling in the collective litigation.

The second part of the Dutch approach to collective action came into force in 2005. It exists in the possibility of having a settlement pronounced legally binding upon parties that have not been involved in the settlement agreement, subject to their exercise of an opt-out option.[38] As a result of this procedure, group litigation has now taken off in Dutch legal culture. In recent years, a number of collective settlements have been pronounced binding[39] and a greater number of foundations[40] have emerged purporting to represent the interests of groups of people affected by perceived injustices. These foundations hope to affect settlements by bringing pressure on the perceived wrongdoer, either by generating media attention or bringing a collective claim. These associations usually charge a limited fee to the persons whose interests they represent. The founders of the association hope to be reimbursed by the proceeds of a settlement that will be pronounced legally binding.

Court or Process Costs

Litigation costs in the Netherlands consist of many different costs. These are (ignoring lawyers' costs, which are dealt with below): court charges, bailiff's services (either in starting the procedure or in enforcing a judgment), witness' costs and experts' costs. In general, these costs can be predicted with some degree of accuracy as most of these costs are calculated on the basis of a tariff. However, in the case of witness' and experts' costs these tariffs are considered to be too low and the commentaries report that the parties often deviate from the tariffs. This naturally diminishes the accuracy of any prediction on the size of the expected costs.

Court Charges

The system of court charges in civil cases in the Netherlands will be soon be modernised. The old law stemming from 1843[41] has been frequently updated but the

[38] Arts 1013 *et seq* Code of Civil Procedure.

[39] Hof Amsterdam 15 Jul 2009, *LJN* BJ2691 (*Vedior*); Hof Amsterdam 29 May 2009, *LJN* BI5744 (*Shell*); Hof Amsterdam 29 Apr 2009, *LJN* BI2717 (*Vie d'Or*); Hof Amsterdam 25 Jan 2007, *LJN* AZ7033 (*Duisenberg regeling*) and Hof Amsterdam 1 Jun 206, *LJN* (*DES*).

[40] From news reports it appears that only foundations and not associations are founded for this purpose. It is likely that this is explained by the fact that members influence a lot the governing bodies within associations, while foundations do not have members.

[41] Wet tarieven in burgerlijke zaken, *Stb* 1843, 37.

government is now proposing a new law.[42] This new law will simplify the old system, but will not constitute a radical break from the old system.

The explanatory documents of the proposed new law illustrate the principles behind the system of court charges. Three guiding motives for the legislator may be discerned: the user pays principle, the principle of access to justice and an ease-of-use principle. The user pays principle speaks for itself: the legislator wants the user of the court system to contribute towards the costs of the system. The legislator also recognises that ensuring that users contribute towards the costs of the system has behavioural effects on users. According to the legislator, a user pays principle encourages parties to carefully consider the need for using the court system. This effect is not the primary objective of the system of court charges, but is considered desirable.[43] The effect is also mentioned as a justification for the higher court charges for the appeals court and the *Hoge Raad*. In applying the user pays principle, the fact that the judiciary is funded though the Council for the judiciary (*Raad voor de rechtspraak*) means that the government has a fair idea of what the average costs of a certain type of case are. However, as stated before, the users of the court system are only required to pay a contribution to these costs. As a result, no great effort is put into calculating these costs exactly, other than ensuring that the revenues of the new system will match the revenues of the old system.[44]

The user pays principle is offset by the access to justice principle. In the explanatory documents, the legislator refers to the case law of the ECHR regarding court charges.[45] The principle of access to justice explains why court charges are intended to cover only part of the costs of litigation in the courts, why legal entities pay a higher court charge than individuals, and why persons qualifying for legal aid pay a fixed low rate.

The third principle that may be discerned is the ease-of-use principle. This principle is new. Under the old law it takes a lot of time to work out the applicable rate for court charges. The objective of the new law is that a court worker or lawyer should be able to see at a glance what court charge is due.

Both under the new as under the old law court charges have to be paid before the case starts.[46] In small claims cases[47] only the plaintive has to pay court charges. In other civil cases both the plaintive and the defendant have to pay court charges.

[42] *Kamerstukken II* 2008–2009, 31 758. The bill is now before the upper house of parliament (*Eerste Kamer*).

[43] *Kamerstukken II* 2008–2009, 31 758, no 6, 3.

[44] *Kamerstukken II* 2008–2009, 31 758, no 3, 3–4.

[45] *Kamerstukken II* 2008–2009, 31 758, no 3, 5–6.

[46] Art 2 Wet tarieven in burgerlijke zaken and art 3 of the proposed law 'Wet griffierechten burgerlijke zaken'.

[47] Small claims cases in the Netherlands are cases with a financial interest of €5,000 or less and certain types of case such as rent and labour related cases independent of the financial interest of the case (art. 93 Rv). At the moment the government is proposing to raise the financial interest threshold to €25,000 and including cases related to sales by professionals to consumers independent of the financial interest of the case. See Evaluatiewet modernisering rechterlijke organisatie, *Kamerstukken II* 2008/09–2009/10, 32 021.

At present, a lot of different rates apply to different types of cases. The most important rate is the rate for cases with a monetary claim. In that case, parties each have to pay 2.2 per cent of the amount claimed with a minimum of €313. The maximum amount that a party has to pay is €4,938. If the defendant is a natural person he pays a maximum of €1,185.

Under the new rules, only three different tariffs will apply in civil cases in the courts of first instance. The first rate is for cases with no clear monetary value or cases where an amount of less than €12,500 is claimed. The second rate will apply for cases where more than €12,500 and less than €100,000 is claimed. The third rate will apply tocases where more than €100,000 is claimed. The first rate will be €255 for individuals and €560 for legal entities. The second rate will be €580 for individuals and €1,165 for legal entities. The third rate will be €1,395 for individuals and €3,490 for legal entities. Higher rates are charged in the courts of appeal and the *Hoge Raad.*

At present, litigants who qualify for legal aid only have to pay one quarter or half of the court charges, depending on their income,[48] but the opponent is required to pay the remainder if he loses the case. The legislature is proposing to change this arrangement and set fixed court charges for people qualifying for legal aid. These charges will be €70 in first instance, €270 for appeal and €280 for cases at the *Hoge Raad.*[49]

Assistance of a Bailiff

In the Netherlands, the assistance of a bailiff is required at two stages of the proceedings. First of all, in most civil cases the bailiff's services are required to serve the summons (*dagvaarding*), the document necessary to start the litigation. Secondly, the services of the bailiff are required to enforce a judgment in the event that the losing party refuses voluntarily to honour the verdict. In that case, the bailiff may be authorised by the prevailing party to, for example, garnish the wages of the losing party by attachment. The price for the *ex officio* services of a bailiff is strictly regulated.[50] The law provides a list of actions conducted by the bailiff with a fixed price.[51] The most important of these actions is undoubtedly the summons that initiates most civil litigation (€72.25). The rate applicable to the enforcement of a verdict varies with the steps the bailiff has to take. For example, attachment of a bank account will cost €151.44, while garnishing wages costs €107.79 plus €9.21 per month.

[48] Arts 17–18a Wet tarieven in burgerlijke zaken

[49] *Kamerstukken II* 2008–2009, 31 758, no 3, 3.

[50] In the Netherlands the bailiffs are also allowed to provide other services, such as extra judicial debt recovery. The prices of these services are not regulated.

[51] Besluit tarieven ambtshandelingen gerechtsdeurwaarders, *Stb* 2001, 325, ammended in *Stb* 2001, 600.

Witness of Fact

A witness of fact is obliged to appear if summoned to give evidence.[52] He is entitled to compensation for his time and for travel expenses.[53] The witness must be paid at the end of his testimony.[54] The law provides for a tariff that applies both in criminal and civil cases.[55] Under this tariff a witness is entitled to €6.81 per hour of travel or testimony.[56] This is a little below the minimum wage for an adult in the Netherlands.[57] However, some commentaries report that these rates are not used in practice as they are considered too low.[58] Indeed, the standard forms that the judiciary make available to claim expenses leave it up to the witness to put down a higher hourly rate.[59]

Expert

Dutch law provides for two ways in which an expert can be employed. First of all there is the court-appointed expert.[60] This expert may be asked to make a report or be called to testify. Secondly, a party can employ an expert to make a report and add the report to his brief. Such an expert may also be called to testify.[61] A court-appointed expert will be reimbursed by the court out of the money that the party who calls the expert is required to deposit. A party-employed expert is reimbursed by the party concerned. For court-appointed experts, the law provides for extensive regulation of the maximum rates that an expert may charge.[62] However, on closer examination, most of the rates that this regulation provides for concern the actions of experts in criminal cases. For civil cases, the most important rate is the general rate for scientific expert, which is set at €81.23 per hour excluding taxes.[63] If a court appointed expert is called to testify, the same rate applies per hour of testimony. These rates do not bind the parties. Parties are allowed to agree higher rates and, since an expert is under no duty to accept his appointment, deviation from the maximum rate is common.[64] No regulation applies to party-appointed

[52] Art 165(2) Rv.

[53] Art 182 Rv.

[54] AIM Van Mierlo and JH Van Dam-Lely, *Procederen bij dagvaarding in eerste aanleg* (Deventer, Kluwer, 2003) 318–19.

[55] Art 1 Besluit tarieven in burgerlijke zaken read in conjuction with Besluit tarieven in strafzaken 2003.

[56] Art 2 Besluit tarieven in burgerlijke zaken read in conjuction with art. 8 Besluit tarieven in strafzaken 2003.

[57] cf art 8 Wet minumumloon en minimumvakantietoeslag.

[58] CJC Van Nispen, 'Aantekening bij art 182' in AIM Van Mierlo, CJJC Van Nispen and MV Polak (eds), *Tekst en Commentaar Burgerlijke rechtsvordering* (Deventer, Kluwer, 2008) no 2.

[59] The form may be found on www.rechtspraak.nl/Naar+de+rechter/Formulieren/.

[60] Art 194 Rv.

[61] Art 200 Rv.

[62] Art 2 Besluit tarieven in burgerlijke zaken read in conjuction with Besluit tarieven in strafzaken 2003.

[63] Art. 8 Besluit tarieven in strafzaken 2003.

[64] GR Rutgers, 'Aantekeningen bij art. 199' in EM Wesseling-van Gent, P Vlas and M Ynzonides (eds), *Burgerlijke Rechtsvordering* (Deventer, Kluwer, 2002) art. 199 aant. 2.

experts. A party may pay them market rates. However, if a party-appointed expert is called to testify, for the purpose of costs, he is treated as the equivalent of an ordinary witness. In all likelihood the party that employs the expert will supplement this rate to achieve a market rate.

Lawyers' Costs

Hourly rates remain the default for lawyer's fees in the Netherlands. However, a lawyer and his client are allowed to make their own arrangements and lawyers will offer other arrangements. A number of fee arrangements are suggested on the bar association website. These are hourly rates, an outcome-based approach where the lawyer charges a lower (hourly) rate if the case is lost and a higher hourly rate if the case is won, a fixed sum for the case, a fixed sum for a year's work, and a special rate for the collection of debts.[65]

The freedom of lawyers to agree to outcome-based fees is limited by the rules of conduct for lawyers. These rules forbid no-win-no-fee arrangements[66] and *quotum pars litis* arrangements.[67] These prohibitions are based on the principle that a lawyer should be independent in executing his office.[68] These prohibitions are subject to some exceptions. First of all, the rules of conduct specifically allow *quotum pars litis* arrangements that fall within the customary practice established in debt collection cases.[69] Secondly, arrangements that provide for a higher fee for a lawyer in the event that a case is won have been allowed by the court of discipline of the bar association (*Hof van Disipline*).[70] In its ruling, the court narrowly construed the prohibition on *quotum pars litis* arrangements. The court ruled that arrangements where the lawyer charges a base rate that applies regardless of the outcome and an uplift on this base rate upon a successful outcome are allowed, provided that base rate will cover the lawyer's expenses and provides for a modest income. The uplift may be expressed as a mark-up on the base fee or as a percentage of the result of the case.[71] Thirdly, the client and the lawyer may agree that they

[65] www.advocatenorde.nl/algemeen/hoe_rekent_een_advocaat.asp.

[66] Rule 26 (2).

[67] Rule 26 (3).

[68] Rule 2 (1).

[69] Within the ambit of the rule of conduct 'debt collection' is the work a lawyer does to collect a package of debts where no legal defence is anticipated. In the explanation of this rule it is noted that *quotum pars litis* agreements where possible for debt collection cases when the bar association still published advisory rates as these rates had a special rate based on a *quotum pars litis* arrangement. When the bar association stopped publishing advisory rates, the rules of conduct were amended to reflect the fact that *quotum pars litis* arrangements are allowed as long as they stay within the boundaries of established practice in debt collection cases. The argument for this exception to the rules is that the *quotum pars litis* arrangements in debt collection cases have never caused any problems.

[70] As expressed by Hof van Dicipline 9 Feb 1998, no 2474, *Advocatenblad* (1999) 346.

[71] In the rules on result-based fees (*Verordening op de praktijkuitoefening (onderdeel Resultaatgerelateerde Beloning)*) the bar association expressly states that the ruling of the disciplinary court is respected and should be considered when applying the rules.

will fix the fee upon the conclusion of the case based on the value of the work of the lawyer for the client.[72] Lastly, a lawyer may limit his fee if a case is lost.

These exceptions notwithstanding, the prohibitions on no-win-no-fee and *quotum pars litis* arrangements are enforced by the bar association. If a party feels his lawyer has violated these prohibitions he may complain to the bar association's disciplinary authorities. The president of the local bar association (*deken*) may also bring a complaint against a lawyer. As mentioned above, no-win-no-fee is offered though claims agencies.

The rules of conduct stipulate that a lawyer should discuss the financial consequences of a commission and explain the way he will charge his client.[73] The lawyer should also inform his client if he foresees that his bill will be in excess of the amount originally estimated. This implies that a lawyer should give an estimate in advance. The bar association website states, with regard this matter, that it is hard to give a precise estimate. Qualitative research suggests that clients are dissatisfied with the vague estimates lawyers give or that no estimate is made.[74]

There is no tariff regulating the size of lawyers' fees in the Netherlands.[75] In the past, the bar association used to publish advisory rates. This practise was abandoned as a result of competition law issues.[76] The only requirement for lawyers' rates may be found in the rules of conduct. These specify that the amount a lawyer charges must be 'reasonable'.[77]

In civil cases, the requirement that a lawyer's fee must be reasonable is enforced through a special procedure. The rules of conduct for lawyers[78] obliges a lawyer to inform his client of the possibility of requesting the supervisory board of the local bar association (*Raad van Toezicht*) to check the lawyer's bill.[79] The idea is that the client should have an easily accessible procedure to verify his lawyer's bills by experts. Although this idea is sympathetic, in practice the existence of this procedure leads to complicated jurisdictional issues in cases where a lawyer tries to collect his bills. The reason is that the competence of the board and of the normal courts is mutually exclusive, and the competence of the board is limited.[80] As a result, the legislator is now proposing to scrap the procedure before the board as soon as legislation has been enacted obliging lawyers to submit to the jurisdiction of a dispute resolution board.[81] These dispute resolution boards will

[72] Vademecum Advocatuur, Wet en Regelgeving, Praktijkvoering, Financiën.

[73] Rule 26 (1).

[74] O Couwenberg, MJ Schol and HB Winter, *Toegang tot advocaten. Een kwalitatief onderzoek naar belemmeringen in de toegang tot advocaten voor betalende particulieren en MKB-bedrijven* (Groningen, RUG Faculteit der Rechtsgeleerdheid & Pro Facto, 2009) 21 and 37.

[75] Strictly speaking this is not true. The law on charges in civil matters (*Wet tarieven in burgerlijke zaken*) still contains some antiquated rates a lawyer is allowed to charge. These rates include the rate of 0.41 euro for writing a letter and an hourly rate of 0.82 euro (art. 29). Obviously these rates are not used. Why the legislator bothered to convert these amounts into euros is anyone's guess.

[76] eg JLRA Huydecoper, 'Big Bang?' (1996) *Advocatenblad* 965.

[77] Rule 25.

[78] Rule 27.

[79] Art 32 Wet tarieven in burgerlijke zaken.

[80] PJM von Schmidt auf Altenstadt, 'Kroniek kosten' (2003) *TCR* 70.

[81] Kamerstukken II 2008–2009 31 758, no 6, 20.

be competent to address all problems in the relationship between a lawyer and his client.

Cost Shifting

Under Dutch law, costs are shifted on the basis of a mitigated loser pays rule. This rule is made up of two parts. First of all, almost all litigation costs, such as bailiff's costs, witness' costs, court fees etc are fully shifted onto the losing party. The one exception is the losing party's lawyer's costs. These costs are calculated on the basis of a tariff, the *liquidatietarief*.[82] Since this tariff leads only to a small percentage of the lawyer's costs being deemed shiftable, and since lawyer's costs make up a large part of the total litigation costs, the effect is a mitigated loser pays rule. The size of the irrecoverability gap will depend on the nature of the lawyer's services. With regards to 'bespoke' lawyering, lawyers estimate the size of the irrecoverability gap to be as large as 90 per cent.[83] For more standard work, such as bulk debt recovery work, the gap may be smaller, ranging from 25 per cent to 50 per cent.

The mitigation of the loser pays rule is based on the way cost shifting is regarded in the Netherlands. Although article 237 of the Code of Civil Procedure expressly stipulates that the losing party has to pay his opponent's costs, Dutch legal doctrine has held since the second half of the nineteenth century that this rule lacks a solid basis in substantive Dutch Law.[84] Under Dutch legal doctrine, the loser of an action is not considered to have acted tortiously by starting litigation or forcing the other side to litigate. The Dutch cost shifting rules are instead held to be based on the principle of fairness (*billijkheid*). This principle is not a very firm foundation on which to base extensive cost shifting. In addition, the legislator has explicitly chosen to protect the interest of the losing party against high shiftable costs.[85]

The reason that only lawyer's fees, out of all litigation costs, are only partially shifted, while other costs are fully shifted, may be explained by a peculiarity of the Dutch legal profession. Until recently, Dutch law distinguished two roles for lawyers. These were the lawyer who would draw up any briefs (*advocaat*) and the lawyer who would file the briefs (*procureur*).[86] The fee of the latter was, until the 1950s, regulated, while the fee of the former was for parties to agree upon. Initially, the cost shifting rules would only allow the fee of the *procureur* to be shifted, since only this fee was considered absolutely necessary for litigation.[87] The fee of the *advocaat* was not shiftable. Later, the regulations for the fee of a *procureur* were

[82] The *Liquidatietarief* may be found on www.rechtspraak.nl under 'landelijke regelingen'.

[83] The author arrived at this figure by informally polling lawyers at post-academic courses he taught in the autum of 2009.

[84] Haardt (n 1) 16–19.

[85] ibid, 9.

[86] A Dutch lawyer was, however, entitled to serve in both capacities, as the law provided that any *advoacaat*, was also a *procureur* (Art 15 (old) *Advocatenwet*).

[87] Haardt (n 1) 89 and 100–101.

withdrawn. However, for the purpose of cost shifting, the bar and the bench agreed upon a tariff to calculate the lawyer's fees for the purpose of cost shifting, the *Liquidatietarief*. Although this tariff now encompasses both the work of the now abolished *porocureur* and of the *advocaat*, the notion that lawyers' fees can only be partially shifted remains.

The *Liquidatietarief* works by assigning points to certain acts a lawyer has to undertake during the course of the litigation. For example, the *Liquidatietarief* assigns one point for composing a brief, one point for attending the examination of witnesses and two points for oral pleadings. The number of points accumulated in a case is then multiplied by the applicable rate for a case. This rate depends on the amount at stake.

The judge may deviate from the mitigated loser pays rules in a number of ways. First, the judge has considerable leeway in determining which party should be considered the winning party (or the losing party).[88] The judge may determine that no party should be considered the winning or losing party. A judge may also rule that a party is only partly to be considered as the winning party.[89] To the extent that a party is not deemed to be the prevailing party, he cannot recover his costs.[90] Although it follows that the judge may apply the loser pays rule anywhere from zero to a hundred per cent, in practice judges either rule that one party is deemed to be the losing party, or that both parties are deemed to be the losing party. The intermediate options remain largely unused. The explanation for this might be that as the irrecoverability gap is already very large, judges do not consider it necessary to 'punish' a partially losing party further. Another explanation might be that because the amount at stake is low, lawyers do not put a lot of effort into trying to assign blame for the litigation for the purpose of cost shifting.

In theory, the judge is also entitled to deviate from the *Liquidatietarief*, since this tariff is only an agreement between the bar and the bench that does not bind the judge in a strictly legal sense.[91] In practice, however, judges hardly ever deviate from the tariff.[92]

Some exceptions to the loser pays rule apply. In some cases, no cost shifting is applied. No cost shifting is the norm for non-contentious cases, ie cases where the intervention of a judge is not needed to resolve a dispute, but only to achieve a certain result. An example is the ruling that a man is not the father of a child.[93] The idea in these cases is that no party can be 'blamed' for the litigation. No cost shifting is also the norm in cases where a close connection exists between the parties, for example between (former) spouses, brothers and sisters, and so on.[94] In these cases, the ground for the absence of cost shifting is found in the relation between

[88] HR 22 Jan 1988, *NJ* 1988, 415 (*Land Aruba/Van Kessel*).

[89] Art 237 Rv and WH Heemskerk, *Hoofdlijnen van Nederlands bugerlijk procesrecht* (Amsterdam, Elsevier Juridisch, 2009) 138.

[90] Art 237 Rv and ibid, 138.

[91] As is expressly recognised in the preamble to the *Liquidatietarief*.

[92] eg Hof Amsterdam 16 Dec 2008, LJN BH8898.

[93] HR 20 Jan 1967, *NJ*, 83 (*Laret qq/X*) and HR 6 Oct 2006, *NJ* 2006 (*Baumgarten qq/X*).

[94] Art 237 Rv.

the parties. The idea is that in such close relations conflicts are not lightly litigated and that cost shifting would impede reconciliation between the parties.[95]

In some instances full costs shifting is applied. First of all, extra-judicial costs are in principle fully shifted.[96] The reason is that these costs are regarded as part of the damages for which the plaintive is claiming compensation. The result of this approach is one-way pro-plaintive costs shifting. Since litigation, or forcing another party to litigate, to give effect to a claim is not regarded as tortious, the extra-judicial costs of the defendant cannot be shifted.

Full cost shifting is also applied in intellectual property (IP) enforcement cases as a result of the implementation of the IP enforcement directive.[97] An interesting development is the fact that for these cases tariffs have also been introduced.[98] However, these tariffs are not used to determine the amount of the costs shifted but only as an indication to determine whether the costs that are made are reasonable and proportional in the sense of article 1019h Rv (article 14 of the directive).

Costs Reduction Strategies

The Netherlands have no cost reduction strategies employed by the courts like cost capping orders or costs protection orders. The Netherlands do, however, try to limit the costs incurred as a result of a trial. The most important way is by limiting the amount of expensive evidence gathering, like the examination of witnesses or the appointment of experts. The judge will only order such procedures if he determines that there is a genuine need for them, such as when the parties disagree on a specific issue and this issue is relevant to adjudicating the case. If there is a genuine need for an evidence gathering procedure, the judge enjoys full discretion as to whether or not to appoint an expert.[99] With regard to witnesses, the judge's discretion is narrower. The judge is obliged to order the examination of a witness if there is a genuine need for such examination and the evidence the witness may bring forward is relevant to deciding the case.[100] The judge is not allowed to speculate on whether a witness would be able to remember the relevant facts or how reliable the evidence a witness would give would be.[101] Parties are free to introduce

[95] Haardt (n 1) 51 and 58; S van der Aa and P Sluijter, 'Belaging ende proceskosten in familierechtelijke relaties. Compensatie als misplaatste compassie?' (2009) *Nederlands Juristenblad* 2480–481 and Hof Leeuwarden 19 Nov 2002, *LJN* AF0713.

[96] See above under 'developments'.

[97] Directive 2004/48/EC of the European Parliament and the Council of 29 April 2004 on the enforcement of intellectual property rights [2004] OJ L 157/32.

[98] Indicatietarieven in IE-zaken to be found on www.rechtspraak.nl under 'Landelijke regelingen'.

[99] Art 194 Rv.

[100] Art 166 Rv.

[101] Eg HR 1 Apr 2005, *NJ* 2006, 5 (*Zeegers/Nieuwkamp*) and HR 6 Apr 2001, *NJ* 2002, 385 (*VNP/Havrij*).

written evidence.[102] The parties may, however, try to circumvent the judge's supervision by requesting provisional evidence gathering procedures. Case law severely limits the judge's discretion to refuse such procedures.[103] The Netherlands has no formal pre-action protocols. Within some areas of the law, such as insurance law, there is some call for such protocols. The role of such protocols is also played by a relatively active judge, who may, after the initial briefs, order the parties to elaborate on certain arguments or introduce certain documents into evidence.[104] After provisional evidence gathering procedures the judge also has an opportunity to give similar instructions, or try to affect a settlement.[105]

Two other ways the Netherlands try to lower litigation costs are the promotion of alternative dispute resolution and maintaining the quality of the law. In the last two decades a great number of laws have been re-codified. As a rule, this process does not result in a radical break from the past, but rather produces systematisation of the law, as well as the incorporation and clarification of case law.

Incentives

Little or no empirical research has been done on the incentives that the Dutch cost rules provide. Based on general law and economics theory, one might conjecture that the lack of full cost shifting lowers the probability that a plaintiff will start a case, since he will have to bear a substantial percentage of his litigation costs. On the other hand, since the plaintiff who loses his case will only have to bear a small percentage of his opponent's litigation costs, a plaintiff might be more willing to start a relatively weak case than under full cost shifting.

The defendant will probably be less inclined to settle a case than under full cost shifting, as he will only have to bear a small part of his opponent's costs. This holds especially true for weak cases, where otherwise the defendant would otherwise be reasonably assured that he would have to bear all his opponent's costs.

The costs rules probably provide both the plaintiff and the defendant with more incentives to monitor their lawyers in order to keep costs down than full cost shifting would do.[106] It also provides them with incentives to take out legal expenses insurance. The low amount at stake and the relatively easily applied laws probably

[102] HR 19 Mar 1999, *NJ* 1999, 496 (*Tankink/Hartman*).

[103] See eg for the provisional examination of witnesses HR 11 Febr 2005, *NJ* 2005, 442 (*Frog People Mover/Floriade 2002*) and HR 21 Nov 2008, *NJ* 2008, 608 (*Udo/Renault*). See eg for the provisional appointment of experts HR 30 Mar 2007, *NJ* 2007, 189 (*Aegon/D*) and HR 19 Dec 2003, *NJ* 2004, 584 (*Wustenhoff/Gebuis*).

[104] Art 23 Rv.

[105] Art 191 Rv.

[106] Some tentative support for this conjecture may be derived from MG Faure and NJ Philipsen, 'Honoraria van belangenbehartigers in letselschadeschadezaken: een dossieranalyse (2001–2006)' (2008) *AV&S* 316–29 who investigate the rise in extra judicial costs. They show that extra judicial costs have risen more as compared to for example inflation or wages. They suggest that this sharper rise may be attributed to the lack of monitoring of cost as extra judicial costs are as a rule fully shifted.

account for the absence of 'costs wars'. The fact that the shiftable costs are relatively low and reasonably predictable means that test cases may be undertaken at relatively low risk.

Duration of Procedures

The duration of a case is obviously largely determined by the complexity of the case. An uncontested small claims case was, on average in 2008, processed within one week. In the same period, a contested uncomplicated small case took 19 weeks to process, while a complicated case took 47 weeks. Normal contested civil cases at the district court level take 61 weeks to process. In the courts of appeal, civil cases take on average 71 weeks to process. [107]

Delay in any cases may marginally raise costs for the parties. Most costs, such as court charges, bailiff's fees and witness's fees, remain fixed. Lawyers' fees may marginally rise as lawyers have to fulfil administrative requirements, such as extra procedural meetings. Delay may also warrant extra contact between client and lawyer.

[107] Jaarverslag 2008 (Raad voor de Rechtspraak, Den Haag 2008) 68.

15

The Netherlands: Policy Observations

PAULIEN M M VAN DER GRINTEN*

Introduction

The Civil Justice Project carried out by the Centre for Social Legal Studies and the Institute of European and Comparative Law at Oxford University is an exciting and stimulating project for everyone involved in the field of Civil Justice. It offers a platform for discussion and an opportunity to exchange information, knowledge and practical experience in Europe and in the rest of the world. All sorts of studies, pilots and other initiatives from around the world inspire both legal practice and policy makers to find solutions for the ever existing difficulties with cost and funding in civil litigation. Tackling only some of the cost and funding issues would already be quite an achievement. We all know how—especially for lower value claims—cost and funding are the main obstacles to access to justice.

One of the main obstacles to access to the courts for both individuals and legal entities is lawyers' fees. Even the highest court fees do not come anywhere near the fees charged by lawyers at an hourly rate. Bearing this in mind, what are the options to reduce lawyers' fees or at least to reduce their burden on litigants? Are there special solutions in mass claims? My observations on behalf of the Dutch government will not provide you with any final answers from the Netherlands. They may just help to give a complete picture by also looking at a government's perspective on some of the issues. The first sections below focus on options directly related to lawyers' fees and the costs and funding of civil procedure. The following sections take a broader perspective and include substantive law, enforcement and further research as options for making civil justice more cost efficient.

Lower Fixed Lawyers' Fees?

Lower fixed fees would have a positive effect both on access to justice and on lowering court awards for legal costs. However, for the Netherlands, statutory lawyers'

* Co-ordinating Legal Adviser, Ministry of Justice of the Netherlands

fees in the 'free market' of legal services are an unlikely option. In recent years a reverse trend towards introduction of free market rates has taken place, even for civil notaries and public enforcement officers whose tasks have a much closer link to the government's public authority. Moreover, it is unlikely to be Europe's way forward in reducing costs, since national competition authorities and the European Commission will not be keen on fixed fees.

Different Types of Contingency Fees for Lawyers?

At the other end of the scale, the option would be to leave the issue of cost and funding completely to the free market, in which lawyers offer their services to clients on the basis of different types of contingency fees. A great variety of those already exist in some countries (success fee, no-win-no-fee, no-cure-no-pay).

In the Netherlands, there is an on-going debate as to whether no-cure-no-pay should be allowed. Lawyers have promoted its use especially in personal injury cases. The Netherlands Bar Association used its regulatory powers to introduce no-cure-no-pay as a possible remuneration method for lawyers' services. However, subsequent Ministers of Justice and Secretaries of State have used their powers first to annul this rule before it could enter into force and then, in 2006, to announce measures to prohibit contingency fees in the Netherlands. Nevertheless, those measures have not been adopted so far and the pros and cons are still being weighted.

The main argument against no-cure-no-pay or similar mechanisms would be that the lawyer's own interest in the outcome of the case creates false incentives for the lawyer's handling of the case. Moreover, if the case is won, a significant part of the actual compensation meant to cover the victim's damage goes to the lawyer instead of the victim. Especially in mass cases (where funding is crucial) no-cure-no-pay leads to the lawyers' interests becoming a central issue in solving the mass dispute and to sometimes disproportionate remuneration for them, which is detrimental to (the amounts of compensation paid to) victims. To put it more bluntly, there is a risk that lawyers in their capacity of litigation funders become too eager and that this may result in a lawyers' paradise rather than a victims' paradise.

At the same time it is entirely clear that parties and their lawyers will look—and must look—for fee arrangements that both enhance access to justice and are commercially attractive. From a policy perspective, we should accept that individual parties will always keep looking at all possible options to fund their litigation.

Special Purpose Vehicles and Third Party Funding?

Another options might be to fund litigation through special purpose vehicles (SPVs) or third party funders. This type of funding is most likely to be found either in very complex and expensive individual litigation or in mass claims. In the Netherlands, some mass claims have been funded by private means, through SPVs acting on behalf of individual claimants. Those individual claimants whose cases are part of the mass claim contribute to the funding of the SPV. The SPVs are usually set up and run by lawyers. Contrary to the general tendency in individual cases, in mass claims we therefore see a tendency towards a more important role for lawyers to co-ordinate and set up a mass litigation. Up to now this has certainly led to better access to justice in those cases. Fairly recently, the first commercial third party funders have also entered the Dutch arena.[1]

But the more mass claims become a 'market', the more questions arise regarding supervision of the SPV (and its means) and of the third-party-funder, mechanisms to prevent the private interests of funding vehicles prevailing over the interest of claimants, and their effect on lawyers' fees, on costs and on settlements and so on. At this stage, I would not dare to predict the effect of third party funding of claims on lawyers' fees. It could result in lower lawyers' fees, because of better control and supervision by the commercial third party funder who protects his own interests. Or it could, on the contrary, lead to extremely high lawyers' fees, as the lawyers may feel a lesser moral obligation to limit their fees, since it is not the client himself who has to pay for them.

It is the task of policy makers to develop a view on this and to take action accordingly. If we fail to do this, the litigation market will find its own answers, whether we like them or not. Innovative entrepreneurs will still try and make a living out of other people's legal problems. Since this is happening right now, and has already led to abusive practices, the question is no longer *whether* we should regulate this, but rather *how* we should do this in order to prevent further abuse.[2] Exchange of knowledge and information and further empirical research, both at national and at European and international levels, can help us here.

[1] In the Airlines cartel case the branch organisation of transport companies announced it was bringing an action against the airlines and mentioned explicitly that a commercial third-party funder (Claims Funding International) would help the to build their claim against the cartelists.

[2] eg in Oct 2009, the bankruptcy of the Dutch *DSB-bank* was caused directly by the call from the spokesman of a claims vehicle, claiming to act on behalf of clients of the bank with a dispute regarding their mortgage, to collect all their savings from that bank *in order* to willingly cause the bank to collapse. In reality the SPV turned out to represent less than one hundred claimants.

Full Legal Costs Awards as a General Rule?

As explained in section 2, we do not have fixed lawyers fees in the Netherlands. What we do have is a 'loser pays' system based on lawyers' costs calculated at a fixed rate (*liquidatietarief*). The fixed rate is based on the value of the claim and the procedural steps taken, for which a writ of summons, statement of claim, oral hearing or pleadings would each represent a procedural stage. For example, for a claim worth €100,000, the winner could claim just over €1,400 per stage from the loser, regardless of the hourly fee and the total sum paid by the winner to his own lawyer. In an average case (writ of summons, oral hearing, further statement of claim, judgment) this would result in a total cost reward for lawyers' fees of less than €4,500.[3] The actual amount charged by the winner's lawyer might be twice as high or more, thus leaving the winner responsible for the greater part of his own costs.

However unfair this may seem, the idea behind it is one of access to justice. By limiting the lawyers' costs to be paid if the case is lost, the risk of litigating the case also becomes limited. This improves the parties' access to the court but at the same time leaves them with a substantial amount of costs they will have to bear themselves, regardless of the outcome of the case.

Full legal costs awards, meaning that the winner is entitled to compensation from the loser for the integral costs paid by the winner to his own lawyer, might seem to improve access to justice, especially from a weaker-party-claimant's perspective. Indeed, if he can litigate his claim successfully, this weaker-party-claimant will not have to worry about the high fees he paid his lawyer. But beware of risks for the claimant who loses his case and then has to bear the actual legal costs of the other party. This might turn out to be a serious hurdle even to starting litigation.

In the Netherlands the need for parties to have predictable costs risks was illustrated fairly recently by intellectual property (IP) lawyers and their clients in the application of the IP Enforcement Directive.[4] This Directive aims at improving the position of rightholders who want to act against piracy and other IP infringements by giving them more tools in civil procedure (seizure of evidence, disclosure and integral costs awards). The introduction of the European rule on integral costs awards in IP infringement cases resulted in a clear decline in IP litigation in the Netherlands and reduced access to justice. Rightholders and their lawyers thought the costs too unpredictable and did not dare take the risk of litigating their infringement cases. According to those involved, the increased settlement rate that followed was not the result of a positive incentive to co-operate but completely

[3] For exact amounts and calculations see http://www.rechtspraak.nl/Naar+de+rechter/Landelijke+regelingen/Sector+civiel+recht/Liquidatietarief+rechtbanken+en+gerechtshoven.htm (last consulted on 20 Oct, 2009).

[4] Directive 2004/48/EC of the European Parliament and the Council of 29 Apr 2004 concerning the Enforcement of Intellectual Property Rights (OJEC L 195).

fear-driven. Within a year of the entry into force of the Directive, courts and IP lawyers agreed on guidelines they would use to calculate the costs and thereby make them more predictable for the parties.

(Compulsory) Insurance for Legal Expenses?

Private insurance for legal expenses is widespread in the Netherlands. This type of insurance usually covers lawyers' fees, court costs and the other party's legal costs if the case is lost by the insured party (at a fixed rate). Internationally, this could be one of the factors that may help to keep the cost of individual parties in civil litigation within acceptable limits (the insurance premium). The Netherlands has considered the possibility of compulsory insurance for expenses. However, this puts a huge and unattractive burden on governments in terms of guaranteeing access for all to an insurance policy, supervising the premiums, supervising the insurers' compliance with the rules for this particular type of compulsory insurance, providing for safeguards if people do not take out the insurance and so on. Direct funding by governments through legal aid might even be cheaper.

Less—Compulsory—Legal Representation Before the Courts?

In the Netherlands, we see a tendency to have less compulsory legal representation. In July 2009, a bill was submitted to Parliament raising the amount above which legal representation is required from €5,000 to €25,000. This could reduce the costs of civil procedure by excluding lawyers' fees. In practice, claimants choose to use a representative in cases below €5,000. But in those cases this representative is often a bailiff and not a lawyer. However, the more complex the case, the more parties need legal expertise to truly enforce their access to justice. The Dutch legal aid scheme provides for legal aid also in cases where there is no requirement for legal representation.[5] I expect the trend towards less compulsory representation by lawyers will continue in individual cases. But this will not lead to substantive costs reduction.

[5] However, there is a relevance test for low value claims below €180, which threshold may possibly be increased to €500 in the near future (Statute on Legal Aid ('*Wet op de rechtsbijstand*), s 12 para 2b. together with Regulation on Legal Aid Criteria ('*Besluit rechtsbijstand- en toevoegcriteria*'), s 4 para 2 and proposed legislation to be known from *Staatscourant* of 9 Oct2009, 15173.

Collective Solutions In Legal Aid

In the Netherlands, we have only just begun to look into the possibilities for collective legal aid as a means of improving access to justice and reducing costs in mass claims. All institutions involved in funding civil litigation, including private insurers of legal expenses and our Legal Aid office, are tentatively looking at the possibility of tenders by our Legal Aid Office for lawyers to deal with a bundle of mass claims instead of providing each individual claimant with his own lawyer. The money saved by having only one or a few lawyers could be used to fund the necessary research or experts.

Another possibility we see is to give more room for the granting of legal aid to legal entities like the Dutch Consumers Organisation to bring a collective action. The Dutch rules on collective action[6] do not allow a collective claim for pecuniary damages. Still, financing a collective action to get a decision of the court on the unlawfulness of the other party's behaviour or his breach of contract would lead to better access to justice and more effective legal aid in mass claims. It could turn out to be highly efficient to finance the collective action by such a legal entity *first*. The outcome in the collective action will usually solve many of the issues to be raised in all the individual cases waiting behind it.

More Accessible, Efficient Courts?

Reducing costs in civil litigation could also start from a different angle. Shaping our rules of civil procedure to make them both access-friendly and efficient will help to make the cost of civil procedures acceptable. If a case goes to court in the Netherlands the courts will try and assist the parties and their lawyers in reaching an early settlement of the case. The settlement rate at the court of first instance is about 50 per cent of all civil cases, most of which are settled at or just after the first oral hearing. Moreover, Dutch civil procedure is based on a funnelmodel. The taking of evidence is only done in as far as a party's statement is both disputed and considered relevant by the court for the outcome of the case, and only after the court has given its view as to which party bears the burden of proof.[7] The intention is to prevent front loading of costs and, thereby, to keep the costs of litigation within acceptable limits. However, improvements can be made here, especially in relation to an appeal to our Appeals Court (*gerechtshof*) or cassation with the Dutch Supreme Court (*Hoge Raad der Nederlanden*) where cost are still a real hurdle.

[6] Dutch Civil Code, art 3:305a

[7] Implicit in the Dutch Code of Civil Procedure, arts 149 and 150.

A recent legislative project concerns access to justice for simple claims with a Wizard-based electronic standard form.[8] The Wizard leads the claimant or the defendant through all the important issues to be completed in the standard form. This should help citizens to litigate their simple disputes without the help of a lawyer. If this procedure proves a success, we will have better access to justice at lower costs in simple cases up to €25,000.[9]

In personal injury cases, a bill on 'partial dispute' procedures will help the parties to solve their dispute out of court.[10] Either party can ask the court to intervene on one or more specific issues that are an obstacle to solving their dispute out of court (eg on liability, or on medical data). The court only intervenes if its intervention can positively affect the out of court resolution of the dispute as a whole. To ensure access for the victim, all the costs of the partial dispute procedure will be borne by the person held liable (his insurer) and can be claimed in full should proceedings on the dispute as a whole follow. Moreover, to help the parties in a personal injury case to solve their dispute, a self-regulatory Code of Conduct exists with rules on a transparent and harmonious compensation scheme.[11]

More Alternatives for Court Proceedings?

Alternatives to court proceedings can help individual claimants to choose the most suitable and efficient type of dispute resolution for their cases, provided that information on the various alternatives is readily available to them. In the Netherlands part of our civil justice approach is to offer a wide range of dispute resolution mechanisms. Our legal front office for citizens (the 'Legal Desk') will refer citizens to the best way to solve their dispute. This can be through mediation, private ADR-mechanisms for consumers, Ombudsman or the courts. The Dutch government co-finances mediation and self-regulatory claims tribunals for consumers, which offer a real alternative to litigating a consumer dispute in court at reasonable cost. We must keep looking for further possibilities to improve and innovate these alternatives to court proceedings.

Better Substantive Laws?

Civil justice starts with clear rights and obligations for citizens. The clearer these are the lower the cost of enforcing individual rights and claims will be. This is why

[8] Simple Proceedings for Simple Claims (*Eenvoudige procedures voor eenvoudige zaken*).

[9] The work on the drafting of the bill to introduce this has started recently.

[10] The bill introducing this possibility for the parties has been adopted by the Dutch Senate (Bill nr. 31 518) and will be published and enter into force in Apr 2010.

[11] However, speaking more generally, from a cost perspective protocols for different types of civil procedure are often perceived as making litigation more costly since they provide parties with further material for debate and may lead away from the actual legal dispute.

our efforts should be aimed at making clear and unambiguous legislation on substantive law, which prevents legal disputes and which enables citizens to help themselves to solve their disputes. A successful example of this type of legislation is the Dutch Statute on Electricity (*Elektriciteitswet*) together with the Dutch Grid Code. These include a provision that puts an obligation on the provider to compensate consumers for a fixed amount for a power failure of more than four hours.[12] Each commercial party on the Dutch energy market is bound by the Grid Code, which is part of his licence. The results are clear rights and obligations for the parties and easier (public) enforcement in case of a dispute. We are currently reviewing whether this type of legislation could also be used in other fields, especially in cases where low value damages are most likely.

The Forgotten Truth About Enforcement

If we look at the cost and funding of civil litigation, we often stop looking at the outcome of the court proceedings. However, any individual claimant with a right he wants to enforce will not perceive civil justice as *justice* if a successful judgment cannot be followed by actual enforcement of his rights. If in the end he does not get paid, it simply means he has wasted a lot of money.

A Dutch pilot study of 2009 shows a 'full enforcement' rate[13] of civil judgments in the Netherlands of around 75 per cent after three years in contested cases and of significantly lower percentages between 31 per cent and 65 per cent after three years in default cases (depending on the value of the claim).[14] In the majority of default judgments the reason for lack of enforcement was the debtor's lack of money and assets.[15] This outcome leaves much to be desired and has a serious impact on civil justice and how it is perceived by citizens.

In cases where a settlement was reached, the percentage of full enforcement after three years is 85 per cent.[16] Should this be regarded as a separate argument to stimulate settlements rather than court decisions? Further research may provide us with more tools for our policy makers in this field.

[12] Dutch Statute on Electricity 1998, Art 31 para 1f together with Dutch Grid Code, para 6.3.

[13] 'Full enforcement' meaning that the civil judgement or settlement has been *entirely* enforced.

[14] The percentage 31% total enforcement refers to default judgments on claims with values of more than € 5,000. In 42% of those cases there has been no enforcement at all. See the report on compliance with and enforcement of civil judgements and settlements by RJJ Eshuis, *De daad bij het woord. Het naleven van rechterlijke uitspraken en schikkingsafspraken. Een pilotstudie binnen het domein van de civiele rechtspleging*, Raad voor de rechtspraak, Research Memoranda no 1/2009, Jul 2009.

[15] See however N Dominy & E Kempson, '*Can't Pay or Won't Pay? A Review of creditor and debtor approaches to non-payment of bills*' (London, DCA, 2003).

[16] With 10% partial enforcement and 5 % where there has been no enforcement at all, see Eshuis, n 14 above.

More (Empirical) Research

Finally, the way forward needs to be supported by a lot of research. This is why it is so important to have the CEPEJ report and all the studies presented in this Civil Justice Project. The Netherlands has planned to carry out an empirical study on the costs of civil litigation and their effect on access to justice. This will be a unique study for the Netherlands, which should provide us with an overall view of the relation between the costs and funding of civil litigation and access to justice. For the first time in the Netherlands, the complete chain of costs will be included in one study. This includes court fees, lawyers' costs and costs awards, legal aid, insurance policies for civil litigation and the costs of funding of the courts. Hopefully, it also includes the costs of actual enforcement.

Why do we need complete picture? An example from the Netherlands may illustrate this. Currently a bill simplifying our court fees system is pending before Parliament. In order to safeguard access to justice for individuals, the bill provides for rather modest fees for individuals as well as a special low–income fee. However, the fees for legal entities are about twice as high as the fees for individuals. In appellate and Supreme Court proceedings they are about ten times as high, up to about €5,000. In our loser-pays system this means that a consumer who starts a procedure against a business bears the risk of having to pay those high court fees paid by the business. In terms of an integral approach to access to justice this may require some further thought.

Hopefully, our integral costs study will provide some answers for us, and maybe even for others facing similar questions about costs and funding of civil litigation. Others will do other studies. Gradually best practices may become apparent and will help us see possible next steps at national and at European or even global level. This Civil Justice Project creates an excellent forum for expert debates, exchange of empirical data and creative thinking about issues of civil justice, which can help us to meet the challenges of a civil justice in the twenty-first century.

16

New Zealand

KIM ECONOMIDES* AND GRAHAM TAYLOR**

Introduction[1]

This chapter summarises and assesses recent experience in New Zealand concerning the cost and funding of civil litigation, and the quest for alternatives outside court that purport to make the civil justice system more accessible. We are particularly concerned to highlight deficiencies that impact on ordinary citizens who, either as actual or potential users, may find it expensive, both in economic and psychological terms, to bring their disputes to civil courts and who therefore may seek redress elsewhere or, indeed, abandon their claim altogether. It is already clear from preliminary findings of the Court User Survey conducted by the University of Otago Legal Issues Centre that there is a perception amongst New Zealanders that litigation costs are too high.[2] Understanding the detail of formal and informal dispute processes, including the social and economic costs and consequences of avoidance, is a complex ongoing task but for now we concentrate on describing the tip of the conflict iceberg. Our focus is on the adequacy of the costs regime and current funding arrangements but, wherever possible, we highlight the potential for exporting innovative solutions developed in New Zealand that might have relevance for jurisdictions enjoying less freedom to experiment with civil procedure.

There is no distinctive national theory of litigation in New Zealand apart from pragmatism. The dominant approach is to seek out simple and sometimes radical solutions to practical problems that work well for ordinary citizens. The Accident Compensation Scheme (ACC), which has effectively removed personal injury work from both lawyers and the courts through a system of comprehensive social insurance, is the envy of many legal systems and is a good illustration of the pragmatic spirit of reform that pervades not only the legal system and its culture,

* Professor of Law, Director, University of Otago Legal Issues Centre, Dunedin, New Zealand.

** Barrister, Wellington, New Zealand.

[1] We should like to thank the following colleagues attached to the University of Otago Legal Issues Centre (UOLIC) for research assistance with the preparation of this chapter: Mark Henaghan, Fanaafi, Aiono-Le Tagaloa, Rachel Souness, and Shana Fonnesbeck. Jim Guest, a Dunedin litigation lawyer, has also assisted us in the latter stages of this report. The usual disclaimer applies.

[2] See www.otago.ac.nz/law/lic/survey.html.

but public life more generally.[3] One consequence of the ACC is to relieve, if not remove, court congestion caused by the traffic in personal injury litigation. New Zealand has made significant investment in other extra-judicial alternatives to formal legal processes while at the same time experimenting with civil procedural rules, the most current example being the introduction of new District Court rules that entered into force on 1 November 2009.[4]

Tribunals are also currently under review and serve to divert cases away from the formal court system toward diverse specialist fields that include the: Copyright Tribunal; Disputes Tribunal; Motor Vehicle Disputes Tribunals; Human Rights Review Tribunal; Waitangi Tribunal; Weathertight Homes Tribunals and the Tenancy Tribunal.[5] As elsewhere, the tribunal system in New Zealand developed not logically but in response to social and economic pressures and without any overall coherent or consistent policy on costs or procedure.[6] Consequently, both fees and procedural formality vary considerably, with some tribunals, such as the Human Rights Review Tribunal, not charging filing or hearing fees.[7] Application fees in other tribunals vary from $20 to about $400, and are generally lower than court fees. Although research by the New Zealand Law Commission indicates there is not much public concern about tribunal fees, an earlier study indicates that fees may discourage public use of the tribunals.[8] Furthermore, the Law Commission notes that the total cost of accessing New Zealand tribunals is not limited to filing and hearing fees, but may include costs associated with hiring lawyers and experts, as well as opportunity costs associated with taking the time from work to attend a hearing. The potential impact of these costs should not be ignored, as a recent survey indicates that the perceived (not actual) costs associated with obtaining a lawyer may inhibit people from pursuing a claim.[9] This

[3] The ACC provides comprehensive, no-fault injury cover to all NZ residents, regardless of the cause of injury and effectively eliminates the market for personal injury legal claims. The scheme was initiated in response to *Woodhouse Report* (1967) at www.library.auckland.ac.nz/data/woodhouse/ and covered 1.76 million claims in 2007–2008. It is funded through a variety of taxes (employer, income, petrol, motor vehicle licensing fees). The care, compensation and administration costs in 2008 totalled $3.65 billion. See further www.acc.co.nz/about-acc/media-centre/frequently-asked-questions/ABA00105.

[4] See www.courtsofnz.govt.nz/about/system/rules_committee/district-courts-revision/Rules-Committee-DCR-overview.pdf.

[5] See www.justice.govt.nz/tribunals and 'Tribunals in New Zealand' NZLC IP 6 Wellington 2008, www.lawcom.govt.nz/UploadFiles/Publications/Publication_131_385_IP6_Tribunals_in_NZ.pdf.

[6] See generally, JA Farmer, *Tribunals and Government* (London, Weidenfeld and Nicholson, 1974).

[7] 'Tribunals in New Zealand' NZLC IP 6 Wellington 2008 (n 5). The filing fee in the Environment Court went from $50 to $500 on 7 May 2009—Resource Management (Forms, Fees, and Procedure) Regulations 2003, reg 35, amended by the Amendment Regulations 2009 (SR 2009/73).

[8] ibid at 53 (citing a 2005 New Zealand Ministry of Consumer Affairs survey where 45% of participants thought tribunal fees might inhibit access to the Disputes Tribunal).

[9] See Legal Services Agency, www.lsa.govt.nz, *Report on the 2006 Survey of Unmet Legal Needs and Access to Services*, Prepared Nov 2006, Wellington, NZ by Ignite Research that considered perceptions of cost on accessibility: Over a quarter of people with problems (27%) felt that the fear of cost had stopped them from approaching a lawyer to help them with their problem or to see if they could get legal aid. This figure represents about 8% of all people aged over 15 years (an estimated 240,000 people). Problem areas where cost was a greater barrier to accessing services from a lawyer were in immigration and family/*whanau* problems or relationship breakdowns. Consumer related issues were much less affected by the cost of lawyers' fees.

suggests that psychological barriers can be just as significant as economic ones in deterring people from using the legal system.

It is hardly surprising then to find that mediation and arbitration appear to be quite popular in New Zealand. A 2004 survey of NZ lawyers showed 93.4 per cent believed that disputants wanted to take up ADR in order to reduce costs.[10] While another 2004 survey, this time of disputants, found that 61.2 per cent believed ADR resulted in cheaper resolution of their dispute.[11] Some NZ lawyers believe that ADR merely frontloads costs and can actually result in longer, more costly disputes if unsuccessful: 17.9 per cent of NZ lawyers reported increased costs as a limitation of mediation; while 40 per cent reported increased costs as a limitation of arbitration.[12]

The Costs Regime—Applying Principles of Predictability And Proportionality

Certain general principles apply to the determination of costs:-

1. the party who fails with respect to a proceeding or an interlocutory application should pay costs to the party who succeeds;
2. an award of costs should reflect the complexity and significance of the proceeding;
3. costs should be assessed by applying the appropriate daily recovery rate to the time considered reasonable for each step reasonably required in relation to the proceeding or interlocutory application;
4. an appropriate daily recovery rate should normally be two-thirds of the daily rate considered reasonable in relation to the proceeding or interlocutory application;
5. what is an appropriate daily recovery rate and what is a reasonable time should not depend on the skill or experience of the solicitor or counsel involved or on the time actually spent by the solicitor or counsel involved or on the costs actually incurred by the party claiming costs;
6. an award of costs cannot exceed the costs incurred by the party claiming costs; and
7. so far as possible the determination of costs should be predictable and expeditious.[13]

[10] 'Alternative Dispute Resolution: General Civil Cases' prepared for the Ministry of Justice by K Saville-Smith and R Fraser, Centre for Research Evaluation and Social Assessment (June 2004), Table 4.2 available at www.justice.govt.nz/publications/global-publications/a/alternative-dispute-resolution-general-civil-cases/publication.

[11] ibid at Table 4.6.

[12] ibid at Table 4.7.

[13] District Court Rule 46 (becomes r 4.2 under new rules taking effect 1 Nov 2009). This is mirrored in High Court Rule 14.2. The general principles are stated in *Holdfast NZ Ltd v Selleys Pty Ltd* (2005)

This final principle of predictability of costs is especially important, and for all key stakeholders involved with litigation: clients, lawyers and court administrators. The number of costs judgments required are now 10–15 per cent of the number before the 2000 costs regime came into operation. To this extent the costs system has to be regarded as highly predictable. Moreover, the case management system requires cases to have their category for costs identified from the outset. This adds a further dimension of predictability in that the (1), (2), (3) classification will seldom be altered at the end of the case.[14] Parties can therefore be advised with reasonable accuracy as to the costs they are likely to be awarded or have to pay, and the amount can be factored into advice on the appropriateness of settlement offers. The occasions on which indemnity (r 14.6(4)), increased (r 14.6(3)) or decreased costs (r 14.7) are awarded are all specified in the rules, though there is discretion in each case to allow for unusual circumstances. The normal classification of a case is Band B. This will be changed to Band C only following an assessment of which particular parts of a case require Band C. A party seeking either Band C or an uplift of costs must show 'why relevant steps should be classified C': 'a blanket banding C is neither desirable nor possible under the Rules.[14a] The approach to increased or reduced costs does not depend on considering actual and reasonable costs, but is based on percentage uplifts or reductions in the Schedule. Normally, the limit is 50 per cent, but that can be exceeded. This contributes to predictability too and, since actual and reasonable costs are not relevant, this helps to offset the burden on parties facing a large law firm 'team' operation or major corporate 'no stone unturned' conduct of a case.[15]

Particular rules apply to special categories of litigant: a lay litigant is entitled to an award for disbursements.[16] A public interest party will commonly be required to pay only modest or even no costs.[17] And special principles apply to costs in

17 PRNZ 897 (CA). On the application of the 'predicable and expeditious' standard, see further R McGechan, *McGechan on Procedure* (Wellington, Thompson Brookers, 2008). Actual costs incurred by a party are usually not taken into account in assessing reasonably daily recovery rate. 46.04 (citing *Health Waikato Ltd* v *Elmsly* (2004) 17 PRNZ 16 (CA)).

[14] *Paper Reclaim Ltd v Aotearoa International Ltd [costs]* (2007) 18 PRNZ 743 (CA), para 30.

[14a] See *Paper Reclaim Ltd v Aotearoa International Ltd* [2007] NZCA 544, (2007) 18 PRNZ 743, at [35] and *Commissioner of Inland Revenue v Chesterfields Preschools Ltd* [2010] NZCA 400, at [161] and [164]–[165].

[15] See Simon France J in *New Zealand Fish and Game Council v Attorney-General* (High Court, Wellington CIV 2008-485-2020, 2 Oct 2009); *Chesterfields Preschools v Commissioner of Inland Revenue* (High Court, Christchurch CIV 2008-409-722, 1 May 2009, per Fogarty J)(overturned on appeal *Commissioner of Inland Revenue v Chesterfields Preschools Ltd* [2010] NZCA 400, see n 14a *above*) on increased and indemnity costs in operation in an unusual situation.

[16] *Re Collier (A Bankrupt)* [1996] 2 NZLR 438 (CA)) which may include the expenses incurred by a 'McKenzie friend': *Knight v Veterinary Council of New Zealand* (High Court, Wellington CIV 2007-485-1300, 31 July 2009, per Clifford J).

[17] The principle was stated in *Ratepayers and Residents Action Association Inc v Auckland City Council* [1986] 1 NZLR 746 (CA). See *Titahi Bay Residents Association Inc v Porirua City Council* (High Court, Wellington CIV-2007-485-1933, 18 Oct 2007, per Simon France J) as a good illustration, where the Judge also commented orally that the cost of judicial review claims was something public authorities should see as something that goes with the territory of being a public authority. The party must wholly have a public interest, not a private interest. Such a party must stay within public interest

habeas corpus and New Zealand Bill of Rights Act 1990 cases.[18] In legal aid cases there is authority that the ordinary award of costs should not be reduced because the legal aid paid was less than the award.[19] However, the Court of Appeal has reduced the award in one case when it was acknowledged that legal aid was less than the award the Court proposed to make. This is in accordance with the basic principle of costs that a party cannot receive more than he, she, or it incurred.

Proportionality is the other guiding principle of the costs regime intended to give 2/3rds of actual and reasonable costs on an average proceeding in the relevant classification and banding. The daily recovery rates (HC Rules, Schedule 2) are based on a 6 hour 'day' (this appears from the 2/3rds objective and the hourly rate on which it is based). The recovery rate is amended each year following a survey of fee rates. The issue of proportionality therefore depends on how realistic the time allowances are. From a practical standpoint, there are two serious underestimates of time allowances (HC Rules, Schedule 3), both relating to preparation time where a case goes to trial. This time allowance is twice the hearing time, or the same as hearing time for appeals and interlocutory applications. Neither is a realistic allowance. For ordinary proceedings, this is demonstrated because where a case is settled before trial, items 7.1–7.4 of the 3rd Schedule total (in a band (B) case) gives 5 days for a Plaintiff and 4 for a Defendant. A trial has to exceed 1½ days to give a greater allowance for preparation and hearing and 2–2½ days to give a greater allowance for preparation taken alone. A policy of encouraging settlement (which may be the reason for the under-allowance) also has the effect of undermining proportionality.[20] The average appeal involves only submissions, but this means that the time going into their preparation bears no real relationship to the time taken to deliver them. It would be more practical to choose a multiplier that will deliver a reasonably accurate time as an average, eg 2½–3 would be appropriate in band (B).

In contrast to these serious under-allowances, there is an over-allowance for case management conferences. The allowances for bands (A), (B) and (C) for memoranda and appearance respectively are:

matters in presenting his, her, or its case to be protected: *Gibbs v New Plymouth District Council (No 2)* (High Court, New Plymouth CIV-2004-443-115, 5 Oct 2006, per Heath J).

[18] Costs will rarely be awarded against an unsuccessful applicant for habeas corpus: *Manuel v Superintendent, Hawkes Bay Regional Prison* [2006] 2 NZLR 63 (CA). Costs were awarded in *Arumalla v Kilari* (Court of Appeal CA 240/2009, 19 Aug 2009 [2009] NZCA 361) because the procedure was inappropriate, being used to expedite a bail application pending judicial review. The Court said that the HC Rules should be used as a guide to exercising the discretion as to quantum. As to NZBORA (New Zealand Bill of Rights Act 1990) cases, see *Attorney-General v Udompun* [2005] 3 NZLR 204 (CA).

[19] *Kawhia Offshore Services Ltd v Rutherford* (High Court, Hamilton CP 61/99, 10 Jul 2002, per Master Faire). Costs above legal aid were paid in *Taunoa v Attorney-General* (2004) 8 HRNZ 53 (without a judicial decision on the point).

[20] A better approach to allowances where the matter is settled would be to have a multiple of the time for which the matter was set down. One needs to recognise that trial preparation under the HC Rules does not start until after setting down, so the trial time is known. Looking just at the preparation and trial time, the idea that preparation of witness statements, documents, authorities, cross-examination and submissions can ever be twice the hearing time is unrealistic. A more realistic figure is probably 4–5 times—except in very long cases where the correlation tends to break down, even on an averaging basis. Again, the time allowance for appeal preparation is unrealistic.

(A)	(B)	(C)
0.2	0.4	1
0.3	0.3	0.7

In practice a memorandum even in a complex case would seldom take 3 hours (half a day) and a band (B) case would seldom take longer than one hour. Where counsel travel from out of town, case management conferences are commonly conducted by telephone and would exceed 10–15 minutes only if an unrepresented party is involved, in which case it may extend to 45 minutes but more commonly they would last 15–30 minutes. Face-to-face case management conferences seldom take more than 10 minutes per hearing as Judges would have longer case management arguments set down for specific interlocutory hearings. One consequence of these under- and over-allowances is that costs on an appeal from a tribunal or district court (which is normally allocated a half day hearing) provide almost as much time for the case management conference as to prepare for and appear in the hearing itself.

Settlement—Some Concerns

The new District Court rules have been designed to encourage 'a logically staged exchange of relevant information which is conducive to exploration of settlement.'[21] Settlement is also encouraged in the High Court.[22] In practice the High Court does not express an opinion at the case management stage on whether the case 'should be settled'. This is because if settlement is to be accepted as fair by the parties it needs to be entered into freely. At later stages, when a judge has gained a sufficient understanding of the facts, issues and context, opinions on desirability, and sometimes parameters of settlement are not uncommon. The latter opinion can be especially effective where counsel see prospects of settlement, but parties often need a nudge that counsel cannot give.

Pre-litigation encouragement of settlement is not institutionalised, save to the extent that the Legal Services Agency (LSA) might agree to fund a party only up to the stage of a negotiated settlement or mediation (private mediation can be covered by a grant for the mediator and counsel, but court ordered mediation or settlement conference has to come within the overall grant of aid). To the extent that preparation for trial or appeal hearing has been under-assessed in the costs regime as an incentive to settle, the costs regime does not itself encourage settlement as such.

[21] Rules Committee Information Paper, www.courtsofnz.govt.nz/about/system/rules_committee/district-courts-revision/Rules-Committee-DCR-overview.pdf).

[22] The HC Rules include an item in the standard case management directions on this: Sch 5 item 10. Sch 6 on appeals has no similar item. This requires counsel and parties to address whether settlement is reasonably likely at an early stage (in practical effect before pleadings are filed). The general understanding is that 90% of civil proceedings filed in the High Court are settled, but the figure varies greatly within areas of proceedings.

Current proposals for compulsory settlement conferences or mediations do not command support from counsel and are seen as undesirable. Unless the parties (a) wish to settle (whether after prodding or not), and (b) are both willing to compromise to do so, settlement is pointless and contrary to the objective of dispute resolution that the parties should go away feeling they have had a fair deal. A party forced to settleand to compromise is unlikely to come away satisfied. In short, access to peace is not synonymous with access to justice.[23]

Private Funding of Litigation

It is a well-established ethical obligation, enshrined in the NZLS Code of Ethics, that lawyers' fees are fair in all the circumstances, taking into account time, skill, urgency, importance to client, value to client and those who chose to ignore this obligation do so at their peril as some have been disciplined.[24] Contingency and conditional fee arrangements are now permitted but are relatively recent, though previously they were in use on an unknown number of occasions.[25] More common are the quasi-*pro bono* arrangements usually with community group clients: here fees are billed on a commercial basis but with the tacit or express understanding that the client will pay what he, she, it feels he, she, it can and any shortfall will not be pursued, but any costs award goes to the lawyer to bring the amount received up to or closer to the commercial fee. Indemnity costs awards are actual and reasonable costs, and there is case law where actual costs held not reasonable cannot be recovered.[26]

A major driver of costs in environmental litigation is expert evidence. The Environment Court tries hard to reduce this problem by taking evidence-in-chief as read and requiring expert witnesses to 'caucus' to prepare statements of common ground among them—which is intended to obviate evidence on these points. The expert evidence problem started in the late 70s and early 80s with the Environmental Defence Society Inc, which had a pool of counsel and expert witnesses willing to offer their services *pro bono*. They presented specialist experts in landscape, traffic, ecology, etc, and won a series of major victories. In consequence authorities presented their own experts, which in turn meant that all parties had to produce experts and even a small subdivision is likely to require planning,

[23] See H Genn, *Judging Civil Justice* (Cambridge, CUP, 2009).

[24] See NZLS Code of Ethics. See also Lawyers and Conveyancers (Conduct and Client Care) Rules listing relevant factors.

[25] See www.lawcom.govt.nz/UploadFiles/Publications/Publication_79_174_R72.pdf.

[26] eg 'over-lawyering' cannot be recovered—*Davis v Independent Newspapers Ltd* (HC, Auckland CP 67-SD02, 16/May/2003, Master Lang) (non-party discovery). Cases before the 2000 costs regime came in, reducing the de facto '2/3rds of actual and reasonable' for taking a 'no stone unturned' approach: *Waiatarua Group v Minister for State-owned Enterprises* (1990) 2 PRNZ 447, 451–452, *Neave v Wordsworth* (1993) 7 PRNZ 352, 359, *North Shore City Council v Local Government Commission* (1995) 9 PRNZ 182, 189, *Legal Services Agency v Haslam* (2007) 18 PRNZ 469, 481 (charging for such an approach may be professional misconduct).

landscape and traffic expert witnesses for all parties. Costs thus create a double disincentive to the parties. The Environment Court's use of caucusing experts has significant flaws which are not inevitable and do not always arise. The first is that some parties (developers normally) send lawyers to the caucus as well as the relevant expert, and the lawyers in practice make the discussion bend to their client's needs or wishes. The second is that in the absence of lawyers to provide a balance, a dominant witness will dragoon the others into acceding to his or her view. This distorts the caucus and, potentially, the hearing as well. The agreed statements are intended to take issues off the disputes table. However, an agreement is only as good as the caucus discussion that precedes it. Thus, if a relevant factor has been left out of the caucus discussion, counsel will examine the experts on the issue because the validity of the agreement is undermined if the factor is truly relevant. Overall, however, these developments in the Environment Court do save time, but without further empirical research we cannot know whether this is at the cost of reaching the correct or preferable decision in the case—an important consideration given that the Environment Court hears the matter *de novo*.

Public Funding of Litigation—Legal Aid

Legal aid remains important to ordinary individuals who lack the means to litigate but is currently subject to a fundamental review under Dame Margaret Bazley following concerns regarding the cost and scope of its operation.[27] One of the interim findings of the Bazley review is that high cost cases have in recent years eaten up a significant portion of the legal aid budget:

> '45 per cent of the legal aid budget goes on 5 per cent of the cases. In 2007/08, the top 100 cases (covering 0.17 per cent of the people receiving grants) received 17 per cent of total expenditure ($18.26 million). In effect, the top 100 cases received 100 times the value of the average for all grants in that year. The top 10 cases received more than 300 times the value of the average for all grants in the 2007/08.'[28]

The government has accepted the recommendations of her report. Once legislation is enacted, the Legal Services Agency will be 'folded into' the Ministry of Justice, where legal aid decisions will be made by a 'statutory officer' not subject to direction by the Minister on individual decisions. How this officer's assistants will relate to the government department of which they will, presumably, be members, so as to preserve their independence, has not been made public. In consequence, it seems to be intended that the Ministry's lawyers and the Crown Law Office will

[27] See Legal Aid Review, *Improving the Legal Aid System. A Public Discussion Paper* (Sept 2009, Wellington); *Transforming the Legal Aid System. Final Report and Recommendations* (Nov 2009, Wellington). See also K Economides, 'Reforming legal aid' [2010] *New Zealand Law Journal* 5,6,9. The Legal Services Bill received its first reading in Parliament on 24 August 2010.

[28] ibid, para 96.

advise the statutory officer on legal matters. How they are to do this when virtually all criminal and a lot of civil proceedings are against the Crown or government departments that the Crown Law Office will also be representing has yet to be revealed. On a substantive level, there are proposed to be simpler processes and no repayments for lesser criminal matters on legal aid and bulk funding to groups of lawyers. Again, the way this is to be achieved has not been announced.

Legal aid is for the most part limited (with exceptions for trustee companies and Waitangi Tribunal matters) to individuals. This creates a distortion in that groups will hunt out someone who has no assets and low income and so is at no real risk of adverse financial consequences to front matters for them where the case will set a precedent from which they can benefit. This tactic has been used in the United States by public interest law firms, which do not exist in New Zealand. However, the Environmental Legal Aid Fund, operated by the Ministry for the Environment, to a limited extent fills this gap in environmental litigation. They have a maximum grant of $30,000 and tend to fund the experts not the lawyers. On the other hand, other groups, such as women, in practice often appear to fall outside the scope of the scheme.[29]

Given the potential of legal aid to address the problem of the cost of civil litigation for ordinary citizens, and the relative scarcity of supplements, it is worth examining more closely the recent history, scope and operation of the scheme.[30] The 2000 Act is the fourth statute dealing with legal aid. The first was the Offenders Legal Aid Act 1954, which dealt only with criminal legal aid. Each of the next three Acts provided for civil legal aid. The second was the Legal Aid Act 1969 (the 1969 Act), which dealt with civil legal aid only. There was a Legal Aid Board, District Legal Aid Committees, and an appellate Legal Aid Appeal Authority. Decisions to grant legal aid were made by the Committees—sections 20, 22—as were decisions on withdrawal—section 24. The Committees consisted of practising lawyers with the High Court Registrar as chairman giving their services voluntarily. Much of their work was done in lunch-hour meetings with, where necessary, a member taking a file to assess and draft decisions in other spare time. Generally speaking, the civil matters for which aid is available,[31] grounds of

[29] Study Paper 1, *Women's Access to Legal Services: Women's Access to Justice*, Joanne Morris OBE (Law Commissioner Mar 1994–Mar 1999, Jun 1999, Wellington, N.Z.) [Refers to Mar 1997 'Women's Access to Civil Legal Aid' NZLC MP8].

[30] See further ILAG Wellington conference, 2009, NZ national report on legal aid: www.ilagconference.org/reports/New_Zealand.pdf. See also, GB Fea, *Legal Aid in New Zealand* (Wellington, Butterworths, 1975).

[31] Legal aid is available for a 'proceeding' in a forum specified in s 7 (2000 Act). Since the 1969 Act was enacted, the major change has been to include the Waitangi Tribunal in 1975. The fora include all the ordinary courts in the New Zealand hierarchy, a number of tribunals, and, where 'the Agency considers that the case is one that requires legal representation (having regard to the nature of the proceedings and to the applicant's personal interest) and considers that the applicant would suffer substantial hardship if aid were not granted' a number of specialist courts and a general class of 'any administrative tribunal or judicial authority'. There has been a list of exclusion of classes of proceedings since then: of relator actions, national and local election petition, and certain immigration proceedings. The 1969 Act (s 16(1)) and the 1991 Act (s 20) set out a description of what was included in legal aid for a civil proceeding: 'Civil legal aid consists of representation, on the terms provided for by

eligibility[32] and grounds for refusing legal aid[33] in the Legal Services Act 2000 as originally enacted (pre-2006 Amendment Act) were those in the 1969 Act. These

this Act, by a solicitor, and, so far as necessary, by counsel, including all assistance usually given by a solicitor or counsel in the steps preliminary or incidental to any proceedings or in arriving at or giving effect to a compromise to avoid or bring to an end any proceedings.' When the 2000 Act was introduced into Parliament, this provision was omitted. The omission was pointed out by the Law Society and, for some reason, the Select Committee resolved the omission by altering the definition of 'legal services' in the definition in section 4 to say 'in relation to legal aid, means legal advice and representation; and includes assistance (i) with resolving disputes other than by legal proceedings; and (ii) with taking steps preliminary or incidental to any proceedings; and (iii) in arriving at or giving effect to any out-of-court settlement that avoids or brings to an end any proceeding'. Placing the provision where it was caused problems of interpretation with the Legal Aid Review Panel holding that if anything on which a lawyer was engaged could, if it was not agreed go to a s 7 forum, legal aid was available. The High Court decision on an application by the Agency for a declaratory judgment (*LSA v New Zealand Law Society* [2004] 3 NZLR 63) raised as many problems as it solved. So a petition to the Governor-General to exercise the prerogative of mercy by referring a matter to the Court of Appeal was held to be eligible for legal aid as a preliminary to the reference or incidental to the preceding conviction: *Yash v LSA* (2006) 18 PRNZ 320. The position is accurately resolved by *LSA v A* (2008) 19 PRNZ 1 with its focus on what is the proceeding and whether the matter is truly for settling that potential proceeding or truly preliminary to it.

[32] From the 1969 Act until amended by the 2006 Act, the limits for financial eligibility were $2,000 disposable income and $2,000 of disposable capital. The failure to adjust this level with inflation was ameliorated by two facts. First was that the definition of income excluded welfare benefits (though this effectively restricted eligibility to beneficiaries), and the discretion in s 9(1) for 'special circumstances' having regard to '(a) the likely cost of the proceedings to the applicant; or (b) the applicant's ability to fund the proceedings if legal aid is not granted'. This discretion was exercised increasingly liberally, though never particularly liberally as time went by. The 2006 Act moved to a sliding scale of income depending on the number of dependents and the existence of a partner. The limit is set at the point where 'Working for Families' negative income tax phases out fully: Legal Services Regulations 2006, reg 5. The discretion has come to be exercised tightly again, though there is a recent LARP decision (091/10) that suggests that if a person is a spendthrift the discretion should be exercised in their favour (the Agency considered whether to appeal this decision on the ground that the income limit is a proxy for ability to pay for legal representation, and actual disposable income is no longer a relevant factor), but decided to leave the point for another case should LARP carry on the approach. So far as capital is concerned, there are legislative deductions in the LSA Regulations 2006 similar to those under previous Acts but after them there is a very steep reduction in allowable capital. The question of interests in trusts, including discretionary trusts, has always been addressed. The definitive High Court decision both on interpretation and on calculating an interest in a trust is *Nicholl v LSA* (2009) 19 PRNZ 668, See also *Headley v LSA* (HC, Hamilton CIV 2008-419-1478, 22 Apr 2009, Andrews J).

[33] The grounds of eligibility relevant to the Litigation Funding are s 9(3) ('The Agency must refuse to grant legal aid if the applicant has not shown that the applicant has reasonable grounds for taking or defending the proceedings or being a party to the proceedings'), in the case of an original proceeding 9(4)(d) ('(i) the applicant's prospects of success are not sufficient to justify the grant of legal aid; or (ii) the grant of legal aid is not justified, having regard to the nature of the proceedings and the applicant's interest in them (financial or otherwise), in relation to the likely cost of the proceedings; or (iii) for any other cause where it appears unreasonable or undesirable that the applicant should receive legal aid in the particular circumstances of the case), and in the case of an appeal (4)(e) ('(whether or not in respect of proceedings in which the applicant has received legal aid), the Agency considers that for any reason the grant of legal aid or further legal aid is not justified'). The test in s 9(4)(d)(i) has become for most cases 'What, if any, legal action would the applicant (assuming they were a reasonable individual) take in the circumstances if paying their own legal costs?'—*Timmins v Legal Aid Review Panel* [2004] 1 NZLR 708 para 35. Although Wild J just referred to this question as a 'helpful' one, LARP has adopted it as standard, and the latest High Court cases have done so too: *LSA v Pickard* (HC, Auckland CIV 2009-404-1230, 3 Jul 2009, Ronald Young J), *LSA v L A E* (HC, Auckland CIV 2009-404-3399, 6 Aug 2009, Dobson J). In *LSA v Russell* (HC, Wellington CIV 2009-404-3107, 2 Sept 2009), Clifford J overruled a dangerous LARP decision that legal aid should be granted for an uneconomic claim because a reasonable defendant would settle rather than face a 'costs protected plaintiff').

are imported into the provisions on withdrawal and amendment of aid in the 2000 Act (s 26(2)(a)).

The 1969 Act contained no provisions for amending a grant of aid. It provided for aid for a proceeding to be withdrawn on the grounds, inter alia, that the Committee: 'is satisfied that the aided person has required the proceedings to be conducted unreasonably so as to incur an unjustifiable expense to the Crown or has required unreasonably that the proceedings be continued' (s 24(1)(e)) or 'considers that the aided person no longer has reasonable grounds for taking, defending, or being a party to the proceedings, or that it is unreasonable or undesirable in the particular circumstances for him to continue to receive legal aid' (s 24(1)(g)). The same provisions are found in the 1991 and 2000 Acts. These were the only grounds for withdrawing aid which touched upon the merits or conduct of the actual legally aided case. All the other grounds related to matters external to the aided proceeding.

The amount of legal aid was 80 per cent of profit costs, which could be taxed by the Registrar secretary of the District Legal Aid Committee (s 9(2)(b)).[34] The Board had power to issue instructions, binding on Committees (s 5(3)), as to general administration of the legal aid scheme and policies to be followed by Committees in carrying out their functions—s 5(2). The Appeal Authority was not limited as to the approach to appeal (the power that the Authority had without any other limit indicates a general appeal). Its membership was limited to seven, all of whom had to hold the normal qualification for judicial office in New Zealand of seven years practice and included the future Ellis, Gendall and Heron JJ. It was chaired by a District Court Judge. The third Act was the Legal Services Act 1991 ('the 1991 Act'), which covered both civil and criminal legal aid. Criminal legal aid was granted by Court Registrars, civil legal aid by District Legal Services Subcommittees—ss 7 and 33–34. The Subcommittees had decision-making powers independent of the Legal Services Board. The only difference in the new Subcommittees from the Committees in the 1969 Act was that the Registrar was now the secretary.

The key relevant changes from the 1969 Act were the departure from a percentage of profit costs in favour of fixing 'total remuneration'. From the power to fix total remuneration flowed the development of standard fees, expressed in the Board's Instructions on Civil Legal Aid Remuneration initially as stated sums and later as hours at guideline rates. These Instructions were deemed to be Regulations—section 97A—and were expressly binding on Registrars, Committees and Subcommittees—section 96(4). Subcommittees also developed a system of 'staged grants' where legal aid was granted not for a single sum for the entire proceeding, but for a sum for certain stages, eg to commencement, or discovery, or setting down. As a matter of normal course, each stage had attached to it a 'total remuneration'.[35] When that stage was completed the grant could be

[34] cf s 32(b) of the 1969 statute which specified 85%.

[35] This change recognised the problems and lack of fiscal control inherent in the 1969 Act's 85% of profit costs taxed by the registrar. Taxation was seldom undertaken so that lawyers on a legal aid case in effect 'wrote their own checks'. This made legal aid a desirable activity for lawyers with almost

extended to the next stage for a further sum.[36] It was possible to have the total remuneration for a particular stage increased, usually if events unexpectedly created extra work. The ease of doing so varied from district to district. Some districts such as Wellington took a strict view on what was unexpected, Auckland a lenient view. The system of staged grants was carried into the 2000 Act.

The other major change was in the appeals area where the new Legal Aid Review Authority (LARA) was restricted to determining appeals 'as if the decision . . . had been made in the exercise of a discretion'—section 132(1). It dealt only with civil legal aid and then only some decisions. LARA consisted of seven members, all of whom had to hold the normal qualification for judicial office in New Zealand. Its membership included the future Gendall and Wilson JJ and District Court Judge Walker. It was chaired by a District Court Judge.

The fourth is the 2000 Act. This represents the last stage in unification. Decisions are now wholly within the LSA for both civil and criminal legal aid. In keeping with the move from autonomous decision-makers exercising statutory powers conferred on them to a bureaucratic or departmental structure, the need for the formal binding instruction process disappeared and was not re-enacted. The senior management as an incident of the statutory powers conferred on the LSA as such, determines policy and the normal administrative law incidents of that process apply. The changes identified in relation to the 1991 Act were carried on. 'Total remuneration' becomes 'maximum grant' (s 14(2)(c)) and the staged grant process becomes formalised in a process of applications for amendment of grants (s 24).[37] 'Grant of aid' is defined to include an amendment to

guaranteed payment of fees—only at a lower rate. Move to a maximum grant process gave control of the amount paid to the Legal Services Board. This was a radical move. By putting control in a government agency, rates of legal aid remuneration became subject to political influence and eventually (in the 2000 Act) to control by the political government. The explanation for the preceding sentence is that the understanding under the 1991 Act (and still under the 2000 Act until almost the present time) was that the granting process and amounts of legal aid would be covered by the Crown through supplementary appropriations. The Board was given a 'letter of comfort' that appropriations would also be adjusted to cover changes in hourly rates of legal aid. This letter of comfort was not provided to the Legal Services Agency. The consequence is that hourly rates are now dependent on the political competition of the budget round. Most recently, hints are starting to emerge that the government may be feeling its way towards a capped budget for legal aid, but this will not be clear until the government reacts to the Bazley review.

[36] The intention of staged grants when introduced by the Legal Services Board was to control the grant by requiring re-approval of the grant at each stage. The model was that of the private client who regularly approves continuing involvement in a proceeding as the 'landscape' changes. There was intended to be no grant for the full case as existed under the 1969 Act. In practice, not too much changed. District Subcommittees tended to continue as under the 1969 Act, just extending an existing grant in stages. Local practice did vary and it was this variation of local practice in granting and administration that led first, soon after the middle of the decade, to Regional Legal Aid Offices which did the administration of grants but had no involvement in decisions themselves. This half way house made insufficient improvements towards consistency and so the policy of a Legal Services Agency that undertook the whole of the legal aid task was accepted as necessary, leading to the structure of the 2000 Act.

[37] In *LSA v Black* (High Court, Wellington CIV 2004-404-2561, 14 Oct 2005, Goddard J) the staged grant argument was made and rejected in favour of an expectation that legal aid once granted would continue to the end, and interpreting the gateway for withdrawing aid in s 26(2)(a) 'no longer' to requiring a change of circumstances since the original grant or that the original grant was made by 'mistake'. 'Mistake' has not been further explored. The expectation of aid continuing was taken byLARP to be a 'legitimate expectation' in terms of administrative law and a change of circumstances

grant–section 4. Provision for amending grants appeared for the first time in the 2000 Act.

With provision for amending grants as well as withdrawing them, the legislation on the grounds for amending or withdrawing was redrafted. Section 26 contains two subsections: subsection (1) provides three mandatory grounds for withdrawing aid, and subsection (2) six discretionary grounds for amending or withdrawing aid. Some grounds that were mandatory in previous Acts have become discretionary, and vice versa. Section 26(2)(a) is new, but the other five discretionary grounds are materially identical with those in previous Acts. Section 26(2)(a) provides that aid may be withdrawn if the LSA is satisfied that 'the aided person is no longer a person who would be entitled to that grant of legal aid, by virtue of any of the provisions of sections 9, 10, or 11'.[38]

So far as appeals are concerned, the LARA (a normal tribunal) becomes LARP which decides 'reviews' (not 'appeals') on the papers (s 56(5)) by assigned teams of 1–3 persons, only one of whom must be a lawyer, but only one member of LARP (the convenor) is required to have the standard New Zealand judicial prerequisite of seven years standing as a barrister and solicitor. Non-lawyers can be members. LARP's jurisdiction is greatly widened to include criminal legal aid decisions, remuneration, and most individualised decisions made by the Agency. A change is made to the function of LARP: it is limited to two grounds of review only: that the decision reviewed was 'manifestly unreasonable' and that it was 'wrong in law'.[39]

was interpreted by LARP as requiring a change in the facts or law applicable. The Agency's position of information or events which cast light on the matters relevant to granting legal aid such as to make a re-assessment of aid appropriate. *LSA v Ogilvie* (High Court, Wellington CIV 20906-404-739, 29 Jun 2006, Clifford J), *LSA v Anderson* (High Court, Auckland CIV 2008-404-5206, 15 Dec 2008, Clifford J), *Pickard* (n 33), and *L A E* (n 33) have brought the position to one more or less as argued by the Agency. See *Ogilvie* for the best formulation, which has not been departed from later. See *Pickard* (n 33) for LARP overturning the Agency's withdrawal of aid made when counsel said the case should not be continued. See *L A E* (n 3) for associated positions adopted by LARP but rejected, particularly that aid could not be withdrawn (or, seemingly, refused) until all the relevant evidence was available.

[38] This should have signalled that there were to be regular reviews of whether the grant should be made if applied for at each stage, but this is not the way it has been treated.

[39] The concept of manifestly unreasonable was before the High Court in a series of cases culminating in *LSA v A & O* (2003) 17 PRNZ 443 where Hansen J summarised the position by reference to earlier cases in para 11:

> There are a number of decisions considering what is meant by 'manifestly unreasonable'. These are *Legal Services Agency v M* (5/8/02, Hansen J, HC Dunedin A 6/02); Legal *Services Agency v Fainu* (2002) 17 PRNZ 433; *Legal Services Agency v Tana* 9/12/02, O'Regan J, HC Whangarei AP 26/02. From these decisions the following propositions can be distilled:
>
> (a) 'Manifestly unreasonable' means something different from what is 'wrong in law'.
> (b) 'Manifestly unreasonable' will be made out where it is shown, clearly and unmistakably, that the decision made by the Agency went beyond what was reasonable, or was irrational or logically flawed.
> (c) 'Manifestly unreasonable' requires not only that the decision be found to be unreasonable, but that LARP forms the view that the decision is so clearly unreasonable that the intervention of the Panel is called for.
> (d) The determination of what is 'manifestly unreasonable' is to be made objectively by the members of LARP, applying their judgment to the matter in accordance with the principles stated earlier. It is not for LARP to substitute its view of what the decision should have been for that of the Agency.

The 2000 Act was expressly an amendment of the organisation of legal aid, not the availability of legal aid. The latter is dealt with in the Legal Services Amendment Act 2006 ('the 2006 Act'). By section 47(2) of the 2006 Act, it applies only to applications or grants made after it came into operation (1 March 2007).

The most important changes in the 2006 Act were to financial eligibility and repayment of legal aid. There was one significant change in other eligibility criteria. The change to financial eligibility has already been noted.[40] The increase in the number of grants of aid has been in the vicinity of 20 per cent.[41] The change in substantive eligibility was in the area of family law. In the decisions appealed by the LSA to the High Court and reported as *LSA v A & O*,[42] LARP had decided that in family matters where children were involved, any solution is a success, so that section 9(4)(d)(i) did not apply. This was rejected, but the 2006 Act added new subsections to section 9, subsections (5) and (6) to cater for family law cases specifically with its own set of criteria in place of section 9(4)(d). Subsection (5) states the test as being whether legal aid is 'justified'. The relevant factors for justification in subections (6) are:

> (a) any previous proceedings in the matter to which the application relates, (b) any personal protection issues such as (without limitation) any orders relating to domestic violence, protection of personal property rights, compulsory treatment, or compulsory care, (c) the interests and welfare of any other person who may be affected by the outcome of the proceedings, (d) whether there are any complex factual, legal, or evidential matters that require the determination of a court, and (e) whether it is in the public interest that legal aid be granted.

The changes to repayments are far-reaching. Under the 1969 Act provision for repayment of aid was normally out of property recovered or retained as a result of the proceeding (s 18(4)).[43] There was an automatic charge on these 'proceeds of proceeding imposed by the Act which could take the form of a charge on property'. The 1991 Act changed this, retaining the charge on proceeds of proceeding in section 40(1) (the 'mandatory charge'), but adding provision for a 'discretionary charge' on property irrespective of the success of the proceeding (s 40(2)). This was carried forward into the 2000 Act with a significant procedural variation. Whereas under the 1991 Act, applicants for aid were told that there 'may' be a charge imposed, the charge was not imposed until the end of the case. This was seen as unfair because people did not take the 'may be imposed notice' as serious and forgot about it. The 2000 Act required charges to be notified and imposed

(e) 'Manifestly unreasonable' is a different statutory formulation from 'plainly wrong' (which focuses attention of whether a decision is correct or incorrect), but rather it focuses attention on whether the decision is unreasonable and not only that but also clearly and unmistakably unreasonable.

LARP's standard statement of the law in its decisions omits sub-para (e). Consequently, it tends to focus on correctness and regularly substitute its assessment of the merits for that of the Agency.

40 cf n 33.

41 For actual figures see Bazley Discussion Paper (n 27) and LSA Annual Reports.

42 cf n 39.

43 The legislation also contemplated repayment from the party's disposable income.

when a grant (including an amended grant) is made. This has been interpreted by the LSA and LARP as meaning that if a charge is not imposed, it cannot be imposed retrospectively, ie, the charge is notified on each grant and amendment in respect of the maximum remuneration provided by that grant or amendment. The Agency requires written acceptance that it may impose a charge before the grant is legally accepted. If the applicant does not sign and return this, there is no lawful grant and should the Agency provide legal aid thereafter, the applicant is under no obligation to repay it.[44] All three Acts provided for applications to exclude property from a charge in whole or part (1969 Act s 18(4A), 1991 Act s 45, 2000 Act s 33).[45] The 2000 Act added the concept of writing off the repayment in whole or part (s 37).[46]

The 2006 Act totally changed the concept of repayment other than on the proceeds of proceedings. The 1991 and 2000 Acts provided by way of contributions or repayments for charges up to the maximum legal aid actually paid—hence the common reference to legal aid being a loan not a grant.[47] The 2006 Act substituted a concept of ability to repay in the form of a Prescribed Repayment Amount (PRA) based around the tables used for eligibility for legal aid.[48] The effect is that in a case where substantial legal aid is paid out, repayment will be much less unless the aided person has significant equity in capital items or high income. The effect of these changes on the operation of exemptions from charges and writing off debt has yet to be worked out in LARP or the High Court. An effect of this change is that the PRA has to be notified with the letter making the grant, even though it may be substantially more than the likely maximum repayment because the amount of legal aid is significantly less. The staged grant process means that commonly only the cost of the stage for which a grant is sought is identified by the provider, so the PRA can have the effect of 'scaring' applicants into refusing aid.[49]

The LSA operates through 11 local offices. The Head Office does not have officers making decisions on individual applications, but is occupied with policy issues and management of the LSA's operation. There are 94 grants officer positions throughout the country making decisions on grants of aid. They are supported by five internal specialist advisers and 35 external specialist advisers. All specialist advisers are experienced lawyers holding practising certificates. Legal aid for Waitangi Tribunal, general civil matters, and appeals are managed centrally

[44] *Johns v LSA* (High Court, Auckland CIV 2006-404-1435 & CIV 2005-404-6373, 9 Oct 2006, Andrews J).

[45] The operation and principles of this under the 1991 Act (and by implication the 2000 Act) are found in *Bates v Legal Services Board* [1999] NZAR 91.

[46] The operation and principles of this are found in *LSA v Sweeney* (2005) 17 PRNZ 767. This concept has proved troublesome as something cannot be written off until it has been incurred and as no payment of legal aid occurs until a claim is made for services rendered in the past (2000 Act, ss 73–76), the Agency has to notify applicants of the maximum they may have to repay at the start. This worked adequately until the 2006 Act.

[47] Found in LARA decisions and repeated in *Clark v Wellington District Legal Services Committee* [1999] NZAR 496, 504.

[48] Legal Services Regulations 2006, regs 10–12.

[49] The Agency has significant anecdotal information to this effect, as do providers.

within the Wellington regional office. The LSA receives about 100,000 applications for legal aid each year and grants aid in about 89,000 of them.[50] On average three decisions are made on each file where legal aid is granted. Thus, conservatively the LSA has to make about 100,000 decisions a year, though the figure is undoubtedly higher and is likely to be in the range of 280,000 or more. That means four decisions per grants officer per working day if only decisions whether or not to grant aid are considered, or up to 11–12 a day if decisions other than granting legal aid ones are included.

Grants officers operate by reference to the LSA's Grants Manual. This is now progressively being folded into the Provider Manual available on the LSA website (www.lsa.govt.nz). Grants officers are also assisted by 'specialist advisers'. These are practitioners who provide advice and recommendations on applications. They fill the need for practical experience of conducting litigation that used to be provided by members of the previous District Legal Services Subcommittees.

As a matter of practice, complex civil litigation involves many amendments to grant. Such a case tends to progress in a legal aid sense in a piecemeal fashion. Opinions from counsel on the prospects of success given at an early stage become less relevant as the case advances. The LSA recognises how onerous it would be if before every amendment to grant in such a complex case a current assessment on the prospects of success were to be required. This point is of some significance because in fact the granting of an amendment to a grant does not necessarily involve a confirmation by the LSA that the matter has sufficient prospects of success to continue. The LSA is also cautious in withdrawing aid, a caution engendered by the approach commonly found in LARP decisions that once legal aid has been granted it should seldom be withdrawn: LARP sees 'a legitimate expectation' that aid once granted will continue to the conclusion of the case.

Supplements to Legal Aid

While many New Zealanders carry professional or trade indemnity insurance, and this is now compulsory for lawyers under the LCCCC Rules, legal expense insurance, after-the-event insurance, or other analogous one-off insurance, currently is unknown in New Zealand as a separate product. We suspect that the absence of personal injury litigation, along with community attitudes and market practices, is likely to result in lower demand for private insurance to cover legal expenses in NZ.[51]

Third party funding does however exist, but it would seem unusual for third parties to take a percentage of 'winnings', though we cannot be sure this does not

[50] See further Bazley Discussion Paper (n 27).

[51] 'Seeking Solutions—Options for change to the New Zealand Court System' NZLC PP52 Wellington 2002 at 100: /www.lawcom.govt.nz/UploadFiles/Publications/Publication_89_218_Part_1_PP52%20Introduction.pdf.

happen and any person or body which provides third party funding for a share of the 'winnings' could well be liable in costs.[52] As recently as 2001, the New Zealand Law Commission recommended preserving the torts of maintenance and champerty.[53] However, recent High Court cases indicate that the courts are not at all hostile to non-party litigation funding.[54] Possibly in response to these recent High Court rulings, litigation funding companies have now entered the New Zealand market, mainly from Australia.[55] Assisted by the downturn in the economy there is also the further possibility that class actions, which have yet to take root in New Zealand, could soon be imported, again along the lines of the Australian model, and the Rules Committee of the Ministry of Justice is currently examining litigation funding in the context of class actions.[56]

Court and Process Costs

Court charges, including fees lists for all courts and fee waivers, are regularly updated for both the District and High Courts.[57] Charges relating to translators,

[52] See *Dymocks Franchise Systems (NSW) Pty Ltd v Todd (No 2)* [2005] 1 NZLR 145 (PC), *Carborundum Abrasives Ltd v Bank of New Zealand Ltd* [1992] 3 NZLR 187, *Hamilton v Papakura District Court* (1997) 11 PRNZ 333, *Kelmarna Properties Ltd v Scenic Developments Ltd* (HC, Christchurch CIV 2003-009-1781, 1 Nov 2004, *per* Hansen J).

[53] 'Subsidising Litigation' NZLC R72 Wellington 2001.

[54] *Houghton v Saunders* (2008) 19 PRNZ 173 ('In an age where the costs of litigation are beyond the means of many people, professional funders undoubtedly have an increasingly important role to play in ensuring that legal obligations and rights are enforced and vindicated') Evidence of champerty alone does not warrant a stay. See also, *Auckland City Council as Assignee of Body Corporate No 16113 et al. v. Auckland City Council* [2008] 1 NZLR 838 (modern interests in access to justice and promoting settlement of litigation trump antiquated concerns re champerty).

[55] See '*Impact Funding*' (now known as '*Ask Funding*')—Australian, primarily T&E (advances on delayed payouts from wills or financing will contests) and family law cases: 'Firm offers loans for lawyers' fees' *Sunday Star-Times* 4 August 2007, available at: www.stuff.co.nz/sunday-star-times/business/money-story-archive/42984. *See also* www.askfunding.com.au; and '*Quantum Litigation*'—Australian, contractual disputes, insolvency, franchising, trade practices, intellectual property, family law. See L Craymer, 'Private funder Quantum Litigation enters NZ market', *National Business Review*, 22 May 2009, www.nbr.co.nz/article/private-funder-quantum-litigation-enters-nz-market-102729; www.quantumlitigation.com.au/.

[56] Legislation on class actions has been proposed but not yet enacted: see *Class Actions for New Zealand—A Second Consultation Paper prepared by the Rules Committee, October 2008* at para 10: www.law.stanford.edu/library/globalclassaction/PDF/New_Zealand_Class_Actions_consultation_paper_Oct2008.pdf.

[57] Fees list for all courts (updated 22 Sep 2009) available at www.justice.govt.nz/services/court-fees/court-fees-and-charges; Application and procedures for fee waiver (regardless of status as a legal aid recipient) at www.justice.govt.nz/services/court-fees. See Working Party on Civil Court Fees (2003), includes Principles for Setting Civil Court Fees www.justice.govt.nz/publications/global-publications/r/review-of-civil-court-fees/appendices and FAQs regarding civil court fees ww.justice.govt.nz/publications/global-publications/r/review-of-civil-court-fees/civil-court-fees-questions-and-answers. District Courts Fees Regulations 2001 (Appx of Dst Ct Rules)–covers power to waive fees, manner in which hearing fees to be prepaid, GST included. High Court Rules re costs and taxation of costs—s 14.11—effect of settlement offer on costs to encourage settlement. See also High Courts Fees Regulations 2001—covers power to waive fees, manner in which hearing fees to be prepaid, GST included.

fact and expert witnesses are covered by secondary legislation.[58] From 1 July 2004 (High Court Fees Amendment Regulations 2004), the Government moved to increase High Court fees to recover 50 per cent of High Court running costs. Filing fees must be paid at the time the documents are filed in order to have them accepted. Some filing fees such as interlocutory applications include the 'setting down' fee that covers organising the hearing and a half day or day's hearing time. The setting down fee for any substantive hearing is to be paid 10 working days after the date of setting down. In practice, failure to pay within 10 days will not cancel the setting down or the date of hearing fixed. The setting down fee must be paid before hearing. The Court stating the setting down date and requiring payment sends out a notice. This is normally preceded by e-mail communications or sometimes telephone to find a convenient day for counsel that is available for hearings that are to take place in a comparatively short time into the future.

Trials of civil proceedings in short trials (1–3 days) are sometimes set down to start the time line for exchanging evidence with the trial date to be set later. Long trials, even if well into the future, will be set down with hearing dates in order to secure major blocks of court time. Further hearing fees for periods beyond that covered by the setting down fee are levied by the half day and are officially to be paid before the Court sits for the period covered. In practice they tend to be paid after the event. A reminder e-mail will go out immediately after the hearing specifying the amount to be paid and the Registry will continue to follow this up. Sometimes it may be weeks or months later that these are paid. Parties may be encouraged to pay the full hearing fee for the trial with the setting down fee.[59] Court fees may also be waived in cases of hardship. The level of non-concession fees are such that they are 243 per cent of the daily recovery rate for costs for Band (A), 162.5 per cent for Band (B) and 109.7 per cent for Band (C). In other words, court fees constitute a significant portion of the total cost of civil litigation in the High Court.

[58] See, 'Witnesses and Interpreters Fees Regulations 1974' setting out fees and allowance schedules for witnesses (fact & expert) and translators, but apparently these only apply to criminal cases and/or fees paid by the Crown unless expressly extended under another act (s 3) See also, A Beck, 'Increased Costs Awards' (2002) *NZLJ* 443–44.

[59] Setting down and hearing fees are paid per case, so if two or more matters are being heard together, each incurs the setting down and hearing fees. In one matter where four appeals involving the same issues and with very similar facts were heard together over one half day four setting down fees were levied. A study preceding these regulations determined the costs involved. The change was vigorously opposed by the New Zealand Law Society, but with limited success. There are 'concession' proceedings at a heavily reduced rate and provision has been made for waiving court fees which benefits all those on legal aid. To benefit from the 'public watchdog' costs protection a party must not have a personal interest: *Chopra v Chief Executive, Department of Labour* (High Court, Wellington CIV 2009-404-911, 14 Aug 2009, per Wylie J).

General Costs Issues

Lawyers' costs have already been described above but today legal fees take a variety of different forms, eg hourly rate, fixed/capped fee, success fee (operated with an initial fee or hourly rate), as well as a percentage of the damages/recovery. The LCCCC Regulations envisage that the full range fee charging is available, but must be set out when the retainer is completed, ie, in advance. It is uncertain what attitude would be taken to changing the fee basis in the course of the retainer, but one imagines that so long as what was done was appropriate and the client was not dragooned into it, the change would be allowed. The hourly rate has been the standard form of charging for some years. More recently, there have been stirrings to change this in the direction of fixed/success fees that are seen by some to enable a higher return to the lawyer. The LCCCC Regulations apply and are subject to the review procedures but the more directive elements of the LCCCC Regulations are new. There is no official or unofficial tariff specifying what you have to pay your lawyer. The survey of fees across New Zealand for purposes of HC Rules Schedule 2 found $270 to be the applicable average. Rates are substantially higher in Auckland than elsewhere. An argument that there should be a special Auckland recovery rate for Schedule 2 has been rejected both at policy and case law level. The rates charged to government (central or local) tend to be lower than normal commercial rates by 20–25 per cent, possibly in recognition of reliability and promptness of payment but also a public interest consideration may be at work.

Cost shifting, as described earlier, is at the discretion of the Court.[60] Since 2000 the costs regime has placed predictability and maintenance of awarding scheduled costs at the centre of practical operation of the regime so that the discretion is reserved for the unusual case that required Schedule 3 to be varied. There is power to make a decision on costs at an early stage of a proceeding but costs are, however, almost invariably determined at the end of the case.[61] If a party is only partly successful a discount from Schedule 3 is made.[62] If the successful party loses some interlocutory steps, the Schedule 3 allowance is simply set off against the amount of the steps and overall success of the successful party. This is normally done without dispute. Where there are several parties on a winning side, the extent to which separate representation is needed and contributes to the case will dictate the extent to which each party receives the Schedule costs. Thus, if a separately represented successful party contributes to the case on one of three causes of action of equal importance, one third of Schedule costs will be awarded. This type of case will require a specific judicial decision if the parties cannot agree. Only where the separately represented successful parties did not contribute separately to the case

[60] See also HC Rule 14.1.

[61] See *Berkett v Cave* [2001] 1 NZLR 667 (CA).

[62] See *Blair v Upper Hutt City Council* (High Court, Wellington CIV 2005-486-2268, 1 Apr 2009, Clifford J) paras 18-20 indicating the courts will take a broad view in assessing the appropriate reduction.

will a single award be made.[63] The aim is for an irrecoverability gap of one third of average reasonable costs. The under- and over-allowances noted earlier mean that the irrecoverability gap can get as high as 80 per cent.

Generally speaking, costs can only be awarded by a court (other than the High Court which has inherent jurisdiction) or tribunal if legislation allows for this. No courts other than the High Court and District Courts have a scale or schedule governing costs, but either by way of practice direction or unofficial practice, experienced counsel know the principles and sometimes the actual amount of costs likely to be awarded. The normal award for a Supreme Court substantive hearing is $15,000 per day plus disbursements. The normal award on a leave application is $2,000 plus disbursements. Prior to the Court of Appeal (Civil) Rules (No 2) 2008, the normal award for a substantive hearing in the Court of Appeal was $6,000 per day or part thereof plus disbursements. The normal award on a leave application was $1,500 plus disbursements. Under the new Rules a slight modification of the High Court rules for costs on appeals have been applied, including classification, banding and daily recovery rate. The under-allowances noted previously apply here, but are exaggerated by not allowing for the greater preparation needed for Court of Appeal hearing nor the greater skill required of counsel. The effect has been substantially to increase the irrecoverability element of costs from what occurred previously, which in turn had involved a greater irrecoverability than in the High Court. Costs in the Environment Court are subject to the Court's practice direction.[64] In practice, costs generally lie where they fall unless there has been some unreasonable conduct affecting the case.

Changes in rules apparently aimed at reducing costs in the superior courts are seen by more experienced counsel as concerned only with reducing court time and can have the effect of increasing cost to the parties. The front-loading of cost in litigation has the effect of requiring the case to be prepared twice. The theory that preparing one's evidence as early as possible promotes settlement and reduces cost is considered to be doubtful in practice. Evidence prepared before discovery, for instance, tends to be unreliable because it is necessarily made in at least partial ignorance of what occurred. The strategy and tactics in a case necessarily evolve as knowledge of it changes but, so far as costs are concerned, focus is the key to their reduction by concentrating on the key issues and essentials and fighting 'brush fires' only when necessary.

Finally, we need to consider the objective of expeditious procedure that clearly will affect the cost of litigation. So far as we are aware, there are no reliable national statistics currently available in New Zealand on the length of civil or criminal trials making it impossible to assess precisely how delay impacts on costs. The University of Otago Legal Issues Centre is currently planning research to investi-

[63] Where there are several losing parties, the successful party receives only one award which is divided between the losing parties, sometimes on a joint and several (such as where there may be doubts whether a party is in fact likely to pay), sometimes on a several basis. This type of case will require a specific judicial decision if the parties cannot agree. *Bullock* and *Sanderson* orders are also made where appropriate.

[64] [1998] NZRMA 282 paras 33–37.

gate this point, as it is a vitally important one. Anecdotally, we can say that the delay between a case being ready for hearing and trial date varies with the length of the hearing (longer hearings are more difficult to schedule) and the number of other cases for hearing. Cases that are genuinely urgent can be fitted in within days (if necessary) to a few weeks. Without urgency, six months seems to be a typical delay for a one-day hearing in Wellington or Auckland. Where the hearing is in a provincial court, even Hamilton, which has at least one High Court Judge sitting every day, hearing delays are affected by the priority given to criminal matters and the number of sitting days. Thus in Rotorua, where there is a lot of 'crime', getting a civil fixture can prove very difficult.

Conclusion

The New Zealand system for funding litigation has been responsive to evolving social and commercial pressures, and some might say too responsive, with the result that it has become very piecemeal. Policymakers have noted this characteristic and the 'lack of a consistent rationale' for court fees:

> 'There is no systematic basis for the existing fee structure in civil courts. Some fees are at or near full cost recovery, while others are only token in nature. At different times policy decisions have been made to keep particular fees low, or not charge for certain services, but there is no comprehensive policy framework for determining what fees should be charged. Current fees differentiate between cases in terms of the type and number of documents filed with the court, rather than the complexity of the issues, or the demands made on the time of court staff or judges. This provides few incentives to economise on the use of court resources. It also results in inequities between users, as some are likely to pay a higher proportion of the actual cost of processing their case than others. There may also be inequity between court users, who on average pay only a small proportion of the cost of processing their cases, and taxpayers, who meet the bulk of the expenses involved. All citizens derive some degree of benefit from the existence of courts, but it is not clear what that benefit is worth in dollar terms, or what share of the cost of processing cases should be met by users in return for the private benefits they receive.'[65]

While it would appear that courts and tribunals are reasonably affordable to the majority of citizens who require these services, it cannot be denied that the twin problems of cost and delay remain and, whether perceived or experienced, frequently undermine accessibility. Whether reformers choose to avoid or adapt the current costs regime, or import or export innovative procedures, it also cannot be denied that promising and often highly imaginative solutions to economic and other problems of access to justice are continually being sought, and discovered, in New Zealand.[66]

[65] See Ministry of Justice, *Equitable Fees in Civil Courts—October 2002* para 1.2.1. www.justice.govt.nz/publications/global-publications/e/equitable-fees-in-civil-courts/background.

[66] See eg, Right Honourable Lord Justice Jackson *Review of Civil Litigation Costs: Preliminary Report* (May 2009, London) Ch 59, NZ Law Commission *Delivering Justice for All* (Report 85, Wellington, 2004).

17

Poland

MAGDALENA TULIBACKA*

General Overview And Trends

The rules on costs and funding need to be seen in the context of very significant and ongoing transformation of the Polish civil justice system as a whole since the end of socialism in 1989.[1] With growing emphasis on access to justice and the rule of law, reforms have attempted to deal with a number of problems: lack of accessible justice, complex and lengthy proceedings, a complex regulatory framework for civil procedure (including the legislation governing costs and funding), and relatively high costs of litigation. These challenges are still widespread in Poland, and are made worse by other characteristic features of post-socialist reality: inefficient law enforcement, bureaucracy, and under-resourced public services. While a coherent regulatory framework has been established, grounded in the principles of effectiveness, efficacy, and equality of access to justice, and is capable of addressing most of these challenges at a systemic level, some problems still remain in practice.

The new legislative framework for costs of litigation in Poland is grounded on the principles of clarity, predictability, proportionality, encouraging settlement, and reducing the costs.[2] A similar approach can be observed in the legislation concerning funding mechanisms. However, reasonably priced justice is still not easy to obtain in Poland. There are many reasons for this. Some reasons are systemic: the inherent nature of the court structure, the structure of the judiciary and the relatively outdated structure of the legal profession.[3] Some reasons are

* Senior Lecturer, Westminster University and Associate Fellow, Centre for Socio-Legal Studies, Oxford.

[1] See M Tulibacka, 'The ethos of the Woolf Reforms in the transformations of post-socialist civil procedures: case study of Poland', in D Dwyer (ed), *The Civil Procedure Rules Ten Years On* (Oxford, Oxford University Press, 2010) ('Tulibacka, 2010') 395–413; and M Tulibacka, 'Poland' in D Hensler, C Hodges and M Tulibacka (eds), *Globalization of Class Actions* (Thousand Oaks, CA, Sage, 2009) The Annals of the American Academy of Political and Social Science, Vol 622 ('Tulibacka, 2009') 190–200.

[2] See K Gonera, *Komentarz do ustawy o kosztach s dowych w sprawach cywilnych* (*Commentary to the Act on court costs in civil cases*) 3rd edn (Warsaw, LexisNexis, 2008) 10–14.

[3] See Tulibacka, 2009 n 1 for a more detailed analysis of the court structure and the structure of the legal profession in Poland: www.law.stanford.edu/display/images/dynamic/events_media/Poland_National_Report.pdf, in particular 19–22, also 7–9, and 12–13.

administrative and organisational: the increasing load of cases produces delays and puts a significant strain on the judiciary.[4] As a consequence, costs have not become as predictable and proportionate as was expected as a result of the reforms. Further, some of the most crucial problems in Polish civil justice relate to legal culture and practice rather than hard letter law. Civil procedure rules are becoming clearer and leave less scope for unnecessary complexity and delays, but judges are as yet unable to make fully effective use of their new powers to manage litigation.[5] The attitudes of the judiciary and the quality of their work continue to be criticised,[6] and civil society has only recently started to mature.[7]

Funding mechanisms also remain a challenge. The rules on availability of legal aid, the main mechanism of funding litigation for those unable to afford it, have been simplified and clarified. Nevertheless, the legal aid system is neither particularly efficient nor particularly transparent and accessible. Other funding methods, such as insurance, are relatively undeveloped. Litigation practice, in the wake of the ever-growing need for access to courts, has developed some ways of helping with the funding of litigation. Thus, while *pacta de quota litis* are prohibited by the rules of lawyers' ethics, they are sometimes offered to clients in practice. Legislation has also been introduced to offer viable alternatives to legal aid: the new Class Actions Law of 2009 (to come into force in June 2010)[8] introduced contingency fees as a method of funding newly introduced class litigation.

Civil Justice and Civil Procedure Reforms

In the socialist period, civil procedure had a clearly inquisitorial character, with judges obliged to 'seek the objective truth', actively assisting the parties by

[4] Since the 1990s, the powers and responsibilities of civil courts in Poland have grown considerably. The number of cases lodged in courts continues to increase each year. There was a 6.1% growth in cases in 2009, from 11,210 cases in 2008 to 11,897: Ministry of Justice website: www.ms.gov.pl/aktualnosci.php#akt100211. This large number of cases has not been accompanied by a proportionate increase in the number of judges, or indeed a proportionate increase in funding for the court system. While the efficiency of courts is improving (Ministry of Justice www.ms.gov.pl/aktualnosci.php#akt100211), there are still significant problems with delays. See the European Commission for the Efficiency of Justice (CEPEJ) (Council of Europe) 'European Judicial Systems. Efficiency and quality of justice', Sept 2008, at www.coe.int/t/dg1/legalcooperation/cepej/.

[5] See Tulibacka, 2010, n 1.

[6] With regard to the quality of adjudication scholars commented on the 'bound judicial decision making' as a reminder of the socialist period (Z Kühn, 'Worlds Apart: Western and Central European Judicial Culture at the Onset of the European Enlargement' (2004) 52 *Am J Comp L* 531), and of lack of initiative and the ability to take decisions based on the judges' own experience and expertise: E Łętowska, *Prawo Umów Konsumenckich, Drugie Wydanie* (*The law of consumer contracts*), 2nd edn (Warszawa, CHBeck, 2002).

[7] The problems with regard to lack of maturity in civil society concern the social trust in the civil justice system, social confidence in the judiciary, and social awareness of their rights. The author of this chapter wrote about these issues elsewhere: M Tulibacka *Product Liability Law in Transition. A Central European Perspective* (Aldershot, Ashgate Publishing, 2009) ('Tulibacka, Product Liability') 149–50.

[8] The Act of 17 Dec 2009 on Class Actions, published in *Dziennik Ustaw* (Journal of Laws) of 2010, no 4, item 44.

instructing them about their substantive and procedural rights. The regulatory framework for costs of litigation was extremely complex, and the costs were high. Funding mechanisms were limited to personal funds and legal aid. Civil litigation was not seen as an effective mechanism for enforcing rights. Indeed, the entire law enforcement framework was ineffective, both in the public sphere (administrative bodies) and private sphere (litigation). There were numerous reasons for this lack of efficacy: the cost, shape and length of civil procedure and the formalistic judicial attitudes, the economic reality of the overwhelming state presence in the market, administrative inefficiencies related to state planning, substantial bureaucracy, and lack of faith by ordinary citizens in the State and in the law.[9]

Following the transition from socialism, Poland is a democratic country complying with international human rights instruments (such as the European Convention of Human Rights)[10] and with the laws of the European Union.[11] These international obligations inform and shape the internal process of transformation. Polish civil procedure has become more adversarial, and the role of the judge is now more clearly defined. The new system is dominated by the principle of 'equality of arms' between the parties, and although civil procedure is still judge-driven, the parties are responsible for the trial and the outcome of the case. Initially, there were plenty of opportunities for the litigating parties to litigation to delay the proceedings, for instance by bringing repeated formal complaints or introducing new factual and legal points on appeal, but these opportunities have gradually been limited. The judge now has much greater control over the proceedings, and his obligations to achieve a swift conclusion of the proceedings have been clearly set out in the Code of Civil Procedure.[12] The challenge that lies ahead is for judges to grasp these new powers effectively and use them to speed up proceedings and increase efficiency. The Polish judiciary is not yet entirely comfortable with taking full charge of litigation, and this feature of Polish legal culture, together with the increased workload of judges, continues to lead to unnecessary delays and complexities in civil proceedings.

Civil procedure used to be regulated in a more systematic, clear manner. Specific stages and procedural steps were drawn very precisely. Polish civil procedure has three stages: in the first two instances courts consider both the factual and the legal elements of the case, and the third stage—cassation—focused only on the legal aspects.[13] Apart from the emphasis on clarity and efficiency in civil proce-

[9] See Tulibacka, 2010, n 1, and Tulibacka, Product Liability, n 7, for a more detailed description of these phenomena.

[10] Available at www.echr.coe.int/ECHR/EN/Header/Basic+Texts/The+Convention+and+additional +protocols/The+European+Convention+on+Human+Rights/.

[11] The European Union puts a great emphasis on access to justice, and the effectiveness and efficiency of justice systems of its Member States: ec.europa.eu/justice_home/fsj/civil/fsj_civil_intro_ en.htm. Civil justice is a relatively new dimension within the EU system, but it is developing very dynamically: see Tulibacka, 'Europeanisation of Civil Procedures: in Search of a Coherent Approach' (2009) 46 *CMLR* 1527 for a critical approach to the European harmonisation in this area.

[12] The Code of Civil Procedure of 1964, published in *Dziennik Ustaw* (Journal of Laws) no 43, item 296, subsequently amended.

[13] Cassations are considered by the Supreme Court and have a public policy, law-shaping role.

dure, settlement and court-based mediation are now encouraged. Judges are to aim at settling every case, if it is possible.[14] Mediation was introduced into the Code of Civil Procedure in 2005.[15] It can take place before the case is brought to court as well as during litigation. The new Act on Court Costs[16] introduced costs benefits for parties who settle their case, and also where the settlement follows mediation. Judges are now being trained in a plethora of new laws and regulations, the institutional framework of courts is being transformed, and the work of the judiciary is assisted by legal clerks. There is an increased emphasis on expertise and specialisation in adjudicating cases, in order to increase both the efficiency and the quality of justice. Numerous specialised civil proceedings have been introduced into the Code of Civil Procedure.[17]

The entire civil justice system is subject to reform. The emphasis on effective and efficient law enforcement entails, on the one hand, the creation of a new institutional framework of public enforcement bodies dealing with civil justice issues and, on the other hand, renewed focus on private enforcement. Apart from the changes to civil procedure rules in individual cases, and the introduction of numerous types of representative proceedings, a class action procedure was also introduced in 2009.[18] ADR mechanisms have gained importance, and new mechanisms are appearing. Arbitration and various other mechanisms of non-judicial dispute settlement are increasingly popular. There are numerous arbitration courts and bodies: including the Arbitration Courts for Consumer Affairs run by the State Inspection Authority.[19] Ombudsmen have been established (including the general Ombudsman, the Insurance Ombudsman, and regional consumer ombudsmen) and entrusted with responsibilities that include negotiating settlements and taking part in litigation.[20] Various business codes of practice are being introduced, many of which have mechanisms for resolving disputes between their members and their customers.

[14] Article 10 of the Code of Civil Procedure.

[15] Act of 28 Jul 2005 on the amendment of the Civil Procedure Code and some other acts introduced mediation into the Code of Civil Procedure.

[16] The Act on Court Costs in Civil Cases (referred to below as the 'Act on Court Costs' or simply 'the Act'), of 28 Jul 2005, was published in *Dziennik Ustaw* (Journal of Laws) no 167, item 1398, later amended.

[17] Among many procedures are those in competition law matters and in matters concerning unfair contractual clauses.

[18] The Act of 17 Dec 2009 on Class Actions, n 8. See Tulibacka, 2009, n 1.

[19] Other arbitration bodies are listed on the website of the Polish Arbitration Association (www.pssp.org.pl/arbitraz.htm), and include the Arbitration Court for the Polish Confederation of Private Employers (Leviatan), the Arbitration Court for the Polish Cotton Chamber and the Arbitration Court for the Polish Banks Association (all of the above are industry bodies, and the Arbitration Courts were established by these bodies). Other bodies that resolve disputes out of court include Settlement Courts for medical cases, or Settlement Courts for pharmacists. These are organised and controlled by the professional associations for doctors and for pharmacists.

[20] The Act on Class Actions empowers the regional consumer ombudsman to bring a class action as class representatives. For further powers of the regional consumer ombudsman and other ombudsmen in civil proceedings (including representative proceedings) see Tulibacka, 2009, n 1.

Funding Methods

Legal Aid

Legal aid has been the most popular method for assisting litigants who would otherwise be unable to bear the costs themselves. The arrangements are set out in the Act on Court Costs in Civil Cases of 2005, which entirely changed the previous system and made it simpler and clearer.[21] Any physical or legal person who is or will be a party to litigation may submit an application to the court for a waiver of court costs and for a nomination of a lawyer *ex officio*.[22] The application can be submitted before the start of litigation (together with the claim) or during the proceedings.[23] It is assessed using a means test and a merits test. The means test is set out in relatively wide terms: the party must document that he or she cannot fund the litigation without significant financial detriment.[24] The merits test is similarly open: the aid will be refused if the claim or defence is clearly unsubstantiated.[25] Polish civil procedure does not always require the presence of a lawyer in litigation, so the court will only appoint a lawyer if it considers this necessary. The court refers its request to the regional barristers or legal advisers' council to nominate the lawyer. It has been estimated that such *ex officio* lawyers appear in 0.3 per cent of court cases.[26] Since March 2010,[27] a party who has not applied for a waiver of court fees can also make an application for appointment of a lawyer.[28] Decisions on granting legal aid are normally made by a court clerk rather than a

[21] An important change introduced by the Act was limiting the possibilities for litigation parties to unreasonably repeat applications for legal aid. Before the introduction of the Act, parties could bring new applications for legal aid immediately after the refusal to grant them aid was final. This was possible even if there were no new circumstances that would justify the grant of legal aid, and led to parties abusing the system in order to delay litigation.

[22] Lawyers appointed for legally aided parties are reimbursed by the state according to a specified tariff system. They can be barristers or legal advisers: see below.

[23] The application should normally be made in writing. While there is no specific form to fill in, the application should be accompanied by information about the applicant's financial status. Before the Act of 14 Dec 2006 *on the amendment of the Act on Court Costs in Civil Cases*, published in *Dziennik Ustaw* (Journal of Laws) of 2007, no 21, item 123, legally aided parties still needed to pay the 'base fee' (30 PLN—see below for an analysis of various types of court fees). This is no longer the case.

[24] Art 102.1 of the Act on Court Costs.

[25] Art 109.2 of the Act on Court Costs.

[26] This figure includes both civil and criminal cases. A Krajewska, 'Projekt Ustawy o Bezplatnej Pomocy Prawnej Jesienia Trafi do Sejmu' (*the draft act on legal aid will reach the Parliament in Autumn*), 30 Jul 2007.
Available at: wiadomosci.ngo.pl/wiadomosci/368239.html.

[27] Art 117.1 of the Code of Civil Procedure was amended by the Act of 17 Dec 2009 on the amendment of the Code of Civil Procedure and some other acts, published in *Dziennik Ustaw* (Journal of Laws) of 2010, No 7, item 43, 1.

[28] Applications may be submitted before the start of the proceedings, or during proceedings. They must be accompanied by similar documents as those needed for waiver of court fees. The information to be submitted concerns the financial position of the applicant. The court must be satisfied that the applicant cannot afford a lawyer without a significant financial detriment to himself and his family.

judge.[29] This transfer of power is part of a wider process of judicial reform aimed at relieving judges of various administrative responsibilities. As a result of numerous amendments of the Code of Civil Procedure and the Act on Court Costs, clerks are now empowered to make decisions on many aspects of cases that do not involve adjudication.[30]

The Act on Court Costs also establishes statutory exemptions from court fees and expenses for certain persons and organisations. Some exemptions depend on the subject matter of the claim (for instance an appeal from the court's decision to refuse legal aid). Others are available to specified persons or institutions, such as prosecutors, the Ombudsman, consumer ombudsmen, and trade inspectors. Following the amendment of the Act in December 2006, non-profit social organisations can be exempted, subject to the court's discretion, from having to pay court costs in a number of specified cases, for instance consumer matters or environment protection.

While the provision of legal aid has become clearer and more predictable, the system remains unsatisfactory because of two remaining fundamental problems. Firstly, legal aid is still inherently court-based: a judge or a clerk makes decisions on provision of aid, and the legal aid budget is part of the courts' budget. Hence, this is not a system that efficiently administers the courts' resources and judicial time. The second problem is that there is no established institutional framework for free legal advice and assistance before litigation is commenced. The availability of any assistance at that stage is random, and the system suffers from the absence of an adequate statutory and organisational footing, and lack of funding. Around 85 legal advice and assistance offices have so far been established in courts, although they are often under-resourced and overwhelmed with work.[31] Lawyers who offer free legal advice and assistance are based in some local and regional social assistance centres and centres for family assistance.[32] Local consumer ombudsmen serve as first points of contact for many consumers, negotiating settlements and advising consumers on other possible courses of action.

Drafts of new legislation dealing with both problems have appeared a number of times, but no legislation has yet been enacted. The latest draft, published on

[29] Art 118 of the Act on Court Costs concerns their powers to grant a waiver of a court fee. Article 123.2 of the Code of Civil Procedure provides that clerks can also make decisions on appointing a lawyer to a legally aided party.

[30] Arts 102 and 118 of the Act on Court Costs. Clerks make decisions granting and refusing legal aid and withdrawing the aid from parties whose circumstances change, and fining parties who gave incorrect information during the application process: Arts 110 and 111 of the Act.

[31] Information from *Rzeczpospolita*, 30 May 2009, I Walencik, 'Organizacje potrzebne do pomocy prawnej' (*organisations needed for legal aid*) quotes Grayna Kołodziejska, director of the Department of Courts at the Ministry of Justice, speaking at a Conference in May 2009 organised by the Institute of Public Affairs: www.rp.pl/artykul/312786.html accessed on 25 Dec 2010.

[32] *Miejskie o rodki pomocy społecznej* and *centra pomocy rodzinie*. See M Szochner-Sieminska, 'B dzie bezpłatna pomoc prawna w o rodkach pomocy społecznej' (*free legal aid in social assistance centres to be introduced*), at the following website: iskb.infor.pl/pomoc-spoleczna/gospodarka-samorzad/wiadomosci/104065,Bedzie-bezplatna-pomoc-prawna-w-osrodkach-pomocy-spolecznej.html.

9 February 2009,[33] envisaged a network of units providing state-funded legal assistance and legal information, to replace the existing legal aid system. Such units would be based in the existing local social assistance centres and centres for family assistance. Legal assistance would cover pre-litigation advice and any other assistance required, as well as preparing formal documents and court representation. It would be provided on the basis of specified financial criteria, and decisions would be made by the local government official (*starosta*), or the head of the Centre where the application was made. Provision of legal information would not be limited by any financial criteria. Funded by the state budget, supervised by the Legal Aid Board, and administered by the local social assistance centres and centres for family assistance, the legal aid units would maintain links with *pro bono* lawyers, non-governmental associations and charities involved in providing legal advice and assistance. They would run lists of such persons and associations and refer people in need of help to them. The draft signifies a very important change in the Polish legal aid system in separating the provision of legal aid from the court system. It is still being considered by the Parliament but since the financial implications are significant, final decisions will take time.

An important point to note is that a legally aided party who loses his case remains liable for the winning party's costs under the 'loser pays rule'.[34] This liability can be limited or waived, subject to judicial discretion. Article 102 of the Code of Civil Procedure specifies that in exceptional cases the court may order that the loser should only cover a part of the winner's costs, or that no costs should be paid. In evaluating the position of legally aided parties, the court can take into account their submissions concerning their difficult financial situation. On the other hand, if a legally aided party wins the case, the loser may be required to bear the costs.[35]

Pro Bono

Pro bono services may be offered by legal advisers, barristers and non-governmental organisations.[36] Lawyers have pointed out on many occasions that the wider popularity of *pro bono* work amongst them is stifled by refusals of consecutive governments to exempt these services from VAT. VAT of 22 per cent is payable by organisations that offer free legal advice and assistance, and recipients are also obliged to declare this as a financial benefit and pay tax on it. A draft act amending the Act on goods and services tax, prepared by the Pro Bono Centre and some law firms in 2009, has not been enacted so far.[37]

[33] See draft and explanatory note published on 16 Feb 2009 on the website of the Ministry of Justice: www.ms.gov.pl/projekty/projekty.php.

[34] Art 98 of the Code of Civil Procedure.

[35] Art 113 of the Code of Civil procedure.

[36] Non-governmental organisations assist more than 100,000 cases annually: see www.ngo.pl and A Krajewska, 30 Jul 2007, available on wiadomosci.ngo.pl/wiadomosci/368239.html.

[37] A Krajewska, 23 Jan 2009, wiadomosci.ngo.pl/wiadomosc/dzialaj/429550.html.

Insurance

Insurance as a mechanism for funding litigation is not widely offered. The Polish insurance market is gradually maturing, although the unpredictability of costs and the delays in litigation which plague Polish civil litigation do not attract insurers to litigation expenses insurance. The only existing form of insurance is BTE insurance, which is not offered as a stand-alone product, but as an attachment to other policies, in particular car insurance or home insurance policies.

Contingency Fees

Members of the Polish legal profession cannot currently officially charge fees that depend on the outcome of a case, and their remuneration cannot constitute a part of the amount awarded. Contingency fees are prohibited by the rules of lawyers' ethics. This clear prohibition has not, however, constituted a complete barrier. Some lawyers have made such informal arrangements with their clients where there was no other way in which litigation could be financed.

The Act on Class Actions of 2009, recognising the fact that funding mass claims could be problematic, has permitted lawyers to agree with the class representative for their remuneration to be a percentage of the amount awarded to the class, although not more than 20 per cent. However, the Act has some interesting and perhaps problematic features. Firstly, the lawyer's remuneration agreement is to be concluded by the class representative (the 'named claimant', who can be either a member of the class or a local consumer ombudsman). The procedure is based on an opt-in model, and the agreement must be part of the documentation to which the prospective class members must have access before making a decision to opt into the procedure. However, it does not seem possible for them to dispute any specific clauses of the arrangement. Indeed, no regulation exists on how these costs would be paid after the proceedings have been completed. The role of the court in overseeing this process is also unclear, although the court has a role in the initial approval of the arrangement, the text of which must accompany the original claim of the class representative. If the case is lost, the class members and/or the class representative will have to pay the winning party's costs, even if they do not need to pay their own lawyers. This may well constitute a barrier to bringing such class actions, especially since ATE insurance is unavailable in Poland.

Court and Proceeds Costs

Court fees are payable when the claim, or any other document or form for which the law specifies a fee, is lodged with the court. They are intended to cover the costs of the operation of the civil justice system.[38] In addition, the 'process costs' cover expenses incurred during litigation, including travel expenses of legally aided parties, travel costs, accommodation and compensation for witnesses, remuneration for experts, translators, and other persons and institutions taking part in litigation, and the costs of gathering further evidence.[39] These costs are paid by the state as they fall due, and the final cost assessment determines which party is liable to reimburse them.

The changes introduced into the system of court and 'process costs' in Poland within the last few years have been very significant. The most important change has been the introduction of the Act on Court Costs. It replaced many other pieces of legislation, simplified the regulatory framework for court costs and adjusted them to the changing reality.

Court Fees

The Act on Court Costs in Civil Cases changed the manner in which fees are charged, reduced the level of fees,[40] and limited the number of cases in which parties would be partly or totally exempted from having to pay the fees.[41] The reforms are aimed at increasing the effectiveness and speed of civil proceedings, and improving access to justice.[42] The guiding principle is that court fees should be relatively easy to establish at the outset of the proceedings. In many cases, the fee is fixed regardless of the value in dispute, and amounts range between 30 and 5,000 PLN.[43] In other cases, a proportionate fee is charged, again relatively straightforward to establish. The claimant or his legal representative is obliged to state the amount of the claim (even if it is only an approximate amount) at the time of lodging the claim,[44] and the proportionate fee is 5 per cent of this amount. In cases where the value of the claim cannot be determined, and in cases involving

[38] No data are available on the extent to which the court fees actually cover the costs of the functioning of the justice system in Poland.

[39] Art 5 of the Act on Court Costs.

[40] Before the Act, there were in fact two parts of a court fee: the 'inscription' and the 'secretarial fee'. The inscription could reach as high as 8% of the value in dispute.

[41] On the other hand, the cases in which such exemptions are granted are now regulated much more clearly. See above for the analysis of the legal aid system.

[42] Uzasadnienie projektu ustawy o kosztach s dowych w sprawach cywilnych (*Explanatory Note to the draft act on court fees in civil cases*) published on the website of the Polish Ministry of Justice –www.ms.gov.pl/kkpc/koszty1_uzas.rtf, p 1. The methods of payment and other detailed conditions for payment of court fees are specified in the Regulation of the Minister of Justice of 31 Jan 2006 on the methods of paying court fees in civil cases (*Dziennik Ustaw* (Journal of Laws) no 27, item 199).

[43] Art 12 of the Act. Types of cases where fees are fixed include property law, marital property, family matters, public procurement, unfair contractual clauses, insolvency, and many others: see Arts 22–76 of the Act.

[44] The clear regulation of costs should mean that the claimant is able to establish the amount payable himself and often simply buy an official stamp for the appropriate amount, to be attached to the claim form. Art 130.2 of the Code of Civil Procedure prescribes that if claims are brought by a barrister, solicitor or a patent ombudsman, and they have not been paid for as required, they are to be sent back by the court without the need to provide a justification. The party then has one week to make the required payment.

non-pecuniary rights where no fixed fee is specified, the court fixes a temporary fee, which can range between 30 and 1,000 PLN. The final fee in such cases is established at the end of the proceedings as part of the final cost assessment.[45] In all cases where neither a fixed fee nor a proportionate fee is payable, parties are required to pay a base fee of 30 PLN.[46] The Act on Court Costs also provides for a secretarial fee (*opłata kancelaryjna*), payable per page for certain official documents, transcripts, or excerpts.[47] As mentioned above, legally aided parties are not required to pay any court fees, and their obligation to pay the base fee was repealed in 2006.

While the much greater use of fixed fees and smaller proportionate fees is a positive development, the level of court fees is still seen as to some extent an obstacle to access to justice. In an interview with Gazeta Prawna, Maciej Dobrowicz—the Head of the National Chamber of Legal Advisers—argued for a further decrease of proportionate fee to three per cent in high value, complex cases.[48] The Class Actions Act of 2009 addresses his postulates to some extent. A court fee in a class action concerning pecuniary claims is to amount to two per cent of the value of the claim, or if the latter is not established at the outset—a temporary fee is to be between 100 and 100,000 PLN.[49] For non-pecuniary claims a fixed fee of 600 PLN is specified.[50]

Witnesses' Expenses

Witnesses are not entitled to remuneration. They receive reimbursement of costs for travel and accommodation, and compensation for loss of remuneration or profit.[51] While it is the court that makes the final decision on the appointment of witnesses, the parties can nominate as many witnesses as they see necessary. Recently, the Supreme Court held that a court in charge of a case can nominate a witness without the parties' request, provided the party in question is not represented by a lawyer.[52]

[45] Art 15 of the Act on Court Costs. It can be a proportionate fee (if the value of the subject of the dispute has been determined) or a fee the amount of which is specified by the court (in which case it cannot exceed 5,000 PLN). In the latter case, the court considers the social implications of the judgment and the complexity of the case.

[46] Art 14 of the Act. This fee is payable in quite a narrow range of cases, for instance those concerning labour relations.

[47] The fee is 6 PLN per page: arts 77 and 78 of the Act on Court Costs.

[48] Gazeta Prawna, 20 Oct 2009, prawo.gazetaprawna.pl/wywiady/362868,wysokie_oplaty_sadowe_w_polsce_ograniczaja_dostep_do_wymiaru_sprawiedliwosci.html.

[49] Arts 13.2 and 15.2 of the Act on Court Costs, amended by the Act on Class Actions 2009.

[50] Art 26.1 of the Act.

[51] Art 85 of the Act. With regard to the remuneration or profit—compensation should amount to their average daily remuneration or business profit (Article 86). Detailed rules concerning compensation of witnesses are contained in the Regulation of the Minister of Justice of 4 Jul 1990 on the compensation for parties and witnesses in civil litigation (*Dziennik Ustaw* (Journal of Laws) no 48, item 284).

[52] Judgment of the Supreme Court of 15 Dec 2005, file no V CK 400/05.

Remuneration of Experts, Translators and Other Persons

Experts are appointed by the court upon the request of the parties.[53] It is specified that the court appoints an expert if there is a need for specialist knowledge during litigation, and whereas the parties can suggest the names of experts the judge makes the final decision. (The parties can consult their own experts, but this is always done at their own expense and the opinions of such experts are not considered as evidence.) The court determines the scope of the expert's opinion, which is normally given in writing. The parties can comment on the opinion and they are also given the opportunity to contest it and question the expert during a formal hearing. The parties requesting their appointment normally make an advance payment to experts.[54] Their remuneration is subsequently established by the court on the basis of their professional knowledge and experience as well as the time and effort spent in preparing the opinion.[55] Experts charge an hourly fee (which covers both preparation of the opinion and the appearance in court), the base amount of which is 22–31 PLN. This rate may be increased, depending on the expert's expertise and seniority (for instance academic experts receive a higher rate), and the complexity of the case. Experts can also claim reimbursement of travel costs, accommodation and other expenses. Translators and other persons who take part in litigation are compensated following the same principles as the experts.[56] Decisions concerning compensation of witnesses, experts, translators and other persons are made by court clerks.[57]

Lawyers' Fees

Lawyers who represent litigation parties are normally barristers (*adwokat)* or legal advisers (*radca prawny*). The amendment of the Act on legal advisers in 1997 introduced a significant level of parity as regards the competences of both professions.[58] It also introduced equality as regards their remuneration. The general

[53] Arts 278–291 of the Code of Civil Procedure regulate appointment of experts.

[54] The court will refuse to appoint an expert if the party does not make an advance payment (art 130.4 of the Code of Civil Procedure). Of course, if the party wins the case, he can recover the costs from the losing party at the end of the proceedings.

[55] The Regulation of the Minister of Justice of 18 Dec 1975 on costs of obtaining expert evidence in civil litigation (*Dziennik Ustaw* (Journal of Laws) no 46, item 254) provides that all experts' remuneration is calculated on the basis of the amount for persons occupying managerial positions in public administration, established annually. In 2009, the basic amount is 1,835.35 PLN—State Budget for 2009 (*Ustawa bud etowa na rok 2009 z dnia 9 stycznia 2009 roku*) (*Dziennik Ustaw* (Journal of Laws) no 10, item 58).

[56] Art 89 of the Act.

[57] Art 93 of the Act.

[58] The Act on legal advisers of 6 Jul 1982, amended by the Act on the reform of the law on barristers, the Act on legal advisers and some other Acts of 22 May 1997 (published in Dziennik Ustaw (Journal of Laws) no 75, item 471).

principle governing the fees for barristers and legal advisers in Poland is freedom of contract.[59] However, for cost-shifting purposes, fees are established by law on a tariff basis as specified in two Regulations of the Minister of Justice of 2002.[60] The tariff that applies depends on the type of case, and on the amount in dispute. In many cases, the minimum fee is specified: this applies in family law disputes,[61] property law disputes, intellectual property and patent cases, criminal cases and many others. In other civil, employment and social insurance cases, fees are specified according to a scale that depends on the value of the case.[62] The general principle is that the fee established by the court for the particular case in the final cost assessment should not be higher or lower than the minimum rate, irrespective of any agreement between the lawyer and the client. However, the Regulations allow exceptions to this principle: the court may establish a fee higher than the minimum rate (although not higher than six times the minimum rate) if the complexity of the case and the barrister or solicitor's amount of work justify this.[63] Further, in exceptional cases, where the financial or family position of the client or the type of case justifies this, the lawyer may agree to a fee which is lower than the minimum rate or even waive the fee entirely. In such cases, the court may establish such agreed lower or waived fee for cost-shifting purposes. The tariffs also apply in cases where the lawyer was appointed by the court for a legally aided party. Lawyers can receive up to 150 per cent of the minimum rate, and such amount is reimbursed by the losing party or, if the legally aided party lost the case or if the opposing party is unable to pay, by the State.[64]

[59] H St pie , *Honorarium adwokata i radcy prawnego w polskim systemie prawnym* (barristers and solicitors' fees in the Polish legal system) (2005) www.oirp.waw.pl/temidium/wynagrodzenie1.htm (*Temidium*—the newsletter of the District Chamber of Legal Advisers in Warsaw).

[60] Regulations of the Minister of Justice of 28 Sept 2002: w *sprawie opłat za czynno ci adwokackie oraz ponoszenia przez Skarb Pa stwa kosztów nieopłaconej pomocy prawnej udzielonej z urz du* (on the remuneration of barristers' services and on the payment by the State Treasury of the costs of unpaid legal assistance nominated *ex officio*), later called 'Regulation on Barristers' Fees'; and *w sprawie opłat za czynno ci radców prawnych oraz ponoszenia przez Skarb Pa stwa kosztów pomocy prawnej udzielonej przez radc prawnego ustanowionego z urz du* (on the remuneration of legal advisers' services and on the payment by the State Treasury of the costs of legal assistance given by a legal adviser nominated *ex officio*), later called 'Regulation on legal advisers' fees'. *Dziennik Ustaw* (Journal of Laws) no 163, items 1348 and 1349.

[61] For instance, a fee in a divorce case is 360 PLN (art 7.1 of the Regulation on Barristers' Fees, and art 6.a of the Regulation on Legal Advisers' Fees).

[62] For cases worth up to 500 PLN the fee is 60 PLN; for cases worth between 500 and 1,500 PLN it is 180 PLN, for cases worth between 1,500 and 5,000 PLN it is 600 PLN; for cases worth between 5,000 and 10,000 PLN it is 1,200 PLN; for cases worth between 10,000 and 50,000–2,400 PLN; for cases worth between 50,000 and 200,000 PLN–3,600 PLN, and for cases above 200,000 PLN–7,200 PLN.

[63] Chapter Two paragraph 2.2 of both Regulations.

[64] Art 19 of the Regulation on Barristers' Fees, and art 15 of the Regulation on Legal Advisers' Fees.

Costs of Mediation and Expenses of Mediators

As mentioned above, mediation was introduced into Polish civil litigation in 2005.[65] Parties can commence mediation on their own initiative, or they can be referred to mediation by a judge in charge of their case.[66] If the court refers parties to mediation, the costs of mediation are seen as part of the overall costs of litigation, and thus the rules governing their assessment and apportionment analysed below will also apply.[67] This will also be the case if parties commence litigation within three months of the completion of unsuccessful mediation, although in this situation only a quarter of the costs of mediation will be calculated as part of the litigation costs.[68] Remuneration for mediators is established according to a tariff set out in the Regulation of the Minister of Justice of 2005.[69] In cases involving pecuniary claims, the remuneration is one per cent of the value in dispute, and in cases where the value cannot be established in advance and non-pecuniary cases it is 60 PLN for the first mediation meeting and 25 PLN for each following meeting. Mediators are also entitled to reimbursement of reasonably incurred and necessary costs of travel, correspondence with the parties, stationery, and hire of premises for mediation meetings (not more than 50 PLN per meeting).

Overall, the costs of mediation are not regulated in as much detail as court and 'process costs'. The parties are given the freedom to agree on the costs with the mediator independently of the rules specified above. These agreements will be upheld if mediation leads to settlement. In such cases, each party will bear its own costs of mediation, unless the parties agree otherwise.[70]

Cost Assessment and Allocation

Cost assessment is done by the court at the conclusion of the litigation in each instance.[71] It can be delegated by a judge to a court clerk. Article 98 of the Code of Civil Procedure clearly sets out that only reasonably incurred costs, those necessary for proceeding with litigation, will be awarded. Article 109 reiterates this rule

[65] Act of 28 July 2005 on the amendment of the Civil Procedure Code and some other acts introduced mediation into the Code of Civil Procedure.

[66] Art 202.1 of the Code of Civil Procedure.

[67] Art 98.1 para 1 of the Code of Civil Procedure.

[68] Art 98.2 para 2 of the Code of Civil Procedure. However, the costs of mediation are not treated as 'court costs'—thus even if a party is legally aided the state is not required to cover them.

[69] Regulation of the Minister of Justice on the remuneration and expenses of mediators in civil litigation (*Rozporzadzenie Ministra Sprawiedliwosci w sprawie wysokosci wynagrodzenia i podlegajacych zwrotowi wydatkow mediatora w postepowaniu cywilnym*) of 30 Nov 2005, *Dziennik Ustaw* (Journal of Laws) no 239, item 2018.

[70] Art 104.1 of the Code of Civil Procedure.

[71] ibid, art 108.1.

for the purposes of cost assessment and allocation. The general rule followed by the Polish Code of Civil Procedure is that the court determines which costs were indeed necessary and reasonably incurred. However, the Code also specifies certain costs which will always need to be covered by the final cost decision: the 'process costs' incurred by the parties, their travel expenses and compensation for lost remuneration or business profit, and the remuneration of one lawyer.[72]

Polish civil procedure follows the 'loser pays' rule,[73] which applies even in cases where the party was in receipt of legal aid.[74] There are exemptions from this rule, most of which are subject to the discretion of the court.[75] If a party to a case was only partially successful, the costs may be apportioned equally or proportionately between the parties.[76] If the defendant accepted the claim immediately and did not wish to prolong litigation, the court may require that the claimant cover the defendant's costs.[77] If the specific circumstances call for it, the court may decide that the loser should only incur a part of the costs or no costs at all.[78] If a winning party behaved in an unreasonable manner during litigation, for instance by refusing to mediate if the parties initially agreed to mediation, the court may make an adverse costs decision.[79] If the parties settled the case, they can agree that each party pays its own costs.[80]

Conclusions

These rules on costs are fairly recent. While the foundations for an accessible, efficient and effective civil justice system have been laid in Poland, the future will show whether they will indeed produce these desired results. As far as the costs of litigation are concerned, the regulatory framework has become more grounded, clearer and transparent. The costs have been reduced. Funding mechanisms are evolving towards greater accessibility, although there is still plenty of scope for improvement (with regard to legal aid and insurance), and for greater clarity (with regard to contingency fees). However, the true costs of litigation reach beyond the officially regulated court costs and lawyers' fees to inefficiencies, delays and complexities of civil procedure. Further, if the quality of civil justice and quality of adjudication are not satisfactory, they may not be seen as 'value for money,' irrespective of the financial cost. Plenty of challenges lie ahead for the Polish civil justice system.

[72] Arts 98.2 and 98.3 of the Code of Civil Procedure. Interestingly, the Code refers to the remuneration of 'one lawyer'—this applies even if the party used a number of lawyers or a large law firm.
[73] Art 98 of the Code of Civil Procedure.
[74] Art 108 of the Act on Court Costs and art 121 of the Code of Civil Procedure.
[75] Arts 100–104 and 106 of the Code of Civil Procedure.
[76] Art 100 of the Code of Civil Procedure.
[77] ibid, art 101.
[78] ibid, art 102—this may be dictated by equity or justice considerations.
[79] ibid, art 103.
[80] ibid, arts 104 and 105.

18

Portugal

HENRIQUE SOUSA ANTUNES*

General Overview and Trends

The system of legal costs in Portugal finances the justice system, guarantees access to the law and discourages frivolous or excessive claims in law and judicial practices which are merely dilatory. From the ideals of the French Revolution, which favoured the free use of justice services, law inherited sensitivity towards a justification for the rules of exemption from costs and legal aid. However, one characteristic of the Portuguese legal system is the participation of the user in the cost of its operation.

Once it has been established that access to the courts implies that the legal costs be assumed, the next task is to define the content of this responsibility. Various principles emerge from the history of Portuguese law, in the period prior to codification. The Philipine Ordinances (in the seventeenth century) represent the final expression of these: the defeated party in the action was responsible for the procedural costs, even if the judge recognized that he had just cause to litigate;[1] the judge had the possibility of exempting the defeated party from payment of personal costs, if he concluded that the grounds on which the latter had to litigate were justified; malice was punished: if the party acted in court in a malicious way, he should pay double or triple the amount of the costs and, in the absence of property, should be imprisoned.

The system described above raises four issues.[2] Firstly, how are procedural costs distinguished from personal costs? Secondly, what constitutes just cause to litigate? Linked to these first two questions, what is the reasoning behind exemption from the payment of personal costs if there are justified grounds to litigate? Lastly, does the application of the punishment of paying double or triple the costs apply to all the costs, just the procedural costs or just the personal costs?[3]

* Professor of Law at the Catholic University of Portugal.

[1] The grounds for the rule are: 'He who needs to use the courts to protect his right may not suffer any disadvantage from taking this course, and must reach the end of the process with his right intact' in: P Costa e Silva, *A Litigância de Má Fé* (Coimbra, Coimbra Editora, 2008) 44.

[2] This issue is dealt with by Costa e Silva (n 1) 47 *et seq*. Our analysis closely follows this text.

[3] Costa e Silva (n 1) 47.

Personal costs included the time invested in the action, assessed according to the quality and social status of the party, food, transport, accommodation, and expenses with people who, in view of the party's social class, necessarily accompanied him. However, the law established maximum limits for compensating certain personal costs.[4] Meanwhile, having outlined the expenses which made up the personal costs, it is possible to conclude, on the one hand, that these were distinct from expenses for lawyer fees, which could be compensated for if the judge ordered the defeated party to pay for losses and harm, and, on the other hand, different from both of these categories was damage which had no intrinsic relationship with the action.[5]

Mere failure to succeed in the action did not exclude just cause to litigate, although it constituted a presumption of its absence. Whenever a founded reason legitimated participation in the suit, there was therefore no reason to attribute compensation to the successful party regarding personal expenses with the suit. In the case of malice, which type of costs were doubled or tripled and who received the resulting punitive sum are controversial issues.[6]

To sum up, three levels of responsibility were defined, depending on the subjective state of the defeated party. In earlier texts other distinctions also applied. In the Manueline Ordenances (sixteenth century), the active procedural position was differentiated from the passive procedural position. If the claimant, being the defeated party in the action, acted in just cause, he benefited from exemption from payment of any of the costs of the successful party. The defendant, on losing the suit, was obliged to pay the procedural costs, even if his participation in the action had justified grounds.[7] The Afonsine Ordenances (fifteenth century) introduced the distinction between objective just cause and subjective just cause, associating exemption from the payment of any costs with the former.[8]

In the draft bill for the first codification on civil procedure in Portugal, the 1876 Code, the author (Alexandre de Seabra) set out that the obligation to pay costs was related to the good or bad faith of the parties in the case, regardless of success or failure in the action (article 46). He later clarified that the principle regarded only the duty to pay costs in the situation of partial failure, and, thus, the rule laid down that the costs would be paid by the defeated party in proportion to his failure. Meanwhile, articles 50 and 51 of the Bill discussed the punishment of a litigant in bad faith with a fine (10 per cent of the value of the case: on revision, the application of a fine of five per cent to the defeated party was included, with autonomy of bad faith) and compensation. Finally, article 52 obliged the parties to pay a sum

[4] ibid, p 49 *et seq.*

[5] See the examples of Almeida e Sousa, quoted by Costa e Silva (n 1) 55: if, on route, the party was robbed or the horse that brought him died. Also if, due to absence, herds of cattle died or ploughing was delayed. In this respect, we may also emphasise, however, that jurisprudence extended the compensation imposed on the defeated party to damage that he caused, with malice, to the honour, liberty or property of the successful party (Costa e Silva (n 1) 73 *et seq*).

[6] Costa e Silva (n 1) 58 *et seq.*

[7] ibid, p 114 *et seq.*

[8] ibid, p 126 *et seq.*

corresponding to 0.5 per cent of the value of the case for the courts' operating and maintenance expenses (on revision, this rule was altered, extending the payment to one per cent of the value of the case, but restricting the duty to pay it to the defeated party). The final text of the Portuguese Civil Procedure Code of 1876 maintained the later versions of the Bill, although with regard to aggravated procedural responsibility, it eliminated the duty to pay a fine of five per cent of the value of the case for mere failure in the action, not depending on the bad faith of the litigant.[9]

Victus Victori Principle

In current Portuguese legislation the option of the principle of *victus victori* (loser pays principle) appears to be clear. One may read, in article 446 (1) and (2) of the Portuguese Civil Procedure Code (approved by Decree-Law no. 44 129, dated 28 December 1961, with the relevant subsequent amendments):

> '1—The decision which judges the action or any of its incidents or appeals shall order costs to be borne by the party which has given rise to them or, where there is no successful party in the action, whoever gains advantage; 2—It is understood that the defeated party gives rise to the costs, in the proportion in which he is so defeated'.

Quoting the Judgment 303/2001, of the Constitutional Court:

> 'The fact that the legislator opted for the principle of correspondence between the responsibility to pay the costs and the result of the procedural activity of those intervening in the case is justified. In fact, the responsibility for the payment of the costs is based on the idea that a case should not cause harm to the party with reason, with the costs being paid by the defeated party, and in proportion to this defeat, or, where there is no winner, by the party that gained advantage from the claim. In general, a sacrifice of patrimony should not be imposed on the party for whose benefit the intervention of the court took place, since it is in the interest of the State that the use of the procedure does not cause harm to the litigant with reason. Thus, and as a rule, the responsibility for the payment of the costs is based on the principle of causality and, additionally, on the principle of the procedural advantage or benefit'.

The rule is not absolute, however, excluding mere failure from constituting the grounds for attributing costs. This fact allows some legal theory to recognise subjective reasons in the responsibility for costs, without the law making that requirement explicit.[10] Fault in the proceedings therefore very often constitutes a justification for the assumption of charging costs, even when the party wins the action.[11] What is at issue, fundamentally, is the lack of procedural interest. The

[9] ibid, p 191 *et seq.*

[10] In a different sense there is the rule for the sharing of costs where the action subsequently becomes impossible or useless not through any fault of the parties, under the terms of art 450 of the Portuguese Civil Procedure Code.

[11] In this sense, Costa e Silva (n 1) 640 *et seq.*

revision brought about by Decree-Law no 34/2008, dated 28 February, to which we shall give detailed attention, added other examples to the list.

Article 448 (Acts and measures which are not included in the general rule on costs) and article 449 (Responsibility of the claimant for the costs) of the Portuguese Civil Procedure Code outline situations of fault in the use of proceedings. One may read in paragraphs 1 and 2 of the first rule:

> '1. The responsibility of the defeated party regarding costs does not cover superfluous acts and incidents . . .; 2. Acts and incidents which are unnecessary for the declaration or defence of the right shall be considered superfluous. The costs of these acts shall be borne by whosoever requested them . . .'.

Article 449 (1) provides:

> 'When the defendant has not given rise to the action and does not contest it, the costs are paid by the claimant'.

Among the facts described in paragraph 2 of this article are situations in which the obligation of the defendant is only due at the time of the summons or after the action has been proposed, or where the claimant, although benefiting from a right which is clearly enforceable, uses declaratory proceedings, or, also, when declarative proceedings are used when simplified proceedings for compliance with pecuniary obligations could be used. Regarding the first situation mentioned, we may also refer to article 662 (Judgment in the case of unenforceable obligation), which establishes that if the obligation is unenforceable when the action is brought and the defendant contests the enforceability of the provision, without litigating with regard to the existence of the duty (2), the claimant shall bear the costs and pay the fees of the defendant's lawyer (3). Thus, both in the provisions of article 449 and underlying that which is laid down in article 662, 'the use of the court proved to be totally unnecessary since the attitude of the defendant suggested that he would have complied with the obligation by which he was bound. The claimant won the action, but since it was unnecessary, he gave rise to the legal costs, and consequently should bear them'[12].

The 2008 reform widened the range of departures from the *victus victori* rule. Thus, in accordance with article 447-C (4) of the Portuguese Civil Procedure Code:

> '[C]harges arising from the carrying out of measures which are clearly unnecessary and dilatory in nature shall be borne exclusively by the claimant, regardless of whether he wins or is ordered to pay costs'.

The other rule is based on the preference for the use of alternative means of dispute resolution. These structures include the Magistrates' Courts (*Julgados de Paz*), the employment mediation system, the family mediation system, the automobile arbitration centre and several consumers' arbitration centres. If the successful party takes legal proceedings, where, however, it was possible to choose

[12] Costa e Silva (n 1) 463.

alternative dispute structures, he shall bear his own costs, except when the counterparty made the use of that alternative means of dispute resolution unfeasible (article 447-D, (4)). The following has been written in this regard:

> 'If the claimant has used judicial action, having been able to resort to mechanisms of alternative dispute resolution, he shall bear the costs of what he has done, with no right to be reimbursed. This penalising measure appears to be excessive, since the claimant may have reasons for opting for the judicial route, if this affords greater legal security. Granting benefits for those who resort to alternative structures . . . seems correct; what should not be applauded is the sacrifice of the successful party, who is deprived of the right to reimbursement for what he has spent, simply due to the fact that he has used the court, when this is a constitutional right . . .'.[13,14]

We are of the same opinion.

Conciliation

The 2008 reform sought, meanwhile, to favour conciliation of the parties in court. Article 446-A(2) of the Portuguese Civil Procedure Code participates in this aim by providing, with regard to joint actions, that 'in cases of settlement of some of the joint parties, those who settle shall benefit from a 50 per cent reduction in the amount of costs', in addition to article 22 (2)(b) of the Regulations on Legal Costs, which determines the conversion of the amount paid as a justice fee in the prior payment of charges in actions in which the parties reach a settlement. We may also mention that article 451 (2) of the Portuguese Civil Procedure Code rules on costs in the situation of settlement in the following terms:

> 'In the case of settlement, the costs are shared in half, unless there is an agreement to the contrary, but when the settlement is made between a party who is exempt or dispensed from paying costs and another who is not exempt or dispensed, the judge, after consultation with the Public Prosecutor's Office, shall determine the proportion in which the costs must be paid'.

Effects of Decree-Law no. 34/2008

Current legal discussion concerning the costs of proceedings takes as its reference the alterations resulting from the aforementioned Decree-Law no 34/2008. The reform introduced a range of measures which, although having different purposes,

[13] E Valles, *Custas Processuais* 2nd edn (Coimbra, Almedina, 2009) 57. However, the legislator established in art 46 of Ministerial Order no. 419-A/2009 that up until the publication of the required implementing rules, 'the costs of the successful part shall be borne by the defeated party and the exemptions and benefits provided for in law are guaranteed, regardless of the use of any structure of alternative dispute resolution'.

[14] The conversion of the justice fee into prior payment of costs has the sense of a positive measure, when there is withdrawal from the action with the purpose of the subsequent use of extra-judicial dispute resolution proceedings (art 22 (2)(c), of the Regulations on Legal Costs).

come together to form an added burden on some users of the judicial system. The discussion among academics and law professionals includes as its central questions the compatibility of the solutions with the constitutional principles of equality, of proportionality and of access to law and to the courts (articles 13, 18(2) and 20 of the Constitution of the Portuguese Republic of 1976, subsequently amended).

We shall therefore take a closer look at the revision in question. Decree-Law no 34/2008 amended, amongst other texts, the Civil Procedure Code, the Criminal Procedure Code, the Tax Procedure and Process Code, approved the new Regulations on Legal Costs, bringing together in this document all the quantitative and procedural rules on the costs due in any case, whether civil, criminal, administrative or fiscal, and repealed a significant number of principles and statutes. One of the aims of the reform was the concentration of the rules. The others may be summarised: '. . . increasing the flexibility of the base of reference for the calculation of justice fees, penalising the intense litigation of companies and the so-called case blocking, and encouragement of the use of means of alternative dispute resolution'.[15]

Regarding the adoption of penalising measures there are clear objections to the new regime adopted. We may firstly provide a description of its content. The preamble reads:

> 'One of the factors which greatly contribute to the congestion within the judicial system is the "colonisation" of the courts by a group of companies whose activity represents a constant and unlimited source of cases for the collection of debts of small monetary value. These collection claims and the respective enforcement, which represent over half of all pending proceedings, illustrate a panorama of abusive use of judicial means without consideration for means of preventive justice. Within this scope, the adoption of some more incisive measures is proposed, which seek to penalise the unnecessary and unjustified use of the courts and "mass litigation"'.

Pursuing this aim, the legislator added to the Portuguese Civil Procedure Code a rule which determines the increase of 50 per cent of the justice fee for commercial companies which, in the previous year, presented an annual volume of entries into the court greater than 200 actions, proceedings or enforcements (article 447-A (6) of the Portuguese Civil Procedure Code, and article 13 (3) and (5) of the Regulations on Legal Costs).[16]

Meanwhile, what is considered to be particularly penalising is the exceptional sanctioning fee applicable to parties in proceedings 'who, for dilatory reasons, "block" the courts with clearly groundless appeals and petitions' (preamble). The law subjects the application of the measure to a decision by the judge stating grounds. It appears appropriate when the petitions, appeals, objections and requests for rectification, reform or clarification, which are clearly unfounded, are

[15] S da Costa, 'Regulamento das Custas Processuais' (2009) 52 *OA—Boletim da Ordem dos Advogados* 26.

[16] The payment of the aggravated justice fee is due from 1 Jan 2010 (art 47 of Ministerial Order no. 419-A/2009, dated 17 Apr 2009).

merely the result of a lack of prudence or diligence by the party, are beyond the discussion of merit and are merely dilatory in character, or, while they seek to discuss the merits of the case, are clearly unfounded due to the existence of jurisprudence in the opposite sense and they are exclusively the result of negligence of the party (article 447-B). It is stated that the decision to apply an exceptional sanctioning fee may be fixed between 2 and 15 units of account (article 10 of the Regulations on Legal Costs), this amount being greater than the fine applied to litigation in bad faith (between 0.5 and 5 units of account, with the possibility of an increase to 10 units of account in particularly serious cases—article 27 (1) and (2) of the Regulations on Legal Costs).[17] We may note that the law omits the criteria to be considered in fixing the exceptional sanctioning fee, whereas with regard to the fine Article 27 (3) of the Regulations on Legal Costs provides:

> 'The amount of the fine or penalty is always fixed by the judge, taking into consideration the effects of the violation of the law on the regular progression of the proceedings and on the correct decision in the case, the economic situation of the agent and the repercussions of the punishment on his patrimony'.

It further laid down (article 27 (4) of the Regulations on Legal Costs):

> 'A fine and an exceptional sanctioning fee may not be simultaneously applied to a party in the same proceedings'.[18]

The measures outlined are included in a 'plan of moralisation and rationalisation . . .' (preamble) of the use of the legal system. Others, however, have afforded it a different reading, in the light of the constitutional protection for equality, proportionality and access to law and to the courts. Regarding the penalising of companies with a high level of litigation, the following has been written:

> 'It is difficult to understand how recourse to judicial means can be punished based on the criteria of the number of cases that a legal subject finds himself forced to instigate in a given year, and even harder to accept is the idea that the need to use the courts for the collection of debts, even if they are of a low value, is considered to be immoral and abusive. Such an understanding (and the measure adopted) is not in line with the principle of equality and the much talked of right of access to the courts, both consecrated in the Constitution as fundamental rights'.[19]

[17] The solution is unjustified. The regime of litigation in bad faith applies to wilful conduct or conduct with gross negligence. Art 456 (2) of the Portuguese Civil Procedure Code describes the behaviour which may be sanctioned with the payment of a fine and compensation to the other party, including in this, amongst other expenses, the fees of the legal representatives: 'A litigant in bad faith is one who, wilfully or with gross negligence: a) has inferred an intention or opposition the lack of grounds for which should not be ignored; b) has altered the truth of the facts or omitted facts which are relevant to the decision in question; c) has practised a gross omission of the duty to cooperate; d) has used the case or the procedural means in a manner which is clearly censurable, with the purpose of achieving an illegal objective, preventing the discovery of the truth, distorting the action of Justice or delaying, with no serious grounds, the *res judicata* of the decision'. There is, indeed, an 'absolute systematic incongruence' (in the words of Costa e Silva (n 1) 288): 'It can be seen . . . that in the current scheme as a reaction to the misuse of proceedings, a more serious sanction corresponds to a lesser deviation from ethical behaviour' (Costa e Silva (n 1) 288).

[18] This rule was, however, repealed by Law 64-A/2008, dated 31 Dec 2008.

[19] A Costa Almeida and M Gonçalves, 'O preço da justiça' (2009) 52 *OA—Boletim da Ordem dos Advogados* 28.

In relation to the exceptional sanctioning fee, we may read:

> '. . . besides the fact that the judicial decision may be based on criteria marked by vagueness and subjectivity, it is unacceptable that the grounds for it may be "the existence of jurisprudence in the opposite sense" to that proposed by the party. This is nothing more than the unfounded restricting and constraining of rights which are legally guaranteed to the parties, an affront to the free exercise of the practice of law and a neglect of the constant progression which characterizes Law and Jurisprudence today'.[20]

We have a different opinion regarding 'mass litigation'. The effect of the use of the legal system by companies which intervene in a large number of actions on the use of the same services by the general public justifies the fact that the companies in question pay a fee which exceeds the proportion of actions, proceedings or enforcements that enter the courts. The fee is a cost, which, in this situation, reflects the scarcity of the means for responding to the intentions of the creditor. We would accept, however, the fixing of the amount of reference of the entries and the aggravation of the justice fee in line with an approximate assessment of the costs and social benefits of the measure.

On the issue of justice fees in general, it has been written:

> 'Given that the user of Justice is a beneficiary of the provision of a service, it is reasonable to require from him the payment of a certain amount for the service provided. However, and in order to be able to say that the principle of proportionality in the fixing of justice fees has been observed, it is not sufficient to conclude that those who use the courts gain a benefit. It is necessary to find criteria that allow for the quantifying of how much it costs to grant this benefit to those who use the court. . . . For this idea to be realized, a first step may not be dispensed with: that of determining the real cost of any proceedings. Only then will we know if the fee applied bears any relation to the value of the service provided, that is, if it is reasonable and appropriate'.[21]

There is a need for a certain proximity to the actual cost of access to the courts, accepting, however, the inexistence of exact correspondence:

> 'The Constitutional Court has accepted that, for the purposes of a judgment of unconstitutionality regarding the amount of costs established, it is not necessary for the justice fee . . . to correspond to the cost of the service of the administration of justice . . ., and that there does not have to be strict economic equivalence between the value of the service and the amount of the sum to be provided by the user of that service. Nevertheless, even if this is understood, it is necessary that the criteria adopted is not disproportionate'.[22]

[20] Costa Almeida (n 19) 29.

[21] Costa e Silva (n 1) 282.

[22] R Medeiros, in J Miranda and R Medeiros *Constituição Portuguesa Anotada*, vol I (Coimbra, Coimbra Editora, 2005) 183. According to the Constitutional Court, quoting G Canotilho and V Moreira, 'the principle of proportionality is divided into three sub-principles: principle of adequacy (measures restricting rights, freedoms and guarantees should prove to be a means for the pursuit of the aims envisaged, safeguarding other constitutionally protected rights or goods); principle of demandability (these restrictive measures must be demanded in order to achieve the ends in view, when the legislator does not have other less restrictive means at its disposal to achieve the same purpose); principle of fair measure, or proportionality in the strict sense (excessive and disproportionate measures may not be adopted to attain the intended aims)' (Judgment 634/93).

The determination of correspondence proves to be difficult, in fact:

> 'This is, basically, the conclusion that can be drawn from the jurisprudence of the Constitutional Court: while this court accepted that some justice fees do not conform to the principle of proportionality, since they appear exorbitant in relation to the service that is provided, the court was not able to declare, assertively, what the parameters of constitutional suitability would be, in its opinion. And it was unable to do so for the simple reason that there is a lack of all the statistical information relevant to the formulation of this decision'.[23]

In our opinion, the criticism of the inappropriateness of the criteria of jurisprudence in the opposite sense as a justification for the exceptional sanctioning fee does seem to be fair. Jurisprudence is denied the character of an immediate source of law. No general binding force is recognised for decisions of the courts. The indirect binding of those intervening in proceedings resulting from the application of the aforementioned sanctioning fee thus appears to be without grounds.

Other Measures of Decree-Law no. 34/2008

Other aspects of the 2008 reform are criticised from the perspective of access to law and the courts. It is worth taking a look at the options taken.

Firstly, Decree-Law no 34/2008 eliminated the payment of the justice fee in two instalments, the initial justice fee and the subsequent justice fee, concentrating this duty into a single moment, the beginning of the proceedings. The legislator justifies this position in the preamble: 'In this way, and since the pursuit of the action, incident or appeal is dependent on the prior payment of the single justice fee, this will equally avoid the numerous cases of non-compliance which have led to the increase of small enforcements for costs instigated by the Public Prosecutor's Office'. Dissenting voices may be heard:

> 'Such an option represents an excessive and unjustifiably burdensome cost for citizens and companies, which in practice will preclude, on the one hand, their right of access to the courts and, on the other, their right to defence and exercise of adversarial proceedings, *conditio sine qua non* of the actual realization of justice. We would also add that such an innovation appears even more incoherent when there is so much talk of "a time of crisis" and when exceptional measures to combat this situation are advocated . . .'.[24]

Secondly, the law restricted the exemption from payment of costs. Indeed, in the words of the legislator itself, there was a 'drastic reduction in exemptions'. In the opinion of some, this choice was not justified in all cases. This is the situation, for example, in appeals with deferred progression which, when they do not progress due to the lack of interest or withdrawal of the claimant, are subject to costs. There

[23] Costa e Silva (n 1) 282 *et seq.*

[24] Costa Almeida (n 19) 28. The legislator, considering the 'difficult economic cycle the country is going through' would later, in the implementing rules, allow for delayed payment of the justice fee in two instalments, up to a time limit of 90 days, during a transitional period ending on 31 Dec 2010 (art 44(2) of Ministerial Order no. 419-A/2009).

is a lack of procedural activity which legitimises the charge.[25] In another sense, the provision of some exemptions is also criticised. This benefit is received by the magistrates and voting members of the Higher Council of the Judiciary who are not judges, in any actions in which they are a party through the exercise of their functions (article 4 (1)(c) of the Regulations on Legal Costs). The lack of a similar benefit for lawyers has warranted criticism from members of that group: 'Such exclusion appears to be clearly in opposition to the constitutional principle of equality, not being based on any legitimate grounds for the different treatment'.[26] Finally, the conditional nature of some exemptions is censured, since it constitutes, in general, 'uncertainty which generates a disturbance in proceedings at the level of the prior payment of the justice fee',[27] and, in particular, exerts 'real pressure to resort to alternative means of dispute resolution. For example, if, regarding an employment issue, the other legal requirements having been confirmed, the workers or family members do not first use an alternative structure for dispute resolution, they will not be entitled to exemption from the payment of costs'.[28]

Thirdly, it is worth mentioning the legislator's decision to disassociate the amount of the justice fee from corresponding with the value of the claim:

> 'It has been seen that the value of the claim is not a decisive element when considering the complexity of the proceedings and in the generation of costs for the legal system. Therefore, seeking to improve the correspondence of the justice fee, a mixed system is now established based on the value of the claim, up to a certain maximum limit, and the possibility of correcting the justice fee in the case of particularly complex proceedings, regardless of the economic value attributed to the case'.

Article 447-A(7) of the Portuguese Civil Procedure Code, with the additions from the 2008 reform, provides that

> 'for the purposes of the decision on the payment of the justice fee, actions considered to be particularly complex are those which: a) relate to issues of high legal specialisation or technical specificity or which require the combined analysis of legal issues of a very varied scope; and b) require that a large number of witnesses be heard, or require the analysis of extremely complex means of evidence or the carrying out of various lengthy actions for the production of evidence'.

On this issue, see article 6 (5) of the Regulations on Legal Costs which indicates the application of a table which fixes the amounts of the justice fee that the judge may determine, finally, in the case of particularly complex actions and appeals. The amount is, however, variable, in the case of temporary injunctions or procedural incidents (article 7 (5) of the Regulations on Legal Costs). If the principle is reasonable, the referral to the power of the judge to assess the higher amount due, although within the legally established limits, certainly narrows the predictability

[25] Costa Almeida (n 19) 29.
[26] Costa Almeida (n 19) 29.
[27] S da Costa, 'Regulamento das Custas Processuais' (n 15) 26.
[28] Costa Almeida (n 19) 29.

of the justice fee for the provision of the service (note that the amount may vary between 7 and 14 units of account for incidents, and 9 and 20 units of account for temporary injunctions). The issue should be seen in the light of the constitutional interpretation of article 20 (1) of the Constitution of the Portuguese Republic:

> 'Everyone is guaranteed access to law and the courts for the defence of his or her rights and legally protected interests; justice may not be withheld from a person for lack of financial means'.

In fact,

> 'the law may not . . . adopt solutions which are so onerous that, in practice, they prevent the average citizen from accessing justice. That is, having safeguarded legal protection for the most needy, the costs should not be unbearable in relation to the capacity to contribute of the average citizen; the adoption of measures regarding costs which, namely in cases of greater uncertainty regarding the outcome of the proceedings, inhibit the interested parties from accessing justice are not constitutionally admissible'.[29]

Reimbursement of Expenses

The rules regarding the reimbursement of expenses, fixing the extent of that restitution and the criteria of division, certainly influence the cost of justice. Portuguese law limits the benefit of the successful party to the justice fees, the charges and a sum equivalent to half of the value of the justice fees paid by both parties, intended to cover the lawyer's fees (Article 26 (3)(c) of the Regulations on Legal Costs). It is a well-known fact that the amounts charged by legal representatives constitute a significant portion of the costs involved in access to justice. This matter therefore deserves serious consideration. Firstly, the legitimacy of the restriction on the reimbursement of lawyer's fees to the aforementioned limit is questioned.[30] Secondly, the possibility of making the payment of these fees conditional upon success in the action should be assessed. It is, perhaps, time to rethink our tradition. In the same way, it is thought to be advisable to promote prior agreements on the fees of the legal representative.

[29] Medeiros (n 22) 183.

[30] In support of the stipulation of the full payment of the successful party's legal representative's fees, E Valles states: 'Should our system be different, and order the defeated party to also pay in full the fees paid by the successful party to his legal representative? There are countries, such as those with the Anglo-Saxonic system, where this is the case. This practice, of forcing the defeated party to also pay the successful party's legal fees, has some grounds. Under the terms of article 562 of the Civil Code, "whosoever is obliged to repair a harm must restore the situation which would have existed had the event which obliged the repair not happened". If the successful party had not been obliged to use the court to see his right enforced, he would not have had to pay fees to his legal representative. For this reason, despite recognizing that the question is rather complex, we agree with the principle that the fees of the legal representative should be the subject of reimbursement by the defeated party' (*Custas Processuais* (n 13) 33).

Writing on legal costs generally includes references to the frequent intervention of higher courts, the absence of clear incentives for alternative dispute resolution, the giving of non-jurisdictional tasks to judges, the scarcity of summary proceedings and, above all, the proliferation of legislative instruments which so often reveal a lack of technical quality.[31]

The absence of the impact of the time and the burden of the legal action with regard to the reimbursement of the successful party, with the exception of the situation of the litigant's bad faith, is an option within our current procedural law that may be criticised. It will be remembered that the historical solution was the compensation for personal costs by the defeated party, from which he was only exempt if he proved justified grounds for the litigation. To sum up, it is considered that negligent conduct by the defeated party would provide reasons for compensation of the loss directly associated with the proceedings.

Funding Claims

Some notes on the subject: cases are usually financed from personal funds. Membership of an organisation, such as a trade union, often confers legal support. Legal expenses insurance is commonly associated with the legal protection provided by different types of insurance, namely car or home insurance. The after-the-event insurance is not part of the Portuguese tradition. Banks or other credit institutions offer loans or grants to finance litigation, but generally at high interest rates. Finally, funding from a third-party investor seems compatible with our legal order.

In Portuguese law, the constitutional guarantee of access to the law and to the courts justifies the creation of a regime of legal aid for those who are unable to bear the costs of a case. It is considered that in compliance with the aforementioned constitutional provision, a serious and deep reflection on the legal expenses insurance, and favouring its expansion, is fully warranted.

The system of access to the law and the courts is regulated by Law no34/2004, dated 29 July 2004, amended and republished by Law no 47/2007, dated 28 August 2007. The regime provides that no person shall have the knowledge, exercise or defence of their rights hindered or denied on the basis of their social or cultural status, or due to a lack of economic funds. The guarantee of access to law includes both access to legal information and access to legal protection. Included within the latter are legal consultation and legal aid. The condition for having access to these facilities is the interested party's lack of funds, that is, that he is unable to pay the costs of a case, considering his income, his property and the permanent expenses of his family unit (article 8 of Law no 34/2004). The right to legal protection

[31] See the studies published in J Álvaro Dias (ed), *Os Custos da Justiça* (Coimbra, Almedina, 2005), in particular the interventions of P Teixeira da Cruz, A Coimbra and E Blankenburg.

applies to all the courts, regardless of the type of case, to all the Magistrates' Courts (*Julgados de Paz*) and to other alternative dispute resolution structures.

Legal aid is frequently identified with the appointment of an official lawyer, paid for by the state. It may, however, take other forms, in particular exemption from payment of the justice fees and other costs of the case. It may be noted that in the regime prior to the 2008 reform, if the defeated party benefited from exemption of costs, the successful party in the case would receive reimbursement of the justice fees paid at the expense of the state. In the law currently in force, due to the absence of any express rule which protects the right to reimbursement of the justice fees, it appears that if the defeated party litigates with legal aid, reimbursement is excluded.[32]

Court or Process Costs

The debate is the classic one:

> 'It may be asked whether or not justice should be free, with some arguing that the collective should bear the cost of justice, since it is through justice that the State achieves its social aim of reintegration of the law, whilst others claim that the citizens to use the courts, having given rise to litigation or benefited from it, should bear the cost of justice'.[33]

The constitutional guarantee of access to law and the courts proves to be compatible with the exclusion of justice that is free of charge, although it requires limits to the court costs: 'the principle of equity thus requires that the service of justice is paid for in part by the collective via taxes, and in part by the respective users via the payment of the justice fee'.[34] The objective of bringing the cost of the service closer to the value of that service, although excluding an absolute economic equivalence between the two amounts, inspires the options of the legislator. In the preamble of the Regulations on Legal Costs reads:

> 'In general terms, it has also been sought to fit the amount of the justice fee to the type of case in question and to the costs which, in concrete terms, each case brings to the legal system, in a philosophy of distributive justice to which the system of legal costs should not be immune, as a model of funding of the courts and passing on of the cost of justice to the respective users'.

Article 16 of the Regulations on Legal Costs provides an extensive list of the types of costs covered within the procedural costs. Included in these, amongst many others, are compensation to witnesses and payment owed to those who accidentally intervene in the case, experts, translators, interpreters and technical

[32] See Valles, (n 13) 32.
[33] S da Costa, *Regulamento das Custas Processuais*, 2nd edn (Coimbra, Almedina, 2009) 130.
[34] da Costa (n 33) 130.

consultants [1(e) and (h)]. Article 17, and the annexed table to which it refers, rule that payments may be variable, although within the limits established by law.

The Portuguese legal system allows the user of the justice system a certain degree of predictability regarding the costs associated with litigation, at least if the costs related to the proceedings are reduced. In fact, except in particularly complex cases, where the law now allows the judge to correct the justice fee applicable, it is the value of the case which determines the amount of the justice fee. The lawyer is also responsible for providing information on the fees the client will be charged. The justice fee, it will be recalled, must be paid at the commencement of proceedings. The charges, or rather, the expenses resulting from the conducting of the case may be required in advance if they exceed a certain amount (articles 21 and 22 of the Regulations on Legal Costs). Otherwise, they are due at the end of the proceedings and, thus, are the responsibility of the defeated party.

Lawyers' Costs

According to article 100 of the Bar Association Statute, the following are criteria for calculating fees: the importance of the services provided, the difficulty and urgency of the matter, the amount of intellectual creativity involved in the service provided by the lawyer, the result obtained, the time spent, the responsibilities taken on by the lawyer and any other professional services (3). The fees should be adequate reward for the services provided and should be paid in cash, with the possibility of the parties agreeing on a fixed sum (1). Payment of an hourly rate, periodic payments or payments per service are therefore accepted. The lawyer should present the client with the fees total divided into a list of the services provided (2).

In his relationship with the client, it is the lawyer's duty to inform him, if he so requests, of the criteria used for calculating his fees, indicating, whenever possible, the approximate total amount (article 95(1)(a) of the Bar Association Statute). Considering the applicable competition rules, a tariff for fees is excluded.

Quota litis (a share of the amount awarded) is prohibited but success fees are given legitimacy. This is set out in article 101 of the Bar Association Statute:

> '1. Lawyers are prohibited from entering into *quota litis* agreements; 2. A *quota litis* agreement is an agreement made by a lawyer and his client, before the final conclusion of the case in which the latter is a party, such that the right to fees is exclusively dependent on the result obtained in the case and as a result of which the client agrees to pay the lawyer a portion of the result that he obtains, whether this consists of a quantity of money or of any good or value; 3. An agreement which consists of the prior calculation of the amount of fees, even if this is a percentage, according to the value of the case entrusted to the lawyer, or through which, in addition to the fees calculated according to other criteria, it is agreed that there shall be a bonus depending on the result obtained, shall not be considered a *quota litis* agreement'.

Cost Shifting

It should be reiterated that, in line with the Civil Procedure Code, the defeated party must pay the costs of the case, in the proportion of which he is so defeated. Where the payment cannot be calculated in the action, as happens for example in inventories or in actions to divide a common good, the criterion of advantage in the proceedings is applied, and the party which benefited from the case must pay the costs (article 446). If, in the case of a joint action, several claimants or several defendants are defeated, these shall be responsible for paying the costs in equal proportions (article 446-A).

The procedural costs include the justice fee, the charges and the party costs. The justice fee is understood to be the amount due for each party's action in becoming involved in the proceedings, and is fixed according to the amount and the complexity of the case. The charges in the case are the expenses that are a result of the development of the case, based on the acts requested by the parties or ordered by the judge in the case. The party costs correspond to the sums spent by the party on the case and which the law states shall be compensated by the other party. Included in these are, namely, the justice fees paid, the charges actually borne by the party, the remuneration of the enforcement agent and any expenses paid by him, and the fees of the legal representative and any expenses paid by him. Regarding the latter two categories, it should be remembered that there is a legal limit of 50 per cent of the sum of the justice fees paid by the defeated party and by the successful party. This is set out in articles 447 and 447-D (2) of the Civil Procedure Code and article 26 (3) of the Regulations on Legal Costs.

Another important rule in this area should be mentioned: according to article 450 of the Civil Procedure Code, where the claim or opposition ceased to be founded due to intervening circumstances which are not the fault of the parties, the costs are shared between them in equal proportions (1). The law lists the situations in which there is a change of circumstances that is not the fault of the parties (2). In other cases where the action subsequently becomes impossible or useless, the responsibility for paying costs remains with the claimant (3).

General Costs Issues

In the Magistrates' Courts, the jurisdiction of which is limited to declarative actions for an amount not exceeding that for which Courts of First Instance have authority (€3,740.98), in matters which basically relate to the compliance or failure to comply with obligations and the exercise of powers which make up rights *in rem*, the law establishes a particularly favourable regime of procedural costs. Some of the rules may be highlighted (under the terms of Ministerial Order no

1456/2001, dated 28 December 2001, amended by Ministerial Order no. 209/2005, dated 24 February 2005): a single fee of €70 is due; payment is in instalments, with an initial payment of €35 and, for the defeated party, a second payment of the same amount; this second portion must be paid within three working days after the date the decision is known; any failure by the unsuccessful party to pay the second portion of €35 results in the application and payment of a surcharge of €10 per day of delay in complying with the obligation, although the total amount of this surcharge may not exceed €140; the magistrate reimburses the successful party in the amount of the €35 initially paid; when the case is concluded following an agreement reached through mediation, the fee is reduced to €50, with €10 being returned to each of the parties.

The use of electronic means during the course of the case allows for a reduction in the costs involved. On this subject see article 6 (3) of the Regulations on Legal Costs:

> 'In cases in which the use of electronic means is not compulsory, the justice fee is reduced to 75 per cent of its total amount when the party delivers the first or only procedural item using the electronic means available',

and article 22 (5) of the same statute:

> 'In cases in which the use of electronic means is not compulsory, when the party delivers all the procedural items to the court using the electronic means available, one third of the amount paid as the justice fee also reverts (in pre-payment of costs), notwithstanding the provisions of article 6(3)'.

The settlement of a case in a First Instance Court usually takes very long (on average, between 10 months and 3.5 years). The delay is mostly reflected on societal or collective costs and on the user personal expenses or damages, rather than on court fees or charges in the case.

19

Russia

DMITRY MALESHIN*

General Overview and Trends

Russian civil procedure is a unique system possessing features that do not exist in traditional continental or Anglo-Saxon approaches. Its unique features include the role of the judge in the process of proof-taking; the role of the procurator; the review of judgments in the 'supervisory' instance; the original status of judicial precedent.

Payment of a duty to the state for use of the courts was introduced in 1930 and has been maintained under the modern Russian legal system. There is no any special theory on costs in the Russian doctrine of civil procedure. However, the purpose of court costs and fines is not only to reimburse the state for the costs, but also to prevent groundless cases from being brought.

Funding Claims

Individuals and companies have to fund litigation from their own resources. There is no ban on obtaining loans from banks or others, nor on attorneys paying the state duty for clients. Legal Expenses Insurance or after-the-event insurance for individuals or companies is not available under Russian legislation.

In general free legal aid is also not available. However, there are some exceptions. Members of the Colleges of Advocates are supposed to give free legal advice in some cases.

The Federal Law on 'Lawyer's activity and the Bar in the Russian Federation' provides that legal aid shall be rendered free of charge, first, to citizens of the Russian Federation the average *per capita* income of whose families is lower than the value of the minimum subsistence level established by law, and, second, to

* Vice-Dean, Associate Professor of Civil Procedural Law, Lomonosov Moscow State University.

citizens of the Russian Federation living alone whose incomes are lower than the indicated value, in the following cases:

—to plaintiffs in cases concerning alimony, damage relating to a breadwinner's death, maiming or another job-related injury to health;
—to veterans of the World War II: on issues not relating to entrepreneurial activity;
—to citizens of the Russian Federation when applications for pensions and benefits are drawn up;
—to the citizens of the Russian Federation who have suffered from political repression on issues relating to rehabilitation.

A person who is granted legal aid is not required to pay the state duty and expenses. Instead, it is to be paid by the defendant if he loses. If both parties are relieved from the payment of the state duty and the expenses, the losses should be compensated from the funds of the federal budget.

In all cases legal assistance shall be rendered free of charge to minors residing in the official institutions for preventing child neglect and minors' offences.

Court or Process Costs

State Duty

Claimants filing a claim with a court shall pay the state duty.[1] The amount depends on the type of court, type of claim and amount of claim. Participants usually engage their own translators if they need translation services. Service of process, enforcement of a judgment and assistance of a bailiff are free of charge.

There are two court systems in Russia that hear civil cases. Courts of general jurisdiction hear normal civil cases involving individuals. State arbitration courts hear commercial civil cases involving legal entities. The state duty for filing a claim with a court of general jurisdiction ranges from four per cent for a small claim to 0.5 per cent for claims amounting to more than 500,000 roubles, but with a limit on the duty of 20,000 roubles. Some categories of plaintiffs are exempt from paying this state duty mainly due to social reasons.

The state duty for filing a claim with a state arbitration court ranges from four per cent for small claim to 0.5 per cent for claims that amounts more than 1,000,000 roubles, with a cap of 100,000 roubles.

[1] Art 333.18 of the Tax Code of the Russian Federation provides that the state duty shall be paid in cash or by way of cashless settlement. The fact of a payment of state duty by way of cashless settlement shall be proved by a payment order bearing the bank's note of execution thereof, and the fact of a payment of state duty in cash shall be proved by the receipt of the established form issued to the taxpayer by the bank.

Witness of fact

Article 95 of the Russian Civil Procedural Code provides:[2]

> 1. Witnesses, experts, specialists and interpreters shall be compensated for the expenses for fares and accommodation incurred in connection with the summons to the court; a daily allowance shall also be paid to them.
>
> 2. Working citizens summoned to a court as witnesses, shall be paid a monetary compensation on the basis of the actual expenditure of time in the performance of the duties of a witness and their average earnings. Non-working citizens summoned to a court as witnesses, shall be paid a monetary compensation on the basis of the actual expenditure of time on the performance of the duties of a witness and the minimum rate, established by a federal law, of the remuneration of labour.

There is a similar rule in the Russian Arbitration Procedural Code. However, in practice the amount of compensation is rather small and the procedure for applying for such compensation is very time-consuming. Therefore, witnesses usually participate in civil hearings due to their relations with parties or at the request of parties in the case.

Expert

There are two types of experts who participate in civil litigation: state experts who work in the Ministry of Justice or in the Ministry of Internal Affairs; and other experts who work in commercial expert organisations. Russian courts most frequently appoint experts from state expert institutions of the Ministry of Justice due to their long-standing and well-known reputation. State experts charge rates from tariffs approved by the Government, depending on the type of expertise.
A party to litigation sometimes obtains expertise from a commercial expert organisation prior to litigation in order to obtain evidence and check whether he has good grounds for bringing a claim. During the litigation, parties might convince a judge to appoint an expert from a commercial expert organisation by showing that state experts do not have appropriate expert equipment or are too expensive. Commercial experts obviously charge commercial rates as agreed with clients.

Lawyers' Costs

Lawyers are free to negotiate their fees with their client. The level of fees charged depends on the lawyer's qualifications. Lawyers' fees for representation in civil litigation can be divided into three main groups:

[2] Sums of Money to Be Paid to Witnesses, Experts, Specialists and Interpreters.

—Fees charged by international law firms;
—Fees charged by Russian law firms;
—Fees charged by Russian advocates.

International law firms usually represent their clients in commercial disputes heard in state arbitration courts, and charge their usual (or slightly reduced) hourly rates. The average hourly rate of an associate of an international law firm in Moscow is currently around €300. Russian law firms usually represent their clients in commercial disputes heard in state arbitration courts, and charge different rates depending on the reputation of the law firm and how rich its client is. Rates of Russian law firms are lower than the rates of international law firms. Russian law firms tend to add a success fee to agreed hourly rates or fixed fee. The success fee is usually in the region of 10 per cent of the amount of the claim.

Russian advocates usually represent their clients in civil disputes heard in courts of general jurisdiction, and their fees depend entirely on the reputation of the individual advocate and how rich his client is. Advocates often work only for a success fee agreed with a client, which will usually be close to 10 per cent of the amount of the claim.

An agreement involving a success fee is not enforceable in Russian courts against clients, because the Russian Constitutional Court has ruled that a success fee could adversely influence proceedings,[3] but clients usually do not refuse to pay an agreed success fee because they have a long-standing relationship with their lawyers.

Times Of Payment and Cost Shifting

The issues related to distribution of court charges are regulated by the Civil Procedure Code of the Russian Federation No 138-FZ dated 14 November 2002, and the Arbitration Procedure Code of the Russian Federation No 95-FZ dated 24 July 2002. Relevant extracts are set out in Appendices 3 and 4. The rules provided for in these Codes are mostly the same and are as follows:

In addition to the state duty, the Codes define as 'court charges':

1. the sums to be paid to the witnesses, experts, specialists and interpreters;
2. the expenses of the interpreter's service used by foreign citizens and by stateless persons, unless otherwise stipulated in an international treaty of the Russian Federation;
3. the coss of the fares and accommodation of third parties in connection with the summons to court;
4. fees for the services of the representatives;
5. expenses for carrying out an examination of evidence *in situ*;

[3] Ruling of the Russian Constitutional Court No 355-O dated 20 Oct 2005.

6. compensation for actual loss of time by the party;
7. postal expenses;
8. other expenses recognised by the court as necessary.

The state duty is to be paid by the applicant when filing a claim with the court. If it is not paid, the Codes provide for the court to discontinue the claim. Where a claimant is exempt from paying the state duty, it has to be paid by the loser at the end of the case, *pro rata* to the claim being satisfied. Where a claim has been partially satisfied and the respondent has been exempt from paying the state duty, the state duty is to be levied against the claimant.

At the time of filing an application for a witness, expert or specialist to be involved, the party applying for their involvement must deposit the relevant sum in the special bank account of the Judicial Department to cover their costs or such other charges as are recognised by the court to be necessary. Where both parties have made the same application, the amount should be deposited in equal parts. No 'legal aid' covers such costs. Where the involvement of the witness, expert or specialist has been initiated by the court, the relevant amount should be paid by the state. Translation charges shall be paid by the state upon the translators' performance of their duties, except where the parties engage translators themselves.

The party considered to be the loser according to the verdict issued by the court has to reimburse the winner the amount of the 'court charges' paid, as defined above. Where the claim has been partially satisfied, the loser has to reimburse the court charges *pro rata* to the amount of the satisfied claim.

If the state grants 'legal aid' to a party, this only exempts them from payment of state duty and expenses. The lawyer is not paid by the state, and the party must either agree to pay the lawyer in civil cases—the state does pay in criminal cases—or the lawyer must agree to act for free. There is no special tariff for fee shifting.

General Costs Issues

Cases in the arbitration court, whether in a court of first instance, appellate court or cassational court, take around nine months. In practice, the court may accelerate the procedures and the claimant may not pass all judicial stages, so cases often take around five or six months. Cases in a court of general jurisdiction take two or three months for a simple case, such as recovery of small amount of damage caused by a car accident, and can take some years for complicated cases, such as inheritance or a real estate dispute, but generally take around six to eight months. Russian judges sitting in courts of general jurisdiction tend to create procedural obstacles for bringing a claim if they find, after a preliminary review, that there is no merit in the claim.

The statistics available for cases in arbitration courts are shown in Table 1.[4]

[4] Official website of the Supreme Arbitration Court www.arbitr.ru.

Table 1: Arbitration Courts Statistics

	2004	2005	2006	2007	2008
Number of Claims	1 340 699	1 628 133	1 080 154	953 045	1 078 481
Number of appeals	100 484	109 190	115 832	129 012	127 627
Number of cassational appeals	77 862	83 867	87 845	93 284	84 529
In exercise of supervisory functions	19 935	19 472	19 460	21 418	21 023

20

Spain

MARIA ARÁNZAZU CALZADILLA MEDINA,*
CARLOS TRUJILLO CABRERA** AND
ALEJANDRO FERRERES COMELLA†

Funding Claims

Personal funding is the most common sort of litigation funding in Spain. Litigation funding by banks, trade associations or similar third party funding does not exist in Spain.

Legal aid

Legal aid is available to parties involved in civil litigation in Spain. The legal aid system is regulated by Act 1/1996, January 10, and is based on the appointment by the Government of a *pro bono* lawyer and the subsidising of the costs of court agents and experts. The Autonomous Communities (Regional Governments) are in charge of organising and supervising the legal aid system with the assistance of the local Bar Associations. The Autonomous Communities fund the Bar Associations for provision of legal aid by its associate lawyers, and the Bar Association pays the lawyers. In 2008, the Governments spent €219.7 million in legal aid litigation, assisting more than 1,400,000 Spanish individuals.[1]

Applicants must meet a financial eligibility requirement. Legal aid covers payment of the applicant's litigation expenses (ie lawyers' legal fees, expert witnesses' fees). If the party with legal aid loses, he does not have to pay the other side's costs, nor does the Government. Thus, one of the benefits of legal aid is that the assisted party cannot be ordered to pay legal costs.

Consumer associations that are declared as having 'public interest' by the Government are awarded legal aid benefits by law. As a result of the implementation of a collective claim regulation (ie class action system), some national

* University of La Laguna, La Laguna (S/C de Tenerife).
** University of La Laguna, La Laguna (S/C de Tenerife).
† Uría Menéndez, Barcelona.

[1] Data provided by the Spanish National Bar Association (*Consejo General de la Abogacía Española*).

consumer associations which comply with certain legal requirements can be a party to proceedings by appearing before the Court as the representative of identified or unidentified consumers in order to claim damages suffered by each and all the consumers who are represented in the collective claim. As a result, collective claims brought by consumer associations on behalf of identified or unidentified consumers result in a new sort of third party litigation funding system.

Legal Expenses Insurance

Civil liability insurance policies normally include legal expenses insurance. The insurance company normally has the right to decide which lawyers (either in-house lawyers of the insurance company or external lawyers proposed by the insured company) will handle the case. As a general rule, insurance companies will try to impose limts on legal fees and will rarely agreet to pay legal fees beyond the amounts recommended by the regulation determined by the different local Bar Associations. There are no insurance policies that only cover legal expenses in Spain. After-the-event insurance does not exist in Spain.

Court Costs

A plaintiff must pay a fee when filing a lawsuit, or an appellant on filing an appeal.[2] The amount of the fee varies depending on the amount of the plea and the type of proceedings. The fee comprises a fixed amount to be paid in each case, and a variable amount that depends on the financial value of the case. For example, in ordinary proceedings, the base amount is €150, and the variable amount is 0.5 per cent of the amount of the plea, subject to a limit of €6,000. If the amount of the plea cannot be determined, the plea is to be valued at €18,000 for the purposes of determining the amount of fee.

Individuals and small companies (with turnover below €8 million) are exempt from this tax. Court fees are not reimbursed to winning parties.

Lawyers' Costs

Lawyers' fees are freely agreed between client and lawyer, and can be based either on fixed amounts or on hourly rates. Charging by hourly rates is normally only done by big law firms.

[2] Art 35 of the Fiscal, Administrative and Social Order Act 53/2002 dated 30 Dec 2002.

Although not legally binding, rules published periodically by local Bar Associations have a clear impact on the level of fees actually charged. Such rules usually include tariffs that are based on the type and complexity of the case and the amount (of the plea) involved. An example of current tariffs published by the Bar Association of Barcelona for ordinary proceedings (*juicio ordinario*), which is the normal procedure for compensation claims, is shown at Table 1.

Table 1: Tariffs published by the Bar Association of Barcelona for juicio ordinario

Amount of the plea		Fees
Up to €3,000	30%	€900
Up to €20,000	20%	€4,300
Up to €50,000	15%	€8,800
Up to €100,000	10%	€13,800
Up to €300,000	7%	€27,800
Up to €600,000	5%	€42,800
Up to €1,500,000	3%	€69,800
More than €1,500,000	An additional 0.60% on the excess	

The tariff rates in Table 1 are to be increased or decreased depending on the complexity of the litigation. They are also to be increased in line with the consumer price index as from January 2005, which was when these rates were established. As a comparison, the tariff rates for ordinary proceedings the Bar Association of Santa Cruz de Tenerife are shown in Table 2.

Table 2: Tariffs published by the Bar Association of Santa Cruz de Tenerife for juicio ordinario

Up to €1,202 (minimum € 240)	32%	€384.64	€384.64
Excess up to €3,005	22%	€396.66	€781.30
Excess up to €18,030	15%	€2,253.75	€3,035.05
Excess up to €30,051	12%	€1,1442.52	€4,477.57
Excess up to €60,101	8%	€2,404.00	€6,881.57
Excess up to €150,253	6%	€5,409.12	€12,290.60
Excess up to €300,506	5%	€7,512.65	€19,803.34

cont.

Table 2: *cont.*

Excess up to €601,012	4%	€12,020.24	€31,823.58
Excess up to €1,202.024	2%	€12,020.24	€43,843.82
Excess up to €3,005.061	1%	€18,030.37	€61,874.19
Excess above €3,005.061	0.5%		

The Bar Association rules also have an impact on the amount that the winning party is entitled to claim from the losing party when a court order to pay legal fees has been issued (see below). Thus, article 246 of the Spanish 1/2000 Civil Procedure Act (CPA) provides that the court will request the local Bar Association to validate the amount that the winning party asks to be reimbursed as legal fees if such amount is challenged by the losing party.

Success fees and *quota litis* agreements (ie contingency fee agreements) are valid in Spain. After some discussion, the Spanish Supreme Court determined the validity of *quota litis* agreements in its decision of 4 November 2008, which declared to be illegal a previous prohibition of *quota litis* agreements that had been specified in Article 16 of the Spanish National Bar Association Rules.

Witness of Fact

If the witness of fact asks for this at the trial, after having been direct- and cross-examined, the party who proposed the witness must compensate the witness with the "costs and damages" that the witness' attendance at the trial may have caused.[3] Such compensation of witnesses to fact is very rare in practice and is normally limited to travel expenses. Thus, in those rare cases in which a fact witness to fact makes a compensation petition, the amount involved is low.

Experts

Expert witnesses are paid on the basis of the tariffs determined by the professional association to which each expert belongs. The tariffs of professional associations set out variable criteria on which fees are based, but these normally include the amount of the plea. An expert witnesses' remuneration is paid by the party who retains that expert, or by the party that requests the court to appoint the expert. The losing party must reimburse the remuneration of the other party's expert if at the end the court orders it to pay the legal fees of the case.

[3] CPA, art 375.

Each party can either nominate its own expert or ask the court to appoint an expert. Whilst each party may attach to its initial brief of allegations (ie particulars of claim or defence) as many expert witness statements on the same issue as it deems necessary, the court will only appoint one expert witness per issue. For example, whilst the claimant or the defendant may each be able to retain two, three or even more expert witnesses to prepare a witness statement on the cause of, for example, the car accident on which the product liability claim is based, the court will only appoint one expert at the request of any of the parties to deal with such issue. The court will not normally agree to appoint an expert witness to report on a specific issue if the party requesting such appointment has already retained an expert witness whose statement is attached to the initial brief of allegations and who has therefore issued an opinion on the matter–although this issue is disputed amongst Spanish civil procedure scholars and case law.

An expert witness statement produced by a physician or by a doctor of medicine on the cause of the disease or on the physical damages suffered by the claimant in a case where the amount of the plea is €600,000 should not normally exceed €11,000.

Court Agent's Costs

Every party must appoint a Court Agent (*Procurador*).[4] The Court Agent is a procedural law specialist who acts as liaison between the parties and the court officials. Thus, interim orders and decisions are notified to the parties through the Court Agent. Each party must pay the fees incurred by its Court Agent. However, the amount that the winning party has paid to its Court Agent can be added to the amount that the party asks to be reimbursed as legal fees.

The Court Agent's fees are a fixed amount, depending on the value of the case, and are set forth in scales published—and periodically updated—by the Court Agent National Council. Both the Spanish and the EU authorities have recently announced that they will review the legality of Court Agent fees, in order to determine whether or not they are consistent with competition regulation. As a result of that review, the 25/2009 Free Access Act, which transposes the Bolkestein Directive,[5] came into force on 27 December 2009 and modifies (among 47 National Acts), article 14 of the 2/1974 Professional Associations Act. From that date, professional associations cannot provide any kind of indicative scales or any other recommendation, directive, guideline or rule regarding professional fees, except for those indicative scales that professional associations may set in order to be used when a costs valuation objection needs to be made by the Court, as mentioned below in relation to cost shifting.

[4] CPA, art 23.

[5] Directive 2006/123/EC of the European Parliament and of the Council of 12 December 2006 on services in the internal market, OJ L 376/36.

Court Agent fees are modest, as can be seen from the Table 3,[6] and normally amount to a maximum of 20 per cent of the lawyers' fees.

Table 3: Tariff of fees for a *Procurador*

Up to €	€	Up to €	€
60.1	9.64	5,409.11	152.05
120.2	17.39	6,010.12	165.27
180.3	21.21	12,020.24	264.44
240.4	26.04	24,040.48	396.67
300.51	29.95	36,060.73	528.89
360.61	34.77	48,080.97	661.11
420.71	42.43	60,101.21	760.27
480.81	46.93	90,151.82	826.39
540.91	49.58	120,202.42	892.50
601.01	52.88	180,303.63	958.61
1,202.02	66.11	240,404.84	1,024.72
1,803.04	79.33	300,506.05	1,090.83
2,404.05	89.25	360,607.26	1,156.94
3,005.06	99.16	420,708.47	1,223.05
3,606.07	112.38	480,809.68	1,355.27
4,207.08	125.60	540,910.89	1,428.00
4,808.1	138.83	601,012.1	1,540.39[7]

If the amount of the plea is unquantified, or in certain other circumstances, the Court Agent's fee is €260.

Cost Shifting

The loser pays rule applies in Spain. Thus, article 394 of the CPA specifies that 'litigation costs . . . will be imposed on the losing party, except where the court holds that the case in hand presented serious doubts of a factual or legal nature.' The loser pays rule is in fact applied by Spanish courts whether the case is fully accepted or fully dismissed. In such cases, a finding by the court that the case at hand presented serious doubts of a factual or legal nature is really very exceptional.

However, the amount that the losing party may finally pay as compensation to the winning party for litigation costs may not cover all the actual costs incurred by the latter. In this regard, the following circumstances must be taken into account:

(i) where the party that has been ordered to pay litigation costs to the counter-party challenges the amount that the counter-party claims as lawyers fees, the

[6] In an ordinary proceeding, each attorney will receive a 10% bonus.
[7] For each €6,010.12 or fraction that exceeds €601,012.10, €11.24 will be added.

amount that the court finally sets as lawyers fees may be lower than the actual fees paid by the winning party to its lawyer. Thus, while the lawyer and client can freely agree on the legal fees that the client must pay, the court may finally order the losing party to reimburse only the amount which results from the application of the rules or indications that are periodically published by the Spanish Bar Associations;

(ii) additionally, article 394 CPA sets a general limit, pursuant to which the losing party will not be ordered to pay as litigation cost reimbursement more than one-third of the value of the litigation;
(iii) while the order to reimburse litigation costs includes the costs of the lawyer, factual and expert witnesses, and court agent's fees, court taxes are not reimbursed to the winning party that benefits from Court order to pay legal fees, as mentioned above.

Orders to pay litigation costs must be included in the decision on the case by the judge or court and can be judicially executed when the decision on the case is final (ie litigation costs orders cannot be provisionally executed while any appeal filed against the decision on the case is pending). The winning party has 15 years to request the court to decide on reimbursement. The parties can object to the court's decision,[8] in which case the court consults the Bar Association to give its decision.

General Costs Issues

The CPA does not permit parties to ask for cost capping orders or cost protection orders from the court. However, as regards the client-attorney relationship, fee estimation and budgeting are becoming very common requests from clients.

On average, legal actions filed before the Courts of First Instance (civil and commercial law jurisdiction) last 10½ (ie from the moment that the claim is filed until the Court of First Instance renders its decision). Although appeals will normally take longer (18 months on average), the fact that the CPA significantly eases the provisional execution of the decisions issued by the Court of First Instances means that the filing of an appeal by the defendant does not delay the legal process. Therefore, except for some specific jurisdictions, delays in the legal process or in a complex procedure are not considered to be an issue in Spain.

The unpredictability of outcomes is more likely to affect potential claimants, but outcomes in Spanish proceedings are not generally thought to be unpredictable.

The proportion of cases that are settled in Spain is very low. This is because the CPA and related regulation do not set out efficient ADR mechanisms (apart from arbitration) As an exception, mediation systems are working satisfactorily in small

[8] Arts 241–246 CPA.

claim consumer cases, since many Autonomous Community Governments have incorporated publicly-funded Consumer Law Mediation Bodies. In some cases, Consumer Law Arbitration Tribunals are linked to the mediation systems, providing an expeditious and effective arbitration proceeding. ADR mechanisms are likely to expand in Spain in the future.

The official statistics available for civil cases in 2008 are at Table 4.

Table 4: Court Case Statistics, 2008[9]

Rates 2008. Civil				
	Disposal rate[10]	Pending rate[11]	Judgment rate[12]	Clearance rate[13]
Courts of First Instance	0.87	0.70	0.22	1.71
Commercial Courts	0.70	1.22	0.42	2.23
Violence against Women Courts	0.91	0.57	0.43	1.59
Family Courts of First Instance	0.98	0.34	0.55	1.35
Courts of First Instance and Enquiry	0.82	0.90	0.27	1.92
Juvenile Courts	3.68	0.67	0.13	1.85
Provincial courts. Civil Division	1.00	0.47	0.69	1.46
Provincial courts.				
Mixed Divisions	109	0.35	0.71	1.36
H.C.J. Civil and Criminal Chamber	0.99	0.26	0.30	1.26
Central Juvenile Courts	1.86	0.97	0.17	1.63
High Court 1st Chamber	0.87	0.70	0.22	1.71
TOTAL	0.87	0.73	0.30	1.75

Another indicator of the quality of justice is the outcome of appeals. The percentage of the judgments of the appellate courts that end with the upholding, full reversion, partial reversion or quashing of decisions is presented for different types of courts is shown in Table 5.

[9] at www.poderjudicial.es/eversuite/GetRecords.

[10] Number of proceedings disposed of, divided by the number of incoming cases related to a certain period of time. It relates the number of incoming cases to the capability to decide on the case.

[11] Number of pending proceedings at the end of the year divided by the number of proceedings disposed of.

[12] Number of judgments divided by the number of procedures disposed of.

[13] A quotient where the numerator is the sum of the pending and incoming proceedings at the beginning of the period and the denominator is the number of cases disposed of in the same period.

Table 5: Statistics on Appeals

	Courts of Civil Jurisdiction				
	Appeals submitted/ Judgments	Upheld in full	Reversed in part	Reversed	Quashed
First Instance Court of and First Instance and Enquiry Courts	16.8	63.3	16.1	19.9	0.7
Commercial Courts	25.5	70.2	15.1	13.8	0.9
Provincial Courts	3.6	92.4	4.8	2.2	0.7

21

Switzerland

WALTER A STOFFEL* AND JAMES F REARDON†

Swiss law imposes a considerable financial burden upon litigation before courts, both in terms of court fees as well as in terms of costs related to counsel. Litigation is risky, financially, for both parties, but especially for the plaintiff, because of the *lose pays* rule and of the prohibition of contingency fees. Costs may be mitigated by voluntary insurance schemes which may include a success fee. Social civil trials, quite important in the fields of landlord and tenant disputes as well as in labour law, are exempted from all costs.

General Overview and Trends

Both as background and context, the first point that attracts the attention of any casual observer of Switzerland is its complexity. Switzerland is a Confederation that comprises twenty-six Cantons (including six half-Cantons). The Cantons have substantive powers in many areas, despite the limits imposed by the Federal Constitution.[1] Thus, there is an inherent tension as to whether the Cantons or the Confederation has authority over any area of law. For over a century,[2] Switzerland has lived with a dual system under which the substantive civil law, debt

* Professor of Commercial Law, Private International Law, and Bankruptcy Law at the University of Fribourg, Switzerland. Former President of the Swiss Competition Commission.

† PhDcandidate at the University of Fribourg; Attorney. Former Academic Visitor at the Centre for Socio-Legal Studies, Oxford University. Former Special Assistant to the President of the Swiss Competition Commission.

[1] Art 3 of the Federal Constitution of the Swiss Confederation (RS 101), dated 18 Apr 1999. English version available at: www.admin.ch/ch/e/rs/c101.html.

[2] The idea of a unified Swiss civil procedure existed at least as early as the beginning of the nineteenth century, ie before the creation of the Swiss Confederation in its historic form in 1848. After initial rejection by the Swiss voters of unification proposals in the mid-nineteenth century, two major events shook the Swiss legal landscape, namely the coming into force of the unified Debt Enforcement and Bankruptcy Act in 1892, and the constitutional revision of 1898 that gave the Confederation the necessary powers to legislate substantive civil law, but not civil procedure law. See the Federal Council's Message regarding the Federal Code of Civil Procedure, dated 28 Jun 2006, ('Federal Council, Message') 6841, 6853, at www.admin.ch/ch/f/ff/2006/6841.pdf.

enforcement, and bankruptcy proceedings fall within the competence of the Confederation, while each Canton legislates its own civil procedure and regulates the organisation of its courts.[3] However, in 2011 Switzerland will experience a new era of federalism, with the coming into force of the new Federal Code of Civil Procedure (FCCP).[4]

Pressure for unification of Swiss civil procedure grew with the Federal International Private Act, which entered into force in 1987, and the Lugano Convention on Jurisdiction and the Enforcement of Judgments in Civil and Commercial Matters, concluded in 1988 and reviewed in 2007. The acceptance by the population of the new Federal Constitution in 1999 conferred upon the Confederation responsibility for civil procedure. Significantly, article 122 § 2 of the Federal Constitution, repeated in article 3 FCCP, states that the Cantons shall be responsible for the organisation of the courts and the administration of justice in civil matters, unless Federal law provides otherwise.[5] Thus, even if there is much talk about 'unification' of the civil procedure, there is nevertheless a dual system according to which the Confederation has the power to legislate over the substantive and procedural laws, and the Cantons may freely—unless Federal law provides otherwise—organise their court system.

In order to achieve a more effective judicial system at the Federal level, the Confederation has for a number of years been adjusting the Federal judicial system. These adjustments included the following proposals, namely the creation of a Federal Criminal Court and of a Federal Administrative Court, the coming into force of the Federal Supreme Court Act in 2007 (FSCA),[6] and with it a simplification of the procedures before the Supreme Court and a number of other smaller issues.[7] Supporting these changes was recognition that the Supreme Court was unable to perform its specific tasks, such as guaranteeing the uniform application of the law, due to the fact that it was submerged in processing cases. One main point of interest—and of federal interventionism within the Cantonal powers—is the requirement for dual jurisdiction at the Cantonal level in civil matters before a litigant can submit his case for review to the Supreme Court.[8] In order to enforce the Federal substantive civil law, the Federal Legislator has quite frequently included certain procedural provisions within the substantive law, such as in divorce law, tenancy agreements for residential property,[9] and labour law.

[3] Federal Council, Message (n 2) 6853, which indicates that such situation is unique in Europe.

[4] *Code de procédure civile* (Federal Code of Civil Procedure, FCCP) (RS 272), dated 19 Dec 2008, at www.admin.ch/ch/f/ff/2009/21.pdf.

[5] Federal Council, Message (n 2) 6875.

[6] *Loi sur le Tribunal fédéral* (Federal Supreme Court Act) (RS 173.110), dated 17 Jun 2005. Available at: www.admin.ch/ch/f/rs/1/173.110.fr.pdf.

[7] This paragraph is derived from the Federal Council's Message regarding the Total Revision of the Federal Judicial Organisation, dated 28 Feb 2001, 4000–280 (especially 4010–41). Available at: www.admin.ch/ch/f/ff/2001/4000.pdf.

[8] Art 75 § 2 FSCA.

[9] In Switzerland, residential property leases is a highly sensitive political issue, due to the fact the number of tenancy agreements for residential property is much greater than in many other industrialised countries.

Sometimes burdensome, prior to the Lawyers' Freedom of Movement Act,[10] which entered into force in 2002, was the task of finding a legal adviser capable of representing or assisting the litigant before the appropriate Cantonal jurisdiction. Another factor the prospective litigant must take into account is the language barrier. Switzerland has four national languages (German, French, Italian and Romansh) and, as stated in article 129 FCCP, a trial is conducted in the language of the jurisdiction. Thus, even before considering the costs of litigation, the litigant has to determine which venue, what language, and which counsel is qualified to assist or represent him. The costs, both in terms of expense and time, may be significant even before an actual trial is commenced.

In relation to the assumption and division of costs for courts, in general the Cantons shoulder most of the expenses, even though the Confederation may have legislated in the area of law in question. This chapter will introduce the basic litigation costs and funding within the new FCCP framework, and but can only generalise about the different position within each Canton.[11]

Funding Claims

Personal Funds

As with many aspects of Swiss law, the prospective litigant enjoys the traditional way of funding his litigation, ie on his own. No public law limit applies to one's own funding. There are no specific loans or grants from banks. The general rules regarding loans and grants (mainly the general terms of the banks, and with them, the specific financial situation of the prospective litigant) apply with respect to the funding of claims.

Benefits of Membership of an Organisation

Benefits deriving from membership depend on the by-laws of the association under scrutiny. An interesting example (and a very popular association) is ASLOCA, the association for the defence of tenants. Indeed, tenancies are widespread in Switzerland, as the level of private ownership is very low in the country, and real estate tenancy law is highly developed (as will be mentioned below with respect to the so-called 'social civil trials'). For example, assistance by ASLOCA (Canton of Vaud) to its members before the conciliation committee concerning

[10] *Loi fédérale sur la libre circulation des avocats* (Lawyers' Freedom of Movement Act) (RS 935.61), dated 23 Jun 2000. Available at: www.admin.ch/ch/f/rs/9/935.61.fr.pdf.

[11] A summary of the Zurich Code of Civil Procedure is P Dickenmann, 'Funding, Costs and Proportionality in Civil Justice Systems—Answers for Switzerland' ('Dickenmann, Report') available at: www.csls.ox.ac.uk/COSTOFLITIGATIONDOCUMENTSANDREPORTS.php.

tenancy agreements[12] issues amounts to CHF 100.[13] More generally, ASLOCA (Canton of Neuchâtel) indicates that it assists its members in the procedures before the conciliation committee concerning tenancy agreements and before the Courts at a reduced fee.[14]

Legal Aid

According to article 29 § 3 of the Federal Constitution, anyone who does not have sufficient means has the right to free legal advice and assistance unless their case appears to have no prospect of success. If it is necessary in order to safeguard their rights, they also have the right to free legal representation in court. According to the Federal Council,[15] legal aid is a pillar of our social procedure. Legal aid comprises different elements, namely the deposit of a guarantee and an advance, legal costs, and the appointment by the court of counsel to assist or represent the needy litigant.[16] Each of these elements may be totally or partially covered by the Canton.

In order to qualify for legal aid, the applicant must fulfil two requirements, namely (1) he must lack sufficient funding to litigate, and (2) his cause does not seem to be without any likelihood of success.[17] To 'lack sufficient funding' means that the litigant's revenue and wealth are insufficient to finance a trial without putting the litigant in financial peril. In practice, a litigant with assets amounting to less than 130 per cent of the minimum living standard (according to article 93 DEBA)[18] would qualify for legal aid.[19] With respect to the likelihood of success, it is generally understood that when the likelihood of success is 20 per cent or less, then legal aid will not be granted.[20]

The needy litigant is required to reimburse to the Canton the amounts received when he is able to do so.[21] The FCCP Draft Project had proposed a statute of

[12] This is the mandatory first step for a trial with respect to tenancy agreements.

[13] Information available at: www.asloca.ch/?q=node/51.

[14] Information available at: www.asloca.ch/?q=node/44.

[15] Federal Council, Message (n 2) 6912.

[16] Art 118 FCCP.

[17] Art 117 FCCP.

[18] *Loi fédérale sur la poursuite pour dettes et la faillite* (Debt Enforcement and Bankruptcy Act, DEBA) (RS 281.1), dated 11 Apr 1889. Available at: www.admin.ch/ch/f/rs/2/281.1.fr.pdf.

[19] According to the *Normes d'insaisissabilité pour l'année 2010* (Minimum Living Standard for the year 2010) of the Canton of Geneva (E 3 60.04), the following elements have to be taken into account (only some illustrative elements will be provided here, all costs are understood as on a monthly basis):

1. A single person: CHF 1,200.
2. A married couple: CHF 1,700.
3. Child care: CHF 400 (child under 10)/CHF 600 (child over 10).
4. Social contributions (invalidity insurance, unemployment insurance, accident insurance, etc.).
5. Rent and mortgage fees.
6. Heating bills and other accessories to living.

See www.ge.ch/legislation/.

[20] There is a lot of case law concerning the likelihood of success. See for example ATF 119 Ia 251 (Supreme Court Decision). Available at: www.bger.ch/fr/index/juridiction/jurisdiction-inherit-template/jurisdiction-recht/jurisdiction-recht-leitentscheide1954.htm.

[21] Art 123 § 1 FCCP.

limitations of five years for such reimbursement.[22] A number of commentators opposed this limit[23] as being too short and contrary to the general rule of 10 years as provided by the Swiss Code of Obligations.[24] The Federal Council revised the proposal and the statute of limitations is now fixed at 10 years commencing as of the end of the trial.[25]

During the FCCP consultation, there was some debate as to whether the Confederation should regulate legal aid. Indeed, some Cantons and other commentators believed that it was unnecessary to transfer the competence to regulate legal aid to the Confederation. According to these critics, legal aid is part of the organisation of the courts, which, as mentioned above, falls as a rule within the competence of the Cantons.[26] Moreover, legal aid before criminal courts and administrative tribunals falls within the competence of the Cantons. Thus, if the FCCP were to create a competence for the Confederation in that area, there would be a Federal competence for civil matters on the one hand, and a Cantonal competence for criminal and administrative matters on the other hand. More controversially, the project under consultation provided that the Canton in which the trial took place would have to pay the appointed counsel 'full-fee',[27] and predictably that suggestion was unpopular with some Cantons, which were concerned to avoid an increase in legal aid spending. Furthermore, the FCCP Draft Project did not define 'full-fee', and the amount of 'full-fee' paid differs from one Canton to another.[28]

The final FCCP draft reached a consensus that created a 'unified' federal legal aid system for civil matters. However, the notion of 'full-fee' was dropped; instead the Cantons are required to pay an 'equitable' amount to the counsel (FCCP).[29] It is generally accepted that most—if not all—of the Cantons will keep their current system of remunerating counsellors who operate under the legal aid system. For example, the Canton of Geneva entitles a partner at a law firm to an hourly fee of CHF 200, an associate CHF 125, and a trainee CHF 65.[30] It should be mentioned that the legal aid services tend to cut costs, and do so by reducing—in a discriminatory manner—the numbers of hours claimed by the lawyers, deemed 'unnecessary' for the case in question.

Article 29 § 3 of the Federal Constitution indicates that 'anyone' has the right to legal aid. It is evident that natural persons could benefit from such programme,

[22] Art 112 §2 of the Preliminary Draft of the Expert Commission on the Federal Code of Civil Procedure ('FCCP Draft Project'), Jun 2003. Available at: www.ejpd.admin.ch/etc/medialib/data/staat_buerger/gesetzgebung/zivilprozess.Par.0002.File.tmp/entw-zpo-f.pdf.

[23] Answers to the Preliminary Draft of the Expert Commission on the Federal Code of Civil Procedure ('FCCP consultation'), pp 306–331, see especially pp 328–331. Available at: www.ejpd.admin.ch/content/dam/data/staat_buerger/gesetzgebung/zivilprozess/ve-ber.pdf.

[24] Art 127 of the *Loi fédérale complétant le code civil Suisse (Livre cinquième: Droit des obligations)* (Swiss Code of Obligations, CO) (RS 220), dated 30 Mar 1911, at www.admin.ch/ch/f/rs/2/220.fr.pdf.

[25] Art 123 § 2 FCCP. Federal Council, Message (n 2) 6915.

[26] Art 3 FCCP.

[27] Art 107 § 3 FCCP Draft Project (n 22).

[28] FCCP consultation (n 23) 316–21.

[29] Art 122 § 1(a) and § 2 FCCP. Federal Council, Message (n 2) 6914.

[30] Art 19 of the *Règlement sur l'assistance juridique* (Legal Aid Ordinance) (E 2 05.04). Available at: www.ge.ch/legislation/.

but what about legal entities? In its Message,[31] the Federal Council says that legal entities could exceptionally benefit from legal aid, and to exclude *de lege* their right to legal aid does not take into account all the plausible scenarios that might present themselves before the courts. The current Zurich Civil Procedure Code forbids legal entities to benefit from legal aid.[32] The FCCP thus widens the scope of potential beneficiaries of legal aid in some Cantons, such as the Cantons of Zurich or Geneva.[33]

Legal Expenses Insurance

It is legal to cover oneself from the vagaries of legal expenses with insurance, as a private person (*Assurance de protection juridique privée*), or as a professional. After-the-event insurance is not known in Switzerland.[34]

Funding from a Lawyer or Other Third Party Investor

The *pactum de quota litis* (contingency fee) is forbidden in Switzerland. Article 12(e) of the Lawyers' Freedom of Movement Act states that the lawyer cannot, before the end of a case, agree with the client to accept to receive his fees depending on the result of the case. Neither can the lawyer waive his fees if he loses the case.[35] Article 19 § 2 of the Swiss Professional Code of Ethics from the Swiss Lawyers' Federation says practically the same,[36] as well as article 12 of the Habits and Customs of the Geneva Lawyers' Association.[37] Such agreement is thus both illegal and unethical. However, a *pactum de palmario* (success fee) is possible, as explained below (at note 99).

No law forbids third party financing in Switzerland, except, as mentioned above, by a lawyer based on the contingency fee system. A key player in litigation funding is Allianz, through its branch Allianz ProzessFinanz.[38] It finances only claimants, not defendants. Only claims of at least CHF 300,000 are considered, and most importantly the defendant must have 'a viable creditworthiness' (in other words, deep pockets). Allianz ProzessFinanz funds pre-trial negotiations and mediations as well as litigation, and can cover lawyers' fees, court fees, the cost of a credit assessment of the opposing party, costs for experts and their opinions,

[31] Federal Council, Message (n 2) 6912.

[32] Art 84 § 3 of the *Zürcher Zivilprozessordnung* (Zurich Code of Civil Procedure, ZCPC) (RS-ZH 271), dated 13 Jun 1976, at www2.zhlex.zh.ch/appl/zhlex_r.nsf/WebView/DBC9D18A4D8F825AC12573B50031449D/$File/271_13.6.76_59.pdf.

[33] Art 2 of the Legal Aid Ordinance (n 30).

[34] Dickenmann, Report (n 11) 12.

[35] Lawyers' Freedom of Movement Act (n 10).

[36] Swiss Professional Code of Ethics from the Swiss Lawyers' Federation. Available at: www.swiss-lawyers.com/fr/04_sav/02_statuten_standesregeln/Schweizerische_Standesregeln.pdf.

[37] Habits and Customs of the Geneva Lawyers' Association. Available at: www.odageneve.ch/index.php?option=com_content&task=view&id=34&Itemid=94.

[38] All the information in this paragraph is derived from Allianz ProzessFinanz' website. Available at: www.allianz-profi.ch/what_is_litigation_funding/how_does_litigation_funding_work/index.html.

coverage of advances/deposits, and other costs related to the case. Allianz's share of the proceeds is 30 per cent, and if the case is settled in the first six months after the signing of the financing agreement, its share is reduced to 20 per cent.

The Swiss Supreme Court decided in late 2004 that a Cantonal Act banning the possibility of third parties funding litigation was against freedom of commerce enshrined in article 27 of the Swiss Constitution.[39] One of the main arguments of the defendant, the Canton of Zurich (against which the parties had appealed), was that by allowing third parties to fund litigation, they would imperil the relationship between the lawyer and his client, which would lead to an '*Interessenkollision*' (conflict of interest). The Supreme Court disagreed and stated that there was no conflict of interest as the client and the funder have in principle the same goal, namely to benefit from the highest return in the case, and the lawyer has to work diligently towards this goal too.[40]

Court or Process Costs

The issues of whether Cantons or Confederation pay for the court system, and regulates fees paid by litigants, remain topical. In the recent debates, Cantons strongly resisted being saddled with further costs related to the judicial system, since they had already had to assume some additional costs resulting from the reform of the judiciary at the Federal level in all the fields of law, and invoked the principle of the neutrality of costs with respect to the unification of the civil procedure.[41] During the FCCP consultation,[42] there was some debate as to whether the Confederation or the Cantons should regulate legal costs payable by litigants. The Cantons were adamant about keeping the necessary powers to regulate such costs, and the outcome was that article 96 FCCP states that the Cantons regulate legal costs.

Article 98 FCCP states that the court may request from the plaintiff an advance corresponding to the totality of the estimated court charges. In contrast, Article 87 § 1 of the FCCP Draft Project indicated that the plaintiff must advance only half of the estimated amount of the court charges. This is the 'middle line' between some Cantons in which an advance amounting to 100 per cent of the court charges needs to be paid and other Cantons in which no such advance is requested at all.[43] In its Message,[44] the Federal Council reports that the Cantons heavily criticised

[39] BGE 131 I 223 (Supreme Court Decision 2P.4/2004 dated 10 Dec 2004) ('BGE 131 I 223'). Available at: www.bger.ch/fr/index/juridiction/jurisdiction-inherit-template/jurisdiction-recht/jurisdiction-recht-leitentscheide1954.htm.

[40] BGE 131 I 223 (n 39) 236–37.

[41] Federal Council, Message (n 2) 6857.

[42] FCCP consultation (n 23) 247–57.

[43] Explanatory Report Accompanying the Preliminary Draft of the Expert Commission on the Federal Code of Civil Procedure ('Explanatory Report'), Jun 2003, 52, at www.ejpd.admin.ch/content/dam/data/staat_buerger/gesetzgebung/zivilprozess/vn-ber-f.pdf.

[44] Federal Council, Message (n 2) 6905–906.

this proposal of the FCCP Draft Project. As mentioned above, the FCCP now contains the provision for an advance of 100 per cent of the court charges. This provision is not mandatory, and the courts may adapt their stance according to the wealth of the plaintiff. Otherwise, such a provision would have a chilling effect on a potential plaintiff and would limit access to justice in many worthy cases. However, those explanations are not reassuring. Indeed, it is our opinion that Article 98 FCCP contributes to legal uncertainty and does not encourage access to justice. Article 98 refers to court charges defined in Article 95 § 2 FCCP which includes, among others, conciliation fees, court fees, evidence fees and translation fees. Moreover, it is not determined whether this advance is solely made for the jurisdiction requesting said advance, in other words, a potential plaintiff may worry that the lower Cantonal court requests an advance if the case is appealed, that is for potential costs before the Cantonal Court, even though it is unclear—before the start of any procedure—whether the case will be appealed at all.

Court Fees

As mentioned above, Switzerland is a Confederation, with each Canton retaining the necessary powers to regulate the legal costs for its own court.[45] The Confederation, on the other hand, has jurisdiction over the federal courts, most notably the Supreme Court and thus sets the legal fees applicable to the Supreme Court. In this section, a brief comparison between the court fees of the Cantons of Zurich and Geneva will be examined, followed by the fees for the Supreme Court.

In the Canton of Zurich, the Zurich Supreme Court Ordinance on Court Fees indicates how much the claimant has to pay as an advance in order to start the procedure.[46] The amounts specified for monetary claims by article 4 § 1 of that Ordinance are at Table 1.

Table 1: Court Fees for monetary claims in the Canton of Zurich

Amount at Issue	Court Fee
up to CHF 1,000	25% of the amount at issue, but at least CHF 150
over CHF 1,000	CHF 250 plus 20% of the amount at issue above CHF 1,000
over CHF 5,000	CHF 1,050 plus 14% of the amount at issue above CHF 5,000
over CHF 20,000	CHF 3,150 plus 8% of the amount at issue above CHF 20,000
over CHF 80,000	CHF 7,950 plus 4% of the amount at issue above CHF 80,000
over CHF 300,000	CHF 16,750 plus 2% of the amount at issue above CHF 300,000
over CHF 1,000,000	CHF 30,750 plus 1% of the amount at issue above CHF 1,000,000
over CHF 10,000,000	CHF 120,750 plus 0.5% of the amount at issue above CHF 10,000,000

[45] Art 96 FCCP.

[46] *Verordnung des Obergerichts über die Gerichtsgebühren* (Ordinance of the Zurich Supreme Court on Court Fees) (RS-ZH 211.11) dated 4 Apr 2007, at www2.zhlex.zh.ch/appl/zhlex_r.nsf/WebView/DE2D1139DF7B06D3C12573B40036C690/$File/211.11_4.4.07_59.pdf.

With respect to non-monetary claims, the court fees will consider the interest of the parties in litigating the case, the time the court has to deal with the case, and the complexity of the case. In principle, the fee should be no less than CHF 300 and no more than CHF 13,000.[47]

By comparison, the court fees in Geneva for monetary claims are at Table 2.[48]

Table 2: Court Fees for monetary claims in the Canton of Geneva

Amount at Issue	Court Fee
up to CHF 2,000	CHF 200
over CHF 2,000	CHF 300
over CHF 4,000	CHF 500
over CHF 6,000	CHF 650
over CHF 8,000	CHF 800
over CHF 10,000	CHF 1,500
over CHF 15,000	CHF 2,000
over CHF 20,000	CHF 2,000 plus CHF 350 for every additional CHF 10,000
over CHF 100,000	CHF 5,000 plus CHF 1,500 for every additional CHF 100,000
over CHF 1,000,000	CHF 20,000 plus CHF 3,000 for every additional CHF 500,000
over CHF 10,000,000	CHF 80,000 plus CHF 2,000 for every additional CHF 1,000,000

The court fees cannot amount to more than CHF 100,000, except (a) when both parties have chosen Geneva as their forum and none of them have their domicile or seat in Switzerland, in which case the costs are doubled, or (b) when there are multiple claimants or defendants, in which case the court fees are increased by 20 per cent.[49] Moreover, when the claimant has not determined the exact amount for his claim, the cost fees amount to CHF 800 subject to subsequent review.[50]

For non-monetary cases, the amount of the court fees varies according to the nature of the claim.[51] For a divorce case for example, the court fees amount to CHF 600, or for competition matters, court fees amount to CHF 4,000.[52]

At the Federal level, the amount due varies between CHF 200 and CHF 100,000 for monetary claims, and between CHF 200 and CHF 5,000 for non-monetary claims.[53] Article 1 of the Swiss Supreme Court Ordinance on Court Fees states that for monetary claims the amount of court fees varies depending on the amount at issue, as shown in Table 3.[54]

[47] Art 4 § 3 Ordinance of the Zurich Supreme Court on Court Fees (n 46).

[48] Art 11 § 1 of the *Règlement fixant le tarif des greffes en matière civile* (Ordinance Setting the Court Fees in Civil Matters) (E 3 05.10) dated 9 Apr 1997. Available at: www.ge.ch/legislation/.

[49] Art 11 § 2 of the Ordinance Setting the Court Fees in Civil Matters (n 48), in connection with Arts 8 and 9 of said Ordinance.

[50] Art 11 § 1(a) Ordinance Setting the Court Fees in Civil Matters (n 48).

[51] Art 12 of the Ordinance Setting the Court Fees in Civil Matters (n 48).

[52] Art 15 §1(b) FCCP, in connection with Art 31 § 1(b)(1) of the *Loi sur l'organisation judiciaire* (Geneva Judiciary Organisation Act) (E 2 05) dated 22 Nov 1941 and Art 12(e) of the Ordinance Setting the Court Fees in Civil Matters (n 48). Available at: www.ge.ch/legislation/.

[53] Art 65 § 3 FSCA.

[54] *Tarif des émoluments judicaires du Tribunal fédéral* (Swiss Supreme Court Ordinance on Court Fees) (RS 173.110.210.1), dated 31 Mar 2006. Available at: www.admin.ch/ch/f/rs/1/173.110.210.1.fr.pdf.

Table 3: Court Fees for monetary claims before the Supreme Court of the Swiss Confederation

Amount at Issue	Court Fee
up to CHF 10,000	CHF 200–5,000
over CHF 10,000	CHF 500–5,000
over CHF 20,000	CHF 1,000–5,000
over CHF 50,000	CHF 1,500–5,000
over CHF 100,000	CHF 2,000–8,000
over CHF 200,000	CHF 3,000–12,000
over CHF 500,000	CHF 5,000–20,000
over CHF 1,000,000	CHF 7,000–40,000
over CHF 5,000,000	CHF 10,000–60,000
over CHF 10,000,000	CHF 20,000–100,000

Within the above mentioned court fees are included the court fee *per se*, the fee for the number of copies, translation fees (except from one official language to another), and the expenses and salaries paid to the witnesses of facts and experts.[55]

The claimant must pay an advance for the estimated court fees. Only for special circumstances can the fees be waived.[56]

Generally, the fees are due at the start of the proceedings; otherwise the court will not consider the claim.[57] The claimant—or the appellant—must make the necessary advance. At the Supreme Court level, the judge in charge of instructing the case sets the deadline within which the appellant must pay the fees.[58] Should the claimant—or appellant—fail to pay the fees in time the court will dismiss the case with a binding judgment.

Other Official Charges

No VAT is levied on the court fees and no specific fees for bailiff exist in the Canton of Zurich or of Geneva, or before the Supreme Court.

As discussed in the section on general cost issues below, conciliation is a necessary first step towards a fully-fledged trial. The Cantons remain competent to set the conciliation fee. For example, Geneva has a conciliation fee amounting to CHF 120.[59]

The provisions related to the enforcement of judgments are articles 335–346 FCCP. There are, however, two different types of enforcement based on whether the claim is of a monetary value or not. With respect to non-monetary claims, the articles 335–346 FCCP apply. As the Cantons remain competent with respect to

[55] Art 65 § 1 FSCA.

[56] Art 62 § 1 FSCA.

[57] Art 3 § 1 of the Ordinance Setting the Court Fees in Civil Matters (n 48).

[58] Art 62 § 3 FSCA.

[59] Art 10 of the Ordinance Setting the Court Fees in Civil Matters (n 48).

the organisation of their justice system, the rules will differ from one Canton to another. For example, the Canton of Zurich has given the necessary competence to the Single Judge at the District Court in summary proceedings,[60] while the Canton of Geneva has given the necessary powers to the Attorney General (article 474 § 1 of the Geneva Civil Procedure Act).[61] Naturally, the general rules on costs and compensation apply to these cases.

With respect to monetary claims, the provisions set out in DEBA, and more specifically in the Ordinance on the Fees Perceived when applying the Debt Enforcement and Bankruptcy Act, are applicable.[62] As mentioned above in the General Overview and Trends section, the Debt Enforcement and Bankruptcy Act was one of the earliest federal acts, and the rules regarding the costs have since then been regulated at the federal level. The costs are in principle not high, since many aspects of DEBA relate to procedural issues, the trials on the merits of the cases were (and are still) handled by Cantonal courts applying federal substantive rules. Indeed, article 50 DEBA Tariff states that the Cantons retain their jurisdiction to set court fees in matters involving the ordinary procedure and the accelerated procedure. Federal jurisdiction regulates thus exclusively summary proceedings, for which the tariff set out in article 48 DEBA Tariff is shown in Table 4.

Table 4: Fees for summary proceedings under the Debt Enforcement and Bankruptcy Act

Amount at Issue	Court Fee
up to CHF 1,000	CHF 40–150
over CHF 1,000	CHF 50–300
over CHF 10,000	CHF 60–500
over CHF 100,000	CHF 70–1,000
over CHF 1,000,000	CHF 120–2,000

This table applies to a limited number of cases, included in article 25 § 2 DEBA, such as cancellation or suspension of the enforcement,[63] of decisions rendered in bankruptcy cases, or seizure. Moreover, these court fees are a set price which includes all costs related to the judicial handling of those above mentioned cases and it must be settled in advance by the party who requires the court to act.[64]

Regarding the fees for the delivery of a summons to pay to the debtor, the costs depend on the amount at issue. Article 16 DEBA Tariff is shown at Table 5.

[60] Arts 300–310—especially art 302—ZCPC (n 32).

[61] *Loi de procédure civile* (Geneva Civil Procedure Act, GCPA) (E 3 05) dated 10 Apr 1987, at www.ge.ch/legislation.

[62] *Ordonnance sur les émoluments perçus en application de la loi fédérale sur la poursuite pour dettes et la faillite* (Ordinance on the fees perceived when applying the Debt Enforcement and Bankruptcy Act, DEBA Tariff) (RS 281.35), dated 23 Sept 1996, at www.admin.ch/ch/f/rs/2/281.35.fr.pdf.

[63] Art 85 DEBA.

[64] Art 49 §§ 1–2 DEBA Tariff.

Table 5: Fees for delivery of a summons to pay under the Debt Enforcement and Bankruptcy Act

Amount at Issue	Fee for the Summons to Pay
up to CHF 100	CHF 7
over CHF 100	CHF 20
over CHF 500	CHF 40
over CHF 1,000	CHF 60
over CHF 10,000	CHF 90
over CHF 100,000	CHF 190
over CHF 1,000,000	CHF 400

In practice, the claimant will first deliver a summons to pay. If the debtor opposes the summons to pay, then the claimant will file an ordinary procedure before the cantonal court and will include the claims. The costs of requesting the summons to pay will be added to the general expenses alongside the claim before the court. Indeed, the costs of enforcement are borne by the debtor, but the claimant has to provide the necessary advance.[65]

Witness of Fact

At the Federal level, there are no specific rules on the costs related to witnesses of facts.[66] The general rules consequently apply to these costs. Article 102 § 1 FCCP declares that each party must make the necessary advances for the administration of the evidence she requires to be given. In Geneva, the parties are invited to indicate who they wish to have as witnesses and must pay a corresponding advance—set by the judge—for the costs related to the subpoenas.[67] If the party does not pay, the witness will not receive the subpoena.[68]

Contrary to what happens in the Canton of Zurich for instance, where the witness automatically receives an allowance for his testimony,[69] the witness appearing before a Court in the Canton of Geneva has to request an indemnity and the judge will then set the amount for the indemnity, taking into account the profession of the witness, the distance from her domicile, and the length of time her

[65] Art 68 DEBA.

[66] Arts 150–167 & 169–176 FCCP.

[67] Art 215 § 2 GCPA.

[68] Art 215 § 3 GCPA.

[69] Art 3 §§ 1–2 of the *Entschädigungsverordnung der obersten Gerichte* (Ordinance of the Zurich Supreme Court on the compensation) (RS-ZH 211.12) dated 11 Jun 2002, at www2.zhlex.zh.ch/appl/zhlex_r.nsf/WebView/C1256C610039641BC1256036003CDB08/$File/211.12_11.6.02_38.pdf. The witnesses may expect an allowance ranging from CHF 20 and CHF 100 (art 3 § 1). However, art 3 § 2 states that the witness may ask for CHF 25 to CHF 150 per hour, in order to compensate 'adequately' the loss incurred.

presence was required.[70] The party who had called her as a witness would have to pay the related expenses.[71]

As a rule in proceedings before the Supreme Court, facts are not discussed except when resulting from manifest inaccuracy of the precedent authority.[72] Moreover, new evidence is equally forbidden before the Supreme Court.[73] Thus, as a rule, witnesses are not heard before the Supreme Court.

The *loser pays* rule is also applicable to the witnesses of facts.[74]

Expert

The judge may, at the request of a party or *ex officio*, appoint an expert.[75] When a party requests an expert, she must pay an advance for the probable costs.[76] The judge assesses the advance that should be paid, and sets a deadline for the party to pay the advance.[77] If the party does not pay the advance in time, the judge sets another deadline for the other party to pay the advance, if she deems it necessary. If the other party does not pay the advance, then the expert's evidence is deemed unnecessary and the judge will follow the line of argument of the party who did not ask for the expert.[78]

The expert has a right to receive a payment for his work.[79] The decision concerning the amount to be paid to the expert may be subject to appeal. The judge decides on the expenses and the salary of the expert, once the expert has accomplished his work and has given the court clerk his list of expenses and salary.[80]

The *loser pays* rule is also applicable to the ruling on the expert's expenses and salary.[81]

Any Other Costs

An unjustified trial may cost a lot, especially for the defendant if he prevails.[82] In most cases that should not be too much of a problem for him, because he will be awarded, especially with respect to his counsel's costs, an amount set out in the Cost Shifting section below. However, when certain conditions are met, he can ask

[70] Art 237 § 1 GCPA.
[71] Art 237 § 2 GCPA.
[72] Art 97 § 1 FSCA.
[73] Art 99 § 1 FSCA.
[74] Art 106 § 1 FCCP.
[75] Art 183 § 1 FCCP.
[76] Art 102 § 1 FCCP.
[77] Art 268 § 2 GCPA.
[78] Art 268 § 3 GCPA.
[79] Art 184 § 3 FCCP.
[80] Art 269 § 2 GCPA.
[81] Art 106 § 1 FCCP.
[82] See D Hofmann and C Lüscher, *Le Code de procédure civile* (Berne, Stämpfli Vertrag AG, 2009) 61–64.

for securities to be deposited by the claimant specifically for his counsel's costs. It is known as the *cautio judicatum solvi* request.[83] The conditions in which a *cautio judicatum solvi* is possible are the following:[84]

a. The claimant does not have his residence or seat in Switzerland;
b. The claimant appears to be insolvent, namely due to a bankruptcy order, a continuing legal settlement (*procédure concordataire*) or the issuance of an act attesting the insufficiency of funds;
c. The claimant owes some court fees from a previous trial;
d. Other reasons indicate that the claimant will not pay such counsel's expenses.

International treaties that forbid a *cautio judicatum solvi* between parties that have their legal residence or seat in the territory of the contracting States, and only for that reason, are reserved.[85]

Article 99 § 3 FCCP excludes some specific types of cases, namely in simplified proceedings,[86] with the notable exception of monetary claims,[87] in divorce cases and in summary proceedings.[88]

A similar article appears in the Federal Supreme Court Act for proceedings before the Supreme Court.[89] If the claimant does not have his residence or seat in Switzerland, or when he is insolvent, then, at the behest of the other party, the Court may request a *cautio judicatum solvi*. As will be shown in the Lawyers' Costs section below, the Supreme Court has a tariff for the legal costs. In such cases, the Supreme Court will apply this tariff to the *cautio judicatum solvi* request.

If the claimant does not pay the advance in time, the court will not judge the case on its merits.[90] This procedural defence may have a crippling effect on the claimant's ability to take his suit forward.

Lawyers' Costs

The agreement between a lawyer and his client is a mandate, as defined by articles 394–406 CO. There are no specific rules as to how much a lawyer may ask for a fee, only guidelines. Once the lawyer accepts a mandate, he informs his client of the invoicing terms and regularly—or at his request—updates him on the amount of fees due.[91] With respect to the ethical rules,[92] the amount of fees must be appropriate and its determination must take into account factors such as the time and

[83] Art 99 FCCP.
[84] Art 99 § 1 FCCP.
[85] Art 2 FCCP. See especially Federal Council, Message (n 2) 6906.
[86] Arts 243–247 FCCP.
[87] Art 243 § 1 FCCP.
[88] Arts 248–251 FCCP, with the exception of clear cases as defined by Art 257 FCCP.
[89] Art 62 § 2 FSCA.
[90] Art 101 § 3 FCCP and art 62 § 3 FSCA.
[91] Art 12(i) of the Lawyers' Freedom of Movement Act.
[92] Art 18 of the Swiss Professional Code of Ethics from the Swiss Lawyers' Federation.

complexity of the case. Moreover, the lawyer must explain how he will calculate the fees. In the Canton of Geneva, the fees are set by the lawyer, with the exception of the taxation commission.[93] He must take into account the same criteria as mentioned above in the Swiss Professional Code of Ethics from the Swiss Lawyers' Federation.[94] Thus, guided by these principles, the lawyer and the client will agree on an hourly rate (at least for the majority of cases), on the terms of payment, and so forth.

In principle, the lawyer is paid on an hourly basis. However, it may be the case that big companies require from their counsel a flat fee, in exchange for handling their whole legal business. Such agreements are much less frequent when the clients are individuals.

The lawyer may freely set his fees in agreement with his client. However, should there be a disagreement between a lawyer and his client over the amount of fees due, a taxation commission exists in Geneva to resolve such issues. The taxation commission comprises two members of the judicial branch and one lawyer.[95] The taxation commission renders a decision solely on the amount of fees due to the lawyer. Should there be an issue over the execution of the mandate, for example, then the parties must address themselves to the ordinary judge.[96] It should be noted that in practice lawyers do not like to show their agreements to the public. That is why (a) the parties tend to negotiate if the client is unwilling to pay the amount requested by the lawyer and (b) the public is excluded from the hearings.[97] This procedure is free of charge.[98]

As mentioned in the Funding Claims section above, the *pactum de quota litis* is considered both illegal and unethical in Switzerland. On the other hand, a *pactum de palmario* may be agreed upon, most notably when the lawyer works for a lower fee than usual.[99] Article 19 of the Swiss Professional Code of Ethics, produced by the Swiss Lawyers' Federation, states that it is acceptable for the parties to allow for a success fee. However, it should be noted that the term used in French is *prime* and in German *Erfolgsprämie*, both of which do not mean 'fee', but rather 'bonus'. Thus, it should be understood as an additional amount, rather than replacing the usual fees.

Regarding the question of the existence of official or unofficial tariffs for what the client must pay his lawyer, such tariffs should not exist, due to the fact (a) an official tariff would put the authority regulating this issue at odds with the Bar and (b) an unofficial tariff (ie a tariff provided by a local Bar association) would be considered a price agreement and would infringe the Cartel Act. Thus, with the exception of legal aid as mentioned above, such tariffs do not exist—or at least should not—in Switzerland.

[93] Art 34 of the *Loi sur la profession d'avocat* (Geneva Lawyers Act) (E 6 10) dated 26 Apr 2002, at www.ge.ch/legislation.

[94] See also art 12 of the Habits and Customs of the Geneva Lawyers' Association, which does not add much to these guidelines.

[95] Art 36 of the Geneva Lawyers Act (n 93).

[96] ibid, art 39 § 1.

[97] ibid, art 37 § 2.

[98] ibid, art 37 § 4.

[99] Art 12 of the Habits and Customs of the Geneva Lawyers' Association mentions the agreement on '*honoraires de diligence*' in order to enjoy a success fee.

Finally, it is very commmon in practice that the lawyer asks for a deposit and that he bills his client on a monthly (or other periodic) basis.

Cost Shifting

The expenses must be borne by the loser.[100] Thus the *loser pays* rule, which includes, among others, the court fees and the successful party's expenses is applicable in Switzerland.

When there is no clear loser or successful party, then the costs are divided between the parties, according to the merits of the case.[101] For example, when the merits (of a simple case) indicate that the claimant has won 60 per cent of his claim and the defendant 40 per cent, then the costs will be divided according to the merits. Thus the claimant will have to bear 60 per cent of the costs while the defendant will be saddled with the rest (40 per cent).

However, one has to mention two exceptions to the general rule, namely fairness and needlessness. The FCCP provides some judicial oversight in case of fairness (*équité*). Indeed, the judge may not apply the *loser pays* rule when (a) the claimants wins on the merits, but not on the exact amount he claimed, due to the fact that the court had discretion over it or the amount was difficult to estimate; (b) a party went to trial in good faith; (c) the trial concerns family law; (d) the trial covers same-sex partnerships; (e) the trial has become without object and the law does not provide for specific remedies; and (f) particular circumstances would seem unfair to apply the usual *loser pays* rule.[102] Furthermore, the legal expenses can be borne by the Canton, if fairness commands it, when they are ascribable neither to the parties nor to third parties.[103] Finally, needless expenses are to be borne by the person (either party or third party) who incurred them.[104]

As mentioned in the first section, a frequent practice of the Federal Legislator is to include procedural provisions in substantive acts. One notable exception to the cost shifting rule relates to the Federal Act on Mergers, Demergers, Transformations and Transfers of Assets and Liabilities.[105] When the bearer of an equity right or of a membership right believes that he has not been adequately protected or compensated, he may request from the judge an adequate compensation.[106] In this case, the 'costs of the proceedings shall be borne by the acquiring legal entity'.[107] If special circumstances justify it, the court may order the plaintiff

[100] Art 106 § 1 FCCP.

[101] Art 106 § 2 FCCP.

[102] Art 107 § 1 FCCP.

[103] Art 107 § 2 FCCP.

[104] Art 108 FCCP.

[105] Federal Act on Mergers, Demergers, Transformations and Transfers of Assets and Liabilities (Merger Act) (RS 221.301), dated 3 Oct 2003, at www.admin.ch/ch/f/rs/2/221.301.fr.pdf.

[106] Art 105 § 1 of the Merger Act.

[107] English translation of Art 105 § 3 1st sentence of the Merger Act in M Bauen et al, *Merger Law* (Zürich/Basel/Genf, Schulthess Juristische Medien, 2005) 496.

to bear the costs of the proceedings, in its entirety or in part.[108] The reasoning behind this exception is that if the general *loser pays* rule were to be applied, small investors would not bother to safeguard their rights.[109]

Some Cantons, such as the Canton of Zurich, calculate according to a tariff the expenses the successful party may ask with respect to his lawyer's fees. The figures set out in article 3 § 1 of the Supreme Court of the Canton of Zurich Ordinance on the Lawyer's Fees,[110] in connection with article 68 § 1 of the Zurich Civil Procedure Code and article 48 §§ 1(c) and 2 of the Lawyers Act are at Table 6.

Table 6: Tariff for reimbursement of lawyer's fees by a losing party in the Canton of Zurich

Amount at Issue	Legal Expenses		
up to CHF 5,000	25% of the amount at issue, but at least CHF 100		
over CHF 5,000	CHF	1,250	plus 23% of the amount at issue above CHF 5,000
over CHF 10,000	CHF	2,400	plus 15% of the amount at issue above CHF 10,000
over CHF 20,000	CHF	3,900	plus 11% of the amount at issue above CHF 20,000
over CHF 40,000	CHF	6,100	plus 9% of the amount at issue above CHF 40,000
over CHF 80,000	CHF	9,700	plus 6% of the amount at issue above CHF 80,000
over CHF 160,000	CHF	14,500	plus 3.5% of the amount at issue above CHF 160,000
over CHF 300,000	CHF	19,400	plus 2% of the amount at issue above CHF 300,000
over CHF 600,000	CHF	25,400	plus 1.5% of the amount at issue above CHF 600,000
over CHF 1,000,000	CHF	31,400	plus 1% of the amount at issue above CHF 1,000,000
over CHF 4,000,000	CHF	61,400	plus 0.75% of the amount at issue above CHF 4,000,000
over CHF 10,000,000	CHF	106,400	plus 0.5% of the amount at issue above CHF 10,000,000

108 Art 105 § 3 2nd sentence of the Merger Act.

109 R Bahar, 'Art 105' in H Peter and R Trigo Trindade (eds), *Commentaire LFus* (Zürich/Basel/Genf, Schulthess Juristische Medien, 2005) 996 para 38.

110 *Verordnung des Obergerichts über die Anwaltsgebühren* (Supreme Court of the Canton of Zurich Ordinance on Lawyer's Fees) (RS-ZH 215.3) dated 21 Jun 2006, at www2.zhlex.zh.ch/appl/zhlex_r.nsf/WebView/CE007E5355E16FDBC125724B002AD9DA/$File/215.3_21.6.06_55.pdf.

When the case is non-monetary, then the expenses may vary between CHF 1,400 and CHF 16,000.[111] Either way, the court will have to determine on a case-by-case basis exactly how much the loser owes to the successful party. Indeed, it will have to take into account the complexity of the case, the number of briefs and hearings, and the overall workload.[112]

Other Cantons, such as the Canton of Geneva, do not have a specific tariff, nor is the notion of 'compensation' as precise as it appears in the Canton of Zurich. Indeed, the successful party will receive an 'indemnity' for the procedure, to be set by the court according to the following criteria, namely the importance of the case, its complexity, the scale of the procedure, as well as costs not included in the general court fees.[113]

Concerning the court fees, the procedure before the Supreme Court follows the *loser pays* rule with similar exceptions.[114] With respect to lawyer's fees, as in the Canton of Zurich, a Supreme Court Ordinance on Legal Expenses due to the Other Party and the Indemnity due to the Attorney under the Legal Aid Regime[115] sets a tariff, to be followed by the Supreme Court under the usual discretionary rules mentioned above.[116] The tariff set out in article 4 FSCA Tariff is at Table 7.

Table 7: Tariff for reimbursement of lawyer's fees by a losing party before the Supreme Court of the Swiss Confederation

Amount at Issue	Legal Expenses
up to CHF 20,000	CHF 600–4,000
over CHF 20,000	CHF 1,500–6,000
over CHF 50,000	CHF 3,000–10,000
over CHF 100,000	CHF 5,000–15,000
over CHF 500,000	CHF 7,000–22,000
over CHF 1,000,000	CHF 8,000–30,000
over CHF 2,000,000	CHF 12,000–50,000
over CHF 5,000,000	CHF 20,000–1%

In non-monetary cases, the Supreme Court may allocate between CHF 600 and CHF 18,000 to the successful party.[117]

[111] Art 3 § 5 of the Supreme Court of the Canton of Zurich Ordinance on the Lawyer's Fees (n 110).
[112] See generally Art 2 of the Supreme Court of the Canton of Zurich Ordinance on Lawyer's Fees (n 110).
[113] Art 181 § 3 GCPA.
[114] Art 66 §§ 1 and 3 FSCA.
[115] *Règlement sur les dépens alloués à la partie adverse et sur l'indemnité pour la représentation d'office dans les causes portées devant le Tribunal fédéral* (Supreme Court Ordinance on Legal Expenses due to the Other Party and the Indemnity due to the Attorney under the Legal Aid Regime, FSCA Tariff) (RS 173.110.210.3) dated 31 Mar 2006, at www.admin.ch/ch/f/rs/1/173.110.210.3.fr.pdf.
[116] As mentioned by art 8 FSCA Tariff (n 115).
[117] Art 6 FSCA Tariff (n 115).

General Costs Issues

In this section, both conciliation and mediation will be presented in light of the FCCP. Indeed, one of the main innovations of the FCCP compared to the Cantonal Codes of Civil Procedure is the recognition of the importance—and consequent increase in the offer—of alternative dispute resolution mechanisms. The underlying concept is that judicial intervention must be the last result in resolving a dispute between parties. Too often parties have resorted to litigation without first trying other mechanisms of dispute resolution. Out-of-court settlements have thus been given priority over litigation, not because it will reduce the number of cases before the court, but, as the Federal Council claims,[118] out-of-court settlements are more likely to be executed by the parties due to the fact that these settlements can take into consideration specific elements that the court can not. The FCCP contains also the necessary provisions for internal arbitration, but this will not be explored, due to the clear separation the FCCP makes between civil trials, including conciliation and mediation, on the one hand and arbitration on the other.

Finally, some very important exceptions with respect to costs are to be found in the so-called 'social civil trials'. These will be briefly presented in this section too.

Conciliation

The authors of the FCCP believe that conciliation is very important both to litigants and to the judicial system as a whole.[119] Indeed, litigants may reach an agreement (a transaction) at an early stage of the trial and thus avoid wasting too much of their resources during the trial. For the system as a whole, this option is very attractive, as conciliation can relieve the judicial system of unnecessary litigation. Given the relative disparity between the Cantonal civil procedures on this issue, the FCCP positions itself in the middle of the various existing rules.[120] One key element is that *lis pendens* is established as soon as the request for conciliation has been filed before the competent authority, so the parties do not need to rush to court.[121] Another element which increases the attractiveness of conciliation is that it is now considered the first step in a trial and is thus mandatory in almost all cases.[122]

[118] Federal Council, Message (n 2) 6860.

[119] See generally Explanatory Report (n 43) 94 and Federal Council, Message (n 2) 6860–861 and 6936–942.

[120] Explanatory Report (n 43) 94.

[121] Art 62 § 1 FCCP.

[122] Art 197 FCCP. The exceptions are presented in Art 198 FCCP and cover limited areas of the law, for example divorce procedures, summary procedures and some actions relating to the Debt Enforcement and Bankruptcy Act. According to Art 199 § 1 FCCP, the parties may also agree to waive the conciliation procedure when the amount at stake is greater than CHF 100,000. Equally important in commercial matters is the possibility for the plaintiff to opt out of the conciliation procedure when the seat of the defendant is located outside of Switzerland (art 199 § 2(a) FCCP); the plaintiff may also opt out in certain other conditions set forth in art 199 § 2(b) & (c) FCCP.

Even though the conciliation authority (as defined by the Cantons) is established by the State (either part of the judicial system or part of the administration), the hearings before the authority are confidential,[123] ie the depositions of the parties are not recorded in the minutes of the conciliation and cannot be used in further stages if a trial is commenced. Moreover, the procedure is informal[124] and generally oral.[125] With this kind of flexible procedure, the conciliation authority may better serve the interests of litigants as well as reducing the overall costs of the judicial system.

The plaintiff bears the costs of the conciliation procedure when he abandons his request, when he fails to appear before the conciliation authority or when he receives the authorisation to proceed before the court of first instance.[126] However, in this latter case, once the plaintiff files the suit before the court of first instance, the costs of the conciliation procedure will be borne by the loser as determined by the verdict of the court.

The existing mechanisms, such as the mandatory conciliation in cases of tenancy agreement for residential and commercial property, will continue in their present form. Indeed, both the authors of the FCCP Draft Project[127] and the Federal Council[128] are satisfied with these current mechanisms.

Mediation

The articles related to mediation were introduced as a consequence of the comments on the FCCP Draft Project. The Federal Council took into account those remarks and introduced a general section on mediation.[129] It thus refused to introduce a complete set of regulations on mediation claiming that the nature of mediation cannot be taken into account in a code of civil procedure. Indeed, the title on mediation comprises only six articles (articles 213–218 FCCP), compared to more than double those on conciliation provisions. The parties can request mediation in order to replace the conciliation proceedings or at any point in the trial.[130] The court can recommend mediation.[131] If a mediation request is made during a trial, the trial is suspended until the end of the mediation or when one party renounces the mediation. The parties have to agree to the procedure before the mediator.[132] Mediation is confidential, independent from the conciliation authority and from the court, and the depositions of the parties cannot be used in other circumstances.[133]

123 Art 205 § 1 FCCP.
124 Art 204 FCCP.
125 Art 202 § 2 FCCP. See generally Federal Council, Message (n 2) 6936–942 and art 212 § 2 FCCP.
126 Art 207 § 1 FCCP.
127 Explanatory Report (n 43), 97.
128 Federal Council, Message (n 2) 6860.
129 Federal Council, Message (n 2) 6943.
130 Art 213 § 2 FCCP.
131 Art 214 § 1 FCCP.
132 Art 215 FCCP.
133 Art 216 FCCP.

The parties bear the costs of mediation.[134] There is no right to free mediation. There is, however, one exception, namely in the case of children's rights that are non-monetary which applies when the parents are in need (the same as the standard for qualifying for legal aid) and when the tribunal encourages the parents to mediate.[135] Indeed, the Federal Council believes that maintaining dialogue between the parties is paramount.[136] Even if there is no specific provision in the FCCP regarding this issue, it seems quite clear that the mediator will be 'compensated' by the Canton. Indeed, the Federal Council states that, similarly to legal aid,[137] the exemption of mediation fees is not definitive, but subject to reimbursement to the Canton according to article 123 FCCP. Again, the Cantons are free to increase the exceptions exempting parties from bearing the responsibility of the costs of mediation.

Social Civil Trials

In Switzerland, some cases are deemed 'social' and thus the parties are not required to pay either the legal costs and/or the legal fees. These cases are based on political criteria existing within the current legal framework (the cases are described below). Thus, the project does not go beyond the current legal framework.[138] However, during the FCCP consultation,[139] some commentators proposed to extend the notion of 'social civil trial' to agreements concluded with consumers, at least for proceedings before the conciliation authority.

During the conciliation procedure,[140] the conciliation authority does not allocate any legal fee, with the exception of legal aid paid by the Canton. Article 113 § 2 FCCP exempts parties from paying legal costs in cases arising out of (a) the Equality Act, (b) the Handicapped Persons Equality Act, (c) tenancy agreements for residential property, (d) labour law, when the amount in dispute does not exceed CHF 30,000, (e) the Information and Consultation of the Workers Within Undertakings Act, and (f) the Disability Insurance Act with respect to Complementary Coverage. During the trial,[141] the parties are responsible for legal

[134] Art 218 § 1 FCCP.
[135] Art 218 § 2 FCCP.
[136] Federal Council, Message (n 2) 6945–946.
[137] Federal Council, Message (n 2) 6946.
[138] Federal Council, Message (n 2) 6911.
[139] FCCP consultation (n 23) 303–306. See especially the comments from the *Associazione Consumatrici della Svizzera italiana* (Consumers' Association from the Italian speaking part of Switzerland) which indicated that '*Questo articolo è chiaramente incompleto. L'ACSI chiede che sia istituita una procedura di conciliazione gratuita in tutte le controversie (indipendentemente cioè dal valore litigioso) inerenti contratti conclusi con consumatori. La gratuità favorisce il ricorso alla conciliazione, a tutto beneficio di un'evasione celere delle vertenze*'. 'Social civil trials' encourage conciliation. Other proponents claimed that consumers are naturally in a weaker position relative to the seller. However, the Cantons rejected this proposal largely because of budgetary concerns. In the end, consumers will not benefit from a free Federal conciliation before the competent authority.
[140] Art 113 § 1 FCCP.
[141] Art 114 FCCP.

fees. However, the court fees will not be borne by the parties in the same cases in which such costs are waived before the conciliation authority, with the exception of rental agreements for residential property.

When a party has acted in a foolhardy manner or in bad faith, then legal fees and costs may be imposed, even if the issue was under the 'social civil trial' provisions.[142] Moreover, the Cantons may choose to extend the notion of 'social civil trial' to other areas of law.[143] Thus, it remains to be seen whether consumers will actually benefit from some Cantons' largesse.

Conclusion

Swiss law imposes a considerable financial burden upon litigation before courts, both in terms of court fees as well as in terms of costs related to counsel. Litigation is financially risky for both parties, but especially for the plaintiff, because of the *loser pays* rule and of the prohibition of contingency fees. Costs may be mitigated by voluntary insurance schemes which may include a success fee. Social civil trials, quite important in the fields of landlord and tenant disputes as well as in labour law, are exempted from all costs.

[142] Art 115 FCCP.
[143] Art 116 § 1 FCCP.

22

Taiwan

KUAN-LING SHEN* AND HELENA H C CHEN**

General Review and Trends

The Taiwanese Code of Civil Procedure was largely modelled on the German Code of 1977, but the 'loser pays' rule that applies to 'litigation expenses' does not apply to lawyers' costs.

In Taiwan, regulations for civil litigation expenses were originally stipulated in the Civil Litigation Expenses Act. In 2003, as a result of law integration, this special law was abolished and integrated into Taiwanese Code of Civil Procedure ('CCP').[1] Civil litigation expenses mainly cover court charges and other costs, including taxable fees for photocopies, video recording, transcripts, translation, daily fees, travel expenses of witnesses and expert witnesses, and other fees and disbursements necessary for the proceeding items, but not lawyer's costs in principle.

To save time and costs, mediation was also introduced into the court system. For certain types of disputes, compulsory mediation is a pre-requisite before a party to the dispute can bring the case to court.[2] For other types of disputes, the parties may also decide to apply for mediation before initiating a lawsuit, and the charges for mediation are lower than court charges.[3] Should mediation fail and the procedure be converted to litigation, the charges for mediation may be counted as part of the court charges for the litigation and the case is deemed initiated with the court at the time when the parties first applied for mediation.[4]

For matters arising from proprietary rights, court charges are based on the price or value of a claim determined by the court. The claim's value will be based on its transaction value at the time when the action is initiated or, in the absence of such a transaction value, the interests in the claim as owned by the plaintiff.[5] The

* Associate Professor of National Taiwan University, College of Law.
** Partner of Formosan Brothers, Attorneys-at-Law; Member of Taiwan and New York bars.

[1] Mingshi susongfa [Code of Civil Procedure of the Republic of China] (promulgated 26 Dec 1930, last amended 8 Jul 2009) (Taiwan).

[2] Art 403 CCP.

[3] Art 404, para 1 CCP. For court charges for mediation, see art 77-20 CCP.

[4] Art 419, para 2 and art 423, para 1 CCP.

[5] Art 77-1, para 1 & 2 CCP.

criterion for calculating court charges is a certain ratio of the claim's price or value, which will decrease with the increase of the claim's value.

Although, the plaintiff bears the initial responsibility for the court charges, Taiwan applies a *loser pays* rule. A party who fails to sustain his position in court must not only pay his own costs of litigation; but must also defray the litigation costs of his victorious opponent. In cases of a partial victory or a partial defeat, the court may, in its discretion, order the litigation expenses to be borne by both parties in a certain proportion or by a particular party alone, or order both parties to separately bear the litigation expenses they incurred respectively. However, the court may, in its discretion, order the prevailing party to bear the litigation expenses incurred in full or in part for an act performed by the prevailing party, which is unnecessary for asserting or defending its rights.

Furthermore, in matters arising from a partition or demarcation of a thing held indivisibly, due to the fact that there is no substantial victory or defeat, although they are processed in the civil procedure, the CCP was amended in 2003 so that where it is manifestly unfair for the defeated party to bear solely the litigation expenses, the court may, in its discretion, order the prevailing party to bear part of the litigation expenses.[6]

In cases of voluntary dismissal, the plaintiff shall bear the litigation expenses. In cases of a settlement, the parties shall respectively bear the expenses of the settlement and the litigation expenses. But in order to encourage parties to settle the disputes, if the plaintiff voluntarily dismisses the action prior to the closure of the oral-argument session in the court of first instance, within three months from the date of voluntary dismissal, the plaintiff may move for the return of two-thirds of the court charges paid.[7] Likewise, if a settlement is reached either during a court session or mediation session referred to by the court, within three months from the date of settlement, the plaintiff may also move for the return of two-thirds of the court charges paid.[8]

Funding Claims

In most cases, the costs of bringing or defending a legal claim are supported by personal funds. If a party lacks the financial means to pay litigation expenses, except in cases where there is manifestly no prospect for a party to prevail in the action, the court shall, by ruling on a motion, grant litigation aid.[9] If a motion for litigation aid is granted by the court, the party receiving litigation aid will be:[10]

[6] Art 80-1 CCP.
[7] Art 83 CCP.
[8] Art 84 and art 420-1, para 3 CCP.
[9] Art 107, para 1 CCP.
[10] Art 110 CCP.

1. temporarily exempt from paying the court charges and other litigation expenses which are to be advanced under applicable laws, and the national treasury shall disburse the litigation expenses for which the party is so temporarily exempt from paying;
2. exempt from providing a security for the litigation expenses, if applicable; and
3. temporarily exempt from paying lawyer's costs when the presiding judge, pursuant to the applicable laws, appoints an attorney to advocate the case for the party.[11]

Legal expenses insurance is commonly seen in liability insurance, for example, product liability insurance, directors', supervisors' and officers' liability insurance and car insurance. Legal expenses coverage, which covers litigation expenses, lawyers' costs and so on, might be provided in a basic insurance agreement or optional. But, in Taiwan, after-the-event (ATE) insurance is very rare, if not unavailable at all, and loans or grants for the purpose of paying legal expenses from banks and trade associations are also rare.

A lawyer may agree to provide legal services to a client at a lower price or for free, if he/she is so willing. Whether a lawyer will agree to fund a client for litigation expenses, charges for enforcement or other costs are subject to the agreement between the lawyer and his/her client. It does not happen often, and only happens when situation requires it.

Whether a third party investor will agree to fund a client for litigation expenses, charges for enforcement or other costs is subject to the agreement between the investor and the client. It is more likely to happen when there is also an arrangement on how to share the benefit resulting from the outcome of the civil litigation, if the client wins.

Court or Process Costs

Court Charges

Court charges are based on the price or value of a claim that has to be determined by the court. The claim's value will be based on its transaction value at the time when the action was initiated or, in the absence of such transaction value, the interests in the claim as owned by the plaintiff. The criterion for calculating court charges is a certain ratio of the claim's price or value, which will decrease with the increase of the claim's value. Article 77-13 provides the necessary details to calculate the amount of court charges due, as shown in Table 1.

[11] See eg pursuant to art 466-2, para 1 CCP, the court may, on the party's motion, appoint an attorney to advocate the case for the party.

Table 1: Court charges

Below NTD 100,000	NTD 1,000
Up to NTD 1,000,000	NTD 110 for each NTD 10,000 inclusive
Up to NTD 10,000,000	NTD 99 for each NTD 10,000 inclusive
Up to NTD 100,000,000	NTD 88 for each NTD 10,000 inclusive
Up to NTD 1,000,000,000	NTD 77 for each NTD 10,000 inclusive
Above NTD 1,000,000,000	NTD 66 for each NTD 10,000 inclusive

These amounts are cumulative. A fraction of NTD 10,000 shall be rounded up to NTD 10,000 for purposes of taxing court costs. If a claim's value cannot be determined, the value shall be deemed as NTD 1,650,000 for the purpose of calculating and levying court charges.[12]

In matters of appeal to a court of second or third instance, an additional five-tenths court charge of first instance shall be taxed in accordance with the provisions of articles 77-13 and 77-14 CCP. No court charges will be taxed on a repeated appeal from a judgment rendered after the case has been remanded or transferred by a superior court or on an appeal from a judgment rendered by the transferee court after the case is transferred in accordance with the provision of the second paragraph of article 452 CCP.

In contrast, the court charge for matters arising from non-proprietary rights is a flat charge at NTD 3,000 for the court of first instance and NTD 4,500 for the court of second or third instance, namely 150 per cent of the court charge for the court of first instance.[13]

Unless otherwise provided in the CCP, a party may appeal against a court ruling.[14] The court charge for making an appeal or re-appeal against a court ruling is NTD 1,000.[15]

In exceptional situations, a party is entitled to request the court to review a final judgment.[16] The court charge for rehearing a case is the same as what the court would charge in ordinary civil litigation cases.[17] A party is entitled to request the court to review a final ruling when the situations stipulated in the CCP are met. As for court rulings, a court charge of NTD 1,000 shall be levied for a motion for a rehearing of a final ruling.[18]

[12] Art 77-12 CCP and Taiwan Gaodeng Fayuan Minshi susong, feisong shijian, qiangzhi zhising ti gao zheng shou eshu biaozhun [Taiwan High Court's Standard for Increasing Court Charges in Civil Litigation, Non-litigation Cases and Compulsory Execution] amended and announced by Taiwan High Court's Letter, No. Yuan-Xin-Wen-Gong-Zi 0940003474, dated 26 May 2005. Fuchien High Court Kinmen Branch Court also promulgated its amendment to 'Fuchien High Court Kinmen Branch Court's Standard for Increasing Court Charges in Civil Litigation, Non-litigation Cases and Compulsory Execution' on 8 Sept 2005.

[13] Arts 77-14 and 77-16 CCP.

[14] Art 482 CCP provides that: 'Except as otherwise provided, an appeal may be taken from a ruling'.

[15] Art 77-18 CCP provides that: 'Court costs of NTD 1,000 shall be taxed on an appeal from a ruling and on each subsequent re-appeal'.

[16] Those exceptional situations are listed in art 496 CCP.

[17] Art 77-17, para 1 CCP.

[18] Art 77-17, para 2 CCP.

As a general rule, no court charges will be levied on filing motions and statements. Nonetheless, a court charge of NTD 500 shall be levied for the motion listed in item one below and a court charge of NTD 1,000 shall be levied for each of the motions listed in items two to seven.[19]

1. A motion for issuance of a payment order;
2. A motion for intervention or for denying intervention;
3. A motion for restoration to *status quo ante*;
4. A motion for pre-action perpetuation of evidence;
5. A motion for provisional attachment, provisional injunction, or revocation of a ruling for provisional attachment or provisional injunction;
6. A motion for declaration of commencement of guardianship or commencement of assistance or a motion for change or revocation of commencement of guardianship or commencement of assistance;
7. A motion for public summons, for a judgment of abridgment of rights, or for declaration of death.

Other Official Charges

Photocopying, printing, photographing, scanning and translation of court files are charged separately at reasonable rates.[20] The courts also charge separately for issuing additional hardcopies of a judgment certificate to certify that the judgment has become final and binding as well as other litigation documents.[21]

According to an amendment to CCP in 2003, Taiwanese courts no longer charge extra for VAT, bailiff and service of process. Nor do Taiwanese courts charge separate fees for meals, accommodation and transportation incurred by the judge, court clerk, executive officer and interpreter for conducting acts of litigation outside the courtroom.[22]

[19] Art 77-19 CCP.

[20] Arts 2, 3, 5 and 6 of Court's Standard to Charge for Photocopying, Photographing, Transcribing and Translating Court Files. See Fayuan banli minshi susong shijian susong wenshu zhi yingyin, sheying, chaolu ji fanyifei zheng shou biaozhun [Court's Standard to Charge for Photocopying, Photographing, Transcribing and Translating Court Files] amended and announced by the Judicial Yuan's Letter, No. Yuan Tai Ting Min Yi Zi 0930017666, dated 7 Jul 2004.

[21] Art 6-1 of Court's Standard to Charge for Photocopying, Photographing, Transcribing and Translating Court Files, see ibid.

[22] Art 77-23, para 4 CCP provides that: 'Fees for service effected by mail or telecommunication, and fees for meals, accommodation and transportation as incurred by the judge, court clerk, executive officer, and interpreter for conducting acts of litigation outside the courtroom shall not be taxed additionally'. Art 28-2, para 4 of Compulsory Execution Act provides that: 'Fees for meals, accommodation and transportation as incurred by enforcement officers shall not be charged'. See Qiangzhi zhising fa [Compulsory Execution Act] (promulgated 19 Jan 1940, last amended 12 Dec 2007) (Taiwan).

Witness of Fact

Except for those who are apprehended to appear or refuse to sign a written oath or testify without giving a justifiable reason, a witness of fact is eligible to receive *per diem* allowances and travelling expenses.[23]

A witness of fact may request compensation for accommodation, meals and miscellaneous expenses at the following standard for the period during which the witness of fact is required to stay for the court hearing and for the period required for the witness of fact to travel between his/her residence and the court.[24]

1. Accommodation: NTD 1,400/day against proof of expenses. If a witness of fact fails to provide proof of such expenses, the witness of fact can only be paid half the amount, namely NTD 700/day.
2. Meals and miscellaneous expenses: NTD 500/day.

In addition to the above, a witness of fact may request a *per diem* allowance of NTD 500 for each day when he/she actually attends court hearings.[25]

Court-Appointed Expert

The standard of *per diem* allowances and travelling expenses applicable to a witness of fact also applies to an expert appointed by court. In addition to *per diem* allowances and travelling expenses, an expert is eligible to request compensation for his service.[26] The compensation for an expert's professional service varies greatly in each case. The amount of compensation requested by an expert is subject to the court's review and approval. When reviewing the amount, the court shall take into consideration the complexity of the case, the efforts to be spent by the expert and their general salary level in society.[27] Because situations in each case

[23] Art 323, para 1 CCP provides that: 'A witness may claim the prescribed daily fees and travel expenses, except for those who are apprehended to appear, or refuse to sign a written oath or testify without giving a justifiable reason'. For details of the travelling expenses, see art 4 of Court's Standard for Handling Compensations to Witness and Expert Witness for Their Services, Travels and Testaments and Table of Compensations for Expenses Incurred by Central Government Officers from Domestic Business Trips attached to Outlines for Compensations for Expenses Incurred from Domestic Business Trips, see Fayuan banli minshi shijian zhengren jiandingren rifei lüfei ji jiandingfei zhigei biaozhun [Court's Standard for Handling Compensations to Witness and Expert Witness for Their Services, Travels and Testaments] amended and announced by the Judicial Yuan's Letter, No. Yuan Tai Ting Min Yi Zi 0980010767, dated 5 May 2009 and Guonei chuchai lüfei baozhi yaodian [Outlines for Compensations for Expenses Incurred from Domestic Business Trips] amended and announced by the Executive Yuan's Letter, No. Yuan Shou Zhhu Zhong Zi 0960000401, dated 19 Jan 2007.

[24] Art 5 of Court's Standard for Handling Compensations to Witness and Expert Witness for Their Services, Travels and Testaments, ibid.

[25] Art 3 of Court's Standard for Handling Compensations to Witness and Expert Witness for Their Services, Travels and Testaments (n 23).

[26] Art 338, para 1 CCP.

[27] Art 10, para 2 of Court's Standard for Handling Compensations to Witness and Expert Witness for Their Services, Travels and Testaments (n 23).

may vary significantly, it is difficult to provide a clear figure for the amount of such compensation.

Other Costs

Charge for Enforcement of a Final Judgment

The charge for enforcement of a final judgment is stipulated in Article 28-2 of the Taiwanese Compulsory Execution Act (Compulsory Execution Act),[28] which was increased by the Taiwan High Court in the 'Taiwan High Court's Standard for Increasing Court Charges in Civil Litigation, Non-litigation Cases and Compulsory Execution' amended in 2005.[29] According to current law, in matters arising from proprietary rights, if the amount or value of the enforcement is less than NTD 5,000, the charge for enforcement of a judgment is waived. If the amount or value of the enforcement is NTD 5,000 or more, the charge for enforcement of a judgment is 0.8 per cent of the amount or value of the enforcement, provided that a fraction of NTD 100 shall be rounded up to NTD 100 for the purpose of calculating and levying the charges for enforcement.

In matters arising from non-proprietary rights, the court levies a fixed charge for enforcement of a judgment at NTD 3,000.[30]

Charge for Enforcement of a Provisional Attachment, Provisional Injunction or Provisional Execution

The charge for enforcement of a provisional attachment, provisional injunction or provisional execution is the same as the charge for enforcement of a final judgment as explained above.

Deposit

When a party applies for a provisional attachment or injunction, the court, at its own discretion, may request the party to provide a deposit to the court.[31] The amount of the deposit is to be determined by the court and, in practice, is usually one-third of the amount claimed, except for in the following two cases:

(1) Article 526, Para. 4 CCP provides that where the creditor claims household living expenses, maintenance, alimony, distribution of the remainder of husband and wife's property, the court-assessed amount of security provided in the preceding paragraph must not exceed one tenth of the amount claimed.[32]
(2) Similarly, article 58 of the Settlement of Labour Disputes Law also provides that when a labourer claims for salary, pension, severance payment or

[28] For Compulsory Execution Act (n 22).
[29] See n 12.
[30] Art 28-2, para 3 of Compulsory Execution Act (n 22).
[31] Arts 526 and 533 CCP.
[32] Art 526, para 4 CCP.

damages or compensation for occupational accidents and applies for provisional attachment or injunction against his/her employer, the deposit ordered by the court shall not be higher than one-tenth of the amount claimed.[33]

Except for lawyers' costs and payments to experts for their professional service, all other costs, including court charges, are specified in law. Therefore, such costs are predictable and assessable in the early stages of a civil procedure. Even when the value of a claim is argued by the parties, the value of a claim will be determined by the court as one of the first issues to be determined in a civil litigation because, as further elaborated below, payment of court charges is one of the requirements of a valid claim.[34]

The general principle is that full payment of court charges to the court is one of the requirements for a plaintiff to begin an action and for an appellant to file a proper appeal. If a plaintiff or appellant fails to pay all or part of the court charges, the court will order the plaintiff or appellant to pay the court charges within a designated period of time.[35] The CCP does not specifically provide a length of the period. In practice, it is usually within five or seven days after the plaintiff's or appellant's receipt of the court's order but can be as long as 15 days in rare cases, especially when the amount involved is large. If the plaintiff or appellant still fails to pay the court charges in full, the action or appeal will be dismissed by the court with a ruling.[36]

Article 77-22 CCP provides two exceptions to the general principle above. First, pursuant to article 77-22, paragraph 1 CCP, when multiple parties, whose common interests have arisen from the same public nuisance, such as a traffic accident or product defect, or the same transaction or occurrence of any kind, appoint one or more persons from among themselves in accordance with the provision of article 41 CCP to sue for the same category of legal claims, if the court charges exceed NTD 600,000, the claimant shall be temporarily exempt from paying the portion of the court charges in excess of NTD 600,000.[37] After the action is concluded and final, the court of first instance shall make a ruling on its own initiative to levy the court charges, which would have been temporarily exempt under article 77-22,

[33] Art 58 of Settlement of Labour Disputes Law, see Laozi zhengyi fa [Settlement of Labour Disputes Law] (promulgated 9 Jun 1928; last amended 1 Jul 2009) (Taiwan).

[34] Art 249, para 1 CCP.

[35] Art 249, para 1 CCP provides that: 'In case of any of the following, the court shall dismiss the plaintiff's action by a ruling, but where the defect is rectifiable, the presiding judge shall order rectification within a designated period of time: '. . . 6. Where the action is not initiated in accordance with the prescribed formality, or lacks other requirements; . . .' Art 442, para 2 CCP provides that: 'Where the appeal fails the prescribed formality or other legal requirements and such failure is rectifiable, the original court of first instance shall order the appellant to rectify such failure within a period to be designated by the court and dismiss such appeal if the appellant fails to do so'. Art. 444, para 1 CCP provides that: 'If an appeal is not in conformity with the law the court of second instance shall dismiss the appeal by a ruling. Notwithstanding, where such defect is rectifiable, the presiding judge shall order rectification within the period he/she designates'.

[36] ibid.

[37] Art 77-22, para 1 and art 44-2, para 1 CCP.

paragraph 1 CCP, against the party that should bear such court charges in accordance with applicable articles in the CCP.[38] Second, pursuant to article 77-22, paragraph 2 CCP, when an incorporated charitable association or a foundation, with the permission of its competent governmental business authority and to the extent permitted by the purposes as prescribed in its bylaws, initiates an action for injunctive relief prohibiting specific acts of a person who has violated the interests of the majority concerned under article 44-3, paragraph 1 CCP, the claimant shall be exempt from paying the court charges.[39]

Per diem allowances and compensation to a witness of fact and an expert are regarded as fees necessary to the conduct of litigation, and the presiding judge may order a party to advance a payment within a designated period of time.[40] The court clerk, with the court's approval, will notify the party introducing a witness of fact or requesting an expert to advance related fees to the court first.[41] If a witness of fact or an expert is called by the court of its own initiative as it deems necessary, the court will order a party to advance related fees or order both parties to bear the related fees evenly.[42] If the party fails to advance the fee, the court may elect not to conduct such act or notify the opponent to disburse the payment. If the proceedings will be prevented from continuing without the advance of payment for such fees and both parties refuse to advance or disburse such fees after being notified to do so within a designated period of time, the proceeding shall be deemed stayed by consent.[43] In this case, the parties shall resume the proceedings within four months by advancing or disbursing the fees to the court. If no advancement or disbursement is made within the four-month period, the action or appeal shall be deemed withdrawn voluntarily.[44]

Lawyers' Costs

Lawyers are free to make various kinds of fee arrangements with their clients with the exception that contingent fees are not allowed in criminal cases, family law cases and juvenile offender cases.[45] In practice, the following arrangements are quite common.

[38] Art 77-22, para 3 CCP.

[39] Art 77-22, para 2 and art 44-3, para 1 CCP.

[40] Art 94-1, para1 CCP.

[41] A party may file a request for an expert but it is the court that has the authority to appoint an expert. Art 326, para 1 CCP.

[42] Art 6 of Court's Standard for Handling Compensations to Witness and Expert Witness for Their Services, Travels and Testaments, *see* above n 23.

[43] Art 94-1, para 1 CCP.

[44] Art 94-1, para 2 CCP.

[45] Art 37 of the Attorney Regulation Act provides that: 'An attorney shall not demand in advance, or receive fees beyond those specified or provided for in Legal Codes, Attorney Code of Ethics or Bar Association Articles of Incorporation'. Art 35, para 2 of the Attorney Code of Ethics further provides that: 'In criminal, family law or juvenile offender cases, lawyers shall not agree on fees contingent upon

1. Hourly fee. Lawyers may charge solely on an hourly basis, or sometimes lawyers will agree on a limit with their clients. Lawyers may also request a deposit or advance payment due at the time when the retainer agreements are concluded or shortly afterwards. The hourly rates range from NTD 4,000 to NTD 12,000 per hour;
2. Lump-sum fee. Lawyers and clients may agree on a lump-sum fee. Alternatively, lawyers and their clients will agree on a lump-sum fee, provided that if the court hearings are held for more than a certain number of times, say five times, the clients have to pay lawyers a certain amount, say NTD 10,000, for the lawyers' attendance to each court hearing afterwards;
3. Contingency fee. The percentage of the contingency fee varies greatly in different cases. The percentage might be as high as 50 per cent of the collected amount of a judgment in some extreme cases and might be as low as two per cent, especially when the amount or value of the claim is gigantic.

In addition, there can also be various combinations of the above, for example, a lump-sum advance payment plus a contingency fee or an hourly fee (usually at lower rates) plus a contingent fee and so on. Not only are the types of fee arrangements different; the amount of lawyers' costs for each case also varies greatly depending on the types, complexities, disputed amount etc of each case. Thus, it is difficult to provide exact figures for lawyers' costs.

In practice, if lawyers charge on an hourly basis, a statement will be sent to the client periodically to request payment. Lawyers might ask their client to pay a deposit and advance payment for disbursements at the time when a retainer agreement is concluded or shortly afterwards. If lawyers charge a lump-sum fee, the fee can be made in advance in full or be made as the litigation progresses, say 50 per cent up front and 50 per cent when a judgment is rendered, or any other combination. If lawyers' costs are contingent, the amount to be paid is uncertain until the outcome of the case is revealed so that contingency fees are collected after the case is closed. However, even when charging by contingency, lawyers may still require their client to advance part of the retainer or disbursement up front.

The Judicial Yuan promulgated a Standard for Determining Lawyers' Costs Paid to Court Appointed Advocates and Lawyers in the Court of Third Instance,[46] which is applicable when the court or the presiding judge appoint an attorney to act as a special representative or advocate for a party.[47] In addition, Article 16 of

the outcome of the cases'. See Lü shi fa [Attorney Regulation Act] (promulgated on 11 Jan 1941 and last amended on 30 Jan 2002) (Taiwan) and Lüshi lunli guifan [Attorney Code of Ethics] (promulgated by Taiwan Bar Association on 18 Dec 1983 and last amended on 19 Sep 2009).

[46] Fayuan xuanren lüshi ji disanshen lüshi choujing heding zhigei biao zhun [Standard for Determining Lawyers' Costs Paid to Court Appointed Advocate and Lawyer in the Court of Third Instance] (promulgated by the Judicial Yuan on 26 Aug 2003 in its Letter, No. 92 Yuan Tai Ting Min Zhi 22046) (Taiwan).

[47] Situations under which a court may appoint a special representative for a party, plaintiff, defendant or appellant, as the case maybe, are specified in art 51, para 1 & 2 and art 374, para 1 CCP. Situations under which a court may appoint a lawyer as a plaintiff's advocate are specified in arts 44-1, 44-2, 44-3 and 44-4 CCP. The situation under which the court may appoint a lawyer as a party's advocate in the court of third instance is specified in art 466-2, para 1 CCP.

the Attorney Regulation Act requires bar associations to specify in their articles of incorporation a standard for lawyers' costs applicable to their members, namely lawyers registered at the bar association.[48] Accordingly, all bar associations in Taiwan include articles on lawyers' costs in their articles of incorporation.[49] In practice, these standards are regarded as guidelines, and lawyers and clients may still reach agreements on costs higher or lower than these standards.

Cost Shifting

Because the Taiwanese Code of Civil Procedure was initially modelled largely on the German Civil Procedure Statute (Zivilprozeß ordnung) of 1877, the *loser pays* rule was adopted. However, differing from the German law, the *loser pays* rule in Taiwan does not apply to the lawyers' costs. Accordingly, although article 78 CCP stipulates a general principle that 'the losing party shall bear the litigation expenses',[50] since lawyers' costs are not considered as part of litigation expenses, each of the parties has to bear his own lawyers' costs, unless any of the following two exceptions is met. First, when the court appoints a lawyer as a party's special representative or advocate,[51] the lawyers' costs to be paid to the special representative or advocate shall be determined by the court or the presiding judge and such lawyers' costs are considered as part of litigation expenses.[52] Second, pursuant to article 466-3, paragraphs 1 and 3 CCP,[53] lawyers' costs paid to an attorney in the court of third instance are regarded as part of the litigation expenses and the maximum amount thereof is prescribed in Article 4 of Standard for Determining Lawyers' Costs Paid to Court Appointed Advocates and Lawyers in the Court of Third Instance.[54]

[48] Art 16 of Attorney Regulation Act provides that: 'Arts of Incorporation of Bar Associations shall include the following clauses: . . . (6) Standards for attorney service fees; . . .'. See n 23.

[49] See eg art 29 of Arts of Incorporation of Taipei Bar Association; see Taipei Lüshi Gonghui Zhangcheng [Arts of Incorporation of Taipei Bar Association] (last amended 9 Sept 2000); Art 29 of Articles of Incorporation of Taichung Bar Association, *see* Taichung Lüshi Gonghui Zhangcheng [Arts of Incorporation of Taichung Bar Association] (last amended 26 Mar 2006) and art 30 of Articles of Incorporation of Kaohsiung Bar Association, *see* Kaohsiung Lüshi Gonghui Zhangcheng [Articles of Incorporation of Kaohsiung Bar Association] (last amended 19 Nov 2005).

[50] Art 78 CCP.

[51] See n 49.

[52] Art 77-25 CCP provides that: 'When the court or the presiding judge has duly appointed an attorney to act as the special representative or advocate for a party, the compensation to be paid to such appointed attorney shall be determined in the discretion of the court or the presiding judge. Both the compensation provided in the preceding paragraph and the compensation provided in the first paragraph of [CCP] art 466-3 shall be included as part of litigation expenses'.

[53] Art 466-3, para 1 & 3 CCP provides that: '(para 1) Compensation paid to the attorney in the court of third instance shall be included as a part of the litigation expenses and the maximum amount thereof shall be prescribed. . . . (para 3) The rules provided in the preceding paragraph shall be prescribed by reference to the opinions of the Ministry of Justice and the Taiwan Bar Association'.

[54] Art 4 of Standard for Determining Lawyers' Costs Paid to Court Appointed Advocates and Lawyers in the Court of Third Instance, see n 46.

The allocation of responsibilities of litigation expenses is stipulated in greater details in articles 79–86, 89, paragraphs 1 and 2 and 95-1 CCP. First, as exceptions to the general rule of *loser pays*, the winning party will have to pay in any of the following situations:

1. In matters arising from a partition or demarcation of a thing held indivisibly or other matters of similar nature, where it is manifestly unfair for the defeated party to bear solely the litigation expenses, the court may, in its discretion, order the prevailing party to bear part of the litigation expenses (article 80-1 CCP).
2. The court may, in its discretion, order the prevailing party to bear the litigation expenses incurred in full or in part in any of the following situations: (1) An act performed by the prevailing party which is unnecessary for asserting or defending its rights; (2) An act performed by the defeated party which is necessary for asserting or defending its rights in accordance with the phase of the proceedings reached at the time (article 81 CCP)
3. Where a party has failed to timely present means of attack or defence, or to meet a specified date or period, or has otherwise delayed the proceeding by reason of whatever cause imputable to such party, the court may order such party to bear the litigation expenses incurred from the delay, in full or in part, irrespective of his/her victory (article 82).

Second, the CCP prescribes the rules of allocation of litigation expenses in cases of a partial victory, voluntary dismissal and settlement. In cases of a partial victory or a partial defeat, the court may, in its discretion, order the litigation expenses to be borne by both parties in a certain proportion; or by a particular party alone, or order both parties to separately bear the litigation expenses they incurred respectively.[55] When a defendant had forthwith admitted to a claim presented by a plaintiff and established that the litigation action was unnecessary, the plaintiff shall bear the litigation expenses.[56] In cases of voluntary dismissal, the plaintiff shall bear the litigation expenses. When the plaintiff voluntarily dismisses the action prior to the termination of the oral-argument session in the first instance, he/she may, within three months of such a dismissal, move for the return of two-thirds of the court costs paid for that instance.[57] In cases of a settlement, unless otherwise agreed by the parties, the parties shall respectively bear the expenses of the settlement and the litigation expenses.[58]

Third, as to co-parties and third parties, article 85 CCP stipulates the allocation of litigation expenses amongst co-parties and article 86 CCP provides for an intervener's responsibility for litigation expenses incurred in relation to the intervention, and as to third parties, article 89, paragraphs 1 and 2 CCP provides that:

[55] Art 79 CCP.

[56] Art 80 CCP.

[57] Art 83, para 1 CCP. In addition, this paragraph shall apply *mutatis mutandis* to cases of voluntary dismissal of an appeal from a judgment or an appeal from a ruling. See art 83, para 2 CCP.

[58] Art 84, para 1 CCP. Para 2 of the same art further provides that: 'When a settlement is reached, the parties may, within three months after the settlement date, move for the return of two-thirds of the court costs paid for the current court action'.

'In cases of meritless litigation expenses incurred by the court clerk, the executive officer, the statutory agent, or the advocate, intentionally or through gross negligence, the court may by a ruling on a motion or its own initiative, order such court officer, statutory agent or advocate to bear the litigation expenses incurred.

Where the party who was permitted to conduct acts of litigation *pro tempore* in accordance with the provisions of Article 49 or the first paragraph of Article 75 failed to correct the remediable defect, the court may rule by an order on its own initiative that such party will bear the litigation expenses incurred by his/her acts of litigation.'

Where a prosecutor is a party and bears litigation expenses in accordance with the provisions of this Section, such litigation expenses shall be disbursed by the national treasury.[59]

These are applicable to all charges and costs listed herein with the exceptions of (1) some court charges for certain motions, which are specifically provided in the CCP;[60] (2) charge for enforcement of a final judgment, a provisional attachment, provisional injunction or provisional execution, which, to the extent necessary, shall be borne by the debtor;[61] and, (3) most lawyers' costs.

General Costs Issues

Except for lawyers' costs and compensation to experts for their professional services, all the other costs are specified in law so that at a very early stage of a civil litigation, an opponent already has information to assess the amount of risk and actual amount of costs for which he/she might have to pay. Even when the value of a claim is not very clear or argued by the parties, the value of a claim will be determined by the court as one of the first issues to be determined in a civil litigation because payment of court charges is one of the requirements of a valid claim.[62]

Lawyers' costs and compensation to experts for their professional services are two major factors that bring substantial impacts on a party's total legal costs and might not be easily assessable at the beginning of a civil litigation. To control legal budgets, especially in economic down times, more and more clients request their lawyers or experts to provide an estimation or cap for legal services. In addition, while there is a need to engage lawyers or experts for their professional services, the client is more likely to shop around for quotations for the same project so as to compare the terms and prices available in the market.

For different cases of the same nature, a party may consider beginning a lawsuit for one claim first to test the water and then file other claims with the court after obtaining a favourable judgment, as long as other claims will not be time barred if

59 Art 95-1 CCP.
60 See eg arts 86, para 1, 549-1, 608 and 622 CCP.
61 Art 28, para 1 of the Compulsory Execution Act, see n 22.
62 Art 249, para 1 CCP.

lodged with the court later. A claimant is more likely to conduct an investigation on a potential defendant's financial status at an acceptable cost before beginning a lawsuit so as to avoid beginning a futile one.

In Taiwan, legal expenses insurance is normally annexed to liability insurance, for example, product insurance, directors', supervisors' and officers' liability insurance and car insurance. A legal expenses insurance system per se is so far not popular. Most ordinary people do not have legal expenses insurance. Because lawyers' costs are not included in the litigation expenses, parties bear their own lawyers' costs in the court of first and second instance. Only indigent people are eligible to apply for legal aid. Those who do not meet the requirements cannot claim a refund of lawyers' costs, even when they obtain favourable judgments. Some advocate amendment of the relevant provisions in order to oblige the plaintiff (or appellant, as the case may be) to appoint an attorney as his/her advocate also in the court of first and second instance, and to include related attorney costs as part of the litigation expenses, which shall be borne by the defeated party. But it is difficult to have such an amendment proposed and ratified by the Legislative Yuan of ROC in a short period of time.

23

The United States of America

DEBORAH R HENSLER*

General Overview and Trends

Most civil litigation in the US is pursued by private parties seeking resolution of private wrongs aided by private lawyers whose services are secured by contract and paid for by the party seeking representation.[1] Viewed thus the US civil litigation system reflects the highly privatised nature of US society whose citizens generally lack a sense of social solidarity, distrust government and public solutions to social problems, and prefer to leave individuals to their own devices.

The US civil justice system is conventionally described as adversarial, conjuring images of parties' lawyers vigorously battling each other to the ultimate stage of litigation, the jury trial. But empirical evidence suggests that experienced lawyers are more likely to adopt collaborative than competitive negotiation strategies,[2] and a vanishingly small percentage of civil lawsuits in the US are resolved by trial, whether by jury or judge.[3] Rather than presenting themselves as institutions

* Judge John W Ford Professor of Dispute Resolution and Associate Dean, Graduate Studies, Stanford Law School

[1] The overwhelming majority of civil cases in state courts of general jurisdiction involve contract, tort or property claims (National Center for State Courts, Examining the Work of State Courts, 2007, Civil Caseloads, p 21, at www.ncsconline.org/D_Research/csp/2007_files/Examining%20Final%20-%202007%20-%205%20-%20Civil.pdf). In 2005, about 42% of civil cases that reached trial in US state courts in large metropolitan counties involved individuals suing other individuals and about 10% involved businesses suing other businesses. Cases involving individuals versus business constituted the overwhelming majority of the remaining cases. Trial cases represent a small fraction of all cases filed in state courts but there is no reason to believe that public party cases are more likely to settle than private party cases. (Bureau of Justice Statistics, Civil Bench and Jury Trials in State Courts, 2005, Tables 1, 3, and 4, available at www.ojp.usdoj.gov/bjs/pub/pdf/cbjtsc05.pdf).

72% of all civil cases filed in US federal district courts in 2008 had private parties on both sides (Administrative Office of the US Courts, Federal Judicial Caseload Statistics, 2008, Table C-2, available at www.uscourts.gov/caseload2008/tables/C02Mar08.pdf).

[2] M Nelkin, 'The Myth of the Gladiator and Law Students' Negotiation Styles' (2005) 7 *Cardozo Journal of Conflict Resolution* 1.

[3] In 2002, the jury trial rate for state court civil cases was 1.8%, and the bench trial rate was 4.3 %; the total trial rate for federal court civil cases was 1.8%, down from 11.5 % twenty five years previous. See G. T Munsterman and S Strickland, 'The Vanishing Trial?' 19 *The Court Manager*, 52, available at www.ncsconline.org/Juries/JuryNews/JuryNewsCM19-2.pdf, and P Higginbotham, 'The Disappearing Trial and Why We Should Care' 2004 Rand Review, available at www.rand.org/publications/randreview/issues/summer2004/28.html.

charged with interpreting the law and articulating social norms, courts describe themselves as 'dispute resolution forums,' and judges are adjured to focus on managing cases, rather than on legal decision-making.[4] Virtually all civil suits are dropped, summarily dismissed or adjudicated by the court, or settled by the parties, either through bi-lateral negotiations or with the assistance of a mediator.[5] More sophisticated portrayals of civil litigation focus on excessive discovery and other pretrial manoeuvring. But most civil suits involve little or no discovery.[6] Protracted discovery characterises only the small percentage of high value cases that dominate the legal media and the attention of Fortune 50 corporate boards.

The popular culture is sceptical about the motives of those who litigate and, contrary to the conventional wisdom, litigation *rates*, measured by the proportion of people who attempt to pursue claims as a proportion of instances in which claims might be litigated, are modest. About ten per cent of those who are injured in accidents consult a lawyer and less than three per cent file lawsuits.[7] The majority of states have standing ADR (alternative dispute resolution) offices,[8] and many state and federal courts mandate mediation for a large fraction of their civil cases. Most mediators are private practitioners, often lawyers who regard mediation as another line of business. Mediators' fees, which are generally split equally among the parties, are not publicly regulated, even in those jurisdictions that mandate that civil litigants attempt to resolve their cases through mediation before proceeding to trial. Mandatory mediation is often regarded by courts as a case management technique, although frequently publicly justified as promoting other values. Evidence of cost-savings and time-saving due to mediation is mixed.[9]

Businesses have long provided for binding arbitration of disputes arising under their contracts with other businesses. Federal and state statutory and case law strongly support enforcement of such contractual provisions and strictly limit appeals of arbitration outcomes. Over the past decade, businesses have attempted to extend the reach of contractual arbitration to employment and consumer contracts. These efforts have only recently encountered obstacles, chiefly because of

[4] D Hensler, 'Our Courts, Ourselves: How the Alternative Dispute Resolution Movement is Reshaping Our Legal System' (2003) 108 *Penn State Law Review* 165.

[5] GK Hadfield, 'Where have all the trials gone? Settlements, non-trial adjudications and statistical artifacts in the changing disposition of federal civil cases' (2004) 1 *Journal of Empirical Legal Studies* 705.

[6] About 55% of all civil suits filed in federal district courts in the early 1990s were either dropped before answer or disposed of within 9 months of the issue being joined; three-quarters of the first group and more than one-third of the second had no discovery. In the remaining 45 % of civil suits, the median number of hours lawyers worked on discovery matters, per client, was 20. Because a small percentage of the cases with longer times to disposition have much more discovery, the mean hours worked on discovery matters per client is four times as large, for a total of 80. See J Kakalik et al, *Discovery Management: Further Analyses of the Civil Justice Reform Act Evaluation Data*, Rand, 1998, Tables S.1 and S.2, xix and xx1. For cases judged highest in 'complexity' the medians and means, respectively, were 42 and 147. Ibid, Table 2.3, 30.

[7] D Hensler et al, *Compensation for Accidental Injuries in the United States*, Rand, 1991, Figure 5.1, 122.

[8] See, courtadr.org/library/links.php#anchord for a list.

[9] J Lande, 'Commentary: Focusing on Program Design Issues in Future Research on Court-Connected Mediation' (2004) 22 *Conflict Resolution Quarterly* 89, 91, 92.

corporations' attempts to use arbitration to preclude class proceedings.[10] Custom-tailored arbitration programmes have been designed for a wide variety of disputes, including those between investors and brokers.[11] Arbitration fees are set by arbitration providers. Arbitration administration costs are frequently higher than court filing fees.

Legal financing rules for ordinary litigation (ie one plaintiff against one or two defendants) reflect the highly privatised nature of the civil legal system. Except in a very limited set of circumstances defined by statute or rule, each side is responsible for paying its own legal fees, win or lose. In class actions and non-class mass actions judges award fees to prevailing plaintiff counsel but the general rule that each side is responsible for paying its own fees prevails.

Funding Claims

Few individual plaintiffs in the US could afford to pay for legal representation out of their own pocket and the evidence is that few do.[12] Individual plaintiffs in tort and other litigation seeking money damages are generally represented by lawyers charging contingency fees, which have long been legal in the US.[13] Trade unions commonly do not assist with legal expenses, although they may assist their members in finding lawyers; in any event, only a small proportion of the US workforce (around 12 per cent) is now unionised. Legal assistance for many routine civil matters–ranging from housing evictions to welfare claims to family law matters—is available to low income Americans from a combination of publicly and privately funded legal service providers but available data suggest that the population is vastly underserved.[14] Publicly funded assistance is not available for class actions. Individual plaintiffs whose cases raise significant issues—eg civil rights

[10] Public Citizen, 'Forced Arbitration: Unfair and Everywhere' Sept 2009, available at www.citizen.org/documents/UnfairAndEverywhere.pdf; Searle Civil Justice Institute, Northwestern University, Consumer Arbitration Task Force, 'Consumer Arbitration Before the American Arbitration Association' Preliminary Report, 2009, available at www.searlearbitration.org/report; K Stone, 'Mandatory Arbitration of Individual Employment Rights: The Yellow Dog Contract of the 1990s' (1996) 73 *Denv UL Rev* 1017; L Maltby, 'Employment Arbitration and Workplace Justice' (2003) 38 *USFL Rev* 105.

[11] General Accounting Office, *How Investors Fare*, Rep No GAO/GGD-92-74 (May 1992).

[12] Some US state courts report upwards of 50% of suits in divorce, landlord-tenant, probate and other civil matters involve one or more unrepresented parties. National Center for State Courts, 'State Court Pro Se Statistics, 2006,' at www.ncsconline.org/wc/publications/memos/prosestatsmemo.htm#statecourt.

[13] There is some controversy over when contingency fees were adopted in the US but most accounts date the practice at least to the turn of the last century. See S Landsman, 'The History of Contingency and the Contingency of History,' (1998) 47 *DePaul Law Review*. A 1989 national survey of accidental injury victims found that 87% of those who hired lawyers to pursue claims were represented on contingency fee contracts. See D Hensler et al, *Compensation for Accidental Injuries in the United States*, Rand, 1991, Table 5.11, 136.

[14] Legal Services Corporation, *Documenting the Justice Gap in America*, (2005), at www.lsc.gov/press/documents/LSC%20Justice%20Gap_FINAL_1001.pdf.

violations—may be able to obtain assistance without a means test from staff lawyers at NGOs or private practitioners serving *pro bono* (who in certain domains may partner with each other). But except in rare cases where new law might be made, if substantial damages are potentially available, it is generally assumed that a plaintiff will be able to find representation on a contingency fee basis. Legal expense insurance is apparently available to some union members but does not otherwise appear to be a factor in funding civil litigation. After-the-event insurance does not appear to be a factor in ordinary individual litigation.

Law firms that represent plaintiffs on a contingency fee basis fund the litigation at the firm's expense, using capital reserves and credit lines. Up front and on-going costs are reimbursed when and only if the firm is successful in obtaining damages for its clients. Leading plaintiff firms, including class action and mass litigation specialists, are said to have access to generous credit, permitting them to take on significant risks. Smaller law firms whose resources are more constrained adopt business models that recognise their financial limitations. Some such firms specialise in high-volume 'cookie cutter' litigation (eg workers compensation claims, 'slip and fall' suits) in which relatively low expected awards are balanced by modest risk and costs of prosecuting. Settlement rather than adjudication is the expected outcome of such cases, to the extent that some firms are described as 'settlement mills.'

In recent years, third-party funders have appeared. Typically, these funders offer plaintiffs who have already filed suit advances against the value of any damages that may ultimately be recovered; if the plaintiff does not prevail she does not need to repay the advance.[15] These funders appear to target lower-income plaintiffs who are willing to trade earlier (and certain) cash payments against an ultimate larger recovery that may not materialise at all or for several years. Some observers have suggested that funders offer 'advances' rather than 'loans' to escape usury restrictions that might otherwise curtail interest charged.[16] By funding parties rather than their attorneys funders may also intend to avoid strictures against 'fee-splitting' between lawyers and non-lawyers. Interest in financing complex litigation appears to be growing, particularly among investors seeking alternatives to traditional financial instruments. A new category of third-party funders, some publicly traded, are targeting business parties who might be incentivised to prosecute high-end commercial cases if they could off-load some of the costs and risk to others.[17] Third-party funders do not yet appear to be a factor in class or non-class mass litigation where procedural rules and judicial oversight impose special challenges for such funding arrangements.

[15] See eg www.fundmysuit.com; www.getlegalfunds.com; www.americanlegalfunding.com; www.anylawsuits.com; www.litigationcapitalinvestors.com).

[16] JL Hyman and P Frumkin, 'Contingent Advances' (2003) 82 *Sep Michigan Bar Journal* 28 available at www.michbar.org/journal/Art.cfm?ArtID=613&volumeID=47.

[17] L Jones, 'Litigation Funding Begins to Take Off' *National Law Journal*, 30 Nov 2009.

Court or Process Costs

The fee to file a civil case in federal court is set by statute;[18] it is currently $350, which can be waived for plaintiffs proceeding *in forma pauperis*. In state courts, fees may be set by state or local statute and may differ across counties and for different kinds of cases as well as among states. For example, in California, there is a fee of $355 for a plaintiff to file a civil complaint and a fee of $355 for a defendant to file an answer and there is a per party premium of $550 on top of the ordinary fee for cases designated as 'complex,' with a cap of $10,000 per side. Additional fees are levied for motions requiring hearing ($40) and special motions, such as a motion for summary judgment ($200). Special fees are incurred for cases that go to trial, including court reporter fees and juror payments; these are set by the local courts. Fees for small claims (up to $7,500) are modest, ranging from $30 to $75 depending on the amount claimed.[19]

Court fees are not expected to cover public expenditures for the court system; indeed, in some jurisdictions where the costs of court operations are charged to multiple sources no one may know with certainty the average public expenditure to process a civil case. By statute, certain fees can be taxed against (charged to) the losing party, including in federal courts, the costs of depositions, trial witnesses, hearing and trial transcripts, court appointed experts and filing fees (if the plaintiff prevails—there is no fee for filing an answer in federal court).[20] However, a judge may waive costs for a losing party whom she deems not to have adequate assets to pay. Experienced counsel would generally be able to estimate likely costs charged against their client, should he fail to prevail. In most instances, court costs will be a fraction of the claim value. In private civil litigation, prevailing plaintiffs can expect that costs will be taxed against corporate defendants; conversely, losing plaintiffs, if they are individuals or small businesses suing large corporations, might expect that costs will not be taxed against themselves.

Lawyers' Fees

In civil litigation, lawyer fees are determined by contract. In suits for tort and tort-like damages, private fee arrangements depend on whether the lawyer is representing plaintiffs or defendants, and in tort litigation especially, there are few firms that represent both. Plaintiffs in ordinary civil damage litigation are represented

[18] 28 USC §1914. The fee was raised to $350 from $250 in 2006.

[19] *See* www.siskiyou.courts.ca.gov/Files/Statewide%20Civil%20Fee%20Schedule%20Effective%208-4-2009.pdf and www.lasuperiorcourt.org/fees/UI/index.aspx.

[20] 28 USC §1920.

most frequently by lawyers charging contingency fees.[21] The typical contingency fee is calculated as one-third of damages obtained by settlement (net of expenses), and 40 –50 per cent of damages obtained by trial. The plaintiff lawyers' expenses (including court costs) will also be reimbursed by the successful plaintiff. Unsuccessful plaintiffs pay nothing in legal costs. There is little evidence of price competition regarding the contingency fee rate.[22] For routine matters that require a court proceeding—for example, an uncontested divorce or representation at an ADR hearing—lawyers may charge flat fees. Individual tort plaintiffs only rarely obtain representation on an hourly fee and expense basis; in high-end commercial damage litigation corporate plaintiffs may also be represented on a contingency fee basis.

Individual and institutional defendants are usually represented by law firms that charge hourly fees plus expenses. At large corporate law firms that specialise in commercial litigation hourly fees range from several hundred dollars for junior associates to one thousand or more for seasoned litigators. Observers predict that hourly fees, especially fees for less experienced lawyers, will decline as a result of the global financial crisis but whether such declines are occurring and, if so, how extensive they are is not yet clear. Services such as copying, treated as 'cost centres,' may also bring sizeable amounts into large law firms. Corporate clients routinely decry the high costs of civil litigation, which many attribute to hourly billing and to the corporate law firm business model it has engendered. There are reports that experimentation with alternative billing structures is accelerating as a result of the global financial crisis. Some large corporations divide their legal business among many providers, handling routine matters in-house, offering bundles of less routine but predictable legal matters to outside counsel on a competitive—perhaps fixed cost—basis, and dividing remaining matters by substantive area (eg intellectual property) or risk exposure (eg 'bet the company' litigation). Predictably, the prices for the latter are higher. Where the outcomes of litigation might challenge general counsel's own position in a corporation, there may be less willingness to rely on cost factors to place legal business. In some instances, defense counsel's fees may have a contingent element, as when a firm agrees to a lower hourly rate in exchange for a share of the difference between potential exposure and actual damages paid (essentially a 'success fee'). In other instances, a law firm and corporation may become co-venturers in litigation, with the successful law firm awarded a share in the client's business if its efforts on the client's behalf are successful. Large corporations have also made efforts to cut legal expenses by outsourcing (or requiring outside counsel to outsource) routine matters such as document review,

[21] A nationally representative survey of accident victims found that 87% of people who hired lawyers to represent them in personal injury litigation signed contingency fee agreements, 4% hired lawyers for a fixed fee, and less than 1% agreed to pay hourly fees and expenses (D Hensler et al, *Compensation for Accidental Injuries in the United States*, (1991), Table 5.11, 136).

[22] In a series of studies of civil litigation costs conducted in the 1980s, Rand Institute for Civil Justice researchers found price competition among plaintiff contingent fee lawyers only in the area of high-value aviation accident litigation. See J Kakalik et al, *Costs and Compensation Paid in Aviation Accident Litigation*, Rand, 1988.

by limiting charges for services such as copying, and by setting litigation budgets that set priorities for and attempt to limit discovery and other pretrial activities.

In ordinary litigation there is virtually no direct public regulation of fee amounts or financing practices.[23] But judges in recent years have attempted to use case management techniques—limiting time for discovery, setting strict trial and pretrial schedules, referring cases to alternative dispute resolution—to control expenses. The best available evidence indicates that these techniques have little effect on costs, although they may produce other benefits for parties.[24]

By contrast to ordinary litigation, in class actions and non-class mass litigation, where a large majority of plaintiffs are absent from the court or represented chiefly in the aggregate, fees are subject to court approval. In class actions, the judge appoints plaintiff class counsel, often from among law firms that vie for the position; in many instances, the counsel position is shared by several firms. In securities class actions, the class member with the largest financial stake is presumptively the class representative, and law firms compete to represent that entity, which is virtually always a public or private financial institution. Like plaintiff counsel in ordinary civil suits, class counsel provides up front and ongoing funding and is reimbursed for expenses and awarded fees at the conclusion of the suit.

Judges use one of two strategies for calculating fees in class actions, depending on what circuit they sit in. Using the 'percentage of fund' approach (POF) the judge awards class counsel a share of the damages won for the class. A common percentage is one-third but some circuits require or advise judges to award a smaller share, and the available evidence indicates that, at least in the federal courts, as the value of settlements increases, the share awarded to class counsel decreases.[25] Using the alternative 'lodestar' approach, the judge requests that class counsel submit a record of their hours, multiplies these hours by the going rate in the jurisdiction (the 'lodestar' rate), and—if the judge thinks it appropriate—multiplies that product by an additional factor (the 'multiplier') that rewards counsel for the risk they undertook, the success they achieved, the competence they displayed and other factors. Some judges carefully scrutinise the hourly records (or appoint a special master to do so) and disallow hours that they believe are excessive. Multipliers range from one (ie no uplift) to more than five but are generally on the order of two to three. The advantage of the POF approach is that it is easy for the judge to administer. But critics argue that the POF approach too often awards windfalls to class counsel whose effort was not commensurate with the fee.

[23] Some statutory alternative compensation programmes, such as state workers' compensation and the federal veterans' compensation programmes, restrict the fees lawyers may charge. Usually these restrictions are in the form of caps on contingency fee percentages. But some statutes include more complex provisions. For example, the California Medical Injury Compensation Reform Act (MICRA) limits contingent fee percentages according to a sliding scale, with decreasing percentages available for larger recoveries. See N Pace, *Capping Non-Economic Awards in Medical Malpractice Trials: California Jury Verdicts under MICRA*, Rand, 2004.

[24] J Kakalik et al, *An Evaluation of Judicial Case Management under the Civil Justice Reform Act*, Rand, 1996.

[25] T Eisenberg and G Miller, 'Attorney Fees in Class Action Settlements: 2003–2008' NYU Law & Economic Research Paper Series, November 2009.

In addition, in class actions where a substantial fraction of the negotiated settlement amount is not claimed by class members and reverts to the defendant, the actual fraction of total dollars expended by the defendant that is paid to class counsel may far exceed the total amount collected by class members,[26] an outcome that seems inappropriate to many and is partially responsible for the claims of class action abuse in the US. The lodestar approach was adopted by courts in response to criticism of the POF approach but it has been criticised itself for encouraging class counsel to pad their hours. Many judges complain that they have neither time nor competence to assess lawyers' reported hours. In practice, most judges now use a blend of both approaches, starting with the approach favoured in their circuit and then assessing the reasonableness of the calculated award by checking it against the alternative calculation. While not required by law, this blended approach is encouraged by the Manual for Complex Litigation,[27] the leading resource for federal (and some state) trial court judges.

Although fees are paid by settling defendants either as a share of the settlement fund or an addition to it, class counsel and defendants are adjured not to negotiate fees because of the concern that class counsel might agree to a smaller than appropriate settlement amount in exchange for a larger fee. In practice, defendants frequently agree not to contest class counsel requests for fees up to a specified amount. However, fee requests are sometimes challenged by defendants and are often challenged by class members or intervenors who claim 'objector' status, as provided by class action rules.

In non-class mass actions, where plaintiff attorneys have entered into individual representation contingency fee agreements with hundred or sometimes thousands of clients pursuing the same litigation, judges may issue fee orders mandating cost-sharing among plaintiff counsel, including special payments to lead counsel (often appointed to serve on a 'plaintiff steering committee'). In some instances, judges have directed that these payments are to be deducted from plaintiff attorneys' share of their individual clients' damages (rather than charged to their clients as an additional expense); in other instances, judges have directed that these special costs be shared equally between plaintiff attorneys and their clients. In a few instances, judges have asserted their authority under equitable fee doctrine to cap the total amount of fees plaintiff attorneys can collect from clients in non-class mass actions, in effect voiding contractual agreements between attorneys and clients.

[26] D Hensler et al, *Class Action Dilemmas: Pursuing Public Goals for Private Gain* (Santa Monica, CA, RAND Institute of Civil Justice, 2000); N Pace et al, *Insurance Class Actions in the United States* (Santa Monica, CA, RAND Institute of Civil Justice, 2007).

[27] Federal Judicial Center, *Manual for Complex Litigation* (Fourth) (2004).

Cost Shifting

A federal judge can tax as costs several different types of fees, including fees for transcripts, compensation of court-appointed experts, and witness fees,[28] but 'costs' generally are understood as a term of art not to include lawyers' fees. Some statutes intended to encourage litigation (chiefly in civil rights and public law cases) authorise one-way cost shifting including attorney fees to prevailing plaintiffs.[29] Other statutes provide for discretionary shifting of attorney fees, as a sanction for misbehavior.[30] In ordinary litigation, parties are free to negotiate payment of attorney fees to a settling party, if they so desire. Class representatives, however, are *not* free to enter into agreements with regard to attorney fees without formal court approval.

Predictability and Proportionality

The absence of publicly administered fee schedules and the rejection of fee-shifting in the US legal system leads to criticisms that the system encourages frivolous litigation and produces unpredictable outcomes and disproportionate legal costs. The debate over the extent of frivolous litigation in the US is long-running and essentially irresolvable, for it rests more on the opposing values of the protagonists—some of whom would prefer to put their faith entirely in the market, some of whom would rely happily on public regulation and some of whom distrust both the market and regulation to protect public health and social welfare—than on objective assessment of empirical evidence. One person's 'frivolous' lawsuit is another's essential challenge to unlawful behaviour. Economic theory produces ambiguous outcomes with regard to the effect of cost-shifting on the amount of litigation (without regard to judgments of its value)[31] and the best empirical test of the effect, the 1980 adoption of fee-shifting for medical malpractices cases in Florida, found that fee-shifting *increased* litigation, leading to the speedy reversal of the statute.[32]

[28] 28 USC §1920.

[29] For example, the Clean Water Act provides that a federal district court may award litigation costs, 'including reasonable attorney and expert fees' to a prevailing or 'substantially prevailing' party, 33 USCS §1365. In 1992 the US Supreme Court held that courts may not apply 'multipliers' when calculating attorney fees in such cases. *City of Burlington v Dague*, 505 US 557 (1992).

[30] For example, the Copyright Act provides that 'in its discretion,' a district court may 'award a reasonable attorney's fee to the prevailing party as part of the costs.' 17 USC §505.

[31] C Beckner & A Katz, 'The Incentive Effects of Litigation Fee-Shifting When Legal Standards are Uncertain' (1995) 15 *International Review of Law & Economics* 205–224.

[32] J Williams, 'Effects of Attorney Fee-Shifting Laws on Claiming Behavior' (2001) 34 *Policy Sciences* 347–356.

Access to jury trial and the availability of punitive damages arguably increase the unpredictability of outcomes of US civil litigation, but analyses of tort data over the past several decades show fairly predictable relationships between severity of injury and economic losses and case outcomes.[33] Perhaps most important for the critique, proportionality of legal costs under the US regime is under the control of the parties themselves. Since there is no fee-shifting, the litigant, once engaged in litigation, has the ability to control its own costs. Repeat parties such as large corporations and insurers—the most vocal critics of the US legal rules—are in a particularly strong position with regard to predictability as they have sufficient previous experience to provide a basis for analysing the cost consequences of adopting different strategies for different categories of cases. Indeed, the largest empirical study of civil litigation ever conducted in the US concluded that the largest portion of variation in federal civil lawsuit costs was explained by non-court factors (eg financial stakes, number of parties, relationships among the parties).[34] As corporate clients have become more concerned about costs and more sophisticated about legal strategy, it seems likely that they will rely increasingly on such cost modeling. In some instances, this might lead to a decision to offer early settlement of a case with large liability and cost exposure. In other instances, it might lead to a decision to invest in multi-million dollar litigation to curb liability exposure.[35] Ironically, the cost of the US legal system imposes the greatest burden on those who have had the least voice in the public policy debate: individuals and small business owners for whom the cost of legal representation often far outweighs the value of resolving justiciable claims in court. The social cost of denying access to public justice forums to a large proportion of citizens and entrepreneurs has often been the subject of policy discourse in the US but rarely the object of real policy reform.

[33] See eg N Vidmar et al, 'Jury Awards for Medical Malpractice and Post-Verdict Adjustments of Those Awards' (1998) 48 *De Paul L Rev* 265.

[34] J Kakalik et al, *An Evaluation of Judicial Case Management under the Civil Justice Reform Act*, Rand, 1996.

[35] R Seidenstein, 'The Vioxx Hit: Merck's Big Ticket Defense' *New Jersey Lawyer*, 10 March 2008 [available at Lexis].

INDEX

Introductory Note

References such as '178–9' indicate (not necessarily continuous) discussion of a topic across a range of pages. Wherever possible in the case of topics with many references, these have either been divided into sub-topics or only the most significant discussions of the topic are listed. Because the entire work is about 'costs', 'funding' and 'civil litigation', the use of these terms and certain others which occur constantly throughout the book as entry points has been minimised. Information will be found under the corresponding detailed topics.

www.ingramcontent.com/pod-product-compliance
Ingram Content Group UK Ltd.
Pitfield, Milton Keynes, MK11 3LW, UK
UKHW020831290926
15470UKWH00009B/1841/J